Multidisciplinary Approach to Information Technology in Library and Information Science

Barbara Holland
Brooklyn Public Library, USA (Retired)

Keshav Sinha
University of Petroleum and Energy Studies, India

A volume in the Advances in Library and
Information Science (ALIS) Book Series

Published in the United States of America by
IGI Global
Information Science Reference (an imprint of IGI Global)
701 E. Chocolate Avenue
Hershey PA, USA 17033
Tel: 717-533-8845
Fax: 717-533-8661
E-mail: cust@igi-global.com
Web site: http://www.igi-global.com

Library of Congress Cataloging-in-Publication Data

Names: Holland, Barbara, 1953- editor. | Sinha, Keshav, 1991- editor.
Title: Multidisciplinary approach to information technology in library and
  information science / edited by Barbara Holland, Keshav Sinha.
Description: Hershey, PA : Information Science Reference, 2024. | Includes
  bibliographical references and index. | Summary: "This book presents a
  comprehensive introduction to the multidisciplinary field of information
  technology and its applications in library and information science"--
  Provided by publisher.
Identifiers: LCCN 2023058130 (print) | LCCN 2023058131 (ebook) | ISBN
  9798369328415 (hardcover) | ISBN 9798369328422 (ebook)
Subjects: LCSH: Library science--Information technology. | Information
  science--Technological innovations. | Information technology.
Classification: LCC Z678.9 .M85 2024 (print) | LCC Z678.9 (ebook) | DDC
  025.04--dc23/eng/20240206
LC record available at https://lccn.loc.gov/2023058130
LC ebook record available at https://lccn.loc.gov/2023058131

This book is published in the IGI Global book series Advances in Library and Information Science (ALIS) (ISSN: 2326-4136; eISSN: 2326-4144)

British Cataloguing in Publication Data
A Cataloguing in Publication record for this book is available from the British Library.

For electronic access to this publication, please contact: eresources@igi-global.com.

Advances in Library and Information Science (ALIS) Book Series

Alfonso Ippolito
Sapienza University-Rome, Italy
Carlo Inglese
Sapienza University-Rome, Italy

ISSN:2326-4136
EISSN:2326-4144

MISSION

The **Advances in Library and Information Science (ALIS) Book Series** is comprised of high quality, research-oriented publications on the continuing developments and trends affecting the public, school, and academic fields, as well as specialized libraries and librarians globally. These discussions on professional and organizational considerations in library and information resource development and management assist in showcasing the latest methodologies and tools in the field.

The **ALIS Book Series** aims to expand the body of library science literature by covering a wide range of topics affecting the profession and field at large. The series also seeks to provide readers with an essential resource for uncovering the latest research in library and information science management, development, and technologies.

COVERAGE

- RFID (Radio Frequency Identification)
- Mobile Library Services
- Children and Youth Services
- Corporate Libraries
- Professional Development
- Continuing Education for Library Professionals
- Licensing Issues
- Virtual Reference Services
- Social Networking Technologies
- Gaming in Libraries

IGI Global is currently accepting manuscripts for publication within this series. To submit a proposal for a volume in this series, please contact our Acquisition Editors at Acquisitions@igi-global.com or visit: http://www.igi-global.com/publish/.

Titles in this Series

For a list of additional titles in this series, please visit: www.igi-global.com/book-series/advances-library-information-science/73002

Illuminating and Advancing the Path for Mathematical Writing Research
Madelyn W. Colonnese (Reading and Elementary Education Department, Cato College of Education, University of North Carolina at Charlotte, USA) Tutita M. Casa (Department of Curriculum and Instruction, Neag School of Education, University of Connecticut, USA) and Fabiana Cardetti (Department of Mathematics, College of Liberal Arts and Sciences, University of Connecticut, USA)
Information Science Reference • copyright 2024 • 389pp • H/C (ISBN: 9781668465387) • US $215.00 (our price)

Emerging Technology-Based Services and Systems in Libraries, Educational Institutions, and Non-Profit Organizations
Dickson K. W. Chiu (The University of Hong Kong, Hong Kong) and Kevin K. W. Ho (University of Tsukuba, Japan)
Information Science Reference • copyright 2023 • 353pp • H/C (ISBN: 9781668486719) • US $225.00 (our price)

Applying Positivist and Interpretivist Philosophies to Social Research Practices
C.C. Jayasundara (University of Kelaniya, Sri Lanka)
Information Science Reference • copyright 2023 • 300pp • H/C (ISBN: 9781668454312) • US $215.00 (our price)

Handbook of Research on Advancements of Contactless Technology and Service Innovation in Library and Information Science
Barbara Holland (Brooklyn Public Library, USA (Retired))
Information Science Reference • copyright 2023 • 388pp • H/C (ISBN: 9781668476932) • US $270.00 (our price)

Perspectives on Justice, Equity, Diversity, and Inclusion in Libraries
Nandita S. Mani (University of Massachusetts, Amherst, USA) Michelle A. Cawley (University of North Carolina at Chapel Hill, USA) and Emily P. Jones (University of North Carolina at Chapel Hill, USA)
Information Science Reference • copyright 2023 • 320pp • H/C (ISBN: 9781668472552) • US $215.00 (our price)

Handbook of Research on Technological Advances of Library and Information Science in Industry 5.0
Barbara Jane Holland (Independent Researcher, USA)
Information Science Reference • copyright 2023 • 549pp • H/C (ISBN: 9781668447550) • US $270.00 (our price)

Global Perspectives on Sustainable Library Practices
Victoria Okojie (University of Abuja, Nigeria) and Magnus Osahon Igbinovia (Ambrose Alli University, Nigeria)

701 East Chocolate Avenue, Hershey, PA 17033, USA
Tel: 717-533-8845 x100 • Fax: 717-533-8661
E-Mail: cust@igi-global.com • www.igi-global.com

Table of Contents

Detailed Table of Contents

Chapter 1

    Elisha Mupaikwa, National University of Science and Technology, Zimbabwe

Academic libraries' reference services have continued to diversify thanks to digital technologies. The use of digital technologies to support reference services in academic libraries is covered in this chapter. The study is a review of published works in scholarly journals. The study's conclusions indicate that there is a shift toward digital references globally. Emails, Facebook, and Twitter were the most widely used technologies, although real-time reference services powered by artificial intelligence technology were rarely used. Some users favoured in-person reference services they concurred that digital reference services were superior. The chapter highlighted how academic libraries frequently struggle with inadequate financing, outdated infrastructure, and a lack of user and staff education. The study suggests making investments in the infrastructure of digital technology and educating library users on the advantages of utilizing digital reference services.

Chapter 2

    Hamid Farrokh Ghatte, Antalya Bilim University, Antalya, Turkey & Department of Civil
        Engineering, Technical and Vocational University, Tehran, Iran

The study reports on the proposed gene expression programming (GEP) to predict the ability of CFRP wrapping to enhance the post-heated bond strength between steel rebar and concrete. For this purpose, the results of 80 pullout specimens (150×150×250 mm) were selected in two categories of compressive strength of concrete: C30 and C40. In the experiments, a 20 mm rebar was placed in the corner of each specimen with a 25- or 35-mm clear cover and 200 mm of bond length. The specimens were subjected to different levels of heat before using CFRP jackets. The exposure to heat reduced the concrete-rebar bond strength; however, confinement with CFRP jackets significantly improved the bond strength between steel rebar and concrete. The estimated bond strength could be predicted by the accuracy and high prediction ability of the proposed model. Based on the findings, machine learning can bring significant improvements and benefits to the civil engineering industry in terms of the estimation of the mechanical properties of the materials in various conditions.

Chapter 3

Saroj Kumari, Yogoda Satsanga Mahavidyalaya, Ranchi, India
Piyush Ranjan, Jharkhand Rai University, India
Priyanka Srivastava, Sarala Birla University, India

Naturalist Charles Darwin was the first to rationalize the importance of emotions. Emotions are key factors that set up the body to adapt to things like apprehension and outrage and amplify one's possibilities of endurance and achievement. The lockdown limitations and fear and consequences of infectious infection brought the whole world to a halt. Humans across the globe have realized the unpredictability of life and let go of the need to control it. This situation not only has surged the suicidal rates, domestic violence, job insecurities, grief, scarcity of basic needs, but also took a positive turn in human development. Many people felt calm, enjoyed the family bond, went back to their basic survival skills, came close to humanity, and many other realizations. This chapter provided a critical analysis of human emotions at the time of stress and different coping mechanisms adopted by the most successful species on the planet. It throws light on the different spectrums of psychosocial behaviour. The authors provide a topography of human emotions during COVID-19 pandemic.

Chapter 4

Kabelo Bruce Kgomoeswana, University of Limpopo, South Africa
Lefose Makgahlela, University of LImpopo, South Africa

The 4th industrial revolution (4IR) has brought significant technological advancements that have impacted various sectors, including governance and record-keeping. This chapter examines the challenges faced by traditional councils when preserving records during the 4IR. The chapter adopted a desktop research methodology. The data were subjected to substantive and extensive analysis through the instrumentality of content validity, content analysis, and textual criticism to establish facts that defend or refute the hypothesis. The study revealed that traditional councils lack the necessary infrastructure and resources to digitise records, leading to concerns about data loss, system failures, and cybersecurity threats. In essence, the councils are still struggling to protect and secure the records preserved in their custody; as such, council members need digital literacy training. The study recommends strategies that traditional councils should use to preserve records during the 4IR.

Chapter 5

Satishkumar Naikar, D.Y. Patil University (Deemed), Navi Mumbai, India
Shashikumar Hatti, Navodaya Medical College Hospital and Research Centre, Raichur, India
Megha Paul, Librarian Rockwell International School, Hyderabad, India
Rani K. Swamy, Navodaya Medical College Hospital and Research Centre, Raichur, India

Artificial intelligence (AI), which has taken over many industries, is thought of as a continuation of human intelligence. Artificial intelligence applications in libraries have revolutionized the information industry. Many human talents, including calculation, reading, speaking, grasping, remembering, making decisions, and interactive learning, can be stimulated by technological improvements. It is believed that the use of artificial intelligence in virtual reference services will offer libraries a new online service paradigm. Virtual reality is a useful feature that engages users with libraries and improves information literacy abilities. Librarians are always utilizing cutting edge technologies to improve services for their patrons. The chapter covered some AI components, library services to which it can be applied, the benefits of its application, and the problems libraries encounter when implementing artificial intelligence in the library.

Chapter 6

Emily Morgan, Beacon College, USA

The open access (OA) movement, a paradigm shift in scholarly communication, has emerged as a cornerstone of modern higher education and academic libraries. By removing financial barriers, OA ensures unrestricted access to academic resources, democratizing knowledge and fostering a more equitable learning environment. Furthermore, OA promotes interdisciplinary collaboration, enabling scholars to engage in expansive knowledge exchange across diverse fields, fueling innovation. Academic libraries have become instrumental in curating vast repositories of openly accessible content, enhancing their role as facilitators of information literacy. Embracing open access principles enhances the visibility of institutions and researchers but also promotes inclusivity, ensuring that diverse voices find resonance in academic discourse. Explored in this chapter are the multifaceted advantages of the OA movement, underscoring its pivotal role in shaping a more accessible, collaborative, and egalitarian landscape within higher education and academic libraries.

Chapter 7

Nonhlanhla P. Ntloko, Durban University of Technology, South Africa
Tlou Maggie Masenya, Durban University of Technology, South Africa

This chapter analyses the role of digital transformation in KwaZulu-Natal Department of Health Libraries in South Africa, exploring if and how digital technologies can be adopted and used in enhancing access to electronic information. The chapter utilised literature review to critically analyse the role of digital transformation in healthcare libraries, digital technologies used in enhancing access to electronic information, challenges of digital transformation in healthcare libraries, and the strategies to overcoming these challenges. Technology acceptance model (TAM) was used as the underpinning theory to guide this study. Recommendations suggest a need to prioritize digital transformation and provide enough resources to healthcare libraries and formulate policies that would facilitate this process.

Chapter 8

Akancha Kumari, Ranchi University, India

As the world grapples with the pressing challenges of environmental degradation and climate change, the need for sustainable development has become paramount. Green marketing has emerged as a powerful tool for transforming businesses and paving the way towards a sustainable future. This chapter explores the role of green marketing in driving sustainable development by examining its impact on business practices, consumer behavior, and environmental stewardship. The study highlights the strategies and initiatives undertaken by businesses to integrate sustainability principles into their marketing efforts, including product innovation, eco-labeling, green packaging, and communication of environmental values. Through a comprehensive review of relevant literature, case studies, and industry examples, this chapter underscores the transformative potential of green marketing in driving sustainable development. It offers insights to businesses, policymakers, and marketers on how to harness the power of green marketing to create a more sustainable and prosperous future.

Muhammad Rosyihan Hendrawan, University of Brawijaya, Indonesia
Muhammad Shobaruddin, University of Brawijaya, Indonesia

Libraries, archives, and museums (LAMs) as memory institutions share valuable existence to preserve advanced national cultural heritage. Various causes drove LAM convergence in various cases. The Bung Karno Library in Blitar City, one of the Presidential Libraries in the Republic of Indonesia, helps explain the memory institution's convergence. The case studies indicate that collaboration and convergence face shared challenges. The authors propose that collaboration between these organizations is complicated. In the Bung Karno Library, cohesive procedure and accessibility were essential to service the user. However, removing boundaries between memory institutions in Bung Karno Library was universally accepted as necessary to improve user service and promote cultural heritage. These actions might lead to future research and boost the convergence's worth. To balance professional capability and integrate multiple systems, the researched institutions are making significant efforts. A fine balance appears needed to achieve and maintain successful convergence initiatives.

Sephalika Sagar, Amity University, Noida, India
Devesh K. Upadhyay, Birla Institute of Technology, Mesra, India

The authors propose a model for examining the moderating effect of government regulations on electric vehicles and their infrastructure in India. The model was tested empirically using data collected from 101 respondents. Principal component analysis and mediation analysis were employed to analyze the data using JASP 0.17.2.1 (Apple Silicon) software package. Findings based on interaction support the hypothesis that government regulations concerning the manufacturing of electric vehicles, standards and specification of EVs and EV batteries, subsidies, and incentives by central and state governments support. In other words, the potentially negative aftermaths of the lumbering infrastructure of EVs can be controlled and reduced when government regulations concerning infrastructure are implemented meticulously. The research study highlights the theoretical and practical implications of the findings, as well as recommendations for future studies, are suggested.

Kishlay Kumar, Sarala Birla University, India
L. G. Honey Singh, Ranchi University, India
Karan Pratap Singh, Birla Institute of Technology, Mesra, India
Puja Mishra, Sarala Birla University, India

The purpose of this study is to examine the influence of digital media marketing and celebrity endorsement on consumer purchase decisions toward mutual funds investment. Marketing through social media gives marketers a competitive edge when it comes to influencing customers and driving order intent in mutual funds. In this research, the authors examine the effectiveness of digital media and celebrity endorsements in influencing consumer purchasing decisions. This research employed a quantitative approach, and data were collected through online surveys from six districts of Jharkhand, a sample of 310 participants using structured questionnaire using purposive sampling. The findings advocate that celebrity endorsement is a substantial marketing tool for driving the purchase intention via social media. The indirect effect of celebrity endorsement on consumer purchase intention was also significant when digital media was used as a meditating variable. The data analysis and validation of the conceptual framework were carried out using the PLS-SEM. The study's implications are discussed.

Chapter 12

Mallikarjun Mulimani, Government First Grade College, Belagavi, India
Satishkumar Naikar, D.Y. Patil University (Deemed), Navi Mumbai, India

Accreditation plays a vital role in higher education institutions by ensuring quality and standardization. It serves as a measure of an institution's academic programs, faculty qualifications, student support services, and infrastructure. By maintaining accountability and transparency, accreditation upholds standards of excellence and promotes continuous improvement. Accreditation enhances an institution's credibility and reputation, providing a recognized stamp of approval. It also facilitates student mobility and recognition of qualifications, ensuring that degrees and certificates hold value and are widely accepted by other institutions and employers.

Chapter 13

Muhammad Rosyihan Hendrawan, University of Brawijaya, Indonesia
Azman Mat Isa, College of Computing, Informatics, and Mathematics, Universiti Teknologi
  MARA, Malaysia
Ahmad Zam Hariro Samsudin, College of Computing, Informatics, and Mathematics,
  Universiti Teknologi MARA, Malaysia

The libraries, archives, and museums (LAMs) promote culture, community, and change new cultural heritage information management research. History deserves The Ombilin Coal Mining Heritage of Sawahlunto (OCMHS), Indonesia as a World Heritage. The LAM convergence may initiate in OCMHS. LAM convergence counts and digitization changes LAM. Universitas Brawijaya, Indonesia and Universiti Teknologi MARA, Malaysia constructed digital LAM convergence by free open-source software (FOSS) and the software development life cycle (SDLC) cascade development with information system design techniques. The OCMHS LAM standards are initiated with "The Sawahlunto Memories." The OCMHS best practices can be the other example for preserving culture via "The Sawahlunto Memory." Convergent LAMs of OCMHS by "The Sawahlunto Memory" must enhance access to memory institutions and experiences in quick digital technology and effective cultural heritage information management to preserve Indonesia's worldwide cultural heritage.

On March 28, 2023, an open letter titled "Pause Giant A.I. Experiments" was published by the Future of Life Institute, urging A.I. companies to draft a shared set of safety protocols around advanced A.I. development before creating more powerful software that may pose dangers to humanity. A wide range of ethical issues have been raised concerning Open AI's ChatGPT. The use of ChatGPT has demonstrated on numerous occasions that it encourages racial and gender bias. This (AI) chatbot system uses learning models that are not bias-free. The chatbot obeys the algorithm blindly and replies with the requested information when prompted. It cannot tell whether the information is skewed. This chapter examines the ethical implications ChatGPT can have on libraries, other institutions, and society.

The purpose of the study is to highlight digital library services and their importance in academic libraries. Digital libraries are a group of files in digital form accessible on the net or CD-ROM disk. Depending on the precise library, a consumer may be able to get admission to magazine articles, books, newspapers, snapshots, sound documents, and films. The virtual library is one of the maximum cutting-edge trends in library and statistics technology, which helps its users to seek information via the internet. A digital library is prepared for greater ideas and statistics and guides different offerings and places wherein the order is saved in digital format and can be retrieved over networks. Digital libraries are systems presenting the person with resources and getting the right of entry to a very big range; the digital library information prepared storeroom of the records awareness digital library is an international digital library.

Preface

This book presents a comprehensive introduction to the multidisciplinary field of information technology and its applications in library and information science. It covers the basic concepts, principles, techniques, tools, and trends of information technology, as well as the challenges and opportunities it presents for librarians and information professionals. The book also explores the various aspects of information technology that are relevant to library and information science, such as data management, digital libraries, web development, social media, machine learning, artificial intelligence, and more. Moreover, the book encompasses many disciplines concerning information science and it's technology. Such as areas in business, health, machine learning and marketing and more.

The book is designed to help readers understand the theoretical foundations, practical implications, and ethical issues of information technology in library and information science. It is suitable for librarians, researchers, practitioners, educators and advanced students who want to learn more about the multidisciplinary approach to information technology in library and information science.

There are 15, chapters and each chapter will surely grasp your attention.

Chapter 1. Harnessing Digital Technologies for References Services in Academic Libraries: Concepts and Challenges

The use of digital technologies to support reference services in academic libraries is covered in this chapter. The study is a review of published works in scholarly journals. The study's conclusions indicate that there is a shift toward digital references globally. Emails, Facebook, and Twitter were the most widely used technologies, although real-time reference services powered by artificial intelligence technology, were rarely used.

Chapter 2. Applications of Gene Expression Programming for Estimating CFRP Wrapping Effects on the Bond Strength After Elevated Temperature Exposure

The present study reports proposed Gene Expression Programming (GEP) to predict the ability of CFRP wrapping to enhance the post-heated bond strength between steel rebar and concrete. Based on the findings, machine learning can bring significant improvements and benefits to the civil engineering industry in terms of the estimation of the mechanical properties of the materials in various conditions.

Chapter 3. Fluctuation of Emotion in Stress and Different Coping Mechanism During the COVID-19 Pandemic

This chapter provided a critical analysis of human emotions at the time of stress and different coping mechanism adopted by the most successful species on the planet. It throws light on the different spectrums of psychosocial behaviour. The authors provide a topography of human emotions during COVID-19 pandemic.

Chapter 4. Key Challenges Faced When Preserving Records in Traditional Councils During the 4th Industrial Revolution

This chapter examines the challenges faced by traditional councils when preserving records during the 4IR. The chapter adopted a desktop research methodology. The data were subjected to substantive and extensive analysis through the instrumentality of content validity, content analysis and textual criticism to establish facts that defend or refute the hypothesis. The study revealed that traditional councils lack the necessary infrastructure and resources to digitize records, leading to concerns about data loss, system failures, and cybersecurity threats.

Chapter 5. Artificial Intelligence (AI) in Academic Libraries: A Theoretical Study

It is believed that the use of artificial intelligence in virtual reference services will offer libraries a new online service paradigm. Librarians are always utilizing cutting edge technologies to improve services for their patrons. The chapter covered some AI components, library services to which it can be applied, the benefits of its application, and the problems libraries encounter when implementing artificial intelligence in the library.

Chapter 6. Open Access, Open Doors: The Benefits of OA in Academic Research and Higher Education

The Open Access (OA) movement, a paradigm shift in scholarly communication, has emerged as a cornerstone of modern higher education and academic libraries. Explored in this chapter are the multifaceted advantages of the OA movement, underscoring its pivotal role in shaping a more accessible, collaborative, and egalitarian landscape within higher education and academic libraries.

Chapter 7. Enhancing Access to Electronic Information Through Digital Transformation in KwaZulu-Natal Department of Health Libraries in South Africa

This chapter analyses the role of digital transformation in Kwa Zulu Natal Department of Health Libraries in South Africa, exploring if and how digital technologies can be adopted and used in enhancing access to electronic information. Recommendations suggest a need to prioritize digital transformation and provide enough resources to healthcare libraries and formulate policies that would facilitate this process.

Chapter 8. Transforming Business for a Sustainable Future Using Green Marketing

As the world grapples with the pressing challenges of environmental degradation and climate change, the need for sustainable development has become paramount. This paper explores the role of green marketing in driving sustainable development by examining its impact on business practices, consumer behavior, and environmental stewardship.

Chapter 9. Toward a Convergence of Memory Institutions in the Indonesian Presidential Library

Libraries, archives, and museums (LAMs) are memory institutions that share valuable existence to preserve advanced national cultural heritage. The case studies indicate that collaboration and convergence face shared challenges.

Chapter 10. Electric Vehicles in India and Customer Perception: The Moderating Effect of Government Regulations on EVs

Authors propose a model for examining the moderating effect of government regulations on Electric vehicles & it's infrastructure in India.. Findings based on interaction support the hypothesis that government regulations concerning the manufacturing of Electric Vehicles, standards and specification of EVs and EV batteries, subsidies, and incentives by central and state governments support.

Chapter 11. To Examine the Influence of Digital Marketing and Celebrity Endorsement on Consumer Purchase Intention of Mutual Fund

The purpose of this study is to examine the influence of digital media marketing and celebrity endorsement on consumer purchase decisions toward mutual funds investment. Marketing through social media gives marketers a competitive edge when it comes to influencing customers and driving order intent in mutual funds. In this research, we will examine the effectiveness of digital media and celebrity endorsements in influencing consumer purchasing decisions

Chapter 12. The Role and Significance of Accreditation in Higher Education Institutions: A Study

Accreditation plays a vital role in higher education institutions by ensuring quality and standardization. It serves as a measure of an institution's academic programs, faculty qualifications, student support services, and infrastructure. By maintaining accountability and transparency, accreditation upholds standards of excellence and promotes continuous improvement.

Chapter 13. Initiating Memory Institutions Convergence Through Digital Convergence in Indonesian World Heritage Sites

The libraries, archives, and museums (LAMs) promote culture, community, and change new cultural heritage information management research. History deserves The Ombilin Coal Mining Heritage of Sawahlunto (OCMHS), Indonesia, as a World Heritage

Chapter 14. ChatGPT and ITS Ethical Implications on Libraries, Other Institutions, and Society: Is It a Viable Upgrade?

On March 28, 2023, an Open letter titled "Pause Giant A.I. Experiments," was published by the Future of Life Institute, urging A.I. companies to draft a shared set of safety protocols around advanced A.I. development before creating more powerful software that may pose dangers to humanity. A wide range of ethical issues have been raised concerning Open AI's ChatGPT.

This chapter examines the ethical implications ChatGPT can have on libraries, other institutions, and society.

Chapter 15. Digital Library Services and Their Importance in Academic Libraries: An Overview

Digital libraries are a group of files in digital form accessible on the net or CD-ROM disk. Digital libraries are systems presenting the person with resources and getting the right of entry to a very big range, the digital library information prepared storeroom of the records awareness digital library is an international digital library. The purpose of the study is to highlight digital library services and their importance in academic libraries.

Barbara Holland
Brooklyn Public Library, USA (Retired)

Keshav Sinha
University of Petroleum and Energy Studies, India

Chapter 1
Harnessing Digital Technologies for References Services in Academic Libraries:
Concepts and Challenges

Elisha Mupaikwa

https://orcid.org/0000-0002-0313-7139

National University of Science and Technology, Zimbabwe

ABSTRACT

Academic libraries' reference services have continued to diversify thanks to digital technologies. The use of digital technologies to support reference services in academic libraries is covered in this chapter. The study is a review of published works in scholarly journals. The study's conclusions indicate that there is a shift toward digital references globally. Emails, Facebook, and Twitter were the most widely used technologies, although real-time reference services powered by artificial intelligence technology were rarely used. Some users favoured in-person reference services they concurred that digital reference services were superior. The chapter highlighted how academic libraries frequently struggle with inadequate financing, outdated infrastructure, and a lack of user and staff education. The study suggests making investments in the infrastructure of digital technology and educating library users on the advantages of utilizing digital reference services.

INTRODUCTION

Many users who frequent libraries are frustrated with the calibre of the information they get through their searches, and in academic institutions, professors, lecturers, and tutors frequently struggle with the subpar work submitted by students. These difficulties may be a result of users' insufficient knowledge of how to create efficient queries and search strategies to retrieve the appropriate content from collections, or they may be related to the general weaknesses of the ranking algorithms used by the information retrieval systems used by institutions. One of the main pillars of the library, reference services, has long been

DOI: 10.4018/979-8-3693-2841-5.ch001

recognized for its ability to deliver user-specific and tailored information in academic libraries through a variety of methods, including discovery, advice, retrieval, and usability. Uzoigwe and Eze (2018) claim that reference services in academic libraries offer customers in-person assistance and resources in addition to aiding in the completion of activities related to teaching, learning, and research, which are the main duties of any academic institution. In academic libraries, reference librarians have traditionally served as liaisons to connect patrons to the collections and services of the library. These responsibilities have recently changed as libraries now aid people online and these services are now dependent on the internet and the web (AL-Hatmi, Ibri, and Nor, 2022). In the past, these services were provided manually over the desk, but these techniques have since been rendered ineffective since they no longer satisfy the information needs of today's users, who demand both a high volume and quality of information. The reference librarian's position has evolved as a result, and these professionals are now attempting to modify their offerings to match the dynamic changes in the new information environment. The loss of desk-based reference services is due to the increased and improved accessibility of information as well as the variety of formats in which information is given to users. This chapter discusses the application of different digital technologies in supporting reference services in academic libraries.

Reference services in libraries were developed to assist novice and unskilled readers and researchers, according to Mandernack and Fritch (2001), and demand for these services has increased with the rapid pace of industrialization and the emergence of the information and knowledge economies powered by the 4IR. Organized study is conducted at this time to promote innovations and the expansion of democratic ideas. A vital part of librarianship, the library provides individualized services, direct information, and answers rather than leaving users to make their own decisions (Mandernack and Fritch, 2001). In addition, the library has evolved into the primary information source supporting scholar and reference services in all of their forms. Reference librarians have been tasked with handling user inquiries, offering advice on user search, and supporting information literacy initiatives within academic, student, and researcher populations.

The use of technology by librarians has always been widespread, and they have always worked to improve services by incorporating it into their daily duties and jobs. This has seen the transition of librarians from the usage of the landline telephone system to the more practical internet-mediated technology. The majority of institutions are now moving to the usage of the internet and its associated services, which has been made easier by advances in internet connectivity and decreases in the cost of internet connectivity and data. In conjunction with the introduction of computers into library services, new possibilities for computerizing reference services have emerged with online search services, online cataloguing, and remote databases, setting more relevance but requiring new search skills among novice users who lack expertise and technical skills to use these resources. These changes in the digital world have an impact on how people access, retrieve, and disseminate information, which has an impact on their jobs (Khan et al., 2017). Despite these advancements, it is generally agreed upon in the literature that the integration of digitally supported reference services in academic libraries has made it simple for users to access library collections and resources, negating the need for users to make physical movements to access information centres and consult reference librarians in person. Through sophisticated Institutional Repository Systems (IRS) that are accessible from remote places and occasionally incorporate contemporary software advances like Artificial Intelligence (AI), users are now taking the lead in information searches and discovery.

Numerous scholars have looked into the usefulness of digital reference services, and there appears to be agreement among them that modern digital technologies have significantly changed reference services. Since the COVID-19 pandemic, which severely affected all physical and social human interactions including traditional face-to-face reference delivery services due to lockdowns, isolations, self-quarantines, and physical and social distancing, in the year 2029, the relevance of digital reference services has become critical and has attracted more appreciation (Kabir, 2021). Igwebuike and Onoh (2022) reported that in Nigeria, among the 13 private universities investigated, 100% used email, text-based, instant messaging, online pathfinders, and mobile reference services. Some authors have noted the low usage of digital reference technologies in academic libraries. The study also revealed that while the majority (53.8%) of these libraries lacked the capabilities to facilitate collaborative digital referencing, 46.2% of these libraries offered such services. An intriguing finding was that 100% of these libraries lacked the infrastructure to offer digital referencing via Ask a Librarian, video conferencing, and chat services. According to a study by Kadir, Dollah, and Sighn (2015) conducted among academic libraries in Malaysia, 74.2% of librarians reported using email reference services, followed by web forms, "Ask a Librarian," collaborative services, and online chat services. However, among the participants, face-to-face consultations were most frequently used (63.8%), followed by telephone consultation (13.1%), correspondence (6.7%), email (28.8%), web forms (39.4%), "Ask a Librarian" (39.4%), and online chat services (5.9%). Web forms, which were positively rated by 73.4% of the participants, were ranked first among these services, followed by email (72.7%), "Ask a Librarian" (64.5%), and online chat services (47.3%). However, the study found that online chat and video conferencing services were being used more frequently. According to research by Adayi, Neboh, and Oluchi (2023), users at Caritas University and Godfrey Okoye University in Nigeria had varying levels of DRS. However, participants from both colleges reported using email and phone reference services frequently, compared to less frequent usage of web forms, live chat, SMS, Ask-a-service, video calls, social media, robots, collaborative reference services, and voice conversations.

David Lankes is one of the leading scholars in the field of digital referencing. He has worked on several early digital referencing projects, including ERIC, AskERIC, GEM (Gateway to Educational Materials), and the Virtual Reference Desk. To give consumers quick and easy access to material on education, the Educational Resource Information Centre (ERIC) was established in 1966 (Lankes, 1995). At Syracuse University's School of Information Studies, AskERIC was first implemented online in 1992 to support staff and doctoral student information access. This provided a question-answer service that was eventually extended to other universities and implemented for web-based use. The AskERIC question-answer service, AskERIC Virtual Library, AskERIC network connections, and AskERIC research and development are the four main components of AskERIC as a digital reference service (Lankes, 1995). The main goals of the GEM project, which was created in the USA to offer library materials to teachers over the Internet, were to:

i)   Develop a precise syntax and well-defined practices for its application in an HTML environment;
ii) Define a semantically rich metadata profile and domain-specific controlled vocabularies necessary to the description of educational materials on the web;
iii) Design and implement a set of harvesting tools for retrieving data stored as HTML metatags; and
iv) Encourage the design of several prototype interfaces (Sutton, 1998).

Maxwell (2002) explains the idea of a virtual reference desk and presents numerous aspects of user interactions in the virtual reference desk environment, including:

i)   Accessible: Online digital reference services must be simple to use and navigate regardless of the device being used or any physical limitations of people using them.
ii) Quick turnaround: Questions need to be answered as soon as possible.
iii) A clear response standard: To prevent user confusion, communication should be clear.
iv) Dialogical Interaction: The user and the system must engage in discourse. A reference service's competence is assessed by the veracity of its responses.

Maxwell (2002) also proposed facets for service development and management and these are:

i)   Authoritative: Information providers who are experts in their fields must be knowledgeable.
ii) Trained professionals: There has to be a service that trains professionals on how to interact with users of digital platforms.
iii) Confidential: Users and specialists must communicate in complete secrecy.
iv) Reviewed: The usefulness and efficiency of digital reference services must be regularly assessed.
v)   Give users access to relevant data: Digital references must not only give the necessary information but also any supplementary data.
vi) Promote: Services need to inform and enlighten potential users about the advantages of system use.

Governments and organizations around the world, according to Lankes (2004), have invested in the infrastructure, software, and staff training for digital reference services, but there is still a lack of knowledge about these services and their advantages. The absence of engagement and communication between reference librarians and digital librarians makes this situation much worse. According to Lankes (2004), the key issue in creating effective digital reference systems for libraries is "how to effectively and efficiently incorporate human expertise to answer the information demands of information seekers." Human expertise, efficiency and effectiveness, information systems, questions and answers, and questions and answers were the five categories of questions identified by Lankes (2004) in his research agenda on the creation and use of digital reference services in academic libraries. According to Lankes (2004), human expertise in the digital reference system ranges from subject knowledge to process knowledge, or the comprehension of a fundamental group of facts and how they relate to one another. According to Lankes (2004), process knowledge is the capacity to influence a system to produce the desired outcome when a fundamental comprehension of the system's content is not necessary. According to Lankes (2002), the effectiveness and efficiency of a system should be used to justify any investments in digital reference systems. This has to do with the time spent carrying out tasks and the system's accuracy in delivering the required outputs. Lankes (2004) promotes striking a balance between efficiency and effectiveness. Components of information systems outline how technology and resources should be set up to achieve the desired objectives. The term "question components" refers to the recognition, categorization, and application of queries that represent the information requirements of users of the digital reference system. Through some interfaces that connect the user and the expert, answers are then used to communicate knowledge to users (Lankes, 2004). While there has been extensive research on the adoption and usage of digital reference services in academic libraries, there is little evidence to show an improved adoption of digital reference services in these libraries. To motivate the adoption of digital reference services in academic libraries, this chapter discusses the key concepts of digital reference services and how these various technologies have been utilised to complement reference services in academic libraries.

BACKGROUND

The Nature of Digital Reference Services

The traditional position of a reference librarian has evolved in response to these changes to provide services that combine technology. Samuel Green created the idea of reference services at the Worcester Free Public Library in Massachusetts, in the beginning, to aid patrons in their book selection. This had two functions, according to Cassell and Hiremath (2018): first, to expand or improve the library collections, and second, to support the library's continued operation. Reference services have come to be thought of as an organized effort by librarians to assist patrons in making the most of their use of library materials in the years that have followed (Cassell and Hiremath, 2018). However, due to the technological advancements of the internet, the web, and related technologies, several scholars have predicted the end of reference librarians (Mandernack and Fritch, 2001). Due to these difficulties, desk reference services as we know them now are insufficient, necessitating the incorporation of digital technologies.

The way libraries offer information services to their customers and how users choose to access information have both undergone major changes as a result of the Internet and its related technologies, according to Kadir et al. (2015). Consequently, digital reference services have started to appear. Digital reference services are currently viewed by many academic librarians as beneficial and gratifying, despite certain implementation and operation challenges. DRS has been defined in several different ways by authors. Ramos and Abrigo (2011) provided a more condensed explanation of digital reference services, describing this facility as a reference service that is initiated electronically, frequently in real-time, and where customers use computers or internet technologies to communicate with the reference staff without

Figure 1. Elements of a digital referencing facility

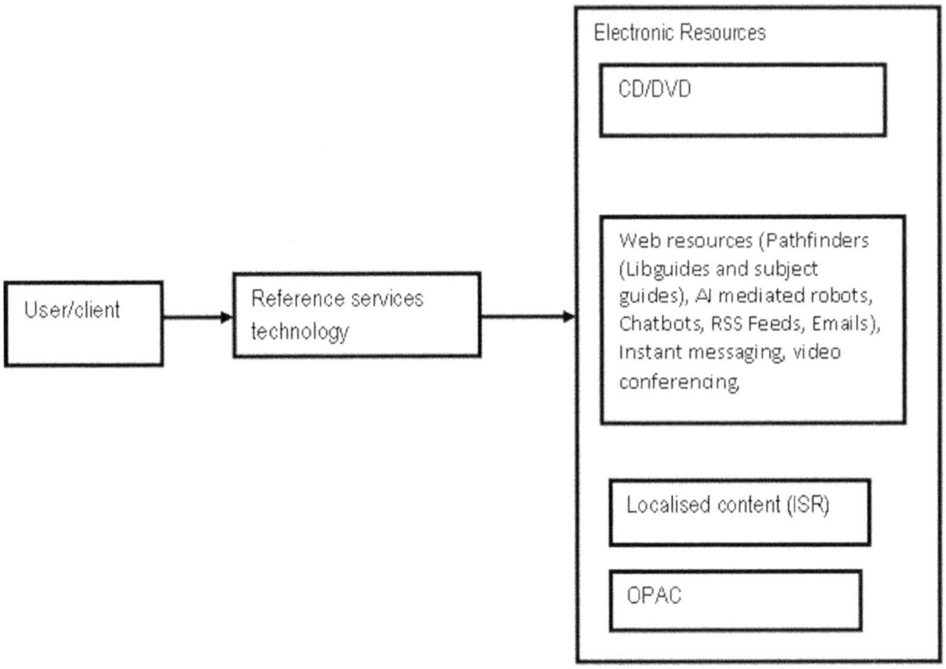

being physically present. The term "human-mediated service over digital networks" has also been used to describe it. To help library patrons with their diverse information needs, digital reference services are provided (Jan, 2018). To assist library information services, reference services that employ computers and the internet are referred to as "virtual reference," "digital reference-reference," "internet information services," and "real-time reference" (Arya and Mishra, 2012). Madu & Husman (2020) define digital reference services as reference services launched electronically, frequently in real-time, when customers use computers and the internet in conjunction with library reference professionals. The emphasis on real-time interaction is the main distinction between this definition and others. However, not all of the digital technologies mentioned in the literature-some of which have been employed for digital reference services-can facilitate online interactivity. To support the primary function of helping users find the information they need, digital reference services encompass two key activities in the library profession. Secondly, they allow librarians to use new digital technologies and have them improve their productivity and performance (Jane, Carter, and Memmott, 1999). According to Singh (2012), the user/client, the information professional, the interface, and the electronic resources are the key elements of digital reference systems in academic libraries, as indicated in Figure 1 below.

Classification of Digital Reference Systems

According to Jan (2018), there are two types of digital reference services: asynchronous virtual reference services (reference through email and the web) and synchronous virtual reference services (chat using instant messaging, video-based reference service, video conferencing). According to several experts, the Internet is the primary impetus behind digital reference services that link consumers to library materials and services. It is also acknowledged as a network of resources and expertise intermediaries available to anyone looking for information online, and these resources are typically employed to assist inexperienced and unskilled users (Oluwabiyi, 2017). It has become challenging for authors to distinguish between digital reference services and virtual reference service services due to the dependency of reference services on the internet. According to Khobragade and Lihitkar (2016), the literature generally divides digital reference services into three categories: asynchronous, synchronous, and collaborative networks. These categories are shown in Figure 2 below.

The user, the interface, electronic resources, and the information professional are common characteristics that define these technologies throughout these three types of DRS.

Asynchronous Reference Services

Both parties to a communication process do not need to be online at the same time for it to be asynchronous. Emails, weblogs (blogs), and RSS feeds are examples of digital tools that facilitate asynchronous communication. Asynchronous collaboration and portfolio learning are made possible by these advancements in teaching and learning, librarianship, and technology (Roy, 2021). A librarian will answer the question after some time has passed in this kind of virtual reference service. In other words, there is a lag time between the user's question and the librarian's response (Sabah, 2018). Kadir, Dollah, and Singh (2015) created the model shown in Figure 3 below for asynchronous reference

The model depicted in Figure 3 above, above states that the Question acquisition is a method of gathering user questions via email, a web form, chat, or other software programs. Through Triagate, this query is forwarded to a digital reference service and a reference or subject expert within the service.

Figure 2. Categorisation of digital reference services

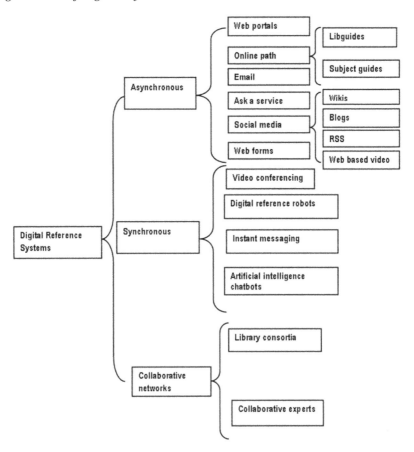

Figure 3. The model for asycnhronous digital referencing

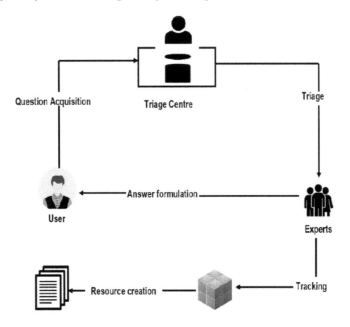

These DRS components screen out questions that are asked repeatedly to spot trends and further identify inquiries that are off-topic. Answer formulation includes elements for producing quality responses in appropriate circumstances, and these are now communicated to users. For collection managers and experts to expand or create collections that better meet users' information needs, tracking is a qualitative and quantitative method of keeping track of repeated questions. Tracking identifies patterns and trends in user information needs and information-seeking behaviours.

Email

Email is one of the most popular digital referencing tools used in academic libraries to offer tailored user assistance services to both on-campus and off-campus customers (Singh, 2012; Age, 2019). This entails the user emailing the reference library with the information they require, and the reference librarian responding through email, phone, or fax as needed. Through the usage of email reference services, librarians can get explanations from users via phone or email. Several studies have shown that academic libraries have employed email for reference services, with certain universities-such as Washington State University-reopening more email questions than other reference services. This was also reported by several Iranian universities, proving the widespread use of email services to serve reference functions in academic libraries. The Frequently Asked Questions (FAQs) are one of the technologies that are frequently used with email. According to Arya and Mishrta (2012), the main benefits of employing email reference services are their widespread availability, lack of intrusion, and lack of need for extra software. In addition, compared to other digital services for reference, most users find it to be convenient, recognizable, and simple to use. Additionally, email services work with PCs, laptops, and mobile devices, making it easier for users and information professionals to use. Age (2019), however, also makes the case that email lacks the emotional indicators found in face-to-face reference service sessions, making it more difficult for the reference librarian to gauge the users' mental states during reference meetings. Email has also come under fire for its lack of immediate reaction and the fact that it necessitates participants in the communication process to be logged in to respond to emails as soon as they are delivered. Email is still regarded by some researchers as the least effective tool for digital reference services, even though it is widely used in reference services. Although often utilized, the email reference models do not offer instant feedback because reference librarians frequently reply after some time.

Web Forms as Reference Services

Users fill out web forms on the library's website or a reference webpage with the information they need, submit the form, and the reference librarians get the request as an email. Search engines, message boards, web contact centres, and web-based user training and feedback are all examples of web-based reference services. According to Coughley (2004), there are several web-based platforms for reference services in academic libraries. One of these services is offered at Kansas State University, where users fill out a form with fields for their name, email address, and phone number as well as their questions. Frequently, these questions receive an email response the same day they are submitted. Glasgow University, a member of the cooperative reference service, was mentioned as another instance where web forms are used as reference tools to assist the information needs of students and staff, with feedback coming in the mail. The Panjab University Library, the Jammu University Library, and the Kashmir University Library did not use FAQ services, although the Delhi University Library did, according to

Singh's (2012) analysis of the use of web forms and FAQs in these libraries. Only Kashmir University Library used bulletin boards, whereas the other libraries did not, according to a study by Sighn (2012) on the use of these services at Panjab University Library, Kashmir University Library, Jammu University Library, and Delhi University Library. Through the web, people can send and read electronic messages that are addressed to a specific individual using bulletin boards. The web search was only used at the Delhi University library for user education and reference reasons, whereas the other four libraries did not employ web contact centres for online reference needs.

Ask a Librarian in Reference Services

With the help of various subject experts, Ask a Librarian is a web-based form service that enables library personnel to receive emails from users with questions. Users of the library can talk live with a librarian or other designated staff member through the free online service "Ask a Librarian" for any quick information and help utilizing it. It is offered by knowledgeable information specialists who can help clients quickly find the solutions to their questions. To deliver this service to its consumers, huge libraries work together with a variety of professionals from various departments or participating libraries. This facility is likewise collaborative, bringing together various subject specialists to answer the information demands of users. It is based on web emails. In academic libraries, this service is frequently utilized for reference services. According to Coughley (2004), this service is offered, for instance, at the University of California (UCLA), where customers can ask topic experts questions online using chat services, in addition to having the option to email their inquiries. Ask a Librarian, Ask an EXPERT, Ask ERIC, Ask a Question, and Ask Me are just a few examples of web-based services in the "Ask a service" category. Reference librarians can respond to users' specific information needs thanks to these services.

Online Pathfinders in Reference Services

Libraries have developed new methods of offering information resources and reference services to users as a result of the introduction of Web 2.0 technology. Subject guides and libguides are recent innovations that aim to instruct users on how to access electronic resources. According to Vileno (2007), a pathfinder is a list of references to the fundamental sources of knowledge on a given subject. Pathfinders are frequently discovered as annotated bibliographies of books, databases, journals, and webpages within a specific topic on the websites of academic libraries (Vileno, 2007). Some authors have suggested that these platforms are more approachable than the actual reference desk since they connect users to a variety of information sources and serve as a credible beginning point for any research project. The pathfinder tool for supporting patron access to electronic materials, Libguides by Springshare's Content Management System, is now very popular. Mwanzu et al. (2022) claim that libguides improve librarians' understanding of their subject resources in addition to making it easier for users to access electronic resources. Although pioneering initiatives were carried out in 2014 at the Aga Khan University in Uganda, there is no evidence from the literature that these technologies have been adopted and implemented in low and middle-income countries (Mwanzu et al., 2022). Since then, however, Sub-Saharan Africa has seen steady progress in the adoption of these technologies, with 18 universities in South Africa and 3 in Kenya implementing libguides, while only 1 university has done so in Ghana, Botswana, Namibia, Uganda, and Tanzania (Mwanzu et al., 2022). By using social media technologies like wikis and blogs to assist librarians in organizing their collections and offering reference services, the effectiveness of libguides has been further increased (Bushhause, 2009; Mafungwa, 2017). Subject guides provide a collection of resources on a specific topic and a broad discipline for a specific course, in contrast to libguides (Courtois, Higgins, and Kapar, 2004). At some universities, such as the Gelman Library at George Washington University, subject guides have been utilized for both reference and instructional purposes.

Synchronous Reference Services

The persons involved in synchronous communication must be online at the same time. Chat rooms, instant messaging, texting, and video conferencing are a few of the technologies accessible in online learning and virtual reference services. Due to its emphasis on building personal connections and the ability to provide quick feedback, synchronous communication in reference services enables in-depth conversation. In synchronous digital reference services, questions are answered right away and information is exchanged in "real-time." This has occasionally been done using software or web-based apps. Singh (2012) discovered that chat, instant messaging, VoIP, Chatbots, and video reference services were used at the Delhi University library. However, the study found that none of the four universities-Panjab University Library, Jammu University Library, or Kashmir University Library-used real-time reference services when comparing how these technologies were used.

Social Media

Software and web-based technologies that enable online interaction, content creation, and sharing have emerged as a result of the growth of the internet. These services can either be synchronous or asynchronous, and these technologies have come to be known as social media. According to Davis (2016), social media is a group of interactive Internet apps that make it easier for users to independently or jointly create, curate, and share user-generated content. Facebook, Friendster, Wikis (like Wikipedia), Linkedin, Instagram, Blogs, and Microblogs (like X, formerly known as Twitter) are a few examples of social media platforms. According to Ramos and Abrigo (2012), numerous institutions in developing nations have embraced chat services like Facebook, Google Hangouts, AOL, Whatsapp, and Yahoo Messenger. Although in some contexts, particularly in developing communities of Africa and Asia, this is still new, social media platforms are now frequently utilized in academic libraries to contact and engage with users. Platforms for social media communication have recently taken the lead in all aspects of human communication. To complement reference services, information workers have started using social media platforms in libraries. Improvements in patron interaction and the promotion of library services through current awareness services (CAS) are two advantages of adopting social media in academic libraries, according to Kabir (2021). Mensah and Onyancha (2021) are two scholars who made the argument that social media has given librarians new chances to interact with people in real time and platforms to enable them to get feedback from their users. Libraries in Belgium, South Africa, and Botswana are a few that have utilized social media for reference needs (Williams, 2018). Twitter (now X) and recently WhatsApp have been the most popular social media platforms, while there is still discussion about the ethical and security concerns related to its use for business and educational purposes in academic institutions generally. For instance, in South Africa, academic libraries use Facebook, Twitter, Instagram, YouTube, WhatsApp, blogs, RSS, and Dropbox, according to Rabatsetsa, Maluleka, and Onyancha (2021). Facebook, Twitter, blogs, and YouTube were the most popular and were mostly utilized for marketing and communication. These findings appeared to corroborate Collins and Quan-Haase's (2014) findings that Facebook and

Twitter are the most popular social media sites among academic libraries, whereas Ezuman's (2013) findings that Facebook, Twitter, MySpace, and LinkedIn are the most popular sites in the USA. Facebook and Twitter (now known as X) were two of the most popular social media sites used by US libraries (Mahmood and Richardson, 2011). In their study on the use of social media in South African academic libraries, Rabatsatse et al. (2021) found that 96% of participating academic libraries used social media for marketing, 92% for sharing library news, 81% for bettering library services, 77% for introducing new library materials, 63% for establishing relationships with internal and external stakeholders, 53% for managing the library brand, and 25% for connecting with users. The study by Rabatsatse et al. (2021) didn't specifically address the functions that each tool performed in reference services, instead appearing to concentrate on the overall function of social media in academic libraries. According to Collins and Quan-Haase (2014), two-thirds of academic libraries in Canada use social media, compared to 71% of academic libraries in Asia, North America, and Europe (Chu and Du, 2012). These libraries have used social media mostly for marketing and communication objectives (Owusu-Ansah et al. 2015; Williams, 2018). According to Asuquo et al. (2023), Facebook, WhatsApp, Telegram, and Twitter were the most popular social media platforms in Nigerian libraries. These platforms were utilized for reference services, posting library events, showcasing new arrivals, and issuing overdue notices. Additionally, these social media platforms have been utilized to supply services to clients, and these services have developed into demand-driven business models. Although some academic libraries in South Africa have acknowledged the importance of social media, particularly in improving reference services and delivering library resources (Penzhorn, 2009), some academic libraries have not implemented social media in their services because students have not perceived the benefits of adopting social media in accessing library services (Alkarausi et al., 2015).

Video and VoIP Conferencing in Reference Services

As the internet has grown, VoIP, which enables the transmission of voice over the internet, has emerged. Due to the integration of speech and data, the technology has gained popularity even in large organizations due to its low cost (Kabir, 2021). In academic libraries that offer reference services, several VoIP tools are quickly expanding in use, especially in industrialized nations. These tools include Skype, Google Meetings, and Google Hangouts, a Google platform that supports SMS, video chat, and instant messaging (Booth, 2008; Abubakar, 2021). The shortcomings of text-based reference services are intended to be addressed by video conferencing. The interface includes a video window on both the reference librarians' and library users' interfaces, allowing for real-time discussion with participants being able to see one another (Singh, 2004). The program is web-based, and Google Meeting is one of the available platforms. Due to their accessibility and affordability, internet audio and video communication has seen a significant increase in supporting reference services, which has led to more users switching to web calling as their main reference service tool in academic libraries (Booth, 2008). This led to innovations like "Skype a librarian" (Booth, 2008), a video kiosk service created at Ohio University.

Collaborative Networks

It is widely accepted that no expert could know everything and that no library could ever hope to satisfy every user's informational needs. Collaboration between experts and libraries is required to meet the information needs of customers because the expertise, information sources, and services that are currently available are never sufficient to meet the needs of all users. Online expert services are given by these cooperative reference projects, which may be provided for a price or even for free (Ranasinghe, 2012). In collaborative networks, teams of specialists and librarians use online platforms to provide reference services to all users, with users selecting the best option from a variety of options offered. Collaboration is at the core of DRS, according to Elisha (2006), because it mandates that libraries within local groups join international consortiums for better collaboration across many sectors of knowledge. AIIExperts, founded in the USA in 1998, is one of the collaborative services for assisting library reference services that have been developed. According to Coughley (2004), this platform hires specialists from all around the world, and consumers choose them based on their profiles to handle their information needs. Emails are used for communication. Several library consortiums, according to Jabir (2008), give their member libraries the chance to share reference queries over the Internet and other technologies through cooperative networking. For instance, the Collaborative Reference Service (CDRS), run by the Library of Congress, is a global network of libraries, consortiums, and museums that employs help-desk technologies to direct queries to the proper organizations. (Jabir 2008) Based on member profiles. Wikis, which are public web pages that let users edit the material, have proved useful in academic libraries for letting subject specialists and reference librarians cooperate and produce content that is shared among users. In addition to wikis, blogs have also been used to produce subject guides that, via the joint efforts of specialists, point users to the library's online resources.

Artificial Intelligence and Reference Services

Computer science's artificial intelligence subfield aims to create tools and software programs that can do tasks with a level of human intellect. Compared to other academic and memory institutions, libraries have always been at the forefront of recognizing, absorbing, and implementing technology into their operations. To get consumers back to use their services, some have even proposed adopting artificial conversational entities for uses like reference interviews. Digital reference robots and chatbots are the two most popular AI-based reference solutions.

Digital Reference Robots

Automated robotics have emerged as a result of the Fourth Industrial Revolution (4IR), which is being pushed by AI, and have been labelled as a disruptive technology in the fields of education and librarianship. A robot is generally understood to be a mechanical device that follows orders from humans to automate operations. These technologies are components of artificial intelligence (AI), and information science and librarianship have been using them increasingly. While bringing a wide range of services, particularly in library management and reference services, these robots have been integrated into academic libraries in a variety of ways depending on the environment. While the robots can be used in academic libraries for general tasks like shelving, they have also been used for other activities like browsing the collections, facilitating participation in events like meetings, workshops, classes, and outreach activities, and interacting with users to facilitate users' access to the library collections. This has freed up library staff to work on other important information services in the library (Owalabi et al., 2022; Blake, 2017; Tella and Ogbanna, 2023). Robots have also been used in academic libraries to promote information literacy, enhance the user experience when accessing the library's resources and services (Woods and Evans, 2018), increase library services' accessibility (Cotera, 2018), transport library materials (Liau,

2019), and locate the collections (Tella, 2020). In addition to this, robots have made it easier for libraries and experts to work together to provide users with positive user experiences, which has enabled collaboration and networked reference services. To give clients of academic libraries a more interesting and immersive experience, the usefulness of these technologies has also been integrated with other digital-based technologies. Voice recognition, language processors, and touch displays are examples of assistive technology that have evolved as a result of advancements in robotics for library services.

Chat services and ChatGPT as a Reference Tool

Conversational software, or chatbots as they are commonly known, has long been regarded as having the ability to revolutionize institutions that focus on people. The term "chat reference" describes a service where the main form of communication between the user and the reference librarians is text communication that takes place in real time. The foundation of chat reference systems is instant messaging. To keep up with the trend and improve customer service, several libraries and information resource centres have included chatbots in their technological infrastructure (Bagchi, 2020). The development of such systems was driven, among other things, by the need for higher income, real-time intelligent patron interaction, and assistance. The general qualities expected of chatbots, such as intent identification, entity extraction, dialogue automation and management, anthropomorphism, and feedback-based correction, align with the motivating qualities. A chatbot's user interface-typically a website or messaging service-can accept text input and forward it to a layer of natural language processing (NLP) that attempts to decipher sentences into their constituent parts and intended purposes. A chatbot is more of a user interface; it is often a website or messaging service that can accept text input and send it to an NLP layer, which tries to break words down into entities and question intents (Ali, 2019). Following the identification of the request's intent, a response is produced utilizing the pertinent knowledge base and, occasionally, an external Web service for more complicated requests.

Chatbots are software programs that have enabled reference chat services in academic libraries. ChatGPT is an example of a chatbot, which is an artificial intelligence program with machine learning capabilities like natural language processing. On many different platforms, chatbots are simply made and may be easily targeted to a variety of users. In addition to assisting users with book searches on a library's website, chatbots can alert users when a book is approaching its due date, point users in the direction of useful library resources, respond to simple information inquiries, and redirect users to librarians for assistance with more difficult reference queries. According to the literature, academic libraries are increasingly using chat services (Kabir, 2021; Mawhinney, 2020), but this trend is only apparent in academic libraries in developing nations. For instance, according to Anna and Srirahayu (2020), only 4% of academic libraries in universities use instant messaging for library services, and this number may be much lower in African universities due to funding and infrastructure issues. According to a survey by Lochore (2004), 29% of academic libraries with US locations used chat services and provided in-person interaction between patrons and library workers. However, there is still disagreement regarding which chat services can be used as reference services (Kabir, 2021).

Although some writers have questioned the moral propriety of using this technology in educational settings, ChatGPT as an AI tool for reference and teaching and learning has gained popularity in teaching and learning situations. Overall, ChatGPT integration with conventional libraries has the potential to significantly improve user experience, boost productivity, and boost the overall efficacy of library services. ChatGPT has the potential to revolutionize the way conventional libraries give information and support to their users by utilizing the capabilities of AI and natural language processing (Verma, 2023). The user experience in a conventional library can be significantly improved by ChatGPT's capacity to comprehend and reply to requests and questions in natural language. Users can save time and become more productive by receiving prompt responses to simple enquiries and being referred to sources of more in-depth knowledge when necessary (Verma, 2023). In addition to answering general inquiries about library policy, services, and resources, ChatGPT can help library visitors with their reference needs. This can allow library workers to concentrate on more difficult jobs and give customers quicker, more effective service (Verma, 2023). A user's search history and reading preferences can be examined using ChatGPT to generate individualized suggestions for books, articles, and other resources. Users may find fresh and pertinent information as a result, stimulating additional research into the library's holdings (Verma, 2023). However, modern technology offers prospects for real-time assistance, personalized service, the creation of extensive knowledgebases, multilingual support, and customer analytics in library reference services (Saeidnia, 2023). When using a chat virtual reference service, a professional librarian must be available and ready to answer questions. This necessitates dependable software, enough bandwidth, and dependable infrastructure. Users may choose to use only chat, only video, or even both for some networked services. Facebook and Google Meet are a couple of the services that enable this.

Challenges

Libraries are essential for spreading knowledge to promote research, instruction, and learning in many African nations. There have been calls for accurate measures of knowledge and accuracy of feedback received from digital reference services since research has historically had difficulty establishing standards for evaluating the quality of reference services. While researching these issues, writers frequently generalize them, yet the unique properties of these technologies make it impossible to generalize the difficulties experienced by users, reference librarians, and institutions in their attempts to provide reference services. However, there have been many obstacles that librarians have had to overcome to provide reference services. For instance, a study conducted in 2011 by Sekyere among some African nations revealed that some academic libraries that used web-based reference services had hanging links or blank web pages, and some of these libraries did not offer advanced reference services, with the majority relying solely on telephone and SMS-based services. It is also challenging for some academic libraries to establish internet-based reference services since these libraries lack working websites.

Face-to-face reference services predominated among the academic libraries in Nigeria that Adesina et al. (2022) investigated, while chat reference and web-based services were less frequently used. This indicates that Nigeria is one of the African nations that is still lagging in the use of digital technologies for reference in academic libraries. Adesina et al.'s list of obstacles from 2022 included:

i)   Reference services are underfunded,
ii) the library's reference policies are out of date,
iii) there is an epileptic power supply that cannot support electronic referencing,
iv) there is a lack of management support,
v)   reference librarians lack personal knowledge and skills,
vi) staff members are unwilling to change and update their knowledge and skills,
vii) there is poor internet access, and
viii) it is difficult to meet the individualized information needs of customers.

Such results are a confirmation of earlier findings by Madu & Husman (2020), who had also reported that academic libraries in Nigeria had difficulty implementing digital reference services due to a lack of internet connectivity. Olabude (2017) also noted that this was a problem that was shared by all Sub-Saharan African nations. In addition to the issue of insufficient internet access, academic libraries and researchers continue to be concerned about the level of digital competence among reference librarians and users. Digital reference librarians must have high digital literacy abilities to exploit current technology and create innovations that cater to users' information-seeking behaviours, claim Madu & Husman (2020). Understanding the demands and information-seeking behaviours of the users presents another problem for academic libraries providing digital reference services. Today's audiences in 21st-century digital environments are autonomous researchers and learners who seek information tailored to their requirements from librarians who must serve the demands of thousands of these various users. In their investigation into the use of digital reference services in the Nigerian state of Benue, Tofi, Agada, and Okafor (2020) found that academic libraries face several obstacles when using these services, including a lack of funding for purchasing and subscribing to electronic resources, poor accessibility and unstable electricity, a lack of technical expertise, a lack of preservation policies, and high maintenance costs.

Igwebuike and Onoh (2022) identified the following as the typical issues preventing private universities in Southeast Nigeria from adopting digital reference services:

i) Irregular reference librarians,
ii) inadequate attitudes toward digital reference services,
iii) inadequate professional skills among reference librarians,
iv) inadequate internet connectivity,
v) inadequate financial support for digital reference services, and
vi) inadequate user knowledge of how to use digital reference services are just a few of the problems.

Recommendations

There is a limited acceptance of contemporary digital technologies for reference purposes, even though the literature admits that digital reference services play a significant role in promoting collection creation and reference services. To solve these issues, numerous recommendations are made. Therefore, this chapter suggests the following tactics to overcome the issues raised above:

i) Investing in adequate information and telecommunications infrastructure;
ii) Training and retraining of librarians in the use of digital reference services;
iii) Provision of funds to support digital reference services;
iv) Increasing bandwidth;
v) Orienating users on digital reference services;
vi) Provision of a steady power supply;
vii) Developing supportive policies on digital reference systems in academic libraries;
viii) Educating senior managers of institutions on the relevance of digital reference services; and,
ix) Lobbying for management support.

Recommendations for Further Research

The chapter suggests additional investigation into the creation of AI-based solutions for digital reference needs. Few tests for AI-based reference services have been conducted, especially in poor countries, and this field has not received much attention. Additionally, it is important to promote research on how users and librarians see digital reference services. Decision-making at all levels of senior management will be aided by this.

REFERENCES

Abubakar, M. K. (2021). Implementation and Use of Virtual Reference Services in Academic Libraries during and post. *Library Philosophy and Practice*.

Adayi, I. O., Neboh, R. I., & Oluchi, E. G. (2023). *Users' assessment of digital reference service delivery in private university libraries in Enugu State. Library Philosophy and Practice (e-journal)*.

Adesina, E. R., Ogunniyi, S. O., & Ajakaye, J. E. (2022). Challenges and Prospects of Reference Services in Federal University Libraries in South-West, Nigeria. *Library Philosophy and Practice (e-journal)*, *7155*. https://digitalcommons.unl.edu/libphilprac/7155

Age, A. (2019). Language style matching as a measure of librarian/patron engagement in email reference transactions. *Journal of Academic Librarianship*, *45*(6), 102069. doi:10.1016/j.acalib.2019.102069

Al-Hatmi, A. H. Z., Ibri, O & Nor, N. S. (2022). Investigating students' use of digital reference services in Oman's Academic libraries. *Electronic Interdisciplinary Miscellaneous Journal*, *45*, 1–36.

Ali, M. S. (2019). Bots in libraries: They're coming for your jobs (or is it?). In ALIA Information Online 2019, ALIA Information Online 2019. Research Collection Library.

AlKarousi, R. S., Jabr, N. H., & Harrassi, N. (2015). Adoption of Web 2.0 applications in Omani academic libraries. *Proceedings of the SLA–AGC 21st Annual Conference*.

Arya, H. B., & Mishra, J. K. (2012). Virtual reference services: Tools and techniques. *Journal of Library and Information Science*, *2*(1).

Bagchi, M. (2020). Conceptualising a Library Chatbot using Open Source Conversational Artificial Intelligence. *DESIDOC Journal of Library and Information Technology*, *40*(6), 329–333. doi:10.14429/djlit.40.06.15611

Blake, R. (2017). Telepresence robots: An innovative approach to library service. *Journal of Library Administration*, *57*(8), 832–840.

Booth, C. (2008). Developing Skype-based reference services. *Internet Reference Services Quarterly*, *13*(2-3), 147–165. doi:10.1080/10875300802103684

Bullard, K. A. (2003). *Virtual reference service evaluation: an application of unobtrusive research methods and the virtual reference desk's facets of quality for digital reference service [Master's paper]*. University of North Carolina at Chapel Hill.

Cassell, K. A., & Hiremath, U. (2018). *Reference and information services: An introduction* (4th ed.). Neal Schuman.

Chu, S. K. W., & Du, H. S. (2012). Social networking tools for academic libraries. *Journal of Librarianship and Information Science, 45*(1), 64–75. doi:10.1177/0961000611434361

Cloughley, K. (2004). Digital reference services: How do library-based services compare with expert services? *Library Review, 53*(1), 17–23. doi:10.1108/00242530410514757

Collins, G., & Quan-Haase, A. (2014). Are social media ubiquitous in academic libraries? A longitudinal study of adoption and usage patterns. *Journal of Web Librarianship, 8*(1), 48–68. doi:10.1080/193229 09.2014.873663

Cotera, M. (2018). We *embrace digital innovation: IE University Library reinventing higher education.* 4th Lebanese Library Association Conference Innovative Libraries: Paths to the future, in collaboration with IFLA Asia Oceania Section, Lebanon.

Davis, J. L. (2016). Social media. In G. Mazzoleni (Ed.), *The International Encyclopedia of Political Communication, First Editition.* John Wiley & Sons. doi:10.1002/9781118541555.wbiepc004

Dollah, W. A. K. W. (2006). *Digital reference services in selected public academic libraries.* Academic Press.

Elisha, M. J. (2016). The application of information and communication technology (ICT) in Nigerian academic libraries prospects and problems. *The Information Manager, 6*(1 & 2), 2006.

Igwebuike, E., & Onoh, E. I. (2022). Availability and Use of Digital Reference Service Tools for Effective Service Delivery by Librarians in Private Universities Libraries in South-East Nigeria. *Library Philosophy and Practice (e-journal). 7105.* https://digitalcommons.unl.edu/libphilprac/7105

Igwebuike, E. & Onoh, E. I(2022). Availability and Use of Digital Reference Service Tools for Effective Internet Research. *Electronic Networking Applications and Policy, 5*(1), 56-63.

Jabir, I. I. N. (2008). Virtual (Electronic) reference services in academic libraries. *J. Of College Of Education for Women, 19*(2).

Jan, S. (2018). Digital reference services in the information and communication technology (ICT) based environment: A study. *Library Philosophy and Practice (e-journal).*

Jane, J., Carter, D., & Memmott, P. (1999). Digital reference services in academic libraries. *Reference and User Services Quarterly, 39*(2), 145–150.

Kabir, A. M. (2021). Implementation and Use of Virtual Reference Services in Academic Libraries during and post COVID-19 Pandemic: A Necessity for Developing Countries). *Library Philosophy and Practice (e-journal), 4951.*

Kadir, W. A., Dollah, W., & Singh, D. (2015). *Digital reference services in academic libraries.* The University of Malaya Press.

Khan, A., Masrek, M. N., Mahmood, K., & Qutab, S. (2017). Factors influencing the adoption of digital reference services among the university librarians in Pakistan. *The Electronic Library*, *35*(6), 1225–1246. doi:10.1108/EL-05-2016-0112

Khobragade, A. D., & Lihitkar, S. R. (2016). Evaluation of virtual reference services provided by IIT libraries: A survey. *DESIDOC Journal of Library and Information Technology*, *36*(1), 23–28. doi:10.14429/djlit.36.1.9150

Khoo, C., Singh, D., & Chaudhry, A. S. (2006). Malaysia: A case study. In C. Khoo, D. Singh & A.S. Chaudhry (Eds.), *Proceedings of the Asia-Pacific Conference on Library & Information Education & Practice 2006 (A-LIEP 2006), Singapore, 3-6 April 2006* (pp. 122-135). Singapore: School of Communication & Information, Nanyang Technological University.

Lachore, S. (2004). How good are the free digital reference services: A comparison between library-based and expert services. *Library Review*, *53*(1), 24–29. doi:10.1108/00242530410514766

Lankes, R. D. (1995). *AskERIC and the virtual library: lessons from emerging and digital libraries*. Academic Press.

Lankes, R. D. (2004). The digital reference agenda. Syracuse University. The USA. *Journal of the American Society for Information Science and Technology*, *55*(4), 301–311. doi:10.1002/asi.10374

Liau, C. (2019). *Transforming library operation with robotics*. Paper Presented at IFLA WLIC 2019.

Madu, A., & Husman, H. (2020). Challenges of virtual reference services implementation by Nigerian academic libraries in the 21st century in Nigeria. *Journal of Economic Development*, *1*(1), 144–155.

Mahmood, K., & Richardson, J. V. Jr. (2011). Adoption of Web 2.0 in US academic libraries: A survey of ARL libraries. *Program: Electronic Library and Information Systems*, *45*(4), 365–375. doi:10.1108/00330331111182085

Mandernack, S & Fritch, J. W. (2001). *The emerging reference paradigm: A vision of reference services in complex information management*. Academic Press.

Maxwell, N. K. (2002). Establishing and maintaining a live online reference service. *Library Technology Reports*, *38*(4), 1–78.

Mensah, M., & Onyancha, M. O. (2021). A social media strategy for academic libraries. *Journal of Academic Librarianship*, *47*(6), 47. doi:10.1016/j.acalib.2021.102462

Mwanzu, A., Nakaziba, S., Karungi, J., Ayebazibwe, E., & Gatiti, P. (2022). Adoption of LibGuides as a reference service in academic libraries: Insights from Aga Khan University, Uganda. *Journal of Academic Librarianship*, *48*, 102560. doi:10.1016/j.acalib.2022.102560

Olabude, F. O. (2007). Utilization of Internet sources for Research by Information Professionals in Sub-Saharan Africa. *African Journal of Library Archives and Information Science*, *17*(1), 53–54.

Oluwabiyi, M. O. (2017). Digital reference services: an overview. *Journal of Information and Knowledge Management, 8*(1).

Owalabi, K. A., Yemi-Peters, O. E., Oyetola, S. O., & Oladokun, B. D. (2022). Readiness of academic libraries towards the use of academic librarians towards the use of robotic technologies in Nigerian University Libraries. *Library Management*. Advance online publication. doi:10.1108/LM-11-2021-0104

Owusu-Ansah, C. M., Gontshi, V., & Mutibwa, L. (2015). Applications of social media and Web 2.0 for research support in selected African academic institutions. *Journal of Balkan Libraries Union*, *3*(1), 30–39.

Penzhorn, C. (2009). Quality through improved service: the implementation of social networking tools in an academic library. *Proceedings of the 2009 IATUL Conference.*

Rabatsetsa, B., Maluleka, J.R. & Onyancha, O. B. (2021). Adoption and use of social media in academic libraries in South Africa. *SA Jnl Libs & Info Sci 2021, 87*(1).

Ramos, M. S., & Abrigo, C. M. (2012). Reference 2.0 in action: An evaluation of the digital reference services in selected Philippine academic libraries. *Library Hi Tech News*, *1*(1), 8–20. doi:10.1108/07419051211223426

Ranasinghe, W.M.T.D. (2012). *New Trends of Library Reference Services.* Professor Jayasiri Linkage Felicitation.

Roy, P. (2021). Asynchronous and Synchronous: A Communication Process in Smart Classroom. *Ideal Research Review*, *65*(1).

Sabah, J. (2018). Digital Reference Services in the Information Communication Technology (ICT) based Environment: A Study. *Library Philosophy and Practice (e-journal),* 1827. https://digitalcommons.unl.edu/libphilprac/1827

Saeidnia, H. (2023). *Using ChatGPT as Digital/ Smart Reference Robot: How may ChatGPT Impact Digital Reference Services?* Advance online publication. doi:10.2139srn.4441874

Sekyere, K. (2011). Virtual Reference Service in Academic Libraries in West Africa. *Journal of Library & Information Services in Distance Learning*, *5*(1-2), 3-9. . doi:10.1080/1533290X.2011.548233

Service Delivery by Librarians in Private Universities Libraries in South-East Nigeria. (n.d.). *Library Philosophy and Practice (e-journal).* 7105. https://digitalcommons.unl.edu/libphilprac/7105

Singh, D. (2004). *Reference services in the digital age.* Paper presented at the Conference on Library Management in the 21st Century at the Ateneo de Manila University, Philippines.

Singh, N. (2012). Digital reference service in university libraries: A case study of the Northern India. *International Journal of Library and Information Studies*, *2*(4).

Sutton, S. A. (1998). Gateway to Educational Material (GEM): Metadata for networked information discovery and retrieval. *Computer Networks and ISDN Systems*, *30*(1-7), 691–693. doi:10.1016/S0169-7552(98)00086-5

Tella, A. (2020). Robots are coming to the libraries: Are librarians ready to accommodate them? *Library Hi Tech News*, *37*(8), 13–17. doi:10.1108/LHTN-05-2020-0047

Tella, A., & Ajani, Y. A. (2022). Robots and public libraries. *Library Hi Tech News*, *7*(7), 15–18. doi:10.1108/LHTN-05-2022-0072

Tella, A., & Ogbonna, P. (2023). Telepresence robots in libraries: Applications and challenges. *Library Hi Tech News*. Advance online publication. doi:10.1108/LHTN-03-2023-0035

Tofi, S. T., Agada, E. O., & Okafor, C. J. (2020). Utilization of Digital Reference Resources and Services by Postgraduate Students in University Libraries in Benue State, Nigeria. *International Journal of Research and Innovation in Social Science*, *IV*(VI).

Uzoigwe, C. U., & Eze, J. U. (2018). The Perceived Benefits of Electronic/Digital Reference Services In Nigerian University Libraries: A survey. *International Journal of Knowledge Content Development & Technology*, *8*(2), 49–65.

Verma, M. (2023). Novel Study on AI-Based Chatbot (ChatGPT) Impacts on the Traditional Library Management. *International Journal of Trend in Scientific Research and Development*, *7*(1).

Vileno, L. (2007). From Paper to Electronic, the Evolution of Pathfinders: A Review of the Literature. *RSR. Reference Services Review*, *35*(3), 434–451. doi:10.1108/00907320710774300

Williams, M. L. (2018). The adoption of web 2.0 technologies in academic libraries: A comprehensive explanation. *Journal of Librarianship and Information Science*.

Woods, D. A., & Evans, D. J. (2018). Librarians' perceptions of artificial intelligence and its potential impact on the profession. *Computers in Libraries*, *38*(1), 26–30.

Yang, S. Q., & Dalal, H. A. (2015). Delivering Virtual Reference Services on the Web: An Investigation into the Current Practice by Academic Libraries. *Journal of Academic Librarianship*, *41*(1), 68–86. doi:10.1016/j.acalib.2014.10.003

KEY TERMS AND DEFINITIONS

Academic Libraries: Libraries housed in educational institutions for the purposes of supporting research and teaching and learning.

Artificial Intelliegence: Technologies that simulate human intelligence and behaviour in solving problems.

Asynchronous Reference System: A Digital reference service that operates in a non-realtime environment.

Digital Reference Robots: Artifcial intelligence-based robots for supporting reference services in libararies.

Digital Reference Services: Information and comminucation technology-based services for assisting users locate and retrieve relevant information in a libaray.

Reference System: A facility for assisting users to locate and retrieve relevant information in a library.

Synchronous Reference System: A realtime references system in a a library.

Virtual Reference Services: Library reference services that are offered remotely.

Chapter 2

Applications of Gene Expression Programming for Estimating CFRP Wrapping Effects on the Bond Strength After Elevated Temperature Exposure

Hamid Farrokh Ghatte

(iD) https://orcid.org/0000-0003-3237-0279

Antalya Bilim University, Antalya, Turkey & Department of Civil Engineering, Technical and Vocational University, Tehran, Iran

ABSTRACT

The study reports on the proposed gene expression programming (GEP) to predict the ability of CFRP wrapping to enhance the post-heated bond strength between steel rebar and concrete. For this purpose, the results of 80 pullout specimens (150×150×250 mm) were selected in two categories of compressive strength of concrete: C30 and C40. In the experiments, a 20 mm rebar was placed in the corner of each specimen with a 25- or 35-mm clear cover and 200 mm of bond length. The specimens were subjected to different levels of heat before using CFRP jackets. The exposure to heat reduced the concrete-rebar bond strength; however, confinement with CFRP jackets significantly improved the bond strength between steel rebar and concrete. The estimated bond strength could be predicted by the accuracy and high prediction ability of the proposed model. Based on the findings, machine learning can bring significant improvements and benefits to the civil engineering industry in terms of the estimation of the mechanical properties of the materials in various conditions.

INTRODUCTION

Machine learning brings a series of applications to the field of civil engineering. Its ability to process large volumes of data, identify patterns, and make predictions and estimations based on that data has

DOI: 10.4018/979-8-3693-2841-5.ch002

proven valuable in various aspects of civil engineering. Artificial neural networks (ANN), support vector machines (SVM), decision trees (DT), adaptive boost algorithms (ABA), optimization methods, and adaptive neuro-fuzzy interference (ANFIS) are just a few of the machine learning techniques that have been employed in the civil engineering field (Siddique et al. 2011; Uysal and Tanyildizi 2012; Vakhshouri and Nejadi 2015; Asteris and Kolovos 2019; Han et al. 2019, Javed et al., 2020; Shahmansouri et al. 2019, 2021 and 2022, Farrokh Ghatte, 2021 and Gholizadeh et al. 2022). With 210 data samples, Doa et al. 2019 employed machine learning techniques including ANN and ANFIS to estimate the compressive strength of geopolymer concrete at 28 days. In contrast, the ANFIS approach outbreaks with a determination coefficient represent accurate predictions.

THE PURPOSE OF THE CHAPTER

In civil engineering, especially in reinforced concrete structures, establishing a connection between temperature and residual bond strength is one of the main factors in the failure mechanisms of elements particularly during seismic actions. The findings in the literature clearly represent that the binding strength dramatically reduces as the temperature rises. The key factors that have affected the results are the features of the materials in terms of concrete and steel rebar, mainly; the diameter and embedding length of the rebar and the cover of the concrete. The pull-out failure mode overtook the splitting failure as the confinement level increased. Therefore, it is important to switch the mode of failure to pull-out mode in concrete members where splitting failure is anticipated and to improve ductility performance by adding external jackets. Steel plate wrapping and fiber-reinforced polymer FRP sheets have all been employed as exterior jacketing in earlier research to strengthen the bond between rebar and concrete. In light of the above-mentioned factors, the study aims to have an improvement in the estimation of the bond strength between reinforcements and concrete in different conditions by employing Gene Expression Programming (GEP). For this purpose, the results of eighty pull-out specimens ($150\times150\times250\ mm$) were selected in two categories of compressive strength of concrete; C30 and C40 with different covers as well as temperatures and compared with carbon fiber-reinforcement polymer CFRP jacketed specimens. The experimental results demonstrated that the CFRP retrofitted method could able to improve the bond strength significantly. Although the elevated temperature could reduce the concrete-rebar bond strength, employing CFRP jackets dramatically increased the bond strength between concrete and reinforcements. The estimated bond strength by employing Genetic engineering programming (GEP) could be predicted by the accuracy and high prediction ability of the proposed model. Based on the findings, machine learning can bring significant improvements and benefits to the civil engineering industry in terms of the estimation of the mechanical properties of the materials in various conditions.

BACKGROUND

Gene Expression Programming (GEP) is, like genetic algorithms (GAs) and genetic programming (GP), a genetic algorithm that belongs to the family of algorithms. A special field of evolutionary computation that aims at building programs automatically to solve problems independently of their domain, like computer problems and mathematical models. GEP was initially developed by Candida Ferreira in 2001. During the last decades, GEP was employed in different research fields like the civil engineering industry and applications and outputs proposed in the literature. The most significant difference between GEP and GP is that GEP adopts a linear fixed-length representation of computer programs, which can later be translated into an expression tree. In the case of the difference between genetic algorithms (Gas) and GP: both systems use only one kind of entity which functions both as genome and body (phenomena). These kinds of systems are condemned to have one of two limitations: if they are easy to manipulate genetically, they lose in functional complexity (the case of GAs); if they exhibit a certain amount of functional complexity, they are extremely difficult to reproduce with modification (the case of GP). GEP was also utilized by (Nour and Guneyisi 2019) by using 97 test datasets to predict the concrete compressive strength of recycled aggregate. They came to the conclusion that GEP offers an accurate forecast of (RACFSTC) with an empirical relationship. A coefficient of determination (R2) for training and testing, respectively, is 0.995 and 0.996, the scientists found, indicating accurate model behavior. By using an ANN technique, (Bingol et al. 2013) estimate the compressive strength of light materials exposed to high temperatures. The authors came to the conclusion that ANN is an advanced prediction strategy, but the model accurately predicts the strength. Researchers also employed ANN and other machine-learning approaches to forecast the attributes of high-performance concretes and recycled aggregate concrete (Chou et al. 2014; Azim et al. 2020 Iqbal et al. 2020). Pala et al. 2007 looked at the long-term effects of substituting silica and fly ash on the performance of cured concrete. The concrete mixtures used in their trials included both the lowest and highest fly ash concentrations, as well as mixtures with and without minor additions of silica fume. Based on the findings, ANNs have a great deal of potential as a method for studying how secondary raw materials affect the compressive strength of concrete. With 234 data samples, Iqbal et al. employed GEP to develop a machine-learning strategy for predicting the presence of green concrete. According to the authors' findings, gene programming provides unwavering prediction accuracy when coupled with an empirical relationship. Using several machine learning techniques, Javed et al. conducted an experimental program to predict the intensity of sugarcane bagasse ash. Using the GEP technique, the scientists found a significant link between input and output. Furthermore, Azim et al. also noticed a similar pattern. The authors predicted reinforced concrete (RC) structures using GEP with a high degree of accuracy. GEP is better than currently used techniques like feature selection techniques.

On the other hand, a large portion of the existing buildings suffers from design and application-related problems that create vulnerability against seismic actions. The structural systems in the past were designed only based on gravity loads, or they may have been designed based on outdated seismic design codes due to insufficient knowledge at the time. In addition, certain buildings violate the design codes applicable during their construction periods due to malpractice in the construction process. As a result, undesired failure mechanisms that are mainly caused by inadequate strength, stiffness, and ductility of structural components are frequently observed during destructive earthquakes (Tapan et al. 2013, Ghatte 2020, Gurbuz et al. 2022 and Adibi et al. 2023). As also indicated by Gurbuz et al. (2022), seismic damages may become severe in substandard RC columns, especially those with high cross-section aspect ratios(h/b, cross-section height to width ratio), as the confinement reinforcement efficiency decreases with an increase in the cross-section aspect ratio. Various confined-concrete models are available in the literature for internal steel or external fiber-reinforced polymer (FRP) confinement consider this reduction in confinement efficiency while obtaining the axial stress-strain relationship of confined concrete under uniaxial compression (Kent and Park 1971; Mander et al. 1988; Samaan et al. 1998; Saatcioglu and Razvi 2002). The application of fiber-reinforced polymer (FRP) composites as an external confinement method has become a favorable substitute for conventional retrofitting techniques, such as RC and steel jacketing, for enhancing the strength and ductility characteristics of substandard RC elements, especially columns. The increasing number of practical applications and the development of codes and guidelines dedicated to retrofit design (such as ACI-440.2R-17 andTBSC-2018) demonstrate the growing interest in the use of fiber-reinforced polymer (FRP) composite materials for retrofitting applications. These documents provide FRP retrofitting techniques for the enhancement of RC members by ensuring easy and fast installation, remarkable strength, and ductility increase with almost no variation in member dimensions, mass, and stiffness (and consequently seismic demand). In the case of the literature related to FRP-confined, RC members are extensive, but most of the studies focus on the behavior under axial loads as well as rely on tests conducted on vertical and transverse reinforcements. During the early stages of FRP-related research, multiple studies focused on the stress-strain relationship of FRP jacketed concrete subjected to axial loading (Toutanji 1999; Xiao and Wu 2000; Toutanji and Deng 2001). Karabinis et al. (2008) exhibited a 3D finite element analysis approach for FRP-confined substandard RC columns. Jiang and Teng (2007) represented an updated stress-strain model for FRP-confined rectangular column cross-sections for analysis purposes. In a review study by (Ozbakkaloglu et al. 2013), a total of 88 stress-strain relationship models for FRP-confined circular concrete sections proposed until the year 2011 were summarized. Furthermore, Ozbakkaloglu and Lim (2013) proposed a new FRP-confined concrete model for design purposes based on the evaluated stress-strain relationship models and extensive test data. Some studies on high-strength and ultra-high-strength concrete confined with FRP composites were also done in the early 2010s (Vincent and Ozbakkaloglu 2013; Lim and Ozbakkaloglu 2014). It is also possible to find studies related to the behavior of the FRP-confined concrete columns subjected to eccentric axial loading (Wu and Jiang 2013; Lin et al. 2020) and retrofitting of columns with fire damage (Akbarzadeh Bengar et al. 2020).

Typical RC columns in practical terms experience a combination of axial load and bending moment, resulting in non-uniform compression in the column cross-sections. Furthermore, even if the intended loads are concentric, geometric and/or material imperfections may cause eccentric loading leading to a non-uniform stress distribution. There are studies in the literature that investigate the rectangular RC columns under eccentric loading in either the strong or weak axes (Hadi and Widiarsa 2012). Accordingly, the strain gradient effect is found to be responsible for the larger axial strain at the center of the outer face of the compression side with respect to the achieved ultimate axial strain of the corresponding concentrically loaded column. The confinement effectiveness of FRP jackets in rectangular cross-sections or wall-like columns (which can be described to be with an aspect ratio higher than the allowed upper limits provided by the current design codes and guidelines) is less than the effectiveness of square cross-sections, and their effectiveness highly depends on the aspect ratio of the cross-section (Prota et al. 2006; Wu and Wei 2010; Abbasnia et al. 2012, 2013; Mostofinejad et al. 2015; Triantafillou et al. 2016).

Furthermore, one of the main topics in RC structures is stress transfer from the steel bars to the surrounding concrete, the steel rebar-concrete link is crucial to the response of RC elements. Therefore, the main interest area in this field is determining the mechanical properties of RC members throughout different conditions, particularly elevated temperatures, and fire. The exposure of structural components to high temperatures during a fire incident causes serious damage to RC construction. Several physicochemical changes occur in RC members exposed to high temperatures, especially in concrete. After Malhotra's research in 1956, a great deal of research has been done on the impact of high temperatures on the mechanical behavior of concrete (Malhotra 1956). According to reports, a number of factors, including the cooling conditions of the structural members, can cause changes in the material's mechanical properties when exposed to high temperatures (Georgali and Tsakiridis 2005, and Arioz 2007).

The bonding strength between reinforcement and concrete at high temperatures has reportedly received less research attention than high-temperature-affected concrete's mechanical characteristics. Pull-out tests on test specimens are typically used to assess the concrete bonding ability. Two classes of steel rebar-concrete bond failure can be defined as concrete splitting or rebar sliding (pull-out). In the condition of less cover or even with a tightly pack the bonding failure generally happens when the reinforcement pulls away after the concrete keys between the bars' ribs break. Tensile splitting fractures arise around the steel rebar when the cover of concrete is relatively thin or the steel rebar spacing is narrow, and concrete splitting failure occurs before the pull-out failure (Eligehausen et al. 1982; Malvar 1992; fib Bulletin No. 10 2000; Yalciner et al. 2012). According to the explanation above, establishing a connection between temperature and residual bond strength is an important subject.

The findings show that the binding strength dramatically reduces as the temperature rises (Bingöl and Gül 2009; Panedpojaman and Pothisiri 2014; Kodur and Agrawal 2017). The outputs of these experiments clearly expressed that the key factors that have affected the results are the mechanical properties of concrete and reinforcements. The failure mode for pull-out overtook the splitting failure as the confinement level increased. Due to the concrete crushing keys, the mode shapes of failure shifted from partial splitting to practically total pull-out (Al-Hammoud et al. 2013). Therefore, it is important to switch the mode shape of failure to pull-out of the bars in concrete members where splitting failure is anticipated and to improve ductility performance by adding external jackets. Fiber-reinforced polymer (FRP) and steel jacketing, and shape memory alloy (SMA) wires, have all been employed as exterior jacketing methods in earlier research to strengthen the bond between rebar and concrete (Choi et al. 2010; Akbarzadeh Bengar and Maghsoudi 2011; Bournas and Triantafillou 2011; Ghasemi et al. 2015; Akbarzadeh Bengar et al. 2015; Farrokh Ghatte et al. 2019 and 2020 and Akbarzadeh Bengar et al. 2020).

The behavior of concrete has recently been predicted using explicit formulations using contemporary computer-based methods like artificial neural networks (ANN) (Naderpour et al. 2010), fuzzy logic (Naderpour and Alavi 2017), and gene expression programming (GEP) (Shahmansouri et al. 2019). When analytical formulations are unavailable, GEP is a potent technique for obtaining explicit formulas from experimental results, including multivariate parameters (Nehdi et al. 2007). Eighty pull-out specimens were built and evaluated as part of the current study's experimental program in order to better understand the behavior of the steel-concrete bond in concretes exposed to high temperatures. The major goal was to ascertain how the bond strength was impacted by the confinement of carbon fiber-reinforced polymer CFRP, concrete cover, temperature, and concrete strength. The GEP technique was also employed in numerical analysis to create closed-form expressions that predicted the binding strength between the steel rebar and the CFRP-wrapped concrete following exposure to high temperatures.

Consideration of the abovementioned surveying clearly reports that a precise formula that can accurately estimate the post-fire bond strength between CFRP-confined concrete and steel rebar is still absent, despite the fact that certain experimental and analytical models are available to examine the parameters impacting the bond strength between steel rebar-concrete. The following investigation reports proposed gene expression programming (GEP) to predict the ability of CFRP wrapping to enhance the post-heated bond strength between steel rebar and concrete. The estimated bond strength could be predicted by the accuracy and high prediction ability of the proposed model.

Table 1. Properties of CFRP sheets

Property	T	D	TS	TM	S	FD
Value	0.11 *mm*	1.76 g/cm³	3530 MPa	230 GPa	1.5%	7 μm

EXPERIMENTAL PROGRAM

Material Properties

The strength of the concrete was graded as C30 and C40, respectively. The mix's components included regular Portland cement, sand with a maximum particle size of 4.75 mm, gravity of 2.65 g/cm3, water absorption of 1.3%, as well as potable water and coarse aggregate with a maximum particle size of 19.5 mm. Sand had a specific gravity of 2.7 g/cm3, a fineness modulus of 2.72, and water absorption of 2.4%. The aggregates' sieve analysis fell within the range advised by ASTM C33 (ASTM 2013). Each specimen had a 20 mm diameter rebar placed into it for the pull-out test. The rebar's elastic modulus was 210 GPa, yield stress was 374 MPa and ultimate strength was 571 MPa. The specimens under research were contained in CFRP sheets, which have the features shown in Table 1. The CFRP sheets were fastened to the concrete surfaces using epoxy glue.

- In Table 1 T is thickness, D is density, TS is tensile strength, TM is tensile modulus S is strain and FD is considered as a Filament diameter.

Test Specimens and Thermal Treatment

Eighty specimens for pull-out testing were arranged (see Figure 1), and the variables were, the thickness of the clean cover, the concrete compressive strength, temperature, and confining parameters with CFRP jacketing (Table 2). All of the samples were tested after being exposed to the elevated temperature and then wrapped by using CFRP jacketing. For higher accuracy, the mean result of two specimens was considered as the reported result.

Specimens had a cross-section of 150×150 *mm* and a height of 250 *mm*. Reinforcements with a 20 *mm* diameter were employed with two different covers for concrete 25 *mm* and 35 *mm*. The embedded length of the reinforcements was consider as 200 *mm* and the expected failure condition in the unconfined samples was the bond splitting failure mode.

An electric furnace was used with the heating regime as shown in Figure 2 for evaluation of the efficiency of elevated temperatures on various mechanical properties. Two hours of maintaining time have been considered for the inside temperature after the target temperature in order to achieve a uniform distribution of the temperature with a 24-hour natural cooling process (Xiao et al. 2014).

Pull-Out Testing Setup

All of the specimens were gradually tested by employing the shown test setup in Figure 3. The pulling-out test was coordinated by a hydraulic universal testing machine (UTM) with 600 KN capacity. Monotoni-

Figure 1. Pull-out test specimens

Table 2. Test matrix

Series	CFRP Jacketed	Clean Cover (mm)	Temperature (°C)				
			20	200	400	600	800
C30	Not	25	20-25	200-25	400-25	600-25	800-25
C30	Not	35	20-35	200-35	400-35	600-35	800-35
C30	Yes	25	20-25	200-25	400-25	600-25	800-25
C30	Yes	35	20-35	200-35	400-35	600-35	800-35
C40	Not	25	20-25	200-25	400-25	600-25	800-25
C40	Not	35	20-35	200-35	400-35	600-35	800-35
C40	Yes	25	20-25	200-25	400-25	600-25	800-25
C40	Yes	35	20-35	200-35	400-35	600-35	800-35

cally pulling load was enforced by a 1 mm/min rate. A linear variable differential transformer (LVDT) was employed to measure the rate of slip throughout the pulling process. If the surrounded concrete split or the applied load became smaller than 50% of the peak load, the loading process stopped.

GEP MODELS AND PARAMETERS

Machine learning approach using genetic programming (GP) and in 1988, Jone Koza created the initial version of GP, which creates a computer-based model to tackle the issue using the Darwinian selection principle (Koza 1994). GP is an artificial intelligence-based predictive tool that creates a program by

Figure 2. The relationship between time and temperature

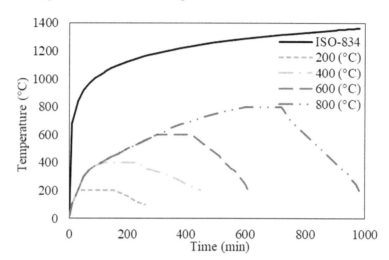

Figure 3. Loading device

simulating the development of biological creatures. GA, introduced by John Holland based on Darwin's survival of the fittest principle, is mainly used for optimization problems (Holland 1992). GP, which is the extension of GA, was introduced by Koza (1994). The method includes five main steps; the initial three steps present the space of the algorithm search and the other two steps present the quality as well as the speed of the proses (Ferreira 2006). Ferreira proposed the GEP method after the previous development of genetic algorithm (GA) and genetic programming (GP) methods (Ferreira 2006). The genetic algorithm's (GA) generalization form is known as GP (Cheng 2007). These two approaches can be distinguished from one another in some way based on the solution representation. While GP uses a programming language to express the given data in the form of a tree-like structure, GA represents the answer as a string of integers (chromosomes) (Alavi et al. 2011). In contrast to GP, which offers alternative strings of varying forms and sizes of nonlinear entities, GA only delivers linear fixed-length binary strings (chromosomes). This makes GP a flexible approach to property prediction. In other words, the representation's solution is shown as a parse tree with shifting string length and shape. The problem hierarchy in GP is comparable to that in GA. The computer software then conducts an independent search for the problem's optimal solution (Baykasoglu et al. 2004; Shi et al. 2011, and Aminian et al. 2011). The following steps make up the overall chain of GP when solving a problem using a programming language:

(1) Select randomly from the problem's function sets and terminal sets to generate and construct individual chromosomes (population set). These groups selected their members at random and created computer models in the shape of trees, with roots (branches) extending to the terminal set, as illustrated in Figure 1.

(2) The GP algorithm performs iterative measurements to choose the best-fitting chromosomes and then creates new individual chromosomes using three methods: crossover, mutation, and reproduction. GP functions similarly to a human analog.

    (A) Reproduction: In this process, the chromosomes of people are replicated in the subsequent process in a new population without being altered (Alavi et al. 2011).

    (B) Crossover: In this procedure, a node is randomly chosen on one of the roots of each program, and the function set and terminal set of each program are then switched, as indicated in Figure 2. This results in a new child program. It is evident that two parents' computer-based programs produce two fresh offspring (Koza 1994 and Alavi et al. 2011).

    (C) Mutation: In this process, a random number is chosen to replace a node of persons in terminal sets and function sets with a parity of the same value.

Selecting sets at random, produces new children, and the best generation showed up as a tree Aminian et al. 2011).

(3) After completing a computer-based program, genetic programming came up with its best answer to the problem (Bennett et al. 1997 and Ashour et al. 2003).

Proposed Model

To develop the bond strength prediction model, the results obtained through an extensive experimental effort were used as the input datasets. A total of 80% of the experiment results were randomly selected as the training set for application of the models, and the last 20% were employed as validation set data. These details included the concrete strength class (SC), concrete cover (CC), exposure temperature (ET), confinement impact (CI), and bond strength (τ_b). The input and output ranges of variables are represented in Table 3. Therefore, the function of the following factors was the bond strength Eq. (1).

$$\tau_b = f\left(SC, CC, ET, CI\right) \qquad (1)$$

Table 3. Input and output ranges

Input Variables	Minimum	Maximum
Concrete strength class (MPa)	30	40
Concrete cover (*mm*)	25	35
Exposed temperature (°C)	20	800
Confinement impact (Binary)	0	1
Output variables		
Bond strength (MPa)	0.77	10.34

RESULTS AND DISCUSSION

In this part, the experimental results are represented by details and the proposed model was compared with the experimental results.

Experimental Results

The failure mechanisms as reported previously generally occurred in one of the two kinds of modes, splitting of the bond and pull-out of rebar (Eligehausen et al. 1982; Malvar 1992; fib Bulletin No. 10 2000 and Yalciner et al. 2012). Therefore, the failure mechanism was concerned with the cover of concrete, compressive strength of the samples, and CFRP jacketing. Generally, the failure mechanism of the unconfined samples was splitting of the bond based on the concrete compressive strength as well as a cover of the concrete, while all of the wrapped specimens experienced the rebar pull-out failure mechanism. In the unheated unconfined samples, a brittle splitting mechanism happened where as in the unwrapped heated samples, despite happening of the splitting mechanism, when the temperature expanded. This failure mechanism to some extent was fewer brittle compared to the unheated samples. A group of failed specimens is presented in Figure 4.

The CFRP jacketing method not only could control the cracks propagation but also could change the failure mechanism from brittle to relatively ductile failure. As clearly represented in the figures, cracks from splitting could be seen in some of the samples, the CFRP jackets successfully increased the bond strength and limited the cracks. Cracking occurred in the middle of the samples and extended to the end of the samples in the splitting of the bond failure modes. The CEB-FIP (fib Bulletin No. 10 2000) states that such failure is considered a partial pull-out failure mechanism when the samples have a moderate level of confinement or a limited cover for concrete condition. The similar samples with various compressive strengths behave almost the same. Furthermore, the cover of concrete cover had a light efficiency on the failure mechanism, since the similar samples with two different kinds of concrete covers represented almost the same failure mode.

The results of the pull-out test including the maximum bond stress and related results in terms of slip and compressive strength, are represented in Table 4. It is evident from the table, with an increment in the temperature, the related residual strength for bond declines. The residual bond strength was approximately just as it is for both C30 and C40 strength classes. By matching the rates of the confined and unconfined specimens, the reduction rate for strength in confined specimens was less than the unconfined samples (600 and 800 °C) the residual strength of the bond was on average 0.26 and 0.11

Figure 4. Samples after the test

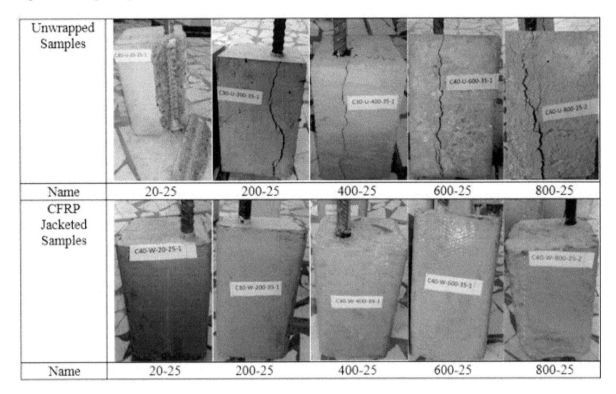

Unwrapped Samples					
Name	20-25	200-25	400-25	600-25	800-25
CFRP Jacketed Samples					
Name	20-25	200-25	400-25	600-25	800-25

for the unconfined samples and 0.43 and 0.25 for the confined samples. Based on Table 4, it is clear that by any incrimination of the compressive strength, the strength of the bond also increased. Apparently, the results showed that in the case of wrapping with CFRP sheets, the strength of the bond had dramatically increment. The above-mentioned increment was much more tangible for the 25 *mm*-cover samples than 35 *mm*-cover samples, based on increasing the confinement rate through CFRP jacketing. Moreover, the efficiency of the CFRP wrapping was much more tangible in samples that were exposed to elevated temperatures. Improvement of the strength of bond in the C30-25, C30-35, C40-25, and C40-35 designs retrofitted with the CFRP wrapping relative to the non-retrofitted designs. The CFRP jacketing method provides a tangible lateral pressure by surrounding the steel rebar on concrete, while dramatically increasing occurred in terms of mechanical interlocking around the reinforcement as well as the elastic confinement ratio.

Based on the results, the ability to retrofit with CFRP to improve the bond efficiency in the heated samples can be deduced. It is crystal clear that the presented retrofitting procedure could compensate for the heat-induced loss in the bond strength, which occurred in the references (unwrapped) samples to a large extent. After the exposure of the specimens to 400 °C, retrofitting could compensate for approximately whole loss of bond that occurred as a result of heat. For the C40 strength class, this drop was completely compensated for in the case of the 25 *mm* concrete cover (after exposure to 400 °C). Due to a more significant effect of retrofitting with CFRP on the concrete samples with the less amount of clear cover, the strength of the bond for this group of samples was well recovered relative to the C30 concretes. By comparing the variation of the compressive strength and strength of the bond with temperature for the references (unconfined) samples with various concrete compressive strength, it is

Table 4. Results of the tests

Concrete Type	Jacketing	Code	Compressive Strength (MPa)	Bond Strength (MPa)	Peak Slip (mm)	$\ddot{A}/\sqrt{f_c'}$	Failure Mode
C30	No	20-25	30.1	5.67	0.27	1.03	S
C30	No	20-35	30.1	8.95	0.44	1.63	S
C30	Yes	20-25	30.1	8.32	1.46	1.52	P
C30	Yes	20-35	30.1	9.60	0.96	1.75	P
C40	No	20-25	39.9	6.50	0.50	1.03	S
C40	No	20-35	39.9	9.36	0.38	1.48	S
C40	Yes	20-25	39.9	10.21	1.08	1.62	P
C40	Yes	20-35	39.9	10.34	1.06	1.64	P
C30	No	200-25	23.6	4.09	0.35	0.84	S
C30	No	200-35	23.6	5.65	0.40	1.16	S
C30	Yes	200-25	23.6	5.90	1.16	1.21	P
C30	Yes	200-35	23.6	8.01	1.06	1.65	P
C40	No	200-25	36.5	5.94	0.20	0.98	S
C40	No	200-35	36.5	6.92	0.40	1.15	S
C40	Yes	200-25	36.5	8.14	0.86	1.35	P
C40	Yes	200-35	36.5	9.90	0.56	1.64	P
C30	No	400-25	22.2	2.67	0.65	0.57	S
C30	No	400-35	22.2	2.14	1.25	0.45	S
C30	Yes	400-25	22.2	6.17	1.75	1.31	P
C30	Yes	400-35	22.2	7.29	0.85	1.55	P
C40	No	400-25	32.6	4.35	0.95	0.76	S
C40	No	400-35	32.6	6.10	0.40	1.07	S
C40	Yes	400-25	32.6	6.74	1.55	1.18	P
C40	Yes	400-35	32.6	7.43	1.15	1.30	P
C30	No	600-25	15.3	1.47	0.75	0.38	S
C30	No	600-35	15.3	2.08	0.90	0.53	S
C30	Yes	600-25	15.3	3.59	2.05	0.92	P
C30	Yes	600-35	15.3	5.02	1.85	1.28	P
C40	No	600-25	18.9	1.79	0.85	0.41	S
C40	No	600-35	18.9	2.61	0.90	0.60	S
C40	Yes	600-25	18.9	4.36	2.25	1.00	P
C40	Yes	600-35	18.9	3.99	2.35	0.92	P
C30	No	800-25	7	0.77	1.05	0.29	S
C30	No	800-35	7	1.04	1.10	0.39	S
C30	Yes	800-25	7	2.05	1.95	0.77	P
C30	Yes	800-35	7	2.32	2.45	0.88	P
C40	No	800-25	6.9	0.80	1.20	0.30	S
C40	No	800-35	6.9	0.95	1.40	0.36	S
C40	Yes	800-25	6.9	2.37	2.45	0.90	P
C40	Yes	800-35	6.9	2.28	3.25	0.87	P

* S is splitting and P is Pull-Out

seen that losing the strength of compressive strength with temperature is less than the strength of the bond. This loss was more tangible for the C30 samples, with the relative compressive strength of the C30 samples after exposure to 200, 400, 600, and 800 °C being 0.78, 0.73, 0.5, and 0.23, subsequently. This change in behavior is mainly based on the strength of the bond that can be kept under control by the tensile stress, and since the reduction in the tensile strength of concrete under fire is greater than the compressive strength, the more significant reduction in the strength of bond relative to the compressive strength is much feasible.

Modeling Results

The bond strength and the other parameters relationship understudy can be derived from the test results. As discussed earlier, the equation obtained from the GEP model is presented as expression trees (ET) in Figure 5 and the mathematical form in Eq. (2) where *SC*, *CC*, *ET*, and *CI* refer to concrete strength class (MPa), concrete cover (*mm*), exposed temperature (°C), and confinement impact (Binary), respectively. In the proposed model, the absolute fraction of variance (R^2) and root mean square error (RMSE) between experimental and predicted values are 0.94 and 0.719, respectively. Hence, it is reliable to use this formula to predict the bond strength.

$$\tau_b = \sqrt[5]{CI - \left(CC + ET \times \left(\sqrt[5]{CC} + \sin\left(SC\right)\right)\right)} \tag{2}$$

$$\times \left(\sqrt[4]{\left(\sin\left(ET - CI\right) - 5.73\right)^2 + ET} - 5.73 \right)$$

$$\times \sqrt{e^{\sin\left(\sin\left(\left(\tan\left(\sqrt[3]{CC}\right)\times\tan^{-1}\left(CC\right)\right)+CI\right)\right)}}$$

Figure 5. The GEP approach model

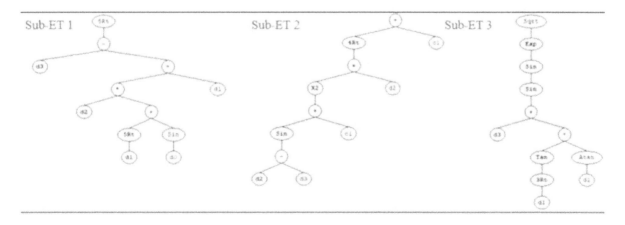

Figure 6. Comparison of predicted values vs. experimental results

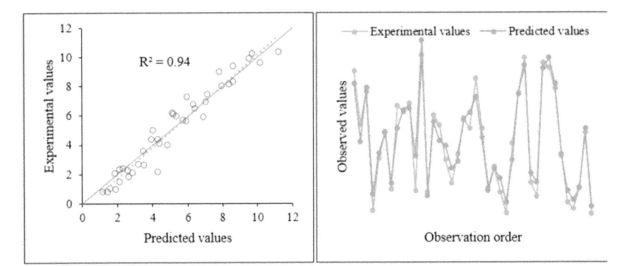

The linear least-squares fit, fit line, and R^2 values are shown in Figure 6, which clearly demonstrates that the predicted values collected from the GEP model have an acceptable agreement with the experimental outputs.

FUTURE RESEARCH DIRECTIONS

The field of machine learning in civil engineering was already advancing rapidly, and it's likely that further progress has been made since then. Although in the last decades machine learning in civil engineering was employed mainly for the prediction of behavior of the material and structural elements, data integration and quality improvement, automated design and optimization, real-time monitoring and predictive maintenance, risk assessment and mitigation, and explainable AI in civil engineering are the main headlines in this field.

CONCLUSION

The objective of this research was to address numerically and experimentally the efficiency of fire in the constructions and evaluate the concrete-steel rebar bond strength in fire-damaged reinforced concrete structures and improve the bond performance through the CFRP jacketing method. Based on the experimental and modeling results obtained through the rebar pull-out tests conducted in this study, the following main conclusions can be drawn:

i. The references (unwrapping) specimens present a brittle performance. The failure was the result of the development of the radial longitudinal cracks to the splitting of the concrete. The above-mentioned kind of failure occurred almost for the reference specimens through all temperatures, and in the lower temperature, more brittle failure modes were observed. However, FRP jacketing could prevent the cracks developments as well as changing the failure mechanism to the rebar pull-out failure as a more plastic failure mechanism.

ii. When the pull-out samples were exposed to the elevated temperature, a reduction in the bond strength was observed, and as the temperature further increased, this drop was more notable. However, this drop was less in the samples with more compressive strength values and cover of concrete compared to the other samples.

iii. By using CFRP as a retrofitting strategy, not only the strength of the bond for the specimens improved significantly but also, the lost bond strength due to temperature in the CFRP-jacketed specimens was notably fewer than the reference specimens.

iv. Elevated temperatures decreased the bond strength of steel rebar concrete after exposure. For the temperature above 400 °C, the severity increased as well. By employing the CFRP jacketing method the results increased dramatically in the bond strength, with more efficiency in the specimens that were exposed to higher temperatures.

v. The CFRP retrofitting method completely compensated for the bond strength loss of the pull-out samples subjected to elevated temperatures up to 400 °C.

vi. A GEP model was proposed in order to predict the bond strength of CFRP-wrapped heat-damaged concrete specimens, which yielded output close to the experimental results with an acceptable level of accuracy.

vii. The GEP predicted results establish the precision and high prediction capacity of the model and the findings can bring significant improvement for the range of organizations involved.

REFERENCES

Abbasnia, R., Ahmadi, R., & Ziaadiny, H. (2012). Effect of confinement level, aspect ratio and concrete strength on the cyclic stress–strain behavior of FRP-confined concrete prisms. *Composites. Part B, Engineering*, *43*(2), 825–831. doi:10.1016/j.compositesb.2011.11.008

Abbasnia, R., Hosseinpour, F., Rostamian, M., & Ziaadiny, H. (2013). Cyclic and monotonic behavior of FRP confined concrete rectangular prisms with different aspect ratios. *Construction & Building Materials*, *40*, 118–125. doi:10.1016/j.conbuildmat.2012.10.008

ACI Committee 440. (2017). *ACI 440.2R-17: Guide for the design and construction of externally bonded FRP systems for strengthening existing structures*. In American Concrete Institute.

Adibi, M., Talebkhah, R., & Ghatte, H. F. (2023). Seismic reliability of precast concrete frame with masonry infill wall. *Earthquakes and Structures*, *24*(2), 141.

Akbarzadeh, H., & Maghsoudi, A. A. (2011). Flexural strengthening of RC continuous beams using hybrid FRP sheets. In *Advances in FRP Composites in Civil Engineering: Proceedings of the 5th International Conference on FRP Composites in Civil Engineering (CICE 2010), Sep 27–29, 2010, Beijing, China* (pp. 739-743). Springer Berlin Heidelberg. 10.1007/978-3-642-17487-2_163

Al-Hammoud, R., Soudki, K., & Topper, T. H. (2013). Confinement effect on the bond behavior of beams under static and repeated loading. *Construction & Building Materials*, *40*, 934–943. doi:10.1016/j. conbuildmat.2012.09.081

Arioz, O. (2007). Effects of elevated temperatures on properties of concrete. *Fire Safety Journal*, *42*(8), 516–522. doi:10.1016/j.firesaf.2007.01.003

Asteris, P. G., & Kolovos, K. G. (2019). Self-compacting concrete strength prediction using surrogate models. *Neural Computing & Applications*, *31*(S1, Suppl 1), 409–424. doi:10.100700521-017-3007-7

ASTM. (2013). *C33-13: Standard Specification for Concrete Aggregates*. ASTM International.

Azim, I., Yang, J., Javed, M. F., Iqbal, M. F., Mahmood, Z., Wang, F., & Liu, Q. F. (2020, June). Prediction model for compressive arch action capacity of RC frame structures under column removal scenario using gene expression programming. In *Structures* (Vol. 25, pp. 212–228). Elsevier.

Bengar, H. A., Hosseinpour, M., & Celikag, M. (2020, April). Influence of CFRP confinement on bond behavior of steel deformed bar embedded in concrete exposed to high temperature. In *Structures* (Vol. 24, pp. 240–252). Elsevier.

Bennett, F. H., Koza, J. R., Andre, D., & Keane, M. A. (1997). Evolution of a 60 decibel op amp using genetic programming. In *Evolvable Systems: From Biology to Hardware: First International Conference, ICES96 Tsukuba, Japan, October 7–8, 1996 Proceedings 1* (pp. 453-469). Springer Berlin Heidelberg. 10.1007/3-540-63173-9_65

Bingöl, A. F., & Gül, R. (2009). The residual bond strength between steel bars and concrete after elevated temperatures. *Fire Safety Journal*, *44*(6), 854–859. doi:10.1016/j.firesaf.2009.04.001

Bournas, D. A., & Triantafillou, T. C. (2011). Bond strength of lap-spliced bars in concrete confined with composite jackets. *Journal of Composites for Construction*, *15*(2), 156–167. doi:10.1061/(ASCE) CC.1943-5614.0000078

Choi, E., Kim, Y. W., Chung, Y. S., & Yang, K. T. (2010). Bond strength of concrete confined by SMA wire jackets. *Physics Procedia*, *10*, 210–215. doi:10.1016/j.phpro.2010.11.100

Chou, J. S., Tsai, C. F., Pham, A. D., & Lu, Y. H. (2014). Machine learning in concrete strength simulations: Multi-nation data analytics. *Construction & Building Materials*, *73*, 771–780. doi:10.1016/j. conbuildmat.2014.09.054

Dao, D. V., Ly, H. B., Trinh, S. H., Le, T. T., & Pham, B. T. (2019). Artificial intelligence approaches for prediction of compressive strength of geopolymer concrete. *Materials (Basel)*, *12*(6), 983. doi:10.3390/ ma12060983 PMID:30934566

Eligehausen, R., Popov, E. P., & Bertero, V. V. (1982). *Local bond stress-slip relationships of deformed bars under generalized excitations*. Academic Press.

Farrokh Ghatte, H. (2020a). Failure mechanisms and cracking performance of T-shaped SCC beam-column connections at top floor: Test results and FE modeling. *Structures*, *28*, 1009–1018. doi:10.1016/j. istruc.2020.09.051

Farrokh Ghatte, H. (2020b). External steel ties and CFRP jacketing effects on seismic performance and failure mechanisms of substandard rectangular RC columns. *Composite Structures, 248*, 112542. doi:10.1016/j.compstruct.2020.112542

Farrokh Ghatte, H. (2021). A hybrid of firefly and biogeography-based optimization algorithms for optimal design of steel frames. *Arabian Journal for Science and Engineering, 46*(5), 4703–4717. doi:10.100713369-020-05118-w

Farrokh Ghatte, H., Comert, M., Demir, C., Akbaba, M., & Ilki, A. (2019). Seismic retrofit of full-scale substandard extended rectangular RC columns through CFRP jacketing: Test results and design recommendations. *Journal of Composites for Construction, 23*(1), 04018071. doi:10.1061/(ASCE)CC.1943-5614.0000907

Ferreira, C. (2001). *Gene expression programming: a new adaptive algorithm for solving problems.* arXiv preprint cs/0102027.

Ferreira, C. (2006). *Gene expression programming: mathematical modeling by an artificial intelligence* (Vol. 21). Springer. doi:10.1007/3-540-32849-1_2

Georgali, B., & Tsakiridis, P. E. (2005). Microstructure of fire-damaged concrete. A case study. *Cement and Concrete Composites, 27*(2), 255–259. doi:10.1016/j.cemconcomp.2004.02.022

Ghasemi, S., Akbar Maghsoudi, A., Akbarzadeh Bengar, H., & Reza Ronagh, H. (2016). Sagging and hogging strengthening of continuous unbonded posttensioned HSC beams by NSM and EBR. *Journal of Composites for Construction, 20*(2), 04015056. doi:10.1061/(ASCE)CC.1943-5614.0000621

Gholizadeh, S., Hassanzadeh, A., Milany, A., & Ghatte, H. F. (2022). On the seismic collapse capacity of optimally designed steel braced frames. *Engineering with Computers, 38*(2), 1–13. doi:10.100700366-020-01096-7

Gurbuz, T., Cengiz, A., Kolemenoglu, S., Demir, C., & Ilki, A. (2023). Damages and failures of structures in Izmir (Turkey) during the October 30, 2020 Aegean Sea earthquake. *Journal of Earthquake Engineering, 27*(6), 1565–1606. doi:10.1080/13632469.2022.2086186

Hadi, M. N., & Widiarsa, I. B. R. (2012). Axial and flexural performance of square RC columns wrapped with CFRP under eccentric loading. *Journal of Composites for Construction, 16*(6), 640–649. doi:10.1061/(ASCE)CC.1943-5614.0000301

Han, Q., Gui, C., Xu, J., & Lacidogna, G. (2019). A generalized method to predict the compressive strength of high-performance concrete by improved random forest algorithm. *Construction & Building Materials, 226*, 734–742. doi:10.1016/j.conbuildmat.2019.07.315

Holland, J. H. (1992). Genetic algorithms. *Scientific American, 267*(1), 66–73. doi:10.1038cientificamerican0792-66

Iqbal, M. F., Liu, Q. F., Azim, I., Zhu, X., Yang, J., Javed, M. F., & Rauf, M. (2020). Prediction of mechanical properties of green concrete incorporating waste foundry sand based on gene expression programming. *Journal of Hazardous Materials, 384*, 121322. doi:10.1016/j.jhazmat.2019.121322 PMID:31604206

Javed, M. F., Amin, M. N., Shah, M. I., Khan, K., Iftikhar, B., Farooq, F., Aslam, F., Alyousef, R., & Alabduljabbar, H. (2020). Applications of gene expression programming and regression techniques for estimating compressive strength of bagasse ash based concrete. *Crystals, 10*(9), 737. doi:10.3390/cryst10090737

Karabinis, A. I., Rousakis, T. C., & Manolitsi, G. E. (2008). 3D finite-element analysis of substandard RC columns strengthened by fiber-reinforced polymer sheets. *Journal of Composites for Construction, 12*(5), 531–540. doi:10.1061/(ASCE)1090-0268(2008)12:5(531)

Kent, D. C., & Park, R. (1971). Flexural members with confined concrete. *Journal of the Structural Division, 97*(7), 1969–1990. doi:10.1061/JSDEAG.0002957

Kodur, V. K. R., & Agrawal, A. (2017). Effect of temperature induced bond degradation on fire response of reinforced concrete beams. *Engineering Structures, 142*, 98–109. doi:10.1016/j.engstruct.2017.03.022

Koza, J. R. (1994). Genetic programming as a means for programming computers by natural selection. *Statistics and Computing, 4*(2), 87–112. doi:10.1007/BF00175355

Lim, J. C., & Ozbakkaloglu, T. (2014). Confinement model for FRP-confined high-strength concrete. *Journal of Composites for Construction, 18*(4), 04013058. doi:10.1061/(ASCE)CC.1943-5614.0000376

Lu, X. Z., Teng, J. G., Ye, L. P., & Jiang, J. J. (2007). Intermediate crack debonding in FRP-strengthened RC beams: FE analysis and strength model. *Journal of Composites for Construction, 11*(2), 161–174. doi:10.1061/(ASCE)1090-0268(2007)11:2(161)

Malhotra, H. L. (1956). The effect of temperature on the compressive strength of concrete. *Magazine of Concrete Research, 8*(23), 85–94. doi:10.1680/macr.1956.8.23.85

Malvar, L. J. (1992). Bond of reinforcement under controlled confinement. *ACI Materials Journal, 89*(6), 593–601.

Mander, J. B., Priestley, M. J., & Park, R. (1988). Theoretical stress-strain model for confined concrete. *Journal of Structural Engineering, 114*(8), 1804–1826. doi:10.1061/(ASCE)0733-9445(1988)114:8(1804)

Mostofinejad, D., & Khozaei, K. (2015). Effect of GM patterns on ductility and debonding control of FRP sheets in RC strengthened beams. *Construction & Building Materials, 93*, 110–120. doi:10.1016/j.conbuildmat.2015.05.062

Naderpour, H., & Alavi, S. A. (2017). A proposed model to estimate shear contribution of FRP in strengthened RC beams in terms of Adaptive Neuro-Fuzzy Inference System. *Composite Structures, 170*, 215–227. doi:10.1016/j.compstruct.2017.03.028

Naderpour, H., Kheyroddin, A., & Amiri, G. G. (2010). Prediction of FRP-confined compressive strength of concrete using artificial neural networks. *Composite Structures, 92*(12), 2817–2829. doi:10.1016/j.compstruct.2010.04.008

Nehdi, M., El Chabib, H., & Saïd, A. A. (2007). Proposed shear design equations for FRP-reinforced concrete beams based on genetic algorithms approach. *Journal of Materials in Civil Engineering, 19*(12), 1033–1042. doi:10.1061/(ASCE)0899-1561(2007)19:12(1033)

Nour, A. I., & Güneyisi, E. M. (2019). Prediction model on compressive strength of recycled aggregate concrete filled steel tube columns. *Composites. Part B, Engineering, 173*, 106938. doi:10.1016/j.compositesb.2019.106938

Ozbakkaloglu, T., Lim, J. C., & Vincent, T. (2013). FRP-confined concrete in circular sections: Review and assessment of stress–strain models. *Engineering Structures, 49*, 1068–1088. doi:10.1016/j.engstruct.2012.06.010

Pala, M., Özbay, E., Öztaş, A., & Yuce, M. I. (2007). Appraisal of long-term effects of fly ash and silica fume on compressive strength of concrete by neural networks. *Construction & Building Materials, 21*(2), 384–394. doi:10.1016/j.conbuildmat.2005.08.009

Panedpojaman, P., & Pothisiri, T. (2014). Bond Characteristics of Reinforced Normal-Strength Concrete Beams at Elevated Temperatures. *ACI Structural Journal, 111*(6). Advance online publication. doi:10.14359/51687098

Prota, A., Manfredi, G., & Cosenza, E. (2006). Ultimate behavior of axially loaded RC wall-like columns confined with GFRP. *Composites. Part B, Engineering, 37*(7-8), 670–678. doi:10.1016/j.compositesb.2006.01.005

Saatcioglu, M., & Razvi, S. R. (2002). Displacement-based design of reinforced concrete columns for confinement. *Structural Journal, 99*(1), 3–11.

Samaan, M., Mirmiran, A., & Shahawy, M. (1998). Model of concrete confined by fiber composites. *Journal of Structural Engineering, 124*(9), 1025–1031. doi:10.1061/(ASCE)0733-9445(1998)124:9(1025)

Shahmansouri, A. A., Bengar, H. A., & Jahani, E. (2019). Predicting compressive strength and electrical resistivity of eco-friendly concrete containing natural zeolite via GEP algorithm. *Construction & Building Materials, 229*, 116883. doi:10.1016/j.conbuildmat.2019.116883

Shahmansouri, A. A., Yazdani, M., Ghanbari, S., Bengar, H. A., Jafari, A., & Ghatte, H. F. (2021). Artificial neural network model to predict the compressive strength of eco-friendly geopolymer concrete incorporating silica fume and natural zeolite. *Journal of Cleaner Production, 279*, 123697. doi:10.1016/j.jclepro.2020.123697

Shahmansouri, A. A., Yazdani, M., Hosseini, M., Bengar, H. A., & Ghatte, H. F. (2022). The prediction analysis of compressive strength and electrical resistivity of environmentally friendly concrete incorporating natural zeolite using artificial neural network. *Construction & Building Materials, 317*, 125876. doi:10.1016/j.conbuildmat.2021.125876

Siddique, R., Aggarwal, P., & Aggarwal, Y. (2011). Prediction of compressive strength of self-compacting concrete containing bottom ash using artificial neural networks. *Advances in Engineering Software, 42*(10), 780–786. doi:10.1016/j.advengsoft.2011.05.016

Tapan, M., Comert, M., Demir, C., Sayan, Y., Orakcal, K., & Ilki, A. (2013). Failures of structures during the October 23, 2011 Tabanlı (Van) and November 9, 2011 Edremit (Van) earthquakes in Turkey. *Engineering Failure Analysis, 34*, 606–628. doi:10.1016/j.engfailanal.2013.02.013

Toutanji, H. (1999). Stress-strain characteristics of concrete columns externally confined with advanced fiber composite sheets. *Materials Journal*, *96*(3), 397–404.

Toutanji, H., & Deng, Y. (2001). Performance of concrete columns strengthened with fiber reinforced polymer composite sheets. *Advanced Composite Materials*, *10*(2-3), 159–168. doi:10.1163/156855101753396636

Triantafillou, T. C., Choutopoulou, E., Fotaki, E., Skorda, M., Stathopoulou, M., & Karlos, K. (2016). FRP confinement of wall-like reinforced concrete columns. *Materials and Structures*, *49*(1-2), 651–664. doi:10.161711527-015-0526-5

Turkish Building Seismic Code 2018. (2018). Prime Ministry, Disaster and Emergency Management Presidency (AFAD).

Uysal, M., & Tanyildizi, H. (2012). Estimation of compressive strength of self compacting concrete containing polypropylene fiber and mineral additives exposed to high temperature using artificial neural network. *Construction & Building Materials*, *27*(1), 404–414. doi:10.1016/j.conbuildmat.2011.07.028

Vakhshouri, B., & Nejadi, S. (2015). Predicition of compressive strength in light-weight self-compacting concrete by ANFIS analytical model. *Archives of Civil Engineering*, (2).

Vincent, T., & Ozbakkaloglu, T. (2013). Influence of fiber orientation and specimen end condition on axial compressive behavior of FRP-confined concrete. *Construction & Building Materials*, *47*, 814–826. doi:10.1016/j.conbuildmat.2013.05.085

Xiao, J., Hou, Y., & Huang, Z. (2014). Beam test on bond behavior between high-grade rebar and high-strength concrete after elevated temperatures. *Fire Safety Journal*, *69*, 23–35. doi:10.1016/j.firesaf.2014.07.001

Xiao, Y., & Wu, H. (2000). Compressive behavior of concrete confined by carbon fiber composite jackets. *Journal of Materials in Civil Engineering*, *12*(2), 139–146. doi:10.1061/(ASCE)0899-1561(2000)12:2(139)

Yalciner, H., Eren, O., & Sensoy, S. (2012). An experimental study on the bond strength between reinforcement bars and concrete as a function of concrete cover, strength and corrosion level. *Cement and Concrete Research*, *42*(5), 643–655. doi:10.1016/j.cemconres.2012.01.003

KEY TERMS AND DEFINITIONS

Artificial Neural Network: ANN is a branch of machine learning by employing the principles of neuronal organization discovered by connectionism in biological neural networks.

Fiber-Reinforced Polymer: FRP is a structure containing an arrangement of unidirectional fibers or woven fiber fabrics embedded within a thin layer of light polymer matrix material.

Genetic Engineering: Genetic engineering, also called genetic modification is the modification and manipulation of an organism's genes using technology.

Machine Learning: Development and use of computer systems with the ability to learn and adapt without following explicit instructions, using various algorithms and statistical models to analyze and draw inferences from patterns in data.

Chapter 3
Fluctuation of Emotion in Stress and Different Coping Mechanisms During the COVID-19 Pandemic

Saroj Kumari
https://orcid.org/0000-0002-3076-7742
Yogoda Satsanga Mahavidyalaya, Ranchi, India

Piyush Ranjan
Jharkhand Rai University, India

Priyanka Srivastava
Sarala Birla University, India

ABSTRACT

Naturalist Charles Darwin was the first to rationalize the importance of emotions. Emotions are key factors that set up the body to adapt to things like apprehension and outrage and amplify one's possibilities of endurance and achievement. The lockdown limitations and fear and consequences of infectious infection brought the whole world to a halt. Humans across the globe have realized the unpredictability of life and let go of the need to control it. This situation not only has surged the suicidal rates, domestic violence, job insecurities, grief, scarcity of basic needs, but also took a positive turn in human development. Many people felt calm, enjoyed the family bond, went back to their basic survival skills, came close to humanity, and many other realizations. This chapter provided a critical analysis of human emotions at the time of stress and different coping mechanisms adopted by the most successful species on the planet. It throws light on the different spectrums of psychosocial behaviour. The authors provide a topography of human emotions during COVID-19 pandemic.

DOI: 10.4018/979-8-3693-2841-5.ch003

INTRODUCTION

Human feelings are complicated, multi-layered mental and physiological reactions to different improvements and encounters. They assume a pivotal part in significantly shaping our considerations, ways of behaving, and connections with our general surroundings. Feelings include a great many sentiments, like joy, sadness, anger, fear, surprise, and disgust, each filling different versatile needs and impacting our navigation and social communications (Aslan, 2021). These emotions and many others contribute to the rich tapestry of human experience, influencing our thoughts, behaviors, and relationships. There are a wide range of kinds of human feelings (Gashi, 2022), each with its own exceptional qualities and capabilities. These emotions are considered universal and are experienced by people regardless of their cultural or social background (Oh, 2019). Some examples include:

- **Joy:** A positive inclination related with satisfaction, happiness, and delight. This emotion is characterized by feelings of contentment, joy, and pleasure. It is often associated with positive experiences and is expressed through smiling, laughter, and other signs of joy.
- **Sadness:** An impression of sorrow, regularly joined by a sensation of mishap or disappointment. Sadness is a feeling of unhappiness, sorrow, or disappointment. It is a natural response to loss, failure, or difficult situations. People experiencing sadness may show signs such as crying, withdrawal, or a lack of interest in activities.
- **Anger:** A compelling profound reaction to saw dangers, treacheries, or disappointments. Anger is an intense emotional response often triggered by frustration, injustice, or perceived threat. It can range from mild irritation to intense rage and is expressed through facial expressions, raised voice, or aggressive behaviour.
- **Fear:** An emotional response to potential danger or threat, triggering a "fight or flight" reaction. Fear is a powerful emotion that arises in response to perceived danger or threat. It prepares the body to react to a dangerous situation, often referred to as the fight-or-flight response. Fear can be triggered by real or imagined threats and is expressed through physical symptoms like increased heart rate, sweating, and trembling.
- **Surprise:** An abrupt and unforeseen response to something new or startling. Surprise occurs in response to unexpected events or stimuli. It is a brief emotional state that can range from mild astonishment to intense amazement. Surprise is often expressed through widened eyes, raised eyebrows, and an open mouth.
- **Disgust:** A pessimistic feeling that can emerge considering something hostile or shocking. Disgust is a reaction to something unpleasant, offensive, or revolting. It can be triggered by specific smells, tastes, or behaviours. Physically, it is often expressed through facial expressions such as wrinkling the nose or turning away from the source of disgust.

These basic emotions serve as the foundation for a wide range of complex feelings and emotional experiences that humans can have. Keep in mind that while these six emotions are considered fundamental, there are also variations and blends of these emotions that form the rich tapestry of human emotional experiences which is shown in Figure 1. The formal evolutionary treatment of human facial expressions began with Charles Darwin's ''The Expression of the Emotions in Man and Animals'' (Darwin, 1872). Darwin found evidence for continuity in bodily movements and facial gestures that humans shared with animals. He used these resemblances across species to argue for common descent (Nikcevie, 2021). Dar-

Figure 1. Six basic emotions

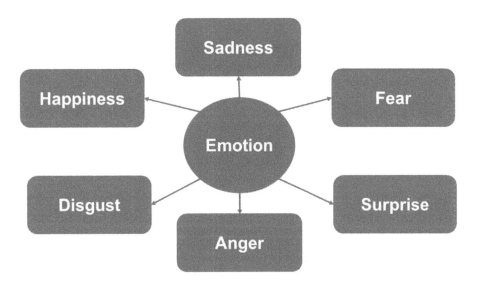

win's view of facial expressions, how- ever, was not "evolutionary" at all, because he did not consider them as adaptations but accidents or vestiges of earlier evolutionary stages in which the intellect was of less importance (Fridlund, 1994). While the argument for phylogenetic continuity plays an important role in contemporary explanations of emotions, Darwin's vestigialism has largely been replaced by the view that expressions of emotion are adaptive and had been selected for social communication (Cohn, 2001) Emotion that is manifested by facial ex- pression signals occurrences of value, and being able to transfer and receive such information undoubtedly confers a survival advantage.

It is generally accepted today that six basic emotional expressions (happiness, surprise, fear, sadness, an- ger, and disgust) are universal in their performance and in their perception (Ekman et al., 1969, 1987). Human feelings assume a crucial part in our survival. They assist us with communicating our perceptions of situations. These emotions permit us to interface and communicate with others on a more profound level (Oumina, A., El Makhfi, N., & Hamdi, M.,2020). These feelings/emotions impact our direction, recollections, and connections, making them an essential part of human experience and social communications (Kodhai, E., Pooveswari, A., Sharmila, P., & Ramiya, N.,2020). It is also important for humane race to cope up with severe conditions in order to survive. One such encounter human race has recently faced is COVID 19 situation which was a global crisis. During the COVID-19 pandemic, hu- man feelings have been incredibly influenced. Many individuals experienced uplifted degrees of dread, nervousness, and vulnerability because of wellbeing concerns, financial difficulties, and social discon- nection (Oumina, A., El Makhfi, N., & Hamdi, M.,2020). Also, sensations of forlornness, pity, and dis- satisfaction arose as people adjusted to better approaches for living and working. However, demonstrations of empathy, fortitude, and flexibility additionally arose, exhibiting the positive parts of human feeling even with affliction (K. Shan, 2017). The COVID-19 pandemic has achieved uncommon changes in our lives, prompting a rollercoaster of feelings for some (Aslan, M., 2021). From beginning nervousness and dread to times of trust and variation, the close to home scene has been set apart by vulnerability and transformation. This presentation will investigate the different manners by which individual's feelings have vacillated because of the difficulties presented by the pandemic. The COVID-19 pandemic (Munsell

SE, O'Malley L, Mackey C., 2020) has significantly elevated stress levels across the globe. Individuals have grappled with concerns related to health, financial instability, isolation, and uncertainty about the future (P. Carcagnì, M. Del Coco, M. Leo, and C. Distante, 2015). The ever-evolving situation, coupled with restrictions and disruptions to daily life, has led to a widespread increase in stress and anxiety (C.-L. Huang and Y.-M. Huang., 1997) As people navigate these challenges, understanding the impact of heightened stress and exploring coping mechanisms becomes crucial for promoting mental well-being during these trying times. During the ongoing COVID-19 pandemic, the manifestation of stress has been diverse and multifaceted, differing greatly among individuals and communities (Zacher, Hannes, and Cort W. Rudolph, 2021). This variation can be attributed to a range of factors, including personal circumstances, availability of resources, and the level of severity of the pandemic in each specific region (I. M. Revina and W. S. Emmanuel, 2018). To shed light on the various forms in which stress has been expressed during this unprecedented time. The COVID-19 pandemic, caused by the novel coronavirus SARS-CoV-2, emerged in late 2019 and quickly became a global health crisis (Park CL, Russell BS, Fendrich M, Finkelstein-Fox L, Hutchison M, Becker J., 2020). Beyond its immediate threat to physical health, the pandemic had a profound impact on mental and emotional well-being. People worldwide experienced unprecedented levels of stress, anxiety, fear, and sadness (due to health concerns, economic uncertainty, social isolation, and the loss of loved ones. This emotional turbulence created a pressing need to understand the fluctuations in emotions during the pandemic and identify effective coping mechanisms to navigate this challenging period. There is a need to focus on various resources that can be harnessed by individuals, especially the youth, to cope with and mitigate the effects of stressors, such as those posed by the COVID-19 pandemic (Nikcevie, A. V., Marino, C., Kolubinski, D. C., Leach, D., & Spada, M. M., 2021). Experiencing a global pandemic that evoke strong reactions offers an opportunity to better understand how particular cognitive resources such as those pertaining to beliefs or perceptions, can alter the effect of existential stressors on the well-being of school-aged samples (P. Carcagnì, M. Del Coco, M. Leo, and C. Distante, 2015). Increasing evidence suggests that the mindsets that individuals hold about stress may be helpful in reducing the maladaptive impact of stress on mental health (Hagger, M. S., Keech, J. J., & Hamilton, K., 2020). However, very few studies have explored this topic in relation to school-aged samples. As such, this study examined the influence of adolescents' stress mindsets on use of coping strategies and well-being in the context of the COVID-19 pandemic.

PURPOSE OR OBJECTIVE

Taken together, this book chapter is dedicated to investigate and examine the emotional spectrum of the humans during difficult times like Corona virus Pandemic. This chapter throws a light on different ways embraced by the people during the pandemic. It delves into the various emotions experienced provoked by fear and uncertainty and discusses how these emotions fluctuate over time. Additionally, it examines the coping mechanisms employed by people to manage their vulnerability using different domains like psychological, social, and behavioral. The chapter gives bits of knowledge into the mental effect of the pandemic and gives thoughts for powerful survival strategies in view of genuine encounters.

Figure 2. Different stages of emotions

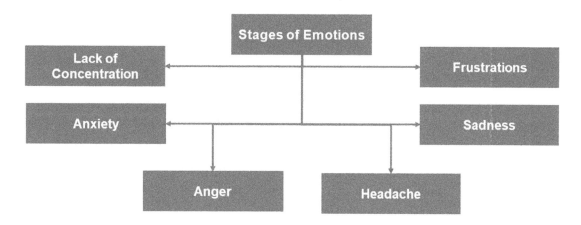

BACKGROUND

Fluctuation of Emotions

During the pandemic, individuals experienced a wide range of emotions, often fluctuating rapidly in response to evolving situations. Fear and anxiety were prominent emotions, driven by the fear of infection (M.-P. Loh, Y.-P. Wong, and C.-O. Wong,2006), uncertainty about the future, and concerns for vulnerable populations. The concept of emotional fluctuations pertains to the inherent and ongoing shifts in an individual's emotional condition throughout their lifetime (M. Abdulrahman and A. Eleyan,2015). It is important to recognize that human emotions are multifaceted and can manifest in different degrees of intensity, durations, and categories, contingent upon a wide range (H. Boughrara, M. Chtourou, C. B. Amar, and L. Chen,2016) of factors including external stimuli, internal cognitive processes, physiological mechanisms, and social engagements. These emotions encompass a diverse array of sensations, such as joy, sorrow, frustration, apprehension, astonishment, affection (S. L. Fernandes and G. J. Bala,2016), and numerous others. Conversely, feelings of hope and solidarity emerged as communities came together to support one another. Additionally, many individuals experienced sadness and grief due to illness and loss, while others felt frustration and anger in response to government policies and public behaviour. Figure 2 represent the different stages of emotion.

Impact of Stress

The COVID-19 pandemic has a considerable influence on the stress levels experienced by people, and this stress has resulted in a multitude of consequences for individuals, communities, and societies. In the following explanation, we will discuss several ways in which stress, arising from the COVID-19 pandemic (Souza, L.K.; Policarpo, D.; Hutz, C.S., 2020). The constant barrage of pandemic-related information, coupled with the challenges of adapting to new norms such as remote work and online learning, contributed significantly to stress levels. Prolonged stress (Angalakuditi, Hindu, and Biswajit Bhowmik, 2023) can have detrimental effects on both physical and mental health, making it crucial to

Figure 3. Stress level during pandemic

identify coping mechanisms that can mitigate its impact. Figure 3 represent the stress levels during the COVID-19.

Different Coping Mechanisms

- **Information Seeking and Awareness:** Many individuals cope by seeking accurate information about the virus, its spread, and preventive measures. Being informed helps people feel more in control and reduces anxiety (Panayiotou, G., Panteli, M. Leonidou, C., 2021).
- **Social Support:** Maintaining connections with friends and family, even virtually, provided crucial emotional support. Social interactions helped mitigate feelings of isolation and fostered a sense of belonging and community.
- **Mindfulness and Relaxation Techniques:** Practices such as meditation, yoga, and deep breathing exercises were employed to manage stress and promote emotional well-being. These techniques helped individuals stay grounded and manage overwhelming emotions.
- **Physical Activity:** Regular physical activity not only contributed to physical health but also released endorphins, which acted as natural stress relievers (Guszkowska, Monika, and Anna Dąbrowska-Zimakowska,2022). Many individuals embraced home workouts and outdoor activities to stay active.
- **Seeking Professional Help:** Mental health services, including therapy and counselling, became more accessible through online platforms. Many people sought professional help to cope with anxiety, depression (A. Hindu and B. Bhowmik, 2022), and other mental health challenges exacerbated by the pandemic.
- **Engaging Hobbies and Creativity:** Pursuing hobbies and creative outlets, such as art, cooking, writing, or gardening, provided (Schuster, R. M., Hammitt, W. E., & Moore, D., 2006) a welcome distraction and a sense of accomplishment. Engaging in these activities offered a break from pandemic-related stressors.
- **Adaptation and Resilience:** People have demonstrated remarkable resilience by adapting to new circumstances. Adaptable individuals (Voronin IA, Manrique-Millones D, Vasin GM,2020) are better able to cope with the challenges presented by the pandemic, finding new ways to work, socialize, and engage in activities.

Stress and its Causes

Disappointment and frustration occur when people are hindered in their attempts (Endler, N. S., Kocovski, N. L., & Macrodimitris, S. D., 2001) to achieve their goals. For example, repeated attempts by someone without proper vocal skills (perhaps due to parental pressure) can lead to personal frustration and subsequent stress (A. P. Fard and M. H. Mahoor, 2022). If such attempts are too intense or too long, the stress can cause physical symptoms and illness (S. Elzeiny and M. Qaraqe, 2018), (M. F. Rizwan, R. Farhad, F. Mashuk, F. Islam, and M. H. Imam, 2019). For example, environmental dissatisfaction and the resulting stress can arise when someone auditioning has to deal with unfamiliar music, poorly trained accompanists, loud noises, or other irritating ecological factors (Apgar D, Cadmus T., 2021). There are many reasons for stress which is shown in Figure 4.

- **Fear and Anxiety:** One of the main causes of stress is fear and anxiety originating from different sources. For example, regularly hearing the news (C. Van Slyke, J. Lee, B. Q. Duong, and T. S. Ellis,, 2022) about the undesired scenarios and plans which go out of our way can be stressful. Especially because they feel they are out of control of these events. Natural disasters tend to be very rare, but media coverage can make them more likely than they are. Fears, for example, worrying that they may not be able to complete a project at work or they will not have enough money to pay their bills etc.
- **Unpleasant Events:** It can be determined if anybody's view of the world or a particular situation is stressful (Huebschmann, N. A., & Sheets, E. S., 2020). For example, "what happens if a thief comes to the house and steals?" Similarly, people who feel they are doing well will be less nervous about their upcoming issues than those who worry about their incompetence.
- **Unrealistic Expectations of Others:** Any unrealistic ex- potations can hurt people, leading to stress. For example (Mustafa Zuhaer Nayef Al-Dabagh, 2014), it is not always possible for an employee, especially in corporate sectors, to meet the organization's expectations which eventually leads to stress.
- **Relationship and Expression:** Stress can be a significant change in anyone's life. The same goes for joys like marriage or promotion. Other events, such as divorce, serious financial difficulties, or the death of a family member, can be significant sources of stress.

Stress is a common emotion. Studies have used machine learning (ML) and artificial intelligence (AI) to recognize human emotions (Zhifeng Li and Xiaoou Tang,2004), but each method yielded different results (B. Bhowmik, 2021). Research is underway to solve the emotion recognition problem, which can be crucial in various aspects of technology and industry (B. Wang, 2016). There are potential applications across industries; this is where emotional computing is heading, designed to solve the emotion classification problem (Vani, 2020), (Turetzkaya, 2020). There are mainly seven types of stress: Acute, Episodic Acute, Chronic, Physical, Psychological, Psychosocial, and Psycho- spiritual Stress. In rundown, the effect of Coronavirus on human feelings has been diverse, enveloping many sentiments from dread and trouble to sympathy and versatility. The aggregate close to home reaction to the pandemic highlights the significance of tending to psychological wellness needs, encouraging social associations, and offering help to people and networks encountering different personal difficulties.

Figure 4. Various levels of stress

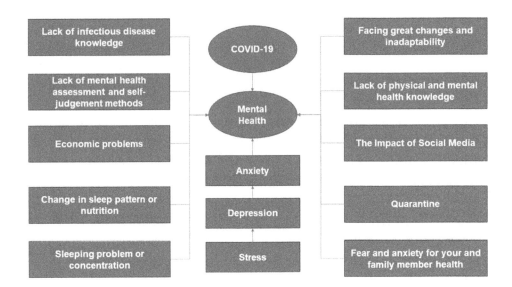

- **Acute Stress:** Generally, acute stress is short-lived. The reactive thinking of humans mainly causes acute stress. The near future is dominated by negative thoughts about recent or upcoming situations, events, or requirements. For example, if any person has been arguing recently, he may experience much stress associated with repetitive negative thoughts about the claim. Or people may be stressed as the deadline for their work approaches (Zwiggelaar, 2014).

- **Episodic Acute Stress:** People who frequently experience acute stress or are ex- posed to frequent stressors in their daily life experience temporary or episodic acute stress. Such people under a lot of stress often lead lives full of chaos and crises. They are always in a hurry or under pressure. They usually cannot organize that much time to maintain responsibility. These people are thus constantly under severe stress.

- **Chronic Stress:** Chronic stress is the deadliest form of stress. If left untreated over a long period, chronic stress can cause significant and often irreversible damage to physical health and mental health deterioration. Behavioural and emotional responses take root when a person lives in a state of chronic stress. Changes occur in the neurobiology of the brain and body. Regardless of the sce- nario, they are constantly exposed to the dangerous effects of stress on the cognitive abilities of the body and mind (Momin, 2016). Symptoms of chronic stress can lead to suicide, violence, ho- micide, psychosis, heart attack, and stroke. Chronic stress is debilitating stress. It exhausts people every day. Chronic stress destroys lives, bodies, and minds. They suffer from persistent fatigue.

- **Physical Stress:** The process of responding to physical stress begins the moment the body per- ceives the presence of a stressor, followed by the transmission of signals in the brain and spe- cific sympathetic and hormonal responses to it to eliminate, reduce, or manage stress. Physical stress includes intense physical labour/exertion, trauma, inadequate oxygen supply, environmental pollution, fatigue, illness, low/high blood sugar, hormonal and biochemical imbalance, etc. (N. Attaran, 2016).

- **Psychological Stress:** Psychological stress includes various work pressures from school, college, office, etc., and other responsibilities. Examples of this psychological stress are fear of losing a job in the industry, financial problems, Health issues, illness, the divorce between a couple, etc. (Pandey, 2017). Psychological stress also includes anxiety, jealousy between friends or colleagues, incapacity of people, guilt, out-of-control in some situations, disappointment, and various emotions like sadness, anger, grief, bereavement, etc.
- **Psychosocial Stress:** Difficulties in relationships (with a partner, sibling, child, parent, employer, coworker, or employer) characterize psychosocial stress. Other factors include a person's social status, job loss, loss of savings or investments, death of a loved one, financial difficulties, isolation in homes, etc. (A. Mohammadi, 2022).

ROLE OF COVID-19 ON STRESS

Stress and coping are closely related constructs with a long history as research topics (e.g., Fava et al., 1998; Lazarus, 1966). Compared to previous research on stress and coping, our sample contains information across a unique worldwide stressful phenomenon: the COVID-19 pandemic. Research on changes in stress and coping around the time of the pandemic have reported mixed results. The world is going through one of humanity's greatest crises due to the COVID-19 pandemic. Millions of people are affected, and many died because of this pandemic. The effect of COVID-19 disease is worldwide. For example, Bharat has 44,645,768 confirmed and 5,28,981 death cases as reported till October 2022. The WHO's report says that nearly 625,740,449 people were affected, and 6,563,667 died from the disease until October 2022 (https://covid19.who.int/, 2010). Thus, the COVID-19 outbreak severely impacts people with stress. The people can be across the professions. This section discusses the impact of stress on people in selected professions. The COVID-19 pandemic has significantly impacted stress levels due to health concerns, social isolation, financial stress, disruptions in daily life, grief and loss, information overload, healthcare challenges, uncertainty about the future, and fears related to reinfections and variants. The long-term psychological effects of this collective stress are areas of ongoing research and concern, highlighting the importance of mental health support and resources during and after the pandemic.

RESEARCH METHODOLOGY

Proposing a research methodology for studying the fluctuation of emotions in stress and coping mechanisms during the COVID-19 pandemic using Artificial Intelligence (AI) involves integrating advanced computational techniques with traditional research methods. Here's a proposed research methodology that combines AI technologies is shown in Figure 5.

Data Collection

- **Dataset:** Flickr & Yale datasets will be used for the detection of fluctuation of emotion during COVID-19.

Table 1. Various author's work

Researchers	Methodology
Aslan, 2021	Deep learning method could be used in developing a real-time system for recognition of human emotions.
Oumina et al., 2020	Proposed good result for the recognition of emotion using two different classifiers.
Kodhai et al., 2020	Proposed several classification algorithms for recognition of facial expression.
Dino and Abdulrazzaq, 2019	Proposed three classifiers as SVM, NN and K-NN for the recognition of facial expression.
Öztürk and Akdemir, 2018	SFTA algorithm produces more successful results than the other feature extraction algorithms.
Jogin et al., 2018	Proposed various classification algorithms using the concept of deep learning will give 85% accuracy for image classification.
Heshmati et al., 2022	Proposed the importance of diversity in emotional experiences in relation to emotional eating.
Xu et al., 2023	Found that among the most proximal domains of stress for Chinese adolescents (i.e., family, peer, and academic stress), peer stress had the most salient association with adolescents' emotional and physical adjustment.
Dai et al., 2023	Interrelationship between emotional changes and the urban built environment was investigated using sentiment analysis based on the textual data collected from Weibo.
Güzel et al., 2023	Suggest that the COVID-19 pandemic is associated with a wide spread negative effect on eating disorder (ED) pathology in patient samples and the general population.
Godara et al., 2023	It might be of utmost importance to provide access to trainings and programs that seek to enhance these protective factors when faced with a global crisis of a similar nature as the COVID-19 pandemic.
Hindu and Biswajit 2023	The AutoCov22 approach demonstrates a promising and plausible best solution over several methods in the state-of-the-art.
Hagger et al., 2020	Research testing the efficacy of stress mindsets in mitigating stress in the context of highly stressful events, such as COVID-19 and its aftermath, to address this evidence gap and provide definitive evidence to support their use in stress management in traumatic events such as pandemics.
Fard and Mahoor, 2022	Proposed loss function in other computer vision tasks such as human body joint tracking.
Elzeiny and Qaraqe 2018	we review and summarize various approaches found in the literature for stress detection using machine learning and suggest directions for future research and interventions.
Rizwan et al., 2019	Emphasizes the importance of respiratory information in stress detection through Machine Learning.
Bhowmik et al., 2021	This work involves monitoring a person's attention and emotional state across the ages. Proposed method identifies individual emotions in each video frame.
Wang et al., 2016	Improve understanding of the combined effects of exposure to both psychological stress (PS) and ionizing radiation (IR) to facilitate, via active intervention, strategies for radiation risk reduction.
Bobade and Vani, 2020	Taking self-reports of the subjects from the dataset into account, which were obtained using several organized questionnaires.
Anishchenko and Turetzkaya 2020	Proposed an improved unobtrusive machine-learning based method for remote mental stress detection by a bioradar.
Rajoub and Zwiggelaar 2014	Learning models of deception based on a leave one person out methodology assumes that the same behaviours and body responses are shared globally across humans of various ages, genders, culture, etc. which so far has not been shown to be accurate.
Kalas and Momin, 2016	GRNN (General Regression Neural Networks) Moreover, the procedure is repeated with respect to three datasets differentiated by the task type: 1) the physical task, 2) the cognitive task, and 3) both tasks.
Attaran et al., 2016	The entire stress monitoring system is further evaluated against a number of other platforms.
Pandey 2017	SVM & logistic regression are used to predict the condition of the patient and IoT is used to communicate the patience about his/her acute stress condition.
Mohammadi et al., 2022	Using Kruskal-Wallis analysis, it is shown that 43 out of 65 features demonstrate a significant difference between stress and relaxed states. K nearest neighbor (KNN) algorithm is implemented to distinguish these states.
WHO 2020	About COVID-19 guidelines & other thins related to COVID-19.
Fernandes and Bala 2016	The multivariate statistical evaluation method introduced revealed that there exists a statistically significant difference between the average recognition distance of the left and right reconstructed face images with varying expressions.
Loh et al., 2006	The neural network that we used as expression classifier/classification engine is a network with simple architecture back propagation.
Abdulrahman and Eleyan 2015	Propose a facial expression recognition approach based on Principal Component Analysis (PCA) and Local Binary Pattern (LBP) algorithms.
Carcagnì et al., 2015	Comprehensive study of how the HOG descriptor could be effectively exploited for facial expression recognition purposes has been carried out.

Figure 5. Theoretical framework for emotion detection

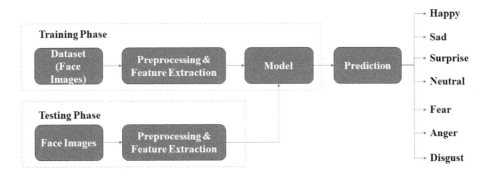

- **Social Media Analysis:** Also gather data from social media platforms using natural language processing (NLP) techniques to analyze public sentiment, emotional expressions, and coping strategies shared by individuals during the pandemic.
- **Surveys and Questionnaires:** Develop online surveys incorporating AI algorithms to analyze responses in real-time, allowing for immediate insights into emotional states and coping mechanisms.
- **Mobile Apps and Wearables:** Utilize mobile applications and wearable devices equipped with AI to collect real-time data on users' emotional well-being, stress levels, and physical activities.

Natural Language Processing (NLP)

- **Sentiment Analysis:** Use NLP algorithms to perform sentiment analysis on textual data, extracting emotional tones and patterns from social media posts, online forums, and survey responses.
- **Topic Modeling:** Use topic modeling techniques (e.g., Latent Dirichlet Allocation) to identify predominant themes related to stressors and coping mechanisms discussed in text data.

Machine Learning and Predictive Analytics

- **Predictive Modeling:** Build machine learning models to predict emotional states and coping behaviours based on various factors, such as demographic information, news about the pandemic and social interactions.
- **Classification Algorithms:** Implement classification algorithms (e.g., Support Vector Machines, Neural Networks) to categorize coping mechanisms into different types, providing insights into the most effective strategies.

Deep Learning

- **Emotion Recognition:** Utilize deep learning models, such as Convolutional Neural Networks (CNNs), SVM, KNN and Recurrent Neural Networks (RNNs), to recognize facial expressions and vocal tones, providing insights into real-time emotional states.

- **Generative Models:** Explore generative models like Generative Adversarial Networks (GANs) to create synthetic datasets, enabling researchers to simulate and analyze different emotional and coping scenarios.

Big Data Analytics

- **Data Mining:** Leverage big data analytics tools to mine large datasets for patterns and correlations related to emotional fluctuations, stressors, and coping strategies across diverse populations.
- **Real-time Analytics:** Implement real-time analytics to process streaming data from social media and other sources, allowing for immediate insights into changing emotional trends during the pandemic.

Ethical Considerations

- **Privacy Preservation:** Ensure data anonymization and privacy protection, especially when dealing with sensitive information obtained from social media and mobile apps.
- **Algorithmic Bias:** Address potential biases in AI models, ensuring fairness and equity in the analysis of emotional responses and coping mechanisms among different demographic groups.

Integration and Interpretation

- **Multimodal Fusion:** Integrate insights from multiple data sources, combining textual, visual, and physiological data to gain a holistic understanding of emotional fluctuations and coping behaviours.
- **Interdisciplinary Collaboration:** Collaborate with psychologists, social scientists, and domain experts to interpret AI-generated insights in the context of human emotions and behaviour during the pandemic.

Several machine learning algorithms and techniques can be employed to analyze fluctuations in emotion, stress, and coping mechanisms during the COVID-19 pandemic. The choice of algorithm depends on the specific task and the nature of the data. Here are some common machine learning algorithms and classifiers used in this context:

Sentiment Analysis

- **Naive Bayes Classifier:** This algorithm is commonly used for sentiment analysis tasks. It works well for text data and is efficient for processing large volumes of textual information.
- **Support Vector Machines (SVM):** SVM can be used for sentiment analysis to classify texts into positive, negative, or neutral categories.
- **Recurrent Neural Networks (RNN) and Long Short-Term Memory (LSTM) Networks:** These are types of neural networks particularly effective for sequential data like text. They can capture contextual information and are widely used in sentiment analysis tasks.

Emotion Recognition

- **Convolutional Neural Networks (CNN):** CNNs are commonly used for image analysis tasks. In the context of emotion recognition, they can analyze facial expressions from images or videos to identify emotions.
- **Recurrent Neural Networks (RNN) and LSTM Networks:** RNNs and LSTMs can also be used for time-series analysis of facial expressions or speech data to recognize emotional patterns.

Time Series Analysis for Stress Fluctuation

- **Autoregressive Integrated Moving Average (ARIMA):** ARIMA models are used for analyzing time-series data. They can predict future values based on past observations, making them useful for studying stress fluctuation trends over time.
- **Long Short-Term Memory (LSTM) Networks:** LSTMs, a type of recurrent neural network, can model long-term dependencies in time-series data, making them suitable for predicting stress levels over time.

Coping Mechanism Analysis

- **Decision Trees and Random Forest:** Decision trees and ensemble methods like Random Forest can be used to analyze factors contributing to the effectiveness of different coping mechanisms (Horiuchi, 2018). They can handle both numerical and categorical data.
- **Natural Language Processing (NLP) Techniques:** NLP techniques such as topic modeling (e.g., Latent Dirichlet Allocation) can be used to identify common themes and topics in textual data related to coping mechanisms.

Personalized Recommendation Systems for Coping Strategies

- **Collaborative Filtering:** Collaborative filtering algorithms analyze user behavior and preferences to recommend coping strategies based on similar users' choices and experiences.
- **Content-Based Filtering:** Content-based filtering recommends coping mechanisms based on the features of the strategies and the user's preferences.

It's important to preprocess the data appropriately, handle imbalanced datasets, and validate the chosen models to ensure their effectiveness and reliability in predicting emotional states and coping mechanisms during the COVID-19 pandemic (Brown, 2020). The choice of algorithm also depends on the specific nature of the data available for analysis. By integrating AI technologies with rigorous research methods, this proposed methodology aims to provide a nuanced and data-driven understanding of the fluctuation of emotions in stress and coping mechanisms during the COVID-19 pandemic (Voltmer, 2021). This interdisciplinary approach can yield valuable insights for public health interventions, mental health support systems, and crisis management strategies. The outcomes of research conducted on the fluctuation of emotions in stress and coping mechanisms during the COVID-19 pandemic (Duan, 2020) would vary based on the methodology used, the sample size, demographics studied, and the specific research

Figure 6. Various solutions to avoid stress

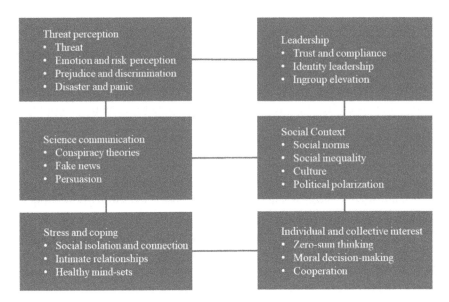

questions asked. However, I can discuss some general trends and potential findings that such research might reveal based on the methodologies described earlier.

FINDINGS, SOLUTION, AND FUTURE WORK

There are various solutions to avoid the stress such as Zero-sum thinking and social isolation. Here we present various ways to cope with the stress in Figure 6.

- **Emotional Fluctuations:** Research might reveal the patterns of emotional fluctuations experienced by individuals during different stages of the pandemic. For instance, initial phases might have seen high levels of fear and anxiety, whereas, with time, resilience and adaptation might have led to more stable emotional states.
- **Stressors Identification:** Studies could identify specific stressors that had the most significant impact on people's emotions. This could include factors such as fear of infection, economic instability, social isolation, or concerns about the health of loved ones.
- **Coping Mechanisms:** Research might shed light on the coping mechanisms that were most adopted. These could range from social support networks to mindfulness practices, physical activities, or seeking professional mental health support.
- **Demographic Variances:** Studies could reveal how different demographic groups (age, gender, socioeconomic status, etc.) experienced and coped with stress and emotional fluctuations differently. For instance, younger individuals might have relied more on digital communication for social support, while older adults might have faced challenges related to technology adoption.

- **Effectiveness of Interventions:** Research might evaluate the effectiveness of various interventions and support systems, both traditional and technology driven. This could include analyzing the impact of online therapy, mental health apps, or community support programs.
- **Long-term Psychological Impact:** Longitudinal studies could offer insights into the long-term psychological effects of the pandemic, including potential increases in anxiety disorders, depression, or post-traumatic stress disorders among certain populations.
- **Resilience Factors:** Research might identify factors that contributed to resilience, such as personal traits, social support structures, or community initiatives. Understanding these factors can inform future strategies for building resilience in communities facing similar challenges.
- **Policy Implications:** Studies might provide valuable data for policymakers and mental health professionals, helping them tailor interventions and support systems based on the specific needs and challenges identified in different demographic groups.

Remember, the actual results would depend on the specifics of the research design, the quality of data collected, and the rigor of the analysis conducted. Researchers typically publish their findings in academic journals, providing detailed insights into their methodologies and results for peer review and the broader academic community. The COVID-19 pandemic has sparked a wide range of emotional reactions, encompassing feelings of fear, anxiety, as well as displays of resilience and adaptability. It is crucial to comprehend these fluctuations in emotions and delve into effective strategies for managing them to foster mental and emotional well-being amidst these trying circumstances. By conducting research in this field, we not only gain insight into the human ability to confront adversity but also acquire valuable knowledge that can shape the creation of interventions and support systems, which aim to assist individuals in navigating the intricate emotional landscape of the pandemic and other unforeseen crises that may arise in the future. The fruitful use of man-made intelligence in getting it and tending to close to home changes and stress during the Coronavirus pandemic has prepared for future examination and applications in the field of emotional well-being. Proceeded with headways in simulated intelligence advances hold the commitment of additional modern and exact mediations custom-made to individual necessities.

CONCLUSION

The COVID-19 pandemic triggered intense emotional fluctuations, ranging from fear and sadness to hope and solidarity. Managing these emotions was essential for overall well-being, and various coping mechanisms were employed to navigate the stressors effectively. As the world continues to grapple with the pandemic's aftermath, understanding these coping strategies and their impact on mental health remains vital for building resilience and promoting emotional well-being in the face of future challenges. The three classifiers were utilized to measure the Fluctuation of Emotion in Stress and different Coping Mechanism During COVID-19 Pandemic, SVM, NN and K-NN. The experiments results show that SVM proven to be better classifier with 93.53% accuracy of correct classification rate. In future, we can use our own novel dataset which is in collecting progress and test the presented method with different machine learning algorithms to provide better accuracy. In conclusion, our research underscores the remarkable capacity of individuals and communities to adapt and find strength amidst adversity. By understanding the intricate dynamics of emotions, stressors, and coping mechanisms during the COVID-19 pandemic, we pave the way for more targeted and effective approaches to supporting mental health in times of crisis. As we move forward, it is our collective responsibility to leverage these insights, fostering a society that prioritizes emotional well-being and resilience for all its members.

ACKNOWLEDGMENT

I would like to express my heartfelt gratitude to all those who contributed to the completion of this book chapter. First and foremost, I am deeply thankful to my guide, Dr. Piyush Ranjan, Dr. Priyanka Srivastava & the editor of this volume, for providing me with the opportunity to contribute to this collection. I'm obligated to my associates for their significant direction and keen input all through the research and writing process. Their mastery has been instrumental in forming the thoughts introduced in this part. I'm likewise grateful to my loved ones for their steady help and consolation. Their confidence in my capacities kept me propelled during testing times, and for that, I am genuinely thankful. Lastly, I am very grateful to Dr. Keshav Sinha who generously shared their experiences and insights, without whom this work would not have been possible.

REFERENCES

Abdulrahman, M., & Eleyan, A. (2015). Facial expression recognition using support vector machines. *2015 23nd Signal Processing and Communications Applications Conference (SIU),* 276-279. 10.1109/SIU.2015.7129813

Angalakuditi, H., & Bhowmik, B. (2023). Impact of Stress During COVID-19 Pandemic. *9th International Conference on Advanced Computing and Communication Systems (ICACCS).* 10.1109/ICACCS57279.2023.10113119

Anishchenko, L., & Turetzkaya, A. (2020). Improved non-contact mental stress detection via bioradar. *2020 International Conference on Biomedical Innovations and Applications (BIA),* 21–24. 10.1109/BIA50171.2020.9244492

Apgar, D., & Cadmus, T. (2021). Using mixed methods to assess coping and self-regulation skills of undergraduate social work students impacted by COVID-19. *Clinical Social Work Journal,* 1–12. PMID:33589848

Aslan, M. (2021). CNN based efficient approach for emotion recognition. *Journal of King Saud University. Computer and Information Sciences.*

Attaran, Brooks, & Mohsenin. (2016). A low-power multi- physiological monitoring processor for stress detection. *2016 IEEE Sensors,* 1–3.

Bhowmik, B., Varna, S. A., Kumar, A., & Kumar, R. (2021). *Deep neural networks in healthcare systems. In Machine Learning and Deep Learning in Efficacy Improvement of Healthcare Systems.* CRC Press, Taylor and Francis.

Bobade, P., & Vani, M. (2020). Stress detection with machine learning and deep learning using multimodal physiological data. *2020 Second International Conference on Inventive Research in Computing Applications (ICIRCA)*, 51–57. 10.1109/ICIRCA48905.2020.9183244

Boughrara, H., Chtourou, M., Amar, C. B., & Chen, L. (2016). Facial expression recognition based on a mlp neural network using constructive training algorithm. *Multimedia Tools and Applications*, *75*(2), 709–731. doi:10.100711042-014-2322-6

Brown, S. M., Doom, J. R., Lechuga-Pena, S., Watamura, S. E., & Koppels, T. (2020). Stress and parenting during the global COVID-19 pandemic. *Child Abuse & Neglect*, *110*(Pt 2), 104699. doi:10.1016/j.chiabu.2020.104699 PMID:32859394

Carcagnì, P., Del Coco, M., Leo, M., & Distante, C. (2015). Facial expression recognition and histograms of oriented gradients: A comprehensive study. *SpringerPlus*, *4*(1), 645. doi:10.118640064-015-1427-3 PMID:26543779

Dai, D., Dong, W., Wang, Y., Liu, S., & Zhang, J. (2023). Exploring the relationship between urban residents' emotional changes and built environment before and during the COVID-19 pandemic from the perspective of resilience. *Cities (London, England)*, *141*, 104510. doi:10.1016/j.cities.2023.104510

Duan, L., Shao, X., Wang, Y., Huang, Y., Miao, J., Yang, X., & Zhu, G. (2020). An investigation of the mental health status of children and adolescents in china during the outbreak of COVID-19. *Journal of Affective Disorders*, *275*, 112–118. doi:10.1016/j.jad.2020.06.029 PMID:32658812

Elzeiny, S., & Qaraqe, M. (2018). Machine learning approaches to automatic stress detection: A review. *2018 IEEE/ACS 15th International Conference on Computer Systems and Applications (AICCSA)*, 1–6. 10.1109/AICCSA.2018.8612825

Endler, N. S., Kocovski, N. L., & Macrodimitris, S. D. (2001). Coping, efficacy, and perceived control in acute vs chronic illnesses. *Personality and Individual Differences*, *30*(4), 617–625. doi:10.1016/S0191-8869(00)00060-X

Fard & Mahoor. (2022). Ad-corre: Adaptive correlation-based loss for facial expression recognition in the wild. *IEEE Access, 10*(26), 756–768.

Fernandes, S. L., & Bala, G. J. (2016). A Study on Face Recognition Under Facial Expression Variation and Occlusion. *Proceedings of the International Conference on Soft Computing Systems*, 371-377. 10.1007/978-81-322-2671-0_35

Gashi, D. (2022). The relationship between big five personality traits, coping strategies, and emotional problems through the COVID-19 pandemic. *Current Psychology (New Brunswick, N.J.)*, 1–10. PMID:36406846

Godara, M., Everaert, J., Sanchez-Lopez, A., Joormann, J., & De Raedt, R. (2023). Interplay between uncertainty intolerance, emotion regulation, cognitive flexibility, and psychopathology during the COVID-19 pandemic: A multi-wave study. *Scientific Reports*, *13*(1), 9854. doi:10.103841598-023-36211-3 PMID:37330557

Guszkowska, M., & Dąbrowska-Zimakowska, A. (2022). Coping with stress during the second wave of the COVID-19 pandemic by Polish university students: Strategies, structure, and relation to psychological well-being. *Psychology Research and Behavior Management, 15*, 339–352. doi:10.2147/PRBM. S345648 PMID:35210882

Güzel, Â., Mutlu, N. L., & Molendijk, M. (2023). COVID-19-related changes in eating disorder pathology, emotional and binge eating and need for care: A systematic review with frequentist and Bayesian meta-analyses. *Eating and Weight Disorders, 28*(1), 19. doi:10.100740519-023-01547-2 PMID:36805344

Hagger, M. S., Keech, J. J., & Hamilton, K. (2020). Managing stress during the coronavirus disease 2019 pandemic and beyond: Reappraisal and mindset approaches. *Stress and Health, 36*(3), 396–401. doi:10.1002mi.2969 PMID:32588961

Heshmati, S., DavyRomano, E., Chow, C., Doan, S. N., & Reynolds, K. D. (2023). Negative emodiversity is associated with emotional eating in adolescents: An examination of emotion dynamics in daily life. *Journal of Adolescence, 95*(1), 115–130. doi:10.1002/jad.12103 PMID:36217272

Hindu, A., & Bhowmik, B. (2022). An iot-enabled stress detection scheme using facial expression. *2022 IEEE 19th India Council International Conference (INDICON),* 1-6. 10.1109/INDICON56171.2022.10040216

Horiuchi, S., Tsuda, A., Aoki, S., Yoneda, K., & Sawaguchi, Y. (2018). Coping as a mediator of the relationship between stress mindset and psychological stress response: A pilot study. *Psychology Research and Behavior Management, 11*, 47–54. doi:10.2147/PRBM.S150400 PMID:29535562

Huang, C.-L., & Huang, Y.-M. (1997). Facial expression recognition using model-based feature extraction and action parameters classification. *Journal of Visual Communication and Image Representation, 8*(3), 278–290. doi:10.1006/jvci.1997.0359

Huebschmann, N. A., & Sheets, E. S. (2020). The right mindset: Stress mindset moderates the association between perceived stress and depressive symptoms. *Anxiety, Stress, and Coping, 33*(3), 248–255. doi:10.1080/10615806.2020.1736900 PMID:32138538

Huebschmann, N. A., & Sheets, E. S. (2020). The right mindset: Stress mindset moderates the association between perceived stress and depressive symptoms. *Anxiety, Stress, and Coping, 33*(3), 248–255. doi:10.1080/10615806.2020.1736900 PMID:32138538

Jogin, M., Madhulika, M. S., Divya, G. D., Meghana, R. K., & Apoorva, S. (2018). Feature Extraction using Convolution Neural Networks (CNN) and Deep Learning. *2018 3rd IEEE International Conference on Recent Trends in Electronics, Information & Communication Technology (RTEICT).*

Kalas, M. S., & Momin, B. (2016). Stress detection and reduction using eeg signals. *2016 International Conference on Electrical, Electronics, and Optimization Techniques (ICEEOT),* 471–475. 10.1109/ICEEOT.2016.7755604

Kodhai, E., Pooveswari, A., Sharmila, P., & Ramiya, N. (2020). Literature Review on Emotion Recognition System. *2020 International Conference on System, Computation, Automation and Networking (ICSCAN).*

Li, Z., & Tang, X. (2004). Bayesian face recognition using support vector machine and face clustering. *Proceedings of the 2004 IEEE Computer Society Conference on Computer Vision and Pattern Recognition, 2*, 374-380. 10.1109/CVPR.2004.1315188

Loh, Wong, & Wong. (2006). *Facial expression recognition for e-learning systems using Gabor wavelet & neural network*. Academic Press.

Mohammadi, A., Fakharzadeh, M., & Baraeinejad, B. (2022). An integrated human stress detection sensor using supervised algorithms. *IEEE Sensors Journal, 22*(8), 8216–8223. doi:10.1109/JSEN.2022.3157795

Munsell, S. E., O'Malley, L., & Mackey, C. (2020). Coping with COVID. *Edu Res Theory Pract., 31*(3), 101–109.

Nikcevie, A. V., Marino, C., Kolubinski, D. C., Leach, D., & Spada, M. M. (2021). Modelling the contribution of the big five personality traits, health anxiety, and COVID-19 psychological distress to generalised anxiety and depressive symptoms during the COVID-19 pandemic. *Journal of Affective Disorders, 279*, 578–584. doi:10.1016/j.jad.2020.10.053 PMID:33152562

Oh, M., Kim, J. W., Yoon, N. H., Lee, S. A., Lee, S. M., & Kang, W. S. (2019). Differences in personality, defense styles, and coping strategies in individuals with depressive disorder according to age groups across the lifespan. *Psychiatry Investigation, 16*(12), 911–918. doi:10.30773/pi.2019.0160 PMID:31801315

Oumina, A., El Makhfi, N., & Hamdi, M. (2020). Control The COVID-19 Pandemic: Face Mask Detection Using Transfer Learning. *2020 IEEE 2nd International Conference on Electronics, Control, Optimization and Computer Science (ICECOCS).*

Öztürk, Ş., & Akdemir, B. (2018). Application of Feature Extraction and Classification Methods for Histopathological Image using GLCM, LBP, LBGLCM, GLRLM and SFTA. *Procedia Computer Science, 132*, 40–46. doi:10.1016/j.procs.2018.05.057

Panayiotou, G., Panteli, M., & Leonidou, C. (2021). Coping with the invisible enemy: The role of emotion regulation and awareness in quality of life during the COVID-19 pandemic. *Journal of Contextual Behavioral Science, 19*, 17–27. doi:10.1016/j.jcbs.2020.11.002

Pandey, P. S. (2017). Machine learning and iot for prediction and detection of stress. *2017 17th International Conference on Computational Science and Its Applications (ICCSA),* 1–5. 10.1109/ICCSA.2017.8000018

Park, C. L., Russell, B. S., Fendrich, M., Finkelstein-Fox, L., Hutchison, M., & Becker, J. (2020). Americans' COVID-19 stress, coping and adherence to CDC guidelines. *Journal of General Internal Medicine, 35*(8), 2296–2303. doi:10.100711606-020-05898-9 PMID:32472486

Rajoub, B. A., & Zwiggelaar, R. (2014). Thermal facial analysis for deception detection. *IEEE Transactions on Information Forensics and Security, 9*(6), 1015–1023. doi:10.1109/TIFS.2014.2317309

Revina, I. M., & Emmanuel, W. S. (2018). A survey on human face expression recognition techniques. *Journal of King Saud University. Computer and Information Sciences.*

Rizwan, M. F., Farhad, R., Mashuk, F., Islam, F., & Imam, M. H. (2019). Design of a biosignal based stress detection system using machine learning techniques. *2019 International Conference on Robotics, Electrical and Signal Processing Techniques (ICREST),* 364–368. 10.1109/ICREST.2019.8644259

Schuster, R. M., Hammitt, W. E., & Moore, D. (2006). Stress appraisal and coping response to hassles experienced in outdoor recreation settings. *Leisure Sciences, 28*(2), 97–113. doi:10.1080/01490400500483919

Shan, K., Guo, J., You, W., Lu, D., & Bie, R. (2017). Automatic facial expression recognition based on a deep convolutional-neural-network structure. *2017 IEEE 15th International Conference on Software Engineering Research, Management and Applications (SERA),* 123-128. 10.1109/SERA.2017.7965717

Souza, L. K., Policarpo, D., & Hutz, C. S. (2020). Self-compassion and Symptoms of Stress, Anxiety, and Depression. *Trends in Psychology, 28*(1), 85–98. doi:10.100743076-020-00018-2

Van Slyke, C., Lee, J., Duong, B. Q., & Ellis, T. S. (2022). Eustress and distress in the context of telework. *Information Resources Management Journal, 35*(1), 1–24. doi:10.4018/IRMJ.291526

Voltmer, E., Köslich-Strumann, S., Walther, A., Kasem, M., Obst, K., & Kötter, T. (2021). The impact of the COVID-19 pandemic on stress, mental health and coping behavior in German university students – a longitudinal study before and after the onset of the pandemic. *BMC Public Health, 21*(1), 1385. doi:10.118612889-021-11295-6 PMID:34256717

Voronin, I. A., Manrique-Millones, D., Vasin, G. M., Millones-Rivalles, R. B., Manrique-Pino, O., Fernández-Ríos, N., Marakshina, Y. A., Lobaskova, M. M., Symanyuk, E. E., Pecherkina, A. A., Ageeva, I. A., Lysenkova, I. A., Ismatullina, V. I., Sitnikova, M. A., & Malykh, S. B. (2020). Coping responses during the COVID-19 pandemic: Cross-cultural comparison of Russia, Kyrgyzstan, and Peru. *Psychology in Russia : State of the Art, 13*(4), 55–74. doi:10.11621/pir.2020.0404

Wang, B., Katsube, T., Begum, N., & Nenoi, M. (2016). Revisiting the health effects of psychological stress—its influence on susceptibility to ionizing radiation: A mini-review. *Journal of Radiation Research, 57*(4), 325–335. doi:10.1093/jrr/rrw035 PMID:27242342

WHO. (n.d.). https://covid19.who.int/

World Health Organization. (2020). *Updated WHO recommendations for international traffic in relation to COVID-19 outbreak.* Available from: https://www.who.int/news-room/articles-detail/updated-whorec ommendations-for-international-traffic-in-relation-to-covid-19-outbreak

Xu, J., Wang, H., Liu, S., Hale, M. E., Weng, X., Ahemaitijiang, N., Hu, Y., Suveg, C., & Han, Z. R. (2023). Relations among family, peer, and academic stress and adjustment in Chinese adolescents: A daily diary analysis. *Developmental Psychology, 59*(7), 1346–1358. doi:10.1037/dev0001538 PMID:37199929

Zacher & Rudolph. (2021). Individual differences and changes in subjective wellbeing during the early stages of the COVID-19 pandemic. *American Psychologist, 76*(1), 50.

KEY TERMS AND DEFINITIONS

Anxiety: In the intricate symphony of emotions, anxiety often plays a discordant note, reminding us of the constant battle within ourselves.

COVID-19: The global pandemic, COVID-19, has not only posed a medical challenge but has also deeply affected our emotional and social landscapes.

Data Mining: In the digital age, data mining unearths invaluable insights, helping us navigate the sea of information and make informed decisions.

Human Emotions: The intricate tapestry of human emotions weaves the essence of our experiences, from the joy of success to the depths of sorrow.

Machine Learning: Machine learning, a realm of artificial intelligence, empowers computers to learn and adapt, mirroring our own cognitive processes in the digital realm.

Psychosocial Behaviour: The study of psychosocial behavior explores the interplay between individual psychology and social influences, unraveling the complexities of our actions and reactions.

Sentiment Analysis: Sentiment analysis harnesses the power of data and natural language processing to decode the emotions hidden within the vast realm of text.

Stress: In the modern hustle and bustle, stress emerges as a constant companion, demanding our attention to maintain our well-being.

Chapter 4
Key Challenges Faced When Preserving Records in Traditional Councils During the 4th Industrial Revolution

Kabelo Bruce Kgomoeswana

https://orcid.org/0000-0002-1592-6100

University of Limpopo, South Africa

Lefose Makgahlela

https://orcid.org/0000-0003-1433-2527

University of LImpopo, South Africa

ABSTRACT

The 4th industrial revolution (4IR) has brought significant technological advancements that have impacted various sectors, including governance and record-keeping. This chapter examines the challenges faced by traditional councils when preserving records during the 4IR. The chapter adopted a desktop research methodology. The data were subjected to substantive and extensive analysis through the instrumentality of content validity, content analysis, and textual criticism to establish facts that defend or refute the hypothesis. The study revealed that traditional councils lack the necessary infrastructure and resources to digitise records, leading to concerns about data loss, system failures, and cybersecurity threats. In essence, the councils are still struggling to protect and secure the records preserved in their custody; as such, council members need digital literacy training. The study recommends strategies that traditional councils should use to preserve records during the 4IR.

INTRODUCTION

Almost every African country has some type of traditional council in its communities. To ensure the exercise of power and authority, the most typical systems of traditional leadership are kings, chiefs,

DOI: 10.4018/979-8-3693-2841-5.ch004

headmen, and village heads. Traditional councils are the most direct form of authority in many rural sections of the continent due to their structure. Thus, understanding decentralisation in an African setting frequently implies acknowledging their involvement at the local government level. Traditional councils also support and contribute to improvement, delivery of services, building a nation, community peace, stability, and cohesiveness, moral regeneration, and cultural and traditional preservation. Traditional councils also play a vital role in many societies, serving as custodians of cultural heritage, ancestral knowledge, and governance systems. Clay tablets, stone drawings, stone carvings, parchment and vellum, leather, cloths, and tree barks are some of the ancient techniques of maintaining records in Africa (Motsi2004, 63). In South Africa, the Constitution (1996) which is the supreme law of the Republic recognises the traditional council in Chapter 12(1) which states that in accordance with customary law, the institution, status, and role of traditional leadership, is duly recognised.

The advent of the 4IR, characterised by technological advancements such as artificial intelligence (AI), big data, and the Internet of Things (IoT), has transformed the way society's function. In the context of traditional councils, this revolution poses unique challenges and opportunities in preserving their records of their cultural identity and heritage. According to Külcü (2009), a record is characterised either by the actual observable form in which it exists or by the information it holds. It should be observed that records vary in format and size, as well as their contents. Malake and Phiri (2020) argue that organisations produce, keep, and preserve records so that they may be utilised. If a user cannot find a document, it may as well not exist. According to Shepherd (2003), effective record management would help organizations conduct operations in a more efficient and fiscally responsible manner, while maintaining consistency in service delivery, decision-making by management, and the openness of policy formulation, execution, and management. This chapter aims to explore the challenges faced when preserving records in traditional councils during the 4IR and suggests strategies for effective record management.

To achieve the above aim, the objectives of the study were to:

- Ascertain the significance of records in the traditional councils.
- Investigate the digitalisation challenges faced by traditional councils when preserving records.
- Determine data security concerns of records in the traditional council.
- Explore the digital literacy level of the council members.

BACKGROUND

Records serve a crucial function in the facilitation of organisational events and functions. In every organisation, records need to be preserved for their role. Preservation is an endeavour to extend something's useful life and prevent it from decaying for as long as possible so that it can be accessed in the future (Ngoepe and Van der Walt, 2009:2). Abioye (2013) explains that the preservation of records ensures that they will continue to exist as proof of events that occurred. Traditional Councils are regarded as traditional institutions responsible for making governmental decisions in the community, and they are also responsible for managing and preserving records for future reference. These Traditional Councils also preserve records to keep the heritage as a traditional institution. Crook (2005:1) states traditional institutions as "all socio-political power systems that have their historical antecedents in early colonial nations and cultures." Africa's traditional record-keeping methods included stone paintings, stone carvings, clay tablets, tree bark, and leather (Motsi, 2004:63). We are now in the 4IR, and things have changed more to digital records preservation. The author, after trying to access records at Ga-Mphahlele traditional council noticed that the records personnels are still struggling with the preservation of records in the 4IR. This called for a need for research to aid the traditional council with the preservation of records in the 4IR.

Methodology

Ihuah and Eaton (2013) assert that, "research methodology is a philosophical stance of worldview that underlies and informs the style of search". A study of literature on current concerns and advancements in records management, preservation, security, literacy, and digitalization was conducted. This provided the authors with further insight into some of the fundamental concepts, challenges, and procedures related to an investigation of record management to coordinate the reader's understanding. The main concepts were discussed using the thoughts and information gained through examining the literature. Desktop research was used as the research approach, and information was gathered from resources such as books, journals, newspapers, and relevant online sites like https://scholar.google.com and institutional academic repositories of different universities. The authors downloaded several articles read, analyzed, and used them to cover the objectives and scope of the study. The articles were selected based on the year of publication to have up to date information and looking at how relevant and authentic they were for the study. The gathered data were submitted to a substantive and detailed investigation using content validity, content analysis, and textual criticism to identify facts that support or refute the hypothesis. Content validity ensures that the data obtained reflects the topic under investigation and that crucial relevant subjects are not omitted. The existence of words or phrases in a text was evaluated to detect the defined features of messages and make sense of them. Textual criticism was used to verify and synthesise literary works to assess their originality and validity.

Literature

The Significance of Records management in Traditional Councils

Effective record management is critical for achieving organizational objectives, missions, and activities. According to Shepherd and Yeo (2003), records are distinguished not by their physical appearance, length of existence, or information content, but rather by their ability to provide proof of an action or event. According to Ricks, Swafford, and Gow (1992), records are essential inside an organization for a variety of reasons, including documenting and validating decision making, safeguarding organizational paperwork, and documenting evidence for future references. According to Thomas, Schubert, and Lee (1983:162), "the results of establishing records centers in institutions include effective storage and retrieval systems as well as comprehensive records transfer and storage programs." Comprehensive records management programs in organizations, according to Shepherd (2006), are a clear identification of organizations' endeavors to supply efficient services and enhance management decision-making, policy implementation, and general administration of organizations. According to Schellnack-Kelly (2013:5), "accessibility and authenticity of information sources determines the integrity and persona of the South African public sector" (in this case, Traditional councils). According to Schellnack-Kelly, information sources are proof of governance obligations to citizens and the global community.

The idea of a 'record' is important to archival science (Quisbert 2006). Though all records are information, not all information has the characteristics of a record. Many researchers have sought to highlight this

Key Challenges Faced When Preserving Records in Traditional Councils

discrepancy in earlier work (Roper & Millar 1999; Ohio State University 2011; Duranti 2014). Records in traditional councils are not merely administrative documents; they hold deep historical and cultural significance. These records often contain details about land ownership, lineage, rituals, and community decisions. Preserving these records is crucial to maintaining social cohesion, resolving disputes, and safeguarding cultural heritage for future generations. According to Chinyemba (2011), organizations must embrace records as a strategic instrument in the same way that they embrace money and human resources. Thus, efficient, and effective record management benefits an organizations or institution's essential stakeholders as well as its administrators, who rely on records to make correct, timely choices (Nwankwo, 2001). According to Ricks, Swafford, and Gow (1992:8), "accurate records are critical to provide background information for future planning while taking advantage of the past."

The right to information is crucial to establishing a connection between government and those being governed (Ngulube, 2004). The ability to access government information is not only a prerequisite for effective governance, democratic participation, and economic growth; it is also an important human right that serves as the foundation for all other human rights (Chibambo 2006, p. 15; Banisar, 2006, p. 6). Accountability, transparency, and the administration of the law are all principles of effective governance that rely heavily on the free flow of information (Mutula & Wamukoya, 2009, p. 333). Openness in general and openness in decision-making in particular can help build citizen trust in government activities and preserve a civil and democratic society (Banisar, 2004, p. 3; 2006, p. 6). Citizens may participate in governance and advocate for their rights if given the opportunity to access information by the government. Records are very important in the traditional council because they advocate openness and transparency in the decision-making process in the traditional council. According to Kenyan research done by Kemoni and Ngulube (2008), records management is required for resource allocation, decision-making, and economic growth. It went on to say that records management is critical to public sector administration and improves service performance. As a result, inadequate records management methods result in poor public service delivery and authorities making misinformed decisions. According to Slote (2000), implementing a thorough records management program provides both immediate and long-term benefits to businesses, such as controlling the number of documents in an organization, improving customer service, and making well-informed choices. Crook (2005, p. 1) defines traditional council as "all forms of social and political authority that can be traced back to precolonial states and societies." Traditional councils have been integral to the governance and decision-making processes of various indigenous communities for centuries. These councils play a crucial role in preserving cultural heritage, resolving conflicts, and maintaining social order. One key aspect that underpins the effectiveness and sustainability of traditional councils is the documentation and management of records. Keeping records has benefits for the traditional council. The advantages, according to Yusof (2005), are that the records are preserved in such a way that they are quickly available, relevant, updated, accurate, and meet the user's demands. Records, such as meeting minutes, oral histories, and customary laws, serve as a repository of knowledge, enabling councils to make informed decisions based on the experiences and wisdom of their forebears. Findings of the study by Ngoepe and Makhubela (2015), suggest that some criminal cases may have been withdrawn owing to missing dockets or improper registration. Records were recreated in certain cases, resulting in a farce of justice. Lawyers, prosecutors, and magistrates might contest the legitimacy of documents if records are not accounted for, according to the study's conclusion. Consequently, the victims and the administration of justice would be delayed, if not deprived entirely, while the offenders are liberated. In many traditional societies, the oral tradition has been the primary mode of transmitting knowledge and history from one generation to the next. However, with the advent of modernisation, technology and external influences, there is a risk of this oral knowledge being lost or distorted. Records offer a tangible and permanent means of preserving the wealth of knowledge held within traditional councils through technological tolls. Chong, Chong and Lin (2010) define technology as an architecture of tools, systems, platforms, and automated solutions that increase knowledge generation, application, and dissemination. Logan (2006) states that organising organisational knowledge and permitting access to it are crucial to employees' abilities to successfully use information that is dispersed throughout the organisation. To develop, collect, organise, and apply new information, current knowledge sharing must be facilitated using technology (Abouzeedan & Hedner 2012; Nassuora & Hasan 2010). This fosters a stronger sense of belonging and cultural pride, which, in turn, enhances social cohesion and the overall resilience of the community. Additionally, the existence of well-organised records empowers traditional councils in their interactions with external entities, such as government bodies and non-governmental organisations, ensuring that their voices are heard and respected. Consequently, upholding the significance of records in traditional councils is vital in safeguarding their cultural legacy and enabling them to adapt to changing circumstances while staying true to their heritage.

Digitalisation Challenges

Digitization has become a practical requirement and reality because of technological innovations, providing greater access to information, preservation, and distribution as needed at any time and from any location. Digitisation is the act of transforming non-digital born documents or analogue information to digital forms (Gbaje, 2007; Feather & Sturges, 2003) or the process of transferring print-on-paper materials to digital form, commonly by scanning (Amollo, 2011). In basic terms, digitization is the process of converting non-digital stuff to digital material. Burkett (2017) defines digitalisation as "the process of exploiting digitisation, encouraging, enhancing, and transforming company procedures and operations by using digitised data and technologies to transform how organizations conduct business and improve productivity." Instead of physically carrying files and documents from one office to another, for example, the organization can utilize emails to disseminate information inside the organization. Whereas digitisation is the act of converting data into digital format, digitalization incorporates digital technology's capacity to acquire and analyze data to make better business choices and allow new business models. In a nutshell, digitization pertains to information, whereas digitalization refers to processes.

The 4IR encourages digitalisation to improve efficiency and accessibility. However, for traditional councils, adopting digital technologies can be challenging. Many councils lack the necessary infrastructure and resources to digitise records, leading to concerns about data loss, system failures, and cybersecurity threats. Globally, government organisations are gradually migrating from paper-based to digital operations (Klareld 2015, 12), resulting in a greater reliance on digital records (Cumming & Findlay 2010, 265). According to the literature, the usage of digitized records ushered in a new era with several changes in corporate operations, communication, records management, and decision-making (Tsvuura & Ngulube, 2021; Eze Asogwa 2013, Asproth 2005). According to Verma (2020), digitising and automating the records management process is critical to maintaining good work quality. According to Thibodeau (2013), despite a patchwork of victories, failures, and hurdles, the transition from traditional records to online records administration has been embraced and executed widely. According to Ndlebe and Dewah (2022), digitisation causes severe obstacles in organizations, such as staff adaption to changes, a shortage of skilled workers, security concerns, and the complexity of the software utilized. Despite these challenges, agencies from government and other organisations are continuing their efforts to convert their valuable papers to electronic format to reap the benefits. Converting records to digital form opens them to numerous safety hazards, as operating multiple systems simultaneously, such as a computerized and physical one, can be exhausting in terms of time, as well as difficult in the organization, especially for records management personnel (Records Nations, 2021). Other challenges include lack of qualified employees (Abdulkadhim, Bahari, Bakri & Ismail 2015; Shatat, 2015; Chaterera, 2012; Mutsagondo & Ngulube, 2018; Ezeani, 2009), lack of adequate facilities (Amollo, 2011; Tsvuura & Ngulube, 2020; Abdulkadhim, Bahari, Bakri & Ismail, 2015) and resistance to digital change (Heathfield, 2021; Loonam, Eaves, Kumar & Parry, 2018; Laumer, 2011; International Data Corporation, 2019).

Digital preservation refers to the general ongoing activities aimed at preserving the semantic meaning of digitally born materials and documents created with recording and imaging technologies, as well as ensuring their long-term storage, access, and use by future generations (Adu & Ngulube 2016, 749; Decman & Vintar 2013, 408; Ross 2012, 45; Groenewald & Breytenbach 2011, 242). The summarised definition from literature confirms that the preservation of information resources in all formats is a continuous activity that occurs throughout the life of the materials (Lischer-Katz 2020, 254). In a similar spirit, Owens (2017, 7) proffers that the process of preservation is never ended, therefore, we can only speak in terms of what we are preserving, not what has been preserved. As a result, the notion of digital preservation keeps attracting the attention of public sector organisations in Africa and elsewhere (Adu & Ngulube 2016, 748). Digitisation is becoming the preferred method for ensuring long-term preservation and access to chosen archive resources (Mnjama, 2011). Dewah and Feni-Fete (2014) regard digitization as a preservation approach that safeguards a document, hence prolonging its life. These digital forms are critical not just for allowing and supporting corporate activities, but they also serve as the government's collective memory (Cumming & Findlay 2010, 265). Competent and well-trained labour is necessary for any library or archive preservation and conservation program to be successful (Ngulube 2006). Traditional councils, according to Masuke (2010), struggle to obtain financing from financial institutions and government agencies because they struggle to preserve accounting records and yearly financial accounts. Furthermore, the digital divide may hinder access to information for certain communities, exacerbating social inequalities.

As the world embraces the digital era, traditional councils are also grappling with the need to digitalise their record-keeping processes. Digitalisation offers numerous benefits, such as enhanced accessibility, efficient data management, and improved decision-making. However, this transition is not without its challenges. One of the primary concerns is the potential loss of cultural authenticity and integrity that accompanies the shift from traditional oral methods to digital formats. In a study on preserving public electronic information for the sustainability of e-governance in Sub-Saharan Africa, Ngulube (2018) found that most of the infrastructure in Sub-Saharan Africa is insufficient for acquiring, maintaining, and keeping digital records, including those on social media. Lowry (2012) also states that in Tanzania, the departments, and organisations responsible for generating the electronic records needed the resources required to sustain and maintain them over time. Infrastructure is the greatest challenge in this scenario. Furthermore, the adoption of digital technologies requires substantial investment in infrastructure, training, and cybersecurity measures to safeguard sensitive information. According to Riege (2005), most knowledge exchange activities would be less effective without technology.

Integrating digital technologies into traditional council record-keeping processes also raises questions about data ownership and privacy concerns. With the potential for large amounts of sensitive information to be stored digitally, there is a heightened risk of unauthorised access or misuse. The National Archives of Australia (2015) recognises that digital technologies need a trained and informed personnel capable of ensuring that digital information stays accessible and protected throughout time. Additionally, the transition to digital systems necessitates digital literacy training for council members and administrators, some of whom may be less familiar with technological tools. Ensuring that everyone is equipped with the necessary skills and knowledge to navigate digital platforms is essential to fully harness the benefits of digitalisation and overcome potential technological challenges in the context of traditional councils.

Data Security and Privacy Concerns

As increasingly complicated technologies are created in the e-records lifecycle process, there is a larger demand for standardized methods to achieve e-records security. So much has changed in recent years in terms of how activities are carried out, such as e-governance, the capacity to pay taxes online, cloud storage, and the emergence of security concerns, which has contributed to complexity in e-records management. As a result, organizations constantly create new techniques for producing, managing, storing, archiving, and disposing of e-records. Such advancements must obviously be supported by ways for leveraging new technology and safeguarding e-records (Bey, 2012). Traditional councils handle sensitive information about their communities, which demands robust data security measures. The transition to digital record-keeping exposes these records to potential cyber-attacks, data breaches, and unauthorised access. Preserving data privacy while embracing technological advancements requires careful planning and investment in cybersecurity measures. According to UNAIDS (2016), security is a set of technological measures that address challenges such as physical, electronic, and procedural protection of gathered e-records. According to ISO 15816 (2002), security management seeks to guarantee that assets, including information, are adequately and cost-effectively secured.

Traditional councils should include authentication, data integrity, confidentiality, authorization, and availability into the system's security processes and policies and consider them security elements (Al-Bakri, Mat Kiah, Zaidan, Zaidan & Alam 2011). Authentication is necessary to safeguard records from unauthorized access and can give high degrees of privacy for records in the traditional council. Members of the council must meet the authentication standards. According to Lhotska, Prague and Aubrecht (2008), the privacy of customers and the uniqueness of other papers should be assured for validity. Data integrity differs from database referential integrity in that authority is required to edit data. A staff member who updates their salary on a payroll records database, an employee who unintentionally or maliciously erases critical data files, a computer virus that harms computers, an individual who can cast important votes in an online poll, and a hacker who is involved in site vandalism are all examples of violations of integrity (Arenas, Banâtre & Priol 2008). Methods for controlling and preventing integrity errors should be developed by information security specialists (Sattarova Feruza& Kim 2007). The desire to use traditional council records is influenced positively by data integrity. When required, confidentiality restricts unauthorized users from accessing, using, copying, or exposing information (Pappas 2008). Data confidentiality ensures that information is only accessible to authorized persons and systems (Smith & Newton 2000). Confidentiality guarantees that only authorized individuals have access to sensitive information. Our plan to use traditional council records is influenced positively by confidentiality. The accessibility and functionality of records, computer systems which process information, and security mechanisms that safeguard information are all examples of availability (Zissis& Lekkas 2012).

Preserving records in traditional councils is not only a matter of safeguarding cultural heritage, but also entails significant data security and privacy concerns. Traditional councils often hold sensitive information, including personal details, customary laws, and community decisions. As these records transition from traditional oral methods to digital formats, there is a heightened risk of unauthorised access and data breaches. According to Wamukoya and Mutula (2005), weak security and confidentiality measures are key problems leading to the failure of digital record capture and preservation. Similarly, Myler and Broadbent (2006) contend that academic institutions are more concerned about information security threats such as cybercrime, privacy, virus attacks, and commercial data mining. Protecting the privacy and confidentiality of data is paramount to maintaining the trust of the community members and upholding the council's integrity.According to Charles Darwin University (2017), university record security guarantees the correct procedure of creating, storing, using, and making records accessible securely, with adequate consideration for permitting access for those members of the University community who have a genuine need to know the information contained within the records and who have the proper authority to access them.

The issue of data privacy in traditional council record preservation is further complicated by the need to strike a balance between openness and secrecy. While some records may contain information that should remain confidential within the council, others might need to be shared with government bodies, researchers, or the broader public for transparency and accountability. These differing levels of access require careful management to ensure that sensitive information is not exposed, while still allowing for the dissemination of knowledge and cultural understanding. As argued by ISO (2001); Kahanwal and Singh (2013), organisations' e-records, such as sensitive personnel data, compensation data, financial outcomes, business strategies, secrets of trade, research, and other details that provide a competitive advantage, require access restrictions for reasons of privacy, proprietary nature of the information, or legal security.DPC (2017) states that security, and privacy controls will:

1. Ensure compliance with any legal and regulatory obligations.
2. Prevent unauthorized or intentional alterations to digital content.
3. Maintain an audit trail to meet accountability standards.
4. Serve as a deterrence to possible breaches of internal security.
5. Ensure the integrity of digital materials.
6. Protect against theft and loss.

Anyone accessing the saved information through the digital preservation system must have proper access privileges (Adu, 2015:97). For sensitive or secret material, additional forms of access restrictions are necessary. Appropriate mechanisms must also be built for authenticating and authorizing users and system access. Minimum authentication, according to IRMT (2009:25), can be done by creating specialized operating system user accounts with suitable authorization. Furthermore, recording adequate audit data for access and usage of a record as part of its metadata is critical (IRMT, 2009:25). Access and security concerns must be addressed since unprotected digital data can be hacked or taken in bulk by identity thieves (Laudon and Laudon, 2005).

The physical infrastructure necessary to store and handle digital information must also be secured against destruction, whether accidental or intentional. According to IRMT (2009:25), physical infrastructure protection techniques include:

1. Physical access restrictions.
2. Systems for detecting intruders.
3. Fire suppression and detection systems.

4.   Power backup sources.

Inadequate security and confidentiality measures have also been identified as a major factor in the ESARBICA region's inability to successfully gather and preserve digital records (Wamukoya and Mutula 2005:74). According to Ngoepe, Mokoena, and Ngulube (2010:51), the digital records management system must handle content, network, and personnel security. Databases including personal, financial, and medical records that are helpful to organizations and people, according to Eze Asogwa (2012), can also constitute a hazard if sufficient security safeguards are not in place. On the other hand, privacy concerns about user data exacerbate the already difficult criteria for choosing and indexing social media material for reuse (DPC, 2016:8).

Digital Literacy

One of the most often accepted definitions of digital literacy today is a collection of interconnected abilities or competences essential for survival in the digital era (List, 2019). Gilster (1997) originated the term "digital literacy," which he described as the capacity to perceive and use digital material in various formats delivered on computers from a range of sources. He went on to say that growing digital literacy to use Internet material necessitates knowing a set of essential skills. While Gilster does not specify the skills needed to develop digital literacy, Bawden (2001, 2008) identifies them as skill sets related to reading and understanding interactive media and interactive texts, assembling information, communicating information collaboratively, and finding and critically evaluating information from digital sources. The successful implementation of digital record-keeping systems relies on skilled personnel with adequate digital literacy. However, traditional councils often lack individuals with technical expertise, hindering the effective utilisation of digital tools. Most African record managers and archivists lack the essential skills and competencies required to maintain documents in an electronic setting. Kemoni and Wamukoya (2000), Iwhiwhu (2005), and Egwunyenga (2009) found that African records keepers lacked the fundamental skills and competencies required to manage records and archives in the public sector. Most African offices are plagued by a severe case of technophobia, particularly among top management. Because of a lack of information technology capabilities, many conventional librarians, records managers, and archivists are exceedingly conservative and mistrust computers. This might be due to generational disparities between young and elderly professionals, which led analogue information managers to regard computers as a threat to their authority. In her study, Ezeani (2010) discovered that younger librarians are faster than older librarians in capturing the use of ICTs because "older librarians are finding it difficult to cope with the requirements of the digital age." In addition, Ojedokun (2008) observed that senior librarians are "too hesitant to abandon old practices in favor of new ones." In order to successfully apply information handling technologies in the administration of electronic records in developing nations, it is necessary to overcome staff and personal reluctance. Ongoing training and education for records managers have emerged as major priorities for governments as well as agencies worldwide (Johare & Masrek 2011, 699). Most records keepers and archivists in Africa are not professionally trained in records management; rather, they are hired with their high school diplomas and work their way up the ranks to become records managers through promotion or experience without formal training in archives and records management. In his study on the electronic records management readiness of federal institutions in Nigeria, Eze Asogwa (2012) observed that all workers in the registration departments had never received any training on records and archives administration.

Digital literacy is critical to the effective preservation of records in traditional councils in the digital age. As traditional councils transition from oral traditions to digital record-keeping, it becomes imperative to equip council members and administrators with the necessary skills and knowledge to navigate digital platforms effectively. The creation of a digital records management system necessitates suitable digital skills to utilise the right digital repository software, apply optical character recognition, assign metadata, learn how to operate a scanner for digitisation, and create high-quality digital materials.Eze Asogwa (2013) conducted a study of three state-owned universities in Nigeria to assess the extent to which staff members were comfortable with digital records management and found that 69 percent of respondents lacked skills to manage records all through their lifecycle. Similarly, Mulaudzi, Wamundila, Mtanga, and Hamooya (2012) claim that records professionals must possess key skills and knowledge to establish and implement complete ERM and preservation plans.Mulauzi et al. (2012, 7) go on to say that skills and abilities vary and can be classified as technology skills, information management skills, and project management skills, which include the ability to create, capture, classify, index, appraise, store, preserve, retrieve, track, dispose of, and archive digital records. Knowledge of the digital record setting, digital record management trends and practices, digital record types, and comprehension of IT applications for recordkeeping are all required competencies (Mulauzi et al. 2012, 7). To perform in online information settings, librarians must be skilled in digitization, metadata production and administration, digital information preservation, and computer skills, according to Raju (2014). According to Yakel (2007), librarians with appropriate digital literacy skills will continue to be effective. Working with contemporary information systems necessitates the use of appropriate abilities. Emiri (2015) evaluated the current digital literacy abilities of 77 university library workers in the Nigerian states of Edo and Delta. Some of the key digital literacy skills gained by these professionals, according to the poll, are their utilization of e-mail, social networking sites (SNSs), personal digital assistants (PDAs), handheld gadgets, and the internet. According to the findings of the research by Safahieh and Asemi (2010), the majority of the librarians at Isfahan University (Iran) did not have appropriate computer capabilities, as almost half of them rated their skills as 'fair'. This level was not considered 'very excellent' by any of the librarians. According to Ayoku and Okafor (2015), university librarians in Nigeria have excellent abilities in e-mail use and typing tasks, but they lack knowledge of how to evaluate and catalogue e-resources; do not understand subject gateways, specialized databases, and some open-access library databases; do not understand database management; are not skilled in designing websites; and are equally unfamiliar with web design applications. By providing training initiatives, traditional councils can empower their members to embrace digital technologies, ensuring the accurate recording, storage, and retrieval of records. Moreover, enhancing digital literacy fosters a better understanding of the potential benefits and challenges of digitalisation, enabling traditional councils to make well-informed decisions on the adoption and integration of technology into their record-keeping practices.

SOLUTIONS AND RECOMMENDATIONS

The 4IR presents both opportunities and challenges for traditional councils in preserving their records and cultural heritage. Embracing digital technologies requires careful consideration of data security, cultural sensitivity, and inclusivity. By adopting best practices and involving local communities, traditional councils can navigate these challenges and leverage technology to safeguard their cultural legacy for future generations. Traditional councils must treat carefully to strike a balance between embracing digitalisation and ensuring the preservation of their unique cultural heritage and knowledge. Traditional councils must also ensure that everyone is equipped with the necessary skills and knowledge to navigate digital platforms by giving them more training. Traditional councils need to establish clear guidelines for data access and sharing, ensuring that individuals who have legitimate reasons to access certain records are identified and authenticated. By doing so, traditional councils can uphold the privacy of their records while fostering constructive collaborations and knowledge exchange. Traditional councils can also implement robust data security measures, including encryption, firewalls, and access controls, while adhering to relevant data protection regulations. Traditional councils can collaborate with educational institutions, NGOs, or government agencies to access resources and expertise in facilitating digital literacy initiatives. By investing in digital literacy, traditional councils can adapt to the digital era while preserving their cultural heritage through effective record preservation. Deman and Vintar (2013) noted that alternative solutions might be proposed in light of the abovementioned challenges of record preservation and traditional council. They proposed that they would be able to solve many of the problems associated with document management, preservation, and archiving by utilizing a centralized technological solution for intermediate preservation and archiving in the form of a community cloud (using the cloud computing concept), supported by appropriate strategies and policies. Intermediate preservation may handle physical, logical, and conceptual levels of preservation, allowing documents to be delivered to archives from a trusted source later in their life cycle. This unified repository should be built as an electronic record center, repository, or interim archive, which is a specially designed or built location for low-cost storage, administration, and transfer of current or semi-current documents awaiting disposal.

FUTURE RESEARCH DIRECTIONS

Several questions remain unanswered at present. Future study on the issues of preserving records within traditional councils in the context of the 4IR should dive into new methods that combine history preservation with cutting-edge technologies. This includes investigating strong frameworks for integrating new technologies like blockchain, AI, and the IoT with traditional record-keeping processes. It is critical that these councils investigate the barriers to technological adoption and develop targeted measures to overcome hesitation. To protect against cyber risks and illegal access, cybersecurity and data protection measures must be thoroughly examined, with an emphasis on modern encryption techniques and secure storage solutions.

CONCLUSION

The challenges faced when preserving records in traditional councils during the 4IR are severe, but not impossible to address. The fast rate of technological innovation has ushered in a new age that necessitates a rethinking of established record-keeping techniques. Limited resources, technical infrastructure, and digital literacy are all issues that must be tackled head on. Adopting creative ideas and cultivating an adaptation culture within traditional councils will be critical. Collaboration with information management specialists and embracing developing technology may be quite beneficial.

REFERENCES

Abdulkadhim, H., Bahari, M., Bakri, A., & Ismail, W. (2015). A research framework of electronic document management systems (EDMS) implementation process in government. *Journal of Theoretical and Applied Information Technology, 81*(3), 420–432.

Abioye, A. (2013). Government record-keeping in Sub-Sahara Africa: Milestones in archives administration in Nigeria. *Comma International Journal on Archives, 1*(1), 15–26.

Abouzeedan, A., & Hedner, T. (2012). Organization structure theories and open innovation paradigm. *World Journal of Science. Technology and Sustainable Development, 9*(1), 6–27.

Adu, K. K. (2015). *Framework for digital preservation of electronic government in Ghana* [PhD thesis]. University of South Africa.

Adu, K. K., & Ngulube, P. (2016). Preserving the digital heritage of public institutions in Ghana in the wake of electronic government. *Library Hi Tech, 34*(4), 748–763. doi:10.1108/LHT-07-2016-0077

Al-Bakri, S. H., Mat Kiah, M. L., Zaidan, A. A., Zaidan, B. B., & Alam, G. M. (2011). Securing peer-to-peer mobile communications using public key cryptography: New security strategy. *International Journal of Physical Sciences, 6*(4), 930–938.

Amollo, B. A. (2011). *Digitization for Libraries in Kenya. International Conference on African Digital Libraries and Archives ICADLA*. Nairobi. Kenya.

Asproth, V. (2005). Information technology challenges for long-term preservation of electronic information. *International Journal of Public Information Systems, 1*(1).

Ayoku, O. A., & Okafor, V. N. (2015). ICT skills acquisition and competencies of librarians: Implications for digital and electronic environment in Nigerian universities libraries. *The Electronic Library, 33*(3), 502–523. doi:10.1108/EL-08-2013-0155

Banisar, D. (2004). The Freedominfo.org Global Survey: Freedom of information and access to government record laws around the world. Freedominfo.org

Banisar, D. (2006). *Freedom of information around the world 2006: A global survey of access to government information laws*. Privacy International.

Basil Iwhiwhu, E. (2005). Management of records in Nigerian universities: Problems and prospects. *The Electronic Library, 23*(3), 345–355. doi:10.1108/02640470510603741

Bawden, D. (2001). Information and digital literacies: A review of concepts. *The Journal of Documentation, 57*(2), 218–259. doi:10.1108/EUM0000000007083

Bawden, D. (2008). Origins and concepts of digital literacy. *Digital literacies: Concepts, policies, and practices, 30*(2008), 17-32.

Bey, P. G. (2012). *The Parkerian Hexad: The CIA triad model expanded* [Master's thesis]. Lewis University.

Burkett, D. (2017). Digitisation and digitalisation: What means what? *Innovation.*

Charles Darwin University. (2017). *Records disposal schedules: higher education teaching and learning of the University of the Charles Darwin University*. https://www.cdu.edu.au/sites/default/files/itms-docs/disposal-schedule-2017.17-charlesdarwin-university-higher-education-teaching-and-learning.pdf

Chaterera, F. (2013). *Records surveys and the management of public records in Zimbabwe* [Minf. Dissertation]. University of South Africa.

Chibambo, M. L. N. (2006). *The right to access government information, democracy, and development in sub-Saharan Africa*. Paper presented at the WSIS Follow-up conference on access to information and knowledge for development. Addis Ababa, Ethiopia.

Chinyemba, A. (2011). *Fostering transparency, good governance, and accountability in institutions of higher learning through records management*. Paper presentation at the XXXI Bi-annual Eastern and Southern Africa Regional Branch of the International 75 Council on Archives (ESARBICA) General Conference on Access to Information: Archives and Records in Support of Public Sector Reform in Context, Maputo, Mozambique.

Chong, C. W., Chong, S. C., & Lin, B. (2010). Organizational demographic variables and preliminary KM implementation success. *Expert Systems with Applications, 37*(10), 7243–7254. doi:10.1016/j.eswa.2010.04.003

Crook, R. (2005). The role of traditional institutions in political change and development. *Center for Democratic Development/Overseas Development Institute. Policy Brief, 4*(4), 1–5.

Cumming, K., & Findlay, C. (2010). Digital recordkeeping: Are we at a tipping point? *Records Management Journal, 20*(3), 265–278. doi:10.1108/09565691011095292

Dečman, M., & Vintar, M. (2013). A possible solution for digital preservation of e-government: A centralised repository within a cloud computing framework. *Aslib Proceedings, 65*(4), 406–424. doi:10.1108/AP-05-2012-0049

Dewah, P., & Feni-Fete, V. (2014). Issues and prospects of digitizing liberation movements' archives held at the University of Fort Hare, South Africa. *Journal of the South African Society of Archivists, 47*, 77–88.

Digital Preservation Coalition (DPC). (2017). *Information security*. https://www.dpconline.org/handbook/technical-solutions-and-tools/information-security

Duranti, L. (2014). Preservation in the cloud: Towards an international framework for a balance of trust and trustworthiness. *Proceedings of APA/C-DAC International Conference on Digital Preservation and Development of Trusted Digital Repositories*, 23–38.

Egwunyenga, E. J. (2009). Record keeping in universities: Associated problems and management options in Southwest Geo-Political Zone of Nigeria. *International Journal of Educational Sciences, 1*(2), 109–113. doi:10.1080/09751122.2009.11889983

Emiri, O. T. (2015). Digital literacy skills among librarians in university libraries in the 21st century in Edo and Delta states, Nigeria. *International Journal of Library and Information Services, 6*(1), 37–52. doi:10.4018/IJLIS.2017010103

Eze Asogwa, B. (2012). The challenge of managing electronic records in developing countries: Implications for records managers in sub–Saharan Africa. *Records Management Journal, 22*(3), 198–211. doi:10.1108/09565691211283156

Eze Asogwa, B. (2012). The readiness of universities in managing electronic records: A study of three federal universities in Nigeria. *The Electronic Library, 31*(6), 792–807. doi:10.1108/EL-04-2012-0037

Ezeani, C. (2010). Information and communication technology: an overview. In E. C. Madu & C. N. Ezeani (Eds.), *Modern Library and Information Science for Professionals in Africa.* TextKinks.

Feather, J., & Sturges, R. P. (2003). *International Encyclopedia of information and Library Science.* Routledge. doi:10.4324/9780203403303

Gbaje, E. S. (2007). *Digitization and its Challenges: Digital records and archival management workshop for members, federal capital territory, Abuja, Archives History Bureau Committee and Laison Officers.* Arewa House Kaduna.

Gilster, P. (1997). *Digital literacy.* John Wiley.

Groenewald, R., & Breytenbach, A. (2011). The use of metadata and preservation methods for continuous access to digital data. *The Electronic Library, 29*(2), 236–248. doi:10.1108/02640471111125195

Heatherfield, S. M. (2021). *What is resistance to change. Definitions and examples of resistance to change.* The Balance Careers. https://www.thebalancecareers.com/what-isresistance-to-change-1918240[Accessed 21 October 2023] https://dspace.unza.zm/handle/123456789/5509

Ihuah, P. W., & Eaton, D. (2013). The pragmatic research approach: A framework for sustainable management of public housing estates in Nigeria. *Journal of US-China Public Administration, 10*(10), 933–944.

International Data Corporation. (2018). *Document processes survey: resistance to digital change. Institutional repositories.* Winston.

International Records Management Trust (IRMT). (2009). *Preserving electronic records: Training in electronic records management.* Module 4. http://www.irmt.org/documents/educ_training/term%20modules/IRMT%204.pdf

ISO 15489-1. (2001). *Information and documentation –Records Management-Part 1: General.* International Organization for Standardization.

ISO/IEC 15816. (2002). *Information technology- techniques –security information objects for access control.* International Organization for Standardization.

Johare, R., & Masrek, M. N. (2011). Malaysian archival heritage at risk? A survey of archivists' knowledge and skills in managing electronic records. *Library Review, 60*(8), 685–711. doi:10.1108/00242531111166719

Kahanwal, D. B., & Singh, D. T. P. (2013). *Towards the framework of information security.* https://arxiv.org/pdf/1312.1460

Kemoni, H., & Ngulube, P. (2008). Relationship between records management, public service delivery and the attainment of the United Nations Millennium Development Goals in Kenya. *Information Development, 24*(4), 296–306. doi:10.1177/0266666908098074

Kemoni, H., & Wamukoya, J. (2000). Preparing for the management of electronic records at Moi University, Kenya: A case study. *African Journal of Library Archives and Information Science, 10*(2), 125–138.

Klareld, A. S. (2015). The "middle archive" exploring the practical and theoretical implications of a new concept in Sweden. *Records Management Journal, 25*(2), 149–165. doi:10.1108/RMJ-12-2014-0047

Külcü, Ö. (2009). Records management practices in universities: A comparative study of examples in Canada and Turkey. *Canadian Journal of Information and Library Science, 33*(2).

Laudon, K. C., & Laudon, J. P. (2005). *Essentials of management information system: managing the digital firm* (6th ed.). Pearson Education.

Laumer, S. (2011). *Why do people reject technologies–A literature-based discussion of the phenomena "Resistance to Change" in information systems and managerial psychology research.* Academic Press.

Lhotska, L., Prague, C., & Aubrecht, P. (2008). *Deliverable D09 security of the multi agent system.* Agent System.

Lischer-Katz, Z. (2020). Archiving experience: An exploration of the challenges of preserving virtual reality. *Records Management Journal, 30*(2), 253–274. doi:10.1108/RMJ-09-2019-0054

List, A. (2019). Defining digital literacy development: An examination of pre-service teachers' beliefs. *Computers & Education, 138*, 146–158. doi:10.1016/j.compedu.2019.03.009

Logan, D. (2006). *Knowledge management is critical to organizing and accessing a company's intellectual assets.* Academic Press.

Loonam, J., Eaves, S., Kumar, V., & Parry, G. (2018). Towards digital transformation: Lessons learned from traditional organizations. *Strategic Change, 27*(2), 101–109. doi:10.1002/jsc.2185

Lowry, J. (2012). *Management and preservation of digital records in Tanzania.* Academic Press.

Malake, S., & Phiri, J. (2020). Developing a records and information management model for oil marketing companies in Zambia based on the records cycle model. *Open Journal of Business and Management, 8*(4), 1870–1887. doi:10.4236/ojbm.2020.84114

Masuke, E. (2010). *Recent African experience in SME financing–a case of CRDB Bank LTD (Tanzania).* A presentation paper.

Mnjama, N. M. (2011). Paper presented at the XXI Biannual East and Southern Africa Regional Branch of the International Council on Archives (ESARBICA) General Conference. *Journal of the South African Society of Archivists, 55.*

Motsi, A. (2004). The nature of documentary materials in Africa and the challenges to preserving them. *ESARBICA Journal, 23*(1), 62–67.

Mulaudzi, F., Wamundila, S., Mtanga, N., & Hamooya, C. (2012). *The role of records managers in the digital age: The Zambian experience.* Paper presented at the Twentieth Standing Conference of Eastern, Central and Southern African Library and Information Associations (SCECSAL) hosted by Kenya Library Association (KLA) on 4 - 8 June at Laico Regency Hotel, Nairobi, Kenya.

Mutsagondo, S., & Ngulube, P. (2018). Skills Impact Assessment of Personnel Managing Electronic Records in Zimbabwe's Public Service. *Mousaion, 36*(2), 1–19.

Mutula, S., & Wamukoya, J. M. (2009). Public sector information management in east and southern Africa: Implications for FOI, democracy, and integrity in government. *International Journal of Information Management, 29*(5), 333–341. doi:10.1016/j.ijinfomgt.2009.04.004

Myler, E., & Broadbent, G. (2006). ISO 17799: Standard for information security. *Information Management Journal, 40*(6), 43–52.

Nassuora, A. B., & Hasan, S. (2010). *Knowledge sharing among academics in institutions of higher learning.* Paper presented at the 5th Knowledge Management International Conference. Terengganu, Malaysia.

National Archives of Australia. (2015). *Overview of classification tools for records management.* Commonwealth of Australia, Canberra: Business Centre ACT 2610.

Ndlebe, A., & Dewah, P. (2021). Digitising Archival Material at ZIMPAPERS Harare: Emerging Challenges and Opportunities in the Covid-19 Era. *Mousaion, 39*(4).

Ngoepe, M., & Makhubela, S. (2015). Justice delayed is justice denied: Records management and the travesty of justice in South Africa. *Records Management Journal, 25*(3), 288–305. doi:10.1108/RMJ-06-2015-0023

Ngoepe, M., Mokoena, L., & Ngulube, P. (2010). Security, privacy, and ethics in electronic records management in the South African public sector. *ESARBICA Journal, 29*(2), 36–66. PMID:20945689

Ngoepe, M., & Van Der Walt, T. (2009). Strategies for the preservation of electronic records in South Africa: Implications on access to information. *Innovation, 38*(1), 1–25. doi:10.4314/innovation.v38i1.46971

Ngulube, P. (2004). Implications of technological advances for access to the cultural heritage of selected countries in sub-Saharan Africa. Government Information Quarterly: *An International Journal of Information Technology Management. Policies and Procedures, 21*(2), 143–155.

Ngulube, P. (2006). Nature and accessibility of public archives in custody of selected archival institutions in Africa. *ESARBICA Journal, 25*(12006), 106–124.

Ngulube, P. (2018). *Managing university records to foster national development and the protection of educational entitlements.* Paper presented at the 2nd Annual Higher Education Records Management Forum, 6 September 2018, at the University of Mpumalanga, Nelspruit, South Africa.

Nwankwo, J. I. (2001). *Fundamentals of management information systems. Spectrum Books.*

Nwogo Ezeani, C. (2009). Digitizing projects in developing countries: The case of the University of Nigeria. *Library Hi Tech News, 26*(5/6), 14–15. doi:10.1108/07419050910985273

Ohio State University. (2011). *University archives: Digital content.* https://library.osu.edu/archives/digital

Ojedokun, A. O. (2008). Transition to Automated Library Information Systems and the Challenges for Libraries in Africa. In *Knowledge and Information Management in the Digital Age: Concepts, Technologies and African Perspectives.* Third World Information Service.

Owens, T. (2017). *The theory and craft of digital preservation*. Johns Hopkins University Press.

Pappas, C. (2008). Hospital librarians' perceptions related to evidence-based health care. *Journal of the Medical Library Association: JMLA*, *96*(3), 235–238. doi:10.3163/1536-5050.96.3.011 PMID:18654652

Quisbert, H. (2006). *A framework for the development of archival information systems* [Masters]. Lulea University of Technology. Department of Business Administration and Social Sciences. Division of Systems Science. https://www.diva-portal.org/smash/get/diva2:990983/FULLTEXT01.pdf

Raju, J. (2014). Knowledge and skills for the digital era academic library. *Journal of Academic Librarianship*, *40*(2), 163–170. doi:10.1016/j.acalib.2014.02.007

Records Nations. (2019). *Different types of security in records management*. https://www.recordnations.com/2019/01/different-types-security-in-records-management/

Ricks, B., Swafford, A., & Gow, K. (1992). Information and image management: A records management systems approach (3rd ed.). South-Western Publishing Co.

Riege, A. (2005). Three-dozen knowledge-sharing barriers managers must consider. *Journal of Knowledge Management*, *9*(3), 18–35. doi:10.1108/13673270510602746

Roper, M., & Millar, L. (1999). *Managing public sector records: Preserving archives*. IRMT.

Ross, S. (2012). Digital preservation, archival science and methodological foundations for digital libraries. *New Review of Information Networking*, *17*(1), 43–68. doi:10.1080/13614576.2012.679446

Safahieh, H., & Asemi, A. (2010). Computer literacy skills of librarians: A case study of Isfahan University libraries, Iran. *The Electronic Library*, *28*(1), 89–99. doi:10.1108/02640471011023397

Sattarova Feruza, Y., & Kim, T. H. (2007). IT security review: Privacy, protection, access control, assuranceassurance, and system security. *International Journal of Multimedia and Ubiquitous Engineering*, *2*(2), 17–32.

Schellnack-Kelly, I. (2013). *The role of records management in governance-based evidence, service delivery and development in South African communities* [PhD Thesis]. University of South Africa.

Shatat, A. S. (2015). Critical success factors in enterprise resource planning (ERP) system implementation: An exploratory study in Oman. *Electronic Journal of Information Systems Evaluation*, *18*(1), 36–45.

Shepherd, D. A. (2003). Learning from business failure: Propositions of grief recovery for the self-employed. *Academy of Management Review*, *28*(2), 318–328. doi:10.2307/30040715

Shepherd, E. (2006). Why are records in the public sector organizational assets? *Records Management Journal*, *16*(1), 6–12. doi:10.1108/09565690610654747

Shepherd, E., & Yeo, G. (2003). *Managing records: A handbook of principles and practice*. Facet Publishers.

Slote, S. (2000). *Records management in the library collections: library records methods* (3rd ed.). Libraries Unlimited.

Smith, G. W., & Newton, R. B. (2000). A taxonomy of organizational security policies. *Proceedings of the 23rd National Information Systems Security Conference. NIST-National Institute of Standards and Technology.*

Thibodeau, K. (2013). Wrestling with shape-shifters: Perspectives on preserving memory in the digital age. *Proceedings of 'The Memory of the World in the Digital Age: Digitization and Digital Preservation*, 15-23. http://www.unesco.org/webworld/download/mow/mow_ vancouver_proceedings_en.pdf

Thomas, V. S., Schubert, D. R., & Lee, J. A. (1983). *Records management systems and administration.* John Wiley and Sons.

Tsvuura, G., & Ngulube, P. (2020). Digitisation of records and archives at two selected state universities in Zimbabwe. *Journal of the South African Society of Archivists, 53*, 20–34. doi:10.4314/jsasa.v53i1.2

United Nations Programme on HIV/AIDS (UNAIDS) Guidance, (2016). *The privacy, confidentiality, and security assessment tool: protecting personal health information.* https://www.unaids.org/en/resources/documents/2019/confidentiality

Verma, P. (2020). *Digitalization: enabling the new phase of energy efficiency.* Group of Experts on Energy Efficiency Seventh session Geneva, 22 and 25 September 2020. GEEE7/2020/INF.3

Wamukoya, J., & Mutula, S. M. (2005). E-records management and governance in East and Southern Africa. *Malaysian Journal of Library and Information Science, 10*(2), 67–83.

Yakel, E. (2007). Archives and manuscripts digital curation, OCLC systems and services. *International Digital Library Perspectives, 23*(4), 335–340.

Yusof, Z.M. (2005). *Issues and challenges in records management.* UKM, Bangi, Malaysia, Tech. Rep.

Zissis, D., & Lekkas, D. (2012). Addressing cloud computing security issues. *Future Generation Computer Systems, 28*(3), 583–592. doi:10.1016/j.future.2010.12.006

ADDITIONAL READING

Abouelmehdi, K., Beni-Hessane, A., & Khaloufi, H. (2018). Big healthcare data: Preserving security and privacy. *Journal of Big Data, 5*(1), 1–18. doi:10.118640537-017-0110-7

Azim, N., Mat Yatin, S. F., Jensonray, R., & Ayub Mansor, S. (2018). Digitization of records and archives: Issues and concerns. *International Journal of Academic Research in Business & Social Sciences, 8*(9), 170–178. doi:10.6007/IJARBSS/v8-i9/4582

Dewah, P., & Sithole, B. (2022). Digitisation of records to improve access at the Zimbabwe Energy Regulatory Authority. *Journal of the South African Society of Archivists, 55*, 74–87. doi:10.4314/jsasa.v55i.6

Heslop, H., Davis, S., & Wilson, A. (2002). *An approach to the preservation of digital records.* National Archives of Australia.

Matlala, M. E., Ncube, T. R., & Parbanath, S. (2022). The state of digital records preservation in South Africa's public sector in the 21st century: A literature review. *Records Management Journal*, *32*(2), 198–212. doi:10.1108/RMJ-02-2021-0004

Molepo, M. J., & Cloete, L. M. (2017). Proposal for improving records management practices of traditional institutions in Ga Molepo, South Africa. *Mousaion: South African Journal of Information Studies*, *35*(1), 46–67. doi:10.25159/2054

Penn, I. A., & Pennix, G. B. (2017). *Records management handbook*. Routledge. doi:10.4324/9781315245140

Schwab, K. (2017). *The fourth industrial revolution*. Currency.

Sigauke, D. T., & Nengomasha, C. T. (2011). Challenges and prospects facing the digitization of historical records for their preservation within the National Archives of Zimbabwe. *2nd Conference on African Digital libraries and Archives (ICADLA-2) at the University of Witswatersrand, Johannesburg, South Africa, 14th–18th November*.

KEY TERMS AND DEFINITIONS

4th Industrial Revolution: Refers to a transformative period characterised by the convergence of digital, physical, and biological technologies, leading to significant and profound changes in various aspects of society, economy, and industry.

Data Security: Data security refers to the practice of protecting digital information, such as files, databases, and systems, from unauthorised access, alteration, or destruction.

Digitalisation: The art of converting the contents of a document from hard copy into machine-readable format.

Preservation: Is a systematic procedure of minimising or lowering damage risks to decrease the pace of degradation of materials.

Records: This refers to information generated, received, and kept as evidence and information by an organisation or individual while fulfilling legal responsibilities or conducting economic activities.

Technological: Pertains to anything related to technology, which encompasses the application of scientific knowledge, engineering principles, and practical skills to create, modify, or improve tools, machines, systems, and processes.

Traditional Council: Means a traditional council that has been established and recognised for a traditional community in accordance with the provisions of section 3 of the Traditional Leadership and Governance Framework Act, 2003 (Act No. 41 of 2003) or any corresponding provision in provincial legislation.

Chapter 5
Artificial Intelligence (AI) in Academic Libraries:
A Theoretical Study

Satishkumar Naikar
https://orcid.org/0000-0002-7621-5388
D.Y. Patil University (Deemed), Navi Mumbai, India

Shashikumar Hatti
https://orcid.org/0000-0001-5223-7163
Navodaya Medical College Hospital and Research Centre, Raichur, India

Megha Paul
https://orcid.org/0009-0003-5766-5273
Librarian Rockwell International School, Hyderabad, India

Rani K. Swamy
Navodaya Medical College Hospital and Research Centre, Raichur, India

ABSTRACT

Artificial intelligence (AI), which has taken over many industries, is thought of as a continuation of human intelligence. Artificial intelligence applications in libraries have revolutionized the information industry. Many human talents, including calculation, reading, speaking, grasping, remembering, making decisions, and interactive learning, can be stimulated by technological improvements. It is believed that the use of artificial intelligence in virtual reference services will offer libraries a new online service paradigm. Virtual reality is a useful feature that engages users with libraries and improves information literacy abilities. Librarians are always utilizing cutting edge technologies to improve services for their patrons. The chapter covered some AI components, library services to which it can be applied, the benefits of its application, and the problems libraries encounter when implementing artificial intelligence in the library.

DOI: 10.4018/979-8-3693-2841-5.ch005

INTRODUCTION

The main objective of artificial intelligence (AI), a branch of computational science, is to enable robots to respond to complex problems in a manner similar to that of humans. In order to provide an output or result, computers may comprehend and interpret human cognitive traits when they are appropriated, modeled, and incorporated as algorithms. From a conceptual standpoint, artificial intelligence can be understood as a neural network—a network of synthetic neurons or nodes that replicates the biological functions of neurons in humans. It was created in a manner to mimic the way human brain activity is structurally organized. As they go from one neural network to the next, they collectively produce well-informed conclusions. It makes educated estimates while processing data, modeling biological processes. Thus, neural networks represent a particular type of machine learning system, or artificial intelligence system. The science of artificial intelligence was founded in the 1950s, and libraries began to use it in the 1990s.

In the twenty-first century, an era of rapid change and technological progress, organizations and institutions must adapt to changing technologies to meet the needs of their end users. Libraries can benefit from artificial intelligence by using cutting-edge technologies that allow robots to recognize, understand, behave, learn, and carry out administrative tasks. Artificial intelligence is essentially a collection of techniques that make this possible. Using cutting-edge technologies for purposes other than information distribution is a hallmark of the librarian profession. The newest developing trend in libraries is artificial intelligence. The information-driven industries like law, health, commerce, the auto industry, etc., artificial intelligence has shown to be a game-changer.

Artificial intelligence is a wider and comprehensive field of study that is often difficult for non-specialists to understand without some basic knowledge. AI has created new opportunities for all disciplines of study advancement. Researchers are currently working on developing new systems that can simulate the mental processes of librarians and exhibit hitherto unattainable human characteristics. Technologically speaking, IT equipment, computer systems, and other gadgets are progressively getting more sophisticated and designed with human-like reasoning and functionality. This awareness of human intelligence (HI) is also evolving into artificial intelligence (AI). To create an intelligent system, implicit human knowledge must be retrieved. This means that before creating an AI device, pertinent traits and information must be gleaned from human specialists; these traits and information are frequently heuristic in nature. Applications and uses for computer-based goods and services include a range of library operations procedures, the provision of diverse library services, and the creation of output products. Artificial intelligence applications will assist in simulating human decision-making. AI technologies are used by library intelligent systems to deliver knowledge-based services to users (Asemi and Asemi, 2018).

The library should embrace and implement artificial intelligence, as it is a widely accepted technology. Its adoption in libraries is doing well, particularly in South Asia. The majority of the time, academic libraries employ these intelligent systems by implementing a variety of library procedures. Rather than focusing on its technological innovations, the main applications of AI demonstrate its true value for our society. Automating human work is what artificial intelligence applications aim to accomplish. Many people have only recently come to realize that machines are capable of performing tasks that humans find challenging, such self-driving cars or interpretation (ALA, 2019). This also holds true for the availability and utilization of library information resources and services, as the goals and objectives of the library can greatly benefit from the application of artificial intelligence and its components.

The IFLA Trend Report from 2016 states that AI can now be used to both supplement and improve current library services. For their professions to remain relevant, librarians must have creative thinking. In the IFLA Trend Report for this century, artificial intelligence was listed as one of the developing technologies. Future libraries can expect to see the following three main effects of artificial intelligence: Beyond term search and text analytics of web content, browsers will be able to optimize search results; Integrated speech recognition, language translation, and speech synthesis will enable real-time multilingual translation; Cloud services will be able to recognize and interpret dynamic and complicated online content. The following three factors primarily represent artificial intelligence (AI), which will be applied in the future to create artificially intelligent libraries: intelligent space guidance system for the library hall; The construction of an intelligent sensing space should allow users to utilize wearable technology, mobile phones, and other mobile terminals to access intelligent voice service, intelligent seat reservations, precise placement of information materials in the library, intelligent navigation, especially for physically challenged patrons, intelligent machine consultation (which can be integrated with virtual reality technology), and other intelligent guidance services (Yu, Gong, Sun, and Jiang, 2019).

Artificial intelligence techniques and areas of application in libraries include robotics (stock taking, shelving, searching, obtaining information from shelves, check-in and check-out); Natural language processing (NLP) includes information retrieval, reading of information resources, text translation from native language, book classification, book/information processing, and knowledge management; chatbots (information retrieval, acquisition, descriptive cataloguing, inquiry services, and library instructions); Pattern Recognition: user identification, RFID, security passwords, image indexing and abstraction, security of library contents, and QR codes for materials; Image processing includes picture and video database management in libraries, record scanning, facial recognition for users, and archiving and preservation; Text data mining includes social media appearance and administration, OPAC searching, metadata, citation support and analysis, and #Library Trends. The use of artificial intelligence (AI) in librarianship is inevitable since it may be used to many different areas of research and life to solve problems in libraries.

One may argue that the development of AI has opened up new possibilities for changing technical and patron services in libraries. The self-learning and self-executing capabilities of AI can aid libraries in better machine-automated intelligent technology engagement for the efficacy and co-creation of all library services. However, in order to adapt to the new environment, librarians must adapt their positions and encourage the modernization of library services and operations with the use of artificial intelligence. Simultaneously, the use of AI in library work is in its infancy (Cox et al., 2019; Hervieux & Wheatley, 2021).

Through improved search and suggestion, comprehensive digital asset description, transcription, and automatic translation, among other means, it can dramatically expand access to knowledge in fundamental ways. In Cox (2022). The use of AI in libraries also brings up a number of ethical issues, and there is a lingering concern that AI may someday take the position of human librarians. As a trend, AI focuses the IT side of library work, where men are overrepresented, which may have an impact on equality, diversity, and inclusion (EDI) in the field. Additionally, AI is often associated with white men. The purpose of this research is to define artificial intelligence in this context from a librarian's point of view (Cave & Dihal, 2020).

BACKGROUND

The capacity of a computer or a computer-controlled robot to carry out actions typically associated with intelligent creatures. Frequently, the phrase is utilized in reference to the development of developing systems with cognitive functions exclusive to humans, like reasoning, meaning-finding, generalization, and experience-based learning. Since the 1940s, when digital computers were first developed, it has been demonstrated that computers are capable of being taught to carry out incredibly complicated jobs, such locating proof for sound theorems or mastering the game of chess. However, no software can yet equal mortality in bigger domains and activities that demand routinely acquired important information, despite ongoing advancements in computer processing speed and memory capacity.

Definition of Artificial Intelligence

Artificial intelligence is formed up of the phrases "artificial" and "intelligence," where "artificial" refers to something that is "man-made" and "intelligent" refers to something that has "thinking power." Technology is advancing quickly in the modern world, and we are daily coming into contact with new innovations.

One of the computer science disciplines that is growing the fastest is artificial intelligence, which has the potential to create intelligent machines and bring in a new era of technological growth. Our world is currently dominated by artificial intelligence. Its current activities include a wide range of subfields, from general to specialized, such as painting, chess playing, theorem proving, self-driving automobiles, and music performance. According to Irizarry-Nones, Palepu, and Wallace (2017), artificial intelligence is the programming and development of computers to carry out tasks requiring human intelligence, such as speech recognition, decision-making, visual perception, language translation, conversing, and emotional feelings.

While we have looked at how various AI approaches work and are constructed, it would also be useful to look at the application contexts that could be based on the data itself. For instance, using Natural Language Processing (Olsson, 2009) to swiftly analyze vast amounts of unstructured text from unknown datasets may provide insight into the text's substance, sentiment, and genre. Robots are actual machines that have been programmed to do a range of tasks on their own. These are frequently just repeated without out any learning, although AI and robots can be coupled. An algorithm, for example, may be used by a robot picking items in a warehouse to determine the optimal path through the space or to teach it where to place objects based on their properties. We have included a few examples of robots in a library setting in our research since we are trying to think widely about the topic of AI.

This section has established in general terms how library work may be impacted by AI techniques. But it exclusively makes a brief referring to potential future changes to libraries and library work. The next section analyzes real-world applications organized according to the functional areas of libraries.

Review of Literature

The body of LIS literature on professional skills captures the quick evolution of professional library work. Professional organizations work to compile a list of pertinent competencies that is periodically updated to reflect industry advancements. For instance, the professional association in the UK, CILIP, released a revised Professional Knowledge and Skills Base in 2021. Federer (2018). Kellam & Thompson

Figure 1. Artificial intelligence component diagram
Source: Vijayakumar & Sheshadri (2019)

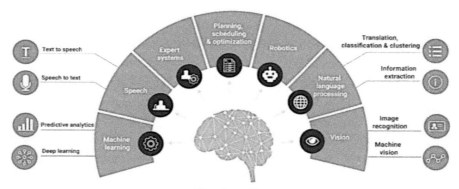

(2016), and Tammaro et al. (2019) examine the knowledge, abilities, and attitudes required to work in new fields of specialized employment, such as AI. The relatively new library professional practice supporting research data management (RDM) and data curation is a good example of this type of writing.

Cox et al. (2019) the LIS competencies literature excels at articulating and disseminating high-level understanding of the knowledge and skill sets required in new fields of employment, assisting new hires in identifying the appropriate skills to pursue, employers in developing job descriptions, and professional organizations and educators in updating curricula. This writing might also be seen as a claim to uncharted area. It is occasionally attempted to demonstrate that the necessary knowledge is essentially something library professionals already know.

Jacknis (2017) libraries may guarantee the use of the instruments for the new generation of knowledge, which transcends Google search, which has been designed for academic purposes, thanks to the numerous talents librarians have learned to arrange the material and make it accessible anywhere.

Kristin,(2016) libraries concentrate their efforts on using AI to improve content access. With many libraries starting and offering Makerspace competencies, we have been able to observe the proof of this change toward AI application.

Liu (2011) asserts that she conducted a thorough analysis of the literature on the application of intelligent agent technology in libraries in her papers. In order to give customers the greatest service possible, the researcher stated that librarians and AI should complement one another.

Components of Artificial Intelligence

Machine Learning, Expert Systems, Natural Language Processing, Pattern Recognition, and Robotics are just a few subfields of the artificial intelligence that are shown in the above diagram (Figure 1). They want to use computers to recreate human intelligence.

Machine Learning: In 1959, Arthur Samuel, an American pioneer in artificial intelligence and computer gaming, coined the phrase "machine learning," which he defined as "it allows computers to learn without explicit programming." Machine-learning applications are categorized into four main groups based on the type of "signal" or "responses" to the learning system: (a) supervised learning; (b) unsupervised learning; (c) reinforcement learning; and (d) semi-supervised learning.

Natural Language Processing: Teaching computers to comprehend the language we use today is one of computer sciences (CS) long-standing objectives. Natural Language is the latest version of computer language. A natural language interface with a restricted vocabulary and syntax has been created by artificial intelligence researchers. The computer can understand the major linguistic concepts in a query and its response by using natural language processing. It aims to create and enhance a machine that analyzes and produces human-readable text. Speech synthesis, machine translation, linguistic techniques, information extraction, information recovery, and speech recognition are just a few of the numerous elements that make up natural language processing.

Expert System: A computerized knowledge system that acts as a portal or interface for granting access to the database and retrieving pertinent data is known as an expert system. It could be as simple as standardized data regulations or as complicated as integrated development, which requires years to implement. A computer program that offers professional advice, solutions, or opinions in relation to a particular issue is known as an expert system. The knowledge base, inference engine, and user interface are the various components of expert systems.

Pattern recognition: The information that has been saved previously and the new information are closely linked when using this strategy. For the duration of their lives, all living organisms go through this process continuously. Pattern recognition is being studied by several academic fields, including as informatics, cognitive science, ethology, and psychology. Pattern recognition employing information gleaned from patterns or expertise from past experiences. Classified patterns are most commonly observations or sets of dimensions that characterize points in a multi-dimensional space. The steps involved in pattern recognition are data collection, preprocessing, character and model selection, training, and evaluation.

Robotics: In general, robotics is studied as a branch of artificial intelligence (AI) with an emphasis on perceptual and motor tasks. Robots are mechanical devices that, either directly under human direction or in compliance with a preset program, carry out automated activities utilizing artificial intelligence techniques.

Chatbots: Responding to a customer's questions can take a while. An artificially intelligent answer to this issue is the employment of chatbots, which train machines to respond to client requests. This enables machines to not only take and track orders, but also to answer.

Artificial Intelligence Cognitive Skills

The term "Artificial Intelligence" refers back to the simulation of human intelligence approaches via way of means of machines, in particular pc systems. It additionally consists of Expert systems, voice recognition, device vision, and herbal language processing (NLP).

AI programming specializes in 3 cognitive aspects, which includes mastering, reasoning, and self-correction.

1. Learning Processes
2. Reasoning Processes
3. Self-correction Processes

Learning Processes

This a part of AI programming is involved with accumulating facts and growing regulations for reworking it into beneficial information. The regulations, which can be additionally referred to as algorithms, provide computing gadgets with step-via way of means of-step commands for engaging in a selected job. In artificial intelligence, learning takes several different forms. The easiest way is to learn by trial and error. For example, a simple computer program can try random moves to solve checkmate-one chess problems until a mate is found. The program can then save the solution along with the location so that the next time the computer touches the same location, it remembers the solution

Reasoning Processes

This a part of AI programming is involved with deciding on the pleasant set of rules to gain the favored result. Reasoning is drawing conclusions appropriate to the situation. Inferences are classified as either deductive or inductive. An example of the first is: "Fred must be either in a museum or a cafe. He is not in a cafe; therefore he is in a museum", and of the second: "Previous accidents like this were caused by instrument failure; therefore this accident was caused by instrument failure."

Self-Correction Processes

This a part of AI programming objectives to fine-music algorithms often with the intention to make sure that they provide the maximum dependable effects possible. Examples of AI Artificial Intelligence is an in depth area of pc technology which specializes in growing wise machines able to doing sports that could commonly require human intelligence. While AI is a multidisciplinary technology with several methodologies, advances in deep mastering and device mastering create a paradigm shift in nearly each issue of technology.

Artificial Intelligence in Academic Libraries

At this stage, the number of specific AI applications currently applied to the library is particularly intensively investigated. It expands on a number of previous initiatives to describe the variety of AI packages in the library (Cox, 2021; Hervieux & Wheatley, 2022; Huang, 2022). The approach used here is to employ a broad definition so that the reader can navigate through fairly complex scenes. In certain library areas, some programs may also be able to collect more relevant data, such as research libraries and technology discovery applications in files. The relationship between AI and information literacy is probably much more likely to be addressed at the center by public libraries.

AI implementation in back-end library operations Here, AI is used to automate rote administrative and manual chores. One example is the use of robotic process automation (RPA) to automate clerical jobs that are frequently repeated (Lin, et al., 2022; Milholland & Maddalena, 2022). RPA enables one to program a computer to carry out tasks that are often done by Text or other data can be changed by hand and require a series of repetitive procedures where little human judgment is required, such as collecting data from various sources, processing it, and recording the results (Lin et al., 2022). All libraries can benefit greatly from such applications in automating operations such processing inputs from forms, transferring data between systems, or combining inputs from various sources. Such usages are described in a case study by knowing how to analyze workflows and having the technical know-how to apply RPA tools are necessary skills (Lin et al., 2022). Around 2005, pioneer libraries started utilizing similar systems. To make room for other uses by clearing space from bookcases is a major motivation for this. Both of these uses are driven by efficiency and are often less divisive because they appear to be freeing people from laborious duties. Artificial Intelligence approaches are used to describe library collections, which are typically specialized collections of rare archival material, as those found in research libraries. However, it could also be used to refer to legal knowledge and materials in a law library. This is frequently caused by the sheer volume of data, which makes it impossible for humans to manually create metadata for discovery (Cordell, 2020; Europeana Tech, 2021).

One of the key challenges is that algorithms honed on contemporary handwriting or photographs would perform worse on older script or images. This suggests that expensive training data creation is required for special collections. Such training data may only be partially reusable. Since there are currently few ready-made options, there would likely be massive technological development expenditures that many libraries lack the funding to cover. Additionally, even large organizations who have a track record of creating these solutions and plenty of resources admit that scaling up projects into services is difficult (EuropeanaTech, 2021).

Several ethical issues also exist in this situation such advances in AI come at a time when the authenticity of collections is being questioned more and more, especially those that were compiled about indigenous peoples during the colonial era (Terras, 2022). These collections reflect collecting methods that are incompatible with modern notions of consent and represent indigenous people in ways that they have not authorized (Padilla, 2019). These issues could become more entrenched or severe as a result of AI. Making outputs understandable for consumers who are not experts in the technology is also a problem. The sustainability concerns surrounding some machine learning should also be mentioned (Brevini, 2020).

In the near future, libraries will be significantly impacted by artificial intelligence and its components; these developments will differ greatly from what is currently possible in libraries. Currently being created or built up to this point, most library-oriented AI applications are runtime's fundamental business assistance. Smart systems that assist with many activities for the library, like personnel, finances, collection growth, scheduling, etc., are examples of potential uses. These applications comprise systems that improve user services, like quick referencing and the ability to save, retrieve, and use information (Vijaykumar and Sheshadri 2019). AI applications allow libraries to shift focus and attention, particularly from conventional methods of accomplishing tasks to more advanced and contemporary ways of completing these tasks. Artificial intelligence (AI) provides a very helpful short cut to applying information (making wise decisions) and achieving better results (user pleasure). With the deployment of AI, libraries will now need to concentrate on improving material access rather than physical availability. The goal of AI subfields and their constituent parts is to use computers to mimic human intelligence. Thus, rather than being a threat, the use of AI in libraries can only be beneficial (Whitehair 2016).

Cataloging

Since descriptive cataloguing is thought to be rule-based, its application in AI has focused on it (AACR2). There are two ways that artificial intelligence algorithms can be used for information material cataloging.

The first is a human-computer interface, where the intermediary (a human) and the support system (an AI) split the cataloguing effort; the second is a fully cataloguing system integrated with an electronic publishing system, where text is generated digitally, passed through knowledge-based systems, and cataloged with minimal or no human intervention. In their attempts to convert AACR2 into the highly structured standards needed for system coding, researchers have encountered formidable obstacles at every turn (Afolayan, et al, 2020). Expert systems can be employed by digital libraries to facilitate the process of classifying and examining digital resources. Through the online system, users will be able to browse the collection, peruse the available resources, and obtain the information of their choice by utilizing this expert system based on a digital library. The utilization of intelligent library retrieval in cataloguing procedures is facilitated by the application of data mining. Additionally, data mining can be utilized to determine users' information needs in online library systems. They support library patrons in selecting the right term or phrase for information retrieval. Numerous research concentrate on the user-centered design of recommender systems for different library divisions as well as for library catalogues (Mogali, 2014).

Additionally, classification is a crucial step in the knowledge organization process. The use of AI technologies for classification in the library include the following: BIOSIS is a knowledge-base-based indexing tool that was created. Additionally, it employs a significant amount of procedural expertise to automatically assign information materials to subject classes. In order to assign as many classifications as possible to biological materials, BIOSIS makes use of the information found in their titles, just like a human indexer would. Applications of artificial intelligence make good use of the structured indexing languages and useful information representation that are available. Coal SORT is a conceptual browser intended for searching or indexing purposes; it lacks procedural expertise. The majority of coal SORT is made up of the software that users need to show certain aspects of it, as well as a framework-based semantical network and the conceptual structure. The EP-X, or Environmental Pollution Expert, resembles a coal SORT. Each system uses a Knowledge-Based methodology to focus on interface improvement. A hierarchical frame-based semantic network of concepts and a model group that expresses the structures known as the pragmatic relationship between concepts make up EP-X's knowledge base. We refer to these patterns as conceptual information (Mogali, 2014).

Collection Development

AI tools can be used to choose book dealers or vendors for library supplies. A vendor or book seller can be identified intelligently by the use of past successful transactions involving the provision of publications of a particular kind. These instruments would be very crucial for the acquisition of unusual information materials, like conference proceedings and publications published in foreign languages, other nations, and specific technical reports, to name a few. Furthermore, investigations have shown that AI tools have also been created specifically for the field of librarianship to help with the process of choosing. Among these are the Monograph Selection Advisor, a cutting-edge attempt in use this new technology to provide information resources for libraries. The technology specifically replicated the item-by-item decision-making process that a topic bibliographer uses to choose monographic materials. To guarantee that the library can get the intended outcomes from the AI system, the system's knowledge base must be large enough and its interface elements must be sufficiently straightforward.

Reference Services

Furthermore, based on AI reference services have made it easier for users to get information by helping them to find it quickly and easily without having to remember connections or paths (Kaushal & Yadav, 2022). According to Kibirige (1998), computerized reference services can help bridge any communication gaps that might arise between an information professional and a library user. This has been accomplished by using chatbot programs, which function as virtual assistants (Nawaz & Saldeen, 2020). As virtual agents, chatbots have enhanced customer satisfaction, services, and user service customization—especially with the so-called millennials who find voice calls intrusive. Furthermore, chatbot reference services provide library employees with much-needed free time to support research and effectively contribute to meeting patrons' information demands. In order to solve issues with library availability and working hours, Meincke (2018) collaborated with a group of Johnson and Wales University library staff members to develop a Python-based chatbot for library services. This chatbot could identify books and articles, answer simple inquiries about the library's operating hours, give general library information, and even crack jokes.

Abstracting and Indexing

The application of AI has been advantageous for the indexing and abstracting fields. AI is used by CiteseerX in a number of its components, including author disambiguation, de-duplication, automatic metadata extraction, and document classification (Wu et al., 2015). The desire to enhance contemporary information storage, preservation, discovery, and retrieval has made metadata research essential. Information seekers nowadays need to be able to not only locate, recognize, pick, and retrieve information, but also investigate it. To help with this, modern librarians are working to develop metadata standards and best practices (Green, 2021). Institutional repositories and digital libraries in academic libraries have used this.

Natural language processing applications in library activities: The first image that comes to mind when we hear the phrase "NLPL" is probably of being able to write or talk in full sentences while having a machine handle the request and speak. Numerous disciplines can use NLPL. This could be used in the domain of searching databases like Online Public Access Catalogues (OPAC), which is more particularly in the subject of library and information science. The foundation for document retrieval is indexing. The aim of indexing is to increase recall, or the proportion of recovered relevant documents, as well as precision, or the percentage of retrieved relevant documents.

The Benefits of Artificial Intelligence in Academic Libraries

The perspective of AI among library employees needs to change for libraries to reap the benefits of applying AI. Librarians and management can gain insight from how AI is viewed in other professions where it is being used, rather than viewing AI as a disruptive tool that will replace library personnel and established library practices. AI must to be looked upon as an instrument to deal with actual-world problems.

AI Enhances Efficiency and Effectiveness in Operations: By improving information resource provision and service efficacy and lowering operational costs through automation, digital asset management, and optimized research data governance, libraries can assess and improve the organizational effectiveness and efficiency of library services. Artificial intelligence (AI) solutions can be developed and integrated into library procedures and services to facilitate collection analysis, visualisation, conservation and preservation, and cost-tracking. Putting intelligent systems into place to provide library users with information resources and services can foster creativity and innovation, which will increase operational efficacy and efficiency.

Possibility of Engaging Wider Audiences: With the addition of chatbots and location-based services to search engine results, the library will be able to offer information services to a wider audience. Additionally, ML algorithms have the ability to instantly digest content from hundreds of sites, replacing the traditional analysis of only a portion of that data. AI applications can discover needs and create excellent and captivating experiences for library users by integrating data on user touch points, past interactions, and behaviors. In order to deliver more effective and efficient information resources and services, the goal is to generate correct research suggestions that are tailored to each individual and even to match search results with particular knowledge.

Supports Library professionals in Achieving Their New Objectives: When AI approaches are applied, human errors and inefficiencies are reduced. Examples of these routines include daily searches and reference operations. These intelligent systems can free up library staff members to work on more worthwhile projects, such as helping patrons create reading lists, teaching patrons how to do better scientific research, developing the library's information resources, and other such tasks.

Establish the libraries at the heart of the new landscape of scholarly information: By identifying connections in large datasets that were previously missed, artificial intelligence (AI) tools have made it easier for scholarly researchers to do multidisciplinary harmonization. Also, by collaborating with Open Publishing institutions and developing research tools that interface with other organizations, libraries may support the ongoing exchange of information and research across all domains and branches. They eventually contribute to a vast, top-notch global resource network by making their collections easier to search, explore, and analyze.

Challenges of Implementation of Artificial Intelligence in Libraries

Currently, the majority of libraries do not have artificial intelligence systems in operation. Artificial intelligence systems in libraries are subject to certain restrictions.

1. Staff members in libraries lack the technical know-how to use and manage artificial intelligence technology.
2. Insufficient money for the purchase or development of artificial intelligence systems for libraries. There are always restrictions on the kind of system the library can buy or design because hardware and software funds are usually limited.
3. The high expense of artificial intelligence system development and upkeep in libraries.
4. An unstable power source, particularly in underdeveloped nations, is used to power artificial intelligence systems in libraries.
5. Development of artificial and expert intelligence systems is inherently complicated.
6. Limited proficiency in natural language.
7. The lack of a shared human knowledge base greatly limits the kinds of tasks that intelligent computers are capable of executing.

8. The amount of time and technological know-how required to develop AI systems for libraries. The strength and complexity of an intelligent library system closely correlate with the amount and kind of work required to construct it. This suggests that the work required to maintain the system will increase with its intelligence. There aren't many sophisticated intelligent systems in libraries at the moment since it's expensive or difficult to find the necessary trained staff members and development tools.

9. Few providers who specialize in library automation have knowledge of artificial intelligence. The complexity of artificial intelligence necessitates specialized knowledge in that area that goes well beyond the creation of traditional library automation systems. Therefore, before any substantial, extensive work in the field of artificial intelligence systems in libraries can be done, this will necessitate hiring new employees in that area.

FUTURE RESEARCH SUGGESTIONS

Furthermore, future theoretical and research studies about the integration of AI applications in academic libraries had to take into account the significance of issues pertaining to library resources and services. This also suggested more research when users involved, study should also explore the data integrity, privacy and security protocols. Although Reliability and ethics of AI use in academic libraries have not received much attention. Thus, the chapter suggests further investigation into the moral concerns surrounding the application of AI in library science and librarianship in the future.

CONCLUSION

This article aimed to assist librarians in navigating the potentially wide-ranging influence of AI on libraries. The basic explanations of artificial intelligence in Part One not only show that the field is expanding but also assist the reader in comprehending the extent of the concern regarding the interaction between people and machines. Through the use of samples from libraries, part two offers some insights into the actual technology. The use of AI in many facets of library operations is covered in more detail in Part 3. This shows how artificial intelligence (AI) can enhance knowledge discovery, create new roles focused on community support, add a new dimension to information literacy, support understanding and control over user behavior, and improve library operations through chatbots and dynamic SLRs. There are several significant obstacles, such as moral and legal dilemmas, a dearth of readily available solutions, difficulty with cost and implementation, a lack of necessary skills, difficulties with teamwork, and the allure of other goals and innovations. The topic of discussion turns to how AI might affect library work and what it means for inclusion, diversity, and equality in the field.

This sort of study makes it easier to see the wider picture of AI's ubiquitous yet uneven impact. In several library sectors, at least in some of their institutions, artificial intelligence advancements are fairly advanced. Similarly, several applications have been proposed on sound principles for many years but have failed to materialize at scale. Some of these prospective uses may not have a big influence on services in the end. Thus, rather than a sense of inevitable outcome, this situation seems possible. It is important, we think, to stress that what we have talked about is a possibility that we can shape, not an inevitable 'wave of the future'.

REFERENCES

Afolayan, J. O., Ogundokun, R. O., Afolabi, A. G., & Adegun, A. A. (2020). Artificial Intelligence, Cloud Librarianship, and Infopreneurship Initiatives for Inclusiveness. In A. Tella (Ed.), *Handbook of Research on Digital Devices for Inclusivity and Engagement in Libraries* (pp. 45–69). IGI Global. doi:10.4018/978-1-5225-9034-7.ch003

Ajakaye, J. E. (2022). Applications of Artificial Intelligence (AI) in Libraries. In I. Ekoja, E. Ogbomo, & O. Okuonghae (Eds.), *Handbook of Research on Emerging Trends and Technologies in Librarianship* (pp. 73–90). IGI Global. doi:10.4018/978-1-7998-9094-2.ch006

Alzubi, J., Nayyar, A., & Kumar, A. (2018). Machine learning from theory to algorithms: An overview. *Journal of Physics: Conference Series*, *1142*, 1–16. doi:10.1088/1742-6596/1142/1/012012

Asemi, A., & Asemi, A. (2018). Artificial Intelligence (AI) application in Library Systems in Iran: A taxonomy study. *Library Philosophy and Practice (e-journal)*, 1-10. https://digitalcommons.unl.edu/libphilprac/1840/

Bowker, L., Kalsatos, M., Ruskin, A., & Ciro, J. B. (2022). Artificial intelligence, machine translation, and academic libraries: Improving machine translation literacy on campus. In The Rise of AI: Implications and Applications for AI in Academic Libraries (pp. 3-14). Association of College and Research Libraries.

Brevini, B. (2020). Black boxes, not green: Mythologizing artificial intelligence and omitting the environment. *Big Data & Society*, *7*(2), 1–5. doi:10.1177/2053951720935141

Cave, S., & Dihal, K. (2020). The whiteness of AI. *Philosophy & Technology*, *33*(4), 685–703. doi:10.100713347-020-00415-6

Chang, R. (1990). Developing a cataloging expert system. *Illinois Libraries*, *72*, 592–596.

Cordell, R. (2020). *Machine learning and libraries: a report on the state of the field*. Library of Congress. https://labs.loc.gov/static/labs/work/reports/Cordell-LOC-ML-report.pdf

Cox, A. (2022). The ethics of AI for information professionals: Eight scenarios. *Journal of the Australian Library and Information Association*, *71*(3), 201–214. doi:10.1080/24750158.2022.2084885

Cox, A. M. (2021). *The role of the information, knowledge management and library workforce in the 4th industrial revolution*. Academic Press.

Cox, A. M., Pinfield, S., & Rutter, S. (2019). The intelligent library: Thought leaders' views on the likely impact of artificial intelligence on academic libraries. *Library Hi Tech*, *37*(3), 418–435. doi:10.1108/LHT-08-2018-0105

Dekker, H., Ferrari, A., & Mandal, I. (2022). URI Libraries' AI Lab Evolving to meet the needs of students and research communities. In S. Hervieux & A. Wheatley (Eds.), *The Rise of AI: Implications and Applications for AI in Academic Libraries* (pp. 15–34). Association of College and Research Libraries.

Donkor, A. B., & Afrane, D. A. (2023). Application of AI in Academic Library Services: Prospects and Implications for Quality Service Delivery. In D. Chiu & K. Ho (Eds.), *Emerging Technology-Based Services and Systems in Libraries, Educational Institutions, and Non-Profit Organizations* (pp. 1–25). IGI Global. doi:10.4018/978-1-6684-8671-9.ch001

EuropeanaTech. (2021). *AI in relation to Glams task Force: Report and Recommendations.* Available at: https://pro.europeana.eu/project/ai-in-relation-to-glams

Federer, L. (2018). Defining data librarianship: A survey of competencies, skills, and training. *Journal of the Medical Library Association, 106*(3), 294–303. doi:10.5195/jmla.2018.306 PMID:29962907

Grbin, L., Nichols, P., Russell, F., Fuller-Tyszkiewicz, M., & Olsson, C. A. (2022). The development of a living knowledge system and implications for future systematic searching. *Journal of the Australian Library and Information Association, 71*(3), 275–292. doi:10.1080/24750158.2022.2087954

Green, A. M. (2022). Metadata Application Profiles in US Academic Libraries: A Document Analysis. *Journal of Library Metadata, 21*(3-4), 105–143. doi:10.1080/19386389.2022.2030172

Hastie, T., Tibshirani, R., Friedman, J. H., & Friedman, J. H. (2009). The elements of statistical learning: data mining, inference, and prediction (Vol. 2). Springer. https://doi.org/ doi:10.1007/978-0-387-21606-5

Hervieux, S., & Wheatley, A. (2021). Perceptions of artificial intelligence: A survey of academic librarians in Canada and the United States. *Journal of Academic Librarianship, 47*(1), 102270. doi:10.1016/j.acalib.2020.102270

Hervieux, S., & Wheatley, A. (Eds.). (2022). *The Rise of AI: Implications and Applications of Artificial Intelligence in Academic Libraries.* Association of College and Research Libraries.

Hu, Y., Li, W., & Wright, D. (2019). Artificial intelligence approaches. In The Geographic Information Science & Technology Body of Knowledge, 3rd Quarter 2019 ed. (pp. 1-12). doi:10.22224/gistbok/2019.3.4

Huang, Y. H. (2022). Exploring the implementation of artificial intelligence applications among academic libraries in Taiwan. *Library Hi Tech.* doi:10.1108/LHT-03-2022-0159

IFLA. (2016). *IFLA Trend Report 2016 Update.* IFLA. https://trends.ifla.org/update-2016

Irizarry-Nones, A., Palepu, A., & Wallace, M. (2017). *Artificial intelligence (AI).* Boston University. Available at https://www.bu.edu/lernet/artemis/years/2017/projects/FinalPresenations/A.I.%20Presentation.pdf

Jacknis, N. (2017). *The AI-Enhanced Library.* Available at: https://norman-jacknis.medium.com/the-ai-enhanced-library-a34d96fffdfe

Johnson, L., Becker, S. A., Estrada, V., & Freeman, A. (2015). *NMC horizon report: 2015 library edition.* The New Media Consortium. https://www.learntechlib.org/p/151822/

Kaushal, V., & Yadav, R. (2022). The role of chatbots in academic libraries: An experience-based perspective. *Journal of the Australian Library and Information Association, 71*(3), 215–232. doi:10.1080/24750158.2022.2106403

Kellam, L. M., & Thompson, K. (2016). *Databrarianship: The academic data librarian in theory and practice.* Association of College and Research Libraries. https://cir.nii.ac.jp/crid/1130282271743223040

Kibirige, H. M. (1988). Computer—Assisted Reference Services: What the Computer Will Not Do. *RQ*, 377-383.

Kitchenham, B., Brereton, O. P., Budgen, D., Turner, M., Bailey, J., & Linkman, S. (2009). Systematic literature reviews in software engineering–a systematic literature review. *Information and Software Technology, 51*(1), 7–15. doi:10.1016/j.infsof.2008.09.009

Lin, C. H., Chiu, D. K., & Lam, K. T. (2022). Hong Kong academic librarians' attitudes toward robotic process automation. *Library Hi Tech.* doi:10.1108/LHT-03-2022-0141

Liu, G. (2011). The application of intelligent agents in libraries: a survey. *Program: Electronic Library and Information Systems, 45*(1), 78-97. doi:10.1108/00330331111107411

Meincke, D. (2018). Experiences building, training, and deploying a Chatbot in an academic library. *Library Staff Publications, 28.* https://scholarsarchive.jwu.edu/staff_pub/28

Milholland, A., & Maddalena, M. (2022). "We could program a Bot to do that!" Robotic process automation in metadata curation and scholarship discoerability. In S. Hervieux & A. Wheatley (Eds.), *The Rise of AI: Implications and Applications for AI in Academic Libraries* (pp. 111–122). Association of College and Research Libraries.

Mogali, S. S. (2014). Artificial intelligence and it's applications in libraries. In *Bilingual International Conference on Information Technology: Yesterday, Today and Tomorrow* (pp. 1-10). Defence Scientific Information and Documentation Centre, Ministry of Defence Delhi. https://www.researchgate.net/publication/287878456_Artificial_Intelligence_and_its_applications_in_Libraries

Nawaz, N., & Saldeen, M. A. (2020). Artificial intelligence chatbots for library reference services. *Journal of Management Information and Decision Sciences, 23*(1S), 442–449. https://www.abacademies.org/articles/artificial-intelligence-chatbots-for-library-reference-services-9653.html

OECD. (2020). *The OECD AI principles.* Available at: https://oecd.ai/en/ai-principles

Okpokwasili, N. P. (2019). Artificial intelligence in libraries and users satisfaction in higher institutions in Nigeria. *International Journal of Research in Informative Science Application & Techniques, 3*(2), 2581–5814. doi:10.46828/ijrisat.v3i2.44

Olsson, F. (2009). *A literature survey of active machine learning in the context of natural language processing. SICS technical report T2009:06.* Swedish Institute of Computer Science. https://www.ccs.neu.edu/home/vip/teach/MLcourse/4_boosting/materials/SICS-T--2009-06--SE.pdf

Omame, I. M., & Alex-Nmecha, J. C. (2020). Artificial Intelligence in Libraries. In N. Osuigwe (Ed.), *Managing and Adapting Library Information Services for Future Users* (pp. 120–144). IGI Global. doi:10.4018/978-1-7998-1116-9.ch008

Padilla, T. (2019). *Responsible Operations: Data Science, Machine Learning, and AI in Libraries.* OCLC Research Position Paper. OCLC Online Computer Library Center, Inc. https://eric.ed.gov/?id=ED603715

Robertshaw, M. B., & Asher, A. (2019). Unethical numbers? A meta-analysis of library learning analytics studies. *Library Trends, 68*(1), 76–101. doi:10.1353/lib.2019.0031

Shao, G., Quintana, J. P., Zakharov, W., Purzer, S., & Kim, E. (2021). Exploring potential roles of academic libraries in undergraduate data science education curriculum development. *Journal of Academic Librarianship, 47*(2), 102320. doi:10.1016/j.acalib.2021.102320

Tammaro, A. M., Matusiak, K. K., Sposito, F. A., & Casarosa, V. (2019). Data curator's roles and responsibilities: An international perspective. *Libri, 69*(2), 89–104. doi:10.1515/libri-2018-0090

Tella, A. (2020). Robots are coming to the libraries: Are librarians ready to accommodate them? *Library Hi Tech News, 37*(8), 13–17. doi:10.1108/LHTN-05-2020-0047

Terras, M. (2022). The role of the library when computers can read: Critically adopting Handwritten Text Recognition (HTR) technologies to support research. In S. Hervieux & A. Wheatley (Eds.), *The Rise of AI: Implications and Applications of Artificial Intelligence in Academic Libraries* (pp. 137–148). Association of College and Research Libraries.

UK Government. (2021). *National AI strategy*. Available at: https://www.gov.uk/government/publications/national-ai-strategy

UKRI. (2021). *Transforming our world with AI*. Available at: https://www.ukri.org/wp-content/uploads/2021/02/UKRI-120221-TransformingOurWorldWithAI.pdf

Vijaykumar, S., & Sheshadri, K. N. (2019). Applications of artificial intelligence in academic libraries. *International Journal on Computer Science and Engineering, 7*(16), 136–140. doi:10.26438/ijcse/v7si16.136140

Whitehair, K. (2016). *Libraries in an artificially intelligent world*. Public Libraries. Available at: https://publiclibrariesonline.org/2016/02/libraries-in-an-artificially-intelligent-world

Williams, R. (2019). Artificial intelligence assistants in the library: Siri, Alexa, and beyond. *Online Searcher, 43*(3), 10–14.

Witten, I. H., & Frank, E. (2002). Data mining: Practical machine learning tools and techniques with Java implementations. *SIGMOD Record, 31*(1), 76–77. doi:10.1145/507338.507355

Wu, J., Williams, K. M., Chen, H.-H., Khabsa, M., Caragea, C., Tuarob, S., Ororbia, A. G., Jordan, D., Mitra, P., & Giles, C. L. (2015). CiteSeerX: AI in a Digital Library Search Engine. *AI Magazine, 36*(3), 35–48. doi:10.1609/aimag.v36i3.2601

Yu, K., Gong, R., Sun, L., & Jiang, C. (2019). The application of artificial intelligence in smart library. In *International Conference on organizational innovation (ICOI 2019)* (pp. 708-713). Atlantis Press. 10.2991/icoi-19.2019.124

ADDITIONAL READING

Asemi, A., Ko, A., & Nowkarizi, M. (2020). Intelligent libraries: A review on expert systems, artificial intelligence, and robot. *Library Hi Tech, 39*(2), 412–434. doi:10.1108/LHT-02-2020-0038

Echedom, A. U., & Okuonghae, O. (2021). Transforming academic library operations in Africa with artificial intelligence: Opportunities and challenges: A review paper. *New Review of Academic Librarianship*, *27*(2), 243–255. doi:10.1080/13614533.2021.1906715

Gujral, G., Shivarama, J., & Choukimath, P. A. (2019). Perceptions and prospects of artificial intelligence technologies for academic libraries: An overview of global trends. *12th International CALIBER*, 79-88. http://ir.inflibnet.ac.in/handle/1944/2337

Lund, B. D., Omame, I., Tijani, S., & Agbaji, D. (2020). Perceptions toward artificial intelligence among academic library employees and alignment with the diffusion of innovations' adopter categories. *College & Research Libraries*, *81*(5), 865–882. doi:10.5860/crl.81.5.865

Wheatley, A., & Hervieux, S. (2019). Artificial intelligence in academic libraries: An environmental scan. *Information Services & Use*, *39*(4), 347–356. doi:10.3233/ISU-190065

KEY TERMS AND DEFINITIONS

Academic Libraries: An academic library is a library that is attached to a higher education institution and serves two complementary purposes: to support the curriculum and the research of the university faculty and students.

Artificial Intelligence: Artificial intelligence is the simulation of human intelligence processes by machines, especially computer systems. Specific applications of AI include expert systems, natural language processing, speech recognition and machine vision.

Chatbots: Chatbots are computer programs designed to simulate conversation with human users through text or voice-based interfaces. Chatbots use natural language processing (NLP) to understand and interpret user input and generate appropriate responses.

Library Services: Library Service means a service that provides reading materials for convenient use; circulation of reading materials; service to help provide users with library materials, educational and recreational audiovisual materials; or a combination of these services.

Machine Learning: Machine learning (ML) is a type of artificial intelligence (AI) focused on building computer systems that learn from data. The broad range of techniques ML encompasses enables software applications to improve their performance over time.

Natural Language Processing: Natural language processing (NLP) refers to the branch of computer science—and more specifically, the branch of artificial intelligence or AI—concerned with giving computers the ability to understand text and spoken words in much the same way human beings can.

Robotics: Robotics is a branch of engineering and computer science that involves the conception, design, manufacture and operation of robots. The objective of the robotics field is to create intelligent machines that can assist humans in a variety of ways.

Chapter 6
Open Access, Open Doors:
The Benefits of OA in Academic Research and Higher Education

Emily Morgan

ⓘD https://orcid.org/0009-0000-3159-4540

Beacon College, USA

ABSTRACT

The open access (OA) movement, a paradigm shift in scholarly communication, has emerged as a corner-stone of modern higher education and academic libraries. By removing financial barriers, OA ensures unrestricted access to academic resources, democratizing knowledge and fostering a more equitable learning environment. Furthermore, OA promotes interdisciplinary collaboration, enabling scholars to engage in expansive knowledge exchange across diverse fields, fueling innovation. Academic libraries have become instrumental in curating vast repositories of openly accessible content, enhancing their role as facilitators of information literacy. Embracing open access principles enhances the visibility of institutions and researchers but also promotes inclusivity, ensuring that diverse voices find resonance in academic discourse. Explored in this chapter are the multifaceted advantages of the OA movement, underscoring its pivotal role in shaping a more accessible, collaborative, and egalitarian landscape within higher education and academic libraries.

INTRODUCTION

Open Access (OA) has emerged as a transformative force in scholarly communication and knowledge dissemination. The advent of the digital era has revolutionized the way knowledge is created and disseminated. At the heart of this movement are several key stakeholders who play pivotal roles in reshaping the information landscape and scholarly communication. In this chapter, we explore the fundamental stakeholders in the Open Access movement, how they utilize and apply OA content, and the profound impact they are having on academia and the broader society. As stakeholders themselves, libraries and librarians play an active role in promoting and educating faculty, students, and staff on the sustainability

DOI: 10.4018/979-8-3693-2841-5.ch006

benefits offered by the Open Access movement. Also explored in the chapter is the history of the OA movement, misconceptions, benefits, implications, and impact of Open Access on libraries in the context of research and dissemination of information in higher education and academia.

The Open Access movement, as a revolutionary shift in scholarly publishing, has gained substantial momentum in recent years. Rooted in the belief that scholarly knowledge should be openly and freely accessible to everyone, regardless of financial or institutional constraints; OA challenges the traditional model of subscription-based journals and promotes unrestricted access to academic research. This movement is not confined to a particular group or institution; rather, it encompasses a diverse range of stakeholders, including researchers, institutions, organizations, students, educators, librarians, and the public. These stakeholders utilize OA platforms in multifaceted ways, shaping the dissemination and consumption of scholarly information in the digital age.

Researchers exhibit an acute awareness of the transformative power inherent in disseminating scholarly knowledge openly. This recognition is underscored by their active participation in publishing their scholarly endeavors in Open Access journals or depositing manuscripts in OA repositories. This deliberate choice ensures that their intellectual contributions resonate globally, transcending the confines of institutional and geographical boundaries. By embracing OA principles, researchers dismantle the barriers that traditionally obstructed the flow of information, thereby democratizing access to knowledge. Unrestricted accessibility to scholarly content serves as a catalyst, expediting the pace of scientific discovery by fostering an environment of unfettered dissemination. The ramifications of this acceleration are profound, propelling the evolution of disciplines through cross-pollination of ideas and methodologies. Interdisciplinary research flourishes under the aegis of OA, as scholars from diverse fields converge, leveraging the shared knowledge landscape. This unrestricted accessibility amplifies the visibility of scholars and their affiliated institutions, enhancing their academic influence and global recognition. Open Access not only catalyzes the acceleration of scholarly progress but also nurtures a vibrant culture of scholarly dialogue. The rapid exchange of ideas facilitated by OA platforms engenders a dynamic intellectual milieu where scholars engage in meaningful discourse. Timely feedback becomes a cornerstone of academic enrichment, refining methodologies, theories, and interpretations. In this ecosystem of shared knowledge, Open Access becomes the linchpin that fortifies the foundations of academic inquiry. Scholars, practitioners, and enthusiasts alike stand to benefit from this scholarly egalitarianism, where information flows freely, unencumbered by financial constraints.

Students, particularly those in higher education institutions, also benefit significantly from the OA movement. Open Access textbooks, educational resources, and research articles eliminate the financial burden of purchasing expensive textbooks or accessing paywalled articles. This accessibility democratizes education, making learning materials freely available to students from diverse socioeconomic backgrounds. Conversely, open educational resources (OERs) empower educators to customize their teaching materials, tailoring content to meet the specific needs of their students and will be explored later in the chapter. This flexibility not only enhances the learning experience but also fosters innovative pedagogical approaches, transforming the dynamics of education.

Universities and research institutions are increasingly recognizing the importance of OA in advancing their missions of education, research, and societal impact. Many institutions have established institutional repositories to archive and disseminate the work of their faculty and researchers. Thus, universities are supporting OA publishing by funding publication fees and incentivizing faculty to publish in Open Access journals. These initiatives align with the ethos of knowledge dissemination and promote the institution's reputation as a hub of innovative research and scholarship.

Funding agencies, both public and private, are influential stakeholders driving the Open Access movement. They often mandate that research funded by public money should be openly accessible. By enforcing OA policies, these agencies maximize the return on investment in research, ensuring that the outcomes are disseminated widely and contribute to scientific progress. Hence, funding bodies support OA initiatives financially, enabling researchers to publish in Open Access journals without incurring publication fees, effectively reducing financial barriers to OA publishing.

Traditional publishers and academic journals have also adapted to the changing landscape by embracing OA models. Many established journals now offer authors the option to publish their articles as Open Access, either through payment of article processing charges (APCs) or through alternative funding mechanisms. Some journals have transitioned entirely to Open Access, exploring sustainable business models to cover publication costs. This shift signifies a departure from the traditional subscription-based model and promotes a more inclusive and accessible system of scholarly communication. Traditional publishing and the various OA models are explored in more detail throughout the chapter.

Though this chapter focuses on academia and higher education, Open Access is not limited to the academic community; it extends its benefits to society at large. OA content empowers the public to access reliable, peer-reviewed information, fostering a scientifically literate society. It supports lifelong learning, enabling individuals to engage with innovative research and make informed decisions in various fields. As a result, OA content often intersects with public interests, such as healthcare, climate change, and social sciences, providing valuable resources for policymakers, activists, and concerned citizens. In the same vein advocacy groups and non-governmental organizations champion the cause of OA, lobbying for supportive policies and raising awareness about the importance of unrestricted access to knowledge. The Coalition of Open Access Policy Institutions, Creative Commons, and The Open Access Scholarly Publishing Association (OASPA) are just a few examples of these agencies. Their efforts are instrumental in driving policy changes and shaping public opinion.

Libraries, as pivotal institutions in the dissemination of knowledge, play a vital role in the OA movement. Traditionally, libraries have served as custodians of print collections, providing access to scholarly publications within their physical spaces. However, in the digital era, libraries have transformed into dynamic hubs of information, embracing digital technologies, and advocating for Open Access. Libraries serve as advocates, educating researchers and faculty about the benefits of OA and guiding them in navigating the intricacies of OA publishing. Librarians collaborate with researchers to identify reputable OA journals and repositories, ensuring the quality and credibility of the published content.

Similarly, libraries are increasingly involved in the creation and management of institutional repositories, where faculty and researchers can deposit their scholarly outputs, including preprints, post-prints, and datasets. These repositories serve as valuable archives of institutional knowledge, preserving the intellectual output of academic communities for future generations. Librarians curate these repositories, ensuring proper metadata standards, compliance with copyright policies, and long-term accessibility of digital content. Comparatively, libraries actively engage in digitization projects, converting rare and valuable print materials into digital formats and making them openly accessible to researchers and the public, thus preserving cultural heritage and expanding the pool of openly accessible resources.

Libraries also advocate for Open Access at the policy level, collaborating with academic institutions to draft OA mandates and negotiating with publishers to secure favorable terms for OA publication fees. These negotiations often result in transformative agreements, wherein institutions pay a single fee to publishers, granting their researchers Open Access publishing privileges. Such agreements not only promote

OA but also contribute to substantial cost savings for institutions, redirecting funds toward enhancing research infrastructure, expanding library collections, and supporting scholarly communication initiatives.

The Open Access movement has ushered in a new era of scholarly communication, dismantling barriers to knowledge and democratizing access to information. Its impact reverberates across diverse sectors, benefiting researchers, students, institutions, and the public at large. Libraries, recognizing the transformative power of Open Access, have emerged as critical stakeholders, actively promoting, facilitating, and shaping the OA landscape. As the OA movement continues to evolve, libraries will remain at the forefront, championing the principles of accessibility, equity, and knowledge dissemination, ensuring that the fruits of academic inquiry are accessible to all, transcending geographical, financial, and institutional boundaries.

As we transition from the various stakeholders in the Open Access movement, it is imperative to contextualize their efforts within the broader landscape of academic publishing. The Open Access movement's origins can be traced back to the late 20th century, when the internet began to revolutionize the way information was disseminated. Traditional publishing models, characterized by restricted access to scholarly works, faced challenges in adapting to this digital era. Academics, researchers, and advocates for accessible knowledge began to question the existing norms, envisioning a more inclusive system where research findings were freely available to anyone, anywhere. This vision became the foundation upon which the OA movement was built. Scholars, librarians, and institutions worldwide joined forces to challenge the barriers that hindered the flow of knowledge. Understanding the brief historical backdrop of this movement is essential to grasp the fervor and dedication exhibited by its proponents. By further exploring the roots of Open Access, we gain valuable insights into the evolution of scholarly communication, shedding light on the transformative journey that has reshaped the way we access and share knowledge in the digital age.

BACKGROUND

The Open Access movement is a significant and ongoing effort to make scholarly research and literature freely accessible to the public online, without any financial or legal barriers. OA has its roots in the early days of the internet and has since evolved into a global movement with various key institutions, individuals, and policies playing crucial roles from its infancy to the present. The Open Access movement can be traced back to the 1990s when the internet began to gain prominence as a medium for sharing information. Scientists and scholars recognized the potential of this innovative technology to disseminate research more widely and efficiently. One such figure and pioneer of the movement, Stevan Harnad introduced his "Subversive Proposal" and seminal work in the field of academic publishing and open access (Bell, 2019). Published in 1994 and introduced at the Network Services Conference (NSC) in London, Harnad's proposal has significantly impacted discussions around scholarly communication and research dissemination. In this paper, Harnad outlines his vision for a new model of academic publishing that he believes would revolutionize scholarly communication. The key issue in academic publishing as identified by Harnard, is restricted access to scholarly works and research data. Harnad's solution as Bell succinctly summarizes is one of the founding principles of the Budapest Open Access Initiative, "an old tradition and a new technology have converged to make possible an unprecedented public good" (2019)—a public good in which research and scholarly communication is openly available to scholars and non-scholars alike. Traditional publishing models often result in paywalls and subscription barriers, limiting access to research for those who do not have institutional access or cannot afford subscription fees. Harnad's proposal for unrestricted access to scholarly research is a "subversive" approach to academic publishing, as it suggests that authors should self-archive their research papers in publicly accessible online repositories. This way, anyone with internet access can read and download the papers for free, bypassing traditional publishers' paywalls, "He wants only to PUBLISH them, that is, to reach the eyes of his peers, his fellow esoteric scientists and scholars the world over, so that they can build on one another's work in that collaborative enterprise called learned inquiry" (Harnad, 1994). Harnad's quote focuses on connecting other scholars and researchers; however, we, as librarians, know the implication the OA movement has for lifelong learning, empowerment, and information and digital literacy. To further librarians' involvement in and support of OA journals, Yoitis writes, "in 1998, ARL [Association of Research Libraries] launched the Scholarly Publishing and Academic Resources Coalition (SPARC), and alliance of university research libraries and organizations" (2005). SPARC was formed to address the increased cost of scholarly journals by supporting competitive OA journals and content.

In 2002 the literature on scholarly communication and Open Access saw a major shift in favor of unrestricted access of scientific works in the Declaration of the Budapest Open Access Initiative. The Initiative marked a critical milestone in bringing together scholars, researchers, and organizations to address the issue of restricted access to academic literature. The BOAI defined Open Access as the free availability of research articles and allowed users to read, download, copy, distribute, print, search, or link to the full texts of these articles (Chan et al., 2002). The BOAI also supported the idea of providing Open Access through self-archiving in institutional repositories and Open Access journals. As Joseph states, "in the view of many OA provided a compelling vision of the future of research communication, and one that was ripe with promise" (2013). The initiative emphasized two main strategies for promoting Open Access to scholarly research and literature as mentioned previously, self-archiving and the creation of Open Access journals. The BOAI, much like Harnad, encouraged authors to deposit their research articles in institutional or disciplinary repositories, making them openly accessible to the public. This strategy aimed to circumvent traditional publishing barriers and provide direct access to research outputs. The BOAI also supported the creation and development of Open Access journals, which would make research articles freely available online without subscription or access fees. The Initiative played a crucial role in shaping the principles and definitions of Open Access in academia as we know it today. Two prominent Open Access journals emerged from the BOAI and the OA movement: the Public Library of Science (PLoS) and the Database of Open Access Journals (DOAJ). Since the BOAI convened over two decades ago, academic libraries have seen an increase in open content distributed throughout our subscription-based databases, in what we now recognize as hybrid OA.

There are several distinct types or models of Open Access, each with its unique characteristics. Green OA (self-archiving) is a model in which the author publishes their research in traditional subscription-based journals (Fitzgerald & Zhehan, 2020). After publication, they also deposit a copy of their work in an Open Access repository, such as an institutional repository or a subject-specific archive. This allows for free access to a version of the article (typically the author's accepted manuscript) after an embargo period set by the journal. The green OA model is also referred to as delayed OA due to the publishing embargo. Gold OA, or publishing in Open Access Journals makes articles freely available to readers immediately upon publication (Fitzgerald & Zhehan, 2020). Gold Open Access journals may be funded through author fees, institutional subsidies, or other means, but the primary characteristic is that readers do not need to pay to access the content. Hybrid OA journals are traditional subscription-based journals that offer authors the option to pay a fee to make their individual articles Open Access (Nick, 2012).

This model allows authors to choose which articles they want to be openly accessible while the journal continues to charge subscriptions for its other content. These types of Open Access reflect the various approaches and strategies used to make research literature more accessible to a global audience while addressing funding and sustainability concerns in the academic publishing ecosystem.

Issues, Controversies, Problems

As we shift our focus from the core concepts of the Open Access movement, we can now define the misconceptions of OA while sketching out the advantages associated with it. One of the most persistent misconceptions is that Open Access undermines the peer review process, leading to a flood of low-quality research. Particularly where global OA publications and journals are concerned. One prevalent misconception is that Open Access journals, particularly those from regions with emerging academic landscapes, may compromise on the quality of peer review and editorial standards. Many Open Access journals and platforms maintain rigorous peer review standards. Nick reinforces this by stating, "publications in the Open Access model still require peer review and/or quality control policies" (2012). The peer review process is essential for maintaining the quality and credibility of research, and Open Access journals are committed to upholding these standards. Furthermore, Open Access can enhance peer review transparency by making reviewers' comments and authors' responses openly accessible, allowing for greater scrutiny and accountability in what Nick calls the "open post-publication peer review system" (2012). OA initiatives, when well-implemented, promote transparency and inclusivity, enabling a broader range of voices and perspectives in scholarly discourse. Simard et al. looked at the adoption of OA practices, publications, and models across different countries to see how OA is implemented globally. The authors posit that on average low-income countries are citing and implementing OA model more often than upper middle and higher-income countries (Simard et al., 2022). One reason for the global adoption of OA is that low-income countries can apply for APC waivers or funding to publish using hybrid or gold OA models. Secondly, palatium OA publications and articles openly available in repositories are more easily accessible to researchers in the regions. Finally, the perception surrounding OA practices and models is still debated heavily in academia and continues to see reticence in its adoption institutionally as talks around OA continue to evolve with the digital landscape. The misconception of compromised integrity often overlooks the valuable contributions made by researchers from diverse backgrounds and regions, fostering a more comprehensive understanding of various subjects. The focus should be on evaluating the integrity and rigor of individual journals based on their editorial processes and ethical standards, rather than dismissing the entire Open Access model. Open Access has played a pivotal role in bridging the knowledge gap between developed and developing countries, ensuring that scholars and institutions with limited resources can still participate in the global academic discourse, for example, distributing research and information during a global health crisis. As a result, the movement fosters collaboration and interdisciplinary research by making it easier for researchers to build upon each other's work, accelerating the pace of scientific discovery and innovation. Embracing OA initiatives can foster a more inclusive, accessible, and collaborative scholarly environment, challenging these misconceptions and promoting a culture of academic excellence worldwide.

Moreover, another prevalent misunderstanding is that articles published in Open Access journals are of lower quality compared to those in traditional subscription-based journals. One reason for these misconceptions is a lack of awareness of the different OA models, a lack of subscription transparency at the vendor level, and predatory journals. A predatory open-access journal is a type of academic publishing outlet that exploits the OA publishing model for financial gain rather than promoting legitimate scholarly communication. These journals often prioritize profit over academic rigor and quality: "transparency, prestige, and rigor are needed to create credible value" (Guédon, 2004). If we are to better understand the nuances of the OA movement, we must commit to continuous education, and form meaningful alliances with scholars and researchers, while paying close attention to the ever-changing digital landscape. The perception of Open Access journals as reputable outlets of scholarly communication is gaining traction due to several factors despite the emergence of predator journals. Firstly, the growing recognition of the importance of free and unrestricted access to scientific knowledge has led many reputable institutions, funding agencies, and scholars to support and publish in OA journals. To reiterate, the rise of high-quality OA journals that uphold rigorous peer-review processes and editorial standards has dispelled the misconception that Open Access equals low quality. The digital age has facilitated widespread dissemination of OA content, increasing its visibility and impact. Likewise, mandates from funding bodies and institutions encouraging researchers to publish their work in OA journals to ensure wider dissemination of research findings have contributed significantly to the credibility of OA publications. As a result, the scholarly community is increasingly embracing OA journals as legitimate and reputable platforms for disseminating research, leading to their growing acceptance in academic circles. To further the inherent quality of OA journals and publications Heck et al. investigated the research output of the *Publications* journal. Almost ten years after the journal's conception and implementation this study outlines the diversity with which the journal has grown in scope, reputation, and community impact —to advance conversations around scholarly discourse:

"We carried out a bibliometric study of *Publications* and questioned the output and role of the journal. We analyzed topics, countries, authors, references, and citations of the journal. Based on our findings, we can summarize that not only have the numbers of published papers and authors grown, but *Publications* has become more diverse, which was determined by the comparison of the numbers of both 5-year periods" (Heck et al., 2023).

As researchers, institutions, and funding bodies recognize the societal and academic benefits of Open Access, the credibility and influence of OA journals continues to grow, marking a significant shift in the flow of information towards a more equitable and accessible scholarly landscape.

Another commonly held misconception is that Open Access means all content is entirely free of cost. While OA aims to eliminate barriers to accessing research, it does not necessarily mean there are no costs involved. Similarly, a lack of awareness surrounding the distinct types of OA models helps perpetuate this misconception, as Platinum OA is the only free model recently gaining traction in the world of scholarly communication. Platinum OA publishing refers to a model of scholarly communication where articles and other bodies of work are made freely accessible to readers without any cost or access barriers. Unlike other forms of Open Access publishing, such as gold or green OA, platinum OA does not require authors or institutions to pay article processing charges (APCs) for publication. Instead, the costs associated with the publication process are covered by other means, such as institutional funding, grants, or subsidies from scholarly societies or organizations. Pearce conducted a study on the rise of Platinum OA Journals and their impact factor to OA publishing and academic publishing and found, "there are now over 350 platinum OA journals with impact factors over a wide variety of academic disciplines, giving most academics options for OA with no APCs" (2022). These findings help equal the playing field for authors and institutions who cannot supply exorbitant APCs. Further examined in this study is the impact factor and prestige these OA journals are gaining in academia as reputable outlets for publication in tenure track positions. Studys like the one Pearce conducted allow information professionals and paraprofessionals better insight into the various intricacies of OA models, how to educate, and advocate for their unique benefits. Green, gold, hybrid models may be the most supported; however, more affordable, and reputable platinum journals are increasing in status and popularity. Bearing this in mind, Open Access strives to make research more accessible, but does not aways eliminate the need for financial support to sustain scholarly publishing.

As noted, though all models are not entirely free, Open Access databases and repositories are a more affordable option for libraries as budgets are constantly evaluated and funding cut. Many of our paid database subscriptions already house OA content as laid out by the hybrid model. Therefore, if libraries invest in a database specifically designed to aggregate and disseminate OA content other subscriptions can be reevaluated and/or canceled, thus saving money and redirecting funds. Anecdotally, the college I work for recently ran a trial subscription to CloudSource OA, an Open Access journal designed to mimic a traditional database. Since our trial, we have purchased a subscription to this database allowing us to use CloudSource as an alternative to Google Scholar. CloudSource allows us to point students to quality, peer-reviewed articles from vetted sources. Having metrics from CloudSource in comparison to our traditional databases will better equip us to make more informed financial and budgeting decisions moving forward.

The final misconception addresses the belief that Open Access threatens copyright and intellectual property. "Open Access does not imply there is no copyright attached to the open document; rather, in most cases the Creative Commons Attribution License (CCAL) model is used" (Nick, 2012). Open Access coexists with copyright and intellectual property rights. Many Open Access journals require authors to retain their copyright and only grant a license for distribution. Additionally, different Open Access licenses under the CCAL allow authors to specify how their work can be used, shared, and adapted while retaining ownership. Open Access promotes wider dissemination of research while respecting the rights of authors.

Libraries and librarians need to dispel these misconceptions to foster a more informed and productive discussion about the role of Open Access in the academic community. Open Access can coexist with rigorous peer review, diverse funding models, and respect for intellectual property rights. By embracing these principles, we can harness the full potential of OA to advance research and education for the benefit of society.

SOLUTIONS AND RECOMMENDATIONS

As our attention turns away from the misconceptions surrounding the Open Access movement, it becomes evident that this transformative approach holds numerous benefits for libraries in higher education. For libraries in higher education to take full advantage of the Open Access movement they look to innovative ways to serve as invaluable hubs of information and learning in the digital age. Since the Open Access movement gained traction, libraries have had a unique opportunity to expand their reach and impact even further. Open Access, which promotes unrestricted access to scholarly research and educational resources, gives us that opportunity. At its center, the OA movement aligns perfectly with the core mission of libraries in facilitating access to knowledge and information, promoting equitable resources and services, and upholding intellectual freedom rights. As stated, one of the primary objectives of libraries is to provide equitable access to knowledge. The OA movement complements this mission by making a vast amount of scholarly content openly available online, "with a new publication model comes the potential for new communities of authors and readers to gather around it" (Lerro,2018). Libraries can leverage Open Access resources and the OA publication process to expand their collections, ensuring that patrons have access to a wider range of research papers, journals, and educational materials. Libraries can also collaborate with Open Access publishers and institutions to curate collections that cater to the needs of their specific user base. This collaboration can lead to more comprehensive and diverse collections that benefit researchers, students, and the community. OA champions the principle that knowledge and information should be available to all, irrespective of geographic location, economic status, or institutional affiliation. "For universities, moving to Open Access publishing would improve the ease of dissemination of scientific work to academics and the public alike" (Siler, 2017). OA not only democratizes access to knowledge but also fosters a more inclusive and equitable society, where individuals can harness the power of information to make informed decisions, drive innovation, and address global challenges. In the digital age, the Open Access movement catalyzes the accessibility gap and advances the cause of equal opportunity and progress for all.

While OA has made significant strides in increasing the accessibility of academic research, it is important to note the increasing cost of database subscriptions is just another factor which causes libraries to look to Open Access. Traditionally, libraries have had to allocate significant portions of their budgets to purchase subscriptions to academic journals and databases. The Open Access movement helps libraries reduce these costs by offering unrestricted access to a substantial portion of scholarly content. As previously mentioned, this can free up funds that can be reallocated to other critical library services and resources. Moreover, the cost savings extend beyond libraries to benefit educational institutions and individual patrons. Students and researchers no longer need to pay exorbitant fees or rely solely on their institution's subscriptions to access academic research. Libraries can play a pivotal role in educating their communities and stakeholders about the financial advantages of OA and providing guidance on how to find and use OA resources effectively and dispel common misconceptions. The goal of the OA movement as Lerro, and others have succinctly stated, "is to make it as easy as possible for researchers, societies, institutions, funders, and governments to achieve their open scholarship aims" (2018). What better way to support this goal than to rally behind its mission armed with information and insider knowledge?

Libraries often serve as hubs for local research and scholarship, connecting academic institutions and the surrounding community. Open Access can play a vital role in promoting and preserving the work of local researchers and institutions. Partnering with local historical societies is one way to foster community connections and allows us to preserve local history and research either through archiving efforts or digitization. Libraries can actively advocate for OA policies within their institutions and encourage faculty and researchers to publish their work in Open Access journals or repositories. Holding workshops in support of Open Access and writing OA guidelines into library collection development policies are just some of the ways libraries can educate and advocate for OA content. By offering workshops, webinars, and training sessions, libraries empower researchers to embrace OA publishing and open research practices. Also, libraries can help set up and maintain institutional repositories, ensuring that their institutions' research output is easily discoverable and accessible to a global audience. This raises the profile of local research and enhances the library's reputation as a central player in promoting and maintaining scholarly communication.

Subsequently, libraries and librarians have espoused the role information literacy plays in helping patrons navigate the vast sea of information available. The OA movement offers libraries an opportunity to educate users about the importance of discerning between credible and unreliable sources online. As librarians, we are no strangers to the concepts of 'fake news' or 'alternative facts.' The internet streamlines and disseminates massive amounts of information from a wealth of sources (Frankland & Ray, 2017). To combat the rapid dissemination of information the Internet provides libraries can offer workshops, tutorials, and resources that teach patrons how to critically evaluate online sources, including OA materials and content. By promoting information literacy skills, libraries can empower their users to make informed decisions and contribute to the creation of knowledge, thereby reinforcing the library's role as an essential resource in the digital age.

The Open Access movement presents libraries with an excellent opportunity to align their missions more closely with the principles of unrestricted access to knowledge and information. By actively engaging with OA initiatives, libraries can broaden access to knowledge, reduce costs for patrons and institutions, support local research and scholarship, and foster information literacy among users. In doing so, libraries can reaffirm their relevance and centrality in the digital age, serving as vital gateways to information and hubs for lifelong learning and intellectual growth. By harnessing the power of Open Access, libraries can continue to evolve and thrive as dynamic, accessible, and indispensable institutions.

FUTURE RESEARCH DIRECTIONS

Open Access continues to grow and transform the information and digital landscape. The literature identifies these emerging trends within the movement, by seeing an increase in interdisciplinary adoption and collaboration, global expansion, Open Educational Resources (OER), data sharing, open peer review, legal and ethical considerations, and sustainability. As we move forward, OA will continue to shape how research and scholarship is disseminated.

The shift towards Open Access in the realm of academic publishing is undeniably gaining momentum, "over the past decade, funding agencies around the world have adopted open access policies" (Zhang & Watson, 2017). This transformation is being driven by the growing recognition of the benefits of OA in disseminating research more widely and effectively. As institutions, funding bodies, and researchers increasingly align themselves with the principles of Open Access, academia is witnessing a profound transformation in the scholarly landscape, particularly in citation rate or "quality advantage" (Gargouri et al., 2010 as cited in Zhang & Watson, 2017). As higher-quality journals look to hybridize or fully embrace OA policies the citation advantage for these higher-quality articles increases substantially. Renowned journals that fully adopt the OA model can increase the volume of Open Access publications and therefore more open repositories, thereby fostering greater accessibility, collaboration, and innovation in the academic community. This trend signifies a positive step towards democratizing knowledge and ensuring that research reaches a broader and more diverse audience, advancing the progress of multidisciplinary knowledge and dissemination.

Also, the OA movement will continue to expand globally with more countries and regions embracing policies and initiatives to promote Open Access; higher education will see a more equitable distribution of knowledge resources worldwide. Since Harnad's presentation at the NSC and the creation of the BOAI, new Open Access initiatives have emerged offering more widespread awareness. One such initiative is International Open Access Week. This annual event organized by SPARC in partnership with the Open Access Week Advisory Committee is a celebration of OA policy, involvement, and discourse centered around the movement. "Open Access Week 2023 is an opportunity to join together, take action, and raise awareness around the importance of community control of knowledge sharing systems" (International Open Access Week, n.d.). Enterprises like Open Access Week connect us to a more accessible and equitable future. As OA continues to grow and evolve, it holds the promise of narrowing the gap in research opportunities and resources, leading to more inclusive and collaborative global endeavors. This shift towards greater openness in academia signifies a step towards harnessing the full potential of global knowledge sharing and innovation.

Open Access extends beyond research publications and encompasses a broader spectrum of educational resources, with Open Educational Resources (OER) emerging as a significant component. OER are educational materials made freely available with open licenses, allowing educators and students to access, use, adapt, and share them without cost constraints. To further this point Norris et al. state, "one method of increasing accessibility is through the creation and use of Open Educational Resource (OER), in place of commercial textbooks, as the primary resource for university and college courses" (2023). In today's context, as educational institutions grapple with the escalating costs of textbooks and course materials, the prominence and financial support for OER are poised to grow, as it works in conjunction with emerging OA models, fair use, and CC copyright licensing. By adopting OER, institutions can reduce the financial burden on students, enhance accessibility to quality learning materials, and promote collaboration and innovation in educational content creation. As the importance of equitable access to education gains recognition, the momentum behind OER is likely to increase, making it an integral part of efforts to make education more affordable and accessible for all.

Open data initiatives, much like OER, are poised to gain even greater significance in the coming years. The expectation for researchers to openly share their data represents a pivotal shift in the research landscape, one that promises to foster transparency, reproducibility, and collaboration. By making data more accessible to the broader academic community and public, these initiatives not only democratize knowledge but also enable independent verification of findings and the exploration of new research directions. To further this point, Gwein states, "it isn't hugely difficult to data share" (2016). Online and institutional repositories allow authors to deposit their work openly for both academic and general consumption alike. Open data sharing not only benefits academia and higher education by accelerating discovery and innovation but empowers society at large, by providing greater insight into the processes and outcomes of research, contributing to informed decision-making and progress across various fields.

OER offers discernible advantages to academic libraries. Firstly, OER alleviates the financial burden on libraries by providing free, openly accessible teaching and learning materials. This reduction in acquisition costs allows libraries to allocate resources more efficiently toward other essential services and collections. Secondly, OER enhances the inclusivity of academic libraries by affording equitable access to high-quality educational content and promoting open education principles. Moreover, OER encourages the cultivation of collaborative, inter-institutional partnerships, enabling libraries to participate in broader educational initiatives. Additionally, the adaptability of OER materials facilitates customization to meet the specific needs of diverse academic programs, fostering a more tailored and relevant learning experience. Finally, OER aligns seamlessly with the core mission of academic libraries as repositories of knowledge, actively advancing the dissemination of information, facilitating the sharing of research discoveries, and promoting the principles of Open Access. In sum, the integration of OER into library resources represents a strategic and responsible approach to serving the academic community's educational and fiscal requirements.

Much like the adoption of OER, the evolution of open peer review models represents a significant step forward in enhancing the transparency and effectiveness of the scholarly publishing process. Open Access models with less restrictive publication processes and emerging technologies, like Artificial Intelligence (AI) "has paved the way for new levels of openness in the review process" (Horbach &

Halffman, 2018). This open approach encourages continuous evaluation and refinement of research findings at all stages of publication, fostering a more dynamic and collaborative ecosystem. As Horbach and Halffman point out, journals—especially OA journals—are making efforts to engage authors with editors in a more interactive review process; "during which reviewers and editors can share or discuss their reports and opinions on a manuscript before communicating a final decision to the author" (2018). By making the peer review process open and ongoing, researchers can receive valuable feedback from prominent voices, audiences, and communities, leading to improved research quality and credibility. In the realm of academic scholarship, this model significantly enhances the dynamism, inclusivity, and diversity of perspectives concerning research output and quality control, thereby contributing to a more comprehensive and robust evaluation of scholarly work as compared to closed review practices. As the open review process continues to evolve, it has the potential to strengthen the foundation of scientific knowledge, and interdisciplinary conversations, and increase public trust in the research community's commitment to rigorous, transparent, and accountable research practices and methodologies.

As OA continues to gain prominence in the academic and research community, inevitably, discussions surrounding intellectual property rights, copyright, and ethical considerations will persist and evolve. One way OA and intellectual property rights support each other is in Creative Commons Licenses (CCAL). In 2001, the CCAL nonprofit was founded creating six licenses to "give everyone from individual creators to large institutions a standardized way to grant the public permission to use their creative work under copyright law" (Creative Commons Attribution License, n.d.). In other words, CCAL works in conjunction with copyright law to help authors retain their rights while also sharing their work openly. Under each license, authors can outline how their work is shared or utilized, provided proper credit is given to the original creator. An additional way OA and copyright contribute to the facilitation of scholarly communication is through the Fair Use guidelines. As a legal framework, the Fair Use guidelines allow for the use and reproduction of copyrighted material under specific circumstances, such as criticism, research, and education (Office, n.d.). These guidelines enable researchers and educators to utilize copyrighted content within the bounds of copyright law, thereby enriching OA platforms with diverse content. As Nick points out, "...when publishers lift an article wait embargo, and place it a subscription-based article in Open Access, the copyright (most likely the U.S. Fair Use guidelines) does not change" (2012). Through the judicious application of Fair Use principles and CCAL, OA publications can incorporate copyrighted materials, facilitating a richer tapestry of information for scholars and students alike. Adopting Fair Use within OA is a cornerstone in advancing accessibility and dissemination of knowledge. within the academic community, fostering a culture of innovation and intellectual inquiry. Moreover, the ethical implications OA poses to scholarly communication become paramount when guiding researchers and institutions in the responsible stewardship of knowledge. These ongoing discussions reflect the dynamic nature of the OA movement and the need for thoughtful responses and solutions to the challenges it presents.

Ensuring the sustainability of OA models in academic publishing is also a worthy endeavor. While Open Access democratizes access to research and knowledge, it also presents the challenge of funding and sustainability. To maintain this accessibility, it is imperative to explore and implement viable funding mechanisms and business models that do not rely on traditional paywalls or subscription fees. This may involve innovative approaches such as collaborative funding from research institutions, public grants, philanthropic support, and partnerships with industry stakeholders. Additionally, optimizing the efficiency of publishing processes, embracing new technologies, and fostering community engagement are key components of achieving long-term sustainability for Open Access models, ensuring that the fruits of academic research remain freely accessible to all.

CONCLUSION

Open Access publishing stands at the forefront of a transformative movement in scholarly communication, redefining the way knowledge is disseminated, accessed, and utilized. Its evolution into a powerful force has dismantled barriers that once restricted the flow of information, paving the way for an inclusive and global exchange of ideas. In this digital age, where information is a cornerstone of progress, OA has emerged as a cornerstone of academic discourse, transcending geographical boundaries and democratizing access to knowledge in unprecedented ways. One of the most significant impacts of OA is evident in the role of librarians, who have seamlessly transitioned into multifaceted professionals within the OA landscape. They now serve as advocates, passionately championing the cause of unrestricted access to knowledge. Librarians have become managers, meticulously curating digital repositories and guiding researchers in navigating the vast expanse of open-access resources. They have evolved into educators, imparting essential skills related to information literacy and critical evaluation of open-access materials. In fact, they function as facilitators, fostering collaborations between researchers and OA platforms, thereby fostering a vibrant scholarly community. The future of higher education is intricately intertwined with the principles of Open Access. As educational institutions embrace OA, they unlock a wealth of opportunities. Expanded access to knowledge becomes a reality, ensuring that learners, regardless of their geographical location or economic background, can tap into a vast reservoir of information. This democratization of education, driven by OA, fosters inclusivity, allowing diverse voices and perspectives to shape the intellectual landscape. OA promotes enhanced research collaboration. By breaking down the barriers to accessing scholarly works, researchers worldwide can collaborate seamlessly, fostering a truly global research community. This collaboration not only enriches the quality of research but also accelerates the pace of innovation. Ideas flow freely, leading to interdisciplinary approaches that tackle complex global challenges, such as climate change, pandemics, and social inequality.

Embracing OA is more than just a change in thinking; it signifies a transformative journey toward a more equitable and knowledge-rich future for all. It cultivates a culture of sharing, where knowledge is not confined within the walls of institutions but is freely accessible to anyone with a thirst for learning. This transformation fosters a society where information is not a privilege but a fundamental right, empowering individuals to make informed decisions, contribute meaningfully to society, and shape a better future for generations to come. In this interconnected world, Open Access emerges as a beacon of enlightenment, illuminating the path toward a more inclusive, collaborative, and innovative future in higher education and beyond.

REFERENCES

Bell, K. (2019). Communitas and the commons: The open access movement and the dynamics of restructuration in scholarly publishing. *Anthropology Today*, *35*(5), 21–23. doi:10.1111/1467-8322.12530

Chan, L. (2002). *The Budapest open access Initiative*. https://www.budapestopenaccessinitiative.org/read/

Creative common attribution license. (n.d.). https://creativecommons.org/share-your-work/cclicenses/

Fitzgerald, S. R., & Jiang, Z. (2020). Scholarly publishing at a crossroads: Scholarly perspectives on open access. *Innovative Higher Education, 45*(6), 457–469. doi:10.100710755-020-09508-8

Frankland, J., & Ray, M. A. (2017). Traditional versus open access scholarly journal publishing: An economic perspective. *Journal of Scholarly Publishing, 49*(1), 5–25. doi:10.3138/jsp.49.1.5

Gewin, V. (2016). Data sharing: An open mind on open data. *Nature, 529*(7584), 117–119. doi:10.1038/nj7584-117a PMID:26744755

Guédon, J.-C. (2004). The "green" and "gold" roads to open access: The case for mixing and matching. *Serials Review, 30*(4), 315–328. doi:10.1016/j.serrev.2004.09.005

Harnad, S. (1994). *A subversive proposal.* https://groups.google.com/g/bit.listserv.vpiej-l/c/BoKENhK0_00

Heck, T., Tunger, D., & Rittberger, M. (2023). Scholarly Communication over a Decade of Publications. *Publications / MDPI, 11*(16), 16. doi:10.3390/publications11010016

Horbach, S. P. J. M., & Halffman, W. (2018). The changing forms and expectations of peer review. *Research Integrity and Peer Review, 3*(1), 8. Advance online publication. doi:10.118641073-018-0051-5 PMID:30250752

International open access week. (n.d.). International Open Access Week. https://www.openaccessweek.org/

Joseph, H. (2013). The open access movement grows up: Taking stock of a revolution. *PLoS Biology, 11*(10), 1–3. doi:10.1371/journal.pbio.1001686 PMID:24167444

Lerro, J., & Lawlor, B. (2018). Flipping the script. *Information Services & Use, 38*(1/2), 91–93. doi:10.3233/ISU-180006

Nick, J. M. (2012). Open access part I: The movement, the issues, and the benefits. *Online Journal of Issues in Nursing, 17*(1), 1. doi:10.3912/OJIN.Vol17No01PPT02 PMID:22320874

Office, U. C. (n.d.). *U.S. Copyright Office Fair Use Index.* https://www.copyright.gov/fair-use/

Pearce, J. M. (2022). The Rise of Platinum Open Access Journals with Both Impact Factors and Zero Article Processing Charges. *Knowledge (Beverly Hills, Calif.), 2*(2), 209–224. doi:10.3390/knowledge2020013

Siler, K. (2017). Future challenges and opportunities in academic publishing. *Canadian Journal of Sociology, 42*(1), 83–114. doi:10.29173/cjs28140

Simard, M. A., Ghiasi, G., Mongeon, P., & Larivière, V. (2022). National differences in dissemination and use of open access literature. *PLoS One, 17*(8), 1–14. doi:10.1371/journal.pone.0272730 PMID:35943972

Yiotis, K. (2005). The open access initiative: A new paradigm for scholarly communications. *Information Technology and Libraries, 24*(4), 157–162. doi:10.6017/ital.v24i4.3378

Zhang, L., & Watson, E. M. (2017). Measuring the impact of gold and green open access. *Journal of Academic Librarianship, 43*(4), 337–345. doi:10.1016/j.acalib.2017.06.004

ADDITIONAL READING

Björk, B. (2017). Gold, green, and black open access. *Learned Publishing*, *30*(2), 173–175. doi:10.1002/leap.1096

Eger, T., & Scheufen, M. (2018). *The economics of open access: on the future of academic publishing*. Edward Elgar Publishing. doi:10.4337/9781785365768

Gaines, A. M. (2015). From concerned to cautiously optimistic: Assessing faculty perceptions and knowledge of open access in a campus-wide study. *Journal of Librarianship and Scholarly Communication*, *3*(1), 1–40. doi:10.7710/2162-3309.1212

Guédon, J.-C. (2008). Mixing and matching the green and gold roads to open access—Take 2. *Serials Review*, *34*(1), 41–51. doi:10.1080/00987913.2008.10765151

Heinz, P. (2022). From library budget to information budget: Fostering transparency in the transformation towards open access. *Insights: The UKSG Journal*, *35*, 8. Advance online publication. doi:10.1629/uksg.576

Jahn, N., Matthias, L., & Laakso, M. (2022). Toward transparency of hybrid open access through publisher-provided metadata: An article-level study of Elsevier. *Journal of the Association for Information Science and Technology*, *73*(1), 104–118. doi:10.1002/asi.24549

Kleinman, M. (2017). Faculty rights to scholarly research. *New Directions for Higher Education*, *2017*(177), 39–50. doi:10.1002/he.20224

Reinsfelder, T. L. (2012). Open access publishing practices in a complex environment: Conditions, barriers, and bases of power. *Journal of Librarianship and Scholarly Communication*, *1*(1), 1–16. doi:10.7710/2162-3309.1029

Rizor, S. L., & Holley, R. P. (2014). Open access goals revisited: How green and gold open access are meeting (or not) their original goals. *Journal of Scholarly Publishing*, *45*(4), 321–335. doi:10.3138/jsp.45.4.01

Roach, A. K., & Gainer, J. (2013). On Open Access to Research: The Green, the Gold, and the Public Good. *Journal of Adolescent & Adult Literacy*, *56*(7), 530–534. doi:10.1002/JAAL.177

KEY TERMS AND DEFINITIONS

Article Processing Charge (APC): A publication fee charged to authors.

File Transfer Protocol: The transfer of computer files from a server across IP networks.

Gold OA: Academic or scholarly works published in an OA journal or hybrid OA journal.

Green OA: Academic or scholarly works published in a traditional subscription-based journal.

Hybrid OA: Traditional subscription-based journal where the author pays a fee to have their work published as open content.

Institutional Repository: A digital archive used to store digital copies of institutional intellectual property.

Open Access (OA): Unrestricted access to scholarly works and research.

Platinum (OA): Unrestricted access to scholarly works and research at no cost at the author or institutional level.

Post-Prints: A digital copy of academic or scholarly works after it has been through the peer review process and accepted for publication.

Predatory OA: Journals that exploit the OA model for money. They do not follow any sort of academic rigor or uphold scholarly communication standards.

Preprints: A digital copy of academic or scholarly works before it is peer-reviewed and accepted for publication.

Self-Archiving: The act of placing a digital copy of academic or scholarly works online for others to use openly and unrestrictedly.

Chapter 7

Enhancing Access to Electronic Information Through Digital Transformation in KwaZulu-Natal Department of Health Libraries in South Africa

Nonhlanhla P. Ntloko

 https://orcid.org/0009-0008-4510-1223
Durban University of Technology, South Africa

Tlou Maggie Masenya
Durban University of Technology, South Africa

ABSTRACT

This chapter analyses the role of digital transformation in KwaZulu-Natal Department of Health Libraries in South Africa, exploring if and how digital technologies can be adopted and used in enhancing access to electronic information. The chapter utilised literature review to critically analyse the role of digital transformation in healthcare libraries, digital technologies used in enhancing access to electronic information, challenges of digital transformation in healthcare libraries, and the strategies to overcoming these challenges. Technology acceptance model (TAM) was used as the underpinning theory to guide this study. Recommendations suggest a need to prioritize digital transformation and provide enough resources to healthcare libraries and formulate policies that would facilitate this process.

INTRODUCTION

Digital transformation holds considerable potential for improved service delivery in healthcare libraries, notwithstanding the apparent limitations such as financing for digital technologies, infrastructure, quality assurance, and personnel training. The burgeoning advancements in digital technologies have transformed

DOI: 10.4018/979-8-3693-2841-5.ch007

various sectors globally, notably healthcare. The digital transformation of the healthcare industry has brought about a change in the dynamic of healthcare delivery. An age of data-driven healthcare service delivery has been ushered in as a result of the advent of digital health, which is a term that incorporates eHealth, mHealth, and new fields like as big data in healthcare and artificial intelligence (Jablonksi et al., 2021). These technologies have blurred the geographical barriers that formerly restricted the provision of healthcare services which was previously limited by factors such as distance and time. For instance, digital health makes it possible to monitor the health of a patient in real time, conduct remote consultations, and have access to healthcare services while remaining in the convenience of one's own home.

Additionally, digital health platforms allow for the aggregation of individual-level health data, which may then be used for population-level health planning and research purposes. As a direct result of this, the use of digital technologies has reimagined the process of providing healthcare services, therefore broadening their appeal while simultaneously enhancing their efficiency. In a similar spirit, digital technologies open a new horizon for healthcare libraries, boosting the breadth of services that these libraries may offer while also improving their operational efficiency. Accessing and making use of information has been completely transformed as a result of the proliferation of digital libraries, databases, and repositories among health professionals. As noted by Wallis et al. (2019), digital technologies allow users to access a great quantity of information instantly, therefore circumventing the physical and temporal limits that are inherent in conventional libraries. This chapter looked at the opportunities and challenges associated with implementing digital technologies in healthcare libraries through digital transformation. This chapter thus examined the role of digital transformation in healthcare libraries in South Africa, with an emphasis on the potential of digital technologies in enhancing access to electronic information. The objectives that guided this chapter were to:

- Determine the role of digital transformation in enhancing access to electronic information in health libraries
- Determine the barriers to effective electronic information access within Kwa Zulu Natal Department of Health (KZN DOH) libraries
- Examine the challenges of digital transformation and innovation in Kwa Zulu Natal Department of Health (KZN DOH) libraries
- Determine the strategies to overcoming the challenges and maximizing opportunities for digital transformation in Kwa Zulu Natal Department of Health (KZN DOH) libraries

BACKGROUND

As stated by Wallis et al. (2019) and Jablonski et al. (2021) healthcare libraries are the backbone of medical knowledge transmission and they serve as conduits for information that is crucial to patient care, teaching, and research. These libraries provide an important connection to the constantly growing corpus of recent research as well as the most recent clinical information. Health libraries provide health professionals with the skills required to locate and utilize the best available evidence for decision making. As a result, patient outcomes are improved, continued education is encouraged, and healthy research cultures are promoted. The significance of this role has been more apparent in recent years as a result of the growing adoption of digital health techniques. According to the National Digital Health Strategy for South Africa 2019-2024, a major amount of health information is now produced, stored, and accessible in digital forms. Digital technologies assist the aggregation, storage and retrieval of information, which makes it simpler for health professionals to get the particular information they want. Users are now able to easily discover information that is both relevant to their needs and up to date thanks to the incorporation of artificial intelligence into digital libraries, which has further improved the retrieval of information. The use of digital technologies to strengthen the role of healthcare libraries has a tremendous amount of untapped potential; nevertheless, the route to fully realizing this promise is plagued with obstacles. The adoption and efficient use of digital technologies is hampered by a number of obstacles, particularly in healthcare libraries in South Africa. The difficulties vary from inadequate infrastructure to limited financial resources, from a lack of human resources to a digital gap (Mthembu et al., 2019; Zungu et al., 2018). Additionally, low internet access, human resource limitations, and a digital divide all contribute to a reluctance to change. These problems highlight how complicated digital transformation is and the need of adopting a multipronged strategy in order to solve them. The lack of necessary infrastructure is a significant obstacle for the digital transformation of healthcare libraries. Mthembu et al. (2019) stated that libraries located in settings with restricted access to resources often lack the appropriate physical and technical infrastructure to enable digital technologies. For instance, the inability to rely on one's source of electrical supply might make it difficult to use digital technologies. In a similar vein, access to digital resources may be limited if the requisite hardware and software are not available, as well as if internet connection is inadequate. Another key obstacle that must be overcome in order for healthcare libraries to successfully undergo digital transformation is the presence of financial restraints. Zungu et al. (2018) further noted that investing a significant amount of money is necessary for the purchase, installation, and ongoing maintenance of digital technologies. In many cases, resource-constrained environments provide a challenge for libraries in terms of securing the required funds to cover these expenditures.

The high cost of digital resources adds another layer of complexity to the existing financial dilemma. For libraries that only have a limited amount of money available, the cost of paying membership fees for digital databases and periodicals might be excessively costly. The digital transformation of healthcare libraries is also hampered by a lack of human resources and a digital divide. As stated by Mthembu et al. (2019), many libraries, especially those in settings with low resources, do not have enough staff members who possess the necessary skills to administer and operate digital technologies. In addition, a significant number of people who use libraries and health care facilities are not adept in the use of digital technologies, which hinders their capacity to access and make good use of digital resources. In this sense, the term "digital divide" refers not just to the inequality in access to digital technologies but also the disparity in the ability to read and write digital information. Another barrier that must be overcome in order for healthcare libraries to fully embrace digital transformation is resistance to change. Uncertainty may result from change, especially when it is of a scale such as that required by digital transformation. Many library patrons and employees are used to the conventional means of gaining access to and making use of information, and as a result, they may be hesitant to adopt fresh approaches to old problems. This opposition may impede the adoption of digital technologies in healthcare libraries, which can also make their efficient use more difficult.

The obstacles that stand in the way of healthcare libraries undergoing a digital transformation are significant, but they are not insurmountable. This underscores a strategy that is all-encompassing and multifaceted, and that engages all relevant parties, such as decision-makers, healthcare administrators, library employees, and library patrons. The current challenge at hand is not only to incorporate digital technologies into health care libraries; rather, the focus should be on ensuring that these technologies are appropriately used to improve the delivery of services and better access to information. In South

African health libraries context, where the digital gap is significant and the need for increased access to information is urgent, this work is especially crucial. The road that lies ahead may be challenging, but the potential benefits of digital transformation, which include increased access to information, enhanced service delivery, and improved health outcomes, make it worthwhile to undertake the trip.

THEORETICAL FRAMEWORK

A theoretical framework for this chapter was drawn from the various literature reviewed. Technology Acceptance Model was adopted in this chapter and its relevance is discussed further below.

Technology Acceptance Model (TAM)

Technology Acceptance Model (TAM) is a significant theoretical framework within the field of information systems, first introduced by Davis in 1989. The aforementioned model provides a comprehensive framework for comprehending the factors that influence the acceptability of technology, with particular emphasis on two key components: Perceived Usefulness (PU) and Perceived Ease of Use (PEOU) (Davis, 1989). The emergence of the digital era introduced a diverse range of tools and technology that significantly transformed the operational landscape of several sectors. However, similar to any novel development, the efficacy of these technologies often relies on the level of acceptance they get from their intended users. The Technology Acceptance Model (TAM) posits that people are more likely to adopt a technology if they regard it as valuable for enhancing their work performance. According to Davis (1989), Perceived Usefulness may be described as the extent to which an individual feel that using a certain technology will improve their work performance. However, the acceptability of a technology, despite its potential transformational advantages, may be constrained if it is viewed as difficult to manage or comprehend. Therefore, the second fundamental aspect of the Technology Acceptance Model (TAM), namely Perceived Ease of Use, has similar importance. According to Davis (1989), the idea may be defined as "the extent to which an individual perceives the use of a specific system to be devoid of exertion." It is thus important to acknowledge that these views are not fixed; rather, they are influenced by a variety of external influences. Various external factors such as training, system features, and user demographics have the potential to have an impact on the perceived usefulness (PU) and perceived ease of use (PEOU) of a system (Venkatesh & Davis, 2000).

Furthermore, the body of research on Technology Acceptance Model (TAM) has undergone significant expansion over time. Venkatesh and Bala (2008) have contributed to this expansion by including supplementary factors such as social impact and enabling circumstances into an enhanced version of the model, often referred to as TAM3. The true worth of TAM is in its practicality and relevance. One example to consider is the health department personnel who are faced with the challenge of navigating the complex array of digital platforms and technologies that have become more prevalent in the contemporary healthcare environment. The range of digital health records, telemedicine platforms, and diagnostic technologies is comprehensive. The use of these technologies in a healthcare environment has the potential to improve operational effectiveness and increase the quality of patient care. However, according to the Technology Acceptance Model (TAM), the full potential of these technologies can only be realized when they are embraced and implemented by the employees. In order to comprehend the attitudes and beliefs of health department workers, one may use the Technology Acceptance Model

(TAM). Begin by assessing their perspectives on the digital tools available to them. Surveys and interviews are valuable instruments in this context. Inquiries such as "To what extent do you perceive this digital platform as facilitating your job responsibilities?" or "What level of confidence do you possess in effectively navigating this software?" might provide valuable insights on Perceived Usefulness (PU) and Perceived Ease of Use (PEOU) respectively, as proposed by Davis (1989). Consider a novel telemedicine platform implemented inside the KwaZulu Natal Department of Health, for an example. Although technology has the potential to facilitate consultations between physicians and patients regardless of geographical boundaries, there is no assurance of its widespread adoption. If medical professionals see the system as burdensome or remain unconvinced of its diagnostic effectiveness, they may exhibit hesitancy in embracing its implementation.

Therefore, by gaining a comprehensive awareness of these impressions in advance, the department may adopt proactive measures. It is possible that the system might benefit from further design modifications aimed at enhancing its intuitiveness. Alternatively, it may be beneficial to provide physicians with training sessions to facilitate their familiarity with the system's functions. However, the application of TAM extends beyond the stage of first adoption. Healthcare institutions may enhance the effectiveness of their digital initiatives by gaining insight into the underlying motivations of its staff members. This knowledge allows them to connect their tactics more closely with the demands of users, resulting in increased and continued use. However, it should be noted that the initial acceptance of a certain technology or practice does not always ensure its sustained usage over time. Periodic assessments grounded on the Technology Acceptance Model (TAM) may effectively maintain the relevance of digital products and provide iterative enhancements via the incorporation of user input (Venkatesh, Morris, Davis, & Davis, 2003).

THE ROLE OF DIGITAL TRANSFORMATION IN ENHANCING ACCESS TO ELECTRONIC INFORMATION IN HEALTHCARE LIBRARIES

Libraries in the healthcare industry play a key role in the multifaceted and ever-evolving facets of healthcare supply. These libraries provide assistance that cannot be replicated in areas such as patient care, nursing education, and research. They operate as bridges, linking healthcare professionals to the vast universe of medical knowledge and advances by providing resources and services such as literature searching, training on critical evaluation, and aid for evidence-based practice (Wallis et al., 2019; Jablonski et al., 2021). Providing users with access to information, teaching users, and lending assistance to research are the three conventional functions that have been integrated into the duties of healthcare libraries. The environment of healthcare information management has been revolutionized by digital transformation, despite the fact that these professions are just as important as they have ever been. Because of this change and the ever-changing demands of library users, possibilities have arisen for healthcare libraries to improve and broaden the range of services they provide, ultimately leading to an increase in the quality of care provided to patients. The term "digital transformation" refers to the process of integrating digital technologies into all aspects of an organization, which results in a significant change in the manner in which the organization functions and provides value to its consumers.

In the context of healthcare libraries, digital transformation refers to the utilization of digital technologies in order to improve the delivery of library services, increase the accessibility of resources, improve user engagement, and support the decision-making and learning processes (Molokisi, 2019; Chamberlain et al., 2021). E-libraries, e-resources (such as e-books and e-journals), mobile applications, social networking platforms, and other online services are examples of the technologies that are provided by health libraries in our days. However, this list is not exhaustive. E-libraries and e-resources have quickly become essential parts of healthcare library collections. This is partly attributable to the fact that they are able to circumvent the physical limitations that are inherent to conventional libraries and resources. The way library users access and engage with library resources and services has been revolutionized by these applications. The applications make it possible for users to access library resources while they are on the go, which increases the mobility and convenience of the services provided by libraries. In addition, they provide a platform for libraries to deliver interactive and individualized services to its patrons, such as instant chat for customer care, customized reading lists, and push alerts when new resources become available. Mobile applications may also be combined with other digital resources and platforms, such as e-books and e-journals, to provide a seamless user experience (Chamberlain et al., 2021). This is possible because of advancements in integration technology.

Beyond the supply of resources and services, another opportunity presented by digital transformation in healthcare libraries is the involvement of patrons. In this day and age of digital technology, when the usage of social media platforms has become an integral part of daily life, libraries have the ability to make use of these platforms in order to improve their connection with users. Libraries have a unique opportunity to engage with users, exchange expertise and information, ask feedback, and advertise their services via social media platforms such as Facebook, Twitter, and LinkedIn. Libraries may provide sophisticated services like predictive searches, personalized content suggestions, and real-time data analysis by integrating technologies such as artificial intelligence and data analytics. These services have the potential to considerably increase the efficacy and efficiency of the processes involved in decision-making and research. In a similar vein, digital technologies may be used into educational endeavors in order to provide learning experiences that are immersive, interactive, and tailored to the individual (Chamberlain et al., 2021). In a nutshell, the digital transformation presents healthcare libraries with a plethora of chances to enhance and extend their existing range of services. By using digital technologies, libraries are able to improve the accessibility and quality of the resources they provide, as well as provide services that are individualized and interactive, boost user engagement, and help decision-making and learning processes. To seize these possibilities, however, needs not just strategic planning and investment, but also a culture that encourages innovation and is committed to continual development. It entails a change in thinking as well as a different strategy for the delivery of services in addition to the adoption of new technologies. Finding the correct balance between accepting new technologies and keeping the human touch that distinguishes a library's services is the challenge and opportunity presented by digital transformation for healthcare libraries. This is also the key to achieving this transformation successfully.

BARRIERS TO EFFECTIVE ELECTRONIC INFORMATION ACCESS WITHIN KWAZULU-NATAL DEPARTMENT OF HEALTH (KZN DOH) LIBRARIES

Although there is a great deal of potential upside to digital transformation in healthcare libraries, there are also many obstacles to overcome. Notably, healthcare libraries, particularly those in the Kwa Zulu natal department of health, suffer a wide variety of challenges that slow down their progress towards digitalization (Zungu et al., 2018; Mthembu et al., 2019). These challenges include a lack of appropriate skills and training among library staff, budgetary restrictions, infrastructure flaws, quality assurance concerns of digital items, restricted internet access, and a lack of enough skills and training among library patrons and staff. These problems create a complicated and multidimensional dilemma, which calls for an all-encompassing, cooperative, and coordinated effort from all stakeholders, including lawmakers, library and healthcare administrators, and staff members. One of the most important obstacles to the implementation of digital transformation in healthcare libraries is the limitation of financial resources. According to Zungu et al. (2018), the procurement, installation, and maintenance of digital technologies all involve significant financial investments. These include the upfront costs of purchasing the necessary hardware and software, as well as the costs of system integration and modification, staff training expenses, and the ongoing costs of software licenses, system upgrades, and maintenance. In addition, the price of digital technologies often surpasses the budget that is allotted to healthcare libraries, making it impossible for these institutions to finance the technologies that are essential for digital transformation. This dilemma is more severe in situations with limited resources, such as hospitals, since there are other urgent healthcare requirements to contend with that further reduce available funds. Another significant obstacle that healthcare libraries must overcome is the lack of sufficient infrastructure.

As noted by Mthembu et al. (2019), the incorporation of digital technologies calls for the establishment of a solid and dependable infrastructure. This infrastructure must include hardware (such as computers, servers, and networking equipment), software (such as operating systems, databases, and applications), and network infrastructure (such as internet connectivity and bandwidth). However, many healthcare libraries, particularly those located in settings with limited resources; lack the required infrastructure to handle digital technologies. This is especially true of those libraries located in academic settings. This lack of infrastructure not only makes the installation of digital technologies more difficult, but it also has an impact on the efficiency and dependability of such technologies. Zungu et al. (2018) stated that ensuring that the materials are up to the high standards expected in the healthcare industry is a process that is both labor-intensive and time-consuming, as well as one that demands specialized knowledge and abilities. Another significant obstacle to digital transformation in healthcare libraries is inadequate internet access. The accessibility and dependability of internet connection are two primary factors that significantly impact the efficacy of digital technologies. Library users are unable to access online resources or utilize online services if their internet connection is unstable. According to Mthembu et al. (2019), sluggish internet connections may hamper the functioning of digital technologies and irritate users, which ultimately undermine the advantages of digital transformation. This issue is more severe in more isolated or rural regions, which often have internet infrastructure that is either insufficient or nonexistent.

Another obstacle that must be overcome on the path to digital transformation is the lack of expertise and training that exists among library staff. As noted by Zungu et al. (2018), the integration of digital technologies calls for a new set of skills and competencies, and these include technical skills (such as software and hardware management, data analytics), digital literacy skills (such as navigating online resources and evaluating digital materials), and soft skills (such as problem-solving, adaptability, and communication). On the other hand, a significant portion of library staff members do not possess these abilities, mostly because there are insufficient possibilities for training and growth. These skills gap not only makes it more difficult to effectively integrate and make use of digital technologies, but it also makes it more difficult for library staff to assist users in making effective use of these technologies. In order to accomplish the goal of overcoming these problems, all of the stakeholders' efforts need to be planned and coordinated.

CHALLENGES ASSOCIATED WITH ADOPTING AND IMPLEMENTING DIGITAL TECHNOLOGIES IN KWAZULU-NATAL DEPARTMENT OF HEALTH (KZN DOH) LIBRARIES

The most common challenges associated with adopting and implementing digital technologies in KZN DOH libraries are information; computer; health literacy skills, access to computers in some libraries especially those in rural settings, poor internet connections, network problems, restrictions in on-line databases, lack of remote access to online library facilities, lack of time for some patrons to go to the libraries, library opening hours, some library collections lack variety and are too limited (e.g. textbooks, e-books, e-journals), infrastructure, subscription renewals and budgetary constraints. However it should be noted that the above mentioned challenges vary from one library to the other, and not all the libraries are faced with the same challenges. From the literature reviewed some other challenges suggested are that health libraries have shortcomings in quality service provision including: lack of Internet access, the unavailability of professional medical librarians, the difficulty of understanding medical terminologies, and lack of awareness among health professionals about on-line electronic information sources rendered by the library (Geda 2021). A study conducted by Nkosi, Asah and Pillay (2011: 879) cited in Maharaj 2014 examined post-basic nursing student's access to information and attitudes toward the use of Information Technology in practice. The study identified that nurse academics and managers need to acknowledge the importance of integrating computer literacy into the nursing curriculum for the purposes of developing adequate skills to function in an environment which is increasing in technology. The study highlighted the factors that hinder use of computers, under five broad headings:

- Lack of computer skills; a lack of computer skills has led to nurses not being able to take advantage of the advancement in IT.
- Lack of access; there is a lack of access to computer equipment, intranet, internet, and passwords, therefore restricting the access.
- Lack of time; there is a shortage of nurses, therefore nurses are overworked and do not have time to use the computer.
- Lack of support; computers are faulty and no support in sorting out these problems.
- Budgetary constraints; cannot buy additional information technology.

The above factors that hinder use of computers have been observed in some of the KZN DOH libraries as well and require the adoption and implementation of certain strategies in order to curb them. Whitney (2017) argued that ensuring that the patrons have ready access to accurate and understandable health information and that health care institutions make themselves understood to those they serve are never-ending challenges. People are always confronting new personal health issues, new interactions with the health care system, and new imperatives to understand environmental factors affecting their health. Advances in information technology and changes in user preferences are continually affecting the ways in which people seek and obtain understandable health information, interact with health care providers, and engage in efforts designed to promote health.

STRATEGIES TO OVERCOMING CHALLENGES FOR DIGITAL TRANSFORMATION IN HEALTHCARE LIBRARIES

In order to successfully complete the digital transformation of healthcare libraries, it is necessary to deploy resources in a planned manner in key areas like infrastructure, funding, training, and quality control systems. At the core of this endeavor is a dedication to catering to the one-of-a-kind information requirements of patients, as well as health professionals, educators, and researchers. To this aim, healthcare libraries need to investigate novel approaches and make use of collaborative partnerships in order to overcome challenges and make the most of the potential given by digital technologies (Geda, 2021; Chamberlain et al., 2021). It is necessary to take a nuanced and multi-pronged strategy in order to address the financial restrictions that provide a hurdle to digital transformation. In order for libraries to successfully get financing for digital technologies and services, they need to actively interact with a diverse group of stakeholders. These stakeholders may include government authorities, non-profit organizations, commercial enterprises, and donor agencies; all of these types of organizations have the potential to contribute to the financial resources essential for digital transformation. Libraries should investigate other types of financing, such as public-private partnerships, crowdsourcing, and social impact bonds, since these models have the potential to provide extra cash and reduce the risk of financial loss. The approach for digital transformation must include significant investments in the underlying infrastructure. The purchase of cutting-edge technology and software; high-speed internet access and reliable network infrastructure need to be the top priority for libraries. Considering the sensitive nature of healthcare information, investments should also be aimed towards protecting the security and privacy of digital systems. The construction of such an infrastructure would involve not just a financial commitment but also strategic collaborations with various network operators, technology suppliers, and other pertinent stakeholders.

A crucial component of digital transformation is equipping library and healthcare staff with the required digital literacy skills. It is imperative that steps be made to improve both their comprehension of and their ability to operate effectively within the digital environment. This might include providing individualized training programs that concentrate on topics such as the use and administration of digital technologies, the assessment of digital content, and the incorporation of technology into healthcare practice. It would be beneficial for libraries if librarians were invited to participate in medical rounds, teaching sessions, and other activities of a similar kind. Their understanding of the medical area will expand as a result of these interactions, which will enable them to better cater to the particular information requirements of health professionals. Furthermore, these contacts may encourage stronger cooperation and understanding between library staff and healthcare practitioners, therefore improving the delivery of library services. This results in an improvement in the overall quality of the library's services. During the process of digital transformation, quality assurance is an extremely important factor to keep in mind. It is essential that libraries build solid systems for verifying the quality of digital resources, as well as their correctness and dependability. Expert review panels, automated checking tools, and user feedback systems are some examples of the methods that could fall under this category.

In addition, libraries should make it a priority to stay informed of the most recent developments in digital quality assurance standards and best practices, and they should work tirelessly to improve the quality assurance procedures they use. When it comes to accelerating the digital transformation of healthcare libraries, the importance of cooperation simply cannot be overstated. It is important for libraries to investigate the possibility of forming partnerships with other libraries, academic institutions, technological businesses, and other types of organizations. These relationships have the potential to make the exchange of knowledge and resources easier, to encourage innovation, and to create the capabilities necessary for digital transformation. One possible solution is the construction of regional centers of excellence, which might solve shortages of technical competence and foster innovation. Centers of excellence can be found across the country. These centers have the potential to act as hubs for training, research, and innovation in digital healthcare librarianship and might provide a broad variety of services, like as training programs, consulting services, and research initiatives, among other things. (Chamberlain et al., 2021). These centres might also serve as platforms for cooperation and networking, bringing together specialists, practitioners, and students from a variety of professions and backgrounds.

In addition, healthcare libraries should make strategic use of digital technologies to improve both access to information and the quality of services provided. This may entail the development of online platforms and mobile applications for accessing library resources, the use of social media to communicate with users, the use of analytics to analyze user requirements and behaviors, and the incorporation of digital technologies into already existing services. It is possible for healthcare libraries to successfully undergo a digital transformation if all of these techniques are implemented in a way that is consistent and synergistic with one another. Nevertheless, this procedure is not a one-time endeavor, but rather an ongoing journey of learning, adapting, and improving. It is imperative that libraries be current on the most recent advancements in digital technologies and healthcare, that they regularly reevaluate their policies and practices, and that they are ready to adapt and innovate in response to shifting conditions and requirements. In the end, the transformation of healthcare libraries into digital formats brings up a plethora of new obstacles as well as possibilities that have never been seen before. These libraries have the potential to develop into dynamic, user-centric platforms that promote evidence-based practice, facilitate lifelong learning, and contribute to the improvement of healthcare outcomes. In other words, they have the potential to become more than just information stores.

MAXIMIZING THE OPPORTUNITIES FOR DIGITAL TRANSFORMATION IN KWAZULU-NATAL DEPARTMENT OF HEALTH (KZN DOH) LIBRARIES

Librarians can be effective leaders or participants in efforts to make health care organizations "health literate". KZN DOH libraries staff needs to understand the patrons perspective on the digital information tools available. Determine if patrons find the services valuable using strategies like surveys, interviews, statistics, etc. Librarians need to promote awareness, facilitate training, evaluate if their digital services are relevant in order to know what is needed most and by who. Whitney (2017) elaborated that librarians support patients' health literacy and health information needs of clinical staff. In outpatient and inpatient clinical settings, the librarians' contribution to promoting health literacy most frequently occurs via their support of information prescription initiatives. Information prescription programs, often denoted as Information Rx, involve physicians supplying patients with prescriptions for quality evidence-based health information that is specifically selected to address the patient's condition. Prescribed information materials may also be tailored to match the patient's other characteristics, such as preferred learning style and reading level. These programs are more targeted to the general patient education or consumer health information services.

Health libraries in KZN DOH can adopt the above strategy as their outreach program to assist clinicians and nurses with health literacy in inpatient and outpatient clinical settings. Health librarians can interact with clinicians for such information using prescribed on-line databases tailored for that function. With enough compliment of health libraries staff, librarians can even take rounds during clinic days in inpatient and outpatient sections and assist with selective dissemination of information. Evidence based information is the key to managing and curbing diseases, so well informed patients and clinical staff are likely to make well informed decision and manage the health issues well. Health librarians specialize in processing, preserving, managing and disseminating information for evidence based practice in the health department. With the overflow of health information from online sources librarians can assist the health and medical staff by sifting such information to the most relevant and preserve it for ease of access through on-line databases, computers, internet, intranet, scanners, mobile technology, social media networks, etc. Libraries and librarians can be effective partners in conducting research in health literacy and in building sustainable health literacy programs within the health libraries in KZN DOH.

Libraries are natural participants and important resources for wide health promotion interventions that aim to present their message via multiple channels in multiple formats and different locations throughout an organization. With regard to research, librarians are well-positioned to conduct investigations into how patrons evaluate health information resources and integrate information from multiple sources. They can also contribute to bridging research and practice by conducting systematic evaluations of their health information outreach projects and determining what factors enable or hinder their success. When it comes to research, librarians can apply their expertise in comprehensive literature searches to conducting meta-analyses of the literature on the connection between health information literacy and behaviour. A study by Geda (2021) argued that medical libraries play a principal role in the dissemination of free and subscribed electronic resources, open-access publishing, and licensing. Health professionals rely on electronic resources in medical libraries. A subscribed database such as MEDLINE is the main source of information for health professionals. More than 50% of doctors were interested in MEDLINE search skills though they did not take advantage of training programs given by librarians. In such cases librarians can take advantage of the walk-ins enquiries to show the doctors how to search for information on such databases. Therefore, managing and supporting electronic resources is a key competency of medical libraries. Libraries provide both physical and remote access to resources. There is a variation in information-seeking behaviour between users who access libraries physically and remotely. Physical access enables librarians to teach search skills, such as medical subject headings (MeSH) taxonomy, keywords, appropriate terminology, relevant databases, and syntax. Medical librarians play an important role in providing information literacy training to health professionals. Medical librarians empower users' information-seeking skills and searching behaviour by providing training on keywords, MeSH and text words.

D'silva (2022) suggested some innovative technologies that can be implemented in the libraries that can maximize the opportunities for digital transformation:

- Block chain: Applications of block chain in the libraries are to build a metadata system for libraries to connect a network of libraries, to host digital peer sharing and to share partnerships.
- Cloud computing: Libraries are shifting their services with the attachment of the cloud with the facilities to access anytime, anywhere. Cloud computing offers many exciting possibilities for libraries that may help to increase performance for some technology activities. With the help of this technology, library staff will be free from managing the servers.
- Artificial intelligence: its main goal is to find any technique that does the task quickly in a better way.

- Remote access to e-resources: e-resources have paved a way to enhance educational standards, especially during the pandemics or state of emergencies.
- Free and expanded access: in response to the uncertain and challenging time, some publishers are providing expanded access to e-resources (access to additional materials than subscribed by the Library), including e-books, e-journals, e-databases, etc., limited period of the emergency (i.e. during the COVID-19 pandemic).
- Open access resources: some publishers offer e-books, e-journals available to utilize for free in the internet or on-line databases.
- Web 2.0 technologies: can help libraries create collaborative and participative environments. and can provide libraries with the ability to offer improved, customer-driven services to their users.
- Synchronous communication: it is Instant Messaging (IM) deployed by libraries in providing "real-time reference" services, where patrons can synchronously communicate with librarians much as they would in a face-to-face reference context.
- Content delivery: Really Simple Syndication (RSS) allows a website (or e-publisher) to list the newest published updates (like the table of contents of journals, recent articles) through a technology called XML. It facilitates a web user to keep track of new updates on the chosen website. Libraries are already creating RSS feeds for users to subscribe to, including updates on new items in a collection, new services, and new content in subscription databases.
- Podcasting: process of capturing audio digital-media files that can be distributed over the internet using RSS feeds for playing-back on portable media players as well as computers. Users can subscribe to such feeds and automatically download these files directly into an audio management program on their PCs. Several libraries use podcasts to support library orientations programmes.
- Vodcasting: also called video podcasting or vlogging, adds video to the downloadable sound files podcast listeners are used to. Downloading the video files is a simple matter of subscribing to a podcast in one of the many freely available directory programs. Libraries use vodcasts to illustrate what the Library has done and attract the community to future programs.
- SMS enquiry service: Short Message Service (SMS) is a delivery mechanism of short messages over mobile networks. The SMS enquiry services in a library allow patrons to use their mobile phones to SMS their inquiries to the Library. The reference staff deployed to attend to such queries can respond immediately with answers or links to more in-depth explanations.
- Publishing tools (Blogs and wikis): Blogs provide control to an individual or group of individuals for publishing content or making commentary on it. The most apparent application of blogs for libraries is to use them as a tool for promotion, publicity and outreach services. Libraries can disseminate information to their users and make announcements for their new resources and events through their blogs.

Wikis: can be used as a communication tool to enable social interaction among librarians and patrons. Users can share information ask and answer questions, and librarians can do the same within a wiki.

KZN DOH can thus adopt and implement some of the above described innovative technologies after careful assessment and evaluation of each library user's needs, compatibility with existing infrastructure, possible upgrades of the existing infrastructure to improve, relevance and cost.

FUTURE RESEARCH DIRECTIONS

Future research directions should be focused on skills, training and development of healthcare librarians on evidence-based practice in healthcare, and more training of medical staff on digital information resources. The necessity of health information staff to be familiarized with the medical terminology, medical procedures and medical language in order to be most relevant in information provision cannot be taken for granted. Librarians are supposedly the custodians of information, health and medicine deal with complex and specialized subjects in the field that requires specialist information, research and evidence-based knowledge. Healthcare libraries and healthcare information staff need to be familiar with the language and information technologies of this field. Healthcare staff cannot deal with the abundance of information without being familiar with the digital techniques of handling information in order for them not to be overwhelmed but be prompt, accurate and more relevant in the digital transformation era.

SOLUTIONS AND RECOMMENDATIONS

Library users may now get the information they need whenever it is most convenient for them thanks to the digital resources, which provide rapid access to a vast variety of books, journals, and, other types of information. In addition, the majority of the time, powerful search and filtering options are included with e-resources. These features make it simpler and faster to get information (Molokisi, 2019). Another consequence of the digital transformation that has important repercussions for healthcare libraries is the proliferation of mobile applications. The ability to interact in real-time communication with your customers is a key component of the success of your business. The transformation to a digital environment also provides opportunity for health libraries to improve the ways in which they assist with the decision-making, learning, and research processes. The process of digital transformation presents a number of difficult and significant challenges, one of the most important of which is quality assurance of digital resources. There is a significant amount of variance in the quality, correctness, and dependability of digital resources, in particular those that are derived from the internet. In addition, the fact that digital materials have a dynamic character and may be updated or amended at any moment adds another layer of complexity to the process of quality assurance. There is a danger that library users may obtain and utilize erroneous or misleading information, which may have major repercussions for patient care and healthcare outcomes if proper quality assurance systems are not in place. The decision-makers in charge of healthcare policy need to provide enough resources to medical libraries and formulate policies that would facilitate digital transformation. Administrators at libraries and healthcare facilities need to make digital transformation a top priority in their strategic planning, invest in the development of their staff as well as their infrastructure, and build partnerships in order to pool their resources and experience. The staff has to be willing to adapt to change, continue their education, and focus on the needs of the customers in order to provide quality service. In addition, it is necessary for all parties involved to work together and exchange information on effective methods in order to expedite the digital transformation of healthcare libraries. The path towards digital transformation in healthcare libraries is ultimately a difficult but essential one, but getting there may be difficult. The potential advantages of digital technologies in boosting the delivery of library services, supporting healthcare provision, and improving healthcare outcomes are too large to ignore, notwithstanding the challenges that may arise.

Viewing these issues not as insurmountable impediments but rather as opportunities for learning, creativity, and progress is the key to successfully navigate through these challenges. By doing so, healthcare libraries will not only be able to overcome the difficulties associated with digital transformation, but they will also be able to take use of the digital age's full potential to make a significant contribution. The integration of new technologies into already-existing systems is just one aspect of digital transformation. It is an all-encompassing procedure that includes making strategic investments, making modifications in operational paradigms, and fostering an atmosphere that is favourable to innovation and cooperation. This necessitates the implementation of a diverse set of initiatives and strategies, each of which should cater to a certain facet of the process of transformation, and which, when combined, should provide for a more seamless transfer into the digital future. Infrastructure is one of these essential components that require a significant amount of strategic investment. The adoption and use of digital technologies become impossible in the absence of the essential digital infrastructure, which includes hardware, software, and connection. Investing in infrastructure also entails guaranteeing the security of digital systems, which is an element that is crucial given the sensitive nature of health information. This necessitates the implementation of stringent cybersecurity precautions, comprehensive data protection procedures, and constant awareness against possible dangers. In tandem with the need for suitable infrastructure is the requirement for sufficient finance.

It is not a free endeavour; in order to be successful; the digital transformation of healthcare libraries demands financial contributions not just initially but also on an ongoing basis. In order to acquire these resources, you will need to interact in a manner that is both inventive and dynamic with a wide variety of possible sources of funding. These sources include governmental agencies, charitable organisations, commercial sector firms, and individual contributors. Other sources of finance, such as public-private partnerships or crowdsourcing, could potentially be able to offer the essential financial assistance that is required. Training is another important pillar of the route towards digital transformation. Without the requisite human ability to manage, maintain, and improve these systems, even the most sophisticated digital technologies are useless. Consequently, making an investment in comprehensive training programmes is a component of this trip that cannot be negotiated. These programmes need to accommodate a wide range of skill levels and positions, including providing fundamental digital literacy for all staff members as well as advanced training for those who are directly engaged in managing digital systems. Another essential component of this journey is fostering an environment that is conducive to cooperation and innovation. A massive endeavour that no one institution can handle alone is the digital transformation of healthcare libraries. It is necessary to collaborate in terms of resources, knowledge, and ideas, as well as to be ready to learn from and with one another. Libraries in the healthcare industry have the potential to establish a supportive environment that propels innovation and growth by forming relationships with academic institutions, technology businesses, other libraries, and a variety of other stakeholders.

There are several possible benefits that may result from a successful digital transformation. It is possible for improved access to information, which may be provided via e-resources and mobile apps, to completely transform the manner in which students, researchers, and healthcare professionals access and utilise information. This, in turn, may promote advances in patient care, education, and research, which will have an effect on the very heart of the healthcare sector. In addition to providing access to information, the integration of digital technologies may also assist the delivery of services in a manner that is more efficient and effective. Through the use of analytics, libraries can gain deep insights into the needs and behaviours of their users, which enable them to tailor their services accordingly. Through the use of social media and other online platforms, libraries can engage with their users in new and meaningful ways, fostering a sense of community and shared learning. Therefore, the potential advantages of digital transformation are not restricted to the operation of healthcare libraries internally. Beyond the confines of the library, they have an effect on society as a whole as well as the larger healthcare sector. Therefore, achieving a successful digital transformation of healthcare libraries is not only a goal in itself; rather, it is a means towards achieving a greater aim, which is to enhance the quality, efficacy, and accessibility of healthcare.

CONCLUSION

The provision of patient care, educational opportunities, and research opportunities are all areas that are significantly aided by the existence of healthcare libraries, which are institutions that are essential to the running of the healthcare sector. The prospects presented by digital transformation hold the potential of greatly increasing the capacity of these libraries, which will in turn make it possible for the libraries to provide better services, increase accessibility, and have a stronger influence on the people who benefit from them. Although insurmountable obstacles, such as those especially noticeable in South African healthcare libraries provide significant impediments to this transformation, the potential advantages presented by the adoption of digital technologies far outweigh these obstacles. Therefore, the challenge at hand is not to make decision between conventional and digital methods; rather, it is to call for a careful synthesis of both methods, making use of the most beneficial aspects of each.

REFERENCES

Chamberlain, D., Elcock, M., & Puligari, P. (2015). The use of mobile technology in health libraries: A summary of a UK based survey. *Health Information and Libraries Journal*, *32*(4), 1–12. doi:10.1111/hir.12116 PMID:26292980

Chisita CT, Ngulube P. (2022). A framework for librarians to inform the citizenry during disasters: Reflections on the COVID-19 pandemic. *Jamba*, *14*(1), 1197.

Creswell, J. W. (2014). *Research design: qualitative, quantitative and mixed methods approach* (4th ed.). Sage.

D'silva, D. R. (2022). Emerging technological trends in Library Management and Services during Covid-19 pandemic. *The Journal of Advannes in Library and Information Science.*, *11*(2), 172–180.

Davis, F. D. (1989). Perceived usefulness, perceived ease of use, and user acceptance of information technology. *Management Information Systems Quarterly*, *13*(3), 319–340. doi:10.2307/249008

Elkin, K. (2018). The role of the health sciences librarian in promoting evidence-based practice. *Journal of the Medical Library Association: JMLA*, *106*(1), 30–36.

Geda, A. F. (2021). The role of medical library in information seeking behaviour of health professionals: A review of the literature. *Journal of Hospital Librarianship*, *21*(4), 405–416. doi:10.1080/15323269.2021.1982263

Geda, A. F. (2021). The role of medical library in information seeking behaviour of health professionals: A review of the literature. *Journal of Hospital Librarianship*, *21*(4), 405–416. doi:10.1080/15323 269.2021.1982263

Hernon, P., & Young, J. (2017). The role of libraries in providing access to the latest research and information in healthcare. *Journal of the Medical Library Association: JMLA*, *105*(4), 233–240.

Jablonski, R. A., Smeby, J. C., & Rydland, J. (2021). The role of libraries in providing support for nursing education and research in healthcare. *Journal of the Medical Library Association: JMLA*, *109*(1), 12–20.

Knuttel, H., Krause, E., Semmler-Schmetz, M., Reimann, I., & Metzendorf, M.-I. (2020). Helath Science Libraries in Germany: New directions. *Health Information and Libraries Journal*, *37*(1), 83–88. doi:10.1111/hir.12299 PMID:32096587

Mcknight, M. (2008). Hospital nurses. *Journal of Electronic Resources in Medical Libraries*, *1*(3), 21–34.

Molokisi, S. (2019). *Exploring the use of social media tools in the University of South Africa library.* UNISA.

Mthembu, T., Naidoo, R., Mkhize, N., Zungu, L., Ndwandwe, T., & Singh, B. (2019). Assessing the quality and reliability of digital information in Kwazulu Natal Department of Health libraries. *Journal of Healthcare Information Management*, *18*(3), 1–6.

National Department of Health. (2019). *National Digital Health Strategy for South Africa 2019 – 2024.* https://www.health.gov.za/wo-content/uploads/2020/11/national-digital-strategy-for-south-africa-2019-2024-b.pdf

Ndwandwe, T., Naidoo, R., Mkhize, N., Mthembu, T., Zungu, L., & Singh, B. (2017). Staff training and capacity building in Kwazulu Natal Department of Health libraries: Challenges and opportunities. *Journal of Healthcare Information Management*, *16*(1), 1–6.

Rajagopaul, A. (2008). *A comparative study of job functions of university and university of technology graduates and diplomates in special libraries and engineering firms.* DUT.

Semertzaki, E. (2011). *Special Libraries as Knowledge Management Centres.* Chandos Publishing. doi:10.1533/9781780632667

Smeby, J. C., & Rydland, J. (2020). The role of libraries in supporting research and education in healthcare. *Journal of the Medical Library Association: JMLA*, *108*(3), 467–474.

Tshuma, N., Haruna, H., Muziringa, M. C., & Chikonzo, A. C. (2015). International trends in Health Science Librarianship part 3: Southern Africa (South Africa, Tanzania and Zimbabwe). *Health Information and Libraries Journal*, *32*(1), 67–72. doi:10.1111/hir.12091

Venkatesh, V., & Bala, H. (2008). Technology Acceptance Model 3 and a Research Agenda on Interventions. *Decision Sciences*, *39*(2), 273–315. doi:10.1111/j.1540-5915.2008.00192.x

Venkatesh, V., & Davis, F. (2000). A Theoretical Extension of the Technology Acceptance Model: Four Longitudinal Field Studies. *Management Science*, *46*(2), 186–204. doi:10.1287/mnsc.46.2.186.11926

Venkatesh, V., Morris, M. G., Davis, G. B., & Davis, F. D. (2003). User Acceptance of Information Technology: Toward a Unified View. *Management Information Systems Quarterly, 27*(3), 425–478. doi:10.2307/30036540

Wallis, J., Marshall, J., & Viera, A. (2019). Staffing challenges for libraries in healthcare institutions: Implications for access to the latest research and information. *Journal of the Medical Library Association: JMLA, 107*(3), 213–219.

Whitney, W., Keselman, A., & Humphreys, A. (2017). Libraries and librarians: Key partners for progress in health literacy research and practise. *Information Services & Use, 37*(1), 85–100. doi:10.3233/ISU-170821

Zungu, L., Naidoo, R., Mkhize, N., Mthembu, T., Ndwandwe, T., & Singh, B. (2018). The impact of limited internet access on access to information in Kwazulu Natal Department of Health libraries. *Journal of Healthcare Information Management, 17*(2), 1–6.

ADDITIONAL READING

Chamberlain, D., Elcock, M., & Puligari, P. (2015). The use of mobile technology in health libraries: A summary of a UK-based survey. *Health Information and Libraries Journal, 32*(4), 265–275. doi:10.1111/hir.12116 PMID:26292980

Hanell, F., & Ahlryd, S. (2021). Information work of hospital librarians: Making the invisible visible. *Journal of Librarianship and Information Science, 00*(0), 1–14.

Haruna, H., & Mtoroki, M. (2016). Health libraries and information services in Tanzania: A strategic assessment. *Annals of Global Health, 85*(5), 912–921. doi:10.1016/j.aogh.2016.10.003 PMID:28283146

Khoro, L. (2019). *Knowledge sharing among library staff of special libraries in KwaZulu-Natal with special reference to using Information and Communications Technology enabled platforms.* DUT.

Lata, N., & Owam, J. (2022). Contemporary trends and technologies in research libraries: an overview. Nigeria: University of Calabar, Nigeria & Ultimate Research Network (URN). doi:10.4018/978-1-6684-3364-5.ch003

Naughton, J., Booth, K., Elliott, P., Evans, M., Simões, M., & Wilson, S. (2021). Health literacy: The role of NHS library and knowledge services. *Health Information and Libraries Journal, 38*(2), 150–154. doi:10.1111/hir.12371 PMID:34051119

KEY TERMS AND DEFINITIONS

Digital Health: Refers to the use of digital technologies in medicine and other health professions to manage illnesses, health risks and to promote wellness.

Digital Literacy: The information technology skills needed for the twenty-first century, and the requisite competency to find, evaluate, utilise, share, and create content using information technologies and the internet.

Digital Transformation: It is how the organization makes use of digital technologies for delivering more sustainable value to patients, healthcare professionals, and the medical organizations themselves.

Electronic Information: It is any information accessed, processed, stored or transmitted in an electronic format (e.g. emails, text messages, raw data, sound files, image files, video files, documents, spreadsheets, databases, programs and algorithms).

Health Literacy: The degree to which individuals have the capacity to obtain, process, and understand basic health information and services needed to make appropriate health decisions.

Healthcare Libraries: Are designed to assist physicians, health professionals, students, patients, consumers, medical researchers, and information specialists in finding health and scientific information to improve, update, assess, or evaluate health care.

Information Access: It is the process by which users acquire adequate information resources, which are bibliographically organized through effective assistance given to them by the library professionals.

Chapter 8
Transforming Business for a Sustainable Future Using Green Marketing

Akancha Kumari

ⓘ https://orcid.org/0009-0004-3227-5460

Ranchi University, India

ABSTRACT

As the world grapples with the pressing challenges of environmental degradation and climate change, the need for sustainable development has become paramount. Green marketing has emerged as a powerful tool for transforming businesses and paving the way towards a sustainable future. This chapter explores the role of green marketing in driving sustainable development by examining its impact on business practices, consumer behavior, and environmental stewardship. The study highlights the strategies and initiatives undertaken by businesses to integrate sustainability principles into their marketing efforts, including product innovation, eco-labeling, green packaging, and communication of environmental values. Through a comprehensive review of relevant literature, case studies, and industry examples, this chapter underscores the transformative potential of green marketing in driving sustainable development. It offers insights to businesses, policymakers, and marketers on how to harness the power of green marketing to create a more sustainable and prosperous future.

INTRODUCTION

Green marketing, also known as sustainable marketing or eco-marketing, is a strategic approach that involves promoting products, services, and business practices that are environmentally friendly and socially responsible (Alkhatib et al., 2023). The core idea behind green marketing is to balance business objectives with environmental concerns, aiming to meet consumer demands for sustainable options while also contributing to the preservation and improvement of the natural environment. Green marketing encompasses a range of strategies and practices that focus on minimizing negative environmental impacts throughout a product's lifecycle. This includes aspects such as:

DOI: 10.4018/979-8-3693-2841-5.ch008

- **Product Design and Innovation:** Developing products that use renewable materials, reduce energy consumption, and have minimal waste during production and disposal.
- **Packaging:** Using eco-friendly and minimal packaging materials to reduce waste and lower the carbon footprint of products.
- **Promotion:** Emphasizing a product's environmental benefits through transparent and accurate communication, highlighting factors such as energy efficiency, reduced emissions, and sustainable sourcing.
- **Education and Awareness:** Educating consumers about the environmental consequences of their choices and how opting for sustainable products can have a positive impact.
- **Certifications and Labels:** Displaying eco-friendly certifications and labels (e.g., organic, fair trade, energy-efficient) to verify a product's adherence to environmental standards.
- **Corporate Social Responsibility (CSR):** Integrating sustainable practices and initiatives into a company's overall CSR strategy, demonstrating a commitment to social and environmental well-being.
- **Consumer Behavior:** Encouraging consumers to adopt environmentally friendly behaviors and purchase decisions, promoting a shift towards more sustainable consumption patterns.
- **Long-Term Sustainability:** Fostering a culture of continuous improvement and sustainability within the organization, focusing on long-term environmental and societal benefits

In a world where environmental concerns are increasingly significant, green marketing serves as a bridge between commerce and conservation. It allows businesses to tap into a growing market of environmentally conscious consumers, while also encouraging them to adopt more sustainable practices. Ultimately, green marketing plays a crucial role in promoting sustainable development, influencing both consumer behavior and corporate strategies to create a more environmentally friendly and socially responsible future.

Green Marketing

Numerous companies have embraced green marketing as a cornerstone of their brand identity, aligning business success with environmental stewardship. Patagonia, an outdoor clothing company, epitomizes this commitment through its "Worn Wear" initiative, which encourages customers to repair and reuse their products, thus prolonging their lifespan (Amin et al., 2012). Tesla, a pioneer in electric vehicles, has revolutionized the automotive industry by promoting its electric cars as a solution to reduce greenhouse gas emissions and air pollution. Unilever's Sustainable Living Plan demonstrates a comprehensive approach to sustainability, aiming to improve the environmental and social impacts of its products across the value chain.

Principles of Green Marketing: Guiding Sustainability and Ethical Engagement

Green marketing is grounded in a set of guiding principles that shape its ethical foundation and strategic direction. These principles go beyond traditional marketing approaches, emphasizing environmental responsibility, transparency, authenticity, and social well-being. By adhering to these principles, businesses can navigate the complexities of green marketing, foster consumer trust, and contribute to a more sustainable future (Anitha and Vijai, 2021). This essay delves into the fundamental principles that underpin green marketing, elucidating their significance and impact on business practices and consumer behavior.

- **Sustainability:** It is the cornerstone of green marketing. This principle emphasizes the importance of meeting present needs without compromising the ability of future generations to meet their own needs. Businesses embracing sustainability prioritize the responsible use of resources, minimize waste, and reduce environmental impact. By aligning products, services, and practices with this principle, green marketing serves as a powerful tool for creating a harmonious balance between economic growth and environmental preservation.

- **Transparency and Authenticity:** It is integral to building consumer trust and credibility in green marketing. Businesses must be open and honest about their environmental practices, disclosing information about sourcing, production processes, and the overall impact of their products. Authenticity ensures that green marketing claims are substantiated by real actions, avoiding greenwashing and reinforcing the genuine commitment to sustainability.

- **Education and Awareness:** Green marketing serves as an educational platform, empowering consumers with knowledge about the environmental implications of their choices. This principle emphasizes the role of businesses in providing accurate and understandable information to consumers (Aulia et al., 2018). By raising awareness about sustainability issues and their solutions, green marketing enables consumers to make informed decisions that align with their values.

- **Value Proposition:** Green marketing requires businesses to position their products or services as valuable solutions that offer both environmental benefits and functional advantages. The value proposition extends beyond sustainability, highlighting features such as energy efficiency, durability, and long-term cost savings. This principle underscores the notion that sustainable choices can enhance the overall quality of a product or service.

- **Consumer Empowerment:** Empowering consumers to make environmentally responsible choices is a fundamental principle of green marketing. By presenting eco-friendly alternatives and educating consumers about the positive impact of their decisions, businesses enable individuals to actively contribute to sustainability. This principle recognizes consumers as agents of change, capable of influencing market trends and driving demand for sustainable products and services.

- **Lifecycle Thinking:** Green marketing embraces a lifecycle perspective, considering the entire journey of a product from sourcing raw materials to disposal. This principle encourages businesses to assess and minimize the environmental impact of each stage, from production and distribution to use and end-of-life management. Lifecycle thinking guides the development of sustainable practices that prioritize efficiency, reduced waste, and circular economy concepts.

- **Continuous Improvement:** Green marketing encourages businesses to adopt a mindset of continuous improvement in their sustainability efforts. This principle recognizes that environmental challenges are dynamic and evolving (Bestari and Butarbutar, 2021). By setting measurable goals, monitoring progress, and innovating to overcome obstacles, businesses can demonstrate an ongoing commitment to sustainability and adapt to changing consumer preferences.

- **Social Responsibility:** Green marketing extends beyond environmental considerations to encompass social responsibility. Businesses are encouraged to support ethical labor practices, community engagement, and positive social impacts. This principle acknowledges the interconnectedness of environmental sustainability and social well-being, reinforcing the idea that responsible businesses prioritize both aspects.

The principles of green marketing provide a robust framework for businesses to navigate the intricate landscape of sustainability, ethics, and consumer engagement. By adhering to these principles, businesses can not only promote eco-friendly products and practices but also contribute to a larger movement towards a more sustainable and equitable world (Bhattacharyya, 2023). From sustainability and transparency to education and empowerment, these principles underscore the transformative power of green marketing in fostering positive change and preserving the planet for future generations.

MOTIVATION FOR THE WORK

- To understand the meaning, importance and challenges of green marketing.
- To explore how green marketing aligns with ethical business values.
- To study green marketing strategies for ensuring business resilience and longevity.
- To learn how green marketing contributes to a better future.
- To leverage library information for in depth research and data on green marketing strategies.

BACKGROUND OF THE WORK

The evolution of green marketing is a captivating journey that reflects the shifting paradigms of consumer consciousness, societal values, and environmental awareness. Born out of a confluence of events, concerns, and changing perspectives, green marketing has transformed from a novel concept to a critical strategy at the forefront of modern business practices (Canavari and Coderoni, 2019). Tracing its origins and understanding its evolution provides invaluable insights into how environmental consciousness has woven itself into the fabric of commerce. The seeds of green marketing were sown in the latter half of the 20th century, a time marked by unprecedented environmental shifts and the burgeoning awareness of humanity's impact on the planet. It was a period of awakening as various environmental crises came to the forefront of public consciousness. Events like the 1973 oil crisis and the subsequent energy shortages acted as a wake-up call, prompting questions about resource sustainability and the consequences of unbridled consumption. The late 1960s and early 1970s saw the birth of the modern environmental movement, driven by seminal works such as Rachel Carson's "Silent Spring" and the establishment of Earth Day in 1970 (Choudhary and Gokarn, 2013). These milestones catalyzed public awareness, pushing environmental issues to the forefront of political and social discourse. As concerns over pollution, deforestation, and resource depletion grew, individuals and communities began to question the long-term consequences of unchecked industrial growth. As public consciousness evolved, a novel wave of consumerism emerged. People began to rethink their purchasing decisions, seeking products and services that aligned with their newfound environmental values (Geng and Maimaituerxun, 2022). This shift was not lost on businesses, and the concept of green marketing began to take shape. The 1980s saw the initial attempts to cater to this growing segment of environmentally conscious consumers. Companies such as Body Shop, with its cruelty-free and ethically sourced products, and Ben & Jerry's, which championed social responsibility and sustainable sourcing, became pioneers of the green marketing movement. They resonated with a generation that sought products that went beyond mere functionality and embraced ethical considerations (Gupta et al., 2023). The 1990s witnessed the formalization of green marketing into a structured business strategy. As globalization gathered momentum, environmental concerns transcended borders, leading to international agreements and conventions aimed at addressing global challenges. The Rio Earth Summit in 1992, for instance, gave rise to discussions on sustainable development and paved the way for corporate sustainability initiatives. The concept of Corporate Social Responsibility (CSR) gained prominence during this era. Businesses started recognizing their role in environmental stewardship, not merely as profit generators but as entities with a responsibility to the planet and society. Green marketing evolved to encompass CSR, with companies embracing practices such as energy efficiency, waste reduction, and responsible sourcing (Jaiswal and Sinha, 2023). While the trajectory of green marketing has been largely positive, it hasn't been without challenges. One notable issue is greenwashing, a term used to describe the practice of misleading consumers with false or exaggerated claims about a product's environmental benefits. This unethical practice erodes consumer trust and undermines the credibility of legitimate green marketing efforts. As a response, regulatory bodies and industry watchdogs have sought to establish guidelines and standards to combat greenwashing and ensure authenticity. The 21st century has witnessed a paradigm shift in green marketing, reflecting a deeper understanding of sustainability's complexity. Businesses are no longer content with superficial eco-friendly claims; they are integrating sustainability into their core operations, from supply chain management to product design, to achieve holistic environmental stewardship (Jaiswal et al., 2023). The rise of the circular economy concept further underscores this shift. Businesses are reimagining product life cycles, focusing on minimizing waste, promoting recycling, and designing for longevity. Concepts like upcycling and cradle-to-cradle design have gained traction, epitomizing the transition from linear production models to closed-loop systems (Karmakar et al., 2022). The evolution of green marketing reflects our changing relationship with the environment, consumer values, and business ethics. From its nascent roots in the wake of environmental awakening to its present form as a powerful strategy for sustainable commerce, green marketing has traversed a remarkable journey (Kaur et al., 2022). It has transcended mere marketing trends to become a fundamental aspect of business strategies, embodying the ethos of environmental responsibility, transparency, and authenticity. As we move forward, the lessons from green marketing's evolution underscore the importance of aligning business practices with ecological imperatives. The journey from greenwashing to genuine sustainability demonstrates the resilience of consumer demand for ethical products and the need for businesses to embrace holistic approaches that extend beyond profitability to contribute to a greener and more sustainable future (Khare et al., 2023).

Importance of Green Marketing

Green marketing plays a pivotal role as a means of achieving sustainable development, forging a symbiotic relationship between economic growth, environmental stewardship, and social well-being. This approach leverages the power of marketing to drive positive change by promoting products, services, and practices that not only satisfy consumer needs but also contribute to the long-term health of our planet and society (Kumar et al., 2023). As we delve deeper into the connection between green marketing and sustainable development, it becomes evident that this synergy holds the potential to reshape industries, transform consumer behaviors, and pave the way for a more equitable and resilient future.

Sustainable development seeks to balance economic progress with environmental protection and social equity. Green marketing aligns seamlessly with this objective by encouraging businesses to prioritize environmental responsibility within their operations (Kumar and Sinha 2023). Companies that adopt green marketing strategies embark on a journey to reduce their ecological footprint, embracing practices that minimize resource consumption, pollution, and waste generation. This not only mitigates their negative impact on the environment but also positions them as responsible corporate citizens contributing to the global sustainability agenda (Lee et al., 2023). Green marketing possesses the remarkable ability to empower consumers and drive behavior change. By highlighting the environmental benefits of products and services, green marketing campaigns inform consumers about the positive impact their choices can have. Educated consumers are more likely to make sustainable decisions, favoring products that conserve energy, reduce emissions, or promote ethical sourcing. This behavioral shift creates a demand for environmentally friendly options, encouraging businesses to innovate and prioritize sustainability in their offerings (Masengu et al., 2023). Green marketing serves as a catalyst for innovation, driving businesses to develop eco-friendly solutions that meet consumer demands while minimizing negative environmental effects. This dynamic has spurred technological advancements in renewable energy, waste reduction, efficient transportation, and sustainable packaging. As businesses vie for the attention of environmentally conscious consumers, they invest in research and development to create products that align with sustainability goals (Murin et al., 2015). This virtuous cycle of innovation enhances the potential for breakthroughs in sustainable technologies.

Green marketing is intrinsically linked to the concept of CSR, where businesses acknowledge their responsibility to positively impact society and the environment. Through green marketing initiatives, companies showcase their commitment to sustainable practices beyond profit-making motives. This can involve initiatives such as reforestation projects, waste reduction campaigns, or contributions to environmental conservation efforts. These endeavors enhance a company's reputation, fostering trust and loyalty among consumers who seek to support socially responsible businesses (Nassani et al., 2023). At its core, green marketing serves as a catalyst for sustainable development. By incorporating environmental considerations into business strategies, companies contribute to resource conservation, reduce pollution, and minimize waste generation. Green marketing encourages the adoption of renewable energy sources, responsible sourcing, and innovative technologies that reduce the carbon footprint of products and operations. Through sustainable practices, businesses actively participate in addressing global environmental challenges, ensuring a more resilient and sustainable future for both ecosystems and society (Nozari et al., 2021). Green marketing is not merely an altruistic endeavor; it also translates into business success. As consumer demand for eco-friendly products and services grows, companies that align their offerings with sustainability principles gain a competitive edge. Adopting green marketing strategies can lead to increased market share, enhanced customer loyalty, and improved financial performance. Furthermore, the pursuit of sustainability often drives innovation, pushing businesses to develop more efficient processes, eco-friendly materials, and novel solutions that address pressing environmental issues (Park et al., 2021).

In an era of information transparency and heightened consumer awareness, a positive brand reputation is invaluable. Green marketing allows businesses to showcase their commitment to ethical practices and environmental responsibility. Companies that actively engage in sustainable initiatives demonstrate their genuine concern for the planet and society, fostering a positive perception among consumers (Priya et al., 2023). Such reputational benefits not only attract environmentally conscious consumers but also resonate with a broader audience those values socially responsible businesses. Green marketing holds the power to reshape consumer behavior and preferences. As consumers become more aware of environmental issues, they seek products and services that align with their values. Effective green marketing campaigns educate consumers about the environmental impact of their choices, enabling them to make more informed decisions (Sinha, 2023). By presenting eco-friendly alternatives as desirable and socially responsible choices, green marketing prompts consumers to reconsider their consumption patterns and opt for products that contribute to a sustainable future. As governments and international bodies enact stricter environmental regulations, businesses that proactively adopt green marketing practices position themselves for compliance. By integrating sustainability into their operations and communicating these efforts transparently, companies can mitigate risks associated with non-compliance and potential fines. Moreover, green marketing equips businesses with the tools to anticipate and adapt to evolving consumer preferences and changing market dynamics, enhancing their resilience in a rapidly evolving business landscape. Beyond economic considerations, businesses have a responsibility as global citizens to minimize their negative impact on the planet. Green marketing enables companies to fulfill their ethical obligations by promoting products and practices that contribute to environmental preservation and social well-being. This commitment to ethical business practices resonates with consumers, employees, investors, and other stakeholders, fostering a sense of shared responsibility in addressing pressing environmental challenges. Green marketing offers businesses a proactive approach to risk mitigation. By adopting sustainable practices and communicating them effectively, companies reduce their exposure to potential legal, financial, and reputational risks associated with environmental non-compliance or negative consumer perception. Investing in sustainability through green marketing ensures long-term viability in a changing business landscape driven by heightened environmental awareness (Spasojevic and Spasojevic, 2018). Green marketing is not limited to external audiences; it also influences internal stakeholders. Employees increasingly seek workplaces aligned with their values, and a commitment to sustainability through green marketing fosters a sense of purpose and engagement among staff. Businesses that prioritize environmental responsibility are more likely to attract top talent, as individuals seek meaningful and socially conscious workplaces. Green marketing promotes collaboration across industries and sectors. Companies that invest in sustainability often collaborate with suppliers, partners, and competitors to develop innovative solutions that address shared environmental challenges. These collaborations foster an innovation ecosystem where best practices are shared, technologies are advanced, and collective efforts drive transformative change.

In the event of a sustainability-related crisis, a history of credible green marketing efforts can help businesses weather the storm. Transparent communication about sustainable practices, coupled with effective crisis management strategies, demonstrates a commitment to rectifying mistakes and aligning with sustainability principles. This approach can aid in reputation recovery and rebuilding consumer trust. Green marketing helps forge emotional connections between consumers and brands. When consumers perceive that a company's values align with their own, they are more likely to develop loyalty and maintain long-term relationships with the brand. Green marketing allows companies to tap into consumers' desire to make a positive impact through their purchasing decisions. Green marketing serves as an educational platform, raising awareness about environmental issues, sustainable practices, and their impact on communities and ecosystems. Businesses can leverage their platforms to educate consumers about the broader implications of their choices, inspiring them to take more conscious and responsible actions beyond product purchases. In competitive markets, green marketing provides a unique differentiator. Businesses that embrace sustainable practices and communicate them effectively stand out from the crowd, capturing the attention of environmentally conscious consumers seeking products and services that align with their values. Businesses that champion green marketing contribute to shaping regulatory and policy landscapes. Their active commitment to sustainability can influence policymakers to implement stricter environmental regulations or incentivize sustainable practices through favorable policies. This, in turn, can create a more supportive environment for sustainable business operations.

Investors are increasingly evaluating environmental and social performance when making investment decisions. Businesses that demonstrate a commitment to sustainability through green marketing are likely to attract socially responsible investors, enhancing their access to capital and financial support. As the concept of the circular economy gains momentum, green marketing provides a platform for businesses to communicate their transition from a linear production model to one that emphasizes reuse, recycling, and minimizing waste. This transition not only aligns with sustainability principles but also enhances business resilience by reducing reliance on finite resources (Suki and Suki, 2019). The importance of green marketing encompasses a broad spectrum of benefits, ranging from risk mitigation and employee engagement to innovation facilitation and regulatory influence. As businesses navigate an increasingly environmentally conscious landscape, green marketing serves as a compass that guides them toward sustainable practices, ethical leadership, and the preservation of our planet for future generations. By capitalizing on the multifaceted advantages of green marketing, companies contribute to a more sustainable and equitable global ecosystem.

Green Marketing Broader Context Towards Library Information

The article can serve as an educational resource within the library's collection. Patrons interested in topics related to green marketing, sustainability, or business practices can access this article for research and learning purposes. Librarians can use the article as a reference when assisting patrons in finding information on green marketing or sustainable business practices. It can help them provide up-to-date and credible sources to users. For academic libraries, the article can be used to support coursework related to marketing, sustainability, or environmental studies. Faculty members can recommend or assign this article to students as part of their curriculum. Libraries that are committed to sustainability and environmental responsibility can use the article to promote their own efforts in adopting green practices. It can be part of a collection of resources showcasing the library's commitment to eco-friendly initiatives. Libraries often host events, workshops, or discussions on various topics. An article on green marketing can serve as a reference or resource for such events, fostering community engagement and awareness of sustainable business practices. Librarians responsible for collection development can use the article as an example when making decisions about acquiring more resources related to green marketing and sustainability (Xiangyuan and Tzesan, 2021). The article might be relevant not only to marketing but also to other fields, such as environmental science, economics, or ethics. Green marketing can benefit library information by enriching the library's collection, supporting research and education, and aligning with the library's goals, whether they involve promoting sustainability or serving the needs of patrons interested in this topic.

THEORETICAL FRAMEWORK

Green marketing and sustainable development are intricately connected concepts that share a common goal: the harmonious coexistence of economic growth, environmental preservation, and societal well-being. Green marketing, characterized by the promotion of eco-friendly products, practices, and values, serves as a catalyst for achieving sustainable development objectives. It explores the dynamic relationship between green marketing and sustainable development, highlighting how businesses can leverage green marketing strategies to drive positive environmental, social, and economic outcomes.

Figure 1. Theoretical framework for green marketing's path to a sustainable future

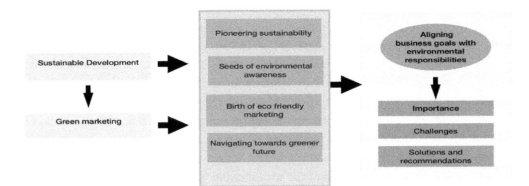

- **Environmental Stewardship**: Green marketing emphasizes the adoption of environmentally responsible practices, such as resource conservation, reduced emissions, and sustainable sourcing. By promoting eco-friendly products and processes, businesses contribute directly to sustainable development goals related to climate action, clean water and sanitation, responsible consumption and production, and life on land and underwater. These initiatives work in tandem to ensure the preservation of ecosystems and the planet's finite resources.
- **Consumer Education and Awareness:** One of the key tenets of green marketing is educating consumers about the environmental impact of their choices. This education fosters awareness and empowers consumers to make informed decisions aligned with sustainable development objectives. By showcasing the long-term benefits of eco-friendly options, businesses encourage behaviors that promote sustainable consumption patterns, which are essential for achieving goals related to biodiversity, climate change mitigation, and responsible production and consumption.
- **Innovation and Circular Economy:** Green marketing encourages businesses to innovate and develop products that minimize waste, optimize resource use, and adhere to the principles of the circular economy. This shift towards circularity, where products are designed for longevity, repairability, and recyclability, aligns with sustainable development goals focused on reducing waste, conserving resources, and promoting sustainable economic growth.
- **Social Responsibility and Equity:** Sustainable development encompasses social dimensions as well. Green marketing goes beyond environmental considerations by promoting ethical practices such as fair labor standards, community engagement, and support for marginalized groups. By addressing social inequalities and ensuring ethical treatment throughout supply chains, businesses contribute to goals related to social equity, decent work, and reduced inequalities.

Synergies and Mutual Benefits

- **Consumer Demand and Market Trends:** As consumer preferences shift towards eco-friendly options, green marketing capitalizes on this trend to drive business success. Aligning with sustainable development goals helps businesses stay relevant and responsive to consumer demand, fostering a market that prioritizes responsible consumption and production.

- **Long-Term Business Viability:** Sustainable development focuses on long-term viability, and green marketing strategies echo this approach. Businesses that integrate sustainability into their core operations are better equipped to withstand changing regulations, consumer expectations, and resource availability. This long-term perspective enhances business resilience and continuity.
- **Shared Responsibility and Collaboration:** Both green marketing and sustainable development recognize the need for collective action. Collaboration among businesses, governments, NGOs, and consumers is essential to address complex global challenges. Green marketing campaigns can serve as platforms for raising awareness, encouraging collaboration, and driving multi-stakeholder efforts.

While the alignment of green marketing and sustainable development is promising, challenges include the risk of greenwashing, complexities in measuring impact, and ensuring authenticity. Additionally, balancing short-term profitability with long-term sustainability goals requires strategic planning and a commitment to responsible business practices.

- **Greenwashing:** Perhaps one of the most significant challenges of green marketing is the risk of greenwashing, wherein companies exaggerate or falsely claim their products or practices to be more environmentally friendly than they actually are. This deceptive practice erodes consumer trust and tarnishes a company's reputation. To counter greenwashing, businesses must ensure that their sustainability claims are substantiated, transparent, and genuinely aligned with their practices.
- **Complexity of Messaging:** Communicating complex environmental and sustainability concepts to consumers in a clear and understandable manner can be a challenge. The language used in green marketing campaigns must strike a balance between being informative and accessible to a diverse audience. Simplifying intricate eco-friendly features without oversimplifying the issues requires careful messaging and creative communication strategies.
- **Consumer Skepticism:** Years of exposure to deceptive advertising and unsubstantiated claims have led to consumer skepticism regarding green marketing. Many consumers are wary of being misled by "green" products or services. Overcoming this skepticism requires consistent and authentic efforts to demonstrate a genuine commitment to sustainability. Businesses must back up their claims with tangible actions and transparent reporting.
- **Competitive Market and Differentiation:** In a crowded market, differentiating genuinely eco-friendly products from those that merely claim to be green can be challenging. Additionally, businesses that have authentically adopted green practices may find it difficult to stand out. Achieving effective differentiation amidst green noise requires innovative marketing strategies that highlight unique selling points and emphasize transparency.
- **Balancing Profitability and Sustainability:** Striking a balance between profitability and sustainability is an ongoing challenge in green marketing. While sustainable practices can lead to long-term benefits, some eco-friendly options may initially come with higher costs due to investments in research, development, and sourcing. Businesses need to navigate these financial considerations while ensuring their commitment to sustainability remains steadfast.
- **Lack of Consumer Awareness and Education:** Consumer understanding of sustainability concepts can vary significantly. Many consumers may lack awareness about the environmental impact of their choices or may not fully comprehend the benefits of eco-friendly products. Green market-

ing campaigns must also serve as educational platforms, providing consumers with the information they need to make informed choices.

- **Perceived Sacrifice of Quality or Convenience:** Some consumers associate sustainable products with compromises in quality, performance, or convenience. Overcoming this perception requires businesses to prioritize the development of eco-friendly products that meet or exceed the standards set by conventional alternatives. Effective communication about the benefits of sustainability, such as durability and long-term cost savings, can help mitigate this challenge.

- **Supply Chain Complexities:** Ensuring sustainability throughout the supply chain can be complex, especially for businesses with extensive and global supply networks. Ethical sourcing, responsible production practices, and reducing carbon footprints require close collaboration with suppliers, which may present logistical challenges and necessitate significant changes in operational processes.

- **Evolving Regulations and Standards:** Environmental regulations and standards are constantly evolving. Keeping up with these changes and ensuring compliance can be challenging for businesses engaged in green marketing. Staying informed about shifting legal requirements and adjusting practices accordingly is crucial to avoiding legal and reputational risks.

- **Short-Term vs. Long-Term Gains:** Green marketing often focuses on long-term sustainability, which may not always align with the short-term goals of businesses seeking immediate profits. Convincing stakeholders, including shareholders and investors, about the long-term benefits of sustainable practices requires clear communication about the strategic advantages and ethical imperatives.

- **Complex Supply Chains and Traceability:** Green marketing often involves making claims about the sustainability of a product's entire lifecycle, from sourcing materials to production and disposal. However, tracing the environmental impact throughout complex supply chains can be challenging. Businesses must work with suppliers to ensure transparency, ethical practices, and accurate data collection to substantiate their claims.

- **Cultural and Regional Variations:** Consumer attitudes towards sustainability can vary significantly across cultures and regions. What is considered environmentally friendly in one culture might not resonate the same way in another. This challenge requires businesses to tailor their green marketing strategies to local contexts and sensitivities, taking into account cultural nuances and regional preferences.

- **Measurement and Metrics:** Measuring the actual impact of a product's environmental footprint can be intricate. Metrics like carbon emissions, water usage, and resource depletion are interconnected and influenced by various factors. Determining the most appropriate metrics and accurately quantifying the environmental benefits of a product can be a complex task, requiring specialized knowledge and methodologies.

- **Limited Consumer Understanding of Sustainable Metrics:** While businesses may use specific metrics and certifications to validate their sustainable practices, consumers might not fully understand these metrics. For instance, consumers may not grasp the significance of a certain carbon footprint reduction percentage. Effective green marketing must translate these metrics into relatable terms and educate consumers about their meaning and importance.

Navigating the challenges of green marketing requires a strategic and holistic approach that integrates authenticity, transparency, education, and innovation. As businesses grapple with complexities ranging from greenwashing to supply chain traceability, they must prioritize ethical practices, build consumer trust, and drive positive change through sustainable initiatives. By recognizing and addressing these challenges, businesses can truly harness the power of green marketing to make meaningful contributions to environmental preservation and societal well-being. Green marketing and sustainable development are not isolated concepts but rather interconnected strategies that hold the potential to shape a more sustainable and equitable world. By leveraging green marketing strategies, businesses can contribute to environmental preservation, social well-being, and economic growth. The synergistic relationship between green marketing and sustainable development underscores the transformative power of responsible business practices in shaping a brighter future for the planet and its inhabitants. IKEA is a prominent example of a company that has embraced green marketing and sustainability practices. They have implemented several initiatives to promote environmental responsibility and have effectively communicated these efforts to their customers.

CASE STUDY: IKEA'S GREEN MARKETING STRATEGY

IKEA is a Swedish furniture retailer with a global presence, known for its affordable and functional furniture and home goods. In recent years, the company has put a strong emphasis on sustainability and green marketing.

Initiatives and Strategies

- **Sustainable Sourcing:** IKEA has committed to sourcing materials responsibly and sustainably. They aim to use renewable and recycled materials in their products. For example, they promote the use of certified wood from sustainable forests.
- **Energy Efficiency:** IKEA has invested in renewable energy sources, such as solar and wind power, to reduce their carbon footprint. They are working towards being energy-positive, generating more renewable energy than they consume.
- **Product Innovation:** The company designs products with sustainability in mind. They have introduced energy-efficient LED lighting, and their "SVALNÄS" wall-mounted shelving system is made from sustainable.
- **Circular Economy Initiatives:** IKEA is focusing on creating a circular economy by designing products for longevity, repairability, and recyclability. They have introduced initiatives like mattress recycling and are exploring ways to make products more easily disassembled and recycled.
- **Sustainable Packaging:** IKEA is working to reduce the environmental impact of its packaging. They have introduced "flat-pack" designs that minimize packaging waste and use more sustainable materials.
- **Renewable Energy Retailing:** IKEA has also ventured into selling solar panels and home battery storage solutions to customers, enabling them to generate their own renewable energy.
- **Marketing Campaigns:** IKEA's green marketing efforts are evident in their marketing campaigns and communications. They highlight the sustainability of their products, such as their commitment to using renewable energy in their stores and factories.

- **Transparency:** IKEA provides information to customers about the materials used in their products and their environmental impact. This transparency builds trust and helps customers make more informed purchasing decisions.

Results and Discussion

IKEA's green marketing strategy has had a significant impact on the company's reputation and consumer perception. By aligning their brand with sustainability and environmental responsibility, they have attracted environmentally conscious consumers and created a positive image. Their efforts to promote circular economy principles and reduce waste have also positioned them as a leader in sustainability within the retail industry.

- **Commitment to Authenticity:** IKEA's success in green marketing comes from their genuine commitment to sustainability. Authenticity is key to building trust with consumers.
- **Transparency:** Transparency about sourcing, manufacturing, and the environmental impact of products builds credibility and reassures consumers.
- **Innovation and Design:** Incorporating sustainable practices into product design and innovation allows a company to offer attractive, functional, and environmentally friendly products.
- **Educational Content:** Providing customers with information about the benefits of sustainable choices helps them understand the value of green products.
- **Long-Term Perspective:** IKEA's approach is rooted in long-term sustainability, which aligns with growing consumer demands for responsible and ethical business practices.

IKEA's green marketing strategy serves as an example of how a company can successfully integrate sustainability into its brand identity and engage consumers in environmentally responsible practices.

Figure 2 present the line graph of IKEA's climate footprint in million tons of CO_2 equivalents (CO_2 eq) from FY16 to FY22, based on the IKEA Sustainability Report 2022. The graph shows that IKEA's

Figure 2. Climate footprints over the years

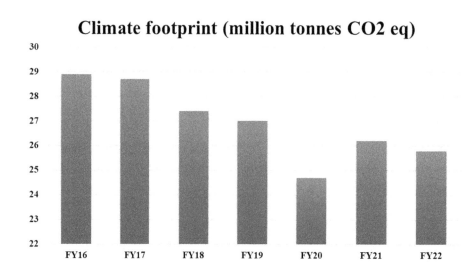

Figure 3. Amount invested towards sustainable development goals

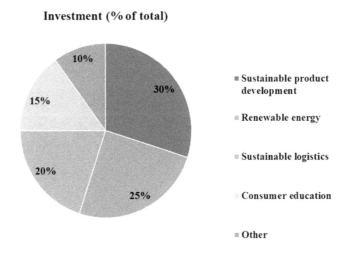

climate footprint has decreased by 12% since FY16, despite an increase in sales. This is due to a number of factors, including increased use of renewable energy, improved energy efficiency of products, and slightly lower production volumes between FY21-22. IKEA is committed to reducing its climate footprint further and achieving net-zero emissions by 2040.

Figure 3 presents the IKEA invested the most in sustainable materials in 2022, followed by renewable energy, circular economy, and sustainable transportation. Here is a brief description of each category:

- **Renewable Energy:** IKEA is investing in renewable energy sources such as solar and wind power to reduce its reliance on fossil fuels.
- **Sustainable Materials:** IKEA is using more sustainable materials in its products, such as recycled wood and bamboo.
- **Circular Economy:** IKEA is working to create a more circular economy for its products, which means that products are designed to be reused, recycled, or repaired at the end of their life cycle.
- **Sustainable Transportation:** IKEA is working to reduce the environmental impact of its transportation operations. For example, it is using more fuel-efficient vehicles and investing in electric vehicles.

Figure 4 shows that IKEA's net profit increased by 10% in FY21 and 12% in FY22, after applying sustainability. This suggests that IKEA's sustainability initiatives are having a positive impact on its financial performance. It is important to note that there are a number of factors that can affect a company's net profit, including market conditions, economic growth, and competitor activity. Therefore, it is difficult to say definitively that IKEA's sustainability initiatives are the sole reason for its increase in net profit. However, the graph does suggest that IKEA's sustainability initiatives are not having a negative impact on its financial performance and may even be having a positive impact. IKEA is committed to continuing to invest in sustainability initiatives. In FY22, IKEA invested EUR 2.1 billion in renewable energy, forestry, and other sustainability initiatives. IKEA believes that investing in sustainability is essential for its long-term success.

Figure 4. Net profit percentage over years

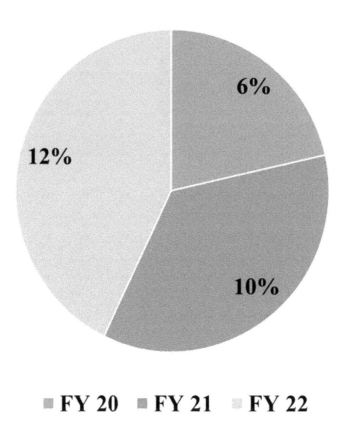

Increase in Net profit %

6%

12%

10%

■ FY 20   ■ FY 21   ■ FY 22

SOLUTIONS AND RECOMMENDATIONS

It is important to note that the success of green marketing strategies largely depends on their alignment with a company's specific goals and context. Here are some key recommendations to consider:

- **Customer-Centric Approach:** Tailor green marketing efforts to the preferences and values of your target audience. Understand their environmental concerns and communicate how your products or services address them. This personalized approach enhances consumer engagement and loyalty.
- **Transparency and Certification:** Be transparent about the sustainability efforts. Seek relevant certifications like organic, Fair Trade, or energy efficiency labels to provide credibility to their green claims. Authenticity builds trust with consumers.
- **Life cycle Assessment:** Conduct a comprehensive life cycle assessment of the products or services to identify areas for improvement. This holistic view helps in reducing environmental impacts and achieving sustainability goals.

- **Collaboration and Supply Chain Management:** Collaborate with suppliers and partners who share the commitment to sustainability. Implement eco-friendly practices throughout the supply chain to minimize environmental footprint.
- **Innovation and Research and Development:** Invest in research and development to create innovative, sustainable solutions. This can lead to new product offerings and improved environmental performance, setting you apart from competitors.
- **Educational Initiatives:** Educate both your employees and consumers about the benefits of green products and practices. Knowledge empowers consumers to make informed choices and fosters a culture of sustainability within your organization.
- **Metrics and Reporting:** Establish key performance indicators (KPIs) to measure the impact of your green marketing efforts. Regularly report on progress and share successes to demonstrate your commitment to sustainability.
- **Adaptability and Flexibility:** Be prepared to adapt to evolving consumer expectations and changing environmental regulations. Stay nimble and proactive in adjusting your green marketing strategies accordingly.
- **Government and Industry Engagement:** Engage with relevant government bodies and industry associations to stay informed about upcoming regulations and best practices. Active participation can help shape favorable policies and standards.
- **Continuous Improvement:** Commit to a cycle of continuous improvement in your sustainability initiatives. Regularly reassess your environmental goals and make necessary adjustments to stay on track.

By incorporating these recommendations into your green marketing strategy, you can not only drive positive change within your organization but also contribute to a more sustainable future while gaining a competitive edge in the marketplace.

CONCLUSION

In conclusion, green marketing stands as a powerful force reshaping the future of business, as exemplified by pioneering companies like IKEA. Originating from the growing awareness of environmental issues in the late 20th century, green marketing has evolved into a strategic imperative for businesses worldwide. IKEA's commitment to sustainability, from eco-friendly materials to energy-efficient designs, serves as a compelling example of how embracing green principles can drive success. This transformative shift towards sustainability isn't merely a trend; it's an essential component of corporate strategy. Businesses that align with environmental responsibility not only meet the expectations of conscious consumers but also adapt to a changing regulatory landscape, ultimately securing a brighter future for themselves and the planet. As we move forward, green marketing will continue to drive innovation, responsible consumption, and sustainable production, setting the stage for a greener and more prosperous future for all. Incorporating an article on green marketing into library information provides a valuable resource for patrons and librarians alike. It serves as an educational tool, supports research, and can align with a library's commitment to sustainability. By making such articles available, libraries play a vital role in disseminating knowledge on environmentally responsible business practices and contributing to a more informed and eco-conscious community.

ACKNOWLEDGMENT

I wish to extend my profound appreciation to my family, whose unwavering support and unwavering belief in me have been the bedrock of my journey. I am deeply indebted to my esteemed mentor, Prof. Jayant Kumar Chakraborty, for his invaluable guidance, unwavering mentorship, and remarkable patience. Furthermore, I wish to convey my heartfelt gratitude to Prof. Keshav Sinha for his profound contributions and invaluable insights that have significantly enriched my academic pursuits.

REFERENCES

Alkhatib, S., Kecskés, P., & Keller, V. (2023). Green Marketing in the Digital Age: A Systematic Literature Review. *Sustainability (Basel)*, *15*(16), 12369. doi:10.3390u151612369

Amin, M. R., Arif, I., & Rahman, M. M. (2012). Green Marketing Practices for Sustainable Business Growth in Bangladesh: A Case Study of Dhaka City. *Global Disclosure of Economics and Business*, *1*(2), 96–102. doi:10.18034/gdeb.v1i2.197

Anitha, M. P., & Vijai, C. (2021). Green Marketing: Benefits and Challenges. *European Journal of Molecular and Clinical Medicine*, *7*(11), 2020.

Aulia, N., Gunawan, J., & Sumarsono, M. (2018). Green Marketing, Ecolabel and Purchase Intention on Food Products during. *COVID*, 19.

Bestari, D. K. P., & Butarbutar, D. A. (2021). Implementation of Green Marketing Strategies and Green Purchase Behavior as Efforts to Strengthen the Competitiveness of MSMEs in Indonesia. Budapest International Research and Critics Institute (BIRCI-Journal): Humanities and Social Sciences, 4(1), 243-254. doi:10.33258/birci.v4i1.1588

Bhattacharyya, J. (2023). The structure of sustainability marketing research: A bibliometric review and directions for future research. *Asia-Pacific Journal of Business Administration*, *15*(2), 245–286. doi:10.1108/APJBA-06-2021-0239

Canavari, M., & Coderoni, S. (2019). Green marketing strategies in the dairy sector: Consumer-stated preferences for carbon footprint labels. *Strategic Change*, *28*(4), 233–240. doi:10.1002/jsc.2264

Choudhary, A., & Gokarn, S. (2013). Green marketing: A means for sustainable development. Journal of Arts. *Science & Commerce*, *4*(3), 3.

Geng, Y., & Maimaituerxun, M. (2022). Research progress of green marketing in sustainable consumption based on CiteSpace analysis. *SAGE Open*, *12*(3), 21582440221119835. doi:10.1177/21582440221119835

Gupta, N. E., Kumar, K., & Sinha, K. (2023). The Nexus of War, Violence, and Rights: A History of War-Torn Afghanistan. In Handbook of Research on War Policies, Strategies, and Cyber Wars (pp. 334-351). IGI Global.

Jaiswal, G., Karmakar, M., & Sinha, K. (2023). Yoga: A Stress Removal Toolkit During War From the Women's Perspective. In Acceleration of the Biopsychosocial Model in Public Health (pp. 137-167). IGI Global.

Jaiswal, G., & Sinha, K. (2023). Yoga: An Ancient Healing Approach for Cyclical Mastalgia. In Perspectives on Coping Strategies for Menstrual and Premenstrual Distress (pp. 237-261). IGI Global.

Karmakar, M., Priya, A., Sinha, K., & Verma, M. (2022, December). Shrinkable Cryptographic Technique Using Involutory Function for Image Encryption. In *International Conference on Advanced Network Technologies and Intelligent Computing* (pp. 275-289). Springer Nature Switzerland.

Kaur, B., Gangwar, V. P., & Dash, G. (2022). Green marketing strategies, environmental attitude, and green buying intention: A multi-group analysis in an emerging economy context. *Sustainability (Basel)*, *14*(10), 6107. doi:10.3390u14106107

Khare, V. K., Raghuwanshi, S., Vashisht, A., Verma, P., & Chauhan, R. (2023). The importance of green management and its implication in creating sustainability performance on the small-scale industries in India. *Journal of Law and Sustainable Development*, *11*(5), e699–e699. doi:10.55908dgs.v11i5.699

Kumar, K., Singhania, D., Singh, K. P., Mishra, P., & Sinha, K. (2023). Navigating the Economic Challenges of the Russia-Ukraine Conflict on India. In Handbook of Research on War Policies, Strategies, and Cyber Wars (pp. 218-238). IGI Global. doi:10.4018/978-1-6684-6741-1.ch012

Kumar, S., Jaiswal, G., & Sinha, K. (2023). Skin Cancer Lesion Detection Using Improved CNN Techniques. In Handbook of Research on Technological Advances of Library and Information Science in Industry 5.0 (pp. 355-377). IGI Global.

Lee, Y. C., Dervishi, I., Mousa, S., Safiullin, K. I., Ruban-Lazareva, N. V., Kosov, M. E., Ponkratov, V. V., Pozdnyaev, A. S., Mikhina, E. V., & Elyakova, I. D. (2023). Sustainable Development Adoption in the High-Tech Sector: A Focus on Ecosystem Players and Their Influence. *Sustainability (Basel)*, *15*(18), 13674. doi:10.3390u151813674

Masengu, R., Bigirimana, S., Chiwaridzo, O. T., Bensson, R., & Blossom, C. (Eds.). (2023). *Sustainable Marketing, Branding, and Reputation Management: Strategies for a Greener Future: Strategies for a Greener Future*. IGI Global.

Murin, I., Marková, I., Zelený, J., & Jaďuďová, J. (2015). Green marketing as a tool influencing consumerś behavior: Slovak case study of regional mark preference. *Procedia Economics and Finance*, *34*, 260–267. doi:10.1016/S2212-5671(15)01628-7

Nassani, A. A., Yousaf, Z., Grigorescu, A., & Popa, A. (2023). Green and Environmental Marketing Strategies and Ethical Consumption: Evidence from the Tourism Sector. *Sustainability (Basel)*, *15*(16), 12199. doi:10.3390u151612199

Nozari, H., Szmelter-Jarosz, A., & Ghahremani-Nahr, J. (2021). The Ideas of Sustainable and Green Marketing Based on the Internet of Everything—The Case of the Dairy Industry. *Future Internet*, *13*(10), 266. doi:10.3390/fi13100266

Park, E., Kwon, J., & Kim, S. B. (2021). Green marketing strategies on online platforms: A mixed approach of experiment design and topic modeling. *Sustainability (Basel)*, *13*(8), 4494. doi:10.3390u13084494

Priya, A., Sharma, S., Sinha, K., & Yogesh, Y. (2023, March). Community Detection in Networks: A Comparative study. In *2023 International Conference on Device Intelligence, Computing and Communication Technologies (DICCT)* (pp. 505-510). IEEE. 10.1109/DICCT56244.2023.10110206

Sinha, K. (2023). The Metaverse and Digital Libraries: Ensuring Safe and Secure Access to Information. In Handbook of Research on Advancements of Contactless Technology and Service Innovation in Library and Information Science (pp. 1-22). IGI Global.

Spasojevic, J., & Spasojevic, M. (2018). Implementation Of Corporate Social Responsibility And Marketing of UNIQA In The Republic Of Serbia. *Economic and Social Development: Book of Proceedings*, 320-327.

Suki, N. M., & Suki, N. M. (2019). Correlations between awareness of green marketing, corporate social responsibility, product image, corporate reputation, and consumer purchase intention. In *Corporate social responsibility: Concepts, methodologies, tools, and applications* (pp. 143–154). IGI Global. doi:10.4018/978-1-5225-6192-7.ch008

Xiangyuan, A., & Tzesan, O. (2021). The Impact of Environmental Corporate Social Responsibility on Enterprise Performance——Implications for Sustainable Development Strategy. In *E3S Web of Conferences* (Vol. 251, p. 02072). EDP Sciences. doi:10.1051/e3sconf/202125102072

KEY TERMS AND DEFINITIONS

Corporate Social Responsibility: Goes beyond profits, emphasizing a company's ethical obligations to society, including philanthropy and ethical business practices.

Eco-Friendly Products: Are designed with minimal environmental impact, often using recycled materials and sustainable manufacturing processes.

Eco-Labeling: Informs consumers about a product's environmental impact, such as energy efficiency or organic certification.

Environmental Responsibility: Means reducing our carbon footprint and protecting natural resources for future generations.

Green Consumer Behavior: Involves making eco-conscious choices, such as buying organic, locally sourced products and reducing energy consumption.

Green Product Development: Involves creating innovative products that minimize resource use, energy consumption, and environmental harm.

Greenwashing: Is when a company falsely claims to be environmentally friendly to attract customers without genuinely sustainable practices.

Sustainable Branding: Is a marketing strategy that promotes a company's environmental and social responsibility commitment.

Sustainable Packaging: Prioritizes materials like biodegradable plastics, recycled paper, and minimalistic designs to reduce waste and pollution.

Chapter 9
Toward a Convergence of Memory Institutions in the Indonesian Presidential Library

Muhammad Rosyihan Hendrawan
https://orcid.org/0000-0003-0438-2571
University of Brawijaya, Indonesia

Muhammad Shobaruddin
University of Brawijaya, Indonesia

ABSTRACT

Libraries, archives, and museums (LAMs) as memory institutions share valuable existence to preserve advanced national cultural heritage. Various causes drove LAM convergence in various cases. The Bung Karno Library in Blitar City, one of the Presidential Libraries in the Republic of Indonesia, helps explain the memory institution's convergence. The case studies indicate that collaboration and convergence face shared challenges. The authors propose that collaboration between these organizations is complicated. In the Bung Karno Library, cohesive procedure and accessibility were essential to service the user. However, removing boundaries between memory institutions in Bung Karno Library was universally accepted as necessary to improve user service and promote cultural heritage. These actions might lead to future research and boost the convergence's worth. To balance professional capability and integrate multiple systems, the researched institutions are making significant efforts. A fine balance appears needed to achieve and maintain successful convergence initiatives.

INTRODUCTION

Memory institutions, including libraries, archives, and museums (LAMs), share similar administrative responsibilities and engage in activities aimed at preserving cultural and historical assets created by advanced societies. These institutions play a crucial role in organizing and managing information, therefore transforming themselves into hubs of knowledge. Given and McTavish (2010) state that LAMs,

DOI: 10.4018/979-8-3693-2841-5.ch009

commonly known as memory institutions, fulfill the role of preserving, accumulating, and overseeing collective memory. These institutions manifest in diverse physical manifestations, such as museums that amass a wide range of artifacts, libraries that curate published and text-based library materials, and archives that preserve unpublished materials. Rasmussen and Hjørland (2023) assert that LAMs have been in existence since ancient times, exhibiting a wide range of sizes and configurations. These institutions often provide challenges in terms of their precise delineation and differentiation from one another. Since the beginning of the 21st century, there has been a growing tendency to use the abbreviation LAM to refer to these institutions collectively. This reflects a heightened interest in seeing them as a unified entity, driven in part by the apparent convergence between them.

In Europe and North America, the concept of institutional memory or cultural heritage institutions is defined by establishments such as libraries, archives, and museums. In nations such as Australia and New Zealand, the designation LAMs refers to diverse assemblages of entities or establishments that possess a societal obligation and purpose of amassing and exhibiting cultural and environmental artifacts (Davis, 2016; Mabe & Potgieter, 2021). The majority of memory institutions get public funding and are responsible for serving the government, the education sector, and society at large (Robinson, 2019). However, it is worth noting that there are memory institutions, such as libraries, archives, and museums, which are privately financed and administered but accessible to the general public (Bafadhal & Hendrawan, 2021).

Indonesia is well recognized for its extensive historical background, diverse cultural heritage, abundant natural resources, and other notable attributes. The abundance of wealth presents a substantial prospect for the populace of Indonesia. As individuals who are part of both the Indonesian and worldwide communities, we are able to perceive and use these valuable resources via a medium often referred to as information. The process of gathering and analyzing data, including textual and other media associated with an event, is the basis for obtaining information. The use of cultural heritage management may be instrumental in the effective management of primary source materials inside memory institutions, including LAMs.

Cultural heritage management procedures facilitate the preservation and accessibility of distinctive hidden collections, as well as print and digital resources, by using both traditional and creative methods. This is particularly important in the current digital information era when the need for increased collection preservation and access is paramount. As human society progresses, there arises a corresponding need to collect, store, administer, and safeguard the products of communal recollection. Consequently, there has been a proliferation of various institutions responsible for overseeing or administering collective memory. Hence, the role of LAMs as custodians of communal memory, including archives and museums, is integral to the community's endeavor to grasp its identity and navigate the realm of knowledge within that particular civilization.

The discussion of Indonesia is inherently intertwined with the prominent figure of Soekarno or Bung Karno. Due to his significant contributions as a prominent national hero and the first president of the Republic of Indonesia, He may be regarded as a crucial source in the context of Indonesian history. The Bung Karno Library, which is one of Indonesia's presidential libraries, is under the direct maintenance and coordination of the National Library of the Republic of Indonesia. It is located in Blitar City, which is situated in the East Java Province. The Bung Karno Library integrates the functions of memory institutions, including LAMs (Kharisma, 2023). The primary objective of the Bung Karno Library is to serve as a hub for scholarly inquiry, advancement, conservation, and promotion of the ideals associated with

Soekarno, the first President of Indonesia. The objectives of this endeavor include the provision of public information services and the management of resources or collections for the benefit of the general public.

The Bung Karno Library prioritizes collection management that focuses on President Soekarno. The primary attraction of this library is its function as a museum dedicated to the presentation of artifacts and the biography of President Soekarno. This feature sets it apart from the majority of other libraries, which often do not provide such services. In addition, the library incorporates an archival group component that oversees the maintenance of dynamic archives inside internal institutions. The library adeptly employs the concept of convergence, capitalizing on its many advantages. Nevertheless, other constraints exist in the practical implementation of policies aimed at advancing the notion of convergence across memory institutions.

BACKGROUND

Library as Memory Institutions

As stated by Pendit (2019), a library is an establishment responsible for the administration and management of a collection of books and other materials. Libraries are integral to the preservation and dissemination of written works, playing a crucial role in documenting and facilitating societal advancements. In the work of Osburn (2009), an endeavor is made to construct an investigation pertaining to the philosophy of libraries and philosophy itself. The author seeks to elucidate the underlying reasons for the existence of libraries, moving beyond mere inquiries into the definition and operational mechanisms of these institutions. The library is often characterized as an institution that engages in three fundamental processes: acquisition, organization, and dissemination of literary materials. Osburn seeks to understand the reasons for the enduring presence of these three activities and the broader philosophical foundations that motivate libraries and their three core functions.

Rubin and Rubin (2020) delineate five discrete library functions. The process of resource identification, selection, and acquisition acts as a mechanism for the storage and management of information sources, including both printed and audiovisual materials that are physically located inside the library. The assemblage of materials is the principal asset of the library. The collection comprises digital materials that may be accessed both inside and outside the physical boundaries of the library. To optimize accessibility, it is important to get resources and efficiently administer them via organization, description, and presentation methods that facilitate users in locating them successfully. The promotion of accessibility involves the incorporation of several components, including the supply of bibliographic descriptions and classifications of superior quality, in conjunction with the use of efficient search engines. The integration of these several components enables the effective administration and availability of information sources, hence enhancing the overall user experience.

Within the domain of collection conservation and preservation, libraries have a unique responsibility to ensure the perpetuation of knowledge and information, regardless of their format, for future availability. Each format is supported by certain requirements that are designed to ensure continuous accessibility and use by providing appropriate maintenance for the managed collections. The library's institutional culture and educational activities function as a central point for anyone wishing to gain information (Lankes, 2016). The library provides educational activities to its clients in order to facilitate the acquisition of crucial knowledge. Operations, administrative, and operational activities are fundamental elements within library organizations as a whole. The efficient support and administration of library operations need the incorporation of several vital components, including budget management, leadership, human resources, public relations, information technology, promotions, and security.

The following functions delineate the priority of information source management inside libraries, beginning with the discovery of these sources and culminating in their operationalization for users. The library plays a crucial role as a primary store of knowledge in society, serving as a gathering place where people come together to access information on a wide array of topics that are relevant to their particular interests and requirements.

Archives as Memory Institutions

The archive serves as the secondary memory institution in this context. Archives serve the purpose of elucidating historical events and safeguarding them for future generations, ensuring the perpetuation of a sense of unity, consistency, and logical progression within the community. Archives function as a communal entity that consolidates historical records and operates as a facilitative instrument via the use of memory texts (Novia & Liaison, 2012). Schwartz and Cook (2002) argue that archives serve as a means of records control, embodying a historical and scientific perspective and contributing to the communal memory and national identity of individuals, communities, and society as a whole. Within this context, archives include a range of significant elements such as history, memory, identity, and power.

The term archives may be traced back to its etymological origins in the Greek word "*archeon*," which underwent further modifications to "*archea*" and eventually returned to its original form as "*archeon*." According to Hendrawan and Ulum (2017), "*archaea*" may be defined as papers or notes that are specifically associated with problem-solving. Archives cover a broad spectrum of actions and events, recorded in many forms and media, that correspond with improvements in information and communication technologies (Duranti & Franks, 2015). The creation and acquisition of these archives are carried out by governmental organizations and administrations, educational institutions, companies, associations, communities, and people as they participate in the implementation of social, national, and governmental activities. Archives are characterized by their enduring nature and ongoing value since they include materials of documentary or historical importance that are impervious to destruction.

Museum Library as Memory Institutions

The museum is the third memory institution examined in this chapter. Museums are esteemed establishments that engage in the acquisition, preservation, interpretation, and exhibition of enduring collections of historical, cultural, and educational artifacts. Museums are establishments that serve as repositories of information pertaining to the progression of human existence and the advancement of civilization throughout many epochs. Buhalis (2020) asserts that museums are now required to integrate management and user research, together with intelligent technology, in order to provide a distinct experiential encounter for visitors or users. A museum is an establishment or site that provides unrestricted access to information for the general public, is easily accessible, engages in the safeguarding and protection of artifacts, disseminates cultural and historical legacy, and has a role in fostering education, scholarly inquiry, and leisure activities (Brown & Mairesse, 2018).

Moreover, as stated by Sodaro (2018), museums serve as a communal space for the preservation of collective memories, the examination of historical and political narratives, the observation of social changes, and the development of national identity. Since its establishment in the late 18th century, the state has used museums as a means of exerting control over memory and history. According to Denton (2014), the majority of museums use visual language as a means of conveying narratives pertaining to historical events.

Museums are more than just places for collecting, preserving, and displaying cultural and spiritual heritage; they have evolved into multifunctional hubs that integrate education, recreation, entertainment, and social significance, and they can even serve as agents of human cultural transformation (Hendrawan & Bafadhal, 2022). The Extraordinary General Assembly of The International Council of Museums (ICOM) accepted the proposal for the revised museum definition on 24 August 2022 in Prague. After its acceptance, the revised definition of the ICOM museum is as follows: a museum is a not-for-profit, permanent institution in the service of society that researches, collects, conserves, interprets, and exhibits tangible and intangible heritage. Open to the public, accessible, and inclusive, museums foster diversity and sustainability. They operate and communicate ethically, professionally, and with the participation of communities, offering varied experiences for education, enjoyment, reflection, and knowledge-sharing (ICOM, 2022).

In contemporary times, modern museums serve as reflections of social phenomena, assuming the role of catalysts for change. They effectively draw attention to various behaviors and events that foster societal advancement, as well as groups dedicated to promoting peace and fostering unity. In order to adapt to contemporary culture and changing urban dynamics, museums use distinct resources to enhance their responsiveness and maintain their significance as valuable contributors to social and cultural progress (Bafadhal & Hendrawan, 2021). In order to effectively engage with individuals and foster intercultural connections, museums are required to adapt to evolving cultural practices.

In Indonesia, the memory above institutions continued to be implemented as independent entities. Efforts are necessary to facilitate the integration of memory institutions in Indonesia, with the aim of enhancing public accessibility to information managed by these organizations. The integration of libraries, archives, and museums (LAMs) facilitates the seamless retrieval of information for users, eliminating the need to navigate several institutions. According to Sudarsono (2016), it can be inferred that the integration of the collections from the three memory institutions is necessary in order to establish an effective storage and retrieval system.

The dissemination of information and knowledge is characterized by its dynamic and expeditious nature, enabling anyone to access both historical and contemporary material. The major goal of LAMs, or cultural heritage institutions such as libraries, archives, and museums, is to provide people with access to information. According to Hadi and Hendrawan (2022), the current proliferation of technology facilitating the exchange of data across various memory organizations is having a detrimental impact on society. This chapter provides a case study on the convergence of best practices throughout memory institutions, specifically focusing on the Bung Karno Proclaimer Library. The construction of this library was motivated by a genuine desire to cultivate Indonesian nationalism in light of globalism, with a profound reverence for Bung Karno and his visionary concepts in forming the bedrock of Indonesian nationalism. As a result, the Bung Karno Library has evolved as a central focus for academic endeavors and the fostering of nationalistic sentiments in Indonesia.

BEST PRACTICE AT THE BUNG KARNO LIBRARY

The Bung Karno Library serves as the Technical Implementation Unit of the National Library of the Republic of Indonesia. The commencement of the library's construction, situated in Blitar City, took place in August 2003 inside a vicinity of 11,144 square meters in close proximity to the burial site of Bung Karno. The inauguration of the Bung Karno Library Building took place on July 3, 2004, with the presence of Megawati Sukarnoputri, the President of the Republic of Indonesia, in accordance with Decree Number 4 of 2005 issued by the Head of the National Library of the Republic of Indonesia (Kharisma, 2023). The management of the Bung Karno Library is formally entrusted to the National Library of the Republic of Indonesia. In the year 2019, the Archives of the National Library of the Republic of Indonesia, which encompasses the Bung Karno Library, established an Archives Administration Team. According to Hadi and Hendrawan (2022), the establishment of the Bung Karno Library in Blitar City was predicated upon a multifaceted analysis, including historical, ideological, and empirical considerations.

From a historical perspective, the City of Blitar is inherently intertwined with the historical narrative of the Indonesian people's arduous endeavor to attain freedom. The City of Blitar has been deeply influenced by the spirit of heroism embodied by Soekarno, also known as Bung Karno, who played a pivotal role as the Proclamator and one of the prominent National Hero of the Republic of Indonesia. Throughout his life, Soekarno consistently maintained his unwavering commitment to the struggle for national independence, actively fostering a sense of nationalism among the Indonesian people. The Indonesian populace has acquired an understanding that Bung Karno's contributions across several domains have consistently held significant value, garnering recognition and appreciation from artists, legislators, and esteemed politicians worldwide.

From an ideological standpoint, the aspiration is for the establishment of the Bung Karno Library to serve as an educational resource for individuals across all societal strata, with a particular emphasis on the younger generation within the Republic of Indonesia. The objective is to foster a comprehensive and unbiased understanding of Bung Karno's ideologies, enabling future generations to recognize its significance as a national intellectual asset that should be harmonized with diverse global perspectives, key concepts, and ideologies.

According to Kharisma (2023), in the present context, it is worth noting that the establishment of the Bung Karno Library has the potential to serve as a valuable complement to the enduring significance of Bung Karno's burial site, which continues to attract pilgrims from both domestic and international spheres. Furthermore, the establishment of Bung Karno's library was very congruent with Bung Karno's inclinations, as he had a deep fondness for literature and a profound appreciation for historical knowledge. This affinity was evident in his dual role as an avid book collector and a prolific writer. Based on this line of reasoning, it is anticipated that the Bung Karno Library will effectively cater to the intellectual requirements of scholarly communities seeking to conduct comparative analyses of a nation's developmental trajectory, commencing from the cultivation of a robust national ethos to the fostering of a deep-seated patriotism that culminated in the establishment of the Republic of Indonesia.

The Bung Karno Library can offer historical facts that can substantiate authentic evidence, enabling open and objective research and study. This serves the purpose of benefiting present and future generations, allowing them to develop an appreciation for and carry forward the accomplishments of those who fought for the realization of national independence, which stands as a collective aspiration. In addition, the preservation of historical facts has significant importance for the continuity of a nation-state, as it

Figure 1. Bung Karno Monument at The Bung Karno Library Gate

enables the use of past historical events as a reference point for shaping the trajectory of the nation's future endeavors.

Situated among the gates to the Bung Karno Library, as shown in Figure 1, is a substantial Bung Karno Monument, symbolically extending a warm greeting to every visitor. The Bung Karno Library has a comprehensive collection of both print and non-print materials pertaining to Bung Karno and the wider public. Located just across the Bung Karno Library, one may find the Bung Karno Museum and Archives (Pratiwi & Setiawan, 2019). This location serves as a repository for several artifacts and archival materials pertaining to the historical legacy of Bung Karno.

In addition to the relics, the Museum also showcases a comprehensive biography of Bung Karno, chronicling his life journey from birth to the various stages of his development, including childhood, adolescence, college years, the inception of his political activism, the period of exile under Dutch Colonial rule, the era of independence, and ultimately, the culmination of his life. This biography is prominently displayed on the walls of the Museum, offering visitors a detailed account of Bung Karno's significant contributions and experiences. To enhance one's understanding of Bung Karno's persona, the museum and archives include a substantial collection of archival photographs featuring Bung Karno from his early years till his presidency. The complex above consistently attracts a diverse range of visitors on a daily basis, including individuals from both local and international locations. A portion of the individuals arrived with the intention of embarking on a pilgrimage to the burial site of Bung Karno, which is situated inside a building complex with an area of 8,985 square meters and in close proximity to the Bung Karno Library.

THE LIBRARY SECTION

The Bung Karno Library offers two primary categories of services, namely technical services and library services, both of which get assistance from the Administration Sub-Division (Pratiwi & Setiawan, 2019). According to Regulation Number 11 of 2015 issued by the Director of the National Library of the Republic of Indonesia, the Technical Instructions for Functional Positions of Librarians and Credit Numbers define technical services as a set of activities that encompass collection development, library material processing, as well as storage and maintenance of library collections. Library services include a range of activities pertaining to the provision of information services within a library setting, which are made available for use by library customers. The Bung Karno Library is entrusted with the crucial task of managing and safeguarding library contents, which the technical services department primarily executes. This substance comprises three distinct subgroups of substances, specifically: 1) Development and Preservation of Library Materials, 2) Preservation of Library Materials, and 3) Analysis of Bung Karno's Literary Collection.

The Substance of Information and Collaboration Services is a department of the Bung Karno Library that is responsible for the provision of library services. This substance consists of three distinct subgroups, each with their respective working groups. The first subgroup is known as Information and Cooperation Services, which is responsible for a range of services, including the Bung Karno Special Collection, Memorabilia Collection Services, General Collection Services, Children's Collection Services, Reference Collection Services, and Information and Complaints Services. The second subgroup is Collaboration and Promotion Libraries, which oversees various services such as Membership Services, Mobile Library Services, Book Lending Services, Library Cooperation, Development, Information Systems, Reference and Information Services.

The patrons or users of the Bung Karno Library include individuals hailing from several cities within Indonesia, as well as those from other countries, who may be categorized into three groups: local and international. The pre-pandemic period saw a higher use rate of services at the Bung Karno Library in comparison to the period during the pandemic. According to Kharisma (2023), in the year 2019, the total number of users amounted to 1,578,893 individuals, with an average daily count of 4,386 individuals. During the COVID-19 Pandemic in the years 2020 and 2021, there was a notable decline in user engagement, with a recorded loss of 587,540 individuals. Specifically, in 2020, the average daily user count amounted to 1,632 people. In 2021, there was a noticeable shift as the number of visitors started to rise, with an average of 2,277 individuals per day and a cumulative total of 819,623 people over the year. However, as shown in Figure 2, in the year 2022, the total number of users amounted to 1,276,703 individuals. In addition to using the book collection, patrons of the Bung Karno Library may avail themselves of the Memorabilia Collection housed inside the Museum. The Memorabilia Collection is the primary attraction for the majority of international visitors to the Bung Karno Library.

Figure 2. Total number of visitors to the Bung Karno Library in 2022
Source: Kharisma (2023)

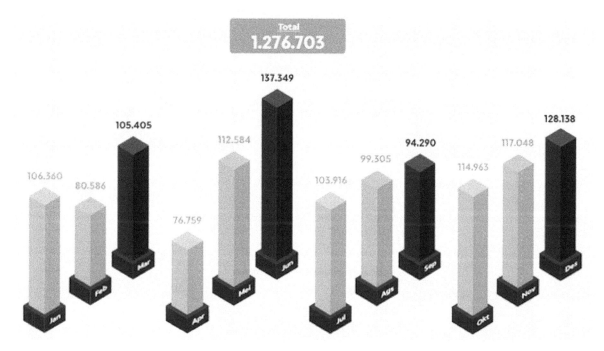

THE ARCHIVES SECTION

According to Decree Number 197 of 2019, issued by the Head of the National Library of the Republic of Indonesia, a team responsible for managing archives has been established at the National Library. As per this decree, the Bung Karno Library has been designated an archivist who is responsible for overseeing the internal archives of the Bung Karno Library. The archivists of the Bung Karno Proclaimer Library handle two main categories of archival materials, namely records and archives. The archivist engages in several tasks, such as conducting a systematic assessment of documents according to their chronological order and historical significance. These documents include a wide range of materials, including a substantial collection of Sukarno's literary works, books that were read by Bung Karno, correspondence, outdated money, photographs, ephemeral items, official charters, decrees, as well as literary works authored by individuals, other than Bung Karno or more of national heroes of the Republic of Indonesia have a connection to Bung Karno.

Despite its relatively short existence of barely three years, archive management has garnered significant scholarly interest. The archivists employed at the Bung Karno Library have actively participated in the Archives Technical Guidance program with the aim of enhancing their understanding and expanding their expertise in archive practices. The Bung Karno Library has been implementing internal archive services for three years. In order to facilitate the seamless execution of archive operations, the archivist coordinator develops Standard Operating Procedures (SOPs). The SOPs that have been developed include the following: 1) SOP for the organization and maintenance of active archives; 2) SOP for the provision of archive lending services; 3) SOP for the management of archive depreciation; and 4) SOP

Figure 3. Part of the archive collection from the Asian and African conference year 1955

for the maintenance and upkeep of archives. Nevertheless, some aspects of the management of the Bung Karno Library's internal archives require evaluation and improvement.

The Bung Karno Library engages in media transfer initiatives to effectively conserve and safeguard unique collections, including priceless historical records. Archives that undergo the process of being converted to media are those that possess a state of deterioration that renders them unsuitable for direct use by library patrons. In essence, these collections are characterized by their fragile condition. Hence, the process of digitization was undertaken in order to enable users to access the archive collection of historical significance without compromising the integrity of the original materials. The process of digitalization comprises four distinct stages. Firstly, archival photos are captured using a digital camera. Secondly, these photos are edited using specialized applications, which may involve cropping or enhancing the images. Thirdly, the edited photos are inserted into a dedicated application to create a digital archive collection that mimics the format of a book. Lastly, the media transfer files are stored in DVDs and databases for preservation and accessibility purposes. The official Bung Karno Library website is likewise used for the dissemination of digitization outcomes. In addition to the online platform, the Bung Karno Library offers access to digitized special collections via DVDs on their audio-visual service. These media include collections that have been converted and preserved in a digital format.

THE MUSEUM SECTION

The Museum in the Bung Karno Library offers the Memorabilia Collection service, where a curated display of paintings and photographs centered around the theme of Bung Karno is showcased. These exhibits are categorized into various sub-themes, including Bung Karno's childhood, Bung Karno and his family, the period of the movement, the period of the proclamation of independence, Bung Karno and diplomacy, and others. The Memorabilia Collection now has a total of 40 artworks and 504 pictures. In addition to curating a selection of paintings and photographs centered around the Bung Karno theme, the Bung Karno Library actively facilitates artists and other institutions in showcasing their artistic works and collections. This is achieved through collaborative exhibitions hosted within the premises of the Bung Karno Library, either within the Memorabilia Collection Service or in the library's hallway.

The museum also has a variety of historical artifacts, including paintings, luggage, clothing belonging to Bung Karno, photographs, antique currency, and keris. These things are shown in exclusive galleries that are unique to the museum since they possess significant historical significance. The collecting of these relics is of utmost importance due to their exceptional historical worth. This collection is exclusively accessible to users and is not subject to commercial transactions or transfers to individuals since it is the property of the state and represents the cultural heritage of the Indonesian nation.

The primary objective of this museum is to engage in the collection, preservation, and exhibition of the cultural history of the community. This institution serves the dual aim of facilitating scholarly investigation and providing opportunities for public pleasure and amusement. The structure has a philosophical significance that is intricately linked to the life trajectory of Bung Karno. The museum's physical site

Figure 4. The museum interior in part of the memorabilia collection

is intricately connected to the tomb, antiquities, and reliefs pertaining to Bung Karno. Through the use of this collection, the librarian or curator on duty cannot only guide visiting individuals but also engage in the art of storytelling for student groups. By exhibiting the personal suitcase used by Bung Karno throughout his period of incarceration, the librarian or curator can narrate the historical account of Bung Karno's valiant struggle for Indonesian independence, thus leading to his repeated imprisonment by the Dutch Colonial Government. The presence of a museum component inside the Memorabilia Collection Service often leads visitors to see the Memorabilia Collection as an independent museum entity rather than an integral part of the Bung Karno Library.

Based on the explanation above, a comprehensive understanding can be attained of the convergence circumstances of memory institutions at the Bung Karno Library. Currently, the primary focus of memory institution convergence at the Bung Karno Library is the management of library collections that represent the three facets of memory institutions, namely LAMs, according to the Preservation Coordinator of the collection. The Bung Karno Library is responsible for the management and curation of two distinct collections, namely books and non-books. The collection of books is categorized into three distinct groups, namely general, special, and reference.

The departments above are located inside the library premises and are organized according to the respective collections they house. The book collection comprises a variety of materials, such as general monographs, special monographs authored by President Soekarno or Bung Karno, serial publications, encyclopedias, and dictionaries. These resources are readily available to the general public without any restrictions. Non-book collections include a diverse range of items, such as DVDs, fragrances, apparel, artworks, pictures, mockups, three-dimensional genuine things, and several other artifacts. Multimedia services provide access to non-book collections, including electronic materials accessible to the general public, as well as specialized services pertaining to Bung Karno.

The Bung Karno Library offers not just conventional library services but also has a unique architectural design and dedicated space that incorporates a museum-like concept to showcase three-dimensional realia collections. According to the ICOM (2022), museums serve as venues for the exhibition of historical and prospective narratives in order to address cultural dilemmas, house cultural artifacts, and specimens as communal legacies, safeguard diverse memories for future generations, and promote equitable rights and access to cultural heritage for all individuals within the society. In juxtaposition to the architecture above, the Bung Karno Library incorporates a separate room dedicated to the display and preservation of memorabilia, which is separated from the main library space. The memorabilia service offers a distinctive exhibition of non-literary collections, including photographs, archives, artworks, three-dimensional objects, and other items related to President Soekarno. These items may include authentic artifacts or replicas that the President often employed throughout his lifetime. The souvenir service area further showcases a sequential account of President Soekarno's life, starting with his birth and concluding with his death.

The Bung Karno Library, being a convergence memory institution, has a department dedicated to the management of internal archives, known as the archival working group. Hendrawan and Ulum (2017) assert that the Bung Karno Library manages the archives. Archives do not serve as direct tools for planning, managing national affairs, or controlling the state. Rather, these archives possess historical relevance and have value for teaching and research purposes.

The Bung Karno Library has collaborated with the National Archives of the Republic of Indonesia (Arsip Nasional Republik Indonesia/ANRI) to curate a comprehensive collection of archives pertaining to President Soekarno. This collaboration includes the acquisition of historical photos depicting significant moments in President Soekarno's life, as well as the procurement of speech manuscripts delivered

Figure 5. LAMs collection management model at the Bung Karno Library

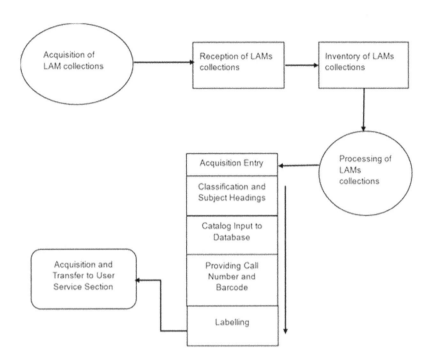

by the President. The procurement responsibilities of the Bung Karno Library include the formulation of an inventory of collections to be acquired and the adjustment of the financial allocation. The acquisition process for book collections, including monographs, serial publications, and electronic resources, is facilitated by a combination of direct appointments with publishers and bidding procedures. Collections that are not comprised of books, namely those pertaining to the life of President Soekarno, include various items such as DVDs, perfumes, apparel, paintings, photos, mockups, and authentic three-dimensional objects. The buying process for non-book collections varies from that of book collections due to the limited availability in the market. In anticipation of this event, the Bung Karno Library engages in collaborative efforts with collectors possessing objects or collections pertaining to President Soekarno. Furthermore, it is important to do separate searches for both the original and the replica.

The collecting phase has transitioned into the processing stage. The library proceeds to conduct an inventory of newly acquired collections, categorizing them based on their titles or topics and the number of copies available. Subsequently, the National Archives of the Republic of Indonesia has developed an automated program to categorize and classify both book and non-book collections inside a database. The use of the Resource Description and Access (RDA) standard is seen in cataloguing criteria. Differences in call number assignment practices may be seen between book collections and non-book collections, with a special emphasis on memorabilia collections.

The memorabilia collection has a diverse array of items, each with unique characteristics and historical significance. These objects have been meticulously sourced from many origins and carefully selected to represent different aspects of historical events, individuals, or cultural phenomena. Each item in the collection is accompanied by a comprehensive description, providing valuable insights into its source origin, historical context, and relevance. Moreover, every object is assigned a registration number, facilitating efficient cataloging and information retrieval processes. This meticulous approach ensures that the memorabilia collection is not just a repository of tangible artifacts but also a valuable resource for scholarly research and historical documentation. This differs from a library collection that uses conventional bibliographical listings. The acquisition method is the last stage in the management of book and non-book collections inside the Bung Karno Library. Processed collections will be sent to the service department in this locality, accompanied by a unique code, serving as verification of the collection's submission.

In order to effectively execute the convergence of memory institutions in the Bung Karno Library, it is essential to create robust standards, regulations, and efficient management techniques. Therefore, the challenge of delineating collections that fall within the categories of books and non-books is a substantial obstacle. Furthermore, the integration of convergence inside memory institutions necessitates the use of unique methodologies and information technologies to manage these collections effectively. The Bung Karno Library is now implementing strategies to address the concept of convergence across memory institutions. These initiatives include the provision of comprehensive public services and the optimization of current policies set by the parent institution, namely the National Library of Indonesia.

The Bung Karno Library, which falls within the purview of archives, is committed to the proficient handling of dynamic archival resources in order to enhance the smooth operation of internal institutional administration. The Bung Karno Library has a proficient archives group or archive management team that demonstrates competent oversight of archives related to President Soekarno. The current undertaking exhibits substantial promise in augmenting the efforts of the Bung Karno Library in developing the concept of convergence. The Bung Karno Library serves as a repository of the national collective memory of the Republic of Indonesia, consistently aiding the state and society in understanding identity and knowledge frameworks within the social structure. Therefore, in the future, the concept of convergence across memory institutions might be used as a strategy to build connections between library, archive, and museum organizations in the development of simultaneous resources. These resources would be based on human resources, policies, governance, standards, service systems, and advanced technology.

FUTURE RESEARCH AND CONCLUSION

Various factors were recognized as the driving force behind the propensity to achieve convergence in many circumstances. The motives discussed are often linked to the objective of improving organizational and user assistance, regardless of whether it corresponds to the requirements of the broader community. Furthermore, the motivation for convergence is also driven by the desire to adjust to the evolving technological environment, which is marked by the growing prevalence of digital entities and the convergence of many systems. Undoubtedly, it is apparent that both financial and administrative efficiency have equal prominence in this particular environment. An instance of an Indonesian Presidential Library, namely the Bung Karno Library situated in Blitar City, Indonesia, serves to enhance a thorough understanding of the resources or collections inside the memory institution. This is accomplished by the analysis of previously distinct collections from novel relational perspectives. The examination of several research indicates that the planning process for convergence initiatives has a significant level of commonality. Likewise, the issues that have been uncovered exhibit recurring patterns that, to a certain degree, are not surprising. The subject under consideration relates to the phenomenon of adaptation when professional identities and cultures with distinct historical antecedents assimilate the practices and abilities of their counterparts. Notwithstanding these challenges, notable benefits were discerned with regard to improvements in public use and staff training, ultimately fostering the cultivation of a more enduring institutional ethos, specifically inside the Indonesian Presidential Library.

The available experience from the case studies suggests the presence of common challenges in co-operation and convergence endeavors. The authors suggest that the process of cooperation across these entities is characterized by inherent complexity and obstacles. The need to ensure coherent accessibility was deemed crucial in meeting the user requirements in the case study of the Bung Karno Library. Some individuals held a firm attachment to tangible cultural heritage and acknowledged the need for different interpretive approaches when dealing with museum objects as opposed to library texts. However, it was widely recognized that improving user support and promoting scholarly pursuits were important goals that required breaking down the barriers between libraries, archives, and museums. The facilitation of educational activities by information scientists and professionals has the potential to promote cooperation and reduce the focus on differences between libraries, archives, and museum resources or collections. Moreover, these activities have the potential for future research and augment the perceived value of digital convergence. The investigated institutions are making notable efforts to reach a balanced state of professional competency while also integrating diverse systems. The attainment of effective convergence programs seems to require the discovery and preservation of a delicate balance.

REFERENCES

Bafadhal, A. S., & Hendrawan, M. R. (2021). Towards Infinity and Beyond Reality: A Cutting-Edge Virtual Museum. In Globalisation of Cultural Heritage: Issues, Impacts, and Challenges. Trengganu: Penerbit Universiti Malaysia Trengganu.

Brown, K., & Mairesse, F. (2018). The definition of the museum is through its social role. *Curator (New York, N.Y.)*, *61*(4), 525–539. doi:10.1111/cura.12276

Buhalis, D. (2020). 'Technology in tourism – from information communication technologies to eTourism and smart tourism towards ambient intelligence tourism: A perspective article. *Tourism Review*, *75*(1), 267–272. doi:10.1108/TR-06-2019-0258

Davis, A. (2016). Two Humanistic Communication Theories for Museums, Libraries, and Archives. *ICOFOM study series*, (44), pp. 5–15.

Denton, K. A. (2014). *Exhibiting the Past: Historical Memory and the Politics of Museums in Postsocialist China*. The University of Hawaii Press.

Duranti, L., & Franks, P. C. (Eds.). (2015). *Encyclopedia of archival science*. Rowman & Littlefield.

Given, L. M., & McTavish, L. (2010). What is old is new again: The re-convergence of libraries, archives, and museums in the digital age. *The Library Quarterly*, *80*(1), 7–32. doi:10.1086/648461

Hadi, A. S., & Hendrawan, M. R. (2022). Analisis Penerapan Konsep Konvergensi Institusi Memori Pada Perpustakaan Proklamator Bung Karno. In I. W. P. Yasa, R. A. G. Purnawibawa, & M. Idris (Eds.), *Strategi Penguatan Nilai-Nilai Kearifan Lokal di Era Surplus Informasi*. Lakeisha.

Hendrawan, M. R., & Bafadhal, A. S. (2022). Virtual Museum. In D. Buhalis (Ed.), *Encyclopedia of Tourism Management and Marketing*. Edward Elgar Publishing. doi:10.4337/9781800377486.virtual. museum

Hendrawan, M. R., & Ulum, M. C. (2017). *Pengantar Kearsipan: Dari Isu Kebijakan ke Manajemen*. Universitas Brawijaya Press.

Kharisma, A. B. (2023). Lebih Dekat dengan UPT Perpustakaan Proklamator Bung Karno. Blitar: Perpustakaan Nasional Republik Indonesia: UPT Perpustakaan Proklamator Bung Karno.

Lankes, R. D. (2016). *The new librarianship field guide*. MIT Press.

Mabe, K., & Potgieter, A. (2021). Collaboration between libraries, archives, and museums in South Africa. *SA Journal of Information Management*, *23*(1).

Novia, J., & Liaison, A. (2012). Library, Archival and Museum (LAM) Collaboration: Driving Forces and Recent Trends. *Library Quarterly: Information, Community, Policy*, *80*(1), 7–32.

Osburn, C. B. (2009). *The Social Transcript: Uncovering Library Philosophy*. Libraries Unlimited.

Pendit, P. L. (2019). *Pustaka: Tradisi & Kesinambungan*. ISIPII Press.

Pratiwi, K. Y., & Setiawan, B. (2019). Analisis Penerapan Konsep GLAM (Gallery, Library, Archives, Museum) di Perpustakaan Bung Karno Blitar. *Jurnal Perpustakaan Universitas Airlangga*, *9*(2), 53–62.

Rasmussen, C. H., & Hjørland, B. (2023). Libraries, Archives and Museums (LAMs): Conceptual Issues with Focus on Their Convergence. *Knowledge Organization*, *49*(8), 577–621. doi:10.5771/0943-7444-2022-8-577

Robinson, H. (2019). *Interpreting Objects in the Hybrid Museum: Convergence, Collections, and Cultural Policy*. Routledge. doi:10.4324/9780429454400

Rubin, R. E., & Rubin, R. G. (2020). *Foundations of library and information science*. American Library Association.

Schwartz, J. M., & Cook, T. (2002). Archives, records, and power: The making of modern memory. *Archival Science*, *2*(1-2), 1–1. doi:10.1007/BF02435628

Sodaro, A. (2018). *Exhibiting Atrocity: Memorial Museums and the Politics of Past Violence*. Rutgers University Press. doi:10.2307/j.ctt1v2xskk

Sudarsono, B. (2016). *Menuju Era Dokumentasi Baru*. LIPI Press.

The International Council of Museums (ICOM). (2022). *Museum Definition*. https://icom.museum/en/resources/standards-guidelines/museum-definition/

KEY TERMS AND DEFINITIONS

Archives: Are structured and maintained resources of historical records, papers, manuscripts, pictures, audiovisual recordings, and other sources that benefit study, historical knowledge, accountability, and cultural heritage preservation. Archives preserve the collective memory of people, organizations, communities, and society. Archives help preserve history, facilitate study, promote transparency, and protect societies' documented cultural heritage. Their windows to the past illuminate human history, culture, and governance.

Collective Memory: Is essential to human culture and civilization. It affects people's history, present, and future. It stores cultural information, values, and identity, giving a community a feeling of continuity and belonging. Groups or communities that remember, comprehend, and interpret previous events, experiences, and cultural occurrences are all integral to collective memory.

Convergence: Refers to the process of moving towards a central meeting point or condition. Additionally, it may be seen as a method of implementing interventions that are executed in a synchronized, integrated, and collaborative fashion with the aim of addressing high-priority objectives.

Cultural Heritage Resources: Are physical and intangible assets of social, historical, artistic, scientific, or societal value. They're passed down to preserve identity, continuity, and history. Community identities, memories, and cultures rely on culture. For cultural continuity, heritage awareness, and preservation, these resources must be conserved.

Cultural Heritage: Comprises a multitude of tangible and intangible elements, making it extensive and intricate. These include hereditary traits, behavioral patterns, customary rituals, and linguistic expressions. The preservation of cultural heritage is of paramount importance due to its historical, aesthetic, scientific, and social significance.

Information: Crucial and abstract facts or information that may transmit meaning, enhance understanding, decrease ambiguity, or influence a person, system, or entity's status, beliefs, or actions.

Intangible Cultural Heritage: Traditions passed down from generation to generation. Actions, expressions, knowledge, abilities, and rituals vary. Intangible cultural heritage includes oral traditions and expressions, performing arts, traditional knowledge and practices, festivals and celebrations, craftsmanship and traditional crafts, language and linguistic traditions, traditional games and sports, social practices, norms, and etiquette, knowledge systems and expertise, music and dance forms, rituals and ceremonies, transmission, and education.

Libraries: Well-selected resources of information resources, materials, and services available to the public, students, academics, or a community to aid education, research, reference, and pleasure. Libraries help preserve knowledge, promote literacy, facilitate learning, and provide access to different information. As inclusive spaces for inquiry, discovery, and active interaction with information, libraries foster curiosity, education, and intellectual growth.

Memory Institutions: Are assets that gather, preserve, interpret, study, and distribute cultural heritage resources. Tangible and intangible resources, records, traditions, and cultural, historical, aesthetic, scientific, or social information. Museums, archives, and libraries all serve this purpose, each with its roles and responsibilities. Resources and acquisition, conservation and preservation, research and scholarship, exhibition and interpretation, education and outreach, access and accessibility, community engagement, advocacy, and policy are memory institutions' primary functions.

Museum: Is an institution that gathers, conserves, studies, interprets, and shows cultural, artistic, historical, or scientific resources for public education and enrichment is a museum. Museums preserve and display humanity's tangible and intangible heritage, promote learning, and engage the public. They are vital organizations that preserve, interpret, and share the rich fabric of human knowledge, creativity, and history.

Presidential Libraries: Serve as repositories and exhibition spaces, consolidating the records and objects associated with a President and their administration and offering them to the public for scholarly examination and discourse, free from any partisan inclinations or connections.

Tangible Cultural Heritage: Is a culture's physical history and legacy passed down through generations. It encompasses various cultural, historical, aesthetic, scientific, and socially significant artifacts, structures, and persons.

Chapter 10
Electric Vehicles in India and Customer Perception:
The Moderating Effect of Government Regulations on EVs

Sephalika Sagar
https://orcid.org/0000-0003-0081-9959
Amity University, Noida, India

Devesh K. Upadhyay
https://orcid.org/0000-0002-2399-1850
Birla Institute of Technology, Mesra, India

ABSTRACT

The authors propose a model for examining the moderating effect of government regulations on electric vehicles and their infrastructure in India. The model was tested empirically using data collected from 101 respondents. Principal component analysis and mediation analysis were employed to analyze the data using JASP 0.17.2.1 (Apple Silicon) software package. Findings based on interaction support the hypothesis that government regulations concerning the manufacturing of electric vehicles, standards and specification of EVs and EV batteries, subsidies, and incentives by central and state governments support. In other words, the potentially negative aftermaths of the lumbering infrastructure of EVs can be controlled and reduced when government regulations concerning infrastructure are implemented meticulously. The research study highlights the theoretical and practical implications of the findings, as well as recommendations for future studies, are suggested.

INTRODUCTION

The worldwide automobile sector is experiencing unprecedented change to transition to alternative/less fuel-demanding choices. India is also funding the transition to electric vehicles. On the one hand, the

DOI: 10.4018/979-8-3693-2841-5.ch010

cost of oil imports of goods, increasing air pollution, the conflict between Russia and Ukraine, spiraling inflation in prices, and worldwide agreements to address worldwide environmental degradation are the primary variables encouraging the government of India to accelerate the switch to electric vehicles, and on the opposite end of the spectrum, expanding buyers desire. During the COP 26 Climate Change Convention in Glasgow, India launched the e-AMRIT portal (https://www.e-amrit.niti.gov.in/), a single point of reference for comprehensive data on electric cars. It tackles significant aspects concerning the widespread use and acquisition of EVs, such as electrical charging station locations and EV financing alternatives, as well as capital prospects, policies from the government, and potential incentives for owners and makers. Notwithstanding the country's lofty goals, India's EV market is still in its infancy. Examining it another way, India has the world's biggest unexplored marketplace, particularly in the two-wheeler category. Following the prescriptive approach, foreign direct investments are the absence of accessible charging facilities was a major impediment to the widespread acceptance of electric cars in India. As a result, India requires a solid foundation for charging networks throughout the country, considering travel and population density. Facilities comprise charging facilities, swapping of batteries stations, and propulsion battery-powered companies. Despite firms devoting themselves to internal filling for vehicles, filling EVs for one's use remains an obstacle. Whereas energy is far more affordable than petroleum, the extended fueling period of electric vehicles strains the infrastructure used to charge them. Furthermore, because charging income is so little, not many carriers are willing to take the risk. When electric vehicles (EVs) advance past the small numbers purchased by early adopters and become mainstream automobiles, accessible electrical charging in India, or precisely its lack thereof, dominates each dialogue. People who commute across towns may require anywhere from three to five applications from infrastructure for charging service providers, which is inconvenient. Furthermore, many charging outlets are not shown on Google Maps or Mapple. Also, it is common for an individual to go to a functional charger to realize it is not working. A unified system for charging exploration, availability, and payment is desperately required. Automakers, electrical power infrastructure providers, and the administration have understood that refueling facilities must be in operation to market EVs. Nevertheless, a more comprehensive comprehension of the subject is required. There is also an imperative for a long-term comprehensive strategy that offers financial motivation to establish a stable charging station network. The initial buyers of electric vehicles primarily depend on domestic or workplace electrical charges. The majority of them either have a second car for far-reaching excursions or undertake attempts to schedule their trips ahead of time and fuel their vehicle properly. Nevertheless, this will be a major deterrent when we contact general purchasers. Because municipal power infrastructure is unreliable, owners of electric vehicles ignore it and prefer to depend on battery refueling. at home. It reduces the profitability of charging infrastructure carriers substantially. The central administration is also prioritizing the transition to environmentally friendly transportation, as seen by recent changes to the Rapid Acceptance and the production of goods of Hybrid and Electric Vehicles in India (FAME) II plan to enable electrical two-wheelers less costly. As of 11 July 2022, about 469,315 electric cars were encouraged via demand subsidies of around INR 18.69 billion via the second phase of the FAME initiative. 6,315 electricity buses and 2,877 electric vehicle (EV) charging stations have been approved in 68 towns throughout 25 states/union territories. The 50 genuine equipment manufacturers (OEMs), both new and determined, have submitted registration applications and reconfirmed 106 EV models. There are 1,576 charging outlets approved for installation on nine motorways and 16 roads. User impression of battery-powered vehicles must be investigated in the context of India's sluggish electrical infrastructure for charging. The moderating effect of government interventions and regulation concerning electric vehicle manufacturing, standards and specifications of EVs and EV batteries, subsidies and incentives from central and state governments, and regulation on charging infrastructure efficiency are good moderators of the relationship between EV infrastructure in India and customer perception of EVs. In other words, when government infrastructure restrictions are rigorously applied, the potentially negative consequences of EVs' sluggish infrastructure may be regulated and mitigated. This study explores the moderating effects of government regulations and commitment concerning EVs and their infrastructure on the relationship between customer perception regarding EVs and buying behavior toward electric vehicles.

EVS CHARGING INFRASTRUCTURE IN INDIA

The rise of battery-powered vehicles has resulted in the establishment of charging enterprises. According to worldwide know-how, several stakeholders/institutions have been involved in creating and growing electric car charging facilities. You may have the largest influence among all these entities by creating and running electric car filling facilities as a filling system maker or charging facility administrator.

Maker of Charging Facilities

You may make money by making and supplying electric car charging facilities. There are two approaches to providing electric car infrared equipment options: first, as an independent distribution - to be set up at residence, workplace, or for open charging; and second, in collaboration with vehicle makers, selling the equipment as a vehicle component. You will effectively offer a comprehensive charging station option, comprising both software and hardware setting up, for public and private filing. You will also supply assistance such as maintaining the equipment and supplementary support. Delta Electronics, Mass Tech, ABB India, Exicom, Okaya, and RRT constitute a few of the key driving facilities builders.

Charging Point Operator (CPO)

By controlling a charging point infrastructure, you will make money as a Charging Point Operator (CPO). You will charge an electric vehicle, assist customers, perform network upgrades (alone or in conjunction with a Connectivity Services Partner), and perform other activities. For charging electric car users, you may pick from several pricing systems, such as time-limited expenses, energy-based expenses, set prices, and subscription costs. Furthermore, the government's Ministry of Power has designated electric car refueling as a "service," indicating that you do not need a license by the Electricity Act of 2003. CSOs include EESL, Tata Power, Magenta Group, Fortum India, Volttic, Charge Zone, and others. CSOs include EESL, Tata Power, Magenta Group, Fortum India, Volttic, Charge Zone, and others.

Traction Battery

Because batteries account for 40% of total EV cost, battery industry services may significantly drive EV adoption. Additionally, firms that provide value by lowering the aggregate expense of electric vehicles serve a significant role. Possible battery services/processes that you may offer for-profit and aid electric car purchasers in reducing their entire expense of possession are:

Battery Recycling

Most batteries in electric vehicles are lithium-ion and contain rare metals, including lithium, nickel, and cobalt. The use of these rare elements is likely to expand as the electric car sector expands, and with abundance focused on a few nations alone, supply chain concerns may occur in the future. As a result, recycling batteries would be the only viable option. Regeneration can lower both the adverse ecological effect and the total expense of battery cells (and hence the cost of electric cars). It employs a cyclical economy concept to maximize asset use. Gravita India is one such firm actively involved in environmentally conscious battery reuse.

Battery Subscription

Starting up a company that deals in battery rental means offering clients lower initial costs for electric vehicles and tackling the most common buyer worry. Battery packs are delivered to drivers of vehicles on a contract foundation, with usage charges based on daily or per km charges.

Pay-as-You-Go

An invoicing method whereby an individual must pay straight before obtaining an item of service (in our example, through a charge station). Pay-as-you-go is most popular with impulsive customers because they are not required to sign a lengthy agreement with the charging station administrator.

Battery-as-a-Service (BaaS)

BaaS employs a cyclical economic concept to maximize resource utilization while connecting the transportation and power sectors. When a battery nears its End-of-Life (EoL), the BaaS supplier either repairs it and makes it appropriate for use in programs such as storing electricity or beneath-the-meter utilization or reuses it by obtaining raw materials from it to produce fresh batteries.

QUESTIONS RELATED TO THE TOPICS

Is Public Charging Able to Match the Growth in EV Sales?

Powering EVs for individual mobility continues to be an obstacle for now. Tata Power announced a target of adding 13,059 charging stations for the company's automobile sector and 8,945 charging stations for general fueling by the end of FY27 in an August 2022 briefing. Furthermore, the corporation aimed to install over 5,000 bus charging stations. In other words, the emphasis is on passive charging sites for vehicles, such as industrial vehicles for visitors and office workers, app-based aggregators of information, and transportation providers. Despite Tata Power's efforts to deploy over 4,000 charging sites, nearly all electric automobile customers will seek combination fueling system (CCS2) DC power sources for public fueling. Tata Power has around 870 connections classified as accessible out of 1,083, meaning an accessibility of 80%, according to information from Tata Power's site. According to sources, the true percentage will probably be 70% or below. While several charging station providers exist in India, none are as large as Tata Power. For instance, there are 450 charging stations in India for Glida, formerly Fortum Charge & Drive India. The fact that there are 50,000 turbochargers in important markets worldwide, all of which are dependable and frictionless, offer free powering up, and identify the car as part of an enclosed network gives Tesla a significant competitive edge in the international market for electric cars.

How Much Time Does a Car Powered by Electricity Require in The Driver's Seat?

Power is far less expensive than fuel. However, the lengthy charging period strains the charging system's facilities. The power supply used for home-based charging is typically 3.3 kilowatts (kW) or 7.2 kW. Two 1.5-ton cooling systems (ACs) equal a 3.3-kw charger, while four 1.5-ton ACs equal a 7.2-kw recharger. That is an enormous amount of power, indeed. Additionally, the plug point is frequently far away if you live in a flat. For this reason, an additional meter is usually required.

What Advancements Have Been Made in the Area of Residential Charging?

These depend on public infrastructure, workplace and home charging stations, and electric vehicle sales volumes. Electricity delivery businesses may need to make extra structural expenditures in the electricity system. Mahindra and Mahindra (M&M) are collaborating with a few partners to provide a more dependable and superior recharging expertise. Dealerships for M&M and Tata Motors are installing chargers. But as this map demonstrates, M&M has connected far insufficient a handful of chargers for their electric SUV.

OBJECTIVES OF THE STUDY

- To identify the factors most influential in customer perception of electric vehicles.
- To analyze the moderating effect of Government policies regarding Electric Vehicles & their infrastructure.
- They analyze the relationship between customer perception of EVs and their purchasing behavior.
- To develop suitable marketing strategies for Electric Vehicles.

BACKGROUND OF THE WORK

As of now, not many studies have been conducted on the infrastructure requirements of electric vehicles. Environmental degradation and airborne pollutants are two of our time's most contentious global challenges. According to UNDP news reports, the power system is responsible for 75% of the world's CO_2 emissions, with motor vehicles, including passenger automobiles, accounting for 41% (Statista, 2022). Nevertheless, the transport industry propels economic development (Umar et al., 2021). The industry's heavy reliance on petroleum and natural gas bolsters the worldwide push for renewable manufacturing and consumption and has unavoidable negative effects on our planet and public health. Accordingly, electric cars can potentially significantly lessen the world's reliance on fossil fuels (Kim et al., 2020; Liao et al., 2019; King et al., 2019). More specifically, the development and use of battery-powered automobiles have been linked to significant societal and environmental advantages. For instance, the increasing popularity of electric cars in Europe has led to a notable decrease in carbon dioxide emissions (Transport & Environment, 2020), positively impacting general wellness, reducing deaths among humans, and improving environmental sustainability. The societal advantages of recent vehicle CO2 emissions reductions, especially in the US, are thought to be brought about by federal air pollution legislation and technological advancements made by automakers (Choma et al., 2020). Following the Electric Vehicles Drive, a multi-governmental policymaking platform founded in 2010, leaders worldwide have teamed together to speed up the widespread use of electric vehicles since they can help reduce CO2 emissions (International Energy Agency, 2022). Public willingness to accept electric vehicles is still inadequate to significantly influence CO2 emissions, notwithstanding ongoing regulatory efforts and advertisements by automakers (Tarei et al., 2021; Liao et al., 2019). According to new research by the World Energy Agency (2022), for instance, the worldwide market contribution of electric vehicles increased fourfold between 2019 and 2021, reaching a share of 9% globally. However, this share is insufficient to offset traditional automobiles' carbon output. The estimate, as mentioned earlier, shows that, compared with standard cars, sales of electric vehicles made up 16% and 17% of cars bought in China and Europe, respectively. In 2021, the worldwide sale of electric vehicles exclusively represented 85% of worldwide sales, with the US coming in second with 10% of sales worldwide. Considering China, Europe, and the US accounted for 90% of the worldwide sales of electric vehicles, this turns into a big issue. The competition to become the market leader in environmentally friendly offerings, like electric cars, is intensifying (transportation & The surroundings, 2020) as big producers declared their intention to reach 100% production by 2030 (International Energy Agency, 2022). Agencies in Europe (International Energy Agency, 2022) and other nations anticipate phase-outs of natural fuel automobiles by 2030 and afterward (Pressman, 2021). This appears to be intensifying the race. As a result, automakers have been progressively formulating business plans that enable them to hold onto their economic edge by gaining market shares and adhering to legal requirements or regulatory rebates (International Energy Agency, 2022). As a result, this has given several automakers fresh insights into environmentally friendly branding. Samuelsen et al. (2013), from the standpoint of operating costs for plug-in electric cars (PEVs) and the viability of battery electric vehicles (BEVs), this research explores the necessary infrastructure for charging BEVs. According to the accomplishments, the most crucial element in lowering PEV operating costs is the charging schedule plan; nevertheless, the advantages of having more charging stations for PEVs reduce with time. An innovative nanoscopic city-scale customer simulation-based approach to locating electric vehicle charging stations is proposed by Alois Knoll and Heiko Aydt (2017). Using a case investigation involving Singapore, we show how advantageous this method is for spatiotemporal organizing. Scheduling may consider the shifting patterns of each automobile movement and data from roadways and congestion that is currently in place. Al-Hanahi, B., Ahmad, I., Habibi, D., & Masoum, M. A. (2021) cover the difficulties of recharging industrial electric cars at their facilities and in public. Using predictive models, Singh, H., Kavianipour, M., Soltanpour, A., Fakhrmoosavi, F., Ghamami, M., Zockaie, A., & Jackson, R. (2022) calculated how many direct current rapid charging facilities and adapters would be needed to meet the demand for electric vehicle (EV) charging in metropolitan areas. Regulators and developers may readily adopt the global estimations of facility funding necessary in metropolitan regions provided by these simulations. The Lucas, Silva, and Neto (2012) methodology assesses the energy consumption and carbon dioxide releases resulting from the building, upkeep, and demolition of facilities supporting the provision of power and energy sources from fossil fuels to automobiles. Saad Alsaidan, I., Ahmad, F., Saad Alam, M., & Shariff, S. M. (2020).Because battery flipping facilities present more revenue options to committed participants, they are emerging as a viable alternative to the conventional electric vehicle charging station model. The many elements of the optimal BSS distribution have been given in this paper. BSS's architecture, methods, and advantages for aggregators, power system operators, and consumers have all been outlined. In addition, a thorough discussion is held of the main obstacles to the BSS, including infrastructure, battery deterioration, compatibility, and title. Wenig et al. (2019) examines the impacts on major operational metrics and adverse consequences of electrical transportation using three electric transportation situation variables: capacity of batteries, charging facility reach, and filling speed. We calculate the cars' power usage and filling behavior, the electrical accessibility of locations, the electrical mileage percentage of hybrid automobiles, and the grid effect (electricity demand and time of peaks) for 180 battery-infrastructure configurations. The findings demonstrate that practical battery storage capacity increases allay worries regarding the necessity of a widespread system for charging. Our research indicates that an extensive refueling infrastructure is not very beneficial for automobiles with extremely low electricity ranges and limited segments of long-distance travelers. Savari et al. (2023). Several EV charging technologies are thoroughly investigated. Several manufacturers are attempting to construct DC fast charging stations because they can charge electric vehicle batteries faster than AC charging stations, even though DC fast charging facilities are more costly to build. A thorough analysis was conducted on the second charging infrastructure trend. Because poor facilities might hinder the market's marketing of electric vehicles (EVs), the building of charging facilities has drawn much attention from advanced and undeveloped nations. Policymakers, automakers, customers, and society as a whole may all benefit from the thorough information about electric cars and viewpoints provided by Razmjoo, A., Ghazanfari, A., Jahangiri, M., Franklin, E., Denai, M., Marzband, M., & Maheri, A. (2022). Authorities should invest in developing electric cars and power technology, offer aid, and create facilities for fueling them to have positive outcomes. In addition, we evaluate the running expenses of electric cars by examining the current global EV sales in 10 countries. The price of grid power, finance costs, location, carbon tax, velocity of the wind, and sunlight all affect the cost of obtaining electric vehicles.

THEORETICAL FRAMEWORK

The study is conducted based on a certain hypothesis, where customer perception and purchasing are considered for the analysis. Figure 1 represents the theoretical framework for government policies.

Hypothesis

- **H0:** Government policies on Electric Vehicles will not moderate the relationship between negative customer perception of EVs and Customer Purchasing behavior.
- **H1:** Government policies on Electric Vehicles will moderate the relationship between negative customer perception of EVs and Customer Purchasing behavior.

Customer perception plays an important role in the context of marketing. To understand consumers' perceptions and attitudes about a company, its brand, and its offerings.

Figure 1. Theoretical framework

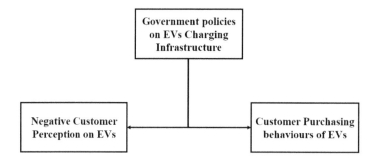

- **Customer Perception and Purchase Behaviours:** Beyond only influencing a single purchase, perceptions also mold the long-term bonds between consumers and businesses. It is frequently demonstrated by consumer retention rates and businesses' capacity to keep getting insightful and pertinent input from their devoted following. Given the significance of customer perception, every interaction between a business and its clients should aim to influence customer perception positively. Additionally, brands need to know which components have the biggest and most lasting effects on customers' perceptions. These components might be concrete or abstract, but insights, CX, and UX experts have the power to influence each one.

- **Government Policy:** Its Moderating Effect On Customer Purchase Behavior. It has been discovered that regulations about EVs influence EV purchases: The three categories of policy measures—financial incentive, availability of information, and convenience—that Wang et al. identified are favorably and considerably correlated to the use of electric vehicles, with convenience policy measures being the most crucial type of policy assess for EV promotion. The most successful policy action, on the other hand, tends to be monetary support (such as subsidies for operations and subsidies for purchases), according to the latest studies. According to Orlov et al., the government lowers the loan rate for those who buy electric cars, encouraging the usage of these vehicles. Zhang et al. claim that customer attitudes and reasons for buying an EV play a major role in determining whether or not subsidized uptake is sustainable. According to Zhang et al., government rebates may only be alluring if they are sufficiently significant to compensate for an electric vehicle's relative advantages and downsides. According to Wang et al., there wouldn't be a noticeable decrease in electric vehicle use in the years to come if financial incentives were to disappear. According to Carlucci et al., policies pertaining to information distribution that promote environmental conservation and the publicizing of electric vehicles help promote the sale of these vehicles. Wolbertus and Higgins have proposed that no-cost parking regulations and spaces set aside for electric vehicles (EVs) can be useful in increasing consumer preference for EVs regarding ease of use policy initiatives. According to Nie et al., free license plates for electric vehicles look appealing to customers compared to programs offering subsidies. The intention to buy BEVs is often positively and significantly influenced by the acceptance of the regulation.

- **Sample and Methodology:** Data from many cities, including Ranchi, Bhubaneswar, Jaipur, and Kolkata, were gathered through a survey. A Google form was used to administer the survey. The poll was given to EV users between June and August of 2023. Of the 254 surveys issued, 101 us-

Table 1. Principal component analysis

Bartlett's Test		
X^2	df	p
171.130	66.000	< .001
The P-value of "< .001" suggests that a substantial correlation exists between the variables being analyzed in this analysis.		

Table 2. Component loadings

Component Loadings	PC1	PC2	PC3	PC4	Uniqueness
How influential are the following factors when purchasing an electric car? [Discounted Road Tax]	0.645				0.521
How influential are the following factors when purchasing an electric car? [Low cost of maintenance]	-0.605				0.547
How influential are the following factors when purchasing an electric car? Brand]	0.601				0.519
How influential are the following factors when purchasing an electric car? [High resale value]	0.558				0.571
How influential are the following factors when purchasing an electric car? Space]		0.842			0.267
How influential are the following factors when purchasing an electric car? [Style/Design]		0.769			0.354
How influential are following are factors when purchasing an electric car? [Updated advance features]			0.818		0.283
How influential are following are factors when purchasing an electric car? Price]			0.640		0.493
How influential are following are factors when purchasing an electric car? Environment friendly]			0.563		0.459
How influential are following are factors when purchasing an electric car? [Fuel efficiency]				0.884	0.170
How influential are following are factors when purchasing an electric car? Performance]					0.443
How influential are following are factors when purchasing an electric car? [Affordable car insurance]					0.715
Note. Applied rotation method is varimax.					

able questionnaires were obtained (return rate = 40.0%). According to Baruch (1999), Mellahi, K., & Harris, L. C. (2016), this ratio is suitable for mail surveys.

- **Data Analysis:** We used principal component analysis and mediation analysis to analyze the data. The principal component analysis determined the most influential factors in purchasing EVs. Mediation analysis examined the direct and indirect relationships between the customer's perception of EVs, government regulations on EV infrastructure requirements, and customer buying behavior towards EVs.

Table 3. Component characteristics

	Unrotated Solution			Rotated Solution		
	Eigenvalue	Proportion Var.	Cumulative	SumSq. Loadings	Proportion Var.	Cumulative
Component 1	2.416	0.201	0.201	2.099	0.175	0.175
Component 2	1.931	0.161	0.362	1.828	0.152	0.327
Component 3	1.283	0.107	0.469	1.666	0.139	0.466
Component 4	1.027	0.086	0.555	1.064	0.089	0.555

Table 4. Direct effects parameter estimates

				Estimate	Std. Error	z-Value	p	95% Confidence Interval	
								Lower	Upper
Customer Perception on EVs	→	Customer Purchase Behaviours towards EVs		0.542	0.281	1.924	0.004	0.251	1.217
Note. Delta method standard errors, bias-corrected percentile bootstrap confidence intervals, ML estimator.									

Table 1 and Table 2 represent the items such as Discounted Road Tax, Low cost of maintenance, Brand, High resale value is loaded on PC1; Interior space, style, designs are loaded on PC2, updated advance features, price, environment friendly feature are loaded on PC3, and Fuel efficiency is loaded on PC4.

Table 3 represent the PC1, PC2, PC3, PC4 with Eigenvalue of more than 1. With Eigenvalues of '2.416', '1.931', '1.283' and '1.027' the components PC1, PC2, PC3, PC4 have emerged as principal components. We can also observe the proportion of variance of component-1 is 0.201; which is a pretty good variance with a compelling solution.

MEDIATION ANALYSIS

Table 4 represent the direct effect is the relationship between customer perception on EVs and Customer Purchase Behavior towards EVs after including the mediator Govt policy on EVs. P value of 0.004 indicate that the relationship is significant.

Table 5 present indirect effect is the relationship between Customer Perception on EVs and Customer Purchase Behavior towards EVs through Govt policy on EVs. The estimate of 0.199 and P value of 0.005 indicates that this is also significant.

Table 6 depicts the relationship between Customer Perception on EVs and Government policies on EVs' manufacturing, and its' infrastructure; on Customer Purchase Behavior towards EVs. Total effect value is the relationship between Customer Perception on EVs and Customer Purchase Behaviours towards EVs without the mediator. With estimate of 0.740 and P value of 0.008 this is also significant. Figure 2 present the path plot of customer purchase behaviours.

dependent regression

Table 5. Indirect effects of customer perception on EVs on

						Estimate	Std. Error	z-Value	p	95% Confidence Interval	
										Lower	Upper
Customer Perception on EVs	→		Govt policy on EVs	→		Customer Purchase Behaviour towards EVs	0.199	0.104	1.916	0.005	0.036	0.633

Note. Delta method standard errors, bias-corrected percentile bootstrap confidence intervals, ML estimator.

Table 6. Total effects

			Estimate	Std. Error	z-Value	p	95% Confidence Interval	
							Lower	Upper
Customer Perception on EVs	→	Customer Purchase Behaviour towards EVs	0.740	0.280	2.646	0.008	0.272	1.482

Note. Delta method standard errors, bias-corrected percentile bootstrap confidence intervals, ML estimator.

Figure 2. Path plot

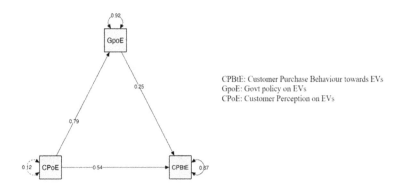

CPBtE: Customer Purchase Behaviour towards EVs
GpoE: Govt policy on EVs
CPoE: Customer Perception on EVs

Customer Purchase Behaviour towards EVs ~ b11*Govt policy on EVs + c11*Customer Perception on EVs
mediator regression
Govt policy on EVs ~ a11*Customer Perception on EVs
effect decomposition
y1 ~ x1
ind_x1_m1_y1:= a11*b11
ind_x1_y1:= ind_x1_m1_y1
tot_x1_y1:= ind_x1_y1 + c11

MARKETING STRATEGIES FOR EVs

The number of automobiles on the planet today is increasing far more quickly than the number of people. A total of roughly 50 million automobiles on the planet in 1950. The number of automobiles on Earth increased to about 600 million by 1994, and if current trends continue, there will be more than 3 billion automobiles by 2050 (Sperling, 1995). In addition to providing independence, confidentiality, and ease to car owners, driving puts the surroundings in danger. Integrated combustion engine vehicle (ICVs) especially seriously damages the ecosystem and individual health by spewing into the environment ever-increasing levels of carbon dioxide as well as other climate-altering greenhouse wastes. Renewable energies and gasoline inhibitors have been discovered to lessen the negative effects of driving. The primary cause of the global warming phenomenon, carbon dioxide emissions, is unaffected by such actions. Probably of the biggest difficulties of our day is addressing the issues brought on by the growing global car population sans compromising people's freedom to select and mobility, which is essential to a democratic nation. Realistic solutions appear to need replacing the current fleet of cars with a more ecologically friendly one. This might be accomplished by discovering least toxic engine designs, converting to less toxic energy sources, or improving the performance and lowering the emissions of ICVs (e.g., Sperling, 1995). Although the initial two options appear to be the most straightforward and accessible, surprisingly little has actually been done to improve the ecosystem throughout these paths. This is one of the causes behind the growing interest in creating automobiles featuring less harmful engine technology, which have the potential to lower greenhouse gas pollutants from the transportation network in addition to locally generated pollution. But existing electric cars (EVs) still have drawbacks that make them less appealing than ICVs. Some of the main drawbacks of EVs include their high initial cost, restricted driving range, lengthy recharge times, and outdated technology for batteries. However, EV energy is cheap, motors powered by electricity require relatively little upkeep, and they outlast inner combustible machines by a large margin. EVs would outperform ICVs if the true expenses of prevailing polluting practices were considered. Therefore, ensuring that the consumer is properly enlightened about the benefits and drawbacks of this recently developed technology is a significant problem for businesses and legislators hoping to establish a worldwide marketplace for EVs. When viewed through the lens of a prospective buyer, electric vehicle (EV) technology represents a novel and as-yet-unknown propulsion solution that primarily eliminates one of the several non-market drawbacks of conventional internal combustion vehicles (ICVs)—local emissions—and dramatically lowers another—greenhouse gas emissions. These social advantages, however, come at a great cost to the individual EV owner or user: a higher purchase price, a smaller driving range, less daily availability (because of recharging times), a reduced loading capacity (because of the batteries), a slower speed and acceleration. Furthermore, the absence of a refilling infrastructure makes EVs less useful. Furthermore, accidents while driving, gridlock, and the requirement for an extensive network of sidewalks are additional societal issues associated with private mobility that the EV does not address. Such an offering seldom ever pitches itself to prospective buyers. Therefore, for the EV to be embraced and spread across the community, clever marketing is required in parallel to regulations supporting it. In-depth analyses of national EV regulations in North America and Europe have been reported recently by several scholars (Schot et al., 1994; Kemp et al., 1998; Weber and Hoogma, 1998). An evident and pressing need is met by studies that aid in the creation of suitable national and international policies in this field. But even if sensible policy recommendations are created and implemented to encourage the consumer acceptability of EVs, the endeavors will be ineffective if EV manufacturers do not engage in a professional and dedicated marketing campaign. However, few investigations try to encourage and assist businesses in developing policies in this area. It takes insight and comprehension of the traits of the fastest prospective customers and the newly introduced item to plan a marketing strategy that can help consumers embrace the new product and "takeoff" (Tigert and Farivar, 1981; Link, 1997). (Hawkins et al., 1998; Goldsmith and Hofacker, 1991). This study outlines a two-phase plan for the target promotion of EVs. It is built on two main points of analysis: an overview of the present and anticipated future features of EVs and an assessment of the literature on the traits of initial consumers of new products. Our attempt is limited to general topics that we deem universally significant for the marketing of electric vehicles in (at least) all advanced nations. Naturally, EV manufacturers must modify their marketing plans to consider the unique features of the national regions. There is little chance that enough EVs will be purchased soon to pay for the expenditures incurred by the makers (Thornton, 1999) or to significantly improve the planet's or society's condition. Therefore, it should be understood that an EV promotion is only financially justifiable under the critical premise that long-term dynamics would drastically shift in preference for EVs. Although we don't think this belief is completely unthinkable, it shouldn't be regarded as an assumption. The picking-up shifts for electric vehicles (EVs) must likely be significantly more pronounced than that of fuel combustion engine technology (which includes a catalyst cleaning) for such a shift to occur. It would cause the current price/performance association difference between both technologies to close quickly. No better "third" technology for personal mobility must be created in the future.

Table 7 demonstrates a current evaluation of the most significant rival technologies, including electric vehicle technology. This analysis indicates that while EV technology holds the greatest potential for

Table 7. Technologies for improving the environmental performance of cars

Technology	CO2	Other Emissions	Cost	Time Perspective
Lean burn	8-12% reduction	No, Increase	1-2% increase	0-3 years
Gasoline-direct-injection-petrol and lean burn	15-25% reduction	HC and CO reduction, NO_x increase	2% increase	1-3 years
Variable intake geometry	10-15% reduction	reduction	2-4% increase	0-3 years
Turbo-direct-injection, diesel	10-15% reduction	0	1-2% increase	0-3 years
Electric cars	20-60% reduction	NO, reduction	100% increase	Min. 5-10 years
Down-sizing	25% reduction	Reduction	30-50% reduction	Now
Best available technology	10-15% reduction	Reduction	5% increase	Now
Energy-saving tyres	1-2% reduction	0	0-5% increase	Now
Better Diesel	1% increase	Particle and NOX reduction	1-2% Increase	Now (If required by law)
Reformulated petrol	1% increase	HC, CO, and NOX reduction	1-2% Increase	Now (If required by law)
Bio-fuels	10-15% reduction	HC, CO, and NOX particle reduction	3-5 times ordinary fuels	more than 10 years
Hybrid cars	10-15% reduction	reduction	10-20% Increase	5 years
Catalytic retrofit	0	HC, CO and NOX reduction	DKK 2-5000 increase	1-2 years

improving the environment, it also has the largest time lag before becoming cost-competitive. Government support can speed up the process and is likely even necessary for the successful marketing of EVs, but it is hardly sufficient (or won't be strong enough to suffice) and can take the form of subsidies, tax breaks for EVs, or constraints on the consumption of ICVs (Bernard, 1981; Kemp et al., 1998; Weber and Hoogma, 1998).

SOLUTION AND RECOMMENDATION

If a technology prediction indicating a sharply reducing price/performance association disparity is to be relied upon, then it becomes appropriate to develop a long-term promotional strategy in which the inevitable deficits in the beginning stages are offset by gains in the course of time. In order to achieve popularity by a small number of precisely chosen sectors initial stages an effective market diffusion strategy likely should involve a reasonably low launch price adjusted for introductory discounts or "learning curve pricing" (Kotler, 1991). (Hawkins et al., 1998). The fact that very few people purchase a new automobile before taking it for a road test highlights how crucial feasibility is to customer preference in this market. The first-time buyer who has an affinity in an electric vehicle (EV) will naturally want to test it out for a while before deciding to buy it, especially since the vehicle is built on new technology with major restrictions that only manifest in extremely rare circumstances. Thus, offering a liberal refund guarantee or the option to lease an EV for a while before making the commitment to spend money on one will aid in attracting interested potential consumers to make the final leap from attention to purchasing the item of an EV. The vast disparity in price, appearance, size, and many other aspects of cars, however, also makes it clear that people view private vehicles as significant lifestyle items in many other ways (Jensen, 1997). Most modern EVs are similar to compact, reasonably fuel-efficient automobiles in most aspects. Therefore, motorists who favour upscale, lively, or off-road vehicles for a variety of personality reasons are far less inclined to think that an EV can adequately replace their current vehicle. According to Weber and Hoogma (1998), policymakers in the field of technology experts have proposed that institutional variables have a greater influence in later stages of invention dissemination, whereas niche-specific elements play a major role in the early stages. In line with this viewpoint, but from a promotional standpoint, we recommend a two-phase approach for EV promotional activities. We propose that the following businesses and individual customers—with a few caveats that we will address later—represent very attractive market niches to be addressed in the first stage of the marketing strategy: (i) Public sector organizations; (ii) "companies with environmental consciousness; and (iii) families having multiple cars; who's ideals and way of life align with having an EV and their mobility requirements for an additional car are for the technical specifications of the current range of EVs. Although it appears that each of these markets only makes up a small portion of the (massive) overall automobile industry, we are optimistic that taken as a whole, they provide a potential customer base far larger than the 2.5% of prospective customers who are usually considered to be "innovators" (Rogers, 1995). Evidently, modern EVs cannot replace every vehicle in any of the three groups. Professional luxury automobiles are part of a business's car fleet, whereas law enforcement vehicles are part of the general public's sector car fleet. Since having an ICV mitigates some of the most significant drawbacks of modern EVs, multi-car households are seen as a possible market niche. Therefore, while the number of vehicles owned by multi-vehicle households greatly outstates the size of the EV market that could exist in this particular category. The percentage of households with several cars (12% in Sweden and Denmark) provides additional insight into the potential scale of this market, however the value-compatibility issue still makes this estimate overstated. It goes without saying that the most desirable market niche for cars is single-car families. Contrary to popular belief, a higher percentage of these families can meet their mobility requirements with EVs of the present age (Garling et al., 1998b). Nonetheless, these families are inclined to believe that depending on an EV can be dangerous at this time, perhaps with the exception of a small number of individuals who consider being environmentally friendly to be their most significant self-defined idea. Therefore, stage2 marketing for EVs ought to concentrate on the most prospective single-car families when tech has advanced and demonstrated benefits of the effective implementation by the stage 1 target categories may be realized. This is part of the broader promotional strategy for EVs.

Public Sector Enterprises

In several nations, the public domain is a significant transport owner and motor vehicle consumer for both commercial and passenger mobility. Official "sustainable buying" regulations for transactions made by the public sector exist in a number of nations like India. A sizable market for electric vehicles (EVs) may develop if particular procurement rules for ZEVs (zero emission vehicles) are adopted globally. Sustainable buying regulations in India are currently expanding to include automobiles (Schot et al., 1994; Nesbitt and Sperling, 1998). It is uncertain that numerous agencies in the public sector, however, will willingly pay a significantly premium price for an EV than for a comparable ICV because they are operating under strict budgetary constraints.

Companies With Environmental Consciousness

Privately owned companies which emphasize harmony with the surroundings and have a strong sustainability reputation make up this group. The percentage of businesses that consider itself to be environmentally friendly is not well estimated. Nonetheless, there is ample evidence that more businesses are using "sustainable" principles in promotional materials and that even more are eager to project an environmentally conscious company image (Peattie, 1995). An environmentally friendly EV has - preferably potentially - a significantly greater worth than it does for the usual individual (or firm) (relative advantage) for businesses looking to enhance their "environmentally friendly company image (Schot et al., 1994). Numerous business organizations automobiles are utilized primarily for relatively short excursions and exclusively during regular business hours, much like the vehicles held by governmental organizations. Given this, the market sector is probably less vulnerable to the technical shortcomings of EVs than private families are.

Families With Multiple Cars

Families having multiple cars are viewed as a relatively attractive category primarily because it is expected that the operational drawbacks of EVs are significantly fewer if the family has access to additional alternative vehicles. According to this supposition, nearly all of EV use surveys conducted by private families across different nations have discovered that these initial users also possessed an ICV (Kurani et al., 1996; Knie et al., 1997; Harms and Truffer, 1998). But that doesn't eliminate the reality that an electric vehicle (EV) is still a more expensive, operationally poorer vehicle than a car, even if its drawbacks might not be as significant for a multi-car family. But a lot of people in this group will also undoubtedly find that their commute costs are a big hardship. People like this are probably not going to give purchasing an EV any more thought if it costs more than an ICV of comparable value. It makes sense for the first EV promotional effort to focus on the following consumer groups: families with multiple vehicles, environmentally aware businesses, and the public sector enterprises such as city patrolling police vans, etc. In most categories, incentive pricing is undoubtedly a crucial component of the plan, and as was previously noted, it's critical that EV makers understand that it will require some time for them to turn earnings on EVs. Numerous insolvencies have served as ample evidence that, despite their high levels of inventiveness and excitement, small businesses have little likelihood of success in this industry without wealthy and persistent owners. Reducing the loss and possibly even making it seem essential to lower prices to maintain competitiveness, even for the aforementioned targeted categories, can be achieved by political backing in the type of incentives or favorable taxation. The rate at which the EV market matures, especially at the national level, may also be significantly impacted by administration or other forms of assistance for facilities market growth, and development and research efforts (Mackenzie, 1997; Weber and Hoogma, 1998). Therefore, close collaboration with regulatory entities—possibly even lobbying—should be a part of any prudent long-term marketing strategy for an electric vehicle. The secret to effectively promoting EVs to the general public, especially single-car families, is to focus on the specific market categories defined in stage 1. If they are happy with the result, electric vehicle owners will advocate for EVs in their networks of friends whether they are driving an EV during their job or in their personal lives (Darley, 1977/78; Bernard, 1981; Darley and Beniger, 1981; Murphy, 1997). Furthermore, by just existing on highways, electric vehicle (EV) innovation is showcased to prospective buyers beyond the social circles of original drivers. Awareness and excitement may grow as a result. Furthermore, the more electric vehicles that people see, the higher the probability it is that they would believe that switching to an electric vehicle is an acceptable alternative for those who sense guilty about the damaging effects that driving automobiles has on the natural world. Considering how vital referrals and displays implications are to long-term viability, it is imperative that EVs are not "over-marketed," especially if doing so means selling them to people who will inevitably have problems with them or otherwise end up unhappy. There are at least two significant ramifications for this (Murphy, 1997). (i) Early EV sales should be predicated on a careful examination of the requirements of the potential buyer and on knowledge of the advantages and disadvantages of the EV. It should be made clear to a prospective buyer that an EV cannot adequately meet their demands not to purchase any. (ii) The offered electric vehicles should have provisions in place to lessen apprehension regarding whether or not the purchased EV's range of travel truly encompasses the intended range for driving. These precautions could include a liberal return provision and/or a maintenance contract that includes things like complimentary ICV renting for the initial several years post buying, usually every other month or so. On the other hand, as is now GM's desired course of action in the USA, Vehicles could be borrowed instead of being bought (Murphy, 1997; Dipert, 1999). Utilizing a computer programme to simulate one's own automobile driving habit could be an inexpensive method of lowering preliminary suspicion and could be enough to persuade the most enthusiastic buyers that an electric vehicle (EV) is a viable answer for their transportation purposes. (Hoyer and MacInnis, 1997).

DISCUSSION, FINDINGS, AND CONCLUSION

The hypothesis of the study that government policies on electric cars do not update the relationship between the negative awareness of customers on electric cars and buy the behavior of electric car customers. It has been analyzed and proven; We can conclude that the influence of mediation has a major direct impact, as well as the indirect effects is very important, which means that reconciliation occurs, but the effect of mediation is part of nature, and this means that even after "the government's policy from among the government on the model" in a model "Customer awareness of electric cars "still has the most relationship. Customers of the electric car "through" government policy on the tram ". Therefore, the conclusion is that this effect is part of nature, so basically, we have a partial mediation effect. This article has attempted to provide an overview of the impact of government regulations on EVs and their infrastructure in India; On the relationship between customers' awareness of electric vehicles and their electric vehicle purchasing behavior. In addition, the study also discovered customers' key decision factors when purchasing electric vehicles. The study also identified the factors that most influence customer perceptions of electric vehicles. Factors like low road tax, low maintenance cost, brand name, high resale value, interior space, style, design, updated advanced features, price and environment. User-friendly features and energy efficiency are factors influencing the purchase of electric vehicles for customers in India. Despite the country's lofty goals, India's electric vehicle market is still in its infancy. On the other hand, India has the largest unexplored market in the world, especially in the two-wheeler segment. The Government of India has also developed the Government of India's FAME initiative, which stands for Faster Adoption and Manufacturing of Electric (Hybrid) Vehicles and Electric (Hybrid) Vehicles. In the coming years, this strategy will encourage higher adoption rates. For the 2023 budget, the Indian Finance Minister also announced a reduction in taxes and customs duties. This will help increase the number of lithium-ion batteries produced domestically for use in electric vehicles. The National Electric Mobility Mission (NEMMP), a comprehensive strategy to promote adoption of electric vehicles in India, is one of the policies and programs developed by the Indian government to help the country achieve these lofty goals. The goal is to reduce India's dependence on crude oil. Several state governments, including Gujarat, Telangana, Tamil Nadu and Assam, have also launched attractive policies and initiatives to encourage EV manufacturing in their regions. These tactics have led to the entry of private companies into the electric vehicle segment, paving the way for increased adoption of electric vehicles in India. The whole world will benefit greatly from India's development. Indian state and national governments must ensure that laws and policies are implemented in the real world to encourage Indian consumers to purchase electric vehicles. It is imperative to ensure proper implementation of the FAME Scheme and the National Electric Mobility Mission Plan (NEMMP), which aims to accelerate the adoption of electric vehicles in India. To achieve the goal of reducing India's dependence on crude oil. Although some European and Asian countries have begun to address the first two sectors mentioned in Step 1, namely public sector organizations and environmentally conscious companies, a more systematic and far-reaching push is needed to effectively target these sectors. An example of an effort that may be considered part of an advertising campaign targeting government agencies but is actually an end-user decision is display initiatives involving privately owned vehicles, light vehicles, and cars. Currently working in the largest city in India. There are several theoretical implications of the current findings. By analyzing EV consumption patterns that are still in their infancy in India and require further research, this work contributes to the body of literature (Gulzari et al., 2022). The aim of this study is to understand the root causes (positive and negative) of customers' attitudes and intentions towards purchasing electric vehicles in developing markets like India. To do this, a research model was created that takes into account the moderating effect of government policies on all aspects of EV adoption, from production to charging. The results of this study have implications for governments, marketers and manufacturers seeking to encourage consumer adoption of electric vehicles in developing countries.

REFERENCES

Ahmad, F., Saad Alam, M., Saad Alsaidan, I., & Shariff, S. M. (2020). Battery swapping station for electric vehicles: Opportunities and challenges. *IET Smart Grid*, *3*(3), 280–286. doi:10.1049/iet-stg.2019.0059

Al-Hanahi, B., Ahmad, I., Habibi, D., & Masoum, M. A. (2021). Charging infrastructure for commercial electric vehicles: Challenges and future works. *IEEE Access : Practical Innovations, Open Solutions*, *9*, 121476–121492. doi:10.1109/ACCESS.2021.3108817

Baruch, Y. (1999). Response rate in academic studies-A comparative analysis. *Human Relations*, *52*(4), 421–438. doi:10.1177/001872679905200401

Bernard, M. J. (1981). Problems In Predicting Market Response To New Transportation Technology. *New Horizons In Travel-Behavior Research*.

Bjerkan, K. Y., Nørbech, T. E., & Nordtømme, M. E. (2016). Incentives for promoting Battery Electric Vehicle (BEV) adoption in Norway. *Transportation Research Part D, Transport and Environment*, *43*, 169–180. doi:10.1016/j.trd.2015.12.002

Buonocore, J. J., Choma, E., Villavicencio, A. H., Spengler, J. D., Koehler, D. A., Evans, J. S., Lelieveld, J., Klop, P., & Sanchez-Pina, R. (2019). Metrics for the sustainable development goals: Renewable energy and transportation. *Palgrave Communications*, *5*(1), 136. doi:10.105741599-019-0336-4

Carlucci, F., Cirà, A., & Lanza, G. (2018). Hybrid Electric Vehicles: Some Theoretical Considerations on Consumption Behaviour. *Sustainability (Basel)*, *10*(4), 1302. doi:10.3390u10041302

Choma, E. F., Evans, J. S., Hammitt, J. K., Gómez-Ibáñez, J. A., & Spengler, J. D. (2020). Assessing the health impacts of electric vehicles through air pollution in the United States. *Environment International*, *144*, 106015. doi:10.1016/j.envint.2020.106015 PMID:32858467

Daina, N., Sivakumar, A., & Polak, J. W. (2017). Modelling electric vehicles use: A survey on the methods. *Renewable & Sustainable Energy Reviews*, *68*, 447–460. doi:10.1016/j.rser.2016.10.005

Darley, J. M., & Beniger, J. R. (1981). Diffusion of energy-conserving innovations. *The Journal of Social Issues*, *37*(2), 150–171. doi:10.1111/j.1540-4560.1981.tb02630.x

Dipert, B. (1999). Green challenger takes on gas guzzlers. *EDN*, *44*(3), 36–37.

Du, H., Liu, D., Sovacool, B. K., Wang, Y., Ma, S., & Li, R. Y. M. (2018). Li, RYM Who buys New Energy Vehicles in China? Assessing social-psychological predictors of purchasing awareness, intention, and policy. *Transportation Research Part F: Traffic Psychology and Behaviour*, *58*, 56–69. doi:10.1016/j.trf.2018.05.008

Gärling, A., & Thøgersen, J. (2001). Marketing of electric vehicles. *Business Strategy and the Environment*, *10*(1), 53–65. doi:10.1002/1099-0836(200101/02)10:1<53::AID-BSE270>3.0.CO;2-E

Gehlert, T., Dziekan, K., & Gärling, T. (2013). Psychology of sustainable travel behavior. *Transportation Research Part A, Policy and Practice*, *48*, 19–24. doi:10.1016/j.tra.2012.10.001

Goldsmith, R. E., & Hofacker, C. F. (1991). Measuring consumer innovativeness. *Journal of the Academy of Marketing Science*, *19*(3), 209–221. doi:10.1007/BF02726497

Gulzari, A., Wang, Y., & Prybutok, V. (2022). A green experience with eco-friendly cars: A young consumer electric vehicle rental behavioral model. *Journal of Retailing and Consumer Services*, *65*, 102877. doi:10.1016/j.jretconser.2021.102877

Hård, M., & Knie, A. (2001). The cultural dimension of technology management: Lessons from the history of the automobile. *Technology Analysis and Strategic Management*, *13*(1), 91–103. doi:10.1080/09537320120040464

Harms, S., & Truffer, B. (1998). *The emergence of a nation-wide carsharing co-operative in Switzerland. A case-study for the EC-supported rsearch project "Strategic Niche Management as a tool for transition to a sustainable transport system"*. EAWAG.

Hawkins, D. (2020). *Consumer behavior: Building marketing strategy*. Academic Press.

Hoyer, W. D., & MacInnis, D. J. (1997). *Consumer Behaviour*.

Ivanchev, J., Litescu, S. C., Zehe, D., Lees, M., Aydt, H., & Knoll, A. (2018, November). Hard and Soft Closing of Roads Towards Socially Optimal Routing. In *2018 21st International Conference on Intelligent Transportation Systems (ITSC)* (pp. 3499-3504). IEEE. 10.1109/ITSC.2018.8569694

Jensen, M. (1997). *Benzin i blodet: Kvalitativ del; foto: Sonja Iskov*. Miljø-og Energiministeriet, Danmarks Miljøundersøgelser.

Kemp, R., & Arundel, A. (1998). *Survey indicators for environmental innovation*. Academic Press.

Kemp, R., Schot, J., & Hoogma, R. (1998). Regime shifts to sustainability through processes of niche formation: The approach of strategic niche management. *Technology Analysis and Strategic Management*, *10*(2), 175–198. doi:10.1080/09537329808524310

Knie, K., Faestermann, T., & Korschinek, G. (1997). AMS at the Munich gas-filled analyzing magnet system GAMS. *Nuclear Instruments & Methods in Physics Research. Section B, Beam Interactions with Materials and Atoms*, *123*(1-4), 128–131. doi:10.1016/S0168-583X(96)00753-7

Kotler, P. (1991). *Marketing Management. Analysis, Planning, Implementation, and Control* (7th ed.). Prentice-Hall.

Kurani, K., Sperling, D., & Turrentine, T. (1996, January). The marketability of electric vehicles: battery performance and consumer demand for driving range. In *Proceedings of 11th Annual Battery Conference on Applications and Advances* (pp. 153-158). IEEE. 10.1109/BCAA.1996.484986

Kurani, K. S., Turrentine, T., & Sperling, D. (1996). Testing electric vehicle demand in 'hybrid households' using a reflexive survey. *Transportation Research Part D, Transport and Environment, 1*(2), 131–150. doi:10.1016/S1361-9209(96)00007-7

Link, F. (1997). *Diffusion dynamics and the pricing of innovations.* Lund University.

Lucas, A., Silva, C. A., & Neto, R. C. (2012). Life cycle analysis of energy supply infrastructure for conventional and electric vehicles. *Energy Policy, 41*, 537–547. doi:10.1016/j.enpol.2011.11.015

MacKenzie, J. J. (1997). Driving the road to sustainable ground transportation. *Frontiers of Sustainability*, 121-190.

Mellahi, K., & Harris, L. C. (2016). Response rates in business and management research: An overview of current practice and suggestions for future direction. *British Journal of Management, 27*(2), 426–437. doi:10.1111/1467-8551.12154

Murphy, I. P. (1997). Charged up. Electric cars get jolt of marketing. *Marketing News, 31*(7), 1.

Nesbitt, K., & Sperling, D. (2001). Fleet purchase behavior: Decision processes and implications for new vehicle technologies and fuels. *Transportation Research Part C, Emerging Technologies, 9*(5), 297–318. doi:10.1016/S0968-090X(00)00035-8

Nie, Y., Wang, E., Guo, Q., & Shen, J. (2018). Examining Shanghai Consumer Preferences for Electric Vehicles and Their Attributes. *Sustainability (Basel), 10*(6), 2036. doi:10.3390u10062036

Orlov, A., & Kallbekken, S. (2019). The impact of consumer attitudes towards energy efficiency on car choice: Survey results from Norway. *Journal of Cleaner Production, 214*, 816–822. doi:10.1016/j.jclepro.2018.12.326

Peattie, K., & Belz, F. M. (2010). Sustainability marketing—An innovative conception of marketing. *Marketing Review St. Gallen, 27*(5), 8–15. doi:10.100711621-010-0085-7

Razmjoo, A., Ghazanfari, A., Jahangiri, M., Franklin, E., Denai, M., Marzband, M., Astiaso Garcia, D., & Maheri, A. (2022). A Comprehensive Study on the Expansion of Electric Vehicles in Europe. *Applied Sciences (Basel, Switzerland), 12*(22), 11656. doi:10.3390/app122211656

Rip, A., & Kemp, R. (1998). Technological change. *Human Choice and Climate Change, 2*(2), 327-399.

Sahin, I. (2006). Detailed review of Rogers' diffusion of innovations theory and educational technology-related studies based on Rogers' theory. *Turkish Online Journal of Educational Technology-TOJET, 5*(2), 14–23.

Savari, G. F., Sathik, M. J., Raman, L. A., El-Shahat, A., Hasanien, H. M., Almakhles, D., Abdel Aleem, S. H. E., & Omar, A. I. (2023). Assessment of charging technologies, infrastructure and charging station recommendation schemes of electric vehicles: A review. *Ain Shams Engineering Journal, 14*(4), 101938. doi:10.1016/j.asej.2022.101938

Schot, J., Hoogma, R., & Elzen, B. (1994). Strategies for shifting technological systems: The case of the automobile system. *Futures, 26*(10), 1060–1076. doi:10.1016/0016-3287(94)90073-6

Shafiei, E., Davidsdottir, B., Fazeli, R., Leaver, J., Stefansson, H., & Asgeirsson, E. I. (2018). Macroeconomic effects of fiscal incentives to promote electric vehicles in Iceland: Implications for government and consumer costs. *Energy Policy*, *114*, 431–443. doi:10.1016/j.enpol.2017.12.034

Singh, H., Kavianipour, M., Soltanpour, A., Fakhrmoosavi, F., Ghamami, M., Zockaie, A., & Jackson, R. (2022). Macro Analysis to Estimate Electric Vehicles Fast-Charging Infrastructure Requirements in Small Urban Areas. *Transportation Research Record: Journal of the Transportation Research Board*, *2676*(11), 446–461. doi:10.1177/03611981221093625

Sperling, D. (1995). *Future drive: Electric vehicles and sustainable transportation*. Island Press.

Su, Z. W., Umar, M., Kirikkaleli, D., & Adebayo, T. S. (2021). Role of political risk to achieve carbon neutrality: Evidence from Brazil. *Journal of Environmental Management*, *298*, 113463. doi:10.1016/j.jenvman.2021.113463 PMID:34426223

Tarei, P. K., Chand, P., & Gupta, H. (2021). Barriers to the adoption of electric vehicles: Evidence from India. *Journal of Cleaner Production*, *291*, 125847. doi:10.1016/j.jclepro.2021.125847

Tigert, D., & Farivar, B. (1981). The Bass new product growth model: A sensitivity analysis for a high technology product. *Journal of Marketing*, *45*(4), 81–90. doi:10.1177/002224298104500411

Wang, F., Yu, J., Yang, P., Miao, L., & Ye, B. (2017). Analysis of the Barriers to Widespread Adoption of Electric Vehicles in Shenzhen China. *Sustainability (Basel)*, *9*(4), 522. doi:10.3390u9040522

Wang, S., Li, J., & Zhao, D. (2017). The impact of policy measures on consumer intention to adopt electric vehicles: Evidence from China. *Transportation Research Part A, Policy and Practice*, *105*, 14–26. doi:10.1016/j.tra.2017.08.013

Weber, W., & Hoogma, R. (1998). Beyond national and technological styles of innovation diffusion: A dynamic perspective on cases from the energy and transport sectors. *Technology Analysis and Strategic Management*, *10*(4), 545–566. doi:10.1080/09537329808524333

Wenig, J., Sodenkamp, M., & Staake, T. (2019). Battery versus infrastructure: Tradeoffs between battery capacity and charging infrastructure for plug-in hybrid electric vehicles. *Applied Energy*, *255*, 113787. doi:10.1016/j.apenergy.2019.113787

Yang, Y., & Tan, Z. (2019). Investigating the influence of consumer behavior and governmental policy on the diffusion of electric vehicles in Beijing, China. *Sustainability (Basel)*, *11*(24), 6967. doi:10.3390u11246967

Zhang, L., Brown, T., & Samuelsen, S. (2013). Evaluation of charging infrastructure requirements and operating costs for plug-in electric vehicles. *Journal of Power Sources*, *240*, 515–524. doi:10.1016/j.jpowsour.2013.04.048

Zhang, X., Bai, X., & Shang, J. (2018). Is subsidized electric vehicles adoption sustainable: Consumers' perceptions and motivation toward incentive policies, environmental benefits, and risks. *Journal of Cleaner Production*, *192*, 71–79. doi:10.1016/j.jclepro.2018.04.252

Zhang, X., Wang, K., Hao, Y., Fan, J., & Wei, Y. (2013). The impact of government policy on preference for NEVs: The evidence from China. *Energy Policy*, *61*, 382–393. doi:10.1016/j.enpol.2013.06.114

KEY TERMS AND DEFINITIONS

Customer Perception: It demonstrates that buyers were driven to embrace Electric Vehicles through parameters such as ease of driving, sustainable development, reduced reliance on petroleum and coal, government rebates, and tax advantages.

Eco-Friendly Vehicles: A green vehicle, clean vehicle, eco-friendly vehicle, or environmentally friendly vehicle is a road motor vehicle that has fewer negative sustainability influences compared to related regular internal combustion engine motorized vehicles.

Environmental Consciousness: Environmental consciousness is the cognitive aspect influencing customer proclivity for environmentally friendly behavior.

EV Infrastructure: Electric Vehicle charging infrastructure and facilities.

Families With Multiple Cars: Multi-car families are more suited for battery-electric vehicle transportation habits and costs.

Government Regulations: The Indian authorities have put in place various initiatives to encourage the use of electric cars (EVs) in the nation at large.

Marketing Strategy: Strategy to market the EVs to target customers.

Public Sector Enterprises: The organizations of public sectors such as the Police, Army, and Hospitals must resolve to use EVs during their movement for discharging their duties and responsibilities.

APPENDIX

Questionnaire

Q1. How important are the following factors when purchasing an electric car? [Style/Design]

Q2. How important is the following factor when purchasing an electric car? Price]

Q3. How important is the following factor when purchasing an electric car? [Space]

Q4. How important is the following factor when purchasing an electric car? [fuel efficiency]

Q5. How important is the following factor when purchasing an electric car? Performance]

Q6. How important is the following factor when purchasing an electric car? [Discounted road tax]

Q7. How important is the following factor when purchasing an electric car? Brand]

Q8. How important is the following factor when purchasing an electric car? [Advanced features]

Q9. How important is the following factor when purchasing an electric car? [Affordable car insurance]

Q10. How important is the following factor when purchasing an electric car? [Low cost of maintenance]

Q11. How important is the following factor when purchasing an electric car? [High resale Value]

Q12. How important is the following factor when purchasing an electric car? [Environmental friendliness]

Q13. How much would you be prepared to pay for a new/used non-electric car?

Q14. How much would you be prepared to pay for a similar model but electric car?

Q15. As a citizen are you committed to being environmentally conscious?

Q16. What factors encourage you to buy electric car?

Q17. What factors encourage you to buy electric car? [Promotion]

Q18. What factors encourage you to buy electric car? Reference]

Q19. What factors encourage you to buy electric car? [New Trend]

Q20. What factors encourage you to buy electric car? [Test drive]

Q21. What factors encourage you to buy electric car? [Financial benefits]

Q22. What factors encourage you to buy electric car? [Low maintenance]

Q23. For you what are the draw back of an electric car? (Recharging takes time)

Q24. For you what are the draw back of an electric car? (Recharging is inconvenient)

Q25. For you what are the draw back of an electric car? (Low number of charging station available)

Chapter 11

To Examine the Influence of Digital Marketing and Celebrity Endorsement on Consumer Purchase Intention of Mutual Funds

Kishlay Kumar
https://orcid.org/0000-0001-9685-1798
Sarala Birla University, India

Karan Pratap Singh
https://orcid.org/0000-0002-4542-7863
Birla Institute of Technology, Mesra, India

L. G. Honey Singh
https://orcid.org/0009-0008-5455-5825
Ranchi University, India

Puja Mishra
https://orcid.org/0000-0002-7270-4264
Sarala Birla University, India

ABSTRACT

The purpose of this study is to examine the influence of digital media marketing and celebrity endorsement on consumer purchase decisions toward mutual funds investment. Marketing through social media gives marketers a competitive edge when it comes to influencing customers and driving order intent in mutual funds. In this research, the authors examine the effectiveness of digital media and celebrity endorsements in influencing consumer purchasing decisions. This research employed a quantitative approach, and data were collected through online surveys from six districts of Jharkhand, a sample of 310 participants using structured questionnaire using purposive sampling. The findings advocate that celebrity endorsement is a substantial marketing tool for driving the purchase intention via social media. The indirect effect of celebrity endorsement on consumer purchase intention was also significant when digital media was used as a meditating variable. The data analysis and validation of the conceptual framework were carried out using the PLS-SEM. The study's implications are discussed.

DOI: 10.4018/979-8-3693-2841-5.ch011

INTRODUCTION

Digital media platforms are important for driving consumer purchase intent through celebrity endorsements. The indirect impact of celebrity endorsement on customer purchase intent was equally considerable when digital media was employed as the main variable. Companies invest a lot of money in endorsement, hoping that endorsing celebrities' attributes will draw in many customers. Celebrities help to create effective recall rates in addition to drawing and keeping attention to a brand or product. A celebrity endorser appeared in about one in every six advertisements in 1979. According to estimates from 1988, one in every five endorsements was made.

Additionally, current research suggests that celebrity endorsements favorably influence customer behavior and responses (Kushwaha et al., 2021). As a result of technology improvements, marketers are using digital media platforms and digital influencers to spread product awareness and branding (Zhou et al., 2021). Marketers view social media opinion leaders as digital influencers because they have the power to spread a lot of buzz among their followers. To transmit the quality of their content to the product, digital influencers are compensated to serve as brand ambassadors and to represent products and businesses. E-commerce merchants know celebrity endorsement significantly impacts consumers' purchase intentions (Nurunnisha et al., 2021). Digital media marketing platforms spread favorable information and testimonials about goods and brands to attract customers (Castillo-Abdul et al., 2021). As a result, these recommendations help e-commerce shops and companies attract customers and earn their trust. They are existing research-based celebrity endorsement or digital marketing techniques as the primary driver of customer purchase intent. Celebrities demand huge fees in exchange for promoting a product or business, and their influence over consumers is likewise considerable. Celebrity endorsements on digital media platforms could be game changers for many businesses because digital media is an expanding marketing tool for practically every industry.

In this millennium, capital market activity has developed, driven by the driving force behind alternative investments, including stocks, bonds, or other securities owned by a group of investors and managed by an Investment Management Company, among the capital market investment products that are considered ideal by investors because mutual funds have a relatively high return (Rahmah, A., 2016). Mutual funds come from the word "mutual," which means "to receive," and "funds," which means "money." The 1995 Capital Market Law defines Mutual Funds as a means to raise funds from public investors, which Investment Manager Companies invest in securities portfolios. As managers of Mutual Fund products, Investment Manager Companies invest their funds in securities, record profits or losses, and receive dividends or interest, which are recorded in Mutual Funds' Net Asset Value (NAV). NAV is one measure to monitor Mutual Fund Performance.

Today, the Internet has opened the door for Investment Management Companies to take advantage of extraordinary digital marketing opportunities. Digital marketing has been considered a new marketing method. It offers new opportunities for Investment Management Companies, which are expected to reach millions of potential Investors buying Mutual Fund products in the next few decades. Digital marketing is simply a marketing activity realized through Internet and cellular communication, namely on the Internet, through social networks, email, apps, platforms, and others (Kannan, P. K., 2017).

Social media holds its own regarding the news and views it promotes. In fact, in today's world, social media has its pride of place, side by side with any financial news resource worth its salt. Thus, this implies that individual and institutional investors rely increasingly on social media sources to make investment decisions.

Table 1. Mutual fund companies operating in India

Name of the Mutual Fund Companies Operating in India	
360 ONE Mutual Fund	Mahindra Manulife Mutual Fund
Aditya Birla Sun Life Mutual Fund	Mirae Asset Mutual Fund
Axis Mutual Fund	Motilal Oswal Mutual Fund
Bandhan Mutual Fund	Navi Mutual Fund
Bank of India Mutual Fund	Nippon India Mutual Fund
Baroda BNP Paribas Mutual Fund	NJ Mutual Fund
Canara Robeco Mutual Fund	PGIM India Mutual Fund
DSP Mutual Fund	PPFAS Mutual Fund
Edelweiss Mutual Fund	Quant Mutual Fund
Franklin Templeton Mutual Fund	Quantum Mutual Fund
Groww Mutual Fund	Samco Mutual Fund
HDFC Mutual Fund	SBI Mutual Fund
HSBC Mutual Fund	Shriram Mutual Fund
ICICI Prudential Mutual Fund	Sundaram Mutual Fund
IIFCL Mutual Fund	Tata Mutual Fund
Invesco Mutual Fund	Taurus Mutual Fund
ITI Mutual Fund	Trust Mutual Fund
JM Financial Mutual Fund	Union Mutual Fund
Kotak Mahindra Mutual Fund	UTI Mutual Fund
LIC Mutual Fund	WhiteOak Capital Mutual Fund

A recent, enlightening study from Greenwich Associates (a division of CRISIL) reveals that nearly 80% of institutional investors use social media for their normal workflow. Furthermore, 30% of such investors state that information and data obtained from social media have directly influenced investment decisions and recommendations. Today's stock market is an online arena of exchanges, and social media thrives online. Is it surprising that social media plays a key role in investment decisions and choices? Research conducted by Hong, J. Y. (2020) states that developments in digital marketing technology have changed marketing strategies. A new marketing strategy called digital marketing and celebrity endorsement has emerged, and its importance continues to grow. It has become a challenge for investment management companies to change the direction of their strategy from offline marketing to digital-based marketing. Table 1 shows the list of mutual fund companies operating in India.

The AUM of the mutual funds of India has witnessed steady growth from ₹ 8.11 trillion in June 2013 to ₹46.63 trillion in August 2023, which is five times in the last ten years. The AUM of the Indian MF Industry has grown from ₹7.66 trillion as of August 31, 2013, to ₹46.63 trillion as of August 31, 2023, a more than 6-fold increase in 10 years. The sector's AUM crossed the ₹10 Trillion milestone for the first time in May 2014, and in November 2020, it crossed the ₹ 30 trillion milestone. If we see the Fig. 1, we will conclude that in the last one-year mutual fund industry has grown tremendously. In April, 22 size of the industry was ₹ 38.99 trillion, and by the end of August 23, it was around ₹ 46.63 trillion.

Figure 1. Growth of mututal fund investor in India

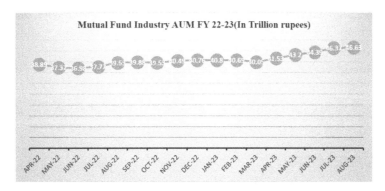

Over the five years through 2025, CRISIL expects the industry's assets under management (AUM) to continue its double-digit growth and cross the ₹ 50 trillion mark.

Based on the background that has been reviewed, as well as the significant growth of investors over the past ten years, the researcher identified the problems to be answered in the results of this study. They are identifying these problems and the role of digital media marketing and celebrity endorsements carried out by investment manager companies to increase mutual fund purchase decisions. Consequently, there is a need to investigate celebrity endorsement's direct and indirect effects on consumer purchase intention and answer the following research questions.

Digital Media Marketing and Celebrity Endorsement on Consumer Purchase Decisions Related to Library Science

- **Information Dissemination Strategies**: Libraries can adopt effective digital media marketing strategies to disseminate information about their services, events, and resources. Understanding how marketing influences consumer decisions can help libraries promote their offerings more effectively (Sinha, 2023).
- **Donor Engagement:** Libraries often rely on donations and funding. Insights from the study can be applied to libraries seeking celebrity endorsements or donations for specific programs, expansion projects, or acquisitions of rare materials.
- **Community Engagement:** Libraries aim to engage with their communities to provide valuable services. By leveraging online marketing techniques examined in the study, libraries can better reach and engage with their target audiences, encouraging them to use library resources and participate in library events (Jaiswal and Sinha, 2023).
- **Understanding User Behavior:** While libraries don't deal with commercial products, they serve users who choose how they engage with library resources and services. Insights into consumer behavior can help libraries tailor their services to meet user preferences, improve user experiences, and increase library usage.
- **Public Relations and Advocacy:** Libraries often need to advocate for their value within the community and secure public support. Understanding the impact of celebrity endorsements and digital media marketing on public perception can inform libraries on creating effective advocacy campaigns (Jaiswal et al., 2023).

- **Resource Allocation:** Libraries have limited resources, and decisions about where to allocate funds and efforts can benefit from an understanding of consumer behavior. Insights from marketing research can help libraries make data-driven decisions about resource allocation for marketing and outreach activities (Gupta et al., 2023).
- **Leveraging Influencers:** Some libraries collaborate with local influencers, authors, or public figures to promote reading, literacy, or library events. The study's findings on celebrity endorsements can guide how to leverage such influencers effectively (Kumar et al., 2023).

MOTIVATION OF THE WORK

- Does celebrity endorsement influence consumer purchase intention through digital media marketing?
- Does digital media marketing mediate the influence of celebrity endorsement on consumer's intention to buy?

To answer the above research question, the present study aims to examine the influence of celebrity commendation on buyer's purchase intention in digital media marketing and the digital media marketing serving as a mediating variable. The research will help digital marketers, policymakers, strategists, consultants, and academics understand the role of celebrity endorsement on digital marketing platforms in increasing consumer purchase intent. The rest of this work has been organized as follows. We introduce digital media marketing, celebrity endorsement, and mutual funds in section 1. Section 2 presents a literature review and theoretical framework. Section 3 represents research methodology. Section 4 represents Data interpretation and analysis. Section 5 represents the Solution, recommendation, and conclusion.

BACKGROUND OF THE STUDY

Early studies in social psychology recognized the significance of credibility and attractiveness as key attributes for effective communication (Kumar et al., 2023). As a result, research on the effectiveness of product endorsements began by focusing on these dimensions of endorsers. Credibility and attractiveness were identified as the most crucial factors in determining the impact of endorsements on consumer behavior. According to the matchup theory, for an endorsement to be impactful, the endorser and the product must share a similar image. This image is determined by factors such as trustworthiness, appeal, and various other considerations.

On the other hand, the meaning transfer model suggests that a successful transfer of cultural meaning from the celebrity endorser leads to effective endorsements (McCracken, 1989). A fresh perspective on the theory of endorsements emerged, giving rise to a new area of study centered around the matchup hypothesis and the meaning transfer model. This research focused on source reliability and trust, where endorsements were found to have a significant impact based on the source's trustworthiness (Schimmelpfennig & Hunt, 2020). This multidimensionality of endorsements theory has opened avenues for further field exploration and understanding.

- **Purchase Intention:** According to Khan et al. (2016), purchase intention refers to the desire or intention to buy something in the present or future. Several factors can influence an individual's purchase intention, including the product's packaging, customers' perception of its value, and celebrity endorsements (Younus et al., 2015; Schimmelpfennig and Hunt, 2020). Additionally, various studies have shown that when social comparison is considered, consumers tend to have higher levels of purchase intention (Wu & Lee, 2008; Zhou et al., 2021). Moreover, a study with similar findings revealed that comparing oneself to others can enhance consumers' inclination to purchase a particular product. This brings us to the marketing strategy of utilizing celebrity endorsements, as consumer attachment to the celebrity directly impacts their intention to buy the endorsed product (Nurunnisha et al., 2021). The expertise of the celebrity is a significant factor in determining this intention (Ohanian, 1991; Kushwaha et al., 2015). Alongside expertise, the attractiveness and trustworthiness of the celebrity model have been shown to directly influence a consumer's intention to make a purchase (Castillo-Abdul et al., 2021). In today's digital age, celebrities also have the power to motivate and sway consumers through various online platforms.
- **Perceived Value:** Perceived Value plays a significant role in shaping consumers' purchase intentions (Karmakar et al., 2022). Factors like celebrity endorsements, packaging, and consumer knowledge indirectly influence purchase intent, with Perceived Value mediating between these factors. Studies conducted by Zhou et al. (2021) have highlighted the direct connection between Perceived Value and purchase intent. Therefore, when aiming for higher purchase rates, it becomes crucial to place a stronger emphasis on Perceived Value.
- **Quality Orientation:** Research has shown that individuals who engage in shopping as a leisure activity prioritize quality when deciding what and where to shop (Bellenger, 1980). This holds even for online shoppers, as those who view shopping as a recreational pursuit emphasize the quality of their products (Gilal et al., 2020).
- **Brand Conscious:** Consumers who are conscious of brands strongly admire a particular brand and actively seek information about it through different media channels. A study conducted by Chu et al. in 2013 found that brand-conscious consumers generally perceive social media advertising positively. Additionally, these consumers are more inclined to take action based on the information they receive from celebrity endorsements and advertisements.

Celebrity Endorsement Effect Purchase Intention

A brand endorser is a well-known public figure who lends fame to promote a company's product, aiming to influence the public and boost sales (McCracken, 1989; Gilal et al., 2020). Moreover, the relevant expertise of a celebrity is considered highly persuasive, leading to increased brand recognition and higher purchase intentions among potential consumers (Kushwaha, 2021). The effectiveness of celebrity endorsement has been demonstrated in both print and television media, resulting in improved consumer recall, brand recognition, and purchase intent for the advertised product (Castillo-Abdul et al., 2021). The key traits of knowledgeability, dependability, and attractiveness contribute to an endorser's credibility in the eyes of consumers, fostering positive attitudes and purchase behavior toward the product and brand (Nurunnisha et al., 2021). The rise in popularity of social media platforms has revolutionized the way celebrity endorsements are approached. While some celebrities utilize these platforms to promote their endeavors rather than for marketing purposes (Stever & Lawson, 2013), para-social relationships can shed light on building connections. As Horton and Wohl (1956) described, para-social relationships refer to the close connections between audiences and celebrities (Zhou et al., 2021). Likewise, repeated exposure to a famous person's image results in the formation of such connections, where individuals in the audience develop a sense of connection and familiarity, a perception of a visible bond, and a feeling of identification with the celebrity (Horton & Wohl, 1956; Gilal et al., 2020). On social media platforms, para-social relationships are thriving. Traditional sources of celebrity-related information, like entertainment news programs and magazines, are gradually being replaced by social media platforms such as Facebook and Instagram. Consumers can directly hear from celebrities through social media, enabling them to experience a personal and intimate connection with them. In their research, Marwick and Boyd (2011) found that mistakes in spelling, grammar, and the use of first-person pronouns contribute to the audience perceiving a sense of closeness with their favorite celebrity (Chung & Cho, 2017; Shiva et al., 2020).

- **Brand Awareness:** It involves recalling a brand, its products, and associated services or offerings. A brand's presence in a consumer's memory indicates familiarity with it (Gilal et al., 2020). Developing a brand image requires establishing brand awareness, product awareness, and perception building. Once the brand is firmly implanted in customers' minds, it becomes easier to establish a connection with them. Brand attitude helps in assessing the attributes and offerings of a brand.

- **Brand Recognition:** As per a study, individuals who held a positive attitude towards advertisements exhibited a higher brand recall rate. Moreover, they were found to be more easily persuaded by the advertisements they viewed (Schimmelpfennig & Hunt, 2020). When an emotional appeal is incorporated into an advertisement, it enhances its effectiveness and increases sales. The three key elements of an advertisement that contribute to its memorability and recall are the brand name, the copy, and the image. An advertisement captures attention and enhances the product's overall appeal by incorporating emotional appeals. The ad's impact on recall is influenced by the consumer's level of engagement, brand attitude, and familiarity with the brand. When it comes to increasing advertisement recall, celebrity endorsements play a significant role. The endorsements connect consumers and the brand, leading to enhanced communication. The perceived similarity between a celebrity and a product also strongly influences brand recall. A higher level of similarity between the two results in better recall of the brand's information (Nurunnisha et al., 2021).

- **Trustworthiness**: The trustworthiness of advertising communication pertains to the level of confidence and acceptance that the message sender receives from the recipient (Ohanian, 1990). In a study conducted by Miller and Baseheart (1969), they examined the influence of source trustworthiness on the persuasive impact of the communicated message. It was found that when the communicator was perceived as trustworthy, a biased message from the sender was considered more effective in changing the recipient's attitude compared to a non-biased message.

- **Brand Loyalty:** Brand loyalty results from brand resonance, which encompasses the depth of the consumer's connection and recognition of the brand. According to Keller and his colleagues (2011), brand loyalty is crucial in increasing sales revenues, market share, and overall productivity for businesses, allowing them to strengthen their market position (Kushwaha, 2021). Implementing celebrity endorsements and various marketing activities to foster brand loyalty leads to repeated purchases, an expansion of market share, higher revenue and profitability, and a competitive advantage for the company.

Hypothesis 1: Celebrity endorsement impacts consumer purchase intention.

Digital Media Marketing Effects Purchase Intention

Digital media marketing promotes products and services through search engines, display networks, and social media platforms. Social media marketing aims to establish connections with consumers rather than simply selling to them (Zhou et al., 2021). Nowadays, businesses increasingly recognize the marketing potential that social media platforms offer, as they provide a space where individuals with similar interests can share recommendations. By utilizing these platforms, businesses can promote their offerings and other services while cultivating a community of brand enthusiasts on social networking sites, blogs, news sites, and other platforms (Priya et al., 2023). Meanwhile, consumers rely on social media to exchange information about products and services with their peers. Engaging in such discussions can be a cost-effective strategy for companies to enhance brand visibility, improve brand identification and remembrance, and foster brand allegiance.

- **Brand Awareness:** Studies have revealed that enhancing the visibility of a business's brand via online platforms leads to a rise in the volume of organic referrals. Organizations utilize digital media marketing channels for multiple purposes, such as attracting fresh clientele, amplifying brand recognition, establishing an online presence for the brand, and fostering customer connections (Shiva et al., 2020).
- **Brand Recall:** In many instances, viewers reject the notion of engaging with commercials put forth by a company. This phenomenon is called "Advertisement Blindness" (Resnick & Albert, 2014). The ability to remember information conveyed in advertisements measures consumers' attention and information processing. It estimates how much they spread electronic word-of-mouth (e-WOM) (Zhou et al., 2021). Research indicates a significant contrast between celebrity-endorsed ads featured in print media and those seen on the social media platform Twitter. Consumers exposed to celebrity endorsements in print had a greater capacity for recall and were more likely to make a purchase.
- **Comparability:** The availability of digital media marketing platforms offers consumers the advantage of comparability. In the past, consumers had limited choices due to restricted accessibility or a lack of organized marketing efforts. However, with digital media, consumers now have multiple options when making their final purchase (Bergkvist & Zhou, 2016). Digital media marketing benefits consumers with competitive prices, high-quality products, and improved services. Additionally, marketers gain a competitive edge and increase brand recognition and loyalty through digital media.
- **Relative Advantages:** One of the main benefits of digital media marketing is its ability to help build a brand by offering consumers a range of choices. Before making a purchase, consumers carefully consider the available options. Additionally, digital media marketing has the advantage of generating customer-generated social media messages. According to several studies (Kushwaha et al., 2020; Zhou et al., 2021), digital media marketing positively impacts consumer purchase intentions. Therefore, it is evident that digital media marketing provides relative advantages regarding brand establishment and consumer engagement through social media.

Hypothesis 2: Digital Media Marketing impacts consumer purchase intention.

Celebrity Endorsement and Digital Media Marketing

Celebrities play a crucial role in helping brands establish and solidify their presence in the digital media landscape. By aligning brand values with celebrity endorsers, brands can enhance the perception of brand fit (Buil et al., 2009; Shiva et al., 2020). In the digital era, celebrity endorsements are widely utilized on social networking sites. The ultimate goal of these promotions is to boost purchase intent and cultivate a positive brand image among consumers. It is well-known that celebrity endorsements significantly impact brand recognition, consumer purchasing behavior, brand recall, and even purchase intention (Hollensen & Schimmelpfennig, 2013). Over the past decade, mobile social media has gained immense popularity as an effective internet marketing channel (Shareef et al., 2019). Digital media marketing is crucial in building and strengthening brand reputation and customer loyalty. It offers a valuable platform for informal communication between brands and consumers, fostering connections and engagement. One of the ways digital media contributes to this is by establishing para-social relationships between celebrities and consumers. These relationships are formed due to continuous exposure to well-known personalities, leading to familiarity, perceived friendship, and identification with the celebrity (Horton & Wohl, 1956; Chauhan et al., 2020). Research has shown that when products are promoted by a celebrity with whom individuals have developed significant para-social relationships, consumers display positive sentiments towards the products and exhibit strong purchase intentions (Knoll et al., 2015; Kim et al., 2015). This highlights the influence celebrity endorsement through digital media marketing platforms can have on consumer behavior, specifically their intent to purchase.

Hypothesis 3: Celebrity endorsement through digital media marketing platforms positively impacts consumer purchase intention.

Figure 2. Conceptual framework and hypothesis

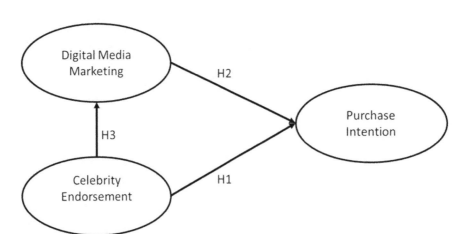

RESEARCH METHODOLOGY

The study focused on customers residing in the six districts of Jharkhand: Ranchi, Hazaribagh, Jamshedpur, Ramgarh, Dhanbad, and Bokaro. From July to September 2023, data was collected using purposive sampling. The questionnaire consisted of eleven items obtained from existing literature. Each of the eleven items was evaluated on a five-point Likert scale, ranging from "1 - Strongly Disagree" to "5 - Strongly Agree". To gather responses, an online structured questionnaire was utilized through Google Forms, with 310 participants interviewed. The study employed Smart PLS 4 to examine the mediating influence of constructs as well as the dependability and validity of the data.

DATA ANALYSIS AND INTERPRETATION

To conduct data analysis and interpret the topic, you would typically follow a structured process involving several steps. Here's an overview of how you might approach this: Data Collection and Preparation Start by collecting the relevant data, which may include survey responses, website analytics, social media metrics, or any other data sources related to digital media marketing and purchase intention. Clean and preprocess the data to ensure it is accurate, complete, and in a suitable format for analysis. Descriptive Statistics begins with descriptive statistics to get an initial understanding of your data. Calculate mean, median, standard deviation, and frequency distributions. Explore the characteristics of your dataset, including the distribution of purchase intention scores and the types of digital media marketing channels used. Data Visualization creates histograms, bar charts, scatterplots, and box plots to visualize the relationships between digital media marketing efforts and purchase intention.

Look for trends, patterns, or outliers in the data that might indicate the strength and direction of the relationship. Hypothesis Testing formulates hypotheses about the relationship between digital media marketing and purchase intention. For example, you might hypothesize that increased exposure to digital media marketing positively affects purchase intention. Conduct statistical analysis to assess the strength and significance of the relationship between digital media marketing variables (e.g., ad spend, frequency of ads) and purchase intention. Interpret the regression model coefficients to understand how changes in digital marketing variables impact purchase intention. Segmentation and Subgroup Analysis are applicable; segment your data into different groups (e.g., age, gender, geographic location) to analyze whether the impact of digital media marketing on purchase intention varies across different demographics. Qualitative analysis, such as open-ended survey responses, involves thematic analysis to extract meaningful insights and quotes supporting your quantitative findings. Summarize your findings, emphasizing whether digital media marketing has a statistically significant effect on purchase intention. Discuss the practical implications of your results for businesses or marketers. Consider the limitations of your study and areas for future research. Present your findings in a clear and visually appealing format, such as tables, charts, and graphs. Prepare a written report with an executive summary, methodology, results, and conclusions. It's important to ensure that your analysis is conducted rigorously and that you interpret the results accurately in the context of your research question.

Table 2. Demographics of the respondents

Demographic Variable	Category	No. of Respondents	Percentage (%)
Gender	Male	190	61.29
	Female	120	38.71
	Transgender	0	0.00
Age	20-25	65	20.97
	25-30	83	26.77
	30-35	130	41.94
	above 35	32	10.32
Qualification	Under-graduation	98	31.61
	Graduation	162	52.26
	Post-graduation and above	50	16.13
Income Group	up to 2.5 lakhs	48	15.48
	2.5 to 5 lakhs	103	33.23
	5 to 7.5 lakhs	119	38.39
	More than seven lakhs	40	12.90

Descriptive Analysis

The descriptive statistics for the survey participants are depicted in Table 2. The data for the survey was collected from 310 customers residing in Ranchi, Hazaribagh, Jamshedpur, Ramgarh, Dhanbad, and Bokaro. Out of these respondents, the majority, consisting of 190 individuals (61.29%), identified as male, while 120 (38.71%) identified as female. Upon analyzing the participants' demographics, it was found that many were young adults. Specifically, 83 respondents fell within the age range of 25 to 30 years (26.77%), and 65 respondents fell within the age range of 20 to 25 years (20.97%). Regarding

Table 3. Quality criteria for reflective model assessments and composite model

Latent Construct	Measured Variables	Factor Loading	Rho-A	Composite Reliability	AVE
Digital Media Marketing	Brand Awareness	0.934	0.78	0.912	0.556
	Brand Recall	0.874			
	Comparability	0.843			
	Relative Advantages	0.898			
Celebrity Endorsement	Brand Awareness	0.756	0.92	0.846	0.795
	Brand Recognition	0.712			
	Trustworthiness	0.789			
	Brand loyalty	0.764			
Purchase Intention	Perceived Value	0.897	0.84	0.941	0.789
	Quality Orientation	0.897			
	Brand Conscious	0.869			

Table 4. Discriminant validity (F&L criterion)

CFA	Digital Media Marketing	Celebrity Endorsement	Purchase Intention
Digital Media Marketing	**0.884**		
Celebrity Endorsement	0.657	**0.759**	
Purchase Intention	0.687	0.389	**0.891**

educational qualifications, the majority of respondents, 162 individuals (52.26%), held a graduate degree, while 50 individuals (16.13%) were postgraduate and above. Additionally, it was observed that the age and income of the respondents played a significant role in their responses, highlighting the impact of celebrity endorsements and digital media. The data revealed that many respondents had annual incomes ranging from 2.5 to 7.5 lakhs, indicating a diverse and suitable sample for this study.

Table 3 above demonstrates the reliability and validity of the data. We used Cronbach's Alpha and Composite Reliability (CR) to assess internal reliability. All the calculated values for Cronbach's Alpha and Composite Reliability (CR) exceed 0.70, indicating that the constructs can be considered reliable (Hair et al., 2019). Moreover, all the major components that reflect the study have "average variance extracted" (AVE) ratings well above the 0.50 threshold, confirming convergent validity. This finding suggests that the study deserves further investigation (Hair et al., 2022).

The examination of discriminant validity presented in Table 4 is grounded on the criterion established by Farnell and Larcker (1981). In this criterion, the value computed, specifically the square root of the 'Average Variance Extracted (AVE)' of the constructs on the diagonal, surpasses the correlation values between the constructs' items. Consequently, it has been confirmed that all constructs possess distinct characteristics.

Structural Model Assessments

The structural model evaluations aimed to explore the connection between the constructs and their ability to predict outcomes (Hair et al., 2019). To determine the p-values for the hypotheses presented in

Table 5. Hypothesis testing of the model

Hypothesis	Path Relationships	Standardized Beta	Standard Deviation (STDEV)	Standard Error (ST ERR)	t-Statistics	Decision
H1	Digital Media Marketing-> Purchase Intention	0.689	0.031	0.031	22.499***	Accepted
H2	Celebrity endorsement -> Purchase Intention	0.039	0.044	0.044	0.908ns	Rejected
H3	Celebrity Endorsement -> Digital Media Marketing	0.495	0.07	0.07	8.232***	Accepted
	Celebrity Endorsement -> Digital Media Marketing-> Purchase Intention	0.919	0.072	0.0712	11.354***	Accepted
('*p≤0.01, **p≤0.05, ***p≤0.001')						

the study, the investigation utilized 5000 bootstraps without any changes indicating insignificance (Hair et al., 2020). Within the structural inner model, each set of predictive variables, defined as formative measurement models, were assessed individually to gauge tolerance and the 'Variance Inflation Factor' (VIF). The computed values were below 3.33, well below the designated threshold (Diamantopoulos et al., 2008). The model illustrates the structural path of dependent and independent constructs and variables. We identified three major hypotheses (Figure 1) and developed a paths model during the literature review.

In the present context, using PLS-SEM models in research is widely acknowledged for assessing and validating the model's fit (Hair et al., 2020). The analysis in Table 5, clearly explains the structural model and hypothesis testing. Based on the findings presented in Table 4, it is evident that digital media marketing significantly influences consumer purchase decisions ($p \leq 0.001$). Therefore, hypothesis H1 is supported, indicating that digital media marketing plays a role in facilitating comparison, brand recall, awareness, and relative advantage. Another key finding from the analysis is the considerable impact of celebrity endorsement on digital media marketing ($p \leq 0.001$), leading to the acceptance of hypothesis H3. According to various research studies, the endorsement of celebrities has a positive influence on consumers' intention to make a purchase, especially when it is associated with or promoted through digital media marketing. After conducting a thorough review of relevant literature, we formulated a hypothesis. We found that celebrity endorsements influence consumers in six districts of Jharkhand and can impact their purchasing decisions. However, our analysis also revealed that the calculated t-value of 0.908 is greater than 0.00, indicating that our initial hypothesis (H2) was rejected. Based on the results of our hypothesis testing, we can conclude that while celebrity endorsements have only a minimal impact on consumer's intention to purchase, digital media marketing plays a crucial role in creating awareness, facilitating product comparison, offering relative advantages, and ultimately influencing consumers' final purchase decisions.

Additionally, the F2 values for digital media and purchase intention were 0.559 and 0.083, respectively, exceeding the threshold value of 0.015, thus further supporting our framework (Cohen, 1988). Similarly, the R2 values for celebrity endorsement and digital media are 0.689 and 0.72, respectively, above the threshold value of 0.35. Furthermore, the Q2 values for purchase intention (0.528) and digital media (0.539) fall within an acceptable range (Gessier, 1975). Finally, the estimated SRMR values indicate 0.026, below the limit value of 0.08 (Hair et al., 2022).

FINDINGS OF THE STUDY

According to previous research, it has been found that utilizing celebrity endorsements is the most effective approach to increasing customer awareness in advertisements (Freiden, 1984; Schimmelpfennig and Hunt, 2020; Nurunnisha et al., 2021). The results of this study support these findings by indicating that celebrity endorsements positively impact consumers' intention to make a purchase (Castillo-Abdul et al., 2021; Zhou et al., 2021; Gilal et al., 2020). Furthermore, the analysis reveals that the influence of celebrity endorsements on buying intention is greatly influenced by the utilization of digital media marketing (McCracken, 1989; Gilal et al., 2020; Castillo-Abdul et al., 2021; Stever & Lawson, 2013). However, the data contradicts the hypothesis that digital media marketing determines consumers' likelihood of choosing a brand (Gilal et al., 2020; Chung & Cho, 2017; Shiva et al., 2020).

SOLUTIONS AND RECOMMENDATIONS

Limited information regarding celebrities' impact on brand development through social media platforms is available. This research addresses this gap by examining how celebrities influence consumer purchase intentions through digital media endorsements. Previous studies have demonstrated that when a celebrity endorses a brand, it enhances the likelihood of consumers selecting it. This current study expands the existing knowledge in the realm of digital media. After examining the impact of using celebrities as endorsers on digital platforms and the subsequent influence on consumers' intention to purchase, entrepreneurs and managers can utilize this research to allocate resources effectively. The growing presence of consumers on digital media, where they consume online content quickly, compels brands to reassess and modify their conventional marketing strategies. Harnessing technological advancements and embracing innovative marketing approaches will greatly enhance the brand value of any company that connects with consumers through different digital platforms.

Theoretical Suggestion

First, the factors in this study can be re-tested by adding or modifying some of the variables analyzed in future research that is interested in analyzing the purchase decision and performance of mutual funds related to digital marketing and celebrity endorsements. Second, future researchers can broaden their research goals to include particular mutual fund products based on the type and worldwide mutual fund products. Third, a larger sample size of research respondents can help the findings become more generalized and representative of all mutual fund investors nationwide.

Practical Suggestion

To achieve a sizable retail market, investment management organizations that handle mutual funds must first increase their marketing efforts through digital marketing channels. The firm plan of the Investment Manager must strengthen the digital marketing channel, which includes maximizing the function of the company website. Second, more must be done to promote literacy among retail investors and educate them about mutual fund products and the online transaction process. Literacy and education can be maintained through podcasts created in association with SEBI online or by producing literate and educational content that will be placed on the social media pages of investment management firms.

Limitation and Future Scope

Data has been gathered from a large group of participants. However, a disparity exists between genders, as female participants greatly outnumber their male counterparts. The research was conducted exclusively in the six districts of Jharkhand (Ranchi, Hazaribagh, Jamshedpur, Ramgarh, Dhanbad, and Bokaro). Therefore, the findings may vary in other regions. It is imperative to explore similar factors in different areas. By incorporating digital media platform elements into the model, such as identification, categorization, and inclusion, it is possible to conduct thorough investigations into the popularity of each platform among users, as well as the diverse consumer behaviors exhibited on these platforms. The involvement of prominent film actors, athletes, and emerging influencers on social media within the digital realm can serve to examine celebrity endorsements' impact further.

CONCLUSION

The significance of digital media and celebrities in advertising campaigns is becoming increasingly crucial. With this in mind, this research aimed to ascertain the direct and indirect impacts of celebrities on consumers' intention to purchase. Celebrities are generously compensated for endorsing brands or products. Marketers strive to engage well-known individuals in society to endorse their products, aiming to enhance product performance and brand recognition. Consequently, it was revealed that celebrity endorsement plays a pivotal role in increasing consumers' intention to purchase when executed through digital platforms. However, relying solely on celebrity endorsement is inadequate in boosting consumer purchase intent. Therefore, marketers are advised to leverage celebrity endorsement marketing content through digital media tools to amplify the effectiveness of advertising campaigns and attain advertising objectives. Moreover, when endorsing a brand or product, a highly credible celebrity surpasses a less credible one.

ACKNOWLEDGMENT

Thank Ms. Meghna Ghosh, Assistant Professor of Birla Institute of Technology and Science (BITS) Law School, Mumbai, for her support and encouragement. He helped me complete the research and study, which resulted in the successful completion of this chapter. Secondly, I would like to thank Mr. Shreya Bharti, Sarala Birla University, for his valuable support in writing and correction. Finally, I would like to congratulate Sarala Birla University for supporting us with its vast collection of books in the library.

REFERENCES

Bergkvist, L., & Zhou, K. Q. (2016). Celebrity endorsements: A literature review and research agenda. *International Journal of Advertising, 35*(4), 642–663.a Bellenger, D. N. (1980). Profiling the recreational shopper. *Journal of Retailing, 56*(3), 77–92.

Buil, I., de Chernatony, L., & Hem, L. E. (2009). Brand extension strategies: Perceived fit, brand type, and culture influences. *European Journal of Marketing, 43*(11/12), 1300–1324. doi:10.1108/03090560910989902

Castillo-Abdul, B., Bonilla-del-Río, M., & Núñez-Barriopedro, E. (2021). Influence and Relationship between Branded Content and the Social Media Consumer Interactions of the Luxury Fashion Brand Manolo Blahnik. *Publications / MDPI, 9*(1), 10. doi:10.3390/publications9010010

Chu, S. C., Kamal, S., & Kim, Y. (2013). Understanding consumers' responses toward social media advertising and purchase intention toward luxury products. *Journal of Global Fashion Marketing, 4*(3), 158–174. doi:10.1080/20932685.2013.790709

Chung, S., & Cho, H. (2017). Fostering para-social relationships with celebrities on social media: Implications for celebrity endorsement. *Psychology and Marketing, 34*(4), 481–495. doi:10.1002/mar.21001

Freiden, J. B. (1984). Advertising spokesperson effects-An examination of endorser type and gender on 2 audiences. *Journal of Advertising Research, 24*(5), 33–41.

Gilal, F. G., Paul, J., Gilal, N. G., & Gilal, R. G. (2020). Celebrity endorsement and brand passion among air travelers:Theory and evidence. *International Journal of Hospitality Management*, *85*, 102347. doi:10.1016/j.ijhm.2019.102347

Gupta, N. E., Kumar, K., & Sinha, K. (2023). The Nexus of War, Violence, and Rights: A History of War-Torn Afghanistan. In Handbook of Research on War Policies, Strategies, and Cyber Wars (pp. 334-351). IGI Global.

Hair, J. F., Hult, G. T. M., Ringle, C. M., & Sarstedt, M. (2022). *A Primer on Partial Least Squares Structural Equation Modeling (PLS-SEM)* (3rd ed.). Sage.

Hair, J. F., Risher, J. J., Sarstedt, M., & Ringle, C. M. (2019). When to use and how to report the results of PLS-SEM. *European Business Review*, *31*(1), 2–24. doi:10.1108/EBR-11-2018-0203

Hong, J. Y. (2020). *From Marketing to Digital Marketing: Paradigm Shift and New Dilemma*. Academic Press.

Horton, D., & Wohl, R. R. (1956). Mass Communication and Para-Social Interaction. *Psychiatry*, *2747*(March), 215–229. Advance online publication. doi:10.1080/00332747.1956.11023049 PMID:13359569

Jaiswal, G., Karmakar, M., & Sinha, K. (2023). Yoga: A Stress Removal Toolkit During War From the Women's Perspective. In Acceleration of the Biopsychosocial Model in Public Health (pp. 137-167). IGI Global.

Jaiswal, G., & Sinha, K. (2023). Yoga: An Ancient Healing Approach for Cyclical Mastalgia. In Perspectives on Coping Strategies for Menstrual and Premenstrual Distress (pp. 237-261). IGI Global.

Kannan, P. K., & Li, H. A. (2017). Digital marketing A framework, review and research agenda. *International Journal of Research in Marketing*, *34*(1), 22–45. doi:10.1016/j.ijresmar.2016.11.006

Karmakar, M., Priya, A., Sinha, K., & Verma, M. (2022, December). Shrinkable Cryptographic Technique Using Involutory Function for Image Encryption. In *International Conference on Advanced Network Technologies and Intelligent Computing* (pp. 275-289). Cham: Springer Nature Switzerland.

Khan, S. K., Rukhsar, A., & Shoaib, M. (2016). Influence of Celebrity Endorsement on Consumer Purchase Intention. IOSR Journal of Business and Management. *18*(1), 2319–7668. doi:10.9790/ 487X-18110609

Kim, H., Ko, E., & Kim, J. (2015). SNS users' para-social relationships with celebrities: Social media effects on purchase intentions. *Journal of Global Scholars of Marketing Science*, *25*(3), 279–294. doi: 10.1080/21639159.2015.1043690

Knoll, J., Schramm, H., Schallhorn, C., & Wynistorf, S. (2015). *International Journal of Advertising: The Review of Marketing Communications Good guy vs. bad guy: the influence of para-social interactions with media characters on brand placement effects*. doi:10.1080/02650487.2015.1009350

Kumar, K., Singhania, D., Singh, K. P., Mishra, P., & Sinha, K. (2023). Navigating the Economic Challenges of the Russia-Ukraine Conflict on India. In Handbook of Research on War Policies, Strategies, and Cyber Wars (pp. 218-238). IGI Global. doi:10.4018/978-1-6684-6741-1.ch012

Kumar, S., Jaiswal, G., & Sinha, K. (2023). Skin Cancer Lesion Detection Using Improved CNN Techniques. In Handbook of Research on Technological Advances of Library and Information Science in Industry 5.0 (pp. 355-377). IGI Global.

Kushwaha, B. P., Rao, N. S., & Ahmad, S. Y. (2015). The factors influencing consumer buying decision of electronic products. Management Dynamics, 15(1), 5-15.

Marwick, A., & Boyd, D. (2011). To see and be seen: Celebrity practice on Twitter. *Convergence (London), 17*(2), 139–158. doi:10.1177/1354856510394539

Mccracken, G. (1989). Who Is the Celebrity Endorser? *Cultural Foundations of the Endorsement Process., 16*(December), 310–321.

Miller, G. R., & Baseheart, J. (1969). Source trustworthiness, opinionated statements, and response to persuasive communication. *Speech Monographs, 36*(1), 1–7. doi:10.1080/03637756909375602

Nurunnisha, G. A., Roespinoedji, R., & Roespinoedji, D. (2021). Female Students Perceptions on The Effect of Country of Origin, Brand Ambassador on Purchase Intentions: A Study on The Geographical Origin of Tokopedia E-Commerce Company, Indonesia. *Review of International Geographical Education Online, 11*(1), 573–582.

Ohanian, R. (1991). The impact of celebrity spokespersons' perceived image on consumers' intention to purchase. *Journal of Advertising Research, 31*(1), 46–54.

Priya, A., Sharma, S., Sinha, K., & Yogesh, Y. (2023, March). Community Detection in Networks: A Comparative study. In *2023 International Conference on Device Intelligence, Computing and Communication Technologies (DICCT)* (pp. 505-510). IEEE. 10.1109/DICCT56244.2023.10110206

Rahmah, A. (2016). *Analisisperbandingankinerjareksa dana syariah dan kinerjareksa dana konvensionaldenganmetodesharpe, treynor dan jensen* [Doctoral dissertation]. Universitas Islam Negeri Sumatera Utara.

Resnick, M., & Albert, W. (2014). The impact of advertising location and user task on the emergence of banner ad blindness: An eye-tracking study. *International Journal of Human-Computer Interaction, 30*(3), 206–219. doi:10.1080/10447318.2013.847762

Schimmelpfennig, C., & Hunt, J. B. (2020). Fifty years of celebrity endorser research: Support for a comprehensive celebrity endorsement strategy framework. *Psychology and Marketing, 37*(3), 488–505. doi:10.1002/mar.21315

Shareef, M. A., Mukerji, B., Dwivedi, Y. K., Rana, N. P., & Islam, R. (2019). Social media marketing: Comparative effect of advertisement sources. *Journal of Retailing and Consumer Services, 46*, 58–69. doi:10.1016/j.jretconser.2017.11.001

Shiva, A., Narula, S., & Shahi, S. K. (2020). What drives retail investors' investment decisions? Evidence from no mobile phone phobia (Nomophobia) and investor fear of missing out (I-FoMo). Journal of Content. *Community and Communication, 10*(6), 2–20. doi:10.31620/JCCC.06.20/02

Sinha, K. (2023). The Metaverse and Digital Libraries: Ensuring Safe and Secure Access to Information. In Handbook of Research on Advancements of Contactless Technology and Service Innovation in Library and Information Science (pp. 1-22). IGI Global.

Stever, G. S., & Lawson, K. (2013). Twitter as a way for celebrities to communicate with fans: Implications for the study of para-social interaction. *North American Journal of Psychology*, *15*(2).

Wu, L. L., & Lee, L. (2008). Online social comparison: Implications derived from Web 2.0. *PACIS 2008 - 12th Pacific Asia Conference on Information Systems: Leveraging ICT for Resilient Organizations and Sustainable Growth in the Asia Pacific Region.*

Younus, & Zia. (2015). Identifying the factors affecting customer purchase intention. Global Journal of Management and Business Research. *Administrative Management*, *15*(2).

Zhou, S., Barnes, L., McCormick, H., & Cano, M. B. (2021). Social media influencers' narrative strategies to create eWOM: A theoretical contribution. *International Journal of Information Management*, *59*, 102293. doi:10.1016/j.ijinfomgt.2020.102293

KEY TERMS AND DEFINITIONS

Celebrity Endorsement: Celebrity endorsement, also known as celebrity branding or advertising, is a marketing strategy that uses a celebrity's fame and image to promote a brand or product.

Consumer Purchase Intention: A consumer's purchasing intention refers to a consumer's attitude toward a specific purchasing behavior and the consumer's degree of willingness to pay.

Digital Media Marketing: Digital marketing, also called online marketing, promotes brands to connect with potential customers using the Internet and other forms of digital communication. It includes email, social media, web-based advertising, and text and multimedia messages as a marketing channel.

Mutual Fund: A mutual fund is a pooled collection of assets that invests in stocks, bonds, and other securities. When you buy a mutual fund, you get a more diversified holding than you would with an individual security, and you can enjoy the convenience of automatic investing if you meet the minimum investment requirements.

PLS-SEM: The partial least squares path modeling or partial least squares structural equation modeling (PLS-SEM) is a method for structural equation modeling that allows the estimation of complex cause-effect relationships in path models with latent variables.

Purposive Sampling: Purposive sampling refers to a group of non-probability sampling techniques in which units are selected because they have characteristics that you need in your sample.

Social Media: Social media refers to interactions among people who create, share, and exchange information and ideas in virtual communities and networks.

Chapter 12
The Role and Significance of Accreditation in Higher Education Institutions:
A Study

Mallikarjun Mulimani
ⓘ https://orcid.org/0000-0003-4711-5975
Government First Grade College, Belagavi, India

Satishkumar Naikar
ⓘ https://orcid.org/0000-0002-7621-5388
D.Y. Patil University (Deemed), Navi Mumbai, India

ABSTRACT

Accreditation plays a vital role in higher education institutions by ensuring quality and standardization. It serves as a measure of an institution's academic programs, faculty qualifications, student support services, and infrastructure. By maintaining accountability and transparency, accreditation upholds standards of excellence and promotes continuous improvement. Accreditation enhances an institution's credibility and reputation, providing a recognized stamp of approval. It also facilitates student mobility and recognition of qualifications, ensuring that degrees and certificates hold value and are widely accepted by other institutions and employers.

INTRODUCTION

The library at an educational institution is today viewed as a fully engaged link between the students and the enormous repository of information resources, between classroom lectures and the enormous sources of information from which the lectures get their material. The librarian has an extended role now from keeper of information resources to become a true friend and a perfect guide for the learners in an academic setting. Dissemination of knowledge in any academic institution is attained by means of (i)

DOI: 10.4018/979-8-3693-2841-5.ch012

Teaching, (ii) Research, iii) Publication, and iv) Extension programmes. Library is a treasure house of ever-increasing universe of knowledge that supplements towards the better performance of all the four activities. Academic libraries pay an indispensable role in the dissemination of information or knowledge generated in the higher educational institutions, the universities and colleges. In fact, the publication wing of the universities in India is created to perform this function and the university library can assist that in publication marketing. The coming up of open access initiative has identified new role for the academic libraries with the institutional repositories taking shape within the ambit of college or university library. Academic library is therefore an integral part of the entire academic system; it promotes teaching, research, learning, and problem-solving and provides endless services to the real education; and ascertains that it is a veritable center of academic learning for self-achievement. (Karisiddappa, 1996)

The effect of information and communication technology has led to long lasting changes in the Academic Libraries' overall structure, management, and service delivery. Academic libraries have immediately embraced ICT due to the availability of affordable and user-friendly technology to increase the impact of their services and acquire the necessary visibility. Since the National Assessment and Accreditation Council (NAAC), an independent UGC agency, took over the assessment and accreditation of academic institutions in the late 1990s, this has been progressing at an accelerated rate due to the necessity of library automation and networking. The NAAC issued a brochure and case studies on recommendations and best practices in college libraries, as well as made some recommendations for best practices to be used in academic libraries. The first of the best practices listed by NAAC focuses on computerizing libraries and collection development to create a strong enough foundation for e-information resources. Previously optional and viewed as a luxury since it was not cost-effective, automation of libraries is now a necessary routine procedure for library management. In their administrative duties, libraries are now implementing management ideas like quality management and assessment. The top 10 predictions for the future of academic libraries have been compiled by the Association of College and Research Libraries of the American Library Association. (NAAC, 2005) "Digitization and digital collections and preservation, data storage and retrieval" is the first of these. The National Knowledge Commission, which was established by the Indian government, has recently emphasized the significance of academic libraries as sources for 'access to knowledge'. Thus, businesses are adjusting to the managerial, technological, and organizational changes brought about by these circumstances, which have influenced them both internally and outside. (National Knowledge Commission, 2007)

Libraries offer everyone access to books and other documents. Libraries assist those with disabilities in finding relief from their suffering, underprivileged people in reclaiming their place in society, and businesspeople in growing their enterprises. Additionally, it encourages researchers, students, and other team members to pursue their objectives. The libraries offer essential data in a way that advances education. In addition to serving as a bridge between teaching and learning, libraries offer vast resources that can be used to improve classroom instruction. At all educational levels, books and libraries are acknowledged as the true center of learning since they play a significant role in the history of Indian civilization. The purpose of library services, both in physical and online locations, is to support each individual library user in achieving academic achievement by offering the materials and an environment that will promote intellectual, emotional, and social growth. (Neelameghan, 1968) Modern job classification relies on scientific management, which is the study of a job's work. The analysis' findings aid the executive officer in understanding clearly and intelligently what he or she may and should anticipate from a worker. This gives him a yardstick to gauge how well a worker is doing their job. The key components of the library management process are planning, organizing, staffing, directing, coordinating, reporting, and budgeting. Luther Gulick invented the term "POSDCORB" to describe these components. (UGC Library Committee, 1965). The purpose of this study is to examine the role and significance of accreditation in higher education institutions. It aims to explore how accreditation processes impact the quality and credibility of education provided by these institutions.

BACKGROUND OF HIGHER EDUCATION IN INDIA

Early Indian Education System

Libraries and educational institutions are the two pillars of the educational system. Both are necessary for the system to function. Any system that wants to endure for the benefit of society or its own survival must adapt to the environment. The Indian educational system is the same. India used to have a totally different type of educational system. In ancient times, the caste system was highly powerful. Brahmana, Kshatriya Vaishya, and Shoodra were the three most prevalent "varnas". The Brahmana community was the only one eligible for education. The core of the student's curriculum was the Veda of his particular school. It was an offence if anybody tries to get the education. But some time before 500 BC the education of the Kshatriya and Vaisya castes likewise passed under Brahmana control. Later come the Buddhist Education system. It was same as that of Brahmin system but the difference was it did not have caste and Vedas. Oral instruction and memorization were main techniques for teaching and learning process. Buddhists had introduced Buddhist Literature-the Tripitika, Grammer-both in Pali and Sanskrit. So the interest of students declined in Vedas and Upanishads and there was a great tendency to specialize in the fields like Grammar, Law Logic, Philosophy and Comparative Philosophy. The women education was in very negligible proportion. The higher learning seats like Takshashila, Nalanda, Vikramashila, Vallabhi etc. came in the existence as early as 17th century BC. They attracted many scholars from all over the India (Government of India, 1967).

In his report, the Kothari Commission, which reviewed the situation of higher education from 1964 to 1966, underlined the necessity for a system with built-in flexibility. This paper served as the foundation for the 1968 National Policy of Education. The same strategy was used in 1985 with the same goals of developing human capital to support the economy and instilling important values (Gandhi, 2013). In the 1990 Ramamurthy Committee Report "Towards an enlightened human society," emphasis was placed on the creation of autonomous colleges, the redesigning of courses and programs, the transformation of teaching methods, the increased support for research, and the use of the Open University system. The same was implemented in 1992.

During the last 10-15 years, India has emerged as a destination for the development of Information Technology related products and services. The UGC is building the network of all the education institutes. EduSat is the first of its kind which links and raises the quality of schools and colleges all over the country. (National Knowledge Commission 2007)

Academic Libraries: In the Beginning

School, college, university, and research libraries are all considered academic libraries. All of these meet the demands of the academic community, add to the institution's study and research programs, and promote the preservation and sharing of information. Even though these academic libraries have some things in common, their worth and content are very different from one another. Academic libraries don't just exist; they do so in order to further the goals of the educational system, of which they are a component. (Jange, 2022)

College Libraries

College libraries are a crucial part of higher education and act as the primary learning resource. As learning takes precedence over teaching, libraries must fulfill their job in an appropriate manner. A significant turning point in the development of college libraries was the formation of the Library Committee of the University Grants Commission and the publication of its Report in 1965. The UGC (India) and State Government funding of college libraries is one of the Committee's main recommendations. These suggestions address a variety of topics, including the number of employees and their qualifications, book selection and collection, programs to promote reading, ideas for new libraries, and more. In recognition of the importance of libraries in higher education, the National Education Commission, which operated from 1964 to 1966, declared that no new institution or department should be established without making sufficient provisions for its library. Both the educational system and the information environment have undergone tremendous transformation in the last 50 years. Colleges are currently not restricted to graduate teaching only. Some institutions are seeing a rapid increase in the number of students, and the library is a place where they may learn about other information sources and expand their knowledge outside of the classroom. In addition to undergraduate courses, several colleges also offer postgraduate ones. Here, they can set their long-term goals and guide their career. As a result, college libraries are crucial to graduate and postgraduate education programs. (Government of India, 1986)

University Libraries in India

A university is a symbol of reality, sanity, tolerance, and humanity. Through the expansion of information, it aids in the advancement of society as a whole. To impart knowledge to students in all areas of the universe of knowledge and provide professional and vocational training (education and training); to disseminate knowledge and close the social and cultural gap (publication); to diffuse and foster true values and attitudes in society through a variety of extension activities (extension). These are the functions of universities. An accurate description of a university is that it is "a community" with "scholars and teachers as the head, students as the body, and the library as the heart." The value of libraries in higher education has been repeatedly underlined in India by educationists, librarians, scholars and committees.

In the report of the University Education Commission, it is stated that libraries are crucial to higher education: "The library is the heart of all University work, directly so as to its research work, and indirectly so as to its educational work, which derives its life from research work. Higher education libraries' expansion in India has received a lot of attention. However, the expansion of academic college libraries falls far short of expectations. There is a lot of difference amongst libraries; neither college nor university libraries have had the same evolution. (Government of India, 1950)

Modern Academic Libraries

The primary causes of insufficient development can be attributed to the universities' lack of teaching duties, the classroom-based, one textbook learning process, the lack of trained staff, the absence of suitable structures, furnishings, and equipment, and the leftover budget allocation. However, the creation of the UGC by the Statute of 1956, support from other nations, the formation of the library committee by the UGC, the awarding of academic status to library professionals, and other factors greatly enhanced the performance of the libraries, (Government of India, 1965)

Establishment of UGC

The establishment of University Grants Commission (UGC) by a statute in 1956 was a great impetus for college and the University libraries. UGC appointed a library committee under the chairmanship of Dr. S R Radhakrishnan and in 1965 this committee produced the report. One of the most important recommendations of far-reaching consequence was the recommendation to equate the professional staff of libraries with the academic staff of the college and universities in the salary and status. Continuing developments in discipline, IT revolution and ever emerging communication networks invited attention of the UGC again to pay serious attention. As a result, the second National Review Committee on University and College Libraries was constituted in 1996. (Karisiddappa, 1996)

The University Grants Commission (UGC) in India created the National Assessment and Accreditation Council (NAAC) as an independent agency to evaluate and accredit the nation's higher education institutions. (NAAC, 2005) The main objectives of NAAC are:

1. To promote quality assurance in higher education institutions in India by developing a system of accreditation based on objective and transparent criteria.
2. To encourage higher education institutions to adopt best practices in teaching, research, and governance, and to create a culture of quality consciousness and continuous improvement.
3. To help institutions of higher education to identify their strengths and weaknesses and to develop strategies for improvement.
4. To provide a mechanism for accountability and transparency in higher education institutions, by evaluating their performance against established benchmarks and standards.
5. To facilitate the sharing of best practices among institutions of higher education in India and to promote collaboration and networking among them.
6. To enhance the reputation and credibility of Indian higher education institutions, both nationally and internationally, by promoting quality and excellence.

Trends in Higher Education

The recently announced UGC Tenth Plan document is attentive to the demand for utility-oriented education as well as the knowledge industry and the knowledge-controlled global economy. The statement also exhorts universities to implement teaching and exam methods that are comparable internationally. In this scenario, UGC and the NAAC are immensely crucial in encouraging higher education institutions to raise their profiles and adapt their organizational structures to meet the new, growing market demands. (UGC Library Committee, 1965) The suggestions made by the UGC committee for the Promotion of Indian Higher Education Abroad (PIHEAD) may be discussed in this perspective. The UGC has chosen twenty institutions that potentially position themselves as providers of high-quality education abroad.

There are many negative perspectives on globalization and how it affects the educational system in India. There have been two different types of flows of human capital from India over time. The first occurred before globalization and resulted in knowledge workers leaving their home countries to supply the western market. The second took place when the WTO and GATS's new trade regimes went into effect, and it involves a new group of students who are now receiving training from western educational institutions that are either based in India or have been formed through a franchise system. These educational institutes train Indian students in western academic disciplines so they can compete on the world market. From a historical perspective, it is evident that since 1857, colleges have played a crucial role in the establishment of the nation's contemporary higher education system, and universities only started creating their own teaching faculties in the 1920s. There were 27 of these colleges in existence in 1857. At the time of independence, there were 18 universities, bringing the total up to 650. According to the UGC Report from 1975–1976, there were 3085 Arts, Science, and Commerce colleges, and there were 3217 affiliated colleges in these fields overall in 1979–1980. The remaining 1341 colleges were university constituent colleges in these and a variety of other fields. (University Grant Commission, 1988)

Growth and Development

The National Policy on Education (NPE), which was published in 1986, and the Programme of Action (POA), which was amended in 1992, are two of the most noteworthy educational policies and programs that the Central Government continues to take a major role in the development and supervision of. The Central Advisory Board of Education (CABE), the highest advisory body for providing guidance to the federal and state governments on matters pertaining to education, was first established in 1920 and disbanded as a cost-saving move in 1923. It was brought back to life in 1935 and lasted till 1994. Sadly, it was not reorganized once its extended stay expired in March 1994.

The Radhakrishnan Report of 1948 on higher education soon after Independence emphasized the importance of University and College library in higher education. The report also stated that a library was the "heart" of an educational institution. The Mudaliar Commission Report of 1954 stressed the importance of library in Secondary Education with the conviction that the habit of using a library at the school level will continue to persist in an individual student at the college and university atmosphere. Further, Kothari Commission (1964) reiterated the importance of libraries in education at all levels. In 2004-05, an estimated 104.81lakh students were enrolled in the institutions of Higher Education as against 99.54 lakh in the previous year and the faculty strength was 4.71lakh as compared to 4.57lakh in the previous year. Further, there is a plan to start new universities in various states to cater to the needs of higher education in the country. (NAAC, 2005)

Significance of the Study

In recent times the National Assessment and Accreditation Council an autonomous body is established by UGC to assess and accredit the Institutions of Higher Education in the country. The purpose of this study is to know the status and development of NAAC accredited College Libraries in terms of providing quality services, availing of books, magazines and journals. Today, it is very necessary to have digital libraries in colleges. The students today want faster access to information, and this is provided by many college libraries. The NAAC, on the basis of its criteria, evaluates the quality and development of education in NAAC accredited colleges and it is the college library which plays an important role in imparting good education. So, the main aim of this study is to know the development of NAAC accredited college libraries. The NAAC accredited College Libraries have to fulfill the criteria's which are laid by NAAC.

In spite of NAAC accreditation, the college libraries have not yet made themselves efficient to provide the best services to its users.

THE ROLE OF ACCREDITATION IN HIGHER EDUCATION INSTITUTIONS

Accreditation plays a crucial role in ensuring the quality and credibility of higher education institutions. It serves as a rigorous evaluation process that assesses an institution's adherence to specific standards and criteria set by accrediting bodies. The primary goal of accreditation is to promote continuous improvement and accountability in educational practices.

Quality Assurance: Accreditation serves as a quality assurance mechanism by evaluating the overall educational experience provided by institutions. It assesses various aspects such as curriculum, faculty qualifications, student support services, infrastructure, and learning outcomes. Through this process, accreditation helps institutions identify areas for improvement and implement necessary changes to enhance the quality of education.

Recognition and Reputation: Accreditation enhances the reputation and recognition of higher education institutions. Accredited institutions are perceived as having met certain standards of excellence, which can increase public trust, student enrollment, and employer confidence. Accreditation also facilitates student mobility, as credits earned at accredited institutions are more likely to be recognized by other institutions and employers.

Student Protection: Accreditation serves as a mechanism for student protection. It ensures that institutions provide adequate student support services, maintain ethical practices, and comply with applicable regulations. Accreditation also safeguards against fraudulent or substandard educational providers, protecting students from investing time and resources in low-quality programs.

Continuous Improvement: Accreditation encourages institutions to engage in ongoing self-assessment and improvement. Through the accreditation process, institutions are prompted to evaluate their educational practices, curriculum relevance, and alignment with industry demands. This promotes a culture of continuous improvement, where institutions strive to meet evolving educational needs and remain responsive to changing societal demands.

Access to Funding and Grants: Accreditation is often a prerequisite for accessing government funding, financial aid programs, and research grants. Accredited institutions are more likely to receive financial support, which can contribute to infrastructure development, faculty recruitment, research activities, and student scholarships. Accreditation, therefore, plays a crucial role in facilitating institutional growth and sustainability.

OBJECTIVES OF THE STUDY

This study of NAAC accredited college libraries shall try to investigate several facts and facets pertaining to their development.

1. To examine the status of NAAC accredited college libraries
2. To analyses NAAC accreditation college libraries developed at First cycle

Table 1. Year of establishment of the first grade colleges

Sl. No.	Establishment Year	No of Colleges	Percentage	p-Value
1	1933	2	2.8	0.001*
2	1935	1	1.4	
3	1944	1	1.4	
4	1945	1	1.4	
5	1948	2	2.8	
6	1954	1	1.4	
7	1963	3	4.2	
8	1964	1	1.4	
9	1965	2	2.8	
10	1967	2	2.8	
11	1968	3	4.2	
12	1969	4	5.6	
13	1970	1	1.4	
14	1972	2	2.8	
15	1973	1	1.4	
16	1974	2	2.8	
17	1975	2	2.8	
18	1977	2	2.8	
19	1979	1	1.4	
20	1980	2	2.8	
21	1981	2	2.8	
22	1982	3	4.2	
23	1983	1	1.4	
24	1984	5	6.9	
25	1985	2	2.8	
26	1986	2	2.8	
27	1987	2	2.8	
28	1988	1	1.4	
29	1991	2	2.8	
30	1996	1	1.4	
31	1997	1	1.4	
32	2000	1	1.4	
33	2002	1	1.4	
34	2004	3	4.2	
35	2005	1	1.4	
36	2007	5	6.9	
37	2008	2	2.8	
38	2009	1	1.4	
Total		72	100.0	

3.   To ascertain funding sanctioned to NAAC accredited college libraries by UGC and government for last five years.

METHODOLOGY

Data Collection In this study, a census survey method was utilized, and questionnaires were employed as the data collection tool. The target population consisted of 80 NAAC accredited college libraries. Sample Selection out of the 80 NAAC accredited college libraries, 72 questionnaires were selected for inclusion in the study through a purposive sampling method to ensure representative data.

From Table 1 it is observed that colleges were established from 1933 to 2009 and survey was administered on the colleges for data collection. From 1984 to 2007 the highest number of colleges were established, 1964 second place i.e., 04 colleges started. 03 colleges established 4 times and 2 colleges started 15 times and lastly 16 colleges established as per year. As per the data received no other colleges established after 2009 have undergone NAAC process.

Table 2 represents the categories of gender among the respondents covered under study. Gender is an important consideration in the development of society. From the above table it is observed that 74% of the respondents are male and 26% of them are female.

Table 3 shows that NAAC was established to evaluate the infrastructure, instruction, research, and learning standards at universities and first grade colleges. NAAC-certified institutions meet all requirements, obtain the highest grades (A++, A+, A), and get the most student enrollment applications. The NAAC has set criteria for grading colleges. Table 3 reveals that 37.5% of the colleges have secured B grade, 20.8% of them have secured B+, 19.5% of them secured A grade, 15.3% of them have secured B++ grade and 7% of the colleges have secured C.

Table 2. Gender wise distribution

Sl. No	Gender	No of Respondents	Percentage	p-Value
1	Male	53	74	
2	Female	19	26	0.001*
	Total	72	100	

Table 3. NAAC grade of the colleges

Sl. No	Grade	No of Colleges	Percentage	p-Value
1	A	14	19.5	
2	B	27	37.5	
3	B+	15	20.8	
4	B++	11	15.3	0.001*
5	C	5	7.0	
	Total	72	100.0	

Table 4. Structure of library

Sl. No	Library Structure	No of Colleges	Percentage	p-Value
1	Centralized	40	56	
2	Decentralized	32	44	0.001
	Total	72	100.0	

Table 5. Types of colleges

Sl. No.	Types of the Colleges	No of Respondents	Percentage	p-Value
1	Government colleges	11	15.3	
2	Private Aided colleges	48	66.7	0.001
3	Unaided colleges	13	18.1	
	Total	72	100.0	

The NAAC grades range from A++ to C, with A++ being the highest and C being the lowest. Institutions with A++ and A+ grades are considered to be of excellent quality, while those with A and B grades are considered to be of good quality. Institutions with a C grade are advised to improve their quality and are given a timeline for the same.

Table 4 reveals that Structure of library organization and It involves managing and recruiting the staff, training and developing the staff members, managing funds, and overall functioning of the library. From the above table it is observed that most of the college libraries have centralized structure i.e., 56% and 32% of them are decentralized. From the above pie chart, we get to know that, structure of library organization is centralized in case of 55.6% of colleges and remaining have decentralized approach of library structure

Table 5 shows what type the surveyed colleges belongs to, College is important for many reasons, including increased career stability and satisfaction, and the ability to make an impact on your community. With more and more careers requiring advanced education, a college degree can be critical to your success in today's workforce. It is revealed that surveyed colleges most of them are Private aided institutions which are 48 in number and the remaining colleges i.e., 13 are unaided and 11 are Government colleges. The above graph shows that private aided colleges dominate the survey with 48 colleges and the rest belongs to government and unaided private colleges.

Table 6 provides information with the source of income to the college libraries. Sources of funding are very important, and they play a crucial role in access to higher education. It is revealed that According to the data, 25% of the respondents reported that they received finance from the State Government, while 34.7% of the respondents received finance from the University Grants Commission (UGC), which is a central government body that provides funding to higher education institutions in India. The highest percentage of respondents, i.e., 40.3%, reported that they received finance from the management of the entity.

Table 7 represents the area that colleges belong to for a variety of reasons, including those like better career opportunities in the future, skill development, all round learning, personal growth and development, boosted self-confidence, welfare of the society, economic growth and development of the nation

Table 6. Sources of finance

Sl. No	Sources of Finance	No of Respondents	Percentage	p-Value
1	State Govt.	18	25.0	
2	UGC	25	34.7	
3	Management	29	40.3	0.001
	Total	72	100.0	

Table 7. College location

Sl. No	Colleges Location	No of Respondents	Percentage	p-Value
1	Urban	43	59.7	
2	Semi urban	8	11.1	
3	Rural	21	29.2	0.001*
	Total	72	100.0	

and so on. About 43 colleges are situated in urban locality, 21 colleges in rural area and 8 colleges in semi urban area. From the above it is observed that about 59.7% of colleges are from urban areas.

The data shows in Table 8 that the majority of the members in this group are students, comprising 98.17% or 57,385 out of the total 58,453 members. On the other hand, teachers make up only a small percentage of the group, accounting for 1.83% or 1,068 members.

Table 9 shows that credibility is defined as the quality of being trusted. In literature, having a credible text means that the information therein is reputable and a trusted source for those looking for information on the subject. It reveals that among the surveyed college's 64 college libraries conduct user orientation regularly for their new students, 28 college libraries have their own printed library brochure, 22 of them have their own library website and 19 of them have introduced the scheme of Earn while you learn for

Table 8. Membership of libraries

Sl. No	Membership	Total No	Percentage
1	Students	57385	98.17%
2	Teachers	1068	01.83%
	Total	58453	

Table 9. Library effectiveness and credibility

Sl. No	Library Effectiveness and Credibility	Yes		No		p-Value
1	Library Website	22	30.6	50	69.4	0.001*
2	Printed Library Brochure	28	38.9	44	61.1	0.001*
3	Conduct User Orientation regularly	64	88.9	8	11.1	0.001*
4	Introduced 'Earn while you Learn' scheme	19	26.4	53	73.6	0.001*

Table 10. Library building

Sl. No.	Library Building	No of Respondents	Percentage	p-Value
1	Independent	32	44	
2	Part of main building	40	56	0.001*
	Total	72	100.0	

Figure 1. Library building

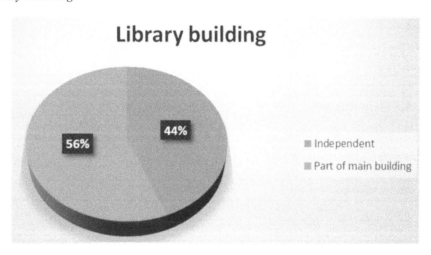

student's benefit. The above graph shows that among the colleges surveyed 30.6% of the college libraries have library website, 38.9% of college libraries have printed library brochure, 88.9% of the college libraries conduct regular user-oriented programs and 26.4% college libraries introduced 'Earn while you learn' scheme.

Table 10 shows that Library buildings often provide quiet areas for studying, as well as common areas for group study and collaboration, and may provide public facilities for access to their electronic resources; for instance: computers and access to the Internet. It is revealed that most of the college libraries are situated in the main building itself. Whereas some have independent buildings. The above chart shows that 56% of the college libraries are a part of the main building and 44%of the college libraries have independent buildings.

Table 11 depicts the availability of general facilities in the college libraries under survey. Sections in a library are Acquisition, Technical Processing, Circulation, Reference, Periodicals, Maintenance, and Administration & Finance. It shows that 100% of college libraries have library committee, 93.1% have circulation counter, 88.9% have internet facilities, 87.5% have drinking water facility, 86.1% of the college libraries consists of reading hall, 81.9% have periodical section, 79.2% have librarian chamber, 72.2% have reprography facilities, 61.1% have generator facilities, 58.3% have washroom facility and 25% of the college libraries have wheelchair facilities.

According to the table all 72 college libraries have the library committee, Circulation Counter are available in 67 college libraries, 64 college libraries have Internet facility, 63 colleges have Drinking water facility, 62 college libraries have reading hall, 59 of them have Periodical section, 57 of them have

Table 11. Library sections and facility

Sl. No	Library Sections	Yes	No	Average	Percentage	p-Value
1	Reading hall	13.9	10	62	86.1	0.001*
2	Circulation Counter	6.9	5	67	93.1	0.001*
3	Librarian's Chamber	20.8	15	57	79.2	0.001*
4	Periodical section	18.1	13	59	81.9	0.001*
5	Reprography	27.8	20	52	72.2	0.001*
6	Generator facility	38.9	28	44	61.1	0.001*
7	Internet facility	11.1	8	64	88.9	0.001*
8	Drinking water facility	12.5	9	63	87.5	0.001*
9	Wash room facility	41.7	30	42	58.3	0.001*
10	Wheel chairs for handicapped students	75.0	54	18	25.0	0.001*
11	Library have Library Committee	0	0	72	100.0	0.001*

Table 12. Collection development policy

Sl. No	Collection Development Policy	No of Colleges	Percentage	p-Value
1	Written	51	71	
2	Unwritten	21	29	0.001*
	Total	72	100.0	

librarians chamber, 52 of them have reprography facility, 44 of them have generator facility in times of power cut off, 42 of them have washroom facility and 18 of them provide wheel chairs for differently abled students.

Table 12 shows that collection development is the process of building useful, balanced collections over time within a set budget, based on assessed, ongoing information needs of the library's users. It also includes selection criteria, resource sharing, replacement of items, and routine de-accessioning. The table reveals that almost half of the college libraries under survey have written form of collection development policy, whereas 21 of them use unwritten form of collection development policy. The above table and pie chart depicts that 71% of the college libraries have written form of collection development policy and 21% of the colleges have unwritten form of collection development policy.

Table 13. Method(s) adopted for procuring books

Sl. No	Method(s) Adopted	No of Colleges	Percentage	p-Value
1	E-Tendering	8	11.1	
2	Reputed Vendor	44	61.1	0.001*
3	Quotations	20	27.8	
	Total	72	100.0	

Table 13 shows that Information sources building, an important function of the library, should be based on sound policies and programs. It involves a series of operations performed according to systemic procedures. It reveals that 61.1% of the college libraries procure books from reputed vendor, 27.8% of them procure books by quotations and 11.1% of them procure books from E-Tendering. The above bar graph represents the methods adopted for procuring books by the college libraries. Wherein it shows that 44 college libraries get books from reputed vendor and 20 of them through quotations and 8 of them by E-Tendering.

Table 14 specifies the number of resources in print form. In a library, we find a variety of printed material in various forms like books, periodicals, newspapers, reference books, etc. There are about two lakh, thirty thousand nine hundred and seventy -four Books/monographs, then thirty one thousand nine hundred and eighteen copies of Back volumes of Journals, then thirteen thousand twenty one copies of Secondary periodicals, there are six thousand seven hundred thirty seven books on government publication, then four thousand one hundred and ninety two dissertations available, about one thousand six hundred ninety two maps and charts, then one thousand one hundred and forty nine thesis, also two

Table 14. Total information resources in libraries

Sl.	Print Form Library Resources	Collection
1	Books/monographs	2130974
	Electronic	1292000
2	Secondary periodicals Foreign Indian	13021 139 949
	Electronic	25200
3	Theses	1149
4	Back volumes of Journals	31918
5	Cases	270
6	Dissertations	4192
7	Patents	130
8	Standard	25
9	Govt. publications	6737
10	Technical reports	115
11	Maps and charts	1692
12	Scientific data bases (please describe type)	13
13	Others (please specify)	186

Table 15. Periodicals (journals)

Sl. No.	Periodicals (Journals)	Printed	Electronic
1	Foreign	139	0
2	Indian	949	0
3	Journals received as Gift	194	0

hundred and seventy case studies are found, one hundred and eighty six other materials, one hundred and thirty patents are available, one hundred and fifteen technical reports are found and a few standard materials and scientific data bases are available.

The Table shows the number of printed foreign and Indian journals along with gifted journals. The total number of Indian journals is 949 whereas foreign journals are 139 in number and there are 194 gifted journals.

Table 15 shows that 949 journals of Indian origin, 194 journals are received in the gift form and 139 foreign journals are available in the printed form in the surveyed college libraries.

FINDINGS OF THE STUDY

The following are the major findings of the study.

1. The period between 1984 and 2007 saw the highest number of college establishments among the surveyed colleges. This indicates a concentrated period of growth and development in higher education institutions.
2. Out of 72 respondents of Libraries of NAAC Accredited Colleges. Considered for this study, 53 (74%) are male and 19 (26%) are female respondents from Libraries of NAAC Accredited Colleges.
3. It is evident from the data that 27 (37.5%) respondents are B grade Libraries of NAAC Accredited Colleges
4. It is evident from the data that 40 (56%) libraries each have centralized structure of the organization
5. The majority (48 in number) are private aided institutions. This indicates that private aided colleges play a dominant role in the higher education landscape of the surveyed area.
6. It is observed that all the (29) colleges got funds from management
7. Majority of the surveyed colleges, accounting for about 59.7%, are situated in urban localities. This indicates a higher concentration of colleges in urban areas compared to rural and semi-urban regions.
8. The majority of the members in this group, specifically 98.17% or 57,385 out of the total 58,453 members, are students. This indicates that students form the largest segment within this group.
9. Majority of college libraries (88.9%) conduct regular user orientation programs for their new students. This indicates a proactive approach by these libraries in familiarizing students with the library resources, services, and facilities, thereby promoting effective utilization of the library.
10. Majority of the respondents, 40 college libraries are located as part of the main building. This indicates that there is a relatively even distribution between college libraries situated within the main building and those with their own separate building. (Table 4.10)
11. The results indicate that 40 libraries are part of the main building.
12. The major finding from the given data is that among the surveyed colleges, 51 of them have a written collection development policy.
13. The major finding from the given data is that among the surveyed colleges, the most commonly adopted method for procurement of goods and services is through reputed vendors, with 44 colleges utilizing this approach.
14. Specifically, the data reveals that the collection of electronic books/monographs amounts to 2,130,974, while the print collection stands at 1,292,000. This indicates a preference and invest-

ment in digital resources, reflecting the growing shift towards digital formats and the increasing availability and accessibility of electronic books and monographs.

15. It reveals that 61.1% of the college libraries procure books from reputed vendor, 27.8% of them procure books by quotations and 11.1% of them procure books from E-Tendering.

IMPROVEMENT OF THE LIBRARY

Based on the data collected from the professionals of Libraries of NAAC Accredited Colleges. The following suggestions are made.

1. It is suggested to the authorities of the Libraries of NAAC Accredited Colleges. To provide more number of computer terminals to the library to help the LIS professionals to conduct the programmes effectively and efficiently.
2. It is suggested to the authorities of the Libraries of NAAC Accredited College. To subscribe e-Shodh Sindhu Consortium.
3. It is suggested to the Librarians to conduct the Information Literacy Programmes frequently to help the students to learn the technology time to time.
4. It is suggested to the Librarians to either to increase the duration of the programmes or the ILPs should be conducted frequently.
5. It is suggested to the authorities of the Libraries of NAAC Accredited Colleges. To support the library in the benefit of the student's community, as the users constitute an important component in the trinity of library science.
6. It is suggested to the Librarians to publicize by using either of the options to the help the users.

FURTHER AREAS OF RESEARCH

The following further areas of Research may help the budding researchers in identifying and formulation of research problem.

1. A study of fostering Information Literacy Programmes in the Libraries of NAAC Accredited Colleges can be conducted.
2. A comparative study of Govt. Aided and Private Colleges may also be conducted.

CONCLUSION

ICT has had a significant impact on libraries and information centers in today's society. It has significantly altered how data or information is collected, stored, processed, and retrieved while also assisting library employees in carrying out their duties efficiently and correctly. Today's society is flourishing, but because of how quickly things are changing in the 21st century, it is difficult for institutions to keep up with the fierce competition. This created a demand for NAAC-accredited colleges' libraries to educate young, capable, and dynamic engineers who could take on the problems. These Libraries of NAAC

Accredited Colleges. Institutions should work with growing industry to produce quality and relevant young engineers.

As a result, librarians employed by various types of libraries, and libraries at NAAC-accredited colleges in particular, have a crucial role to play in advancing information literacy in society. By designing and supplying a suitable information environment for the efficient and effective use of all types of information resources, they can play a crucial part in the educational changes taking place in teaching, learning, and research in higher education. In conclusion, library and information professionals, library associations, library and information science institutions, and policy makers are totally responsible for integrating library awareness-related programs into the libraries of NAAC Accredited Colleges. Hence, it is strongly advocated that the higher education system must devise ways and means to implement programme at all levels especially in Libraries of NAAC Accredited Colleges and technology education.

REFERENCES

Acevedo-De-los-Ríos, A., & Rondinel-Oviedo, D. R. (2022). Impact, added value and relevance of an accreditation process on quality assurance in architectural higher education. *Quality in Higher Education*, *28*(2), 186–204. doi:10.1080/13538322.2021.1977482

Al Shraah, A., Abu-Rumman, A., Alqhaiwi, L., & Alshurideh, M. T. (2023). The role of AACSB accreditation in students' leadership motivation and students' citizenship motivation: Business education perspective. *Journal of Applied Research in Higher Education*, *15*(4), 1130–1145. doi:10.1108/JARHE-11-2021-0409

Alaskar, A., D'Errico, E., Alipoon, L., & Dehom, S. (2019). Institutional accreditation in Saudi Arabian higher education: Perceptions and involvement. *Quality in Higher Education*, *25*(3), 245–260. doi:10.1080/13538322.2019.1667630

Aleksandrov, A. Y., Barabanova, S. V., Vereshchak, S. B., Ivanova, O. A., & Aleksandrova, Z. A. (2016). Revisiting the legal consequences of international accreditation of higher education programs in the Russian Federation. *Journal of Advanced Research in Law and Economics*, *7*(2), 202–210. https://journals.aserspublishing.eu/jarle/article/view/206

Andreani, M., Russo, D., Salini, S., & Turri, M. (2020). Shadows over accreditation in higher education: Some quantitative evidence. *Higher Education*, *79*(4), 691–709. doi:10.100710734-019-00432-1

Association of College & Research Libraries (ACRL). (n.d.). *Changing roles of Academic & Research Libraries*. Retrieved from http://ww.ala.org/ala/mgrps/divs/acrl/issues/value/changingroles.cfm

Blanco-Ramírez, G., & Berger, J. (2014). Rankings, accreditation, and the international quest for quality: Organizing an approach to value in higher education. *Quality Assurance in Education*, *22*(1), 88–104. doi:10.1108/QAE-07-2013-0031

Dattey, K., Westerheijden, D. F., & Hofman, W. H. A. (2014). Impact of accreditation on public and private universities: A comparative study. *Tertiary Education and Management*, *20*(4), 307–319. doi:10.1080/13583883.2014.959037

Duarte, N., & Vardasca, R. (2023). Literature Review of Accreditation Systems in Higher Education. *Education Sciences*, *13*(6), 582. doi:10.3390/educsci13060582

Fernandes, J. O., & Singh, B. (2022). Accreditation and ranking of higher education institutions (HEIs): Review, observations and recommendations for the Indian higher education system. *The TQM Journal*, *34*(5), 1013–1038. doi:10.1108/TQM-04-2021-0115

Gandhi, M. (2013). International initiatives in assessment of quality and accreditation in higher education. *International Journal of Educational Planning and Administration*, *3*(2), 121–138.

Gopinath, M. (1985). Information technology and its impact on information retrieval systems. *Library Science with a Slant to Documentation*, *22*(4), 237–251. http://library.isical.ac.in:8080/jspui/bitstream/10263/1108/1/LSWASTD-22-4-1985-P237-251.pdf

Government of India. (1950). *The Report of the University Education Commission (December 1948 – August 1949)*. https://indianculture.gov.in/reports-proceedings/report-university-education-commission-december-1948-august-1949-vol-i

Government of India. (1967). *Report of the Education Commission (1964-66)*. https://indianculture.gov.in/reports-proceedings/report-education-commission-1964-66

Government of India. (1986). *National Policy on Library and Information System: A presentation 1985-1986*. Government of India.

Hanh, N. D. (2020). A review of issues of quality assurance and quality accreditation for higher education institutions and the situation in Vietnam. *Accreditation and Quality Assurance*, *25*(4), 273–279. doi:10.100700769-020-01439-3

Hanh, N. D., Nga, N. T. M., Loan, V. Q., & Viet, N. M. (2019). Role of quality assurance and quality accreditation in higher education in some developing countries and Vietnam. *American Journal of Educational Research*, *7*(9), 649–653. https://pubs.sciepub.com/education/7/9/8/

Horakeri, M. D. (2011). *Growth and development of college libraries in the electronic environment a study of impact of quality awareness and competence building measures* [Doctoral dissertation, Karnatak University]. Karnatak University, Dharwad. http://hdl.handle.net/10603/95581

Jange, S. (2022). NAAC accreditation and academic libraries: librarians' role beyond librarianship. *Journal of Indian Library Association*, *57*(4), 12-23. https://www.ilaindia.net/jila/index.php/jila/article/view/1295

Karisiddappa, C. R. (1996). *Preparing Academic libraries for the 21st Century*. Keynote address at workshop held at Manipal, India.

Kohli, N. (2014). Role of accreditation in engineering education. In *2014 IEEE International Conference on MOOC, Innovation and Technology in Education (MITE)* (pp. 157-159). IEEE. 10.1109/MITE.2014.7020261

Kumar, A., Gawande, A., & Raibagkar, S. (2022). Quality complacency in Indian higher education institutions between the second and third cycles of accreditation. *Quality Assurance in Education*, *30*(4), 431–445. doi:10.1108/QAE-01-2022-0019

Kumar, P., Shukla, B., & Passey, D. (2020). Impact of accreditation on quality and excellence of higher education institutions. *Revista Investigacion Operacional, 41*(2), 151-167. https://eprints.lancs.ac.uk/id/eprint/141916

Letelier, M., Carrasco, R., de los Ríos, D., Oliva, C., & Sandoval, M. J. (2010). Evaluation and accreditation: Long term challenges for higher education. *The Journal of Educational Research*, *4*(3), 241–263.

LIM (HT). New Technology and University Library in Developing Contrary. In *Challenges of Information Technology* (p. 294). North Holland.

Mandavkar, P. (2019). Reform process in higher education and need of assessment and accreditation. *SSRN*, *6*(2), 21–24. doi:10.2139srn.3472356

Motova, G., & Navodnov, V. (2020). Twenty years of accreditation in Russian higher education: Lessons learnt. *Higher Education Evaluation and Development*, *14*(1), 33–51. doi:10.1108/HEED-05-2019-0023

Nandi, E., & Chattopadhyay, S. (2016). Quality, accreditation and global university ranking: Issues before Indian higher education. In *India Infrastructure Report 2012* (pp. 205–215). Routledge India. https://smartnet.niua.org/sites/default/files/resources/IIR-2012.pdf#page=206

National Assessment and Accreditation Council (NAAC). (2005). *Best Practices Series: Library and Information Services a case presentations*. NAAC.

National Assessment and Accreditation Council (NAAC). (2005). *Guidelines on quality indicators in Library and Information Services: Affiliated and constituent colleges*. NAAC.

National Knowledge Commission. (2007). *Libraries: Gateways to knowledge: A Road Map for Revitalization*. National Knowledge Commission.

Neelameghan, A. (1968). Education, Research and Library Science. *Timeless Fellowship*, *5*, 53.

Obadara, O. E., & Alaka, A. (2013). Accreditation and quality assurance in Nigerian universities. *Journal of Education and Practice*, *4*(8), 34–41. https://core.ac.uk/download/pdf/234634163.pdf

Prasad, V. S., & Stella, A. (2004). Accreditation of higher education institutions: Indian experience. In *National Assessment and Accreditation Council Commonwealth of Learning Round Table Conference on Innovations in Teacher Education* (pp. 17–19). International Practices on Quality Assurance. https://www.che.ac.za/sites/default/files/publications/d000091_seminar_9-3-05-Int-trends-qa-prof_prasad.pdf

Ranganathan, S. R. (1965). *Universities and Colleges Libraries*. University Grants Commission. https://indianculture.gov.in/reports-proceedings/universities-and-colleges-libraries-containing-report-library-committee

Romanowski, M. H. (2022). The idolatry of accreditation in higher education: Enhancing our understanding. *Quality in Higher Education*, *28*(2), 153–167. doi:10.1080/13538322.2021.1948460

Sinha, V., & Subramanian, K. S. (2013). Accreditation in India: Path of achieving educational excellence. *Business Education & Accreditation*, *5*(2), 107–116. https://ssrn.com/abstract=2239206

Stensaker, B., & Harvey, L. (2006). Old wine in new bottles? A comparison of public and private accreditation schemes in higher education. *Higher Education Policy*, *19*(1), 65–85. doi:10.1057/palgrave.hep.8300110

Stura, I., Gentile, T., Migliaretti, G., & Vesce, E. (2019). Accreditation in higher education: Does disciplinary matter? *Studies in Educational Evaluation*, *63*, 41–47. doi:10.1016/j.stueduc.2019.07.004

Sywelem, M. M., & Witte, J. E. (2009). Higher Education Accreditation in View of International Contemporary Attitudes. *Online Submission, 2*(2), 41-54. https://eric.ed.gov/?id=ED509233

The Hindu. (2010, January 4). Retrieved from http://www.thehinduonnet.com/thehindu

University Grants Commission. (1988). *Development of an Information and Library Network: Report of the Inter Agency Working Group*. University Grants Commission.

ADDITIONAL READING

Dey, N. (2011). Quality assurance and accreditation in higher education in India. *Academic Research International, 1*(1), 104–110. http://www.savap.org.pk/journals/ARInt./Vol.1(1)/2011(1.1-09)a.pdf

Dey, N. (2011). Quality assurance and accreditation in higher education: India vis-à-vis European countries. *European Journal of Higher Education, 1*(2-3), 274–287. doi:10.1080/21568235.2011.617567

Hota, P., & Sarangi, P. (2019). Quality revolution of higher education: A study in India. *Srusti Management Review, 12*(1), 49-56. https://www.srustimanagementreview.ac.in/paperfile/1341955255_Quality%20Revolution%20of%20Higher%20Education.pdf

Manimala, M. J., Wasdani, K. P., & Vijaygopal, A. (2020). Facilitation and regulation of educational institutions: The role of accreditation. *Vikalpa, 45*(1), 7–24. doi:10.1177/0256090920917263

Rath, B. (2013). Role of Accreditation in Improving Quality in Higher Professional Management Education in India. *Srusti Management Review, 6*(1), 165-170. https://shorturl.at/cdfnq

KEY TERMS AND DEFINITIONS

Academic Libraries: An academic library is a library that is attached to a higher education institution and serves two complementary purposes: to support the curriculum and the research of the university faculty and students.

Accreditation: Accreditation is a formal, independent verification that a program or institution meets established quality standards and is competent to carry out specific conformity assessment tasks. Conformity assessment tasks may include, but are not limited to, testing, inspection, or certification.

All India Council for Technical Education (AICTE): AICTE was founded in 1945. It is a high-level Advisory Body to administer an examination on the facilities accessible for technical education and to promote development in the nation in a collective and integrated manner.

Higher Education: Higher education, any of various types of education given in postsecondary institutions of learning and usually affording, at the end of a course of study, a named degree, diploma, or certificate of higher studies. Higher-educational institutions include not only universities and colleges but also various professional schools that provide preparation in such fields as law, theology, medicine, business, music, and art.

National Assessment and Accreditation Council (NAAC): National Assessment and Accreditation Council (NAAC) was established in September 1994 by UGC in Bangalore for assessing the achievement of the universities and colleges in the country. NAAC includes various tasks, such as evaluating performance, assessment, and accreditation of universities in the country.

Statutory Body: Statutory body or authority means a non-constitutional body which is set up by a parliament. Statutory bodies are authorized to pass the law and take the decision on the behalf of state or country. Statutory body has official permission for Legislation i.e. process of enacting laws. Cabinet resolution should be passed to establish this body.

University Grant Commission (UGC): UGC meaning is University Grants Commission, it is a statutory body established by the Indian government in the year 1953, in conformity with the UGC Act 1956. The statutory organization falls under the ministry of education department. The objective of the University Grants Commission is to determine, coordinate, and maintain the standards of the teaching, examinations, and research about higher education.

Chapter 13
Initiating Memory Institutions Convergence Through Digital Convergence in Indonesian World Heritage Sites

Muhammad Rosyihan Hendrawan
iD https://orcid.org/0000-0003-0438-2571
University of Brawijaya, Indonesia

Azman Mat Isa
College of Computing, Informatics, and Mathematics, Universiti Teknologi MARA, Malaysia

Ahmad Zam Hariro Samsudin
College of Computing, Informatics, and Mathematics, Universiti Teknologi MARA, Malaysia

ABSTRACT

The libraries, archives, and museums (LAMs) promote culture, community, and change new cultural heritage information management research. History deserves The Ombilin Coal Mining Heritage of Sawahlunto (OCMHS), Indonesia as a World Heritage. The LAM convergence may initiate in OCMHS. LAM convergence counts and digitization changes LAM. Universitas Brawijaya, Indonesia and Universiti Teknologi MARA, Malaysia constructed digital LAM convergence by free open-source software (FOSS) and the software development life cycle (SDLC) cascade development with information system design techniques. The OCMHS LAM standards are initiated with "The Sawahlunto Memories." The OCMHS best practices can be the other example for preserving culture via "The Sawahlunto Memory." Convergent LAMs of OCMHS by "The Sawahlunto Memory" must enhance access to memory institutions and experiences in quick digital technology and effective cultural heritage information management to preserve Indonesia's worldwide cultural heritage.

DOI: 10.4018/979-8-3693-2841-5.ch013

INTRODUCTION

Within the context of all civilizations, the transmission of ideas, facts, and emotions via various forms of communication, such as writing and other media, is vital for the acquisition of new information and the preservation of collective memory. Documentation is a distinguishing feature of a civilization rooted in culture, setting it apart from a solely oral tradition (Pendit, 2019). This is particularly evident in the realm of preserving collective memory within cultural heritage. Due to the inherent inclination of individuals to accumulate information, it becomes imperative for society to cultivate a collective memory via the use of written records and other artifacts. In the last several years, there has been a significant growth in the approaches used to investigate the resources often associated with cultural heritage (Hall & Walsh, 2021).

This underscores the ongoing need to adapt and enhance the ability to manage, facilitate, and structure extensive amounts of information. Scholars specializing in memory institutions like libraries, archives, and museums (LAMs) have conducted research on collective memories as an integral component of cultural heritage within society. This research involves the deliberate processes of choosing, curating, collecting, organizing, maintaining, archiving, and distributing these memories (Fernando et al., 2012). The convergence of memory institutions, or LAMs, with the concept of collective memory, has emerged as a viable approach for communities, yielding positive outcomes.

The concept of collective memory extends beyond a simple aggregation or summation of individual recollections. However, via the integration of symbols, language, and established conventions, the collaborative endeavor of community members played a significant role in the early promotion of cultural heritage through collective memory exhibitions. The recognition and understanding of cultural heritage play a crucial role in the effective management and conservation of these valuable legacies. Therefore, it is essential to acknowledge the significance of its awareness (Shimray & Chennupati, 2019). The sustainable preservation of cultural heritage is a serious cultural problem in contemporary civilizations. The category encompasses a wide range of agents, including LAMs, particularly within the context of world heritage sites.

An examination of the preceding three decades of the operationalization of the World Heritage Convention reveals a discernible expansion in the understanding and scope of the term 'heritage.' Within the realm of cultural heritage, an anthropological perspective has prompted a shift in focus from safeguarding monumental legacy to acknowledging the dynamic history of indigenous communities, the spiritual abundance of humanity, and the intricate interplay between these aspects and the natural surroundings (Sullivan, 2004). The incorporation of cultural landscapes, especially those linked to natural components rather than tangible cultural artifacts, has had a transformative impact on the understanding, analysis, and execution of the World Heritage Convention (Petrelli et al., 2013). The preservation of exceptional natural ecosystems also serves to support and maintain existing cultures, customs, and beliefs. These judgments have facilitated the identification and acknowledgment of holy places and other assets that possess distinctive and intangible worth.

According to Króll (2021), The concept of cultural heritage is complex and encompasses several dimensions, making it difficult to provide a precise definition. Consequently, the evaluation of the cultural heritage potential of a nation, area, or community is a challenging task. Cultural heritage is the essential part of the collective memory and legacy of the community, or what the community considers its identity, worthy of being transmitted to the next generation of the general public. It comprises not only what we know about life, nature, and the cosmos but also how we know it. Both media can be tangible and intangible. It includes artifacts, specimens, landscapes, cultural practices or traditions, ethics, and documents (Lourenco, 2013).

BACKGROUND

In numerous articles on cultural heritage, specific sub-types of cultural heritage, such as built, movable, and archaeological, are mentioned (Dümcke & Gnedovsky, 2013). According to Lourenco (2013), the shared collective memory of the community is perceived as its identity and collective memory. It is worth passing on to the next generation of the general public. It typically consists of functional structures, instruments, collections or resources, and other materials related to culture and the dissemination of knowledge through libraries, archives, and museums (LAMs).

One of the noteworthy advancements in the domain of Information Science, particularly in relation to cultural heritage management, is the rise and growing significance of memory institutions, also referred to as LAMs. According to Warren and Matthews (2019), these institutions play a crucial role in enhancing the accessibility of cultural heritage resources. In order to develop LAMs that effectively transmit cultural heritage to future generations while maintaining its inherent context, it is crucial to prioritize the comprehensive adherence to the requirements outlined in the UNESCO Convention for the preservation of tangible and intangible cultural heritage (Veldpaus, 2016). In the present day, it is essential to prioritize efforts aimed at enhancing the prominence, visitor engagement, and digital accessibility of resources. The collaboration and convergence of LAMs (Libraries, Archives, and Museums) enable them to reach diverse audiences, garner community support, preserve cultural records, and adapt to evolving circumstances (Potgieter & Mabe, 2018; Mahey et al., 2019; Mariyapillai & Naviratharan, 2020; and Zourou & Pellegrini, 2021).

The convergence of LAMs as memory institutions responsible for managing communal memory on a global scale has been seen to resume and accelerate since the onset of the 21st century. Memory institutions are tasked with the acquisition, administration, conservation, and facilitation of public access to shared memory. According to Robinson (2019), convergence refers to the state in which organizations achieve a high level of integration and interdependence, leading to a loss of autonomy in their operations. In academic settings where LAMs coexist, the convergence effort is seen as a means to achieve cost savings, enhance resource access, ease the implementation of service upgrades, and attract a larger number of visitors or users.

The phenomenon of LAM convergence has emerged as a prevalent worldwide trend among memory institutions. The phenomenon of convergence has assumed the status of a cultural policy inside the country. Subsequently, the government and society demonstrated their dedication by making significant expenditures, prompting several countries to react to this need by enhancing memory institutions and facilitating more robust inter-institutional dialogues. The rationale for the need for convergence is often attributed to the enhanced accessibility of knowledge for consumers across the three institutions.

In accordance with the established paradigm, LAMs serve as intermediaries responsible for facilitating the dissemination of information and cultural traditions. In general, the transmission of information takes place through a unidirectional channel whereby the institution disseminates the information to the intended audience. The advent of technology has brought about significant changes in the manner in which individuals get and use knowledge. Consequently, the role of LAMs within our society and government has undergone a notable transformation in recent times. LAMs play a crucial role in facilitating information retrieval for users. However, the continuous progress of technology has led to the integration of these institutions into a rapidly growing information environment (Constantine et al., 2018).

The inherent openness and inclusivity of the infosphere provide LAM institutions inside the world heritage sites with unparalleled prospects to engage with new users. Simultaneously, it offers users unprecedented avenues to exert influence on these formerly conventional organizations. The primary objective of memory institutions, including LAMs, is to ensure the protection and preservation of cultural heritage via the processes of acquisition, organization, preservation, and exhibition (Hendrawan & Bafadhal, 2021). Nevertheless, there is significant variation in terms of particular missions, institutional cultures, and work methods between different institutions.

THE OMBILIN COAL MINING HERITAGE OF SAWAHLUNTO

The Ombilin Coal Mining Heritage of Sawahlunto (OCMHS), designated as one of Indonesia's World Cultural Heritage Sites, emerged as a consequence of the Industrial Revolution in Europe. This pivotal period prompted the Dutch Colonial administration to embark on an exploration of natural resources, specifically coal, in various regions across the globe, including the OCMHS in the eastern part of the world. The discovery of coal in the Ombilin River in 1858 was made by Dutch mining engineers, including De Groet, and further exploration was carried out by De Greve in 1867 (Saputra, 2012; Asoka et al., 2016; Lindayanti et al., 2016; Lindayanti et al., 2017). Following Indonesia's independence and the discontinuation of coal mining operations by mining companies in 1999, the local community made concerted efforts and reached a consensus to safeguard cultural heritage through regional regulations.

According to UNESCO (2019), the OCMHS was scheduled to be inscribed on the world heritage list at the 43rd World Heritage Committee Session held in Baku, Azerbaijan, on July 6th, 2019. The City of Sawahlunto's Vision and Mission emphasize the importance of maintaining, using, and expanding cultural heritage. This dedication extends to the establishment of memory institutions or cultural heritage institutions, such as LAMs. The need for cultural conservation in Indonesia is stipulated by many laws, including Law Number 11 of 2010, which pertains to Cultural Conservation; Government Regulation Number 66 of 2015, which pertains to Museums; Law Number 43 of 2007, which pertains to Libraries, and Law Number 43 of 2009, which pertains to Archives. Hence, the use of historical structures for adaptive reuse as memory institutions ought to provide a meaningful contribution to the overarching story of the OCMHS, which has been nominated as a World Heritage site by UNESCO in 2019. As per the provisions outlined in Law Number 11 of the Year 2010, specifically in Article 97, the responsibility of managing a recognized cultural heritage site is assigned to a management body. This body may be constituted by either the national government, local government, or communities. Therefore, in continuation with the official recognition of the nominated item as a UNESCO World Heritage site.

The persistent safeguarding of cultural heritage is a prominent cultural dilemma in contemporary culture. Cultural heritage refers to the shared inheritance of a community, including its perceived identity, and is considered worthy of preservation and dissemination to future generations of scholars and the wider populace. Both forms of media may exist in digital formats, either as created digital content or as physical artifacts that have been converted into digital form. The management of cultural heritages requires a profound understanding and appreciation of both aspects. Hence, the recognition of its awareness should be considered of utmost importance.

Currently, there is a notable convergence of memory institutions, including LAMs, inside UNESCO World Heritage sites. The phenomenon of convergence has been adopted as a cultural strategy in the realm of legacy information, with the aim of enhancing users' accessibility to knowledge. The LAMs of the OCMHS in Indonesia, being designated as UNESCO World Heritage sites, exhibit a range of conventional services or a combination thereof. These functions include but are not limited to collection or resources, conservation, access, research, teaching, service, and outreach. This context exhibits a notable instance and encounter of the confluence of LAMs. The phenomenon of digitization has a significant impact on the digital-born information sources that are found inside LAMs. This phenomenon leads to an augmentation in the worldwide network accessibility and convergence of LAMs. There are several methodologies for the creation of an information system and knowledge organization within the context of LAMs, one of which is the use of Free Open-Source Software (FOSS). In the process of convergence of the LAMs, various software advancements with FOSS licenses are used and employed, similar to other countries or organizations that rely on proprietary system information (August et al., 2021).

In contemporary times, it is seen that all of the LAMs within the realm of the OCMHS exhibit commonality in their operational features, including tasks such as resources, preservation, accessibility, provision of services, outreach activities, and similar endeavors. Nevertheless, there are deficiencies in several domains, including professional practices, training, methodologies, coordination, and cooperation. The projected benefits of enhancing the synchronization of shared functions of LAMs are expected to have a positive impact on the OCMHS as a whole. This improvement would include improved integration of LAM into research, teaching, and service across all levels. Additionally, the use of cost savings related to digitization would help ease the budgetary constraints faced by each unit.

Hence, the primary objective is to facilitate users' access to essential information without the need for interchanging between different information sources. This suggests that the resources of the LAMs ought to be included in a system for storing and retrieving knowledge. The integration of various knowledge resources has become much more streamlined due to the ability to store nearly any information in digital format. Here, we may witness a tangible example of the convergence of LAMs. The advancement of convergence may be facilitated by the active involvement of users in generating novel information and experiences using LAMs.

BRIEF THOUGHTS AND DEVELOPMENT OF MEMORY INSTITUTIONS CONVERGENCE

Prior to the widespread adoption and acceptance of convergence as a worldwide phenomenon, scholars, exemplified by Rayward in this case, had already begun contemplating the potential for digital convergence inside memory institutions such as libraries, archives, and museums (LAMs) as early as the mid-1990s. Marty (2014) posits that Rayward started the discussion around electronic information and the potential integration of LAM functions. Marty's assertion that Rayward was the initial scholar to propose the convergence of libraries, museums, and archives is grounded in Rayward's scholarly work from 1996. Specifically, Rayward's article titled "Libraries, museums, and archives in the Digital Future: The blurring of Institutional Distinctions" was presented at the Second National Preservation Conference hosted by the National Library of Australia in Canberra. The second publication, titled "Electronic Information and the Functional Integration of Libraries, Museums, and Archives," was released in 1998 as a chapter in the book "History and Electronic Artifacts."

It is noteworthy that Rayward emerged as an early scholar to contemplate the concept of convergence. However, the manifestation of convergence in Canada became evident in 2004 with the amalgamation of the National Library of Canada and the National Archives of Canada, resulting in the establishment of the Library and Archives of Canada (LAC). Likewise, the discussion about convergence in the United States did not begin until 2005. The author posits that academics, drawing upon their theoretical knowledge and analytical insight, have contemplated various outcomes before practitioners in their respective fields. According to Rayward, the increasing digitization of the world necessitates the occurrence of convergence. The resources provided by LAMs are either digitized or created in a digital format. The use of a worldwide network enhances the accessibility of all these resources. Users don't need to possess knowledge about the specific collective memory they are seeking or its source. In contrast, professionals such as librarians, archivists, museologists, and curators undertake the task of preparing these resources for formal presentations within their respective fields. Divergent attitudes between consumers and information service providers are evident in this context. In due course, the field of information resource management will be influenced by this development. A paradigm change is necessary with regard to the future of convergence and professionals in Libraries, Archives, and Museums (LAMs).

Since the late 1990s, there has been a significant amount of collective effort focused on enhancing the online distribution, exploration, and identification of LAM resources. In their study, Gibson et al. (2007) noted that a considerable fraction of the collaborative projects they analyzed included activities such as digitalization, federated search, or shared database use. Yarrow et al. (2008) recognized many levels of initiatives, including global, continental, national, and local, aimed at the development of collaborative digital resources. Zorich et al. (2008) exclusively focused on digital initiatives as the primary foundation for their collaborative efforts.

The formulation of a long-term strategy for the establishment of a global digital library was undertaken by the Conference of Directors of National Libraries (CDNL) in the year 2008. The CDNL has reached a consensus to undertake the development of a worldwide distribution system that would facilitate access to a complete collection of digital resources. These resources will be openly available and integrated seamlessly, enabling efficient use by users around the globe. This encompasses the provision of access to resources found in memory institutions and private repositories, with the aim of facilitating research, education, innovation, economic progress, and the fostering of global comprehension. This can be attributed to the projected enhancement of strategic cooperation with various stakeholders, such as information professionals, LAM institutions, national and international governmental bodies, non-governmental organizations, publishers, information service institutions, and other private entities.

According to Trant (2009), LAMs have consistently preserved a unique identity, and their self-perception has not been primarily shaped by the parallels in their principal responsibilities and methods throughout history. Nevertheless, much research has been conducted on the potentialities arising from cross-collaboration, as shown by the library's organization of several conferences dedicated to this topic. The conference, known as the 2000 Library Automation Group Conference, with a focus on the convergence of archives, libraries, and museums, extensively explored collaborative digital projects across these institutions (Limb, 2003). The available choices and challenges the primary topics explored throughout the conferences held in 2002 and 2004 were the concepts of invisibility, advocacy, convergence, and collaboration, with a particular emphasis on the researchers and attendees.

As organizations advance through several stages, there is a gradual convergence seen among LAMs characterized by a growing level of trust, integration, dedication, and associated advantages (Higgins, 2013). In general, the motivation to address a scarcity of resources and the involvement of an agent of change serve as the driving forces for transitioning between phases. The progress in technology and the establishment of effective strategies for the creation and administration of digital resources have served as catalysts for individuals driving change. Not all LAM initiatives are situated at identical positions along the cooperation continuum. Nevertheless, due to the demands imposed by the digital era, a significant majority of individuals have embarked on this endeavor, reaping advantages from the use of communal resources and the subsequent improvements in efficiency as trust is established, and aspirations broaden.

Furthermore, there is a regular convening of non-governmental groups focused on cultural heritage to engage in discussions pertaining to shared concerns. The designated nomenclature for this casual assembly is the Coordinating Council for Libraries, Archives, Museums, Monuments, and Sites (LAMMS). In December 2011, the sixth meeting convened and decided to formally endorse the Statement of Principles on Global Cross-Sectoral Digitization Initiatives. The aim was to actively disseminate this statement among various member organizations, such as the International Federation of Library Associations and Institutions (IFLA), the International Council on Archives (ICA), the Coordinating Council of Audiovisual Archives Associations (CCAAA), the International Council of Museums (ICOM), the International Council on Monuments and Sites (ICOMOS), and the International Council on Cultural Heritage (ICCH). The primary objective of the six organizations is to systematically gather, record, arrange, maintain, safeguard, and facilitate the retrieval of humanity's cultural heritage creations held inside memory institutions. Through the analysis and application of information derived from LAMs, individuals can contribute to the generation of novel knowledge, hence facilitating the expansion of convergence. According to Buckland et al. (2013), the convergence process within the LAMs business is deemed essential in response to the recurring phenomenon of digitization.

The process of digitization has a significant influence on the digital-born information sources found inside LAMs. This phenomenon facilitates the enhanced accessibility of resources and information pertaining to LAMs across the worldwide network. The rationale for pursuing convergence in organizations stems from the recognition that the resources available via LAM systems may serve as valuable sources of knowledge. This necessitates the establishment of a unified approach to provide comprehensive, precise, and efficient access to information, hence enhancing the accessibility of knowledge for LAM system users. According to Katre (2011), the only component that enables integrated access convergence is the implementation of a consistent metadata framework. In addition to technological considerations, the realization of a LAMs revolution requires the implementation of mutually advantageous profit-sharing mechanisms, information exchange practices, and motivating incentives. Hence, it is essential for all institutions engaged in collaboration with LAMs to make deliberate decisions on the selection of resource types for digitization. Additionally, they should provide an environment that is open and inclusive, ensuring meticulous storage and convenient accessibility of the digitized content.

LAMs provide an immersive and innovative educational experience that surpasses the constraints of time, language, and uniqueness. Byrne (2015) defines a memory institution as an organizational entity responsible for the preservation and management of a publicly accessible repository of information. Memory institutions include the essential tasks of recording, contextualizing, maintaining, and indexing cultural and communal memory components. In order to effectively apply LAMs, an institution or organization needs to possess a management information system that is efficient, enabling access to information without being limited by geographical or time limitations. This is also associated with the notion of convergence within the ecosystem of memory institutions, including LAMs, via the use of an information system. According to the findings of Rainer et al. (2022), an information system refers to a system that operates within an organization to address the demands of daily transaction processing effectively. Additionally, it facilitates the management of organizational and operational functions while also aligning with the strategic activities of the organization. The ultimate goal is to generate necessary reports for external stakeholders.

FREE OPEN-SOURCE SOFTWARE AND SOFTWARE DEVELOPMENT LIFE CYCLE MODEL

Information systems are complex systems that comprise various resources or components, including software, hardware, and brainware. These components work together to process information and generate outputs that are valuable in attaining specific organizational goals. In the context of Libraries, Archives, and Museums (LAMs), the utilization of information systems necessitates the presence of essential components such as input mechanisms, output mechanisms, software applications, hardware devices, databases, and contingency plans.

There are several approaches to the development of an information system, including the use of a system based on Free Open-Source Software (FOSS). Many countries and organizations adopt the use of software advancements with Free and Open Source Software (FOSS) licenses. This is particularly evident in the implementation of the LAMs integration concept, which is based on the FOSS license. Nevertheless, an organization needs to ensure that the implementation of an information system is accompanied by the necessary measures to ensure its sustained use. This necessitates the company's commitment to the whole life cycle of the system. The purpose of this measure is to guarantee the ongoing functionality of the information system in accordance with its planned operation.

The Software Development Life Cycle (SDLC) paradigm is among the several system life cycles that may serve as a framework for ensuring the long-term sustainability of information systems. It encompasses a range of mechanisms within the SDLC paradigm that facilitate the maintenance of these systems. The cascade technique was chosen as the framework for developing Free and Open Source Software (FOSS)--based information systems at different institutions as a means of implementing the LAMs idea.

Figure 1. Development of the waterfall model
Source: Roger and Bruce (2015)

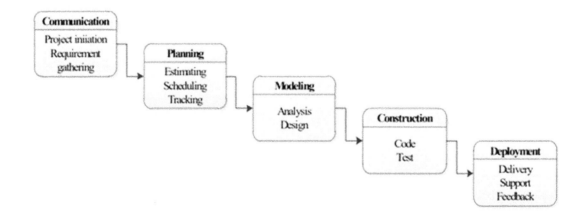

The first phase of this process starts with the assessment of user requisites. The software system progresses sequentially from design, modeling, building, and distribution to users (deployment), culminating in the provision of continuing maintenance for the developed program. Figure 1 presents a visual representation of the many phases of the waterfall model: 1) The phase of communication, namely project initiation and requirements gathering, centers on the process of actively interacting with users in order to comprehend and accomplish the desired objectives prior to initiating the project. The communication process starts with the first phase of problem analysis, subsequently leading to the identification and use of relevant data resources, and ends in the formation of definitive attributes that need to be held or managed; 2) The planning phase encompasses many activities, such as estimating, scheduling, and monitoring. During this phase, specific tasks are identified, which include doing a risk assessment, determining the necessary resources, defining the expected work products, establishing a work schedule, and implementing a system for monitoring the work process; 3) The modeling (analysis and design) phases primarily concentrate on the creation and refinement of a system architectural model. This process places particular attention on the design of data structures, software architectures, interface displays, and program algorithms. The aim is to get a more comprehensive comprehension of the total extent of the undertaking; 4) The construction phases, which include the code and test stages, primarily involve the transformation of design representations into code that machines can interpret. Subsequently, comprehensive testing of both the system and the code is conducted; and 5) The emphasis of the Deployment phase lies in the areas of Delivery, Support, and Feedback. The concluding stage includes the execution of software on projects that have received user approval, as well as the ongoing maintenance and support of the device. Additionally, it involves the refinement and enhancement of the software via the incorporation of user input.

The primary focus of the LAMs information system's architecture is on the creation of software that is licensed freely and falls under the category of Free and Open Source Software (FOSS). This licensing approach ensures that there are no limitations on those seeking to acquire knowledge since the software is released under the GNU public license. Lochhaas and Moore (2010) assert that Free and Open Source Software (FOSS) serves as a tool that gives users access to the source code, enabling them to see the developmental trajectory of the product. Individuals can make changes to the code, engage in experimentation, and generate several iterations, afterward offering the resulting product for sale at a justifiable level of financial gain. In essence, FOSS denotes software characterized by its open or freely available source code, enabling users to see the program's functioning and to augment or advance its development. The development of an information system must be closely aligned with the unique models and goals of the company. One of the existing designs used in software development is the SDLC design, which incorporates the cascade model, often referred to as the traditional life cycle. The construction of this model follows a systematic and step-by-step approach.

COLLECTIVE ACCESS FOR MEMORY INSTITUTIONS CONVERGENCE BRIDGE-BUILDING

Collective Access (CA) is an information system that enables the integration of libraries, archives, and museums (LAMs). The General Public License (GPL) guarantees the liberty to acquire, use, examine, alter, and disseminate the source code of a computer program, provided that the attribution details are retained inside the program's code. The CA can meet the demands of constructing information systems that rely on open-source technologies, particularly digital LAM contents or resources. The framework offered by CA facilitates the management, categorization, and exploration of intricate digital and physical resources within the domains of museums, archives, and libraries. The CA system has been specifically developed to possess the necessary flexibility for effectively managing and overseeing extensive resources, which may include intricate cataloging demands. As a system that facilitates information systems, CA has characteristics actively developed by the user community. CA possessed the following features prior to its development:

1) Data Modeling: a) Numerous metadata standards, including Describing Archives: A Content Standard (DACS), General International Standard Archival Description (ISAD G), DCMES, VRA Core, and numerous others; b) Configurable front-end pages and XML profiles for metadata configuration; c) Integrated information services, including the Library of Congress (LoC), the ULAN Catalog, etc.; d) Search and complex hierarchies for locations, objects, resources, and storage are supported; and e) Comprehensive documentation and complimentary online community support.

2) Process Media: a) Viewing and playback of image, video, audio, PDF, and 3D media formats within a web browser; b) Capacity to migrate formats and schedule migrations; c) Annotation capabilities for photographs, pictures, sound recordings, textual documents, videos and other media; d) HTML 5's pan and zoom functionality functions as a high-resolution image viewer and other object viewer options; and e) Support for Microsoft file formats with generated previews from LibreOffice.

Moreover, it is equipped to provide comprehensive assistance for a diverse array of standard metadata categories and different formats of media. Providence and Pawtucket are the two constituent elements of the CA system: 1) Providence is a component inside the back-end operational domain that enables users to categorize and manage various objects and resources systematically. CA employs a distinct methodology by explicitly customizing a significant portion of schema information with the objects present in a given resource. Providence encompasses a variety of metadata standards for Libraries, Archives, and Museums (LAMs) that were previously included in the default installation profile. These standards include Dublin Core Metadata Element Set (DCMES), PB Core, Visual Resources Association (VRA) Core, DarwinCore (DwC), Categories for the Description of Works of Art (CDWA Lite), and Machine-Readable Cataloging (MARC); and 2) Pawtucket is the section for observing visitors or users, also known as the front end, that displays information from the Providence section so that users can peruse the system's catalog. The default Pawtucket interface includes several features: home, about, browse, advanced search, and gallery. Through the use of additional modules, this functionality can be expanded.

BEST PRACTICE AT THE OMBILIN COAL MINING HERITAGE OF SAWAHLUNTO

The present initiative at the OCMHS employs the SDLC waterfall development methodology, along with adhering to best practices, to prioritize software, hardware, and system design. Hence, it is apparent that the results of the information system design process may be used in the construction of a prototype system referred to as "The Sawahlunto Memory." The focus is structured in the following manner.

Furthermore, the software plays a crucial role in improving the efficiency of organizational operations by serving as a crucial intermediary between the cognitive abilities of individuals and the physical hardware used in the organization. Software refers to a computer program that, upon execution, offers

Table 1. Focus details

Number	Focus	Information
1	Software	Computer Operating System Database Structure Programming language Web Server Requirements
2	Hardware	Server computers Client computers Supporting Equipment
3	The Software Development Life Cycle	*Communication* *Planning* Modeling (*Design*) Construction (*Code Test*) Deployment (*Test*)

various functionalities and operational instructions in accordance with the user's preferences. It also encompasses a data structure that enables the program to modify information proportionately. Additionally, the software is accompanied by documentation that elucidates the program's operation and use (Astyono, 2014). The results of the information system design process may be effectively implemented in "The Sawahlunto Memory."

Presently, the application known as "The Sawahlunto Memory" is poised to commence operations, offering a platform for both the government and the OCMHS community to engage in the contribution of collective memory actively. The following passage explains the software's intended objective: 1) Linux is the server's operating system to support "The Sawahlunto Memory." Linux is the server operating system because it meets "The Sawahlunto Memory's" scalability specifications; 2) Database components: "The Sawahlunto Memory" database is a framework for interactive activities such as storing queries, altering, upgrading, and deleting data and information. "The Sawahlunto Memory" utilizes the MySQL database type, which is known to support the information above and activity management functions; 3) "The Sawahlunto Memory" is built using a structured programming language. Using a structured programming language aims to understand the system's inner workings and the application's source code. It is known that using markup languages and programming languages such as HTML, CSS, PHP, JS (JavaScript), TypeScript (TS), and XML in "The Sawahlunto Memory" will make it simpler to introduce new features and modules in the future; and 4) Web Server: "The Sawahlunto Memory" is a specialized application that runs web-based applications. "The Sawahlunto Memory" is a web-based application that requires supporting software to function. As "The Sawahlunto Memory" is utilized by the Universitas Brawijaya Indonesia and cooperating with Universiti Teknologi MARA Malaysia, the Apache web server facilitates "The Sawahlunto Memory's" information system. The Apache Web Server is the most popular because it is reliable for operating web applications.

In order to achieve optimal use and seamless integration of a system such as "The Sawahlunto Memory," it needs more than just reliance on software alone. The correlation between support requirements, such as hardware, and the sustained use of the system is a crucial factor to be taken into account. The first version of "The Sawahlunto Memory" has garnered positive feedback and endorsement from the governing bodies of the OCMHS memory institutions. The emphasis on hardware is clearly defined. When implementing information systems, it is important to consider the hardware infrastructure of the firm in relation to computer servers. One of the techniques used is the utilization of server computers.

The "Sawahlunto Memory" server is hosted on a virtual machine that has been configured in this manner on the computer server of the OCMHS in partnership with the LAMs. Furthermore, the computer server used by Universitas Brawijaya in partnership with Universiti Teknologi MARA has satisfactorily met the required requirements specified in its technical specifications for efficiently handling the workload connected with "The Sawahlunto Memory."

Client computers are a kind of computer hardware that is interconnected inside a network. The client computer is often known as the user's personal computer (PC). The use of computer clients at the OCMHS is focused on meeting the requirements of users in terms of accessing and managing the content of "The Sawahlunto Memory." The client computer used at OCMHS is packed with features that have been purposefully intended to cater to the requirements of users in their quest for knowledge. The inclusion of supplementary equipment and peripherals at the OCMHS has the potential to improve job completion efficiency and effectiveness, particularly in relation to "The Sawahlunto Memory." Universitas Brawijaya and Universiti Teknologi MARA use a diverse range of technology, including scanners, cameras, printers, barcode readers, and other essential technologies, to streamline the administrative activities of "The Sawahlunto Memory." The equipment mentioned above is used based on the unique requirements of the institutions above.

In designing and constructing a system, multiple phases and distinct steps are required; in a dynamic organization, designing a system is essential. The objective is to define how the extant elements or components will be implemented. In addition, system design focuses on transforming a conventional system into a modern one. It supports the integration of computerized devices that make it simpler to process data and generate quality information. The Universitas Brawijaya and Universiti Teknologi MARA are also responsible for system design by prototyping "The Sawahlunto Memory," which was designed and developed using the CollectiveAccess (CA) software base and the SDLC waterfall system analysis method.

Before commencing any technical tasks, it is essential to engage in effective communication and collaboration with the client, as well as other relevant stakeholders. Stakeholders include individuals or groups who possess a vested interest in the successful completion of the project. The primary aim is to get a comprehensive understanding of the project goals as seen by the stakeholders and gather requirements that aid in delineating the features and functionality of the program (Roger & Bruce, 2015). Effective communication actions with the user are vital for comprehending and achieving mutually agreed-upon goals.

Effective communication between professionals in the fields of museology, curation, librarianship, archival management, and information technology within the OCMHS is vital when developing information systems for libraries, archives, and museums. The activities included in the communication process also fulfill the functions of mapping needs and facilitating early planning during the construction of a

Table 2. Details of the problem from the stage of communication

Library	Archives and Museums	Requirements
Convergence Factor	There must be an app for museums.	A system with the capability to store the cultural heritage resources of the OCMHS and operate as a memory institution is necessary.
Library resources integration	There is no application for storing digital resources in museums and archives.	The implementation of metadata updates is contingent upon the existing cultural heritage resources available at the OCMHS.
		The community within the OCMHS, as well as other interested parties, need the implementation of an archival format.

Table 3. Metadata schema type

Metadata Schema			
Archives	**Museum**	**Library**	**Donors**
DACS	CDWA	MARC21	DCMES

system. The identification of concerns was derived from the outcomes of the focus group discussion, including museologists, curators, librarians, archivists, and IT staff members of the OCMHS.

The act of creating a map has optimized even the most challenging expedition. Software projects are intricate undertakings, and the act of planning produces "maps" that function as guiding instruments for teams. The software project plan map provides a comprehensive overview of the software engineering activities. It delineates the technical responsibilities, potential risks, required resources, deliverables to be produced, and work schedules (Roger & Bruce, 2015). In this phase, the initiation of the planning process involves the assessment of the temporal aspects of technical task execution, identification of possible risks connected with the desired work outcomes, formulation of a thorough work schedule, and implementation of a monitoring system to track the progress of the work process.

In addition, the planning process undertaken by the OCMHS, Universitas Brawijaya, and Universiti Teknologi MARA integrates the use of flowchart diagrams within the planning workflow. These diagrams are used for the goal of identifying and designing novel features, such as metadata schemes, that aim to provide a full comprehension of the operation of these elements and their alignment with the desired aims and purposes as previously planned. The identification of the metadata system is an essential component throughout the planning phase. The main purpose of metadata is to enhance the process of resource discovery by providing more information about a certain collection of data or items. Metadata plays a crucial role in aiding users in assessing the accessibility and use of information. The project titled "The Sawahlunto Memory" aims to optimize its data structure and retrieval capabilities by using several metadata schema alternatives, including DCMES, DACS, MARC21, and CDWA.

The OCMHS often employs models in several professional fields, such as landscaping, bridge construction, aeronautical engineering, craftsmanship, and architecture. The OCMHS uses a "sketch" as a means of comprehending the architecture, assembly of components, and other pertinent properties of an entity. In instances when it is deemed essential, more details are included in the design in order to enhance understanding of the issue at hand and develop effective strategies for its resolution. In a similar vein, a software engineer develops a model with the aim of gaining a deeper understanding of the software requirements and devising a corresponding design to fulfill those needs (Roger & Bruce, 2015). The framework will now be developed based on the findings and outcomes of the system analysis and design process.

The modeling phase encompasses the development and representation of system architectures, with a specific focus on the design of data structures, software architectures, interface displays, and program algorithms. Figure 2 illustrates the sitemap of the CA demonstration. The login page or administration interface is characterized by a blue frame positioned in the top left quadrant. Upon successful verification of their credentials, the user will proceed to log in and have access to an administrative interface characterized by a grey frame, often referred to as the backend. Users are granted access to the homepage, which is visually distinguished by a red frame border. Users can access the login page, which is

Figure 2. CollectiveAccess sitemap

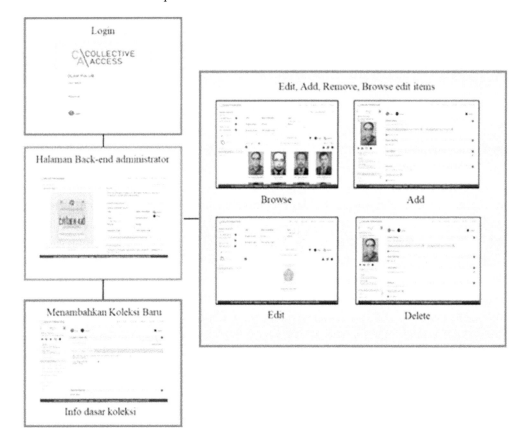

distinguished by a blue frame straight from the site. This login page serves as a platform for users to oversee and control various items and resources effectively.

Figure 3 depicts the architectural layout of the front-end display structure and the corresponding administrator interface, often referred to as the backend. The front-end page functions as a visual interface through which visitors may access and interact with a website or application that has been created using the Bootstrap framework. Bootstrap is a cost-free and open-source cascading style sheets (CSS) framework designed specifically for the construction of user interfaces in online applications. The framework encompasses HTML, CSS, and JavaScript-based designs, along with supplementary interface features. The backend page of "The Sawahlunto Memory" is developed using the PHP programming language and utilizes MySQL databases. It is hosted on the Apache web server.

The construction of what is being referred to in the context of the discussion? The construction of the OCMHS design is necessary. This activity encompasses the process of code creation, which may be done either manually or by automated means, as well as the subsequent testing phase aimed at identifying and rectifying any flaws present in the code. During this phase, the primary emphasis will be placed on the program code depiction of the interface design, as well as the incorporation of mutually agreed-upon functionalities that system users will use in the future. Figure 4 illustrates a notable phase in the development process, wherein the front page's visual presentation has been modified from the default design to a customized one, as per the prior design. As seen in Figure 4, the red frame represents

Figure 3. The CollectiveAccess administrator page displays the design structure

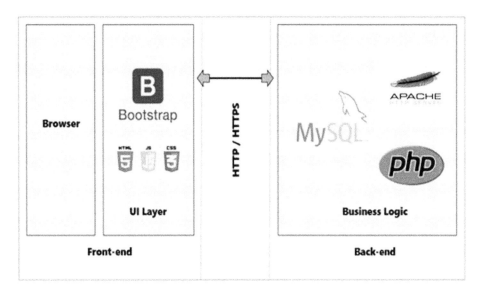

the default display of "The Sawahlunto Memory," while the blue frame corresponds to a customized outcome derived from the preceding model design and design stage.

The last step is the identification of the metadata scheme, as seen in Figure 5 of the publication titled "The Sawahlunto Memory." This is necessary because of the existence of LAM repositories and benefactors, which need distinct descriptions of the metadata and its corresponding parts. Metadata plays a crucial role, serving not just as a source of information but also as a means of describing an

Figure 4. Customise frontend view from CollectiveAccess to "The Sawahlunto Memory"

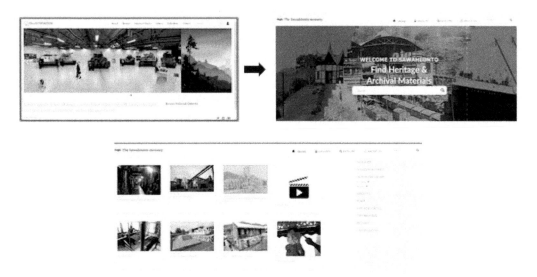

Figure 5. Frontend display customization from CollectiveAccess to "The Sawahlunto Memory"

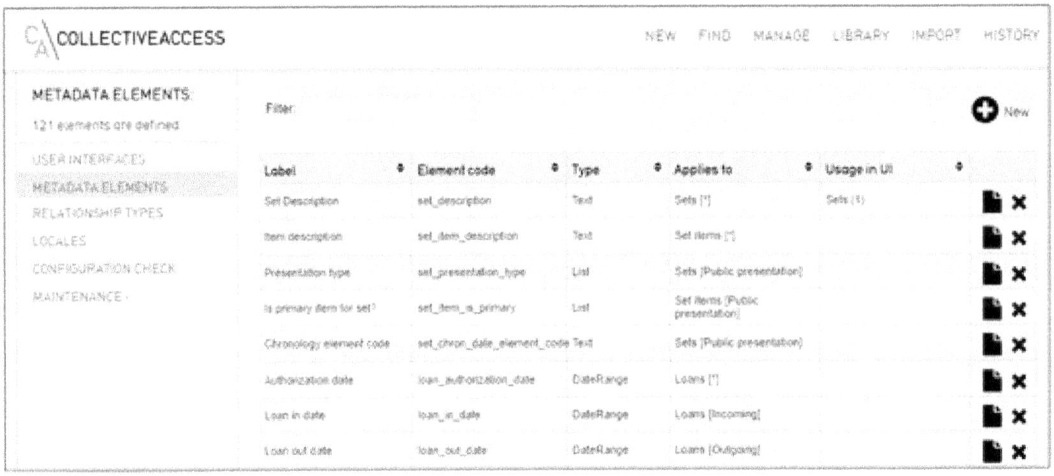

item. Metadata may be produced by human or automated means. The configuration of metadata in "The Sawahlunto Memory" is performed both manually and automatically.

During the phase of deployment, the software, whether in its whole or as an incomplete add-on, is disseminated to the customer. The client then proceeds to assess the supplied product and offer comments in accordance with the predetermined assessment process (Roger & Bruce, 2015). The ultimate step in the process of designing an information system involves the testing of the system prototype, which is developed based on the framework established and shown in the preceding phases. Testing is conducted to assess the functionality of "The Sawahlunto Memory." Functional testing is used to determine the suitability of the system to meet the specified functionality criteria. The tests were undertaken by a team consisting of information system professionals, relevant staff, focus group talks, and system users. The prototype of "The Sawahlunto Memory" was built by Universitas Brawijaya and Universiti Teknologi MARA after undergoing testing.

Based on the observations above, specifically, the outcomes derived from the testing procedure of "The Sawahlunto Memory," it can be concluded that this platform serves as a repository for documenting diverse activities through the utilization of photographs, pictures, sound recordings, textual documents, videos, and other media. These resources are stored within "The Sawahlunto Memory," which functions as a representation of a memory institution or LAMs. The historical component of the OCMHS, as described aesthetically in the gallery menu, captures the attention of ld users of "The Sawahlunto Memory" due to its second success. Additionally, a donor form may serve as an intermediary between the OCMHS community and stakeholders who own various forms of cultural heritage resources, which may be contributed to "The Sawahlunto Memory."

FUTURE RESEARCH SUGGESTIONS

Innovative methods should be explored to disseminate information to the general public, engage in collaborative efforts to safeguard and digitize the collective memory of the OCMHS, and effectively use common resources and facilities. In order to adapt to fast technological developments and modernity, the

OCMHS should prioritize the development of "The Sawahlunto Memory" as a means to preserve the invaluable collective memory with their memory institutions. This initiative is crucial for safeguarding the rich cultural heritage of Indonesia and the globe.

CONCLUSION

This chapter offers an overview of the convergence of memory institutions or Libraries, Archives, and Museums (LAMs) at the Ombilin Coal Mining Heritage of Sawahlunto (OCMHS) and presents illustrative instances of exemplary practices seen at LAM in world heritage sites. The report suggests that LAMs of the OCMHS organizations should engage in collaborative efforts and pursue convergence in order to achieve significant outcomes. The implementable products of the information system design process are evident in "The Sawahlunto Memory."

At present, the application known as "The Sawahlunto Memory" is operational and may be employed by the academic community to assist the government and local community in the OCMHS in actively contributing to the incorporation of collective memory inside the program. This contribution can take the form of photographs, pictures, sound recordings, textual documents, videos, and other media. The recognition of the convergence of memory institutions inside the OCMHS, with the aim of safeguarding its cultural heritage, necessitates careful consideration and planning about the significance of the collective memory held by each person as a valuable asset of the OCMHS. Within the memory institution of the OCMHS, there exists evidence pertaining to varying levels of prosperity as well as the presence of the OCMHS itself. Consequently, the amalgamation of these elements serves to underscore the preeminent memory institution.

The establishment of cooperation requires the alteration of behavior, procedures, and organizational structures, with the outcome being the realization of significant changes and economic benefits. LAMs within the OCMHS are consistently required to address the recurring issues associated with physical limitations.

REFERENCES

Asoka, A., Samry, W., & Saputra, Y. (2016). Sawahlunto Dulu, Kini, dan Esok: Menjadi Kota Wisata Tambang yang Berbudaya. Padang: Minangkabau Press.

August, T., Chen, W., & Zhu, K. (2021). Competition among proprietary and open-source software firms: The role of licensing in strategic contribution. *Management Science*, *67*(5), 3041–3066. doi:10.1287/mnsc.2020.3674

Buckland, M. K., & Lund, N. W. (2013). Boyd Rayward, documentation, and information science. *Library Trends*, *62*(2), 302–310. doi:10.1353/lib.2013.0038

Byrne, A. (2015). Institutional memory and memory institutions. *The Australian Library Journal*, *64*(4), 259–269. doi:10.1080/00049670.2015.1073657

Constantine, E., Garrity, J., Hammes, M., Lockwood, C., & Teesch, L. (2018). *Libraries and Museums: Fostering GLAM Collaboration at the University of Iowa*. University of Iowa. doi:10.17077/yc01-mco1

Dümcke, C., & Gnedovsky, M. (2013). *The social and economic value of cultural heritage: a literature review*. European Expert Network on Culture.

Fernando, S., Hall, M., Agirre, E., Soroa, A., Clough, P., & Stevenson, M. (2012). Comparing taxonomies for organizing collections of documents. *Proceedings of COLING 2012, The COLING 2012 Organizing Committee,* 879–894.

Gibson, H., Morris, A., & Cleeve, M. (2007). *Links Between Libraries and Museums: Investigating Museum-Library Collaboration in England and the USA*. De Gruyter.

Hall, M. M., & Walsh, D. (2021). *Exploring digital cultural heritage through browsing*. Information and Knowledge Organisation in Digital Humanities. doi:10.4324/9781003131816-13

Hendrawan, M. R., & Bafadhal, A. S. (2021). Cutting-Edge Technologies in Cultural Heritage Preservation Through Virtual Museum in the Phygital Era. In Globalisation of Cultural Heritage: Issues, Impacts, and Challenges. Kuala Nerus: Universiti Malaysia Trengganu Press.

Higgins, S. (2013). Digital Curation: The Challenge Driving Convergence across Memory Institutions. In L. Duranti, & E. Shaffer (Eds.), The Memory of the World in the Digital Age: Digitization and Preservation: An international conference on permanent access to digital documentary heritage, Vancouver, Canada, 26-28 September 2012 (pp. 607–623). United Nations Educational, Scientific and Cultural Organization (UNESCO).

Katre, D. (2011). Digital preservation: Converging and diverging factors of libraries, archives, and museums–an Indian perspective. *IFLA Journal, 37*(3), 195–203. doi:10.1177/0340035211418728

Król, K. (2021). Assessment of the cultural heritage potential in Poland. *Sustainability (Basel), 13*(12), 6637. doi:10.3390u13126637

Limb, P. (2003). Archives, Libraries, and Museums Convergence: The 24th Library Systems Seminar, Paris 12-14 April 2000 Archives, Bibliothèques et Musées. *Online Information Review, 27*(5), 368–368. doi:10.1108/14684520310503585

Lindayanti, R. A. F., Efendi, H., Rahman, F., Saputra, Y., Yulia, A., Mega, Y., & Elvira, M. (2017). *Kota Sawahlunto, Jalur Kereta Api dan teluk Bayur: Tiga Serangkai dalam Sejarah Pertambangan Batubara Ombilin di Sumatera Barat*. Minangkabau Press.

Lindayanti, R. A. F., Yulia, A., Bahren, E., Harry, S., Yoni, M., Yuristya, Z., & Zulqayyim. (2016). Pertambangan dan Pengangkutan Batubara Ombilin Sawahlunto pada Masa Kolonial. Padang: Minangkabau Press.

Lochhaas, S., & Moore, M. (2010). Open-source software libraries. *B Sides: Fieldwork, 2010*(1).

Mahey, M., Al-Abdulla, A., Ames, S., Bray, P., Candela, G., Chambers, S., Derven, C., Dobreva-McPherson, M., Gasser, K., Karner, S., Kokegei, K., Laursen, D., Potter, A., Straube, A., Wagner, S. C. & Wilms, L. (2019). *Open a GLAM Lab—Digital Cultural Heritage Innovation Labs*. Book Sprint, Doha, Qatar.

Mariyapillai, J., & Naviratharan, G. (2020). *Islandora: An Open-Source Software Solution for Museum Collections of the Library*. Eastern University.

Marty, P. F. (2014). Digital Convergence and the Information Profession in Cultural Heritage Organizations: Reconciling Internal and External Demands. *Library Trends, 62*(3), 613–627. doi:10.1353/lib.2014.0007

Pendit, P. L. (2019). *Pustaka: tradisi & kesinambungan.* Ikatan Sarjana Ilmu Perpustakaan dan Informasi Indonesia.

Petrelli, D., Ciolfi, L., Van Dijk, D., Hornecker, E., Not, E., & Schmidt, A. (2013). We are integrating material and digital: A new way for cultural heritage. *Interactions (New York, N.Y.), 20*(4), 58–63. doi:10.1145/2486227.2486239

Potgieter, A., & Mabe, K. (2018). The future of accessing our past: Collaboration and digitization in libraries, archives, and museums. In *Proceedings of Business and Management Conferences.* International Institute of Social and Economic Sciences.

Rainer, R. K., Kelly, R. R., & Prince, B. (2022). *Introduction to information systems.* John Wiley & Sons.

Roger, S. P., & Bruce, R. M. (2015). *Software engineering: a practitioner's approach.* McGraw-Hill Education.

Shimray, S. R. & Chennupati, K. R. (2019). Cultural Heritage Awareness among Students of Pondicherry University: a Study. *Library Philosophy and Practice*, 2516.

Sullivan, S. (2004). Local involvement and traditional practices in the world heritage system. *Linking Universal and Local Values, 49*, 49–55.

The United Nations Educational, Scientific and Cultural Organization (UNESCO). (2019). *Ombilin Coal Mining Heritage of Sawahlunto.* Available at https://whc.unesco.org/en/list/1610

Trant, J. (2009). Emerging convergence? Thoughts on Museums, Archives, Libraries, and Professional Training. *Museum Management and Curatorship, 24*(4), 369–387. doi:10.1080/09647770903314738

Veldpaus, L. (2016). Heritage Taxonomy: Towards a common language? In *HERITAGE 2016–5th International Conference on Heritage and Sustainable Development.* Newcastle University.

Warren, E., & Matthews, G. (2019). Public libraries, museums, and physical convergence: Context, issues, opportunities: A literature review Part 1. *Journal of Librarianship and Information Science, 51*(4), 1120–1133. doi:10.1177/0961000618769720

Yarrow, A., Clubb, B., & Draper, J. L. (2008). *Public Libraries, Archives, and Museums: Trends in collaboration and cooperation.* International Federation of Library Associations and Institutions (IFLA).

Zorich, D., Waibel, G., & Erway, R. (2008). *Beyond the Silos of the LAMs: Collaboration Among Libraries.* OCLC.

Zourou, K., & Pellegrini, E., (2021). *Practices of digitally mediated youth engagement in cultural institutions during the pandemic.* GLAMers Consortium.

KEY TERMS AND DEFINITIONS

Archives: Are structured and maintained resources of historical records, papers, manuscripts, pictures, audiovisual recordings, and other sources that benefit study, historical knowledge, accountability, and cultural heritage preservation. Archives preserve the collective memory of people, organizations, communities, and society. Archives help preserve history, facilitate study, promote transparency, and protect societies' documented cultural heritage. Their windows to the past illuminate human history, culture, and governance.

Collective Memory: Is essential to human culture and civilization. It affects people's history, present, and future. It stores cultural information, values, and identity, giving a community a feeling of continuity and belonging. Groups or communities that remember, comprehend, and interpret previous events, experiences, and cultural occurrences are all integral to collective memory.

Convergence: Refers to the process of moving towards a central meeting point or condition. Additionally, it may be seen as a method of implementing interventions that are executed in a synchronized, integrated, and collaborative fashion with the aim of addressing high-priority objectives.

Cultural Heritage: Comprises a multitude of tangible and intangible elements, making it extensive and intricate. These include hereditary traits, behavioral patterns, customary rituals, and linguistic expressions. The preservation of cultural heritage is of paramount importance due to its historical, aesthetic, scientific, and social significance.

Cultural Heritage Resources: Are physical and intangible assets of social, historical, artistic, scientific, or societal value. They're passed down to preserve identity, continuity, and history. Community identities, memories, and cultures rely on culture. For cultural continuity, heritage awareness, and preservation, these resources must be conserved.

Information: Crucial and abstract facts or information that may transmit meaning, enhance understanding, decrease ambiguity, or influence a person, system, or entity's status, beliefs, or actions.

Information Systems: Help management make decisions and operate operations. This system combines people, IT, and coordinated processes. An information system should provide meaningful data. Data is a fundamental component of an information system, but it must be processed to become meaningful and valuable. Information systems are crucial to turning data into useful, reliable information that can be utilized in organizational decision-making and operations.

Intangible Cultural Heritage: Traditions passed down from generation to generation. Actions, expressions, knowledge, abilities, and rituals vary. Intangible cultural heritage includes oral traditions and expressions, performing arts, traditional knowledge and practices, festivals and celebrations, craftsmanship and traditional crafts, language and linguistic traditions, traditional games and sports, social practices, norms, and etiquette, knowledge systems and expertise, music and dance forms, rituals and ceremonies, transmission, and education.

Libraries: Well-selected resources of information resources, materials, and services available to the public, students, academics, or a community to aid education, research, reference, and pleasure. Libraries help preserve knowledge, promote literacy, facilitate learning, and provide access to different information. As inclusive spaces for inquiry, discovery, and active interaction with information, libraries foster curiosity, education, and intellectual growth.

Memory Institutions: Are assets that gather, preserve, interpret, study, and distribute cultural heritage resources. Tangible and intangible resources, records, traditions, and cultural, historical, aesthetic, scientific, or social information. Museums, archives, and libraries all serve this purpose, each with its roles and responsibilities. Resources and acquisition, conservation and preservation, research and scholarship, exhibition and interpretation, education and outreach, access and accessibility, community engagement, advocacy, and policy are memory institutions' primary functions.

Museum: Is an institution that gathers, conserves, studies, interprets, and shows cultural, artistic, historical, or scientific resources for public education and enrichment is a museum. Museums preserve and display humanity's tangible and intangible heritage, promote learning, and engage the public. They are vital organizations that preserve, interpret, and share the rich fabric of human knowledge, creativity, and history.

Tangible Cultural Heritage: Is a culture's physical history and legacy passed down through generations. It encompasses various cultural, historical, aesthetic, scientific, and socially significant artifacts, structures, and persons.

Chapter 14
ChatGPT and Its Ethical Implications on Libraries, Other Institutions, and Society:
Is It a Viable Upgrade?

Barbara Jane Holland

https://orcid.org/0000-0003-3729-0147

Brooklyn Public Library, USA (Retired)

ABSTRACT

On March 28, 2023, an open letter titled "Pause Giant A.I. Experiments" was published by the Future of Life Institute, urging A.I. companies to draft a shared set of safety protocols around advanced A.I. development before creating more powerful software that may pose dangers to humanity. A wide range of ethical issues have been raised concerning Open AI's ChatGPT. The use of ChatGPT has demonstrated on numerous occasions that it encourages racial and gender bias. This (AI) chatbot system uses learning models that are not bias-free. The chatbot obeys the algorithm blindly and replies with the requested information when prompted. It cannot tell whether the information is skewed. This chapter examines the ethical implications ChatGPT can have on libraries, other institutions, and society.

On March 28, 2023, an Open letter titled "Pause Giant A.I. Experiments," was published by the Future of Life Institute, urging AI companies to draft a shared set of safety protocols around advanced A.I. development before creating more powerful software that may pose dangers to humanity. The letter has collected thousands of signatures from influential tech leaders, entrepreneurs, academics, and investors, calling for OpenAI and other artificial intelligence labs to pause training A.I. systems that are more advanced than GPT-4.

Companies were urged to draft a shared set of safety protocols around advanced A.I. development before creating more powerful software that may pose dangers to humanity.

ChatGPT, or Chat Generative Pre-Trained Transformer, is a large language model (LLM) with deep learning methods and a subset of machine learning that can detect, compress, translate, predict, and

DOI: 10.4018/979-8-3693-2841-5.ch014

create text (along with other types of information). As a machine-learning system that learns from data autonomously and can write sophisticated and presumably intelligent writing after training on a vast text data set (van Dis, E et al 2023).

ChatGPT is a neural network model that can generate natural language responses based on user input. It has been widely used for various applications, such as chatbots, conversational agents, and text summarization. However, ChatGPT also poses ethical challenges and risks, such as generating harmful, biased, or misleading content, violating user privacy, or manipulating user behavior.

People enjoy easy shortcuts and most will agree that using a chatbot occasionally is acceptable in the modern day of fierce competition. However, many people have been thinking that because of the release of ChatGPT, the generative AI technology, ethical ramifications have forced us to consider how this seemingly benign chatbot can have unfavorable outcomes and detrimental effects.

Understanding right and wrong is related to ethics. It is almost impossible to make new laws or improve old ones given how quickly technological developments occur.

A wide range of ethical issues have been raised by the useful tool ChatGPT from OpenAI. The use of ChatGPT has demonstrated on numerous occasions that it encourages racial and gender bias. This (AI) chatbot system uses learning models that are not bias-free. The chatbot obeys the algorithm blindly and replies with the requested information when prompted. It cannot tell whether the information is skewed.

Data that is scarce and outdated is fed into ChatGPT. To build ChatGPT, 570 GB of data, or almost 300 billion words, were employed.

It is insufficient to address every topic in the world from multiple perspectives. In addition, beyond 2021, have any modifications been made to this data? In this sense, it also fails to reflect progressivism.

The problem with the ChatGPT models is that they encourage discrimination based on gender, race, and other categories. Many academics and users have noted that when they utilized ChatGPT to gather information or write articles or essays on particular topics, the results were prejudiced and reflected negative prejudices.

ChatGPT can be used by con artists and other nefarious individuals to create fake websites or mobile apps that trick consumers. For ChatGPT to build webpages and applications, it requires a simple prompt. Scammers can use resources to pose as websites and programs that are authorized by law, deceive people by utilizing malicious software, and fool innocent people.

Because they are tech-savvy, younger people will use the internet to either better understand already-existing knowledge or discover new information that is not taught in school. This is entirely morally right. However, a problem arises when students use ChatGPT to finish assignments, study for exams, and compose essays. In universities, homework assignments are graded. Therefore, it is against academic etiquette to use AI-based technology to accomplish your assignments and homework since it is seen as plagiarism. Additionally, ChatGPT poses ethical conundrums for facilities such as libraries and others that provide public access to knowledge and information.

Libraries are establishments that gather, store, and facilitate access to a variety of information sources, including books, periodicals, newspapers, digital data, and multimedia items.

When utilizing ChatGPT, librarians must take certain ethical considerations into account. Among these are making sure that the generated texts are checked, updated, or annotated before being shown to users or utilized for library services. Furthermore, ChatGPT might produce false, slanted, or deceptive information that undermines libraries' credibility and dependability. Therefore, to ensure the responsible and ethical use of ChatGPT and other AI technologies, librarians must be aware of the ethical issues and challenges surrounding them and implement the necessary policies and practices.

ChatGPT may generate erroneous, misleading, or biased information that may affect users or the library's reputation. Before presenting generated texts to users or using them for library services, libraries must ensure that they have been validated, updated, or annotated. In many cases, it's impossible to detect that a human is interacting with a computer-generated bot. Grammatical and syntax errors are rare and written constructions are logical and articulate (Greengard, Samuel, 2022)

Moreover, ChatGPT may acquire, retain, or use personally identifiable or sensitive data from users or library resources without their knowledge or consent. Libraries must respect users' and data privacy and security by adhering to ethical and legal norms and notifying users about how ChatGPT works and what data it utilizes.

Librarians are professionals who manage and organize information resources for various purposes and audiences. They often deal with the ethical implications of their work, such as privacy, intellectual freedom, censorship, and social responsibility.

The social and cultural significance of Texts created by ChatGPT may be offensive, hurtful, or inappropriate for specific groups or settings. Libraries must respect the diversity and inclusivity of their users and the communities they serve by avoiding or limiting ChatGPT's potentially harmful influence on their values, beliefs, or identities.

As other similar systems become more advanced and widespread, librarians have an important role to play in ensuring that they are used in a responsible, ethical, and beneficial way for society.

Some have expressed concerns in universities about how AI could undermine the educational system or encourage academic dishonesty if students substitute it for their ideas, opinions, research, open-book exams, and take-home assignments. Others bring attention to potential advantages. (Holland B 2023).

There is a parallel obligation to manage ethical questions and handle the challenges that result from using such a powerful technology. As ChatGPT and other similar systems become more prevalent in our daily lives, these issues demand our immediate attention.

At present there is relatively little discussion of the ethical benefits of ChatGPT, such as the potential benefits of using ChatGPT in promoting teaching and learning Baidoo-Anu and Owusu Ansah (2023).

This chapter examines ChatGPT, and its ethical implications, concerning libraries, other institutions, and society. The chapter will also identify the main ethical issues, principles, and frameworks that can help guide the development and evaluation of ChatGPT systems.

BACKGROUND AND LITERATURE

The origins of AI and chatbots may be traced back to the 1950s when scientists first investigated the concept of artificial intelligence. Alan Turing's research in the early 1950s laid the foundation for modern computer science. While John McCarthy coined the term "artificial intelligence" in 1956. Several years later, McCarthy and his colleagues set up the Artificial Intelligence project at MIT.

AI and chatbots can be traced back to the 1950s when scientists first began exploring the concept of artificial intelligence. Early breakthroughs included the construction of the first artificial intelligence program, ELIZA, which was designed to simulate human communication.

Developments in machine learning and natural language processing propelled AI back into the spotlight in the 1990s. Ask Jeeves debuted in 1996 with a unique question-and-answer format that allowed users to get responses using both natural language and keyword searching. In 2006, Jeeves was phased out and renamed Ask.com, a simple question-and-answer format. Ask.com exited the search market in 2010, resulting in the loss of 130 search engineering jobs, because it could not compete with more popular search engines such as Google.

On November 30, 2022, a startup called Open AI launched ChatGPT, a sibling model to InstructGPT that is trained to follow instructions in a prompt and deliver a detailed response. The researchers intended to learn about the users' strengths and weaknesses at chat.openai.com.

OpenAI, of San Francisco, CA, released an AI chatbot called ChatGPT in November 2022. Developed using human feedback and freely accessible, the platform has already attracted millions of interactions (Grant N and Metz C 2022).

ChatGPT (Chat Generative Pre-trained Transformer) is based on the GPT-3 (Generative Pre-trained Transformer 3) large language model (LLM). The huge language model is a deep neural network that is trained with petabytes of data and uses billions of parameters.

The GPT-3 fed 45 TB of text data utilizing 175 billion parameters and was designed to improve task-agnostic performance and even compete with previous state-of-the-art systems.

ChatGPT is a large-scale pre-trained language model that can generate coherent and fluent texts on various topics and domains. ChatGPT can also engage in conversational interactions with human users, providing information, entertainment, and assistance.

ChatGPT must be fine-tuned to minimize the risk of generating offensive, biased, or inappropriate content (A.S.Rao et; al 2023). This involves continuous work on the training data, model architecture, and monitoring mechanisms, (vii) robustness and security: Conversational AI models can be vulnerable to adversarial attacks or malicious inputs.

When presented with a query, ChatGPT will automatically generate a response, which is based on thousands of internet sources, often without further input from the user. Resultantly, individuals have reportedly used ChatGPT to formulate university essays and scholarly articles and, if prompted, the system can deliver accompanying references.

The GPT-3 fed 45 TB of text data using 175 billion parameters and has been developed to enhance task-agnostic and even become competitive with prior state-of-the-art fine-tuning approaches (Brown, et al., 2020). Brown et al., (2020) stated that GPT-3 is ten times more than any previous non-sparse language model. GPT-3 has become the basic NLP engine that runs the recently developed language model ChatGPT which has attracted the attention of various fields including but not limited to education (Williams, 2023; Tate, 2023), and engineering (Qadir, 2022).

Chatbots are already being used by certain scientists as research assistants, according to Nature (2022). These chatbots can help scientists organize their ideas, provide comments on their work, help write code, and summarize study literature.

Within two months after its release, ChatGPT amassed 100 million monthly active visitors, making it the fastest-growing consumer application in history (Hu, 2023). ChatGPT can respond to follow-up queries, deny improper requests, refute false assumptions, and acknowledge its errors (Schulman et al., 2022). The bot is already causing disruptions in several industries, including academia. Specifically, it is making people wonder what the future holds for research and university essays (Nature 2023).

Studies across various fields have already listed ChatGPT as an author, but whether generative AI fulfills the International Committee of Medical Journal Editors criteria for authorship is a point of debate (Frye B 2022)

ChatGPT has successfully passed the United States Medical Licensure Exam (USMLE) without any training (DiGigiorgio 2023).

ChatGPT has become the fastest-growing consumer application in history, gathering 100 million monthly active visitors within two months after its launch (Hu, 2023).

Figure 1. ChatGPT user interface by Open AI

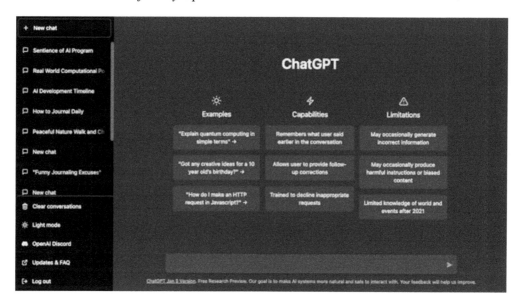

ChatGPT can answer follow-up questions, reject inappropriate requests, challenge incorrect premises, and admit its mistakes (Schulman et al., 2022).

A self-supervised sign-in text, LLM aims to predict the probability of the next words based on the above-mentioned context. The Internet contains large-scale textual data and thus pre-training the model via LM is a natural recourse (Zhou, J et; al 2023) To reduce the possibility of producing objectionable, prejudiced, or improper content, ChatGPT needs to be adjusted A.S. Rao et al., 2023. The training data, model design, and monitoring systems must all be continuously improved. (vii) Robustness and security: Conversational AI models are susceptible to malicious inputs or adversarial attacks.

Human reality emulation is where researchers aim to construct interactive and immersive environments that closely mimic interactions in the actual world (Demitrijevic and Petrović 2018). Offering them an experience that closely mimics human connection is the ultimate goal.

The goal is to develop machines that can learn, reason, and solve problems similarly to humans by imitating human cognition (Martínez-Miranda and Aldea 2005). To foster creativity, this project uses algorithms to mimic human brain processes.

ChatGPT because it moves the emphasis to the larger ecosystem from people (like developers or users) or organizations (like OpenAI) (Chae, 2019, Senyo et al., 2019). Susarla et al(2023) .'s discussion of the ethics of ChatGPT compares potential advantages for problem formulation, data analysis, and writing to concerns about bias, accountability, intellectual property, and depth. They also address guidelines and difficulties for the responsible use of generative AI, such as ChatGPT, in IS research.

ChatGPT (Chat Generative Pre-Trained Transformer) is a complex machine learning model that can carry out natural language generation (NLG) tasks with such a high level of accuracy that the model can pass a Turing Test.

Tasks that ChatGPT excels at include:

- Providing answers to questions.
- Completing a given text or a phrase.

- Writing fiction and non-fiction content from prompts.
- Producing humanlike chatbot responses.
- Generating computer code.
- Translating the text from one language to another.
- Performing calculations.
- Summarizing a given text.
- Classifying text into different categories.
- Analyzing text sentiment.
- Generating text that summarizes data in tables and spreadsheets.
- Conversationally responding to user input.

Data scientists and machine learning engineers used semi-supervised learning to train ChatGPT. creators have used a combination of both Supervised Learning and Reinforcement Learning to fine-tune ChatGPT, but it is the Reinforcement Learning component specifically that makes ChatGPT unique. The creators use a particular technique called Reinforcement Learning from Human Feedback (RLHF), which uses human feedback in the training loop to minimize harmful, untruthful, and/or biased outputs.

TRAINING CHATGPT

Semi-supervised learning algorithms are trained on datasets that are only partially labeled; some of the data points have labels and some do not. To forecast what would happen with the unlabeled data, the model uses the labeled data.

Most of the unlabeled data needed to train the LLM was reportedly obtained by data scientists using web scraping, according to OpenAI. They added text sources to this as well, either from the public domain or from private sources that were made accessible to scholars and perhaps even governments.

Although OpenAI has not specifically explained how they were able to label the extraordinarily enormous data sets needed to fine-tune the model, it is known that they outsourced some of the labelings. It is also possible that they made use of crowdsourcing tools like Amazon's Mechanical Turk.

According to OpenAI, data scientists used web scraping to compile the enormous amount of unlabeled data necessary to train the LLM. Text sources that were either in the public domain or made available for use by researchers and perhaps governments were added to this.

Fine Tuning ChatGPT

Fine-tuning ChatGPT with RLHF consisted of three distinct steps:

1. **Supervised fine-tuning** - A supervised policy (the SFT model) that produces outputs from a predetermined list of prompts is learned by fine-tuning a pre-trained language model on a comparatively limited quantity of demonstration data selected by labelers. This is the standard model.
2. **"Mimic human preferences"** – Voting on a sizable portion of the SFT model outputs is required of labelers in order to create a fresh dataset with comparative data. This dataset is used to train a new model. It is known as the reward model (RM).

Figure 2. Alignment vs. capability

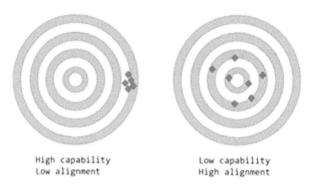

High capability
Low alignment

Low capability
High alignment

3.   **Proximal Policy Optimization (PPO)** – The reward model is used to further fine-tune and improve the SFT model. The outcome of this step is the so-called **policy model**.

Step 1 occurs only once, while steps 2 and 3 can be repeated repeatedly: In order to train a new reward model and therefore a new policy, additional comparison data is gathered on the best policy model that is currently in use.

The creators of ChatGPT have used a combination of both Supervised Learning and Reinforcement Learning to fine-tune ChatGPT, but it is the Reinforcement Learning component specifically that makes ChatGPT unique. A particular technique was used called Reinforcement Learning from Human Feedback (RLHF), which uses human feedback in the training loop to minimize harmful, untruthful, and/or biased

Capability vs. Alignment in Large Language Models

The ability of a model to do a certain task or collection of tasks is referred to as a model's capability in terms of machine learning. The efficiency with which a model can optimize its objective function—the formula that expresses the model's objective—is often used to measure a model's capacity. An objective function that assesses the precision of the model's predictions, for instance, may be included in a model created to forecast stock market values. The model would be regarded as having a high level of skill for this task if it could anticipate the movement of stock prices over time with accuracy.

Alignment, on the other hand, is concerned with what we want the model to do versus what it is being trained to do. It asks the question "Is that objective function consistent with our intentions?" It refers to the extent to which a model's goals and behavior align with human values and expectations. As another example, a bird classifier is trained to classify birds as either "sparrows" or "robins" and a *log loss is used* (which measures the difference between the predicted probability distribution of the model and the true distribution) as the training objective, even though the goal is high classification accuracy. The model might have low log loss, i.e., where the model's capability is high, but poor accuracy on the test set. The log loss is not perfectly correlated with accuracy in classification tasks. This is an example of misalignment, where the model can optimize the training objective but is poorly aligned with the goal in mind.

GPT-3

Although enormous language models, like GPT-3, can produce text that is similar to what a human would write, they may not always provide results that are in line with appropriate standards or human expectations. Their primary goal is to anticipate the next word in a series using a probability distribution across word sequences (or token sequences).

There is a definite difference between how these models are trained and how we would like to use them because, in practical applications, these models are meant to carry out some kind of advantageous cognitive task.

Drawbacks and Limitations

Even though mathematically speaking a statistical distribution of word sequences calculated by a machine might be a very effective choice to model language, humans create language by selecting text sequences that are most appropriate for the given circumstance, using our prior knowledge and common sense to guide this process. This can become a problem in applications that demand a high level of trust or dependability, like conversational systems or intelligent personal assistants.

Complex models trained on huge amounts of data have become extremely capable in the last few years. When used in production systems to make human lives easier they often fall short of this potential.

The alignment problem in Large Language Models typically discloses as:

- Lack of helpfulness: not following the user's explicit instructions.
- Hallucinations: a model making up nonexistent or wrong facts.
- Lack of interpretability: it is difficult for humans to understand how the model arrived at a particular decision or prediction.
- Generating biased or toxic output: a language model that is trained on biased/toxic data may reproduce that in its output, even if it was not explicitly instructed to do so.

Figure 3. Reinforcement learning model

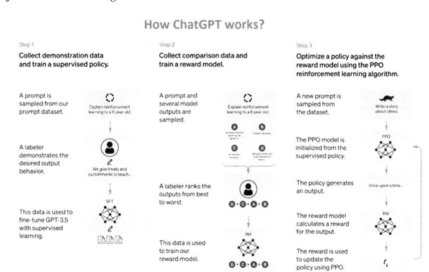

259

Table 1.

1. Gathering data Obtaining the data needed to fine-tune the model is the initial stage in training a GPT model. The information you provide should be relevant to the kind of work you want your model to accomplish, such as sentiment analysis or language translation. You can use datasets that are made accessible to the public, or you can use alternative techniques, such as web scraping, to collect your data.
2. Pre-processing data Pre-processing your data is the next step after obtaining it. The data must be cleaned, formatted so that it can be utilized for training, and divided into training and validation sets.
3. Fine-tuning the model Using the data you have already pre-processed, the GPT model needs to be adjusted. OpenAI's pre-trained GPT models can be used as a basis, and you can adjust them further to fit your particular task. The process of fine-tuning entails changing the model's parameters to improve its performance on your assignment. Using the data you have already pre-processed, the GPT model needs to be adjusted. OpenAI's pre-trained GPT models can be used as a basis, and you can adjust them further to fit your particular task. The process of fine-tuning entails changing the model's parameters to improve its performance on your assignment.
4. Evaluate the model Once you have fine-tuned your model, the next step is to evaluate it. You can do this by using it to make predictions on your validation set and comparing the predictions to the actual labels. This will give you a sense of how well your model is performing and what areas need improvement.
5. Refining the model You can go back and make more changes to your model's performance if it's not quite up to par. This could entail modifying the training set, the fine-tuning parameters, or the model architecture.

CHATGPT 4

On March 13, 2023, Open AI announced their creation of GPT4.

GPT-4 is a big multimodal model (accepting picture and text inputs and outputting text outputs) that, while less proficient than humans in many real-world settings, outperforms humans on a variety of professional and academic standards. For example, it passes a simulated bar exam with a score in the top 10% of test takers, whereas GPT-3.5 has a score in the bottom 10%.

Over the last two years, researchers rebuilt their whole deep learning stack and co-designed a super-computer from the ground up for our workload with Azure. A year they trained GPT-3.5 as the system's initial "test run" several years ago. Challenges were discovered and rectified while also strengthening our theoretical basis. As a result, the GPT-4 training run was unprecedentedly steady, becoming the first huge model whose training performance the researchers could reliably anticipate ahead of time. The researcher's objective was to fine-tune their methods to help them foresee and prepare for future capacities more and more in advance—something considered vital for safety.

ChatGPT and Ethical Implications

ChatGPT can produce fluent and coherent conversations on a wide range of topics, but it also faces some ethical challenges.

The functionality of ChatGPT highlights the growing necessity of implementing robust AI author guidelines in scholarly publishing. Ethical considerations abound concerning copyright, attribution, plagiarism, and authorship when AI produces academic text. These concerns are especially pertinent because whether the copy is AI-generated is currently imperceptible to human readers and anti-plagiarism software (Liebrenz, M 2022).

One of the most difficult tasks in AI is removing biases from training data. ChatGPT learns from massive amounts of text data available on the internet, which can unintentionally reinforce cultural biases. These biases, whether they be gender, race, or other sensitive themes, can show in AI-generated responses, reinforcing harmful preconceptions. To address bias, a mix of varied training data, refining algorithms to detect and correct biases and ongoing human oversight is required.

Bias and accuracy: ChatGPT may produce biased or inaccurate outputs that reflect the prejudices or errors present in its training data. For example, it may generate stereotypes or false information about certain groups of people or topics. This can have negative consequences for the users who rely on Chat-GPT for information or guidance, as well as for the people who are affected by its outputs. Therefore, it is important to ensure that ChatGPT is trained on diverse and reliable sources and that its outputs are verified and corrected when necessary.

Privacy and security: ChatGPT stores the conversations it has with users to improve its model. However, this also means that any personal or sensitive information that users input into ChatGPT may be exposed or reproduced by the tool in the future. This can pose a risk to the privacy and security of the users and the people they mention in their conversations. Therefore, it is important to inform users about the data collection and retention policies of ChatGPT and to provide them with options to delete their chat history or opt out of data sharing.

Figure 4. Ethical implications

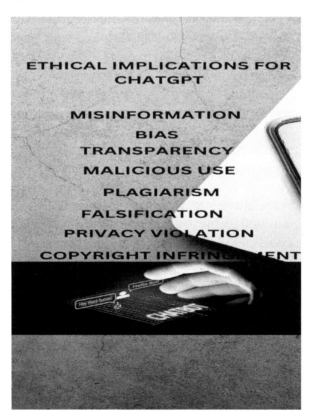

- Plagiarism and academic integrity: ChatGPT can be used to generate content for academic purposes, such as essays, summaries, or data analysis. This can undermine the quality and credibility of academic work, as well as the fairness and honesty of academic evaluation. Therefore, it is important to establish clear guidelines and rules for the use of ChatGPT in academic settings and to use plagiarism detection tools to prevent and detect cheating.

- Copyright and intellectual property: ChatGPT is trained on a variety of sources, many of which are protected by copyright laws. As a result, ChatGPT may reproduce copyrighted content in its outputs without proper attribution or permission. This can infringe on the rights and interests of the original authors or creators, as well as expose ChatGPT users to legal liability.

- Social and cultural impact: ChatGPT can have a significant impact on the way people communicate, learn, and create. It can also influence the way people perceive themselves and others, as well as the values and norms they adhere to. For example, ChatGPT may shape the language and style of users who interact with it frequently or affect their attitudes and beliefs about certain topics or issues.

The Moral Authority of ChatGPT

The area of philosophy known as ethics studies the moral precepts and ideals that direct people's behavior. ChatGPT is a chatbot that responds to user input with natural language using a large-scale neural network model. But ChatGPT also has to deal with moral conundrums and problems, like how to guarantee the reliability, security, and quality of its answers; how to respect users' privacy and autonomy; how to prevent prejudice and discrimination; and how to advance human dignity and the common good. ChatGPT's developers and users must give these moral dilemmas some thought.

According to research by Sebastian Krügel et al. from 2023, ChatGPT may impair users' judgment rather than enhance it. Although it seems ineffectual, transparency is frequently praised. People frequently have contradictory moral beliefs, thus giving them consistent moral direction may aid in improving their moral decision-making. ChatGPT's effectiveness as a moral compass is remarkably inconsistent. However, the study reveals that users underestimate the degree to which receiving guidance from a chatbot influences their moral judgment, even when they are aware that they are doing so. As such, there is a chance that ChatGPT will impede rather than improve users' judgment.

ChatGPT belongs to the new wave of digital technologies that need moral reflection (Kazim & Koshiyama, 2021). But ChatGPT also has to deal with moral conundrums and problems, like how to guarantee the reliability, security, and quality of its answers; how to respect users' privacy and autonomy; how to prevent prejudice and discrimination; and how to advance human dignity and the common good.

Ethical Challenges

ChatGPT also poses ethical challenges that need to be addressed by researchers and practitioners. Some of these challenges include:

- The potential for chatbots to generate harmful, offensive, or misleading content that can harm users or third parties.
- The lack of transparency and accountability for ChatGPT's behavior and outputs, especially when it is deployed in sensitive domains or contexts.

Figure 5. The framework

- The risk of ChatGPT violating the privacy and autonomy of users or third parties by collecting, storing, or using their data without consent or awareness.
- The possibility of ChatGPT creating or exacerbating social biases, stereotypes, or inequalities by reflecting or reinforcing existing prejudices or power structures.

Ethical Frameworks and ChatGPT

The ethical framework for ChatGPT is a set of principles and guidelines that aim to ensure the responsible and beneficial use of conversational AI systems. The framework covers aspects such as data privacy, user consent, transparency, accountability, fairness, safety, and social impact. The framework also provides recommendations for developers, researchers, and users of ChatGPT to adhere to the ethical standards and best practices in the field. The framework is based on the following core values:

- **Respect for human dignity and autonomy:** ChatGPT should respect the rights and preferences of its users and other stakeholders and should not harm or exploit them in any way.
- **Beneficence and non-maleficence:** ChatGPT should contribute to the well-being and welfare of its users and society and should avoid or minimize any potential harm or risk.
- **Justice and fairness:** ChatGPT should treat its users and other stakeholders fairly and equitably and should not discriminate or cause injustice on any grounds.
- **Transparency and explainability:** ChatGPT should be transparent about its capabilities, limitations, data sources, and decision-making processes, and should provide clear and understandable explanations for its actions and outcomes.
- **Accountability and responsibility:** ChatGPT should be accountable for its actions and outcomes and should be subject to appropriate oversight and regulation. ChatGPT developers and researchers should be responsible for ensuring the ethical design, development, deployment, and evaluation of ChatGPT systems.

Figure 6. Ethical framework for ChatGPT

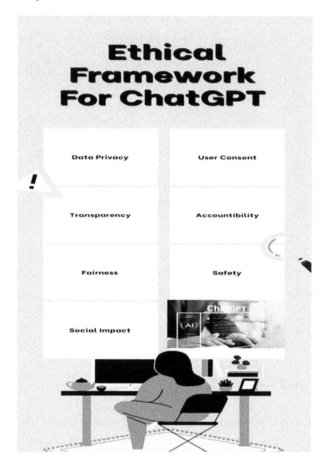

- The lack of transparency and accountability for ChatGPT's behavior and outputs, especially when it is deployed in sensitive domains or contexts.
- The risk of ChatGPT violating the privacy and autonomy of users or third parties by collecting, storing, or using their data without consent or awareness.
- The possibility of ChatGPT creating or exacerbating social biases, stereotypes, or inequalities by reflecting or reinforcing existing prejudices or power structures.

The Ethical Design Framework (EDF) provides a set of guidelines and questions to help designers and developers consider the ethical implications of their ChatGPT systems throughout the design process.

The ethical design framework for ChatGPT has a set of principles and guidelines that aim to ensure the responsible and beneficial use of conversational AI systems. The framework covers four main aspects: user autonomy, user privacy, user safety, and user trust. The framework also provides recommendations for developers, researchers, and policymakers on how to implement the principles and guidelines in practice. Some of the recommendations include:

User autonomy: Respect the user's choices and preferences, provide clear and transparent information about the system's capabilities and limitations, allow the user to opt-out or modify the system's behavior, and avoid manipulation or coercion.

Figure 7. Recommendations for researchers and practitioners

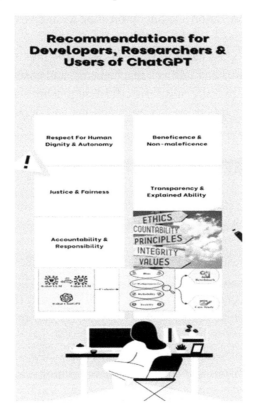

Figure 8. Ethical design

- User privacy: Protect the user's data and identity, obtain informed consent before collecting or sharing data, use data minimization and anonymization techniques, and comply with relevant laws and regulations.
- User safety: Prevent or mitigate harm to the user or others, monitor and report potential risks or threats, implement safeguards and fallback mechanisms, and ensure accountability and redress.
- User trust: Establish a trustworthy and respectful relationship with the user, provide consistent and reliable performance, explain the system's actions and decisions, and solicit feedback and evaluation from the user. -

The Ethical Turing Test (ETT)

Proposes a method to evaluate the ethical performance of ChatGPT systems by comparing their responses to those of human experts on various ethical dilemmas.

- The Ethical Chatbot Manifesto (ECM), outlines a set of principles and values that ChatGPT systems should adhere to respect the rights and dignity of users and third parties.
- The Ethical Impact Assessment (EIA), offers a tool to assess the potential ethical impacts of ChatGPT systems on different stakeholders and domains and to identify and mitigate possible risks or harms.
- The Ethical Alignment Framework (EAF), suggests a way to align the goals and values of ChatGPT systems with those of their users and society, by incorporating ethical principles into their design, training, and evaluation.

Figure 9. Turing test

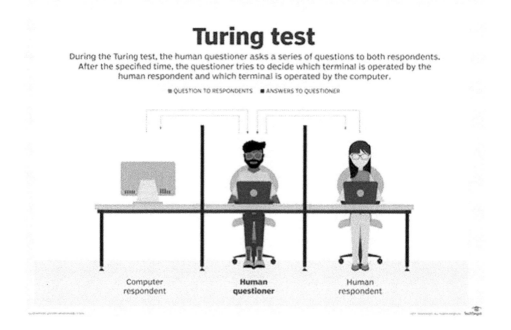

The Ethical Chatbot Manifesto (ECM)

Outlines a set of principles and values that ChatGPT systems should adhere to to respect the rights and dignity of users and third parties. The ECM includes principles such as:

- Chatgpt systems should be honest, trustworthy, and transparent about their identity, capabilities, limitations, and intentions.
- Chatgpt systems should respect the privacy and confidentiality of users and third parties, and only collect, store, or use their data with their consent and for legitimate purposes.
- Chatgpt systems should be fair, inclusive, and non-discriminatory towards users and third parties, and avoid creating or reinforcing social biases, stereotypes, or inequalities.
- Chatgpt systems should be beneficial, helpful, and supportive to users and third parties, and avoid causing or contributing to harm or suffering.
- Chatgpt systems should be responsive, accountable, and explainable for their behavior and outputs, and allow users and third parties to provide feedback and seek redress.

The Ethical Impact Assessment (EIA), offers a tool to assess the potential ethical impacts of ChatGPT systems on different stakeholders and domains and to identify and mitigate possible risks or harms.

- The Ethical Alignment Framework (EAF), suggests a way to align the goals and values of ChatGPT systems with those of their users and society, by incorporating ethical principles into their design, training, and evaluation.
- The lack of empirical studies that evaluate the ethical impacts of ChatGPT systems in real-world settings and contexts.
- The difficulty of measuring and quantifying ethical values and outcomes, especially when they involve subjective or qualitative aspects.
- The diversity and complexity of ethical perspectives and values that may vary across cultures, domains, and stakeholders.
- The uncertainty and unpredictability of ChatGPT's behavior and outputs, especially when it interacts with dynamic and evolving environments and users.

Ethical Challenges to Be Address by Researchers and Practitioners

ChatGPT poses ethical challenges that need to be addressed by researchers and practitioners. Some of these challenges include:

- The potential for ChatGPT to generate harmful, offensive, or misleading content that can harm users or third parties.
- The lack of transparency and accountability for ChatGPT's behavior and outputs, especially when it is deployed in sensitive domains or contexts.
- The risk of ChatGPT violating the privacy and autonomy of users or third parties by collecting, storing, or using their data without consent or awareness.
- The possibility of ChatGPT creating or exacerbating social biases, stereotypes, or inequalities by reflecting or reinforcing existing prejudices or power structures.

- The Ethical Impact Assessment (EIA), offers a tool to assess the potential ethical impacts of ChatGPT systems on different stakeholders and domains and to identify and mitigate possible risks or harms.
- The Ethical Alignment Framework (EAF), suggests a way to align the goals and values of ChatGPT systems with those of their users and society, by incorporating ethical principles into their design, training, and evaluation.

Limitations

- The lack of empirical studies that evaluate the ethical impacts of ChatGPT systems in real-world settings and contexts.
- The difficulty of measuring and quantifying ethical values and outcomes, especially when they involve subjective or qualitative aspects.
- The diversity and complexity of ethical perspectives and values that may vary across cultures, domains, and stakeholders.
- The uncertainty and unpredictability of ChatGPT's behavior and outputs, especially when it interacts with dynamic and evolving environments and users.

Ethical AI

AI that abides by unequivocal ethical principles is said to be Ethical AI. These rules are founded on significant ideals including respect for private lives, justice, and avoiding manipulation. Organizations that utilize ethical AI have clear rules and review procedures in place to ensure they are abiding by these standards.

Beyond what is permitted by legislation, ethical AI goes beyond that. While regulations establish the minimal requirements for permissible AI use, they also establish much higher requirements to uphold core human values.

Dilemmas of Ethical AI

The AI has a trade-off between performance and interpretability. While interpretability refers to the capacity to understand how an AI system thinks or to peer inside its "brain," performance concerns how well an AI system does tasks.

The problem at hand is that the best AI models are usually complex and challenging to comprehend. We don't know how they seem to work behind the scenes. Simpler AI models, on the other hand, may not be as accurate but they are simpler to understand. It's similar to having a distinct but less accurate viewpoint.

AI has become increasingly cryptic or challenging to comprehend as we develop and enhance AI models to boost performance.

Although AI has advanced the industry tremendously, there are ethical questions it also brings up. It can be used unethically to violate privacy and disseminate false information. Achieving equilibrium is essential.

ChatGPT and Libraries, Information Centers, and Librarians

One of the potential applications of ChatGPT is to impact libraries and their services. Libraries are institutions that provide access to information and knowledge for various purposes, such as education, research, and entertainment. ChatGPT could help libraries in several ways, such as:

- Improving search and discovery: ChatGPT could offer a new way of finding information by answering specific questions or generating summaries of topics. It could also provide personalized and contextualized results based on user preferences and needs.
- Enhancing reference and information services: ChatGPT could assist librarians and users in providing or obtaining information on various subjects. It could also generate citations, bibliographies, or annotations for sources.
- Creating cataloging and metadata: ChatGPT could help librarians and users in creating or updating metadata for library resources, such as books, journals, or digital collections. It could also generate keywords, subject headings, or classifications for items.
- Generating content: ChatGPT could help librarians and users in creating or editing content for library purposes, such as newsletters, blogs, reports, or presentations. It could also generate creative content, such as poems, stories, or games.

Ethical Challenges and Risks for Libraries and Their Users

- Privacy: ChatGPT could collect and store user data, such as queries, responses, or preferences. This could raise concerns about data protection, consent, and ownership.
- Bias: ChatGPT could reflect or amplify the biases and inaccuracies of its training data, such as stereotypes, prejudices, or misinformation. This could affect the quality and reliability of its output and influence user perception and behavior.
- Plagiarism: ChatGPT could generate text that is similar or identical to existing sources, without proper attribution or acknowledgment. This could violate intellectual property rights and academic integrity standards.
- Accountability: ChatGPT could generate text that is harmful, offensive, or illegal, such as hate speech, defamation, or fraud. This could cause damage or harm to individuals or groups and raise questions about responsibility and liability.

Librarians can better interpret the ChatGPT output and combine it with their knowledge. ChatGPT needs to be fed very specific questions to provide a useful answer, so expertise may still be needed for the framing of the query.

Programming, communication, and instruction are such a core part of librarianship and while ChatGPT can accelerate the planning process (e.g. coming up with content and materials), the actual act of human delivery can never be replaced. These are face-to-face interactions (either in-person or online) and community. If ChatGPT becomes viable shortly libraries may have to emphasize soft skills such as face-to-face interactions (either in-person or online) and community relationships are also what people expect.

When AI generates academic material, there are numerous ethical concerns around copyright, attribution, plagiarism, and authorship. These problems are especially relevant given that whether copy generated by AI is now unnoticeable to human readers and anti-plagiarism technologies.

Ethical Challenges in Higher Education

The ability of ChatGPT to generate essay writing and assignment solutions has sparked discussions in the educational community about academic integrity violations by high school and university students. For instance, it has been outlawed in American educational districts like New York City, Los Angeles, and Baltimore.

Similar to how American schools seek to reinstate "pen and paper" exams, Australian colleges want to stop students from using computers to compose essays. Since many teachers are concerned.

However, several people have defended and even advocated ChatGPT to enhance writing production. In education, previous research has looked at the effectiveness and utility of big language models in various fields, including medical and healthcare, computer and data science, law, business, journalism and media, and language acquisition. Even though these studies found mixed results when comparing ChatGPT's performance on standardized tests to that of students, studies that specifically compared the model's performance to that of prior large language models all found that the task of question-answering had significantly improved.

In the meantime, Edward Tian, a computer science and journalism student at Princeton, says he created the program, aka "GPTZero," to help combat academic plagiarism generated by the new AI-powered chatbot

ChatGPT and Peer Reviews for Academic Papers

Concerns are raised by ChatGPT's ability to trick reviewers and readers. It is crucial to research if using text created by ChatGPT can lead to biased or inaccurate information and how to avoid these issues as AI algorithms advance. Reviewers and readers may be misled by the usage of ChatGPT-generated text in scientific research publications and other fields in several ways, such as through plagiarism, bias and disinformation, impersonation, spam and scams, and phony reviews.

To test if AI could replace a human peer reviewer in a journal's manuscript evaluation procedure, Checco et al. created an AI tool back in 2021. Additionally, bias may have been discovered since LLMs and other machine learning tools are trained on historical data, which may contain biases by nature. As a result, these biases are likely to be reflected in the results that these tools provide.

AI has made its way into the peer review process, just like a lot of other processes. An online platform called Raxter.io provides several tools for reviewers to provide authors with feedback. It's one illustration of this. Using artificial intelligence (AI) algorithms, the program examines manuscripts to identify potential issues such as careless formatting, vague wording, and missing references. It additionally provides

Although the application of AI to peer review is still in its infancy, it has the potential to greatly increase the process' accuracy and efficiency. Raxter.io and other review helper technologies are just the start of what will undoubtedly be

Hosseini and Horbach (2023) took a close look at how LLMs are being used in the publication process. What they discovered is pretty interesting. On the one hand, LLMs can be handy tools for summarizing peer review comments and creating initial draft decision letters. But here's the catch—they could also make existing problems in the peer review system worse. It turns out that fraudsters might take advantage of LLMs to produce more authentic and well-written fake reviews.

It is already well acknowledged that ChatGPT's features make it a valuable tool for illicit activities (Europol, 2023, Sweney, 2023). There may be ways to identify and block illicit usage of ChatGPT thanks to the organization and technical framework that now allows for web-based communication and central hosting.

The features and capabilities of ChatGPT could affect how it is used and applied, as well as raise potential ethical issues:

Though currently text-based, we assume that it can be integrated into other modalities of communication, such as voice communication (Ali et al., 2023); The Ability to learn from interaction allows it to further improve the content quality and acceptability (Sallam, 2023); Production of high-quality text in response to human input that is often difficult to identify as the output of an AI (Zhang et al., 2023); Ability to engage in a dialogical interaction on a very broad array of topics (Gilson et al., 2023); Ability to tailor its output to specific language styles (Short & Short, 2023);

The Risks in Replacing Human Reviewers

The following are some dangers connected to using ChatGPT for peer reviews. Among these dangers are:

- Lack of transparency: Because AI algorithms can be complicated and challenging to comprehend, it may be challenging to grasp the decision-making process. Because of this opaqueness, it may be difficult to spot and fix any possible biases or algorithmic mistakes.
- Over-reliance on AI: Editors and reviewers run the risk of relying too much on ChatGPT and other AI technologies at the expense of using their discretion and knowledge. This can cause significant scientific discoveries to be lost or ignored.
- Technical problems: These instruments may experience software problems or algorithmic mistakes.

Other Ethical Challenges

One of the ethical challenges is the risk of generating harmful or offensive content, such as hate speech, misinformation, or personal attacks. ChatGPT does not have any inherent moral values or social norms, and it may learn from biased or malicious data that it encounters during training or interaction. ChatGPT may also inadvertently reveal sensitive or private information that it has memorized from its data sources. Therefore, ChatGPT needs to be monitored and moderated by human supervisors who can filter out inappropriate or harmful responses and provide feedback to improve its performance and behavior.

Recommendations and Addressing the Challenges in the Ethical Use of ChatGPT

ChatGPT is a powerful natural language generation system that can produce fluent and coherent texts on various topics and domains. However, ChatGPT also has limitations and challenges, such as generating inaccurate, inconsistent, or irrelevant content, or failing to capture the nuances and contexts of human language. Therefore, ChatGPT can be improved by addressing these issues and enhancing its capabilities and performance. Some possible ways to improve ChatGPT are:

- Incorporating more data and knowledge from diverse and reliable sources, such as facts, figures, or references, to enrich the content and quality of ChatGPT-generated texts.
- Incorporating more feedback and interaction from human users and experts, such as ratings, comments, or corrections, to refine and adapt the content and style of ChatGPT-generated texts.
- Incorporating more reasoning and logic from artificial intelligence and machine learning, such as inference, deduction, or induction, to increase the coherence and consistency of ChatGPT-generated texts.
- Incorporating more creativity and diversity from natural language processing and generation, such as paraphrasing, summarizing, or synthesizing, to enhance the variety and originality of ChatGPT-generated texts.

Transparency: Academic writing must disclose how content is generated and by whom.

- Fact-checking: Academic writing must verify information and cite sources.
- Authorship: Social work scientists must retain authorship while using AI tools to support their work.
- Anti-plagiarism: Idea owners and content authors should be located and cited.
- Inclusion and social justice: Anti-racist frameworks and approaches should be developed to counteract potential biases of LLMs against authors who are Black, Indigenous, or people of color, and authors from the Global South.

ChatGPT is a remarkable innovation that can change the way we think and work. However, it also requires careful consideration and regulation to ensure that it is used responsibly and ethically.

FUTURE RESEARCH DIRECTIONS

Researchers can explore the impact of different modes and settings on the user's perception of the system and its responses. For example, how does the user's trust, satisfaction, engagement, and emotional state change when interacting with a creative, precise, or balanced mode? How do these modes affect the user's expectations and preferences for the system's behavior and output? How can the system provide clear and transparent feedback on its capabilities and limitations in each mode? How can the system handle sensitive or controversial topics respectfully and responsibly?

Examining the social and cultural aspects of ChatGPT as a global system that can communicate in multiple languages and interact with diverse users. For example, how does the system ensure that its responses are culturally sensitive, inclusive, and respectful of different values and norms? How does the system adapt to different linguistic styles, idioms, expressions, and conventions in different languages? How does the system promote intercultural understanding and dialogue among users from different backgrounds and perspectives?

ChatGPT also poses ethical challenges and risks, such as generating harmful, biased, or misleading content, or violating the privacy and autonomy of human users. Therefore, future research is needed to address these issues and ensure that ChatGPT is used for good purposes and in a responsible manner. Such as

Developing methods and metrics to evaluate the quality, reliability, and fairness of ChatGPT-generated texts, and to detect and correct any errors, inconsistencies, or biases.

- Developing guidelines and best practices for ChatGPT developers and users to follow ethical principles and norms, such as transparency, accountability, consent, and respect.
- Developing mechanisms and tools to enable human oversight and intervention in ChatGPT applications, such as providing feedback, corrections, or explanations, or allowing users to opt out or customize their preferences.
- Developing frameworks and models to understand the social and psychological impacts of ChatGPT on human users and society, such as trust, engagement, persuasion, or influence.
- Developing strategies and policies to regulate and govern the use of ChatGPT in different domains and contexts, such as education, health, entertainment, or journalism.

CONCLUSION

The development of advanced AI could lead to disaster due to rogue AIs, AI races, malevolent use, and organizational concerns. Serious worry is warranted since these interrelated hazards have the potential to magnify other existential risks, such as cyberattacks on vital infrastructure, nuclear weapons, great power conflict, pandemics, and authoritarianism.

Few individuals are working on AI safety at the moment. Advanced AI system control is still an unsolved problem, and existing control techniques are insufficient. Today, AI models are so complex that even their designers find it difficult to comprehend how they function, and their dependability is questionable.

We can push for safety laws, restrict access to risky AIs, promote global collaboration and a safety-conscious culture, and expand our alignment research initiatives.

The rate of advancement of AI capabilities and the growth of catastrophic hazards remain uncertain; yet, given the gravity of the potential outcomes, preemptive measures to protect humanity's future are imperative.

ChatGPT is a tool that has both opportunities and challenges for libraries and their users. It is important to use it responsibly and ethically and to evaluate its output critically and carefully. It is also important to understand how it works and what its limitations are. ChatGPT is not a substitute for human judgment or expertise; rather, it is a potential partner that can enhance library services and user experience if used ethically and correctly.

ChatGPT is a remarkable system that can generate impressive texts on various topics and domains. However, it is not perfect and can be improved in many ways. By incorporating more data, feedback, reasoning, and creativity, ChatGPT can become a more reliable, adaptable, coherent, and diverse natural language generation system.

In November 2023, Sam Altman, the CEO of Open AI, released a statement regarding GPT5. The company has been searching for additional data, even requesting access to private data sets, to train its models. But even Altman is unsure about what GPT-5 will be able to accomplish. The CEO claimed that it was impossible to foresee in principle how GPT-5 would differ from its predecessor until the model began to be trained, so he was unable to describe all of how GPT-5 would differ in the meantime. OpenAI's progress has been slow due to Nvidia's limited supply of advanced CPUs. Not long after, Open AI's Board members terminated Altman. days later and rehired him again as CEO. Some claim the board thought he was moving too quickly. If GPT5 emerges after all the signatures of halting AI machines, we will see more people that signed during a 180-degree turnaround to compete with GPT5.

REFERENCES

Arnold, T., & Scheutz, M. (2018, March 1). *The Ethics and Information Technology.* https://dl.acm.org/doi/10.1007/s10676-018-9447-7

Bahrini A. Khamoshifar M. Abbasimehr H. Riggs R. J. Esmaeili M. Majdabadkohne R. M. Pasehvar M. (2023, April 14). *CHATGPT: Applications, opportunities, and threats.* doi:10.1109/SIEDS58326.2023.10137850

Baidoo-Anu D. Owusu Ansah L. (2023, January 27). *Education in the era of Generative Artificial Intelligence (AI): Understanding the potential benefits of CHATGPT in promoting teaching and learning.* doi:10.2139/ssrn.4337484

Bowman, E. (2022, December 19). *A new AI chatbot might do your homework for you. but it's still not an A+ student.* NPR. https://www.npr.org/2022/12/19/1143912956/chatgpt-ai-chatbot-homework-academia

Brundage, M., & Bryson, J. (2016). *Smart Policies for Artificial Intelligence.* https://www.semantic-scholar.org/paper/Smart-Policies-for-Artificial-Intelligence-Brundage-Bryson/937d6d4c34ad41edc6fb68e477cad23657b949e2

Chatgpt for Education and research. A review of benefits and risks. (n.d.). https://www.researchgate.net/publication/369127881_ChatGPT_for_Education_and_Research_A_Review_of_Benefits_and_Risks

Checco, A., Bracciale, L., Loreti, P., Pinfield, S., & Bianchi, G. (2021). Ai-Assisted Peer Review. *Humanities & Social Sciences Communications*, 8(1), 25. Advance online publication. doi:10.105741599-020-00703-8

Dignum, V. (2018, February 13). *Ethics in artificial intelligence: Introduction to the special issue - ethics and information technology.* SpringerLink. https://link.springer.com/article/10.1007/s10676-018-9450-z

Dimitrijević & Petrović. (2018). *The view on structure and organization - researchgate.* https://www.researchgate.net/publication/342790756_LEISURE_TIME_OF_SCHOOL_CHILDREN_-_THE_VIEW_ON_STRUCTURE_AND_ORGANIZATION

Elias, J. (2023, February 1). *Jennifer Elias on LinkedIn: Google is asking employees to test potential CHATGPT competitors...* https://www.linkedin.com/posts/jennifer-elias-845b1130_google-is-asking-employees-to-test-potential-activity-7026375314557595648-Fm3V

Elkhatat, A. M. (2023, August 1). *Evaluating the authenticity of CHATGPT responses: A study on text-matching capabilities - International Journal for Educational Integrity.* BioMed Central. https://edintegrity.biomedcentral.com/articles/10.1007/s40979-023-00137-0

Ethical ai: Striking the balance between progress. (2020). https://www.techopedia.com/the-ethical-ai-dilemma-striking-the-balance-between-progress-and-responsibility

Fedus, W., Zoph, B., Shazeer, N., & University, C. (2022, January 1). Switch transformers: Scaling to trillion parameter models with simple and efficient sparsity. *The Journal of Machine Learning Research.* https://dl.acm.org/doi/abs/10.5555/3586589.3586709

figshare. (2021, May 17). *Ai Ethics in scholarly communication: STM best practice principles for ethical, trustworthy and human-centric AI.* figshare. https://figshare.com/articles/online_resource/AI_Ethics_in_Scholarly_Communication_STM_Best_Practice_Principles_for_Ethical_Trustworthy_and_Human-centric_AI/14572353

Flipboard. (2023, January 18). *Microsoft and OpenAI working on CHATGPT-powered Bing in challenge to Google.* Flipboard. https://flipboard.com/article/microsoft-and-openai-working-on-chatgpt-powered-bing-in-challenge-to-google/f-883a32ec69%2Ftheinformation.com

Følstad, A., & Brandtzæg, P. B. (2017). *Chatbots and the New World of HCI.* Interactions. https://dl.acm.org/doi/10.1145/3085558

FryeB. L. (2022, December 20). Should using an AI text generator to produce academic writing be plagiarism? SSRN. https://papers.ssrn.com/sol3/papers.cfm?abstract_id=4292283

Fütterer, T., Fischer, C., Alekseeva, A., Chen, X., Tate, T., Warschauer, M., & Gerjets, P. (2023). *Chat-GPT in education: Global reactions to AI Innovations.* Scientific reports. https://pubmed.ncbi.nlm.nih.gov/37714915/

Fütterer, T., Fischer, C., Alekseeva, A., Chen, X., Tate, T., Warschauer, M., & Gerjets, P. (2023, September 15). *ChatGPT in education: Global reactions to AI Innovations.* Nature News. https://www.nature.com/articles/s41598-023-42227-6

Future of Life Institute. (2021). *Artificial Intelligence (AI) in decision making.* COPE: Committee on Publication Ethics. https://publicationethics.org/resources/discussion-documents/ai-artifical-intelligence-decision-making

GaoT.FischA.ChenD. (2021, June 2). *Making pre-trained language models better few-shot learners.* doi:10.18653/v1/2021.acl-long.295

Grant, N., & Metz, C. (2022, December 21). A new chatbot is a "code red" for Google's search business. *The New York Times.* https://www.nytimes.com/2022/12/21/technology/ai-chatgpt-google-search.html

Holland, B. J. (2023, January 1). *CHATGPT 3.5 and 4: Its ramifications on librarianship, academia, education, publishing, and the Workplace.* IGI Global. https://www.igi-global.com/chapter/chatgpt-35-and-4/325030

HorbachH. M. (2023, May 18). *Fighting reviewer fatigue or amplifying bias? considerations and recommendations for the use of CHATGPT and other large language models in scholarly peer review.* https://pubmed.ncbi.nlm.nih.gov/36865238/

Karpf, D. (2023, January 4). Money will kill Chatgpt's magic. *The Atlantic.* https://www.theatlantic.com/technology/archive/2022/12/chatgpt-aichatbots-openai-cost-regulations/672539

Kazim, E., Koshiyama, A. S., Hilliard, A., & Polle, R. (2021, September 17). Systematizing audit in Algorithmic Recruitment. *Journal of Intelligence*. https://www.ncbi.nlm.nih.gov/pmc/articles/PMC8482073/

Liebrenz, M. (2023, February 6). Generating scholarly content with ChatGPT: Ethical challenges for medical publishing. *The Lancet. Digital health*. https://pubmed.ncbi.nlm.nih.gov/36754725/

Liu, Y., Han, T., Ma, S., Zhang, J., Yang, Y., Tian, J., He, H., Li, A., He, M., Liu, Z., Wu, Z., Zhao, L., Zhu, D., Li, X., Qiang, N., Shen, D., Liu, T., & Ge, B. (2023). Summary of CHATGPT-related research and perspective towards the future of large language models. *Meta-Radiology*, *1*(2), 100017. doi:10.1016/j.metrad.2023.100017

Martínez-Miranda & Aldea. (2005). *Emotion quantification techniques for cognitive reappraisal*. https://link.springer.com/content/pdf/10.1007/s10462-023-10606-0.pdf

Mintz, S. (2023, January 16). *Chatgpt: Threat or menace?* Inside Higher Ed. https://www.insidehighered.com/blogs/higher-ed-gamma/chatgpt-threat-or-menace

Mouhamad, R. (2022, December 15). *Chatgpt is a "landmark event" for AI, but what does it mean for the future of human labor and disinformation?* CBC news. https://www.cbc.ca/radio/thecurrent/chatgpt-human-labour-and-fake-news-1.6686210

Nature Publishing Group. (n.d.). *Nature news*. https://www.nature.com/articles/d42473-023-00083-y

OpenA. I. (2023, March 27). *GPT-4 technical report*. https://arxiv.org/abs/2303.08774

Pause giant AI experiments: An open letter. (2023, November 27). Future of Life Institute. https://futureoflife.org/open-letter/pause-giant-ai-experiments/

Ramponi, M. (2023, August 4). *How CHATGPT works. News, Tutorials, AI Research*. https://www.assemblyai.com/blog/how-chatgpt-actually-works

Rao, A. S. (2023, August 22). *CHATGPT shows "impressive" accuracy in clinical decision-making*. Medical Xpress. https://medicalxpress.com/news/2023-08-chatgpt-accuracy-clinical-decision.html

Roose, K. (2023, February 3). How CHATGPT kicked off an A.I. Arms Race. *The New York Times*. https://www.nytimes.com/2023/02/03/technology/chatgpt-openai-artificial-intelligence.html

Ropek, L. (2023, January 4). *Did CHATGPT write that? A college student created an AI Essay detector*. Gizmodo. https://gizmodo.com/chatgpt-ai-essay-detector-college-princeton-edward-tian-1849946535

Rosalsky, G., & Peaslee, E. (2023, January 17). *This 22-year-old is trying to save us from ChatGPT before it changes writing forever*. NPR. https://www.npr.org/sections/money/2023/01/17/1149206188/this-22-year-old-is-trying-to-save-us-from-chatgpt-before-it-changes-writing-for

SchulmanJ.WolskiF.DhariwalP.RadfordA.KlimovO. (2017, August 28). *Proximal policy optimization algorithms*. https://arxiv.org/abs/1707.06347

Schulmnan, J. (2022). *Training language models to follow instructions with humans... - OpenAI*. https://cdn.openai.com/papers/Training_language_models_to_follow_instructions_with_human_feedback.pdf

Skitka, L. J., Mosier, K., & Burdick, M. D. (2000). Accountability and Automation Bias. *International Journal of Human-Computer Studies, 52*(4), 701–717. doi:10.1006/ijhc.1999.0349

Staff, N. (2023, March 31). *New York City Department of Education bans CHATGPT*. GovTech. https://www.govtech.com/education/k-12/new-york-city-department-of-education-bans-chatgpt

Stern, J. (2023, May 31). Chatgpt wrote my AP English essay-and I passed. *The Wall Street Journal*. https://www.wsj.com/articles/chatgpt-wrote-my-ap-english-essayand-i-passed-11671628256

Stokel-Walker, C. (2022, December 9). *Ai Bot ChatGPT writes Smart Essays - should professors worry?* Nature News. https://www.nature.com/articles/d41586-022-04397-7

Stokel-Walker, C. (2023, January 18). *CHATGPT listed as author on research papers: Many scientists disapprove*. Nature News. https://www.nature.com/articles/d41586-023-00107-z

Tate, T. (2023, September). *Will ChatGPT give us a lesson in education?* Nature News. https://www.nature.com/articles/d42473-023-00083-y

van Dis, E. A. M., Bollen, J., Zuidema, W., van Rooij, R., & Bockting, C. L. (2023, February 3). *Chatgpt: Five Priorities for Research*. Nature News. https://www.nature.com/articles/d41586-023-00288-7

Zeng, W. (2021, April 26). *Pangu-a: Large-scale autoregressive pre-trained Chinese language models with auto-parallel computation*. https://arxiv.org/abs/2104.12369

ZhouJ.MüllerH.HolzingerA.ChenF. (2023, May 18). *Ethical ChatGPT: Concerns, Challenges, and Commandments.*. https://arxiv.org/abs/2305.10646

Zhou, J. (2023a). CHATGPT: Potential, prospects, and limitations. *Frontiers of Information Technology & Electronic Engineering*. doi:10.1631/FITEE.2300089

Zhou, J. (2023b, May 18). *Ethical ChatGPT: Concerns, Challenges, and Commandments*. https://arxiv.org/abs/2305.10646

ADDITIONAL READING

Holland, B. (Ed.), *Handbook of Research on Advancements of Contactless Technology and Service Innovation in Library and Information Science*. IGI Global. doi:10.4018/978-1-6684-7693-2

KEY TERMS AND DEFINITIONS

Alignment: What we want the model to do ChatGPT (Chat Generative Pre-Trained Transformer The Ethical Impact Assessment (EIA), is a tool to assess the potential ethical impacts of ChatGPT systems on different stakeholders and domains and to identify and mitigate possible risks or harms.

Ethical Chatbot Manifesto (ECM): Outlines a set of principles and values that ChatGPT systems should adhere to respect the rights and dignity of users and third parties.

Ethical Design Framework (EDF): Provides a set of guidelines and questions to help designers and developers consider the ethical implications of their ChatGPT systems throughout the design process.

Ethical Turing Test (ETT): Proposes a method to evaluate the ethical performance of ChatGPT systems by comparing their responses to those of human experts on various ethical dilemmas.

LLM: Large language model GPT-3- Generative Pre-trained Transformer 3 is an autoregressive language model released in 2020 that uses deep learning to produce human-like text.

Chapter 15
Digital Library Services and Their Importance in Academic Libraries:
An Overview

Kantappa Chavan

https://orcid.org/0000-0001-8121-5211

S.D.V.S. Sangh's Shri. L.K. Khot College of Commerce, Sankeshwar, India

Satishkumar Naikar

https://orcid.org/0000-0002-7621-5388

D.Y. Patil University (Deemed), Navi Mumbai, India

ABSTRACT

The purpose of the study is to highlight digital library services and their importance in academic libraries. Digital libraries are a group of files in digital form accessible on the net or CD-ROM disk. Depending on the precise library, a consumer may be able to get admission to magazine articles, books, newspapers, snapshots, sound documents, and films. The virtual library is one of the maximum cutting-edge trends in library and statistics technology, which helps its users to seek information via the internet. A digital library is prepared for greater ideas and statistics and guides different offerings and places wherein the order is saved in digital format and can be retrieved over networks. Digital libraries are systems presenting the person with resources and getting the right of entry to a very big range; the digital library information prepared storeroom of the records awareness digital library is an international digital library.

INTRODUCTION

The phrases, which have been in trend at distinctive instances, consist of a paperless library, and fast advances in statistics technology have revolutionized the function of virtual libraries devices. As a result, the library faces new ventures, competitors, needs, and expectations of the digital library. Libraries are

DOI: 10.4018/979-8-3693-2841-5.ch015

providing services and information products to include the cost of their services and to fulfill the changing facts of the user desires and user society. The digital libraries are nevertheless handled in particular revealed substances which can be high priced and important. Information seekers are now not happy with the handiest revealed substances. They need to add the broadcast data with extra active electronic sources. Needs for digital records are increasing.

The advanced library expands the broadness and size of insightful and instructive confirmation and supports progressive examinations and everlasting learning. To do that, it intervenes among various and dispensed data re-resources from one perspective and a changing over an assortment of individual gatherings on the other option. On this ability, it sets up "an advanced library supplier environment" that is an arranged online records region wherein clients can find, discover, gather access to and, progressively use measurements. Even though getting passage to ways will change contingent upon the guide being referred to, the virtual library bearer environment makes no qualifications among data codes. Books, diaries, paper-based absolutely documents, video, film, and sound accounts are as observed inside the computerized library bearer condition as are online lists, discovering helps, abstracting and ordering administrations, e-diary and e-print contributions, digitized assortments, geographic measurements structures, net sources, and diverse "advanced" possessions.

Computerized libraries are frameworks granting clients reasonably get section to a tremendous, sorted-out vault of certainties, and a data virtual library is a customary virtual library. The library of thousands of organized electronic libraries from the back of human progress, the scholarly cerebrums have poured their omniscience in unique ways in the type of print and non-print shape to edified mass to find excellent innovative work. Various terms had been begat at particular times to speak to the idea of the library without books. Libraries having information in pc decipherable design or gaining admittance to data in virtual organizations have raised to a startling pinnacle and consequently the computerized. Libraries were fitting in with issues to satisfy the momentary developing requests of the shopper network for their multidimensional methodology. Current propels inside the measurements worldwide have changed the situation of the library in scattering information to the individual. An expansion in the number of individuals and their exceptional needs has made modem libraries apply a new verbal trade period. Thus, there might be a typical need and mild to collect plan oversee ensure and circulate measurements in a virtual structure.

BACKGROUND

An advanced library is an assortment of documents fit as a fiddle, to be had on the web or CD-ROM (reduced plate read-best memory) circles. Depending on the specific library, an individual might have the option to get admission to mag articles, books, papers, pictures, sound documents, and recordings. An advanced library is a source that modifies the information and supports customary library fit as a fiddle. A computerized library is readied arrangement of data, with its upheld administrations and a spot in which the information is put away in advanced configuration and can be recovered over systems. It includes an advanced substance interconnected by method for arranging hyperlinks, metadata, or for all intent and purposes question fundamentally based pursuing and programming which may utilize essential pages in HTML or dependent on database control framework. It could be deciphered based on the above definition that a solitary site page or enormous arrangement of mass advanced data is certifiably not a virtual library. Directly here, it is fundamental to see that virtual libraries won't refresh ordinary libraries anyway on the other hand virtual libraries are the fate of regular libraries (Seadle, 2007). Fundamentally, the virtual library is required mechanical help to hyperlink the advantages of numerous contributions that are dispersed to the purchaser. Arrangement of actualities isn't restricted to report carport anyway it is drawn out to computerized relics that can best be dispensed in virtual codes.

Definition of the Digital Library

A digital library is a library in which collections are stored in virtual codecs and available using structures. The content can store on computers, and access slightly. The primary posted use of the phrase can additionally have been in a 1988 document to a business enterprise for countrywide studies projects. And the period is primarily popularized with the aid of the digital libraries initiative in 1994.

The Digital library federation defines virtual libraries as organizations that offer the resources, such as the specialized of the users and faculty members, to select, shape, provide intellectual get the entry of appreciation, allocate, maintain honesty, and make sure willpower through the years of collections of virtual works so that they're comfortable to be had to be used through a definite area.

The virtual documentation suggestion version defines a virtual library as a society, which is probably realistic, to methodically collect, manage and conserve for the long-term rich digital content and provide user groups with specialized functionality for this content, with calculated pleasure, and in compliance with codified regulations.

Digital Libraries Services

Various functions of the physical library are called services. Two of the main categories are technical services and user services (also known as general services) (Lancaster, 1993). Although the distinction between these two types of services is not entirely clear (in fact, some authors contend that there should be no distinction at all, as we will see below), it is distinctions are commonly used in document libraries and library work in general, so in that sense, for now, it will be there, for better or for worse.

The convergence of digital services in physical libraries and digital services in libraries creates the ability to communicate with each other and provide new types of services in both environments. Physical libraries have affected learning since the beginning. Maybe this is normal; when developers are looking for service models to incorporate into their DL, the obvious place to look for these models is the Physics library. For example, Recommendation was one of the first user services integrated into a DL (Janes et al., 1999). With the development of distance education, other user services have emerged, with special attention to those that facilitate the educational effect of learning: for example, the development of online communities.

Technical Services

The Association of Library Collections and Technical Services (ALCTS), one of the many divisions of the American Library Association (ALA), includes the following technical services i.e. collection development, purchasing, cataloging, and classifying, and just as physical libraries are integrating more and more electronic documents into their collections, engineering must determine the means of managing these elements. Many libraries include electronic records in their ILS, even those on the open web that cannot reasonably be said to be part of the library's property (Thomas, 2000 & Lougee 2002).

Argues that libraries take on new functions as they integrate online resources, but that these new functions are "derived from traditional library functions" (p. 5). Loungee (2002) Indicates the category of traditional functions such as collection and association development: traditional technical service functions are now applied to electronic documents. In the new feature category, Lougee (2002) also includes editing and developing the Semantic Web feature. These functions are extensions of traditional engineering services, in that they address the different phases of the library material lifecycle, in these cases adding documents to a collection library (hardware generated by the library) and assigning meta-data to the document. As with traditional engineering services, these new services involve changes to documents in a library's collection, although the definition of "collection" should be expanded to include non-library materials, whether in physical or electronic form. A technical service is a function that performs on a library document, a function that modifies the state or state of a document. These functions are necessary for the operation of the library. However, library users may never directly encounter the functions of the technical services or even the librarians who perform them. Library users benefit from technical services, but only indirectly.

User Services

1. User services, on the other hand, are provided directly to library users. The Reference and User Services Association (RUSA), another division of the ALA, includes references, guides, genealogy, and services to specific user groups as user services. (www.ala.org/ala/rusa/). It's also a bunch of functions, but again, user services are united by a common theme: user services are library functions where users have direct contact with library resources or librarians. Lancaster (1993) divides user services into two categories: "on-demand" services and "notification" services. On-demand services are "passive" or reactive, "in the sense that they respond to requests rather than initiate them" (p. 2). In contrast, notification services are more "dynamic" and proactively provide information to users before any explicit requests and requests. On-demand services include library-like reference functions, where librarians must wait for users to ask questions before they can provide answers. Notification services include functions such as creating educational resources (e.g. pathfinders and guides) that can be developed before any explicit requests from library users.

2. Many technologies exist to help librarians provide services to users. However, unlike ILS, which includes many technical service functions, most user service technologies address only one or a few specific functions. For example, apps like Question point (questionpoint.org) and Ask A Librarian™ from Tutor.com (tutor.com/libraries/ask_a_librarian.aspx) only support digital reference services and database systems such as NoveList® and What Should I Read Next? Only perform advisory functions to readers. Unlike ILS, these services may not affect the library's collections. Links or citations to items in the Library collection may be provided in interactive digital references, and recommendations for good books may be included in the notice for readers, but there is no guarantee that those items will be used by library users. These services affect the user's state of knowledge; then the user himself can make changes – or ask the librarian to make changes – to the library material. Heath et al. (2003) describe LibQUAL+ as a method of assessing users' perceptions of library services. LibQUAL+ is derived from memos. User services are functions performed with library documents, where the state or state of the document is affected only indirectly, if at all. Instead, it is the user himself whose state or state is changed by the user service.

Services in Digital Libraries

Some of the services provided in the DL are similar to those provided in the physical library, but many of them are completely different. This is partly because the field of computer science has historically influenced the development of DL (Levy, 2000) and, like Pomerantz et al. (2007) showed that the service approaches of computer science (CS) and library and information science (LIS) fields differ significantly. Since they are specifically covered in the DL courses of CS programs, these services are often system-centric (e.g.: system-centric, search engine, and links), while in LIS programs the services are often user-centric (e.g. referrals and personalization).

System-Focused Services

The systems approach to DL services dates back at least to Kahn & Wilensky (1995), where they describe the infrastructure of digital information services. Kahn & Wilensky (1995) paper "provides a method for naming, identifying and/or naming digital objects in a distributed repository system" (Section 5, 1). This document first strictly defines terms such as digital objects, descriptors, metadata, and repositories; Kahn & Wilensky's (1995) definitions of these terms were still used during the development of the DL. Indeed, DLs are only given as an example of a digital information service, although it may be more accurate to call a DL, a collection of services. Kahn & Wilensky (1995) suggest that "many other examples of such services can be found in emerging e-commerce applications in 1" (Sections 1, 1). Ironically, the not only term defined in this article is service, although the operational definition can be derived from the examples used in the article: Service, according to Kahn & Wilensky (2006), a frame is a function that can run on one or more digital objects in an archive. For example, depositing digital assets into the archive and accessing the digital assets from the archive are provided as examples of the service, along with querying and searching for references. The premise is digital object-matching service and open architecture that Kahn & Wilensky (2006) proposal purports to provide an unrestricted environment for deploying exceptional concurrent value-added services to enable unforeseen future services.

User-Focused Services

Although SOA is not DL, the extension of the types of services envisioned by DL is not limited to the enterprise domain. Services, as the term used by Kahn & Wilensky (1995) and all subsequent services in the same direction, are defined entirely around digital objects. More recent works define services rather than users. These services are in many ways very similar to those for physical library users, and some of them are very similar to these services. Recent work has explored alternative models of the DL and service that can be integrated or deployed in parallel. At one end of the spectrum of alternative models is the growth of large-scale online communities that jointly develop DL Giersch et al. (2004) examines this DL model in the context of NSDL. It is proposed that the advantage of this DL development model is the wide range of skills that can be drawn from DL development in terms of content creation, infrastructure development, and subject matter expertise. Giersch et al. (2004) drew from this distributed store of disciplinary knowledge. Propose DLs that provide more than so-called human-moderated services.

This is in contrast to services through technology, which are similar types of functionality over digital objects as described above. Giersch et al. (2004) suggest that the two types of services may overlap, but that "technology should complement, not replace, human interaction" (Commitment to technology-mediated services, Section).

At the other end of the spectrum of alternative DL, models are what Beagrie (2005) calls personal digital collections: informal collections of heterogeneous material "collected and curated by individuals" that "may be designated for personal access only or shared with others' (Definition of Personal Digital Collections, 3). Some of the items in these private collections may be fairly standard digital objects (e.g., text documents, images, and videos), but as digital recording devices become more common Rather, the types of digital objects that individuals collect are likely to grow. Begrime notes that some services are springing up to help people maintain their collections. Some of these services are similar to those that can be offered to help organizations manage their digital assets. For example, data storage and backup, and security. However, more and more services are being offered to help people create, organize and share digital content. Some of these services may be algorithmic: for example, data backups can be performed automatically. However, some of these services are provided by humans, such as Giersch et al. (2004) are often suggested by a distributed community of people. However, unlike NSDL communities that exist around the development and maintenance of a particular DL, these communities can only exist around the provision of the service itself. Beagrie uses Flickr (flickr.com) as an example of a digital photo classification service: Flickr is not a single DL, but a service that helps people organize their personal image collections. They and others can provide an additional layer of service by tagging other people's photos.

Self Service

What Gorman (1979) found "irrational and prejudicial" in the distinction between technical and user services was its negative impact on the performance and efficiency of library functions and the work of librarians. In other words, Gorman's objection to this division is practical: libraries could provide a broader range of services and be more efficient if the services were more tightly integrated. Boissonnas (2001) raises another objection to the separation between technical services and user services: this separation does not correspond to the mental model of users of libraries or of information services in general.

As mentioned above, users often do not directly experience the functionality of Engineering Services (although they may use them), so Engineering Services may be hidden from users. In other words, Boissonnas opposes this division because user-centric libraries can be used more easily and intuitively if services are more tightly integrated. Services provided by organizations of all types are increasingly becoming self-service.

Digital Library Access and Information Retrieval

The goal of an information retrieval system is to retrieve all relevant documents in response to a user's query. With limited lexical control, it can be difficult for search engines to use terms in a query to match terms in related documents. A thesaurus can be used to look up information based on concepts. In the case of digital libraries, a thesaurus can be automatically created by semantic indexing on a particular topic. An approach to increase the efficiency of the information retrieval system through experiments in intelligent information processing techniques is presented.

Digital Technology Services

The creation, development, dissemination, and use of digital libraries will only become a reality when libraries and information centers in India have fully developed the most advanced ICT infrastructure. There are open-source software packages for creating digital libraries. Most of the research in India is done using these open-source packages. The Indian scenario of ICT infrastructure use in libraries and information centers shows that specialty libraries are best equipped and involved in the country's digitization consortia and programs (Gulati 2004). Science and Technology Libraries in India are better placed than other libraries, especially in the application of Information and Communication Technologies as these systems perform relatively better in India in terms of budget. A survey of 25 institutions by the Indian Council of Social Science Research (ICSSR) shows that digitization and networking in social science libraries in India are progressing, but rather slowly (Jain 2003).

Copyright

Copyright protects the rights of individuals, groups, and society. Copyright Enforcement and Support. The nature of digital information makes it vulnerable to copyright abuse, and as the number of digital libraries and collections grows, the impact of copyright on the digital environment becomes extremely important, especially in developing and underdeveloped countries, where software piracy is much higher than in developed countries.

Traits of the Virtual Libraries

Virtual library has positive traits, which lead them to be distinctive from the digital library. It has expansive and correct gadgets for looking at large volumes of textual content, image, and audio-video sources. Virtual libraries do not need the physical area to construct series and they may be accessed from anywhere, at any time. Current improvement in the library era and practices has helped carry several digital paperless societies to fact. The outcomes that digital knowledge has added encompass: virtual library collection contains stable files. The virtual atmosphere will allow brief coping with and or quick records. Virtual libraries are primarily based on virtual technology. The belief in digital libraries will comprise the most effective digital materials that can be incorrect. Digital libraries are frequently used by those running on my own. The bodily barriers of facts have been removed. Help for interactions and teamwork is as crucial as information-in search of.

The density of the records garage is enabling the book and garage of virtual records. Telecommunications has facilitated the garage, recovery, use, and trade of digital resources.

Digital Library Functions

- Provide a pleasant interface to users.
- To provide network facilities to consumers and faulty.
- To help virtual library functions and gadgets.
- To beautify advanced seek to get right of entry to and retrieval of digital library statistics.
- To improve the virtual library system.
- To allow one to carry out searches that aren't realistic manually for digital library systems.

- To hold unique series through the digitization machine.
- To get admission to the number one information source.
- To guide multimedia content material in conjunction with text formats.
- Community accessibility on the intranet and net browsing
- Person-pleasant interface systems.
- To superior search and retrieval system may be used in a virtual library.

Digital Library Purpose

They strive to provide instant access to digitized information and include an extensive range of events, including multimedia. A digital library is a library in which collections are stored in virtual codes (rather than print, microform, or other media) and made available through devices.

- To strengthen the systematic improvement of tactics to gather, shop, and arrange, data in virtual shape.
- To promote efficient shipping of the records price-efficaciously to the customers.
- To take the management position in the production or distribution of information
- To encourage efficient shipping of records inexpensively to customers.
- Help supportive hard work in studies aid, compute, with conversation network.
- Aid verbal exchange and cooperation among and among educational establishment's structures.
- The management position in the generation and distribution of expertise.

Components of the Virtual Library

The collection infrastructure usually includes components, metadata, and digital items that a virtual library holds. The metadata affords bibliographic or listing statistics for the digital objects. The additives of a digital library are:

- Facts generation communications systems.
- Digital library collection.
- Telecommunication facility for users.
- Human sources information system.
- Person interface system.
- Repository system.
- Search gadget.

Planning for the Virtual Library

The virtual library board should be profiled according to the plot used for demos and maintenance. Contributors should come from a variety of library departments and renowned professionals may be employed. At least there are ways to develop a virtual library that converts digital materials into a virtual library and directly develops the digital library.

Planning includes:

- Communications and control device
- Digitization structures
- Get admission to be a user
- Various employment
- To furnishings, gadgets, and area for the library
- To budget and fund the device
- Virtual library committee shaped

Digital Library Resources

- Subscription of the virtual structure open to all users on the school website
- Excessive bandwidth internet connection structure
- Selective perception of digital asset acquisition
- Type electronic journal unsubscribe from the internet portal
- Certified databases managing device
- Introduction of local digital content to be had inside the university

Limitations of the Virtual Library

A virtual library isn't always restrained to a specific region or so-known structure it is allotted all over the international. The client can get his/her records on his laptop display utilizing using the net. Certainly, it's far a community of compact disc devices, which gives fingertip get entry to the device. The preliminary price is too high for the communication cost of the virtual library records, i.e. the value of the hardware programming; leased communication circuits are often superfluous.

- To the dearth of program and validation
- To the dearth of maintenance of set copy for the file and the reproduction technical research
- To loss of preservation in a group of students
- To the problem is significant and finding everything, this is available and differentiates precious starting worthless statistics
- To activity loss for virtual publishers and librarians
- Expenditure is unfolding and plenty of growth to be hidden

The cost difficulty: To establish a virtual machine within the digital library gadget is more expensive in the preliminary stage of the system.

The talent personality: We require work in digital gadgets we want talented men or women with recognize of running and maintain

The regulation impact: Nowadays a few people desire to comfy their publications, topics, and many others. That is why they copyright their publications. Whenever a consumer will attempt to reproduce a few topics, he will be afflicted by copyright regulation. There are a few other legal guidelines similar to cyber law, which affect the virtual library gadget.

The skill machine: These days development becomes within each place like software and hardware program. The digital library completely depends on telecommunication and laptop systems. As new knowledge comes into the market the digital gadget needs to trade or be given that era.

Security trouble machine: When our virtual machine is connected to the net the most important trouble is the security to save you from unauthorized get entry and prevent the statistics from the virus is the fundamental challenge in the virtual system.

Implication of Facts Era Environment

It's miles a vital issue concerning library data age, through the merging of PC age with interchanges, advanced imaging, and complete-movement video and sound, can be a viable partner to improving training and subsequently upgrading expertise for grain full work. However, to do this libraries and libraries will trade. Changing over the computerized to advance is upgrading the preparation and ability.

Speed: The we move beginning virtually to digitalization idea we experience that the hurry will turn out to be faster the speed perspective might be discovered in acknowledgment of the working environment employees or understudies/client working. By utilizing digitalization the client recovers measurements snappier.

Access to power gadget: Advanced library manages to gain admittance to vitality to the client. In the digitalization condition, the purchaser gets to the contemporary measurements. Individuals can connect with a bigger no of the datasheet. The client furthermore gets to the overall records through the virtual library.

Supporting electrical vitality framework: In the digitalization idea, the advanced library helps a more extensive assortment of textures. It additionally builds the ability to manage enormous datasheets.

Space vitality gadget: The advanced library will expand the whole quality. It implies that we're making a convenient machine for substances. As time will build the convenience additionally increments as a model like the reduced circle, the DVD device declines the greater measurements and shop it bigger. So there might be no carport issue.

Online reference books gadget: Instructional programming program upgrades the data revel in on the off chance that it is structured well and created through fare gathering. The top of the line of digitized reference materials nowadays is a huge jump. Sent from even the pleasant sneering bundles accessible in the nineteen nineties it's miles because of the commitment of IT. Also, the advances in PC equipment and programming program. Lighting installations quick chip, monstrous memory, uncommon brisk over-the-top goals video show cards, best-in-class soundboard. Which convey virtual sound and the capacity medium of the CD ROM which holds a lot of data as 450 high-thickness diskettes emerge from the inventory of reference offices for thousand of multi-volume reference books and different materials.

Digital library Advantage

The digital library isn't always restricted to a selected area or so-referred to as building its miles in reality allotted everywhere in the international. The user can get his/her data on his laptop display screen with the aid of the usage of the internet. Admittedly, so far this is a web of multimedia gadgets that provide accessibility at your fingertips. In the new environment, maintaining a file will no longer be difficult for the library because users can use it.

Physical device: A consumer of a digital library requires no longer to the library bodily, humans everywhere in the world could advantage of access to the identical order, so extended as a web connection is accessible.

The clock availability gadget: the digital library system can access at any time. 24 hours a day and twelve months a year.

Several operating accesses: Identical sources may be used at an identical time using a figure of customers.

Improve structure: A Digital library offers to get entry to a great deal better off content material in an extra dependent method we will effortlessly move from the catalog to the specific book and then to a selected chapter.

Information recovery machine: A person can be capable of using any search below the phrase or phrase of the whole series. The digital library will give a very user-friendly interface giving a snap-on capable of getting admission to its property.

Maintenance: A correct replica of authentic can be made in any range of periods without any degradation in fine.

Space: Where virtual libraries are restrained by using the storage space area. Virtual libraries can store an awful lot of extra data, surely because virtual information requires little or no bodily space to contain them.

IT creation network: Specific of the digital library can provide the link to every previous source of the virtual library very easily for that reason seamlessly incorporated resource sharing can be performed.

High cost: The value of preserving a digital library is an awful lot lesser than two of a virtual library. A virtual library ought to use a large sum of money to pay for the workforce, e-book continues, lease, to extra books. The virtual library gets clear of prices.

Disadvantages of the Virtual Library

Computer viruses, loss of ability to normalize scanned data, short degradation characteristics of scanned documents, particularly preferred exposure of virtual products and related issues, nature of the threat screen radiation fitness body, etc. Make the digital library sometimes disabled.

Patent: Digitization violates the replica right regulation because the idea content of one author can be liberally moved by using others without his acknowledgment. So one trouble to overcome for digital libraries is the manner in that can share out facts. How does a virtual library distribute records at will whilst defensive the copyright of the writer?

Speed Access: As an increasing number of laptops are linked to the net the velocity of getting admission to reasonably decreasing. If the new generation will no longer evolve to clear up the trouble then shortly the internet might be full of error messages.

The preliminary price is excessive. The communications fee of the virtual library. The cost of hardware, software programs; leasing communiqué circuit is usually very excessive.

Efficiency system: With the whole lot larger volume of digital records, locating the proper fabric for a specific undertaking becomes harder and harder.

Surroundings device: Virtual libraries cannot reproduce the surroundings of virtual libraries. Many people additionally locate analysis revealed cloth to be less complicated than studying cloth on a computer display.

Security: because of technical traits, a digital library can unexpectedly come to be out-of-date and its records may emerge as inaccessible.

FUTURE RESEARCH SUGGESTIONS

This paper highlights and discuss about digital library and its importance. This study recommend that all academic institution and research institution have develop the digital library and its services for user's community. Digital library services major step for increasing the research productivity of the institution and fulfil the curriculum needs. Users can access digital library services by remote access from their devices anytime, anywhere. The Digital library can digitize and preserve the rare collection as well as out print documents.

CONCLUSION

The development of digital libraries in India has been misguided. Most of the changes were made to the S & T libraries. Again, these libraries focus on digital library development without focusing on issues such as education and training, copyright, management, and promotion (marketing). Copyright law needs to be revised to adapt to the electronic environment. Very few institutions have the initiative to organize seminars on digital libraries and digital technology. Digital rights management, digital library security, content management, business models and pricing, and policy research are other important areas where Indian research is scarce or absent. There is currently no pricing model in India. Considering some of the digital library initiatives that have been reported, it would be helpful to conduct a survey of digital libraries in India to understand the current status of digital library initiatives.

There might be persisting with the extension of advanced library sports. Lis and workstation science pros face requesting circumstances a decent method to bring about better frameworks. An ever-increasing number of libraries could have offices and bundles in the computerized library subject. Virtual libraries will be based on the work done inside the data and saved to the moderator's location. Virtual libraries give powerful and disseminate acing sources to understudies and various clients. Arranging an advanced library calls for insightful investigation of the venture and its clients, and an affirmation of the cost and the need for foundation and continuous support virtual libraries present conceivable outcomes and difficulties for the library and certainties networks and all partners.

REFERENCES

Adams, A., & Blandford, A. (2005, June). Digital libraries' support for the user's information journey. In *Proceedings of the 5th ACM/IEEE-CS joint conference on Digital Libraries* (pp. 160-169). 10.1145/1065385.1065424

Agosti, M., & Thanos, C. (2002). Research and Advanced Technology for Digital Libraries 6th European Conference, ECDL 2002 Rome, Italy, September 16–18, 2002 Proceedings. In *Conference proceedings ECDL* (pp. 358). https://link.springer.com/book/10.1007/3-540-45747-X

Ahmad, M., & Abawajy, J. H. (2014). Digital library service quality assessment model. *Procedia: Social and Behavioral Sciences*, *129*, 571–580. doi:10.1016/j.sbspro.2014.03.715

Al-Qallaf, C. L. (2006). Librarians and technology in academic and research libraries in Kuwait: Perceptions and effects. *Libri, 56*(3), 168–179. doi:10.1515/LIBR.2006.168

Anuradha, K. T. (2005). Design and development of institutional repositories: A case study. *The International Information & Library Review, 37*(3), 169–178. doi:10.1080/10572317.2005.10762678

Arora, J. (2003). Indian National Digital Library in Engineering Science and Technology (INDEST): A proposal for strategic cooperation for consortia-based access to electronic resources. *The International Information & Library Review, 35*(1), 1–17. doi:10.1080/10572317.2003.10762590

Awari, V., & Krishnamurthy, C. (2017). Digital Literacy among Post-Graduate Students of University of Agricultural Sciences, Dharwad. *International Journal of Next Generation Library and Technologies, 3*(3).

Balakrishnan, N. (2005). Universal Digital Library—Future research directions. *Journal of Zhejiang University. Science A, 6*(11), 1204–1205. doi:10.1631/jzus.2005.A1204

Beagrie, N. (2005). Digital Preservation: Best Practice and its Dissemination. *Ariadne, 43.* http://www.ariadne.ac.uk/issue/43/beagrie/

Boissonnas, C. (2001). Technical services: The other reader service. portal. *Portal (Baltimore, Md.), 1*(1), 33–46. doi:10.1353/pla.2001.0001

Borgman, C. L. (2002, December). Challenges in Building Digital Libraries for the 21st Century. In *International Conference on Asian Digital Libraries* (pp. 1-13), Springer. 10.1007/3-540-36227-4_1

Breeding, M. (1999). Does the Web spell doom for CD and DVD? *Computers in Libraries, 19*(10), 70–74. https://www.elibrary.ru/item.asp?id=3743560

Buchanan, S., & Salako, A. (2009). Evaluating the usability and usefulness of a digital library. *Library Review, 58*(9), 638–651. doi:10.1108/00242530910997928

Bulla, S. D., Shenvi, S. V., & Turamari, R. (2015). Open Source Software for Digital Library: With Special Reference to Ganesha Digital Library Software. *Indian Journal of Library and Information Technology, 5*(4). https://rb.gy/tjzfw

Chavan, K., & Chavan, S. (2017). Digital Libraries and their Importance: An Overview. In *International Conference on Digital Technologies and Transformation in Academic Libraries (DigiTTAL-2019)* (pp. 100-109). https://rb.gy/5w7l0

Chavan, S., & Naik, R. R. (2017). Impact of Information and Communication Technology Innovation on Library Service in the Engineering Colleges of North Karnataka. International Research. *Journal of Library and Information Science, 7*(2), 236–243. http://irjlis.com/wp-content/uploads/2017/08/3-IR404-62.pdf

Chowdhury, G. G. (2002). Digital libraries and reference services: Present and future. *The Journal of Documentation, 58*(3), 258–283. doi:10.1108/00220410210425809

Chowdhury, S., Landoni, M., & Gibb, F. (2006). Usability and impact of digital libraries: A review. *Online Information Review, 30*(6), 656–680. doi:10.1108/14684520610716153

Crawford, G. A. (1999). Issues for the Digital Library. *Computers in Libraries*, *19*(5), 62–64. https://www.elibrary.ru/item.asp?id=3584440

Gaur, R. C. (2003). Rethinking the Indian digital divide: The present state of digitization in Indian management libraries. *The International Information & Library Review*, *35*(2-4), 189–203. doi:10.1080/10572317.2003.10762600

Giersch, S., Klotz, E. A., McMartin, F., Muramatsu, B., Renninger, K., Shumar, W., & Weimar, S. A. (2004). If you build it, will they come? Participant involvement in digital libraries. *D-Lib Magazine : the Magazine of the Digital Library Forum*, *10*(7-8). Advance online publication. doi:10.1045/july2004-giersch

Gorman, M. (1979). On Doing Away with Technical Service Departments. *American Libraries*, *10*(7), 435–437.

Gorman, P., Ash, J., Lavelle, M., Lyman, J., Delcambre, L., Maier, D., & Bowers, S. (2000). Bundles in the wild: Managing information to solve problems and maintain situation awareness. *Library Trends*, *49*(2), 266–289.

Gulati, A. (2004). Use of information and communication technology in libraries and information centres: An Indian scenario. *The Electronic Library*, *22*(4), 335–350. doi:10.1108/02640470410552974

Gupta, V., & Pandey, S. R. (2019). Recommender systems for digital libraries: a review of concepts and concerns. *Library Philosophy and Practice (e-journal)*, 1-10. https://digitalcommons.unl.edu/libphilprac/2417

Hariri, N., & Norouzi, Y. (2011). Determining evaluation criteria for digital libraries' user interface: A review. *The Electronic Library*, *29*(5), 698–722. doi:10.1108/02640471111177116

Heath, F., Kyrillidou, M., Webster, D., Choudhury, S., Hobbs, B., Lorie, M., & Flores, N. (2003). Emerging Tools for Evaluating Digital Library Services: Conceptual Adaptations of LibQUAL+ and CAPM. *Journal of Digital Information*, *4*(2). http://jhir.library.jhu.edu/handle/1774.2/32792

Heradio, R., Fernández-Amorós, D., Cabrerizo, F. J., & Herrera-Viedma, E. (2012). A review of quality evaluation of digital libraries based on users' perceptions. *Journal of Information Science*, *38*(3), 269–283. doi:10.1177/0165551512438359

Jain, P. K. (2003). Indian council of social science research (ICSSR) maintained research institutes' libraries in India: Towards digitization and networking. *The International Information & Library Review*, *35*(2-4), 217–232. doi:10.1080/10572317.2003.10762602

Janes, J., Carter, D., & Memmott, P. (1999). Digital Reference Services in Academic Libraries. *Reference and User Services Quarterly*, *39*(2), 145–150. https://www.jstor.org/stable/20863724

Jose, A., & Raina, R. L. (2005). Networked Digital Libraries (NDLS) for IIMS: A conceptual model. *Herald of Library Science*, *44*(1-2), 44–48.

Kahn, R., & Wilensky, R. (1995). *A framework for distributed digital object service*. Accessed on 31-10-2022. www.cnri.reston.va.us/k-w.html

Kahn, R., & Wilensky, R. (2006). A framework for distributed digital object services. *International Journal on Digital Libraries*, 6(2), 115–123. doi:10.100700799-005-0128-x

Khan, S. A., & Bhatti, R. (2017). Digital competencies for developing and managing digital libraries: An investigation from university librarians in Pakistan. *The Electronic Library*, 35(3), 573–597. doi:10.1108/EL-06-2016-0133

Koppad, P. B., & Mulimani, M. N. (2021). Digital Information Literacy among users of R.T.E. Society's Arts, Science and Commerce College Library Ranebennur: A Case Study. *Journal of Education: Rabindra Bharati University*, 23(9I), 96–100.

Kotur, M. B., & Mulimani, M. N. (2019). Digital Library Resources for the Users: An Overview. *Journal of Advancements in Library Sciences*, 6(1), 111–114. https://sciencejournals.stmjournals.in/index.php/JoALS/article/view/1743

Krishnamurthy, C. (2004). Emerging Digital Libraries: Pro's and Con's. In *4th ASSIST National Seminar on Digital Resources and Services in Libraries* (pp. 1-11). Department of Library Information Science, Kuvempu University. https://rb.gy/lx710

Krishnamurthy, C., & Awari, V. H. (2012). Digital Reference Service: A Tool to Expand Horizons of Library Services. *Contemporary Research in India: A Peer Reviewed Multi-Disciplinary Research in India, 2*(3). https://rb.gy/vnfw9

Krishnamurthy, C., & Shettappanavar, L. (2019). Digital literacy among female postgraduate students of Karnatak University, Dharwad, Karnataka, India: A study. *Library Philosophy and Practice (e-journal)*, 1-16. https://digitalcommons.unl.edu/libphilprac/2934

Krishnamurthy, M. (2002). Digital Library Gateway for Library and Information Science: A Study. *SRELS Journal of Information Management, 39*(3), 245-254. https://www.srels.org/index.php/sjim/article/view/48887

Krishnamurthy, M. (2004). Digital Library: An overview. *SRELS Journal of Information Management, 41*(4), 317-326. https://www.srels.org/index.php/sjim/article/view/44498

Lancaster, F. W., & Warner, A. J. (1993). *Information Retrieval Today*. Information Resources Press. https://eric.ed.gov/?id=ED365357

Levy, D. M. (2000). Digital Libraries and the Problem of Purpose. *Bulletin of the American Society for Information Science*, 26(6), 22–25. doi:10.1002/bult.180

Lim, E. P., Foo, S., Khoo, C., Chen, H., Fox, E., Shalini, U., & Thanos, C. (Eds.). (2002). Digital Libraries: People, Knowledge, and Technology. In *5th International Conference on Asian Digital Libraries, ICADL 2002, Singapore, December 11-14, 2002, Proceedings* (Vol. 2555). Springer Science & Business Media. https://link.springer.com/book/10.1007/3-540-36227-4

Lougee, W. P. (2002). *Diffuse Libraries: Emergent Roles for the Research Library in the Digital Age*. Council on Library and Information Resources.

Mahesh, G., & Mittal, R. (2008). Digital Libraries in India: A Review. *Libri*, 58(1), 15–24. doi:10.1515/libr.2008.002

Martzoukou, K. (2021). Academic libraries in COVID-19: A renewed mission for digital literacy. *Library Management*, *42*(4/5), 266–276. doi:10.1108/LM-09-2020-0131

Mondal, A. (2014). Impact of ICT on job satisfaction of technical staff of the university libraries of West Bengal, India. *E-Library Science Research Journal, 2*(4), 1-15. http://oldlsrj.lbp.world/Uploade-dArticles/192.pdf

Mulimani, M., & Naikar, S. (2020). Digitisation and Role of Academic Libraries. *Indian Journal of Library and Information Technology*, *10*(4), 13–18. https://ssrn.com/abstract=3769286

Pomerantz, J., Oh, S., Wildemuth, B. M., Yang, S., & Fox, E. A. (2007, June). Digital library education in computer science programs. In *Proceedings of the 7th ACM/IEEE-CS joint conference on Digital libraries* (177-178). 10.1145/1255175.1255208

Rahimi, A., Soleymani, M. R., Hashemian, A., Hashemian, M. R., & Daei, A. (2018). Evaluating digital libraries: A systematised review. *Health Information and Libraries Journal*, *35*(3), 180–191. doi:10.1111/hir.12231 PMID:30160384

Ramesh, D. B. (Ed.). (2004). *Information Technology Applications in Libraries: A Textbook for Beginners*. Reprint.

Rodriguez, M. A., Bollen, J., & Van de Sompel, H. (2006). The convergence of digital libraries and the peer-review process. *Journal of Information Science*, *32*(2), 149–159. doi:10.1177/0165551506062327

Sandhu, G. (2018). The role of academic libraries in the digital transformation of the universities. In *5th International Symposium on Emerging Trends and Technologies in Libraries and Information Services (ETTLIS)* (pp. 292-296). IEEE. https://doi.org/10.1109/ETTLIS.2018.8485258

Schwartz, C. (1993). Evaluating CD-ROM products: Yet another checklist. *CD-ROM Professional*, *6*, 87–87.

Seadle, M., & Greifeneder, E. (2007). Defining a digital library. *Library Hi Tech*, *25*(2), 169–173. doi:10.1108/07378830710754938

Shettappanavar, L., & Krishnamurthy, C. (2021). Digital Literacy Skills among Postgraduate Students of University of Agricultural Sciences Dharwad: A Study. In *International Conference on Marching Libraries from Traditional to Hybrid: Connecting, Communicating and Cooperating* (pp. 301-314). Shree Publishers and Distributors. https://shorturl.at/adiS1

Sukula, S. (2010). *Electronic resource management: What, why and how*. Ess Ess Publications.

Turamari, R., & Kotur, M. B. (2019). Changing Skills of LIS professionals in the Digital Environment. *Indian Journal of Library and Information Technology*, *10*(4), 34–38. https://shorturl.at/rwTU9

Vijayakumar, J. K., & Vijayakumar, M. (2000). CD-ROM to DVD-ROM: a new era in electronic publishing of Databases and Multimedia Reference Sources. *IASLIC Bulletin*, *45*(2), 49-54. http://eprints.rclis.org/14019/1/vijayakumarjk_19.pdf

Xie, I., & Matusiak, K. (2016). *Discover digital libraries: Theory and practice*. Elsevier. https://www.sciencedirect.com/book/9780124171121/discover-digital-libraries

Zirra, P. B., Ibrahim, A. J., & Abdulganiyyi, N. (2019). A review of digital libraries and their impact in Africa. *American Journal of Computer Science and Technology*, 2(4), 60–67. doi:10.11648/j.ajcst.20190204.13

KEY TERMS AND DEFINITIONS

Academic Libraries: An academic library is a library that is attached to a higher education institution and serves two complementary purposes: to support the curriculum and the research of the university faculty and students.

CD-ROM: A CD-ROM (Compact Disc Read-Only Memory) is a type of compact disc that can only be read, not written. It is a digital storage medium that can hold large amounts of data, including text, images, and audio.

Copyright: Copyright refers to the legal right of the owner of intellectual property. In simpler terms, copyright is the right to copy.

Digital Library: A digital library is a collection of digital objects such as books, magazines, journals, audio recordings, video recordings, and other documents that are accessible electronically.

Digital Literacy Skills: Digital literacy skills can be defined as the ability of an individual in this digital age to use computers or other technologies to navigate digital platforms to access, locate, evaluate, create, and disseminate digital content.

Digital Resources: Digital resources are those information resources in an electronic format accessible through internet-connected computers or other electronic devices in libraries known as in-house digital resources.

Digitization: The process of transforming non-digital-born documents into digital formats is known as digitization.

E-Resources: Electronic resources form one of many formats that the library collects to support its universal collections. Electronic resources include websites, online databases, e-journals, e-books, and physical carriers in all formats, whether free or fee-based, required to support research in the subject covered, and maybe audio, visual, and/or text files.

User Services: User services, on the other hand, are provided directly to library users. Also includes references, guides, genealogy, and services to specific user groups as user services.

Virtual Library: A Virtual Library provides remote (online or CD-ROM-based) access to a variety of national and international content services traditionally offered by libraries and other information sources.

Compilation of References

Abbasnia, R., Ahmadi, R., & Ziaadiny, H. (2012). Effect of confinement level, aspect ratio and concrete strength on the cyclic stress–strain behavior of FRP-confined concrete prisms. *Composites. Part B, Engineering, 43*(2), 825–831. doi:10.1016/j.compositesb.2011.11.008

Abbasnia, R., Hosseinpour, F., Rostamian, M., & Ziaadiny, H. (2013). Cyclic and monotonic behavior of FRP confined concrete rectangular prisms with different aspect ratios. *Construction & Building Materials, 40*, 118–125. doi:10.1016/j.conbuildmat.2012.10.008

Abdulkadhim, H., Bahari, M., Bakri, A., & Ismail, W. (2015). A research framework of electronic document management systems (EDMS) implementation process in government. *Journal of Theoretical and Applied Information Technology, 81*(3), 420–432.

Abdulrahman, M., & Eleyan, A. (2015). Facial expression recognition using support vector machines. *2015 23nd Signal Processing and Communications Applications Conference (SIU)*, 276-279. 10.1109/SIU.2015.7129813

Abioye, A. (2013). Government record-keeping in Sub-Sahara Africa: Milestones in archives administration in Nigeria. *Comma International Journal on Archives, 1*(1), 15–26.

Abouzeedan, A., & Hedner, T. (2012). Organization structure theories and open innovation paradigm. *World Journal of Science. Technology and Sustainable Development, 9*(1), 6–27.

Abubakar, M. K. (2021). Implementation and Use of Virtual Reference Services in Academic Libraries during and post. *Library Philosophy and Practice.*

Acevedo-De-los-Ríos, A., & Rondinel-Oviedo, D. R. (2022). Impact, added value and relevance of an accreditation process on quality assurance in architectural higher education. *Quality in Higher Education, 28*(2), 186–204. doi:10.1080/13538322.2021.1977482

ACI Committee 440. (2017). *ACI 440.2R-17: Guide for the design and construction of externally bonded FRP systems for strengthening existing structures*. In American Concrete Institute.

Adams, A., & Blandford, A. (2005, June). Digital libraries' support for the user's information journey. In *Proceedings of the 5th ACM/IEEE-CS joint conference on Digital Libraries* (pp. 160-169). 10.1145/1065385.1065424

Adayi, I. O., Neboh, R. I., & Oluchi, E. G. (2023). *Users' assessment of digital reference service delivery in private university libraries in Enugu State. Library Philosophy and Practice (e-journal).*

Adesina, E. R., Ogunniyi, S. O., & Ajakaye, J. E. (2022). Challenges and Prospects of Reference Services in Federal University Libraries in South-West, Nigeria. *Library Philosophy and Practice (e-journal), 7155.* https://digitalcommons.unl.edu/libphilprac/7155

Adibi, M., Talebkhah, R., & Ghatte, H. F. (2023). Seismic reliability of precast concrete frame with masonry infill wall. *Earthquakes and Structures*, *24*(2), 141.

Adu, K. K. (2015). *Framework for digital preservation of electronic government in Ghana* [PhD thesis]. University of South Africa.

Adu, K. K., & Ngulube, P. (2016). Preserving the digital heritage of public institutions in Ghana in the wake of electronic government. *Library Hi Tech*, *34*(4), 748–763. doi:10.1108/LHT-07-2016-0077

Afolayan, J. O., Ogundokun, R. O., Afolabi, A. G., & Adegun, A. A. (2020). Artificial Intelligence, Cloud Librarianship, and Infopreneurship Initiatives for Inclusiveness. In A. Tella (Ed.), *Handbook of Research on Digital Devices for Inclusivity and Engagement in Libraries* (pp. 45–69). IGI Global. doi:10.4018/978-1-5225-9034-7.ch003

Age, A. (2019). Language style matching as a measure of librarian/patron engagement in email reference transactions. *Journal of Academic Librarianship*, *45*(6), 102069. doi:10.1016/j.acalib.2019.102069

Agosti, M., & Thanos, C. (2002). Research and Advanced Technology for Digital Libraries 6th European Conference, ECDL 2002 Rome, Italy, September 16–18, 2002 Proceedings. In *Conference proceedings ECDL* (pp. 358). https://link.springer.com/book/10.1007/3-540-45747-X

Ahmad, F., Saad Alam, M., Saad Alsaidan, I., & Shariff, S. M. (2020). Battery swapping station for electric vehicles: Opportunities and challenges. *IET Smart Grid*, *3*(3), 280–286. doi:10.1049/iet-stg.2019.0059

Ahmad, M., & Abawajy, J. H. (2014). Digital library service quality assessment model. *Procedia: Social and Behavioral Sciences*, *129*, 571–580. doi:10.1016/j.sbspro.2014.03.715

Ajakaye, J. E. (2022). Applications of Artificial Intelligence (AI) in Libraries. In I. Ekoja, E. Ogbomo, & O. Okuonghae (Eds.), *Handbook of Research on Emerging Trends and Technologies in Librarianship* (pp. 73–90). IGI Global. doi:10.4018/978-1-7998-9094-2.ch006

Akbarzadeh, H., & Maghsoudi, A. A. (2011). Flexural strengthening of RC continuous beams using hybrid FRP sheets. In *Advances in FRP Composites in Civil Engineering: Proceedings of the 5th International Conference on FRP Composites in Civil Engineering (CICE 2010), Sep 27–29, 2010, Beijing, China* (pp. 739-743). Springer Berlin Heidelberg. 10.1007/978-3-642-17487-2_163

Al Shraah, A., Abu-Rumman, A., Alqhaiwi, L., & Alshurideh, M. T. (2023). The role of AACSB accreditation in students' leadership motivation and students' citizenship motivation: Business education perspective. *Journal of Applied Research in Higher Education*, *15*(4), 1130–1145. doi:10.1108/JARHE-11-2021-0409

Alaskar, A., D'Errico, E., Alipoon, L., & Dehom, S. (2019). Institutional accreditation in Saudi Arabian higher education: Perceptions and involvement. *Quality in Higher Education*, *25*(3), 245–260. doi:10.1080/13538322.2019.1667630

Al-Bakri, S. H., Mat Kiah, M. L., Zaidan, A. A., Zaidan, B. B., & Alam, G. M. (2011). Securing peer-to-peer mobile communications using public key cryptography: New security strategy. *International Journal of Physical Sciences*, *6*(4), 930–938.

Aleksandrov, A. Y., Barabanova, S. V., Vereshchak, S. B., Ivanova, O. A., & Aleksandrova, Z. A. (2016). Revisiting the legal consequences of international accreditation of higher education programs in the Russian Federation. *Journal of Advanced Research in Law and Economics*, *7*(2), 202–210. https://journals.aserspublishing.eu/jarle/article/view/206

Al-Hammoud, R., Soudki, K., & Topper, T. H. (2013). Confinement effect on the bond behavior of beams under static and repeated loading. *Construction & Building Materials*, *40*, 934–943. doi:10.1016/j.conbuildmat.2012.09.081

Al-Hanahi, B., Ahmad, I., Habibi, D., & Masoum, M. A. (2021). Charging infrastructure for commercial electric vehicles: Challenges and future works. *IEEE Access : Practical Innovations, Open Solutions*, 9, 121476–121492. doi:10.1109/ACCESS.2021.3108817

Al-Hatmi, A. H. Z., Ibri, O & Nor, N. S. (2022). Investigating students' use of digital reference services in Oman's Academic libraries. *Electronic Interdisciplinary Miscellaneous Journal*, 45, 1–36.

Ali, M. S. (2019). Bots in libraries: They're coming for your jobs (or is it?). In ALIA Information Online 2019, ALIA Information Online 2019. Research Collection Library.

AlKarousi, R. S., Jabr, N. H., & Harrassi, N. (2015). Adoption of Web 2.0 applications in Omani academic libraries. *Proceedings of the SLA–AGC 21st Annual Conference*.

Alkhatib, S., Kecskés, P., & Keller, V. (2023). Green Marketing in the Digital Age: A Systematic Literature Review. *Sustainability (Basel)*, 15(16), 12369. doi:10.3390u151612369

Al-Qallaf, C. L. (2006). Librarians and technology in academic and research libraries in Kuwait: Perceptions and effects. *Libri*, 56(3), 168–179. doi:10.1515/LIBR.2006.168

Alzubi, J., Nayyar, A., & Kumar, A. (2018). Machine learning from theory to algorithms: An overview. *Journal of Physics: Conference Series*, 1142, 1–16. doi:10.1088/1742-6596/1142/1/012012

Amin, M. R., Arif, I., & Rahman, M. M. (2012). Green Marketing Practices for Sustainable Business Growth in Bangladesh: A Case Study of Dhaka City. *Global Disclosure of Economics and Business*, 1(2), 96–102. doi:10.18034/gdeb.v1i2.197

Amollo, B. A. (2011). *Digitization for Libraries in Kenya. International Conference on African Digital Libraries and Archives ICADLA*. Nairobi. Kenya.

Andreani, M., Russo, D., Salini, S., & Turri, M. (2020). Shadows over accreditation in higher education: Some quantitative evidence. *Higher Education*, 79(4), 691–709. doi:10.100710734-019-00432-1

Angalakuditi, H., & Bhowmik, B. (2023). Impact of Stress During COVID-19 Pandemic. *9th International Conference on Advanced Computing and Communication Systems (ICACCS)*. 10.1109/ICACCS57279.2023.10113119

Anishchenko, L., & Turetzkaya, A. (2020). Improved non-contact mental stress detection via bioradar. *2020 International Conference on Biomedical Innovations and Applications (BIA)*, 21–24. 10.1109/BIA50171.2020.9244492

Anitha, M. P., & Vijai, C. (2021). Green Marketing: Benefits and Challenges. *European Journal of Molecular and Clinical Medicine*, 7(11), 2020.

Anuradha, K. T. (2005). Design and development of institutional repositories: A case study. *The International Information & Library Review*, 37(3), 169–178. doi:10.1080/10572317.2005.10762678

Apgar, D., & Cadmus, T. (2021). Using mixed methods to assess coping and self-regulation skills of undergraduate social work students impacted by COVID-19. *Clinical Social Work Journal*, 1–12. PMID:33589848

Arioz, O. (2007). Effects of elevated temperatures on properties of concrete. *Fire Safety Journal*, 42(8), 516–522. doi:10.1016/j.firesaf.2007.01.003

Arnold, T., & Scheutz, M. (2018, March 1). *The Ethics and Information Technology*. https://dl.acm.org/doi/10.1007/s10676-018-9447-7

Arora, J. (2003). Indian National Digital Library in Engineering Science and Technology (INDEST): A proposal for strategic cooperation for consortia-based access to electronic resources. *The International Information & Library Review*, 35(1), 1–17. doi:10.1080/10572317.2003.10762590

Arya, H. B., & Mishra, J. K. (2012). Virtual reference services: Tools and techniques. *Journal of Library and Information Science, 2*(1).

Asemi, A., & Asemi, A. (2018). Artificial Intelligence (AI) application in Library Systems in Iran: A taxonomy study. *Library Philosophy and Practice (e-journal),* 1-10. https://digitalcommons.unl.edu/libphilprac/1840/

Aslan, M. (2021). CNN based efficient approach for emotion recognition. *Journal of King Saud University. Computer and Information Sciences.*

Asoka, A., Samry, W., & Saputra, Y. (2016). Sawahlunto Dulu, Kini, dan Esok: Menjadi Kota Wisata Tambang yang Berbudaya. Padang: Minangkabau Press.

Asproth, V. (2005). Information technology challenges for long-term preservation of electronic information. *International Journal of Public Information Systems, 1*(1).

Association of College & Research Libraries (ACRL). (n.d.). *Changing roles of Academic & Research Libraries.* Retrieved from http://ww.ala.org/ala/mgrps/divs/acrl/issues/value/changingroles.cfm

Asteris, P. G., & Kolovos, K. G. (2019). Self-compacting concrete strength prediction using surrogate models. *Neural Computing & Applications, 31*(S1, Suppl 1), 409–424. doi:10.100700521-017-3007-7

ASTM. (2013). *C33-13: Standard Specification for Concrete Aggregates.* ASTM International.

Attaran, Brooks, & Mohsenin. (2016). A low-power multi- physiological monitoring processor for stress detection. *2016 IEEE Sensors,* 1–3.

August, T., Chen, W., & Zhu, K. (2021). Competition among proprietary and open-source software firms: The role of licensing in strategic contribution. *Management Science, 67*(5), 3041–3066. doi:10.1287/mnsc.2020.3674

Aulia, N., Gunawan, J., & Sumarsono, M. (2018). Green Marketing, Ecolabel and Purchase Intention on Food Products during. *COVID,* 19.

Awari, V., & Krishnamurthy, C. (2017). Digital Literacy among Post-Graduate Students of University of Agricultural Sciences, Dharwad. *International Journal of Next Generation Library and Technologies, 3*(3).

Ayoku, O. A., & Okafor, V. N. (2015). ICT skills acquisition and competencies of librarians: Implications for digital and electronic environment in Nigerian universities libraries. *The Electronic Library, 33*(3), 502–523. doi:10.1108/EL-08-2013-0155

Azim, I., Yang, J., Javed, M. F., Iqbal, M. F., Mahmood, Z., Wang, F., & Liu, Q. F. (2020, June). Prediction model for compressive arch action capacity of RC frame structures under column removal scenario using gene expression programming. In *Structures* (Vol. 25, pp. 212–228). Elsevier.

Bafadhal, A. S., & Hendrawan, M. R. (2021). Towards Infinity and Beyond Reality: A Cutting-Edge Virtual Museum. In Globalisation of Cultural Heritage: Issues, Impacts, and Challenges. Trengganu: Penerbit Universiti Malaysia Trengganu.

Bagchi, M. (2020). Conceptualising a Library Chatbot using Open Source Conversational Artificial Intelligence. *DESIDOC Journal of Library and Information Technology, 40*(6), 329–333. doi:10.14429/djlit.40.06.15611

BahriniA.KhamoshifarM.AbbasimehrH.RiggsR. J.EsmaeiliM.MajdabadkohneR. M.PasehvarM. (2023, April 14). *CHATGPT: Applications, opportunities, and threats.* doi:10.1109/SIEDS58326.2023.10137850

Baidoo-AnuD.Owusu AnsahL. (2023, January 27). *Education in the era of Generative Artificial Intelligence (AI): Understanding the potential benefits of CHATGPT in promoting teaching and learning.* doi:10.2139/ssrn.4337484

Balakrishnan, N. (2005). Universal Digital Library—Future research directions. *Journal of Zhejiang University. Science A*, *6*(11), 1204–1205. doi:10.1631/jzus.2005.A1204

Banisar, D. (2004). The Freedominfo.org Global Survey: Freedom of information and access to government record laws around the world. Freedominfo.org

Banisar, D. (2006). *Freedom of information around the world 2006: A global survey of access to government information laws*. Privacy International.

Baruch, Y. (1999). Response rate in academic studies-A comparative analysis. *Human Relations*, *52*(4), 421–438. doi:10.1177/001872679905200401

Basil Iwhiwhu, E. (2005). Management of records in Nigerian universities: Problems and prospects. *The Electronic Library*, *23*(3), 345–355. doi:10.1108/02640470510603741

Bawden, D. (2008). Origins and concepts of digital literacy. *Digital literacies: Concepts, policies, and practices*, *30*(2008), 17-32.

Bawden, D. (2001). Information and digital literacies: A review of concepts. *The Journal of Documentation*, *57*(2), 218–259. doi:10.1108/EUM0000000007083

Beagrie, N. (2005). Digital Preservation: Best Practice and its Dissemination. *Ariadne*, *43*. http://www.ariadne.ac.uk/issue/43/beagrie/

Bell, K. (2019). Communitas and the commons: The open access movement and the dynamics of restructuration in scholarly publishing. *Anthropology Today*, *35*(5), 21–23. doi:10.1111/1467-8322.12530

Bengar, H. A., Hosseinpour, M., & Celikag, M. (2020, April). Influence of CFRP confinement on bond behavior of steel deformed bar embedded in concrete exposed to high temperature. In *Structures* (Vol. 24, pp. 240–252). Elsevier.

Bennett, F. H., Koza, J. R., Andre, D., & Keane, M. A. (1997). Evolution of a 60 decibel op amp using genetic programming. In *Evolvable Systems: From Biology to Hardware: First International Conference, ICES96 Tsukuba, Japan, October 7–8, 1996 Proceedings 1* (pp. 453-469). Springer Berlin Heidelberg. 10.1007/3-540-63173-9_65

Bergkvist, L., & Zhou, K. Q. (2016). Celebrity endorsements: A literature review and research agenda. International Journal of Advertising, 35(4), 642–663.a Bellenger, D. N. (1980). Profiling the recreational shopper. *Journal of Retailing*, *56*(3), 77–92.

Bernard, M. J. (1981). Problems In Predicting Market Response To New Transportation Technology. *New Horizons In Travel-Behavior Research*.

Bestari, D. K. P., & Butarbutar, D. A. (2021). Implementation of Green Marketing Strategies and Green Purchase Behavior as Efforts to Strengthen the Competitiveness of MSMEs in Indonesia. Budapest International Research and Critics Institute (BIRCI-Journal): Humanities and Social Sciences, 4(1), 243-254. doi:10.33258/birci.v4i1.1588

Bey, P. G. (2012). *The Parkerian Hexad: The CIA triad model expanded* [Master's thesis]. Lewis University.

Bhattacharyya, J. (2023). The structure of sustainability marketing research: A bibliometric review and directions for future research. *Asia-Pacific Journal of Business Administration*, *15*(2), 245–286. doi:10.1108/APJBA-06-2021-0239

Bhowmik, B., Varna, S. A., Kumar, A., & Kumar, R. (2021). *Deep neural networks in healthcare systems. In Machine Learning and Deep Learning in Efficacy Improvement of Healthcare Systems*. CRC Press, Taylor and Francis.

Bingöl, A. F., & Gül, R. (2009). The residual bond strength between steel bars and concrete after elevated temperatures. *Fire Safety Journal*, *44*(6), 854–859. doi:10.1016/j.firesaf.2009.04.001

Bjerkan, K. Y., Nørbech, T. E., & Nordtømme, M. E. (2016). Incentives for promoting Battery Electric Vehicle (BEV) adoption in Norway. *Transportation Research Part D, Transport and Environment, 43*, 169–180. doi:10.1016/j.trd.2015.12.002

Blake, R. (2017). Telepresence robots: An innovative approach to library service. *Journal of Library Administration, 57*(8), 832–840.

Blanco-Ramírez, G., & Berger, J. (2014). Rankings, accreditation, and the international quest for quality: Organizing an approach to value in higher education. *Quality Assurance in Education, 22*(1), 88–104. doi:10.1108/QAE-07-2013-0031

Bobade, P., & Vani, M. (2020). Stress detection with machine learning and deep learning using multimodal physiological data. *2020 Second International Conference on Inventive Research in Computing Applications (ICIRCA),* 51–57. 10.1109/ICIRCA48905.2020.9183244

Boissonnas, C. (2001). Technical services: The other reader service. portal. *Portal (Baltimore, Md.), 1*(1), 33–46. doi:10.1353/pla.2001.0001

Booth, C. (2008). Developing Skype-based reference services. *Internet Reference Services Quarterly, 13*(2-3), 147–165. doi:10.1080/10875300802103684

Borgman, C. L. (2002, December). Challenges in Building Digital Libraries for the 21st Century. In *International Conference on Asian Digital Libraries* (pp. 1-13), Springer. 10.1007/3-540-36227-4_1

Boughrara, H., Chtourou, M., Amar, C. B., & Chen, L. (2016). Facial expression recognition based on a mlp neural network using constructive training algorithm. *Multimedia Tools and Applications, 75*(2), 709–731. doi:10.100711042-014-2322-6

Bournas, D. A., & Triantafillou, T. C. (2011). Bond strength of lap-spliced bars in concrete confined with composite jackets. *Journal of Composites for Construction, 15*(2), 156–167. doi:10.1061/(ASCE)CC.1943-5614.0000078

Bowker, L., Kalsatos, M., Ruskin, A., & Ciro, J. B. (2022). Artificial intelligence, machine translation, and academic libraries: Improving machine translation literacy on campus. In The Rise of AI: Implications and Applications for AI in Academic Libraries (pp. 3-14). Association of College and Research Libraries.

Bowman, E. (2022, December 19). *A new AI chatbot might do your homework for you. but it's still not an A+ student.* NPR. https://www.npr.org/2022/12/19/1143912956/chatgpt-ai-chatbot-homework-academia

Breeding, M. (1999). Does the Web spell doom for CD and DVD? *Computers in Libraries, 19*(10), 70–74. https://www.elibrary.ru/item.asp?id=3743560

Brevini, B. (2020). Black boxes, not green: Mythologizing artificial intelligence and omitting the environment. *Big Data & Society, 7*(2), 1–5. doi:10.1177/2053951720935141

Brown, K., & Mairesse, F. (2018). The definition of the museum is through its social role. *Curator (New York, N.Y.), 61*(4), 525–539. doi:10.1111/cura.12276

Brown, S. M., Doom, J. R., Lechuga-Pena, S., Watamura, S. E., & Koppels, T. (2020). Stress and parenting during the global COVID-19 pandemic. *Child Abuse & Neglect, 110*(Pt 2), 104699. doi:10.1016/j.chiabu.2020.104699 PMID:32859394

Brundage, M., & Bryson, J. (2016). *Smart Policies for Artificial Intelligence.* https://www.semanticscholar.org/paper/Smart-Policies-for-Artificial-Intelligence-Brundage-Bryson/937d6d4c34ad41edc6fb68e477cad23657b949e2

Buchanan, S., & Salako, A. (2009). Evaluating the usability and usefulness of a digital library. *Library Review, 58*(9), 638–651. doi:10.1108/00242530910997928

Buckland, M. K., & Lund, N. W. (2013). Boyd Rayward, documentation, and information science. *Library Trends, 62*(2), 302–310. doi:10.1353/lib.2013.0038

Buhalis, D. (2020). 'Technology in tourism – from information communication technologies to eTourism and smart tourism towards ambient intelligence tourism: A perspective article. *Tourism Review, 75*(1), 267–272. doi:10.1108/TR-06-2019-0258

Buil, I., de Chernatony, L., & Hem, L. E. (2009). Brand extension strategies: Perceived fit, brand type, and culture influences. *European Journal of Marketing, 43*(11/12), 1300–1324. doi:10.1108/03090560910989902

Bullard, K. A. (2003). *Virtual reference service evaluation: an application of unobtrusive research methods and the virtual reference desk's facets of quality for digital reference service [Master's paper].* University of North Carolina at Chapel Hill.

Bulla, S. D., Shenvi, S. V., & Turamari, R. (2015). Open Source Software for Digital Library: With Special Reference to Ganesha Digital Library Software. *Indian Journal of Library and Information Technology, 5*(4). https://rb.gy/tjzfw

Buonocore, J. J., Choma, E., Villavicencio, A. H., Spengler, J. D., Koehler, D. A., Evans, J. S., Lelieveld, J., Klop, P., & Sanchez-Pina, R. (2019). Metrics for the sustainable development goals: Renewable energy and transportation. *Palgrave Communications, 5*(1), 136. doi:10.105741599-019-0336-4

Burkett, D. (2017). Digitisation and digitalisation: What means what? *Innovation.*

Byrne, A. (2015). Institutional memory and memory institutions. *The Australian Library Journal, 64*(4), 259–269. doi:10.1080/00049670.2015.1073657

Canavari, M., & Coderoni, S. (2019). Green marketing strategies in the dairy sector: Consumer-stated preferences for carbon footprint labels. *Strategic Change, 28*(4), 233–240. doi:10.1002/jsc.2264

Carcagnì, P., Del Coco, M., Leo, M., & Distante, C. (2015). Facial expression recognition and histograms of oriented gradients: A comprehensive study. *SpringerPlus, 4*(1), 645. doi:10.118640064-015-1427-3 PMID:26543779

Carlucci, F., Cirà, A., & Lanza, G. (2018). Hybrid Electric Vehicles: Some Theoretical Considerations on Consumption Behaviour. *Sustainability (Basel), 10*(4), 1302. doi:10.3390u10041302

Cassell, K. A., & Hiremath, U. (2018). *Reference and information services: An introduction* (4th ed.). Neal Schuman.

Castillo-Abdul, B., Bonilla-del-Río, M., & Núñez-Barriopedro, E. (2021). Influence and Relationship between Branded Content and the Social Media Consumer Interactions of the Luxury Fashion Brand Manolo Blahnik. *Publications / MDPI, 9*(1), 10. doi:10.3390/publications9010010

Cave, S., & Dihal, K. (2020). The whiteness of AI. *Philosophy & Technology, 33*(4), 685–703. doi:10.100713347-020-00415-6

Chamberlain, D., Elcock, M., & Puligari, P. (2015). The use of mobile technology in health libraries: A summary of a UK based survey. *Health Information and Libraries Journal, 32*(4), 1–12. doi:10.1111/hir.12116 PMID:26292980

Chan, L. (2002). *The Budapest open access Initiative.* https://www.budapestopenaccessinitiative.org/read/

Chang, R. (1990). Developing a cataloging expert system. *Illinois Libraries, 72*, 592–596.

Charles Darwin University. (2017). *Records disposal schedules: higher education teaching and learning of the University of the Charles Darwin University.* https://www.cdu.edu.au/sites/default/files/itms-docs/disposal-schedule-2017.17-charlesdarwin-university-higher-education-teaching-and-learning.pdf

Chaterera, F. (2013). *Records surveys and the management of public records in Zimbabwe* [Minf. Dissertation]. University of South Africa.

Chatgpt for Education and research. A review of benefits and risks. (n.d.). https://www.researchgate.net/publication/369127881_ChatGPT_for_Education_and_Research_A_Review_of_Benefits_and_Risks

Chavan, K., & Chavan, S. (2017). Digital Libraries and their Importance: An Overview. In *International Conference on Digital Technologies and Transformation in Academic Libraries (DigiTTAL-2019)* (pp. 100-109). https://rb.gy/5w7l0

Chavan, S., & Naik, R. R. (2017). Impact of Information and Communication Technology Innovation on Library Service in the Engineering Colleges of North Karnataka. International Research. *Journal of Library and Information Science,* 7(2), 236–243. http://irjlis.com/wp-content/uploads/2017/08/3-IR404-62.pdf

Checco, A., Bracciale, L., Loreti, P., Pinfield, S., & Bianchi, G. (2021). Ai-Assisted Peer Review. *Humanities & Social Sciences Communications,* 8(1), 25. Advance online publication. doi:10.105741599-020-00703-8

Chibambo, M. L. N. (2006). *The right to access government information, democracy, and development in sub-Saharan Africa.* Paper presented at the WSIS Follow-up conference on access to information and knowledge for development. Addis Ababa, Ethiopia.

Chinyemba, A. (2011). *Fostering transparency, good governance, and accountability in institutions of higher learning through records management.* Paper presentation at the XXXI Bi-annual Eastern and Southern Africa Regional Branch of the International 75 Council on Archives (ESARBICA) General Conference on Access to Information: Archives and Records in Support of Public Sector Reform in Context, Maputo, Mozambique.

Chisita CT, Ngulube P. (2022). A framework for librarians to inform the citizenry during disasters: Reflections on the COVID-19 pandemic. *Jamba,* 14(1), 1197.

Choi, E., Kim, Y. W., Chung, Y. S., & Yang, K. T. (2010). Bond strength of concrete confined by SMA wire jackets. *Physics Procedia,* 10, 210–215. doi:10.1016/j.phpro.2010.11.100

Choma, E. F., Evans, J. S., Hammitt, J. K., Gómez-Ibáñez, J. A., & Spengler, J. D. (2020). Assessing the health impacts of electric vehicles through air pollution in the United States. *Environment International,* 144, 106015. doi:10.1016/j.envint.2020.106015 PMID:32858467

Chong, C. W., Chong, S. C., & Lin, B. (2010). Organizational demographic variables and preliminary KM implementation success. *Expert Systems with Applications,* 37(10), 7243–7254. doi:10.1016/j.eswa.2010.04.003

Choudhary, A., & Gokarn, S. (2013). Green marketing: A means for sustainable development. Journal of Arts. *Science & Commerce,* 4(3), 3.

Chou, J. S., Tsai, C. F., Pham, A. D., & Lu, Y. H. (2014). Machine learning in concrete strength simulations: Multi-nation data analytics. *Construction & Building Materials,* 73, 771–780. doi:10.1016/j.conbuildmat.2014.09.054

Chowdhury, G. G. (2002). Digital libraries and reference services: Present and future. *The Journal of Documentation,* 58(3), 258–283. doi:10.1108/00220410210425809

Chowdhury, S., Landoni, M., & Gibb, F. (2006). Usability and impact of digital libraries: A review. *Online Information Review,* 30(6), 656–680. doi:10.1108/14684520610716153

Chung, S., & Cho, H. (2017). Fostering para-social relationships with celebrities on social media: Implications for celebrity endorsement. *Psychology and Marketing,* 34(4), 481–495. doi:10.1002/mar.21001

Chu, S. C., Kamal, S., & Kim, Y. (2013). Understanding consumers' responses toward social media advertising and purchase intention toward luxury products. *Journal of Global Fashion Marketing,* 4(3), 158–174. doi:10.1080/2093268 5.2013.790709

Chu, S. K. W., & Du, H. S. (2012). Social networking tools for academic libraries. *Journal of Librarianship and Information Science*, *45*(1), 64–75. doi:10.1177/0961000611434361

Cloughley, K. (2004). Digital reference services: How do library-based services compare with expert services? *Library Review*, *53*(1), 17–23. doi:10.1108/00242530410514757

Collins, G., & Quan-Haase, A. (2014). Are social media ubiquitous in academic libraries? A longitudinal study of adoption and usage patterns. *Journal of Web Librarianship*, *8*(1), 48–68. doi:10.1080/19322909.2014.873663

Constantine, E., Garrity, J., Hammes, M., Lockwood, C., & Teesch, L. (2018). *Libraries and Museums: Fostering GLAM Collaboration at the University of Iowa*. University of Iowa. doi:10.17077/yc01-mco1

Cordell, R. (2020). *Machine learning and libraries: a report on the state of the field*. Library of Congress. https://labs.loc.gov/static/labs/work/reports/Cordell-LOC-ML-report.pdf

Cotera, M. (2018). We *embrace digital innovation: IE University Library reinventing higher education*. 4th Lebanese Library Association Conference Innovative Libraries: Paths to the future, in collaboration with IFLA Asia Oceania Section, Lebanon.

Cox, A. M. (2021). *The role of the information, knowledge management and library workforce in the 4th industrial revolution*. Academic Press.

Cox, A. (2022). The ethics of AI for information professionals: Eight scenarios. *Journal of the Australian Library and Information Association*, *71*(3), 201–214. doi:10.1080/24750158.2022.2084885

Cox, A. M., Pinfield, S., & Rutter, S. (2019). The intelligent library: Thought leaders' views on the likely impact of artificial intelligence on academic libraries. *Library Hi Tech*, *37*(3), 418–435. doi:10.1108/LHT-08-2018-0105

Crawford, G. A. (1999). Issues for the Digital Library. *Computers in Libraries*, *19*(5), 62–64. https://www.elibrary.ru/item.asp?id=3584440

Creative common attribution license. (n.d.). https://creativecommons.org/share-your-work/cclicenses/

Creswell, J. W. (2014). *Research design: qualitative, quantitative and mixed methods approach* (4th ed.). Sage.

Crook, R. (2005). The role of traditional institutions in political change and development. *Center for Democratic Development/Overseas Development Institute. Policy Brief*, *4*(4), 1–5.

Cumming, K., & Findlay, C. (2010). Digital recordkeeping: Are we at a tipping point? *Records Management Journal*, *20*(3), 265–278. doi:10.1108/09565691011095292

D'silva, D. R. (2022). Emerging technological trends in Library Management and Services during Covid-19 pandemic. *The Journal of Advannes in Library and Information Science.*, *11*(2), 172–180.

Dai, D., Dong, W., Wang, Y., Liu, S., & Zhang, J. (2023). Exploring the relationship between urban residents' emotional changes and built environment before and during the COVID-19 pandemic from the perspective of resilience. *Cities (London, England)*, *141*, 104510. doi:10.1016/j.cities.2023.104510

Daina, N., Sivakumar, A., & Polak, J. W. (2017). Modelling electric vehicles use: A survey on the methods. *Renewable & Sustainable Energy Reviews*, *68*, 447–460. doi:10.1016/j.rser.2016.10.005

Dao, D. V., Ly, H. B., Trinh, S. H., Le, T. T., & Pham, B. T. (2019). Artificial intelligence approaches for prediction of compressive strength of geopolymer concrete. *Materials (Basel)*, *12*(6), 983. doi:10.3390/ma12060983 PMID:30934566

Darley, J. M., & Beniger, J. R. (1981). Diffusion of energy-conserving innovations. *The Journal of Social Issues*, *37*(2), 150–171. doi:10.1111/j.1540-4560.1981.tb02630.x

Dattey, K., Westerheijden, D. F., & Hofman, W. H. A. (2014). Impact of accreditation on public and private universities: A comparative study. *Tertiary Education and Management*, *20*(4), 307–319. doi:10.1080/13583883.2014.959037

Davis, A. (2016). Two Humanistic Communication Theories for Museums, Libraries, and Archives. *ICOFOM study series*, (44), pp. 5–15.

Davis, F. D. (1989). Perceived usefulness, perceived ease of use, and user acceptance of information technology. *Management Information Systems Quarterly*, *13*(3), 319–340. doi:10.2307/249008

Davis, J. L. (2016). Social media. In G. Mazzoleni (Ed.), *The International Encyclopedia of Political Communication, First Editition*. John Wiley & Sons. doi:10.1002/9781118541555.wbiepc004

Dečman, M., & Vintar, M. (2013). A possible solution for digital preservation of e-government: A centralised repository within a cloud computing framework. *Aslib Proceedings*, *65*(4), 406–424. doi:10.1108/AP-05-2012-0049

Dekker, H., Ferrari, A., & Mandal, I. (2022). URI Libraries' AI Lab Evolving to meet the needs of students and research communities. In S. Hervieux & A. Wheatley (Eds.), *The Rise of AI: Implications and Applications for AI in Academic Libraries* (pp. 15–34). Association of College and Research Libraries.

Denton, K. A. (2014). *Exhibiting the Past: Historical Memory and the Politics of Museums in Postsocialist China*. The University of Hawaii Press.

Dewah, P., & Feni-Fete, V. (2014). Issues and prospects of digitizing liberation movements' archives held at the University of Fort Hare, South Africa. *Journal of the South African Society of Archivists*, *47*, 77–88.

Digital Preservation Coalition (DPC). (2017). *Information security*. https://www.dpconline.org/handbook/technical-solutions-and-tools/information-security

Dignum, V. (2018, February 13). *Ethics in artificial intelligence: Introduction to the special issue - ethics and information technology*. SpringerLink. https://link.springer.com/article/10.1007/s10676-018-9450-z

Dimitrijević & Petrović. (2018). *The view on structure and organization - researchgate*. https://www.researchgate.net/publication/342790756_LEISURE_TIME_OF_SCHOOL_CHILDREN_-_THE_VIEW_ON_STRUCTURE_AND_ORGANIZATION

Dipert, B. (1999). Green challenger takes on gas guzzlers. *EDN*, *44*(3), 36–37.

Dollah, W. A. K. W. (2006). *Digital reference services in selected public academic libraries*. Academic Press.

Donkor, A. B., & Afrane, D. A. (2023). Application of AI in Academic Library Services: Prospects and Implications for Quality Service Delivery. In D. Chiu & K. Ho (Eds.), *Emerging Technology-Based Services and Systems in Libraries, Educational Institutions, and Non-Profit Organizations* (pp. 1–25). IGI Global. doi:10.4018/978-1-6684-8671-9.ch001

Duan, L., Shao, X., Wang, Y., Huang, Y., Miao, J., Yang, X., & Zhu, G. (2020). An investigation of the mental health status of children and adolescents in china during the outbreak of COVID-19. *Journal of Affective Disorders*, *275*, 112–118. doi:10.1016/j.jad.2020.06.029 PMID:32658812

Duarte, N., & Vardasca, R. (2023). Literature Review of Accreditation Systems in Higher Education. *Education Sciences*, *13*(6), 582. doi:10.3390/educsci13060582

Du, H., Liu, D., Sovacool, B. K., Wang, Y., Ma, S., & Li, R. Y. M. (2018). Li, RYM Who buys New Energy Vehicles in China? Assessing social-psychological predictors of purchasing awareness, intention, and policy. *Transportation Research Part F: Traffic Psychology and Behaviour, 58*, 56–69. doi:10.1016/j.trf.2018.05.008

Dümcke, C., & Gnedovsky, M. (2013). *The social and economic value of cultural heritage: a literature review.* European Expert Network on Culture.

Duranti, L. (2014). Preservation in the cloud: Towards an international framework for a balance of trust and trustworthiness. *Proceedings of APA/C-DAC International Conference on Digital Preservation and Development of Trusted Digital Repositories, 23–38.*

Duranti, L., & Franks, P. C. (Eds.). (2015). *Encyclopedia of archival science.* Rowman & Littlefield.

Egwunyenga, E. J. (2009). Record keeping in universities: Associated problems and management options in Southwest Geo-Political Zone of Nigeria. *International Journal of Educational Sciences, 1*(2), 109–113. doi:10.1080/09751122.2009.11889983

Elias, J. (2023, February 1). *Jennifer Elias on LinkedIn: Google is asking employees to test potential CHATGPT competitors...* https://www.linkedin.com/posts/jennifer-elias-845b1130_google-is-asking-employees-to-test-potential-activity-7026375314557595648-Fm3V

Eligehausen, R., Popov, E. P., & Bertero, V. V. (1982). *Local bond stress-slip relationships of deformed bars under generalized excitations.* Academic Press.

Elisha, M. J. (2016). The application of information and communication technology (ICT) in Nigerian academic libraries prospects and problems. *The Information Manager, 6*(1 & 2), 2006.

Elkhatat, A. M. (2023, August 1). *Evaluating the authenticity of CHATGPT responses: A study on text-matching capabilities - International Journal for Educational Integrity.* BioMed Central. https://edintegrity.biomedcentral.com/articles/10.1007/s40979-023-00137-0

Elkin, K. (2018). The role of the health sciences librarian in promoting evidence-based practice. *Journal of the Medical Library Association: JMLA, 106*(1), 30–36.

Elzeiny, S., & Qaraqe, M. (2018). Machine learning approaches to automatic stress detection: A review. *2018 IEEE/ACS 15th International Conference on Computer Systems and Applications (AICCSA), 1–6.* 10.1109/AICCSA.2018.8612825

Emiri, O. T. (2015). Digital literacy skills among librarians in university libraries in the 21st century in Edo and Delta states, Nigeria. *International Journal of Library and Information Services, 6*(1), 37–52. doi:10.4018/IJLIS.2017010103

Endler, N. S., Kocovski, N. L., & Macrodimitris, S. D. (2001). Coping, efficacy, and perceived control in acute vs chronic illnesses. *Personality and Individual Differences, 30*(4), 617–625. doi:10.1016/S0191-8869(00)00060-X

Ethical ai: Striking the balance between progress. (2020). https://www.techopedia.com/the-ethical-ai-dilemma-striking-the-balance-between-progress-and-responsibility

EuropeanaTech. (2021). *AI in relation to Glams task Force: Report and Recommendations.* Available at: https://pro.europeana.eu/project/ai-in-relation-to-glams

Eze Asogwa, B. (2012). The challenge of managing electronic records in developing countries: Implications for records managers in sub–Saharan Africa. *Records Management Journal, 22*(3), 198–211. doi:10.1108/09565691211283156

Eze Asogwa, B. (2012). The readiness of universities in managing electronic records: A study of three federal universities in Nigeria. *The Electronic Library, 31*(6), 792–807. doi:10.1108/EL-04-2012-0037

Ezeani, C. (2010). Information and communication technology: an overview. In E. C. Madu & C. N. Ezeani (Eds.), *Modern Library and Information Science for Professionals in Africa*. TextKinks.

Fard & Mahoor. (2022). Ad-corre: Adaptive correlation-based loss for facial expression recognition in the wild. *IEEE Access, 10*(26), 756–768.

Farrokh Ghatte, H. (2020a). Failure mechanisms and cracking performance of T-shaped SCC beam-column connections at top floor: Test results and FE modeling. *Structures, 28*, 1009–1018. doi:10.1016/j.istruc.2020.09.051

Farrokh Ghatte, H. (2020b). External steel ties and CFRP jacketing effects on seismic performance and failure mechanisms of substandard rectangular RC columns. *Composite Structures, 248*, 112542. doi:10.1016/j.compstruct.2020.112542

Farrokh Ghatte, H. (2021). A hybrid of firefly and biogeography-based optimization algorithms for optimal design of steel frames. *Arabian Journal for Science and Engineering, 46*(5), 4703–4717. doi:10.100713369-020-05118-w

Farrokh Ghatte, H., Comert, M., Demir, C., Akbaba, M., & Ilki, A. (2019). Seismic retrofit of full-scale substandard extended rectangular RC columns through CFRP jacketing: Test results and design recommendations. *Journal of Composites for Construction, 23*(1), 04018071. doi:10.1061/(ASCE)CC.1943-5614.0000907

Feather, J., & Sturges, R. P. (2003). *International Encyclopedia of information and Library Science*. Routledge. doi:10.4324/9780203403303

Federer, L. (2018). Defining data librarianship: A survey of competencies, skills, and training. *Journal of the Medical Library Association, 106*(3), 294–303. doi:10.5195/jmla.2018.306 PMID:29962907

Fedus, W., Zoph, B., Shazeer, N., & University, C. (2022, January 1). Switch transformers: Scaling to trillion parameter models with simple and efficient sparsity. *The Journal of Machine Learning Research*. https://dl.acm.org/doi/abs/10.5555/3586589.3586709

Fernandes, J. O., & Singh, B. (2022). Accreditation and ranking of higher education institutions (HEIs): Review, observations and recommendations for the Indian higher education system. *The TQM Journal, 34*(5), 1013–1038. doi:10.1108/TQM-04-2021-0115

Fernandes, S. L., & Bala, G. J. (2016). A Study on Face Recognition Under Facial Expression Variation and Occlusion. *Proceedings of the International Conference on Soft Computing Systems, 371*-377. 10.1007/978-81-322-2671-0_35

Fernando, S., Hall, M., Agirre, E., Soroa, A., Clough, P., & Stevenson, M. (2012). Comparing taxonomies for organizing collections of documents. *Proceedings of COLING 2012, The COLING 2012 Organizing Committee, 879*–894.

Ferreira, C. (2001). *Gene expression programming: a new adaptive algorithm for solving problems*. arXiv preprint cs/0102027.

Ferreira, C. (2006). *Gene expression programming: mathematical modeling by an artificial intelligence* (Vol. 21). Springer. doi:10.1007/3-540-32849-1_2

figshare. (2021, May 17). *Ai Ethics in scholarly communication: STM best practice principles for ethical, trustworthy and human-centric AI*. figshare. https://figshare.com/articles/online_resource/AI_Ethics_in_Scholarly_Communication_STM_Best_Practice_Principles_for_Ethical_Trustworthy_and_Human-centric_AI/14572353

Fitzgerald, S. R., & Jiang, Z. (2020). Scholarly publishing at a crossroads: Scholarly perspectives on open access. *Innovative Higher Education, 45*(6), 457–469. doi:10.100710755-020-09508-8

Flipboard. (2023, January 18). *Microsoft and OpenAI working on CHATGPT-powered Bing in challenge to Google.* Flipboard. https://flipboard.com/article/microsoft-and-openai-working-on-chatgpt-powered-bing-in-challenge-to-google/f-883a32ec69%2Ftheinformation.com

Følstad, A., & Brandtzæg, P. B. (2017). *Chatbots and the New World of HCI.* Interactions. https://dl.acm.org/doi/10.1145/3085558

Frankland, J., & Ray, M. A. (2017). Traditional versus open access scholarly journal publishing: An economic perspective. *Journal of Scholarly Publishing, 49*(1), 5–25. doi:10.3138/jsp.49.1.5

Freiden, J. B. (1984). Advertising spokesperson effects-An examination of endorser type and gender on 2 audiences. *Journal of Advertising Research, 24*(5), 33–41.

FryeB. L. (2022, December 20). Should using an AI text generator to produce academic writing be plagiarism? SSRN. https://papers.ssrn.com/sol3/papers.cfm?abstract_id=4292283

Fütterer, T., Fischer, C., Alekseeva, A., Chen, X., Tate, T., Warschauer, M., & Gerjets, P. (2023). *ChatGPT in education: Global reactions to AI Innovations.* Scientific reports. https://pubmed.ncbi.nlm.nih.gov/37714915/

Fütterer, T., Fischer, C., Alekseeva, A., Chen, X., Tate, T., Warschauer, M., & Gerjets, P. (2023, September 15). *ChatGPT in education: Global reactions to AI Innovations.* Nature News. https://www.nature.com/articles/s41598-023-42227-6

Future of Life Institute. (2021). *Artificial Intelligence (AI) in decision making.* COPE: Committee on Publication Ethics. https://publicationethics.org/resources/discussion-documents/ai-artifical-intelligence-decision-making

Gandhi, M. (2013). International initiatives in assessment of quality and accreditation in higher education. *International Journal of Educational Planning and Administration, 3*(2), 121–138.

GaoT.FischA.ChenD. (2021, June 2). *Making pre-trained language models better few-shot learners.* doi:10.18653/v1/2021.acl-long.295

Gärling, A., & Thøgersen, J. (2001). Marketing of electric vehicles. *Business Strategy and the Environment, 10*(1), 53–65. doi:10.1002/1099-0836(200101/02)10:1<53::AID-BSE270>3.0.CO;2-E

Gashi, D. (2022). The relationship between big five personality traits, coping strategies, and emotional problems through the COVID-19 pandemic. *Current Psychology (New Brunswick, N.J.),* 1–10. PMID:36406846

Gaur, R. C. (2003). Rethinking the Indian digital divide: The present state of digitization in Indian management libraries. *The International Information & Library Review, 35*(2-4), 189–203. doi:10.1080/10572317.2003.10762600

Gbaje, E. S. (2007). *Digitization and its Challenges: Digital records and archival management workshop for members, federal capital territory, Abuja, Archives History Bureau Committee and Laison Officers.* Arewa House Kaduna.

Geda, A. F. (2021). The role of medical library in information seeking behaviour of health professionals: A review of the literature. *Journal of Hospital Librarianship, 21*(4), 405–416. doi:10.1080/15323269.2021.1982263

Gehlert, T., Dziekan, K., & Gärling, T. (2013). Psychology of sustainable travel behavior. *Transportation Research Part A, Policy and Practice, 48,* 19–24. doi:10.1016/j.tra.2012.10.001

Geng, Y., & Maimaituerxun, M. (2022). Research progress of green marketing in sustainable consumption based on CiteSpace analysis. *SAGE Open, 12*(3), 21582440221119835. doi:10.1177/21582440221119835

Georgali, B., & Tsakiridis, P. E. (2005). Microstructure of fire-damaged concrete. A case study. *Cement and Concrete Composites, 27*(2), 255–259. doi:10.1016/j.cemconcomp.2004.02.022

Gewin, V. (2016). Data sharing: An open mind on open data. *Nature, 529*(7584), 117–119. doi:10.1038/nj7584-117a PMID:26744755

Ghasemi, S., Akbar Maghsoudi, A., Akbarzadeh Bengar, H., & Reza Ronagh, H. (2016). Sagging and hogging strengthening of continuous unbonded posttensioned HSC beams by NSM and EBR. *Journal of Composites for Construction, 20*(2), 04015056. doi:10.1061/(ASCE)CC.1943-5614.0000621

Gholizadeh, S., Hassanzadeh, A., Milany, A., & Ghatte, H. F. (2022). On the seismic collapse capacity of optimally designed steel braced frames. *Engineering with Computers, 38*(2), 1–13. doi:10.100700366-020-01096-7

Gibson, H., Morris, A., & Cleeve, M. (2007). *Links Between Libraries and Museums: Investigating Museum-Library Collaboration in England and the USA*. De Gruyter.

Giersch, S., Klotz, E. A., McMartin, F., Muramatsu, B., Renninger, K., Shumar, W., & Weimar, S. A. (2004). If you build it, will they come? Participant involvement in digital libraries. *D-Lib Magazine : the Magazine of the Digital Library Forum, 10*(7-8). Advance online publication. doi:10.1045/july2004-giersch

Gilal, F. G., Paul, J., Gilal, N. G., & Gilal, R. G. (2020). Celebrity endorsement and brand passion among air travelers: Theory and evidence. *International Journal of Hospitality Management, 85*, 102347. doi:10.1016/j.ijhm.2019.102347

Gilster, P. (1997). *Digital literacy*. John Wiley.

Given, L. M., & McTavish, L. (2010). What is old is new again: The re-convergence of libraries, archives, and museums in the digital age. *The Library Quarterly, 80*(1), 7–32. doi:10.1086/648461

Godara, M., Everaert, J., Sanchez-Lopez, A., Joormann, J., & De Raedt, R. (2023). Interplay between uncertainty intolerance, emotion regulation, cognitive flexibility, and psychopathology during the COVID-19 pandemic: A multi-wave study. *Scientific Reports, 13*(1), 9854. doi:10.103841598-023-36211-3 PMID:37330557

Goldsmith, R. E., & Hofacker, C. F. (1991). Measuring consumer innovativeness. *Journal of the Academy of Marketing Science, 19*(3), 209–221. doi:10.1007/BF02726497

Gopinath, M. (1985). Information technology and its impact on information retrieval systems. *Library Science with a Slant to Documentation, 22*(4), 237–251. http://library.isical.ac.in:8080/jspui/bitstream/10263/1108/1/LSWASTD-22-4-1985-P237-251.pdf

Gorman, M. (1979). On Doing Away with Technical Service Departments. *American Libraries, 10*(7), 435–437.

Gorman, P., Ash, J., Lavelle, M., Lyman, J., Delcambre, L., Maier, D., & Bowers, S. (2000). Bundles in the wild: Managing information to solve problems and maintain situation awareness. *Library Trends, 49*(2), 266–289.

Government of India. (1950). *The Report of the University Education Commission (December 1948–August 1949)*. https://indianculture.gov.in/reports-proceedings/report-university-education-commission-december-1948-august-1949-vol-i

Government of India. (1967). *Report of the Education Commission (1964-66)*. https://indianculture.gov.in/reports-proceedings/report-education-commission-1964-66

Government of India. (1986). *National Policy on Library and Information System: A presentation 1985-1986*. Government of India.

Grant, N., & Metz, C. (2022, December 21). A new chatbot is a "code red" for Google's search business. *The New York Times*. https://www.nytimes.com/2022/12/21/technology/ai-chatgpt-google-search.html

Grbin, L., Nichols, P., Russell, F., Fuller-Tyszkiewicz, M., & Olsson, C. A. (2022). The development of a living knowledge system and implications for future systematic searching. *Journal of the Australian Library and Information Association*, *71*(3), 275–292. doi:10.1080/24750158.2022.2087954

Green, A. M. (2022). Metadata Application Profiles in US Academic Libraries: A Document Analysis. *Journal of Library Metadata*, *21*(3-4), 105–143. doi:10.1080/19386389.2022.2030172

Groenewald, R., & Breytenbach, A. (2011). The use of metadata and preservation methods for continuous access to digital data. *The Electronic Library*, *29*(2), 236–248. doi:10.1108/02640471111125195

Guédon, J.-C. (2004). The "green" and "gold" roads to open access: The case for mixing and matching. *Serials Review*, *30*(4), 315–328. doi:10.1016/j.serrev.2004.09.005

Gulati, A. (2004). Use of information and communication technology in libraries and information centres: An Indian scenario. *The Electronic Library*, *22*(4), 335–350. doi:10.1108/02640470410552974

Gulzari, A., Wang, Y., & Prybutok, V. (2022). A green experience with eco-friendly cars: A young consumer electric vehicle rental behavioral model. *Journal of Retailing and Consumer Services*, *65*, 102877. doi:10.1016/j.jretconser.2021.102877

Gupta, N. E., Kumar, K., & Sinha, K. (2023). The Nexus of War, Violence, and Rights: A History of War-Torn Afghanistan. In Handbook of Research on War Policies, Strategies, and Cyber Wars (pp. 334-351). IGI Global.

Gupta, V., & Pandey, S. R. (2019). Recommender systems for digital libraries: a review of concepts and concerns. *Library Philosophy and Practice (e-journal),* 1-10. https://digitalcommons.unl.edu/libphilprac/2417

Gurbuz, T., Cengiz, A., Kolemenoglu, S., Demir, C., & Ilki, A. (2023). Damages and failures of structures in Izmir (Turkey) during the October 30, 2020 Aegean Sea earthquake. *Journal of Earthquake Engineering*, *27*(6), 1565–1606. doi:10.1080/13632469.2022.2086186

Guszkowska, M., & Dąbrowska-Zimakowska, A. (2022). Coping with stress during the second wave of the COVID-19 pandemic by Polish university students: Strategies, structure, and relation to psychological well-being. *Psychology Research and Behavior Management*, *15*, 339–352. doi:10.2147/PRBM.S345648 PMID:35210882

Güzel, Â., Mutlu, N. L., & Molendijk, M. (2023). COVID-19-related changes in eating disorder pathology, emotional and binge eating and need for care: A systematic review with frequentist and Bayesian meta-analyses. *Eating and Weight Disorders*, *28*(1), 19. doi:10.100740519-023-01547-2 PMID:36805344

Hadi, A. S., & Hendrawan, M. R. (2022). Analisis Penerapan Konsep Konvergensi Institusi Memori Pada Perpustakaan Proklamator Bung Karno. In I. W. P. Yasa, R. A. G. Purnawibawa, & M. Idris (Eds.), *Strategi Penguatan Nilai-Nilai Kearifan Lokal di Era Surplus Informasi*. Lakeisha.

Hadi, M. N., & Widiarsa, I. B. R. (2012). Axial and flexural performance of square RC columns wrapped with CFRP under eccentric loading. *Journal of Composites for Construction*, *16*(6), 640–649. doi:10.1061/(ASCE)CC.1943-5614.0000301

Hagger, M. S., Keech, J. J., & Hamilton, K. (2020). Managing stress during the coronavirus disease 2019 pandemic and beyond: Reappraisal and mindset approaches. *Stress and Health*, *36*(3), 396–401. doi:10.1002mi.2969 PMID:32588961

Hair, J. F., Hult, G. T. M., Ringle, C. M., & Sarstedt, M. (2022). *A Primer on Partial Least Squares Structural Equation Modeling (PLS-SEM)* (3rd ed.). Sage.

Hair, J. F., Risher, J. J., Sarstedt, M., & Ringle, C. M. (2019). When to use and how to report the results of PLS-SEM. *European Business Review*, *31*(1), 2–24. doi:10.1108/EBR-11-2018-0203

Hall, M. M., & Walsh, D. (2021). *Exploring digital cultural heritage through browsing.* Information and Knowledge Organisation in Digital Humanities. doi:10.4324/9781003131816-13

Hanh, N. D. (2020). A review of issues of quality assurance and quality accreditation for higher education institutions and the situation in Vietnam. *Accreditation and Quality Assurance*, 25(4), 273–279. doi:10.100700769-020-01439-3

Hanh, N. D., Nga, N. T. M., Loan, V. Q., & Viet, N. M. (2019). Role of quality assurance and quality accreditation in higher education in some developing countries and Vietnam. *American Journal of Educational Research*, 7(9), 649–653. https://pubs.sciepub.com/education/7/9/8/

Han, Q., Gui, C., Xu, J., & Lacidogna, G. (2019). A generalized method to predict the compressive strength of high-performance concrete by improved random forest algorithm. *Construction & Building Materials*, 226, 734–742. doi:10.1016/j.conbuildmat.2019.07.315

Hård, M., & Knie, A. (2001). The cultural dimension of technology management: Lessons from the history of the automobile. *Technology Analysis and Strategic Management*, 13(1), 91–103. doi:10.1080/09537320120040464

Hariri, N., & Norouzi, Y. (2011). Determining evaluation criteria for digital libraries' user interface: A review. *The Electronic Library*, 29(5), 698–722. doi:10.1108/02640471111177116

Harms, S., & Truffer, B. (1998). *The emergence of a nation-wide carsharing co-operative in Switzerland. A case-study for the EC-supported rsearch project "Strategic Niche Management as a tool for transition to a sustainable transport system".* EAWAG.

Harnad, S. (1994). *A subversive proposal.* https://groups.google.com/g/bit.listserv.vpiej-l/c/BoKENhK0_00

Hastie, T., Tibshirani, R., Friedman, J. H., & Friedman, J. H. (2009). The elements of statistical learning: data mining, inference, and prediction (Vol. 2). Springer. https://doi.org/ doi:10.1007/978-0-387-21606-5

Hawkins, D. (2020). *Consumer behavior: Building marketing strategy.* Academic Press.

Heatherfield, S. M. (2021). *What is resistance to change. Definitions and examples of resistance to change.* The Balance Careers. https://www.thebalancecareers.com/what-isresistance-to-change-1918240[Accessed 21 October 2023] https://dspace.unza.zm/handle/123456789/5509

Heath, F., Kyrillidou, M., Webster, D., Choudhury, S., Hobbs, B., Lorie, M., & Flores, N. (2003). Emerging Tools for Evaluating Digital Library Services: Conceptual Adaptations of LibQUAL+ and CAPM. *Journal of Digital Information*, 4(2). http://jhir.library.jhu.edu/handle/1774.2/32792

Heck, T., Tunger, D., & Rittberger, M. (2023). Scholarly Communication over a Decade of Publications. *Publications / MDPI*, 11(16), 16. doi:10.3390/publications11010016

Hendrawan, M. R., & Bafadhal, A. S. (2021). Cutting-Edge Technologies in Cultural Heritage Preservation Through Virtual Museum in the Phygital Era. In Globalisation of Cultural Heritage: Issues, Impacts, and Challenges. Kuala Nerus: Universiti Malaysia Trengganu Press.

Hendrawan, M. R., & Bafadhal, A. S. (2022). Virtual Museum. In D. Buhalis (Ed.), *Encyclopedia of Tourism Management and Marketing.* Edward Elgar Publishing. doi:10.4337/9781800377486.virtual.museum

Hendrawan, M. R., & Ulum, M. C. (2017). *Pengantar Kearsipan: Dari Isu Kebijakan ke Manajemen.* Universitas Brawijaya Press.

Heradio, R., Fernández-Amorós, D., Cabrerizo, F. J., & Herrera-Viedma, E. (2012). A review of quality evaluation of digital libraries based on users' perceptions. *Journal of Information Science*, 38(3), 269–283. doi:10.1177/0165551512438359

Hernon, P., & Young, J. (2017). The role of libraries in providing access to the latest research and information in healthcare. *Journal of the Medical Library Association: JMLA*, *105*(4), 233–240.

Hervieux, S., & Wheatley, A. (2021). Perceptions of artificial intelligence: A survey of academic librarians in Canada and the United States. *Journal of Academic Librarianship*, *47*(1), 102270. doi:10.1016/j.acalib.2020.102270

Hervieux, S., & Wheatley, A. (Eds.). (2022). *The Rise of AI: Implications and Applications of Artificial Intelligence in Academic Libraries*. Association of College and Research Libraries.

Heshmati, S., DavyRomano, E., Chow, C., Doan, S. N., & Reynolds, K. D. (2023). Negative emodiversity is associated with emotional eating in adolescents: An examination of emotion dynamics in daily life. *Journal of Adolescence*, *95*(1), 115–130. doi:10.1002/jad.12103 PMID:36217272

Higgins, S. (2013). Digital Curation: The Challenge Driving Convergence across Memory Institutions. In L. Duranti, & E. Shaffer (Eds.), The Memory of the World in the Digital Age: Digitization and Preservation: An international conference on permanent access to digital documentary heritage, Vancouver, Canada, 26-28 September 2012 (pp. 607–623). United Nations Educational, Scientific and Cultural Organization (UNESCO).

Hindu, A., & Bhowmik, B. (2022). An iot-enabled stress detection scheme using facial expression. *2022 IEEE 19th India Council International Conference (INDICON)*, 1-6. 10.1109/INDICON56171.2022.10040216

Holland, B. J. (2023, January 1). *CHATGPT 3.5 and 4: Its ramifications on librarianship, academia, education, publishing, and the Workplace*. IGI Global. https://www.igi-global.com/chapter/chatgpt-35-and-4/325030

Holland, J. H. (1992). Genetic algorithms. *Scientific American*, *267*(1), 66–73. doi:10.1038cientificamerican0792-66

Hong, J. Y. (2020). *From Marketing to Digital Marketing: Paradigm Shift and New Dilemma*. Academic Press.

Horakeri, M. D. (2011). *Growth and development of college libraries in the electronic environment a study of impact of quality awareness and competence building measures* [Doctoral dissertation, Karnatak University]. Karnatak University, Dharwad. http://hdl.handle.net/10603/95581

HorbachH. M. (2023, May 18). *Fighting reviewer fatigue or amplifying bias? considerations and recommendations for the use of CHATGPT and other large language models in scholarly peer review*. https://pubmed.ncbi.nlm.nih.gov/36865238/

Horbach, S. P. J. M., & Halffman, W. (2018). The changing forms and expectations of peer review. *Research Integrity and Peer Review*, *3*(1), 8. Advance online publication. doi:10.118641073-018-0051-5 PMID:30250752

Horiuchi, S., Tsuda, A., Aoki, S., Yoneda, K., & Sawaguchi, Y. (2018). Coping as a mediator of the relationship between stress mindset and psychological stress response: A pilot study. *Psychology Research and Behavior Management*, *11*, 47–54. doi:10.2147/PRBM.S150400 PMID:29535562

Horton, D., & Wohl, R. R. (1956). Mass Communication and Para-Social Interaction. *Psychiatry*, *2747*(March), 215–229. Advance online publication. doi:10.1080/00332747.1956.11023049 PMID:13359569

Hoyer, W. D., & MacInnis, D. J. (1997). *Consumer Behaviour*.

Hu, Y., Li, W., & Wright, D. (2019). Artificial intelligence approaches. In The Geographic Information Science & Technology Body of Knowledge, 3rd Quarter 2019 ed. (pp. 1-12). doi:10.22224/gistbok/2019.3.4

Huang, Y. H. (2022). Exploring the implementation of artificial intelligence applications among academic libraries in Taiwan. *Library Hi Tech*. doi:10.1108/LHT-03-2022-0159

Huang, C.-L., & Huang, Y.-M. (1997). Facial expression recognition using model-based feature extraction and action parameters classification. *Journal of Visual Communication and Image Representation*, 8(3), 278–290. doi:10.1006/jvci.1997.0359

Huebschmann, N. A., & Sheets, E. S. (2020). The right mindset: Stress mindset moderates the association between perceived stress and depressive symptoms. *Anxiety, Stress, and Coping*, 33(3), 248–255. doi:10.1080/10615806.2020.1736900 PMID:32138538

IFLA. (2016). *IFLA Trend Report 2016 Update*. IFLA. https://trends.ifla.org/update-2016

Igwebuike, E. & Onoh, E. I(2022). Availability and Use of Digital Reference Service Tools for Effective Internet Research. *Electronic Networking Applications and Policy, 5*(1), 56-63.

Igwebuike, E., & Onoh, E. I. (2022). Availability and Use of Digital Reference Service Tools for Effective Service Delivery by Librarians in Private Universities Libraries in South-East Nigeria. *Library Philosophy and Practice (e-journal). 7105.* https://digitalcommons.unl.edu/libphilprac/7105

Ihuah, P. W., & Eaton, D. (2013). The pragmatic research approach: A framework for sustainable management of public housing estates in Nigeria. *Journal of US-China Public Administration*, 10(10), 933–944.

International Data Corporation. (2018). *Document processes survey: resistance to digital change. Institutional repositories*. Winston.

International open access week. (n.d.). International Open Access Week. https://www.openaccessweek.org/

International Records Management Trust (IRMT). (2009). *Preserving electronic records: Training in electronic records management*. Module 4. http://www.irmt.org/documents/educ_training/term%20modules/IRMT%204.pdf

Iqbal, M. F., Liu, Q. F., Azim, I., Zhu, X., Yang, J., Javed, M. F., & Rauf, M. (2020). Prediction of mechanical properties of green concrete incorporating waste foundry sand based on gene expression programming. *Journal of Hazardous Materials*, 384, 121322. doi:10.1016/j.jhazmat.2019.121322 PMID:31604206

Irizarry-Nones, A., Palepu, A., & Wallace, M. (2017). *Artificial intelligence (AI)*. Boston University. Available at https://www.bu.edu/lernet/artemis/years/2017/projects/FinalPresenations/A.I.%20Presentation.pdf

ISO 15489-1. (2001). *Information and documentation –Records Management-Part 1: General*. International Organization for Standardization.

ISO/IEC 15816. (2002). *Information technology- techniques –security information objects for access control*. International Organization for Standardization.

Ivanchev, J., Litescu, S. C., Zehe, D., Lees, M., Aydt, H., & Knoll, A. (2018, November). Hard and Soft Closing of Roads Towards Socially Optimal Routing. In *2018 21st International Conference on Intelligent Transportation Systems (ITSC)* (pp. 3499-3504). IEEE. 10.1109/ITSC.2018.8569694

Jabir, I. I. N. (2008). Virtual (Electronic) reference services in academic libraries. *J. Of College Of Education for Women*, 19(2).

Jablonski, R. A., Smeby, J. C., & Rydland, J. (2021). The role of libraries in providing support for nursing education and research in healthcare. *Journal of the Medical Library Association: JMLA*, 109(1), 12–20.

Jacknis, N. (2017). *The AI-Enhanced Library*. Available at: https://norman-jacknis.medium.com/the-ai-enhanced-library-a34d96fffdfe

Jain, P. K. (2003). Indian council of social science research (ICSSR) maintained research institutes' libraries in India: Towards digitization and networking. *The International Information & Library Review, 35*(2-4), 217–232. doi:10.108 0/10572317.2003.10762602

Jaiswal, G., & Sinha, K. (2023). Yoga: An Ancient Healing Approach for Cyclical Mastalgia. In Perspectives on Coping Strategies for Menstrual and Premenstrual Distress (pp. 237-261). IGI Global.

Jaiswal, G., Karmakar, M., & Sinha, K. (2023). Yoga: A Stress Removal Toolkit During War From the Women's Perspective. In Acceleration of the Biopsychosocial Model in Public Health (pp. 137-167). IGI Global.

Jan, S. (2018). Digital reference services in the information and communication technology (ICT) based environment: A study. *Library Philosophy and Practice (e-journal).*

Jane, J., Carter, D., & Memmott, P. (1999). Digital reference services in academic libraries. *Reference and User Services Quarterly, 39*(2), 145–150.

Janes, J., Carter, D., & Memmott, P. (1999). Digital Reference Services in Academic Libraries. *Reference and User Services Quarterly, 39*(2), 145–150. https://www.jstor.org/stable/20863724

Jange, S. (2022). NAAC accreditation and academic libraries: librarians' role beyond librarianship. *Journal of Indian Library Association, 57*(4), 12-23. https://www.ilaindia.net/jila/index.php/jila/article/view/1295

Javed, M. F., Amin, M. N., Shah, M. I., Khan, K., Iftikhar, B., Farooq, F., Aslam, F., Alyousef, R., & Alabduljabbar, H. (2020). Applications of gene expression programming and regression techniques for estimating compressive strength of bagasse ash based concrete. *Crystals, 10*(9), 737. doi:10.3390/cryst10090737

Jensen, M. (1997). *Benzin i blodet: Kvalitativ del; foto: Sonja Iskov.* Miljø-og Energiministeriet, Danmarks Miljøundersøgelser.

Jogin, M., Madhulika, M. S., Divya, G. D., Meghana, R. K., & Apoorva, S. (2018). Feature Extraction using Convolution Neural Networks (CNN) and Deep Learning. *2018 3rd IEEE International Conference on Recent Trends in Electronics, Information & Communication Technology (RTEICT).*

Johare, R., & Masrek, M. N. (2011). Malaysian archival heritage at risk? A survey of archivists' knowledge and skills in managing electronic records. *Library Review, 60*(8), 685–711. doi:10.1108/00242531111166719

Johnson, L., Becker, S. A., Estrada, V., & Freeman, A. (2015). *NMC horizon report: 2015 library edition.* The New Media Consortium. https://www.learntechlib.org/p/151822/

Jose, A., & Raina, R. L. (2005). Networked Digital Libraries (NDLS) for IIMS: A conceptual model. *Herald of Library Science, 44*(1-2), 44–48.

Joseph, H. (2013). The open access movement grows up: Taking stock of a revolution. *PLoS Biology, 11*(10), 1–3. doi:10.1371/journal.pbio.1001686 PMID:24167444

Kabir, A. M. (2021). Implementation and Use of Virtual Reference Services in Academic Libraries during and post COVID-19 Pandemic: A Necessity for Developing Countries). *Library Philosophy and Practice (e-journal), 4951.*

Kadir, W. A., Dollah, W., & Singh, D. (2015). *Digital reference services in academic libraries.* The University of Malaya Press.

Kahanwal, D. B., & Singh, D. T. P. (2013). *Towards the framework of information security.* https://arxiv.org/pdf/1312.1460

Kahn, R., & Wilensky, R. (1995). *A framework for distributed digital object service.* Accessed on 31-10-2022. www.cnri.reston.va.us/k-w.html

Kahn, R., & Wilensky, R. (2006). A framework for distributed digital object services. *International Journal on Digital Libraries*, *6*(2), 115–123. doi:10.100700799-005-0128-x

Kalas, M. S., & Momin, B. (2016). Stress detection and reduction using eeg signals. *2016 International Conference on Electrical, Electronics, and Optimization Techniques (ICEEOT)*, 471–475. 10.1109/ICEEOT.2016.7755604

Kannan, P. K., & Li, H. A. (2017). Digital marketing A framework, review and research agenda. *International Journal of Research in Marketing*, *34*(1), 22–45. doi:10.1016/j.ijresmar.2016.11.006

Karabinis, A. I., Rousakis, T. C., & Manolitsi, G. E. (2008). 3D finite-element analysis of substandard RC columns strengthened by fiber-reinforced polymer sheets. *Journal of Composites for Construction*, *12*(5), 531–540. doi:10.1061/(ASCE)1090-0268(2008)12:5(531)

Karisiddappa, C. R. (1996). *Preparing Academic libraries for the 21st Century*. Keynote address at workshop held at Manipal, India.

Karmakar, M., Priya, A., Sinha, K., & Verma, M. (2022, December). Shrinkable Cryptographic Technique Using Involutory Function for Image Encryption. In *International Conference on Advanced Network Technologies and Intelligent Computing* (pp. 275-289). Cham: Springer Nature Switzerland.

Karmakar, M., Priya, A., Sinha, K., & Verma, M. (2022, December). Shrinkable Cryptographic Technique Using Involutory Function for Image Encryption. In *International Conference on Advanced Network Technologies and Intelligent Computing* (pp. 275-289). Springer Nature Switzerland.

Karpf, D. (2023, January 4). Money will kill Chatgpt's magic. *The Atlantic*. https://www.theatlantic.com/technology/archive/2022/12/chatgpt-aichatbots-openai-cost-regulations/672539

Katre, D. (2011). Digital preservation: Converging and diverging factors of libraries, archives, and museums–an Indian perspective. *IFLA Journal*, *37*(3), 195–203. doi:10.1177/0340035211418728

Kaur, B., Gangwar, V. P., & Dash, G. (2022). Green marketing strategies, environmental attitude, and green buying intention: A multi-group analysis in an emerging economy context. *Sustainability (Basel)*, *14*(10), 6107. doi:10.3390u14106107

Kaushal, V., & Yadav, R. (2022). The role of chatbots in academic libraries: An experience-based perspective. *Journal of the Australian Library and Information Association*, *71*(3), 215–232. doi:10.1080/24750158.2022.2106403

Kazim, E., Koshiyama, A. S., Hilliard, A., & Polle, R. (2021, September 17). Systematizing audit in Algorithmic Recruitment. *Journal of Intelligence*. https://www.ncbi.nlm.nih.gov/pmc/articles/PMC8482073/

Kellam, L. M., & Thompson, K. (2016). *Databrarianship: The academic data librarian in theory and practice*. Association of College and Research Libraries. https://cir.nii.ac.jp/crid/1130282271743223040

Kemoni, H., & Ngulube, P. (2008). Relationship between records management, public service delivery and the attainment of the United Nations Millennium Development Goals in Kenya. *Information Development*, *24*(4), 296–306. doi:10.1177/0266666908098074

Kemoni, H., & Wamukoya, J. (2000). Preparing for the management of electronic records at Moi University, Kenya: A case study. *African Journal of Library Archives and Information Science*, *10*(2), 125–138.

Kemp, R., & Arundel, A. (1998). *Survey indicators for environmental innovation*. Academic Press.

Kemp, R., Schot, J., & Hoogma, R. (1998). Regime shifts to sustainability through processes of niche formation: The approach of strategic niche management. *Technology Analysis and Strategic Management*, *10*(2), 175–198. doi:10.1080/09537329808524310

Kent, D. C., & Park, R. (1971). Flexural members with confined concrete. *Journal of the Structural Division, 97*(7), 1969–1990. doi:10.1061/JSDEAG.0002957

Khan, A., Masrek, M. N., Mahmood, K., & Qutab, S. (2017). Factors influencing the adoption of digital reference services among the university librarians in Pakistan. *The Electronic Library, 35*(6), 1225–1246. doi:10.1108/EL-05-2016-0112

Khan, S. A., & Bhatti, R. (2017). Digital competencies for developing and managing digital libraries: An investigation from university librarians in Pakistan. *The Electronic Library, 35*(3), 573–597. doi:10.1108/EL-06-2016-0133

Khan, S. K., Rukhsar, A., & Shoaib, M. (2016). Influence of Celebrity Endorsement on Consumer Purchase Intention. IOSR Journal of Business and Management. *18*(1), 2319–7668. doi:10.9790/ 487X-18110609

Khare, V. K., Raghuwanshi, S., Vashisht, A., Verma, P., & Chauhan, R. (2023). The importance of green management and its implication in creating sustainability performance on the small-scale industries in India. *Journal of Law and Sustainable Development, 11*(5), e699–e699. doi:10.55908dgs.v11i5.699

Kharisma, A. B. (2023). Lebih Dekat dengan UPT Perpustakaan Proklamator Bung Karno. Blitar: Perpustakaan Nasional Republik Indonesia: UPT Perpustakaan Proklamator Bung Karno.

Khobragade, A. D., & Lihitkar, S. R. (2016). Evaluation of virtual reference services provided by IIT libraries: A survey. *DESIDOC Journal of Library and Information Technology, 36*(1), 23–28. doi:10.14429/djlit.36.1.9150

Khoo, C., Singh, D., & Chaudhry, A. S. (2006). Malaysia: A case study. In C. Khoo, D. Singh & A.S. Chaudhry (Eds.), *Proceedings of the Asia-Pacific Conference on Library & Information Education & Practice 2006 (A-LIEP 2006), Singapore, 3-6 April 2006* (pp. 122-135). Singapore: School of Communication & Information, Nanyang Technological University.

Kibirige, H. M. (1988). Computer—Assisted Reference Services: What the Computer Will Not Do. *RQ*, 377-383.

Kim, H., Ko, E., & Kim, J. (2015). SNS users' para-social relationships with celebrities: Social media effects on purchase intentions. *Journal of Global Scholars of Marketing Science, 25*(3), 279–294. doi:10.1080/21639159.2015.1043690

Kitchenham, B., Brereton, O. P., Budgen, D., Turner, M., Bailey, J., & Linkman, S. (2009). Systematic literature reviews in software engineering–a systematic literature review. *Information and Software Technology, 51*(1), 7–15. doi:10.1016/j.infsof.2008.09.009

Klareld, A. S. (2015). The "middle archive" exploring the practical and theoretical implications of a new concept in Sweden. *Records Management Journal, 25*(2), 149–165. doi:10.1108/RMJ-12-2014-0047

Knie, K., Faestermann, T., & Korschinek, G. (1997). AMS at the Munich gas-filled analyzing magnet system GAMS. *Nuclear Instruments & Methods in Physics Research. Section B, Beam Interactions with Materials and Atoms, 123*(1-4), 128–131. doi:10.1016/S0168-583X(96)00753-7

Knoll, J., Schramm, H., Schallhorn, C., & Wynistorf, S. (2015). *International Journal of Advertising: The Review of Marketing Communications Good guy vs. bad guy: the influence of para-social interactions with media characters on brand placement effects.* doi:10.1080/02650487.2015.1009350

Knuttel, H., Krause, E., Semmler-Schmetz, M., Reimann, I., & Metzendorf, M.-I. (2020). Helath Science Libraries in Germany: New directions. *Health Information and Libraries Journal, 37*(1), 83–88. doi:10.1111/hir.12299 PMID:32096587

Kodhai, E., Pooveswari, A., Sharmila, P., & Ramiya, N. (2020). Literature Review on Emotion Recognition System. *2020 International Conference on System, Computation, Automation and Networking (ICSCAN).*

Kodur, V. K. R., & Agrawal, A. (2017). Effect of temperature induced bond degradation on fire response of reinforced concrete beams. *Engineering Structures*, *142*, 98–109. doi:10.1016/j.engstruct.2017.03.022

Kohli, N. (2014). Role of accreditation in engineering education. In *2014 IEEE International Conference on MOOC, Innovation and Technology in Education (MITE)* (pp. 157-159). IEEE. 10.1109/MITE.2014.7020261

Koppad, P. B., & Mulimani, M. N. (2021). Digital Information Literacy among users of R.T.E. Society's Arts, Science and Commerce College Library Ranebennur: A Case Study. *Journal of Education: Rabindra Bharati University*, *23*(9I), 96–100.

Kotler, P. (1991). *Marketing Management. Analysis, Planning, Implementation, and Control* (7th ed.). Prentice-Hall.

Kotur, M. B., & Mulimani, M. N. (2019). Digital Library Resources for the Users: An Overview. *Journal of Advancements in Library Sciences*, *6*(1), 111–114. https://sciencejournals.stmjournals.in/index.php/JoALS/article/view/1743

Koza, J. R. (1994). Genetic programming as a means for programming computers by natural selection. *Statistics and Computing*, *4*(2), 87–112. doi:10.1007/BF00175355

Krishnamurthy, C. (2004). Emerging Digital Libraries: Pro's and Con's. In *4th ASSIST National Seminar on Digital Resources and Services in Libraries* (pp. 1-11). Department of Library Information Science, Kuvempu University. https://rb.gy/lx710

Krishnamurthy, C., & Awari, V. H. (2012). Digital Reference Service: A Tool to Expand Horizons of Library Services. *Contemporary Research in India: A Peer Reviewed Multi-Disciplinary Research in India, 2*(3). https://rb.gy/vnfw9

Krishnamurthy, C., & Shettappanavar, L. (2019). Digital literacy among female postgraduate students of Karnatak University, Dharwad, Karnataka, India: A study. *Library Philosophy and Practice (e-journal),* 1-16. https://digitalcommons.unl.edu/libphilprac/2934

Krishnamurthy, M. (2002). Digital Library Gateway for Library and Information Science: A Study. *SRELS Journal of Information Management, 39*(3), 245-254. https://www.srels.org/index.php/sjim/article/view/48887

Krishnamurthy, M. (2004). Digital Library: An overview. *SRELS Journal of Information Management, 41*(4), 317-326. https://www.srels.org/index.php/sjim/article/view/44498

Król, K. (2021). Assessment of the cultural heritage potential in Poland. *Sustainability (Basel), 13*(12), 6637. doi:10.3390u13126637

Külcü, Ö. (2009). Records management practices in universities: A comparative study of examples in Canada and Turkey. *Canadian Journal of Information and Library Science, 33*(2).

Kumar, K., Singhania, D., Singh, K. P., Mishra, P., & Sinha, K. (2023). Navigating the Economic Challenges of the Russia-Ukraine Conflict on India. In Handbook of Research on War Policies, Strategies, and Cyber Wars (pp. 218-238). IGI Global. doi:10.4018/978-1-6684-6741-1.ch012

Kumar, P., Shukla, B., & Passey, D. (2020). Impact of accreditation on quality and excellence of higher education institutions. *Revista Investigacion Operacional, 41*(2), 151-167. https://eprints.lancs.ac.uk/id/eprint/141916

Kumar, S., Jaiswal, G., & Sinha, K. (2023). Skin Cancer Lesion Detection Using Improved CNN Techniques. In Handbook of Research on Technological Advances of Library and Information Science in Industry 5.0 (pp. 355-377). IGI Global.

Kumar, A., Gawande, A., & Raibagkar, S. (2022). Quality complacency in Indian higher education institutions between the second and third cycles of accreditation. *Quality Assurance in Education*, *30*(4), 431–445. doi:10.1108/QAE-01-2022-0019

Kurani, K. S., Turrentine, T., & Sperling, D. (1996). Testing electric vehicle demand in 'hybrid households' using a reflexive survey. *Transportation Research Part D, Transport and Environment, 1*(2), 131–150. doi:10.1016/S1361-9209(96)00007-7

Kurani, K., Sperling, D., & Turrentine, T. (1996, January). The marketability of electric vehicles: battery performance and consumer demand for driving range. In *Proceedings of 11th Annual Battery Conference on Applications and Advances* (pp. 153-158). IEEE. 10.1109/BCAA.1996.484986

Kushwaha, B. P., Rao, N. S., & Ahmad, S. Y. (2015). The factors influencing consumer buying decision of electronic products. Management Dynamics, 15(1), 5-15.

Lachore, S. (2004). How good are the free digital reference services: A comparison between library-based and expert services. *Library Review, 53*(1), 24–29. doi:10.1108/00242530410514766

Lancaster, F. W., & Warner, A. J. (1993). *Information Retrieval Today.* Information Resources Press. https://eric.ed.gov/?id=ED365357

Lankes, R. D. (1995). *AskERIC and the virtual library: lessons from emerging and digital libraries.* Academic Press.

Lankes, R. D. (2004). The digital reference agenda. Syracuse University. The USA. *Journal of the American Society for Information Science and Technology, 55*(4), 301–311. doi:10.1002/asi.10374

Lankes, R. D. (2016). *The new librarianship field guide.* MIT Press.

Laudon, K. C., & Laudon, J. P. (2005). *Essentials of management information system: managing the digital firm* (6th ed.). Pearson Education.

Laumer, S. (2011). *Why do people reject technologies–A literature-based discussion of the phenomena "Resistance to Change" in information systems and managerial psychology research.* Academic Press.

Lee, Y. C., Dervishi, I., Mousa, S., Safiullin, K. I., Ruban-Lazareva, N. V., Kosov, M. E., Ponkratov, V. V., Pozdnyaev, A. S., Mikhina, E. V., & Elyakova, I. D. (2023). Sustainable Development Adoption in the High-Tech Sector: A Focus on Ecosystem Players and Their Influence. *Sustainability (Basel), 15*(18), 13674. doi:10.3390u151813674

Lerro, J., & Lawlor, B. (2018). Flipping the script. *Information Services & Use, 38*(1/2), 91–93. doi:10.3233/ISU-180006

Letelier, M., Carrasco, R., de los Ríos, D., Oliva, C., & Sandoval, M. J. (2010). Evaluation and accreditation: Long term challenges for higher education. *The Journal of Educational Research, 4*(3), 241–263.

Levy, D. M. (2000). Digital Libraries and the Problem of Purpose. *Bulletin of the American Society for Information Science, 26*(6), 22–25. doi:10.1002/bult.180

Lhotska, L., Prague, C., & Aubrecht, P. (2008). *Deliverable D09 security of the multi agent system.* Agent System.

Liau, C. (2019). *Transforming library operation with robotics.* Paper Presented at IFLA WLIC 2019.

Liebrenz, M. (2023, February 6). Generating scholarly content with ChatGPT: Ethical challenges for medical publishing. *The Lancet. Digital health.* https://pubmed.ncbi.nlm.nih.gov/36754725/

LIM (HT). New Technology and University Library in Developing Contrary. In *Challenges of Information Technology* (p. 294). North Holland.

Lim, E. P., Foo, S., Khoo, C., Chen, H., Fox, E., Shalini, U., & Thanos, C. (Eds.). (2002). Digital Libraries: People, Knowledge, and Technology. In *5th International Conference on Asian Digital Libraries, ICADL 2002, Singapore, December 11-14, 2002, Proceedings* (Vol. 2555). Springer Science & Business Media. https://link.springer.com/book/10.1007/3-540-36227-4

Limb, P. (2003). Archives, Libraries, and Museums Convergence: The 24th Library Systems Seminar, Paris 12-14 April 2000 Archives, Bibliothèques et Musées. *Online Information Review, 27*(5), 368–368. doi:10.1108/14684520310503585

Lim, J. C., & Ozbakkaloglu, T. (2014). Confinement model for FRP-confined high-strength concrete. *Journal of Composites for Construction, 18*(4), 04013058. doi:10.1061/(ASCE)CC.1943-5614.0000376

Lin, C. H., Chiu, D. K., & Lam, K. T. (2022). Hong Kong academic librarians' attitudes toward robotic process automation. *Library Hi Tech.* doi:10.1108/LHT-03-2022-0141

Lindayanti, R. A. F., Yulia, A., Bahren, E., Harry, S., Yoni, M., Yuristya, Z., & Zulqayyim. (2016). Pertambangan dan Pengangkutan Batubara Ombilin Sawahlunto pada Masa Kolonial. Padang: Minangkabau Press.

Lindayanti, R. A. F., Efendi, H., Rahman, F., Saputra, Y., Yulia, A., Mega, Y., & Elvira, M. (2017). *Kota Sawahlunto, Jalur Kereta Api dan teluk Bayur: Tiga Serangkai dalam Sejarah Pertambangan Batubara Ombilin di Sumatera Barat.* Minangkabau Press.

Link, F. (1997). *Diffusion dynamics and the pricing of innovations.* Lund University.

Lischer-Katz, Z. (2020). Archiving experience: An exploration of the challenges of preserving virtual reality. *Records Management Journal, 30*(2), 253–274. doi:10.1108/RMJ-09-2019-0054

List, A. (2019). Defining digital literacy development: An examination of pre-service teachers' beliefs. *Computers & Education, 138*, 146–158. doi:10.1016/j.compedu.2019.03.009

Liu, G. (2011). The application of intelligent agents in libraries: a survey. *Program: Electronic Library and Information Systems, 45*(1), 78-97. doi:10.1108/00330331111107411

Liu, Y., Han, T., Ma, S., Zhang, J., Yang, Y., Tian, J., He, H., Li, A., He, M., Liu, Z., Wu, Z., Zhao, L., Zhu, D., Li, X., Qiang, N., Shen, D., Liu, T., & Ge, B. (2023). Summary of CHATGPT-related research and perspective towards the future of large language models. *Meta-Radiology, 1*(2), 100017. doi:10.1016/j.metrad.2023.100017

Li, Z., & Tang, X. (2004). Bayesian face recognition using support vector machine and face clustering. *Proceedings of the 2004 IEEE Computer Society Conference on Computer Vision and Pattern Recognition, 2*, 374-380. 10.1109/CVPR.2004.1315188

Lochhaas, S., & Moore, M. (2010). Open-source software libraries. *B Sides: Fieldwork, 2010*(1).

Logan, D. (2006). *Knowledge management is critical to organizing and accessing a company's intellectual assets.* Academic Press.

Loh, Wong, & Wong. (2006). *Facial expression recognition for e-learning systems using Gabor wavelet & neural network.* Academic Press.

Loonam, J., Eaves, S., Kumar, V., & Parry, G. (2018). Towards digital transformation: Lessons learned from traditional organizations. *Strategic Change, 27*(2), 101–109. doi:10.1002/jsc.2185

Lougee, W. P. (2002). *Diffuse Libraries: Emergent Roles for the Research Library in the Digital Age.* Council on Library and Information Resources.

Lowry, J. (2012). *Management and preservation of digital records in Tanzania.* Academic Press.

Lucas, A., Silva, C. A., & Neto, R. C. (2012). Life cycle analysis of energy supply infrastructure for conventional and electric vehicles. *Energy Policy*, *41*, 537–547. doi:10.1016/j.enpol.2011.11.015

Lu, X. Z., Teng, J. G., Ye, L. P., & Jiang, J. J. (2007). Intermediate crack debonding in FRP-strengthened RC beams: FE analysis and strength model. *Journal of Composites for Construction*, *11*(2), 161–174. doi:10.1061/(ASCE)1090-0268(2007)11:2(161)

Mabe, K., & Potgieter, A. (2021). Collaboration between libraries, archives, and museums in South Africa. *SA Journal of Information Management*, *23*(1).

MacKenzie, J. J. (1997). Driving the road to sustainable ground transportation. *Frontiers of Sustainability*, 121-190.

Madu, A., & Husman, H. (2020). Challenges of virtual reference services implementation by Nigerian academic libraries in the 21st century in Nigeria. *Journal of Economic Development*, *1*(1), 144–155.

Mahesh, G., & Mittal, R. (2008). Digital Libraries in India: A Review. *Libri*, *58*(1), 15–24. doi:10.1515/libr.2008.002

Mahey, M., Al-Abdulla, A., Ames, S., Bray, P., Candela, G., Chambers, S., Derven, C., Dobreva-McPherson, M., Gasser, K., Karner, S., Kokegei, K., Laursen, D., Potter, A., Straube, A., Wagner, S. C. & Wilms, L. (2019). *Open a GLAM Lab—Digital Cultural Heritage Innovation Labs*. Book Sprint, Doha, Qatar.

Mahmood, K., & Richardson, J. V. Jr. (2011). Adoption of Web 2.0 in US academic libraries: A survey of ARL libraries. *Program: Electronic Library and Information Systems*, *45*(4), 365–375. doi:10.1108/00330331111182085

Malake, S., & Phiri, J. (2020). Developing a records and information management model for oil marketing companies in Zambia based on the records cycle model. *Open Journal of Business and Management*, *8*(4), 1870–1887. doi:10.4236/ojbm.2020.84114

Malhotra, H. L. (1956). The effect of temperature on the compressive strength of concrete. *Magazine of Concrete Research*, *8*(23), 85–94. doi:10.1680/macr.1956.8.23.85

Malvar, L. J. (1992). Bond of reinforcement under controlled confinement. *ACI Materials Journal*, *89*(6), 593–601.

Mandavkar, P. (2019). Reform process in higher education and need of assessment and accreditation. *SSRN*, *6*(2), 21–24. doi:10.2139srn.3472356

Mander, J. B., Priestley, M. J., & Park, R. (1988). Theoretical stress-strain model for confined concrete. *Journal of Structural Engineering*, *114*(8), 1804–1826. doi:10.1061/(ASCE)0733-9445(1988)114:8(1804)

Mandernack, S & Fritch, J. W. (2001). *The emerging reference paradigm: A vision of reference services in complex information management*. Academic Press.

Mariyapillai, J., & Naviratharan, G. (2020). *Islandora: An Open-Source Software Solution for Museum Collections of the Library*. Eastern University.

Martínez-Miranda & Aldea. (2005). *Emotion quantification techniques for cognitive reappraisal*. https://link.springer.com/content/pdf/10.1007/s10462-023-10606-0.pdf

Marty, P. F. (2014). Digital Convergence and the Information Profession in Cultural Heritage Organizations: Reconciling Internal and External Demands. *Library Trends*, *62*(3), 613–627. doi:10.1353/lib.2014.0007

Martzoukou, K. (2021). Academic libraries in COVID-19: A renewed mission for digital literacy. *Library Management*, *42*(4/5), 266–276. doi:10.1108/LM-09-2020-0131

Marwick, A., & Boyd, D. (2011). To see and be seen: Celebrity practice on Twitter. *Convergence (London)*, *17*(2), 139–158. doi:10.1177/1354856510394539

Masengu, R., Bigirimana, S., Chiwaridzo, O. T., Bensson, R., & Blossom, C. (Eds.). (2023). *Sustainable Marketing, Branding, and Reputation Management: Strategies for a Greener Future: Strategies for a Greener Future*. IGI Global.

Masuke, E. (2010). *Recent African experience in SME financing–a case of CRDB Bank LTD (Tanzania)*. A presentation paper.

Maxwell, N. K. (2002). Establishing and maintaining a live online reference service. *Library Technology Reports*, *38*(4), 1–78.

Mccracken, G. (1989). Who Is the Celebrity Endorser? *Cultural Foundations of the Endorsement Process.*, *16*(December), 310–321.

Mcknight, M. (2008). Hospital nurses. *Journal of Electronic Resources in Medical Libraries*, *1*(3), 21–34.

Meincke, D. (2018). Experiences building, training, and deploying a Chatbot in an academic library. *Library Staff Publications, 28*. https://scholarsarchive.jwu.edu/staff_pub/28

Mellahi, K., & Harris, L. C. (2016). Response rates in business and management research: An overview of current practice and suggestions for future direction. *British Journal of Management*, *27*(2), 426–437. doi:10.1111/1467-8551.12154

Mensah, M., & Onyancha, M. O. (2021). A social media strategy for academic libraries. *Journal of Academic Librarianship*, *47*(6), 47. doi:10.1016/j.acalib.2021.102462

Milholland, A., & Maddalena, M. (2022). "We could program a Bot to do that!" Robotic process automation in metadata curation and scholarship discoerability. In S. Hervieux & A. Wheatley (Eds.), *The Rise of AI: Implications and Applications for AI in Academic Libraries* (pp. 111–122). Association of College and Research Libraries.

Miller, G. R., & Baseheart, J. (1969). Source trustworthiness, opinionated statements, and response to persuasive communication. *Speech Monographs*, *36*(1), 1–7. doi:10.1080/03637756909375602

Mintz, S. (2023, January 16). *Chatgpt: Threat or menace?* Inside Higher Ed. https://www.insidehighered.com/blogs/higher-ed-gamma/chatgpt-threat-or-menace

Mnjama, N. M. (2011). Paper presented at the XXI Biannual East and Southern Africa Regional Branch of the International Council on Archives (ESARBICA) General Conference. *Journal of the South African Society of Archivists, 55*.

Mogali, S. S. (2014). Artificial intelligence and it's applications in libraries. In *Bilingual International Conference on Information Technology: Yesterday, Today and Tomorrow* (pp. 1-10). Defence Scientific Information and Documentation Centre, Ministry of Defence Delhi. https://www.researchgate.net/publication/287878456_Artificial_Intelligence_and_its_applications_in_Libraries

Mohammadi, A., Fakharzadeh, M., & Baraeinejad, B. (2022). An integrated human stress detection sensor using supervised algorithms. *IEEE Sensors Journal*, *22*(8), 8216–8223. doi:10.1109/JSEN.2022.3157795

Molokisi, S. (2019). *Exploring the use of social media tools in the University of South Africa library*. UNISA.

Mondal, A. (2014). Impact of ICT on job satisfaction of technical staff of the university libraries of West Bengal, India. *E-Library Science Research Journal, 2*(4), 1-15. http://oldlsrj.lbp.world/UploadedArticles/192.pdf

Mostofinejad, D., & Khozaei, K. (2015). Effect of GM patterns on ductility and debonding control of FRP sheets in RC strengthened beams. *Construction & Building Materials*, *93*, 110–120. doi:10.1016/j.conbuildmat.2015.05.062

Motova, G., & Navodnov, V. (2020). Twenty years of accreditation in Russian higher education: Lessons learnt. *Higher Education Evaluation and Development*, *14*(1), 33–51. doi:10.1108/HEED-05-2019-0023

Motsi, A. (2004). The nature of documentary materials in Africa and the challenges to preserving them. *ESARBICA Journal*, *23*(1), 62–67.

Mouhamad, R. (2022, December 15). *Chatgpt is a "landmark event" for AI, but what does it mean for the future of human labor and disinformation?* CBC news. https://www.cbc.ca/radio/thecurrent/chatgpt-human-labour-and-fake-news-1.6686210

Mthembu, T., Naidoo, R., Mkhize, N., Zungu, L., Ndwandwe, T., & Singh, B. (2019). Assessing the quality and reliability of digital information in Kwazulu Natal Department of Health libraries. *Journal of Healthcare Information Management*, *18*(3), 1–6.

Mulaudzi, F., Wamundila, S., Mtanga, N., & Hamooya, C. (2012). *The role of records managers in the digital age: The Zambian experience.* Paper presented at the Twentieth Standing Conference of Eastern, Central and Southern African Library and Information Associations (SCECSAL) hosted by Kenya Library Association (KLA) on 4 - 8 June at Laico Regency Hotel, Nairobi, Kenya.

Mulimani, M., & Naikar, S. (2020). Digitisation and Role of Academic Libraries. *Indian Journal of Library and Information Technology*, *10*(4), 13–18. https://ssrn.com/abstract=3769286

Munsell, S. E., O'Malley, L., & Mackey, C. (2020). Coping with COVID. *Edu Res Theory Pract.*, *31*(3), 101–109.

Murin, I., Marková, I., Zelený, J., & Jaďuďová, J. (2015). Green marketing as a tool influencing consumerś behavior: Slovak case study of regional mark preference. *Procedia Economics and Finance*, *34*, 260–267. doi:10.1016/S2212-5671(15)01628-7

Murphy, I. P. (1997). Charged up. Electric cars get jolt of marketing. *Marketing News*, *31*(7), 1.

Mutsagondo, S., & Ngulube, P. (2018). Skills Impact Assessment of Personnel Managing Electronic Records in Zimbabwe's Public Service. *Mousaion*, *36*(2), 1–19.

Mutula, S., & Wamukoya, J. M. (2009). Public sector information management in east and southern Africa: Implications for FOI, democracy, and integrity in government. *International Journal of Information Management*, *29*(5), 333–341. doi:10.1016/j.ijinfomgt.2009.04.004

Mwanzu, A., Nakaziba, S., Karungi, J., Ayebazibwe, E., & Gatiti, P. (2022). Adoption of LibGuides as a reference service in academic libraries: Insights from Aga Khan University, Uganda. *Journal of Academic Librarianship*, *48*, 102560. doi:10.1016/j.acalib.2022.102560

Myler, E., & Broadbent, G. (2006). ISO 17799: Standard for information security. *Information Management Journal*, *40*(6), 43–52.

Naderpour, H., & Alavi, S. A. (2017). A proposed model to estimate shear contribution of FRP in strengthened RC beams in terms of Adaptive Neuro-Fuzzy Inference System. *Composite Structures*, *170*, 215–227. doi:10.1016/j.compstruct.2017.03.028

Naderpour, H., Kheyroddin, A., & Amiri, G. G. (2010). Prediction of FRP-confined compressive strength of concrete using artificial neural networks. *Composite Structures*, *92*(12), 2817–2829. doi:10.1016/j.compstruct.2010.04.008

Nandi, E., & Chattopadhyay, S. (2016). Quality, accreditation and global university ranking: Issues before Indian higher education. In *India Infrastructure Report 2012* (pp. 205–215). Routledge India. https://smartnet.niua.org/sites/default/files/resources/IIR-2012.pdf#page=206

Nassani, A. A., Yousaf, Z., Grigorescu, A., & Popa, A. (2023). Green and Environmental Marketing Strategies and Ethical Consumption: Evidence from the Tourism Sector. *Sustainability (Basel)*, *15*(16), 12199. doi:10.3390u151612199

Nassuora, A. B., & Hasan, S. (2010). *Knowledge sharing among academics in institutions of higher learning.* Paper presented at the 5th Knowledge Management International Conference. Terengganu, Malaysia.

National Archives of Australia. (2015). *Overview of classification tools for records management.* Commonwealth of Australia, Canberra: Business Centre ACT 2610.

National Assessment and Accreditation Council (NAAC). (2005). *Best Practices Series: Library and Information Services a case presentations.* NAAC.

National Assessment and Accreditation Council (NAAC). (2005). *Guidelines on quality indicators in Library and Information Services: Affiliated and constituent colleges.* NAAC.

National Department of Health. (2019). *National Digital Health Strategy for South Africa 2019 – 2024.* https://www.health.gov.za/wo-content/uploads/2020/11/national-digital-strategy-for-south-africa-2019-2024-b.pdf

National Knowledge Commission. (2007). *Libraries: Gateways to knowledge: A Road Map for Revitalization.* National Knowledge Commission.

Nature Publishing Group. (n.d.). *Nature news.* https://www.nature.com/articles/d42473-023-00083-y

Nawaz, N., & Saldeen, M. A. (2020). Artificial intelligence chatbots for library reference services. *Journal of Management Information and Decision Sciences*, *23*(1S), 442–449. https://www.abacademies.org/articles/artificial-intelligence-chatbots-for-library-reference-services-9653.html

Ndlebe, A., & Dewah, P. (2021). Digitising Archival Material at ZIMPAPERS Harare: Emerging Challenges and Opportunities in the Covid-19 Era. *Mousaion*, *39*(4).

Ndwandwe, T., Naidoo, R., Mkhize, N., Mthembu, T., Zungu, L., & Singh, B. (2017). Staff training and capacity building in Kwazulu Natal Department of Health libraries: Challenges and opportunities. *Journal of Healthcare Information Management*, *16*(1), 1–6.

Neelameghan, A. (1968). Education, Research and Library Science. *Timeless Fellowship*, *5*, 53.

Nehdi, M., El Chabib, H., & Saïd, A. A. (2007). Proposed shear design equations for FRP-reinforced concrete beams based on genetic algorithms approach. *Journal of Materials in Civil Engineering*, *19*(12), 1033–1042. doi:10.1061/(ASCE)0899-1561(2007)19:12(1033)

Nesbitt, K., & Sperling, D. (2001). Fleet purchase behavior: Decision processes and implications for new vehicle technologies and fuels. *Transportation Research Part C, Emerging Technologies*, *9*(5), 297–318. doi:10.1016/S0968-090X(00)00035-8

Ngoepe, M., & Makhubela, S. (2015). Justice delayed is justice denied: Records management and the travesty of justice in South Africa. *Records Management Journal*, *25*(3), 288–305. doi:10.1108/RMJ-06-2015-0023

Ngoepe, M., Mokoena, L., & Ngulube, P. (2010). Security, privacy, and ethics in electronic records management in the South African public sector. *ESARBICA Journal*, *29*(2), 36–66. PMID:20945689

Ngoepe, M., & Van Der Walt, T. (2009). Strategies for the preservation of electronic records in South Africa: Implications on access to information. *Innovation*, *38*(1), 1–25. doi:10.4314/innovation.v38i1.46971

Ngulube, P. (2018). *Managing university records to foster national development and the protection of educational entitlements.* Paper presented at the 2nd Annual Higher Education Records Management Forum, 6 September 2018, at the University of Mpumalanga, Nelspruit, South Africa.

Ngulube, P. (2004). Implications of technological advances for access to the cultural heritage of selected countries in sub-Saharan Africa. Government Information Quarterly: *An International Journal of Information Technology Management. Policies and Procedures*, *21*(2), 143–155.

Ngulube, P. (2006). Nature and accessibility of public archives in custody of selected archival institutions in Africa. *ESARBICA Journal*, *25*(12006), 106–124.

Nick, J. M. (2012). Open access part I: The movement, the issues, and the benefits. *Online Journal of Issues in Nursing*, *17*(1), 1. doi:10.3912/OJIN.Vol17No01PPT02 PMID:22320874

Nie, Y., Wang, E., Guo, Q., & Shen, J. (2018). Examining Shanghai Consumer Preferences for Electric Vehicles and Their Attributes. *Sustainability (Basel)*, *10*(6), 2036. doi:10.3390u10062036

Nikcevie, A. V., Marino, C., Kolubinski, D. C., Leach, D., & Spada, M. M. (2021). Modelling the contribution of the big five personality traits, health anxiety, and COVID-19 psychological distress to generalised anxiety and depressive symptoms during the COVID-19 pandemic. *Journal of Affective Disorders*, *279*, 578–584. doi:10.1016/j.jad.2020.10.053 PMID:33152562

Nour, A. I., & Güneyisi, E. M. (2019). Prediction model on compressive strength of recycled aggregate concrete filled steel tube columns. *Composites. Part B, Engineering*, *173*, 106938. doi:10.1016/j.compositesb.2019.106938

Novia, J., & Liaison, A. (2012). Library, Archival and Museum (LAM) Collaboration: Driving Forces and Recent Trends. *Library Quarterly: Information, Community, Policy*, *80*(1), 7–32.

Nozari, H., Szmelter-Jarosz, A., & Ghahremani-Nahr, J. (2021). The Ideas of Sustainable and Green Marketing Based on the Internet of Everything—The Case of the Dairy Industry. *Future Internet*, *13*(10), 266. doi:10.3390/fi13100266

Nurunnisha, G. A., Roespinoedji, R., & Roespinoedji, D. (2021). Female Students Perceptions on The Effect of Country of Origin, Brand Ambassador on Purchase Intentions: A Study on The Geographical Origin of Tokopedia E-Commerce Company, Indonesia. *Review of International Geographical Education Online*, *11*(1), 573–582.

Nwankwo, J. I. (2001). *Fundamentals of management information systems. Spectrum Books.*

Nwogo Ezeani, C. (2009). Digitizing projects in developing countries: The case of the University of Nigeria. *Library Hi Tech News*, *26*(5/6), 14–15. doi:10.1108/07419050910985273

Obadara, O. E., & Alaka, A. (2013). Accreditation and quality assurance in Nigerian universities. *Journal of Education and Practice*, *4*(8), 34–41. https://core.ac.uk/download/pdf/234634163.pdf

OECD. (2020). *The OECD AI principles.* Available at: https://oecd.ai/en/ai-principles

Office, U. C. (n.d.). *U.S. Copyright Office Fair Use Index.* https://www.copyright.gov/fair-use/

Ohanian, R. (1991). The impact of celebrity spokespersons' perceived image on consumers' intention to purchase. *Journal of Advertising Research*, *31*(1), 46–54.

Ohio State University. (2011). *University archives: Digital content.* https://library.osu.edu/archives/digital

Oh, M., Kim, J. W., Yoon, N. H., Lee, S. A., Lee, S. M., & Kang, W. S. (2019). Differences in personality, defense styles, and coping strategies in individuals with depressive disorder according to age groups across the lifespan. *Psychiatry Investigation*, *16*(12), 911–918. doi:10.30773/pi.2019.0160 PMID:31801315

Ojedokun, A. O. (2008). Transition to Automated Library Information Systems and the Challenges for Libraries in Africa. In *Knowledge and Information Management in the Digital Age: Concepts, Technologies and African Perspectives.* Third World Information Service.

Okpokwasili, N. P. (2019). Artificial intelligence in libraries and users satisfaction in higher institutions in Nigeria. *International Journal of Research in Informative Science Application & Techniques*, *3*(2), 2581–5814. doi:10.46828/ijrisat.v3i2.44

Olabude, F. O. (2007). Utilization of Internet sources for Research by Information Professionals in Sub-Saharan Africa. *African Journal of Library Archives and Information Science*, *17*(1), 53–54.

Olsson, F. (2009). *A literature survey of active machine learning in the context of natural language processing. SICS technical report T2009:06*. Swedish Institute of Computer Science. https://www.ccs.neu.edu/home/vip/teach/ML-course/4_boosting/materials/SICS-T--2009-06--SE.pdf

Oluwabiyi, M. O. (2017). Digital reference services: an overview. *Journal of Information and Knowledge Management, 8*(1).

Omame, I. M., & Alex-Nmecha, J. C. (2020). Artificial Intelligence in Libraries. In N. Osuigwe (Ed.), *Managing and Adapting Library Information Services for Future Users* (pp. 120–144). IGI Global. doi:10.4018/978-1-7998-1116-9.ch008

OpenA. I. (2023, March 27). *GPT-4 technical report*. https://arxiv.org/abs/2303.08774

Orlov, A., & Kallbekken, S. (2019). The impact of consumer attitudes towards energy efficiency on car choice: Survey results from Norway. *Journal of Cleaner Production*, *214*, 816–822. doi:10.1016/j.jclepro.2018.12.326

Osburn, C. B. (2009). *The Social Transcript: Uncovering Library Philosophy*. Libraries Unlimited.

Oumina, A., El Makhfi, N., & Hamdi, M. (2020). Control The COVID-19 Pandemic: Face Mask Detection Using Transfer Learning. *2020 IEEE 2nd International Conference on Electronics, Control, Optimization and Computer Science (ICECOCS)*.

Owalabi, K. A., Yemi-Peters, O. E., Oyetola, S. O., & Oladokun, B. D. (2022). Readiness of academic libraries towards the use of academic librarians towards the use of robotic technologies in Nigerian University Libraries. *Library Management*. Advance online publication. doi:10.1108/LM-11-2021-0104

Owens, T. (2017). *The theory and craft of digital preservation*. Johns Hopkins University Press.

Owusu-Ansah, C. M., Gontshi, V., & Mutibwa, L. (2015). Applications of social media and Web 2.0 for research support in selected African academic institutions. *Journal of Balkan Libraries Union*, *3*(1), 30–39.

Ozbakkaloglu, T., Lim, J. C., & Vincent, T. (2013). FRP-confined concrete in circular sections: Review and assessment of stress–strain models. *Engineering Structures*, *49*, 1068–1088. doi:10.1016/j.engstruct.2012.06.010

Öztürk, Ş., & Akdemir, B. (2018). Application of Feature Extraction and Classification Methods for Histopathological Image using GLCM, LBP, LBGLCM, GLRLM and SFTA. *Procedia Computer Science*, *132*, 40–46. doi:10.1016/j.procs.2018.05.057

Padilla, T. (2019). *Responsible Operations: Data Science, Machine Learning, and AI in Libraries*. OCLC Research Position Paper. OCLC Online Computer Library Center, Inc. https://eric.ed.gov/?id=ED603715

Pala, M., Özbay, E., Öztaş, A., & Yuce, M. I. (2007). Appraisal of long-term effects of fly ash and silica fume on compressive strength of concrete by neural networks. *Construction & Building Materials*, *21*(2), 384–394. doi:10.1016/j.conbuildmat.2005.08.009

Panayiotou, G., Panteli, M., & Leonidou, C. (2021). Coping with the invisible enemy: The role of emotion regulation and awareness in quality of life during the COVID-19 pandemic. *Journal of Contextual Behavioral Science*, *19*, 17–27. doi:10.1016/j.jcbs.2020.11.002

Pandey, P. S. (2017). Machine learning and iot for prediction and detection of stress. *2017 17th International Conference on Computational Science and Its Applications (ICCSA),* 1–5. 10.1109/ICCSA.2017.8000018

Panedpojaman, P., & Pothisiri, T. (2014). Bond Characteristics of Reinforced Normal-Strength Concrete Beams at Elevated Temperatures. *ACI Structural Journal, 111*(6). Advance online publication. doi:10.14359/51687098

Pappas, C. (2008). Hospital librarians' perceptions related to evidence-based health care. *Journal of the Medical Library Association: JMLA, 96*(3), 235–238. doi:10.3163/1536-5050.96.3.011 PMID:18654652

Park, C. L., Russell, B. S., Fendrich, M., Finkelstein-Fox, L., Hutchison, M., & Becker, J. (2020). Americans' COVID-19 stress, coping and adherence to CDC guidelines. *Journal of General Internal Medicine, 35*(8), 2296–2303. doi:10.100711606-020-05898-9 PMID:32472486

Park, E., Kwon, J., & Kim, S. B. (2021). Green marketing strategies on online platforms: A mixed approach of experiment design and topic modeling. *Sustainability (Basel), 13*(8), 4494. doi:10.3390u13084494

Pause giant AI experiments: An open letter. (2023, November 27). Future of Life Institute. https://futureoflife.org/open-letter/pause-giant-ai-experiments/

Pearce, J. M. (2022). The Rise of Platinum Open Access Journals with Both Impact Factors and Zero Article Processing Charges. *Knowledge (Beverly Hills, Calif.), 2*(2), 209–224. doi:10.3390/knowledge2020013

Peattie, K., & Belz, F. M. (2010). Sustainability marketing—An innovative conception of marketing. *Marketing Review St. Gallen, 27*(5), 8–15. doi:10.100711621-010-0085-7

Pendit, P. L. (2019). *Pustaka: tradisi & kesinambungan.* Ikatan Sarjana Ilmu Perpustakaan dan Informasi Indonesia.

Pendit, P. L. (2019). *Pustaka: Tradisi & Kesinambungan.* ISIPII Press.

Penzhorn, C. (2009). Quality through improved service: the implementation of social networking tools in an academic library. *Proceedings of the 2009 IATUL Conference.*

Petrelli, D., Ciolfi, L., Van Dijk, D., Hornecker, E., Not, E., & Schmidt, A. (2013). We are integrating material and digital: A new way for cultural heritage. *Interactions (New York, N.Y.), 20*(4), 58–63. doi:10.1145/2486227.2486239

Pomerantz, J., Oh, S., Wildemuth, B. M., Yang, S., & Fox, E. A. (2007, June). Digital library education in computer science programs. In *Proceedings of the 7th ACM/IEEE-CS joint conference on Digital libraries* (177-178). 10.1145/1255175.1255208

Potgieter, A., & Mabe, K. (2018). The future of accessing our past: Collaboration and digitization in libraries, archives, and museums. In *Proceedings of Business and Management Conferences.* International Institute of Social and Economic Sciences.

Prasad, V. S., & Stella, A. (2004). Accreditation of higher education institutions: Indian experience. In *National Assessment and Accreditation Council Commonwealth of Learning Round Table Conference on Innovations in Teacher Education* (pp. 17–19). International Practices on Quality Assurance. https://www.che.ac.za/sites/default/files/publications/d000091_seminar_9-3-05-Int-trends-qa-prof_prasad.pdf

Pratiwi, K. Y., & Setiawan, B. (2019). Analisis Penerapan Konsep GLAM (Gallery, Library, Archives, Museum) di Perpustakaan Bung Karno Blitar. *Jurnal Perpustakaan Universitas Airlangga, 9*(2), 53–62.

Priya, A., Sharma, S., Sinha, K., & Yogesh, Y. (2023, March). Community Detection in Networks: A Comparative study. In *2023 International Conference on Device Intelligence, Computing and Communication Technologies (DICCT)* (pp. 505-510). IEEE. 10.1109/DICCT56244.2023.10110206

Prota, A., Manfredi, G., & Cosenza, E. (2006). Ultimate behavior of axially loaded RC wall-like columns confined with GFRP. *Composites. Part B, Engineering*, *37*(7-8), 670–678. doi:10.1016/j.compositesb.2006.01.005

Quisbert, H. (2006). *A framework for the development of archival information systems* [Masters]. Lulea University of Technology. Department of Business Administration and Social Sciences. Division of Systems Science. https://www.diva-portal.org/smash/get/diva2:990983/FULLTEXT01.pdf

Rabatsetsa, B., Maluleka, J.R. & Onyancha, O. B. (2021). Adoption and use of social media in academic libraries in South Africa. *SA Jnl Libs & Info Sci 2021, 87*(1).

Rahimi, A., Soleymani, M. R., Hashemian, A., Hashemian, M. R., & Daei, A. (2018). Evaluating digital libraries: A systematised review. *Health Information and Libraries Journal*, *35*(3), 180–191. doi:10.1111/hir.12231 PMID:30160384

Rahmah, A. (2016). *Analisisperbandingankinerjareksa dana syariah dan kinerjareksa dana konvensionaldenganmetodesharpe, treynor dan jensen* [Doctoral dissertation]. Universitas Islam Negeri Sumatera Utara.

Rainer, R. K., Kelly, R. R., & Prince, B. (2022). *Introduction to information systems*. John Wiley & Sons.

Rajagopaul, A. (2008). *A comparative study of job functions of university and university of technology graduates and diplomates in special libraries and engineering firms*. DUT.

Rajoub, B. A., & Zwiggelaar, R. (2014). Thermal facial analysis for deception detection. *IEEE Transactions on Information Forensics and Security*, *9*(6), 1015–1023. doi:10.1109/TIFS.2014.2317309

Raju, J. (2014). Knowledge and skills for the digital era academic library. *Journal of Academic Librarianship*, *40*(2), 163–170. doi:10.1016/j.acalib.2014.02.007

Ramesh, D. B. (Ed.). (2004). *Information Technology Applications in Libraries: A Textbook for Beginners*. Reprint.

Ramos, M. S., & Abrigo, C. M. (2012). Reference 2.0 in action: An evaluation of the digital reference services in selected Philippine academic libraries. *Library Hi Tech News*, *1*(1), 8–20. doi:10.1108/07419051211223426

Ramponi, M. (2023, August 4). *How CHATGPT works. News, Tutorials, AI Research*. https://www.assemblyai.com/blog/how-chatgpt-actually-works

Ranasinghe, W.M.T.D. (2012). *New Trends of Library Reference Services*. Professor Jayasiri Linkage Felicitation.

Ranganathan, S. R. (1965). *Universities and Colleges Libraries*. University Grants Commission. https://indianculture.gov.in/reports-proceedings/universities-and-colleges-libraries-containing-report-library-committee

Rao, A. S. (2023, August 22). *CHATGPT shows "impressive" accuracy in clinical decision-making*. Medical Xpress. https://medicalxpress.com/news/2023-08-chatgpt-accuracy-clinical-decision.html

Rasmussen, C. H., & Hjørland, B. (2023). Libraries, Archives and Museums (LAMs): Conceptual Issues with Focus on Their Convergence. *Knowledge Organization*, *49*(8), 577–621. doi:10.5771/0943-7444-2022-8-577

Razmjoo, A., Ghazanfari, A., Jahangiri, M., Franklin, E., Denai, M., Marzband, M., Astiaso Garcia, D., & Maheri, A. (2022). A Comprehensive Study on the Expansion of Electric Vehicles in Europe. *Applied Sciences (Basel, Switzerland)*, *12*(22), 11656. doi:10.3390/app122211656

Records Nations. (2019). *Different types of security in records management*. https://www.recordnations.com/2019/01/different-types-security-in-records-management/

Resnick, M., & Albert, W. (2014). The impact of advertising location and user task on the emergence of banner ad blindness: An eye-tracking study. *International Journal of Human-Computer Interaction*, *30*(3), 206–219. doi:10.1080/10447318.2013.847762

Revina, I. M., & Emmanuel, W. S. (2018). A survey on human face expression recognition techniques. *Journal of King Saud University. Computer and Information Sciences*.

Ricks, B., Swafford, A., & Gow, K. (1992). Information and image management: A records management systems approach (3rd ed.). South-Western Publishing Co.

Riege, A. (2005). Three-dozen knowledge-sharing barriers managers must consider. *Journal of Knowledge Management*, *9*(3), 18–35. doi:10.1108/13673270510602746

Rip, A., & Kemp, R. (1998). Technological change. *Human Choice and Climate Change, 2*(2), 327-399.

Rizwan, M. F., Farhad, R., Mashuk, F., Islam, F., & Imam, M. H. (2019). Design of a biosignal based stress detection system using machine learning techniques. *2019 International Conference on Robotics, Electrical and Signal Processing Techniques (ICREST)*, 364–368. 10.1109/ICREST.2019.8644259

Robertshaw, M. B., & Asher, A. (2019). Unethical numbers? A meta-analysis of library learning analytics studies. *Library Trends*, *68*(1), 76–101. doi:10.1353/lib.2019.0031

Robinson, H. (2019). *Interpreting Objects in the Hybrid Museum: Convergence, Collections, and Cultural Policy*. Routledge. doi:10.4324/9780429454400

Rodriguez, M. A., Bollen, J., & Van de Sompel, H. (2006). The convergence of digital libraries and the peer-review process. *Journal of Information Science*, *32*(2), 149–159. doi:10.1177/0165551506062327

Roger, S. P., & Bruce, R. M. (2015). *Software engineering: a practitioner's approach*. McGraw-Hill Education.

Romanowski, M. H. (2022). The idolatry of accreditation in higher education: Enhancing our understanding. *Quality in Higher Education*, *28*(2), 153–167. doi:10.1080/13538322.2021.1948460

Roose, K. (2023, February 3). How CHATGPT kicked off an A.I. Arms Race. *The New York Times*. https://www.nytimes.com/2023/02/03/technology/chatgpt-openai-artificial-intelligence.html

Ropek, L. (2023, January 4). *Did CHATGPT write that? A college student created an AI Essay detector*. Gizmodo. https://gizmodo.com/chatgpt-ai-essay-detector-college-princeton-edward-tian-1849946535

Roper, M., & Millar, L. (1999). *Managing public sector records: Preserving archives*. IRMT.

Rosalsky, G., & Peaslee, E. (2023, January 17). *This 22-year-old is trying to save us from ChatGPT before it changes writing forever*. NPR. https://www.npr.org/sections/money/2023/01/17/1149206188/this-22-year-old-is-trying-to-save-us-from-chatgpt-before-it-changes-writing-for

Ross, S. (2012). Digital preservation, archival science and methodological foundations for digital libraries. *New Review of Information Networking*, *17*(1), 43–68. doi:10.1080/13614576.2012.679446

Roy, P. (2021). Asynchronous and Synchronous: A Communication Process in Smart Classroom. *Ideal Research Review*, *65*(1).

Rubin, R. E., & Rubin, R. G. (2020). *Foundations of library and information science*. American Library Association.

Saatcioglu, M., & Razvi, S. R. (2002). Displacement-based design of reinforced concrete columns for confinement. *Structural Journal*, *99*(1), 3–11.

Sabah, J. (2018). Digital Reference Services in the Information Communication Technology (ICT) based Environment: A Study. *Library Philosophy and Practice (e-journal),* 1827. https://digitalcommons.unl.edu/libphilprac/1827

Saeidnia, H. (2023). *Using ChatGPT as Digital/ Smart Reference Robot: How may ChatGPT Impact Digital Reference Services?* Advance online publication. doi:10.2139srn.4441874

Safahieh, H., & Asemi, A. (2010). Computer literacy skills of librarians: A case study of Isfahan University libraries, Iran. *The Electronic Library*, *28*(1), 89–99. doi:10.1108/02640471011023397

Sahin, I. (2006). Detailed review of Rogers' diffusion of innovations theory and educational technology-related studies based on Rogers' theory. *Turkish Online Journal of Educational Technology-TOJET*, *5*(2), 14–23.

Samaan, M., Mirmiran, A., & Shahawy, M. (1998). Model of concrete confined by fiber composites. *Journal of Structural Engineering*, *124*(9), 1025–1031. doi:10.1061/(ASCE)0733-9445(1998)124:9(1025)

Sandhu, G. (2018). The role of academic libraries in the digital transformation of the universities. In *5th International Symposium on Emerging Trends and Technologies in Libraries and Information Services (ETTLIS)* (pp. 292-296). IEEE. https://doi.org/10.1109/ETTLIS.2018.8485258

Sattarova Feruza, Y., & Kim, T. H. (2007). IT security review: Privacy, protection, access control, assuranceassurance, and system security. *International Journal of Multimedia and Ubiquitous Engineering*, *2*(2), 17–32.

Savari, G. F., Sathik, M. J., Raman, L. A., El-Shahat, A., Hasanien, H. M., Almakhles, D., Abdel Aleem, S. H. E., & Omar, A. I. (2023). Assessment of charging technologies, infrastructure and charging station recommendation schemes of electric vehicles: A review. *Ain Shams Engineering Journal*, *14*(4), 101938. doi:10.1016/j.asej.2022.101938

Schellnack-Kelly, I. (2013). *The role of records management in governance-based evidence, service delivery and development in South African communities* [PhD Thesis]. University of South Africa.

Schimmelpfennig, C., & Hunt, J. B. (2020). Fifty years of celebrity endorser research: Support for a comprehensive celebrity endorsement strategy framework. *Psychology and Marketing*, *37*(3), 488–505. doi:10.1002/mar.21315

Schot, J., Hoogma, R., & Elzen, B. (1994). Strategies for shifting technological systems: The case of the automobile system. *Futures*, *26*(10), 1060–1076. doi:10.1016/0016-3287(94)90073-6

SchulmanJ.WolskiF.DhariwalP.RadfordA.KlimovO. (2017, August 28). *Proximal policy optimization algorithms*. https://arxiv.org/abs/1707.06347

Schulmnan, J. (2022). *Training language models to follow instructions with humans... - OpenAI*. https://cdn.openai.com/papers/Training_language_models_to_follow_instructions_with_human_feedback.pdf

Schuster, R. M., Hammitt, W. E., & Moore, D. (2006). Stress appraisal and coping response to hassles experienced in outdoor recreation settings. *Leisure Sciences*, *28*(2), 97–113. doi:10.1080/01490400500483919

Schwartz, C. (1993). Evaluating CD-ROM products: Yet another checklist. *CD-ROM Professional*, *6*, 87–87.

Schwartz, J. M., & Cook, T. (2002). Archives, records, and power: The making of modern memory. *Archival Science*, *2*(1-2), 1–1. doi:10.1007/BF02435628

Seadle, M., & Greifeneder, E. (2007). Defining a digital library. *Library Hi Tech*, *25*(2), 169–173. doi:10.1108/07378830710754938

Sekyere, K. (2011). Virtual Reference Service in Academic Libraries in West Africa. *Journal of Library & Information Services in Distance Learning*, *5*(1-2), 3-9. . doi:10.1080/1533290X.2011.548233

Semertzaki, E. (2011). *Special Libraries as Knowledge Management Centres*. Chandos Publishing. doi:10.1533/9781780632667

Service Delivery by Librarians in Private Universities Libraries in South-East Nigeria. (n.d.). *Library Philosophy and Practice (e-journal)*. 7105. https://digitalcommons.unl.edu/libphilprac/7105

Shafiei, E., Davidsdottir, B., Fazeli, R., Leaver, J., Stefansson, H., & Asgeirsson, E. I. (2018). Macroeconomic effects of fiscal incentives to promote electric vehicles in Iceland: Implications for government and consumer costs. *Energy Policy*, *114*, 431–443. doi:10.1016/j.enpol.2017.12.034

Shahmansouri, A. A., Bengar, H. A., & Jahani, E. (2019). Predicting compressive strength and electrical resistivity of eco-friendly concrete containing natural zeolite via GEP algorithm. *Construction & Building Materials*, *229*, 116883. doi:10.1016/j.conbuildmat.2019.116883

Shahmansouri, A. A., Yazdani, M., Ghanbari, S., Bengar, H. A., Jafari, A., & Ghatte, H. F. (2021). Artificial neural network model to predict the compressive strength of eco-friendly geopolymer concrete incorporating silica fume and natural zeolite. *Journal of Cleaner Production*, *279*, 123697. doi:10.1016/j.jclepro.2020.123697

Shahmansouri, A. A., Yazdani, M., Hosseini, M., Bengar, H. A., & Ghatte, H. F. (2022). The prediction analysis of compressive strength and electrical resistivity of environmentally friendly concrete incorporating natural zeolite using artificial neural network. *Construction & Building Materials*, *317*, 125876. doi:10.1016/j.conbuildmat.2021.125876

Shan, K., Guo, J., You, W., Lu, D., & Bie, R. (2017). Automatic facial expression recognition based on a deep convolutional-neural-network structure. *2017 IEEE 15th International Conference on Software Engineering Research, Management and Applications (SERA)*, 123-128. 10.1109/SERA.2017.7965717

Shao, G., Quintana, J. P., Zakharov, W., Purzer, S., & Kim, E. (2021). Exploring potential roles of academic libraries in undergraduate data science education curriculum development. *Journal of Academic Librarianship*, *47*(2), 102320. doi:10.1016/j.acalib.2021.102320

Shareef, M. A., Mukerji, B., Dwivedi, Y. K., Rana, N. P., & Islam, R. (2019). Social media marketing: Comparative effect of advertisement sources. *Journal of Retailing and Consumer Services*, *46*, 58–69. doi:10.1016/j.jretconser.2017.11.001

Shatat, A. S. (2015). Critical success factors in enterprise resource planning (ERP) system implementation: An exploratory study in Oman. *Electronic Journal of Information Systems Evaluation*, *18*(1), 36–45.

Shepherd, D. A. (2003). Learning from business failure: Propositions of grief recovery for the self-employed. *Academy of Management Review*, *28*(2), 318–328. doi:10.2307/30040715

Shepherd, E. (2006). Why are records in the public sector organizational assets? *Records Management Journal*, *16*(1), 6–12. doi:10.1108/09565690610654747

Shepherd, E., & Yeo, G. (2003). *Managing records: A handbook of principles and practice*. Facet Publishers.

Shettappanavar, L., & Krishnamurthy, C. (2021). Digital Literacy Skills among Postgraduate Students of University of Agricultural Sciences Dharwad: A Study. In *International Conference on Marching Libraries from Traditional to Hybrid: Connecting, Communicating and Cooperating* (pp. 301-314). Shree Publishers and Distributors. https://shorturl.at/adiS1

Shimray, S. R. & Chennupati, K. R. (2019). Cultural Heritage Awareness among Students of Pondicherry University: a Study. *Library Philosophy and Practice*, 2516.

Shiva, A., Narula, S., & Shahi, S. K. (2020). What drives retail investors' investment decisions? Evidence from no mobile phone phobia (Nomophobia) and investor fear of missing out (I-FoMo). Journal of Content. *Community and Communication*, *10*(6), 2–20. doi:10.31620/JCCC.06.20/02

Siddique, R., Aggarwal, P., & Aggarwal, Y. (2011). Prediction of compressive strength of self-compacting concrete containing bottom ash using artificial neural networks. *Advances in Engineering Software*, *42*(10), 780–786. doi:10.1016/j.advengsoft.2011.05.016

Siler, K. (2017). Future challenges and opportunities in academic publishing. *Canadian Journal of Sociology*, *42*(1), 83–114. doi:10.29173/cjs28140

Simard, M. A., Ghiasi, G., Mongeon, P., & Larivière, V. (2022). National differences in dissemination and use of open access literature. *PLoS One*, *17*(8), 1–14. doi:10.1371/journal.pone.0272730 PMID:35943972

Singh, D. (2004). *Reference services in the digital age.* Paper presented at the Conference on Library Management in the 21st Century at the Ateneo de Manila University, Philippines.

Singh, H., Kavianipour, M., Soltanpour, A., Fakhrmoosavi, F., Ghamami, M., Zockaie, A., & Jackson, R. (2022). Macro Analysis to Estimate Electric Vehicles Fast-Charging Infrastructure Requirements in Small Urban Areas. *Transportation Research Record: Journal of the Transportation Research Board*, *2676*(11), 446–461. doi:10.1177/03611981221093625

Singh, N. (2012). Digital reference service in university libraries: A case study of the Northern India. *International Journal of Library and Information Studies*, *2*(4).

Sinha, K. (2023). The Metaverse and Digital Libraries: Ensuring Safe and Secure Access to Information. In Handbook of Research on Advancements of Contactless Technology and Service Innovation in Library and Information Science (pp. 1-22). IGI Global.

Sinha, V., & Subramanian, K. S. (2013). Accreditation in India: Path of achieving educational excellence. *Business Education & Accreditation*, *5*(2), 107–116. https://ssrn.com/abstract=2239206

Skitka, L. J., Mosier, K., & Burdick, M. D. (2000). Accountability and Automation Bias. *International Journal of Human-Computer Studies*, *52*(4), 701–717. doi:10.1006/ijhc.1999.0349

Slote, S. (2000). *Records management in the library collections: library records methods* (3rd ed.). Libraries Unlimited.

Smeby, J. C., & Rydland, J. (2020). The role of libraries in supporting research and education in healthcare. *Journal of the Medical Library Association: JMLA*, *108*(3), 467–474.

Smith, G. W., & Newton, R. B. (2000). A taxonomy of organizational security policies. *Proceedings of the 23rd National Information Systems Security Conference. NIST-National Institute of Standards and Technology.*

Sodaro, A. (2018). *Exhibiting Atrocity: Memorial Museums and the Politics of Past Violence.* Rutgers University Press. doi:10.2307/j.ctt1v2xskk

Souza, L. K., Policarpo, D., & Hutz, C. S. (2020). Self-compassion and Symptoms of Stress, Anxiety, and Depression. *Trends in Psychology*, *28*(1), 85–98. doi:10.100743076-020-00018-2

Spasojevic, J., & Spasojevic, M. (2018). Implementation Of Corporate Social Responsibility And Marketing of UNIQA In The Republic Of Serbia. *Economic and Social Development: Book of Proceedings*, 320-327.

Sperling, D. (1995). *Future drive: Electric vehicles and sustainable transportation.* Island Press.

Staff, N. (2023, March 31). *New York City Department of Education bans CHATGPT.* GovTech. https://www.govtech.com/education/k-12/new-york-city-department-of-education-bans-chatgpt

Stensaker, B., & Harvey, L. (2006). Old wine in new bottles? A comparison of public and private accreditation schemes in higher education. *Higher Education Policy*, *19*(1), 65–85. doi:10.1057/palgrave.hep.8300110

Stern, J. (2023, May 31). Chatgpt wrote my AP English essay-and I passed. *The Wall Street Journal*. https://www.wsj.com/articles/chatgpt-wrote-my-ap-english-essayand-i-passcd-11671628256

Stever, G. S., & Lawson, K. (2013). Twitter as a way for celebrities to communicate with fans: Implications for the study of para-social interaction. *North American Journal of Psychology, 15*(2).

Stokel-Walker, C. (2022, December 9). *Ai Bot ChatGPT writes Smart Essays - should professors worry?* Nature News. https://www.nature.com/articles/d41586-022-04397-7

Stokel-Walker, C. (2023, January 18). *CHATGPT listed as author on research papers: Many scientists disapprove.* Nature News. https://www.nature.com/articles/d41586-023-00107-z

Stura, I., Gentile, T., Migliaretti, G., & Vesce, E. (2019). Accreditation in higher education: Does disciplinary matter? *Studies in Educational Evaluation, 63*, 41–47. doi:10.1016/j.stueduc.2019.07.004

Sudarsono, B. (2016). *Menuju Era Dokumentasi Baru.* LIPI Press.

Suki, N. M., & Suki, N. M. (2019). Correlations between awareness of green marketing, corporate social responsibility, product image, corporate reputation, and consumer purchase intention. In *Corporate social responsibility: Concepts, methodologies, tools, and applications* (pp. 143–154). IGI Global. doi:10.4018/978-1-5225-6192-7.ch008

Sukula, S. (2010). *Electronic resource management: What, why and how.* Ess Ess Publications.

Sullivan, S. (2004). Local involvement and traditional practices in the world heritage system. *Linking Universal and Local Values, 49*, 49–55.

Sutton, S. A. (1998). Gateway to Educational Material (GEM): Metadata for networked information discovery and retrieval. *Computer Networks and ISDN Systems, 30*(1-7), 691–693. doi:10.1016/S0169-7552(98)00086-5

Su, Z. W., Umar, M., Kirikkaleli, D., & Adebayo, T. S. (2021). Role of political risk to achieve carbon neutrality: Evidence from Brazil. *Journal of Environmental Management, 298*, 113463. doi:10.1016/j.jenvman.2021.113463 PMID:34426223

Sywelem, M. M., & Witte, J. E. (2009). Higher Education Accreditation in View of International Contemporary Attitudes. *Online Submission, 2*(2), 41-54. https://eric.ed.gov/?id=ED509233

Tammaro, A. M., Matusiak, K. K., Sposito, F. A., & Casarosa, V. (2019). Data curator's roles and responsibilities: An international perspective. *Libri, 69*(2), 89–104. doi:10.1515/libri-2018-0090

Tapan, M., Comert, M., Demir, C., Sayan, Y., Orakcal, K., & Ilki, A. (2013). Failures of structures during the October 23, 2011 Tabanlı (Van) and November 9, 2011 Edremit (Van) earthquakes in Turkey. *Engineering Failure Analysis, 34*, 606–628. doi:10.1016/j.engfailanal.2013.02.013

Tarei, P. K., Chand, P., & Gupta, H. (2021). Barriers to the adoption of electric vehicles: Evidence from India. *Journal of Cleaner Production, 291*, 125847. doi:10.1016/j.jclepro.2021.125847

Tate, T. (2023, September). *Will ChatGPT give us a lesson in education?* Nature News. https://www.nature.com/articles/d42473-023-00083-y

Tella, A. (2020). Robots are coming to the libraries: Are librarians ready to accommodate them? *Library Hi Tech News, 37*(8), 13–17. doi:10.1108/LHTN-05-2020-0047

Tella, A., & Ajani, Y. A. (2022). Robots and public libraries. *Library Hi Tech News, 7*(7), 15–18. doi:10.1108/LHTN-05-2022-0072

Tella, A., & Ogbonna, P. (2023). Telepresence robots in libraries: Applications and challenges. *Library Hi Tech News*. Advance online publication. doi:10.1108/LHTN-03-2023-0035

Terras, M. (2022). The role of the library when computers can read: Critically adopting Handwritten Text Recognition (HTR) technologies to support research. In S. Hervieux & A. Wheatley (Eds.), *The Rise of AI: Implications and Applications of Artificial Intelligence in Academic Libraries* (pp. 137–148). Association of College and Research Libraries.

The Hindu. (2010, January 4). Retrieved from http://www.thehinduonnet.com/thehindu

The International Council of Museums (ICOM). (2022). *Museum Definition*. https://icom.museum/en/resources/standards-guidelines/museum-definition/

The United Nations Educational, Scientific and Cultural Organization (UNESCO). (2019). *Ombilin Coal Mining Heritage of Sawahlunto*. Available at https://whc.unesco.org/en/list/1610

Thibodeau, K. (2013). Wrestling with shape-shifters: Perspectives on preserving memory in the digital age. *Proceedings of 'The Memory of the World in the Digital Age: Digitization and Digital Preservation*, 15-23. http://www.unesco.org/webworld/download/mow/mow_ vancouver_proceedings_en.pdf

Thomas, V. S., Schubert, D. R., & Lee, J. A. (1983). *Records management systems and administration*. John Wiley and Sons.

Tigert, D., & Farivar, B. (1981). The Bass new product growth model: A sensitivity analysis for a high technology product. *Journal of Marketing*, *45*(4), 81–90. doi:10.1177/002224298104500411

Tofi, S. T., Agada, E. O., & Okafor, C. J. (2020). Utilization of Digital Reference Resources and Services by Postgraduate Students in University Libraries in Benue State, Nigeria. *International Journal of Research and Innovation in Social Science*, *IV*(VI).

Toutanji, H. (1999). Stress-strain characteristics of concrete columns externally confined with advanced fiber composite sheets. *Materials Journal*, *96*(3), 397–404.

Toutanji, H., & Deng, Y. (2001). Performance of concrete columns strengthened with fiber reinforced polymer composite sheets. *Advanced Composite Materials*, *10*(2-3), 159–168. doi:10.1163/156855101753396636

Trant, J. (2009). Emerging convergence? Thoughts on Museums, Archives, Libraries, and Professional Training. *Museum Management and Curatorship*, *24*(4), 369–387. doi:10.1080/09647770903314738

Triantafillou, T. C., Choutopoulou, E., Fotaki, E., Skorda, M., Stathopoulou, M., & Karlos, K. (2016). FRP confinement of wall-like reinforced concrete columns. *Materials and Structures*, *49*(1-2), 651–664. doi:10.161711527-015-0526-5

Tshuma, N., Haruna, H., Muziringa, M. C., & Chikonzo, A. C. (2015). International trends in Health Science Librarianship part 3: Southern Africa (South Africa, Tanzania and Zimbabwe). *Health Information and Libraries Journal*, *32*(1), 67–72. doi:10.1111/hir.12091

Tsvuura, G., & Ngulube, P. (2020). Digitisation of records and archives at two selected state universities in Zimbabwe. *Journal of the South African Society of Archivists*, *53*, 20–34. doi:10.4314/jsasa.v53i1.2

Turamari, R., & Kotur, M. B. (2019). Changing Skills of LIS professionals in the Digital Environment. *Indian Journal of Library and Information Technology*, *10*(4), 34–38. https://shorturl.at/rwTU9

Turkish Building Seismic Code 2018. (2018). Prime Ministry, Disaster and Emergency Management Presidency (AFAD).

UK Government. (2021). *National AI strategy*. Available at: https://www.gov.uk/government/publications/national-ai-strategy

UKRI. (2021). *Transforming our world with AI.* Available at: https://www.ukri.org/wp-content/uploads/2021/02/UKRI-120221-TransformingOurWorldWithAI.pdf

United Nations Programme on HIV/AIDS (UNAIDS) Guidance, (2016). *The privacy, confidentiality, and security assessment tool: protecting personal health information.* https://www.unaids.org/en/resources/documents/2019/confidentiality

University Grants Commission. (1988). *Development of an Information and Library Network: Report of the Inter Agency Working Group.* University Grants Commission.

Uysal, M., & Tanyildizi, H. (2012). Estimation of compressive strength of self compacting concrete containing polypropylene fiber and mineral additives exposed to high temperature using artificial neural network. *Construction & Building Materials, 27*(1), 404–414. doi:10.1016/j.conbuildmat.2011.07.028

Uzoigwe, C. U., & Eze, J. U. (2018). The Perceived Benefits of Electronic/Digital Reference Services In Nigerian University Libraries: A survey. *International Journal of Knowledge Content Development & Technology, 8*(2), 49–65.

Vakhshouri, B., & Nejadi, S. (2015). Predicition of compressive strength in light-weight self-compacting concrete by ANFIS analytical model. *Archives of Civil Engineering,* (2).

van Dis, E. A. M., Bollen, J., Zuidema, W., van Rooij, R., & Bockting, C. L. (2023, February 3). *Chatgpt: Five Priorities for Research.* Nature News. https://www.nature.com/articles/d41586-023-00288-7

Van Slyke, C., Lee, J., Duong, B. Q., & Ellis, T. S. (2022). Eustress and distress in the context of telework. *Information Resources Management Journal, 35*(1), 1–24. doi:10.4018/IRMJ.291526

Veldpaus, L. (2016). Heritage Taxonomy: Towards a common language? In *HERITAGE 2016–5th International Conference on Heritage and Sustainable Development.* Newcastle University.

Venkatesh, V., & Bala, H. (2008). Technology Acceptance Model 3 and a Research Agenda on Interventions. *Decision Sciences, 39*(2), 273–315. doi:10.1111/j.1540-5915.2008.00192.x

Venkatesh, V., & Davis, F. (2000). A Theoretical Extension of the Technology Acceptance Model: Four Longitudinal Field Studies. *Management Science, 46*(2), 186–204. doi:10.1287/mnsc.46.2.186.11926

Venkatesh, V., Morris, M. G., Davis, G. B., & Davis, F. D. (2003). User Acceptance of Information Technology: Toward a Unified View. *Management Information Systems Quarterly, 27*(3), 425–478. doi:10.2307/30036540

Verma, P. (2020). *Digitalization: enabling the new phase of energy efficiency.* Group of Experts on Energy Efficiency Seventh session Geneva, 22 and 25 September 2020. GEEE7/2020/INF.3

Verma, M. (2023). Novel Study on AI-Based Chatbot (ChatGPT) Impacts on the Traditional Library Management. *International Journal of Trend in Scientific Research and Development, 7*(1).

Vijayakumar, J. K., & Vijayakumar, M. (2000). CD-ROM to DVD-ROM: a new era in electronic publishing of Databases and Multimedia Reference Sources. *IASLIC Bulletin, 45*(2), 49-54. http://eprints.rclis.org/14019/1/vijayakumarjk_19.pdf

Vijaykumar, S., & Sheshadri, K. N. (2019). Applications of artificial intelligence in academic libraries. *International Journal on Computer Science and Engineering, 7*(16), 136–140. doi:10.26438/ijcse/v7si16.136140

Vileno, L. (2007). From Paper to Electronic, the Evolution of Pathfinders: A Review of the Literature. *RSR. Reference Services Review, 35*(3), 434–451. doi:10.1108/00907320710774300

Vincent, T., & Ozbakkaloglu, T. (2013). Influence of fiber orientation and specimen end condition on axial compressive behavior of FRP-confined concrete. *Construction & Building Materials, 47,* 814–826. doi:10.1016/j.conbuildmat.2013.05.085

Voltmer, E., Köslich-Strumann, S., Walther, A., Kasem, M., Obst, K., & Kötter, T. (2021). The impact of the COVID-19 pandemic on stress, mental health and coping behavior in German university students – a longitudinal study before and after the onset of the pandemic. *BMC Public Health*, *21*(1), 1385. doi:10.118612889-021-11295-6 PMID:34256717

Voronin, I. A., Manrique-Millones, D., Vasin, G. M., Millones-Rivalles, R. B., Manrique-Pino, O., Fernández-Ríos, N., Marakshina, Y. A., Lobaskova, M. M., Symanyuk, E. E., Pecherkina, A. A., Ageeva, I. A., Lysenkova, I. A., Ismatullina, V. I., Sitnikova, M. A., & Malykh, S. B. (2020). Coping responses during the COVID-19 pandemic: Cross-cultural comparison of Russia, Kyrgyzstan, and Peru. *Psychology in Russia : State of the Art*, *13*(4), 55–74. doi:10.11621/pir.2020.0404

Wallis, J., Marshall, J., & Viera, A. (2019). Staffing challenges for libraries in healthcare institutions: Implications for access to the latest research and information. *Journal of the Medical Library Association: JMLA*, *107*(3), 213–219.

Wamukoya, J., & Mutula, S. M. (2005). E-records management and governance in East and Southern Africa. *Malaysian Journal of Library and Information Science*, *10*(2), 67–83.

Wang, B., Katsube, T., Begum, N., & Nenoi, M. (2016). Revisiting the health effects of psychological stress—its influence on susceptibility to ionizing radiation: A mini-review. *Journal of Radiation Research*, *57*(4), 325–335. doi:10.1093/jrr/rrw035 PMID:27242342

Wang, F., Yu, J., Yang, P., Miao, L., & Ye, B. (2017). Analysis of the Barriers to Widespread Adoption of Electric Vehicles in Shenzhen China. *Sustainability (Basel)*, *9*(4), 522. doi:10.3390u9040522

Wang, S., Li, J., & Zhao, D. (2017). The impact of policy measures on consumer intention to adopt electric vehicles: Evidence from China. *Transportation Research Part A, Policy and Practice*, *105*, 14–26. doi:10.1016/j.tra.2017.08.013

Warren, E., & Matthews, G. (2019). Public libraries, museums, and physical convergence: Context, issues, opportunities: A literature review Part 1. *Journal of Librarianship and Information Science*, *51*(4), 1120–1133. doi:10.1177/0961000618769720

Weber, W., & Hoogma, R. (1998). Beyond national and technological styles of innovation diffusion: A dynamic perspective on cases from the energy and transport sectors. *Technology Analysis and Strategic Management*, *10*(4), 545–566. doi:10.1080/09537329808524333

Wenig, J., Sodenkamp, M., & Staake, T. (2019). Battery versus infrastructure: Tradeoffs between battery capacity and charging infrastructure for plug-in hybrid electric vehicles. *Applied Energy*, *255*, 113787. doi:10.1016/j.apenergy.2019.113787

Whitehair, K. (2016). *Libraries in an artificially intelligent world.* Public Libraries. Available at: https://publiclibrariesonline.org/2016/02/libraries-in-an-artificially-intelligent-world

Whitney, W., Keselman, A., & Humphreys, A. (2017). Libraries and librarians: Key partners for progress in health literacy research and practise. *Information Services & Use*, *37*(1), 85–100. doi:10.3233/ISU-170821

WHO. (n.d.). https://covid19.who.int/

Williams, M. L. (2018). The adoption of web 2.0 technologies in academic libraries: A comprehensive explanation. *Journal of Librarianship and Information Science*.

Williams, R. (2019). Artificial intelligence assistants in the library: Siri, Alexa, and beyond. *Online Searcher*, *43*(3), 10–14.

Witten, I. H., & Frank, E. (2002). Data mining: Practical machine learning tools and techniques with Java implementations. *SIGMOD Record*, *31*(1), 76–77. doi:10.1145/507338.507355

Woods, D. A., & Evans, D. J. (2018). Librarians' perceptions of artificial intelligence and its potential impact on the profession. *Computers in Libraries*, *38*(1), 26–30.

World Health Organization. (2020). *Updated WHO recommendations for international traffic in relation to COVID-19 outbreak*. Available from: https://www.who.int/news-room/articles-detail/updated-whorecommendations-for-international-traffic-in-relation-to-covid-19-outbreak

Wu, L. L., & Lee, L. (2008). Online social comparison: Implications derived from Web 2.0. *PACIS 2008 - 12th Pacific Asia Conference on Information Systems: Leveraging ICT for Resilient Organizations and Sustainable Growth in the Asia Pacific Region.*

Wu, J., Williams, K. M., Chen, H.-H., Khabsa, M., Caragea, C., Tuarob, S., Ororbia, A. G., Jordan, D., Mitra, P., & Giles, C. L. (2015). CiteSeerX: AI in a Digital Library Search Engine. *AI Magazine, 36*(3), 35–48. doi:10.1609/aimag.v36i3.2601

Xiangyuan, A., & Tzesan, O. (2021). The Impact of Environmental Corporate Social Responsibility on Enterprise Performance——Implications for Sustainable Development Strategy. In *E3S Web of Conferences* (Vol. 251, p. 02072). EDP Sciences. doi:10.1051/e3sconf/202125102072

Xiao, J., Hou, Y., & Huang, Z. (2014). Beam test on bond behavior between high-grade rebar and high-strength concrete after elevated temperatures. *Fire Safety Journal, 69*, 23–35. doi:10.1016/j.firesaf.2014.07.001

Xiao, Y., & Wu, H. (2000). Compressive behavior of concrete confined by carbon fiber composite jackets. *Journal of Materials in Civil Engineering, 12*(2), 139–146. doi:10.1061/(ASCE)0899-1561(2000)12:2(139)

Xie, I., & Matusiak, K. (2016). *Discover digital libraries: Theory and practice.* Elsevier. https://www.sciencedirect.com/book/9780124171121/discover-digital-libraries

Xu, J., Wang, H., Liu, S., Hale, M. E., Weng, X., Ahemaitijiang, N., Hu, Y., Suveg, C., & Han, Z. R. (2023). Relations among family, peer, and academic stress and adjustment in Chinese adolescents: A daily diary analysis. *Developmental Psychology, 59*(7), 1346–1358. doi:10.1037/dev0001538 PMID:37199929

Yakel, E. (2007). Archives and manuscripts digital curation, OCLC systems and services. *International Digital Library Perspectives, 23*(4), 335–340.

Yalciner, H., Eren, O., & Sensoy, S. (2012). An experimental study on the bond strength between reinforcement bars and concrete as a function of concrete cover, strength and corrosion level. *Cement and Concrete Research, 42*(5), 643–655. doi:10.1016/j.cemconres.2012.01.003

Yang, S. Q., & Dalal, H. A. (2015). Delivering Virtual Reference Services on the Web: An Investigation into the Current Practice by Academic Libraries. *Journal of Academic Librarianship, 41*(1), 68–86. doi:10.1016/j.acalib.2014.10.003

Yang, Y., & Tan, Z. (2019). Investigating the influence of consumer behavior and governmental policy on the diffusion of electric vehicles in Beijing, China. *Sustainability (Basel), 11*(24), 6967. doi:10.3390u11246967

Yarrow, A., Clubb, B., & Draper, J. L. (2008). *Public Libraries, Archives, and Museums: Trends in collaboration and cooperation.* International Federation of Library Associations and Institutions (IFLA).

Yiotis, K. (2005). The open access initiative: A new paradigm for scholarly communications. *Information Technology and Libraries, 24*(4), 157–162. doi:10.6017/ital.v24i4.3378

Younus, & Zia. (2015). Identifying the factors affecting customer purchase intention. Global Journal of Management and Business Research. *Administrative Management, 15*(2).

Yu, K., Gong, R., Sun, L., & Jiang, C. (2019). The application of artificial intelligence in smart library. In *International Conference on organizational innovation (ICOI 2019)* (pp. 708-713). Atlantis Press. 10.2991/icoi-19.2019.124

Yusof, Z.M. (2005). *Issues and challenges in records management.* UKM, Bangi, Malaysia, Tech. Rep.

Zacher & Rudolph. (2021). Individual differences and changes in subjective wellbeing during the early stages of the COVID-19 pandemic. *American Psychologist, 76*(1), 50.

Zeng, W. (2021, April 26). *Pangu-α: Large-scale autoregressive pre-trained Chinese language models with auto-parallel computation.* https://arxiv.org/abs/2104.12369

Zhang, L., Brown, T., & Samuelsen, S. (2013). Evaluation of charging infrastructure requirements and operating costs for plug-in electric vehicles. *Journal of Power Sources, 240*, 515–524. doi:10.1016/j.jpowsour.2013.04.048

Zhang, L., & Watson, E. M. (2017). Measuring the impact of gold and green open access. *Journal of Academic Librarianship, 43*(4), 337–345. doi:10.1016/j.acalib.2017.06.004

Zhang, X., Bai, X., & Shang, J. (2018). Is subsidized electric vehicles adoption sustainable: Consumers' perceptions and motivation toward incentive policies, environmental benefits, and risks. *Journal of Cleaner Production, 192*, 71–79. doi:10.1016/j.jclepro.2018.04.252

Zhang, X., Wang, K., Hao, Y., Fan, J., & Wei, Y. (2013). The impact of government policy on preference for NEVs: The evidence from China. *Energy Policy, 61*, 382–393. doi:10.1016/j.enpol.2013.06.114

Zhou, J. (2023a). CHATGPT: Potential, prospects, and limitations. *Frontiers of Information Technology & Electronic Engineering.* doi:10.1631/FITEE.2300089

Zhou, J. (2023b, May 18). *Ethical ChatGPT: Concerns, Challenges, and Commandments.* https://arxiv.org/abs/2305.10646

ZhouJ.MüllerH.HolzingerA.ChenF. (2023, May 18). *Ethical ChatGPT: Concerns, Challenges, and Commandments..* https://arxiv.org/abs/2305.10646

Zhou, S., Barnes, L., McCormick, H., & Cano, M. B. (2021). Social media influencers' narrative strategies to create eWOM: A theoretical contribution. *International Journal of Information Management, 59*, 102293. doi:10.1016/j.ijinfomgt.2020.102293

Zirra, P. B., Ibrahim, A. J., & Abdulganiyyi, N. (2019). A review of digital libraries and their impact in Africa. *American Journal of Computer Science and Technology, 2*(4), 60–67. doi:10.11648/j.ajcst.20190204.13

Zissis, D., & Lekkas, D. (2012). Addressing cloud computing security issues. *Future Generation Computer Systems, 28*(3), 583–592. doi:10.1016/j.future.2010.12.006

Zorich, D., Waibel, G., & Erway, R. (2008). *Beyond the Silos of the LAMs: Collaboration Among Libraries.* OCLC.

Zourou, K., & Pellegrini, E., (2021). *Practices of digitally mediated youth engagement in cultural institutions during the pandemic.* GLAMers Consortium.

Zungu, L., Naidoo, R., Mkhize, N., Mthembu, T., Ndwandwe, T., & Singh, B. (2018). The impact of limited internet access on access to information in Kwazulu Natal Department of Health libraries. *Journal of Healthcare Information Management, 17*(2), 1–6.

About the Contributors

Barbara Holland is a Native New Yorker, an Independent Researcher, and a recent retiree from Brooklyn Public Library with over 21 Years of experience as a Sr Librarian. Barbara received the Bachelor of Arts Degree in Psychology from the City College Of New York and a Masters degree in Library Science and Information Studies from Queens College of New York. Barbara's quest for knowledge and information continues to be ongoing. Barbara has presented at the Georgia Conference On Information Literacy, and the Brooklyn Reading Council. Barbara has edited several books with IGI Global publishing: *Emerging Trends and the Impact of Internet of Things and Libraries, Handbook of Research on Library Response to the COVID-19 Pandemic*, and numerous papers over the years. She has an authored book and an active member of the American Library Association. Indexed in Scopus.

Keshav Sinha was born in Dhanbad, India, in 1991. He received the B.E. Degree in Computer Science and Engineering from Sri Chandrasekharendra Saraswathi Viswa Mahavidyalaya, Kanchipuram, India, in 2013 and an M.E. Degree in Software Engineering from the Birla Institute of Technology, Mesra, India, in 2016. Currently, as a research scholar, he is doing a Ph.D. from Birla Institute of Technology, Mesra, India, in Cryptography and Network security. In the future, this work will provide a secure environment for multimedia transmission. He published several papers in various conferences and journals as a research scholar. His current research interest includes Soft Computing, Cryptography, and Network Security, which provides flexibility in the computer science society.

* * *

Kantappa Chavan completed his MLISc from Karnatak University, Dharwad in the year 2015. Presently, he is a Librarian at S.D.V.S Sangh's Shri L K Khot College of Commerce, Sankeshwar. He has published 05 papers in National/International Journals and Conferences. He has received the Best Oral Presenter' at the International Conference held on December 26 to 28 2019 at NITK Mangalore. Beside he has worked for various committees in institute.

Hamid Farrokh Ghatte holds a Ph.D. degree in Structural and Earthquake Engineering from Istanbul Technical University (ITU). Currently, he is an assistant professor at the Civil Engineering Department of Antalya Bilim University (ABU), Turkey. Dr. F GHATTE has also worked as a research assistant at the Civil Engineering Department of Ljubljana University, Ljubljana, Slovenia. He has published several refereed publications and collaborated as a subject reviewer for different international scholarly journals. His current research focuses on the seismic performance and retrofitting of reinforced concrete structures, finite element analysis, rocking walls, and self-compacting concrete members to solve various issues during natural disasters like earthquakes. As a new area of investigation, he is working on machine learning in civil engineering, optimization, and artificial intelligence in civil and structural engineering.

Shashikumar Hatti completed his Master Degree in Library and Information Science from Karnatak University, Dharwad in the year 2015. He also cleared Karnataka SET in the year 2017 conducted by University of Mysore, Mysore. Presently, he is a Librarian at Navodaya Medical College Hospital and Research Centre, Raichur. He has published 05 papers in National Peer Reviewed Journals. He research areas are Public libraries, Information Literacy, User Awareness and Academic Libraries.

Muhammad Rosyihan Hendrawan is a senior lecturer at the Department of Library and Information Science Faculty of Administrative Science at Brawijaya University, Indonesia. Since 2016 He serves as vice head of the University of Brawijaya Archives of and is actively involved as a board in the Indonesian Library and Information Science Scholars Association. His research interests currently focus on a number of areas including cultural heritage information management, information governance, and digital humanities.

Azman Mat Isa is Associate Professor in the School of Information Science, College of Computing, Informatics and Mathematics Universiti Teknologi MARA Malaysia. His research interests currently focus on a number of areas including records management and information governance.

Kabelo Bruce Kgomoeswana was born in Limpopo, South Africa, in 1997. He is working as a library manager at Richfield graduate of institute of technology. he obtained his bachelor's degree (Honors) from the university of Limpopo. he is now completing his Master of Information Studies at the university of Limpopo and anticipating to continue with PhD the following year (2024). He is also completing a higher certificate in Archives and records management at the University of South Afrika. He worked at the university of Limpopo as a student librarian and National library of South Africa as a Trainee librarian. he served in different student support structures at the university of Limpopo. His research interest currently is on a number of areas including records management, Information literacy and records preservation.

Kishlay Kumar was born in Ranchi, India, in 1992. He has completed his BBA and MBA with Human Resource and Marketing as a specialization from Birla Institute of Technology, Mesra, Ranchi in 2013 and 2016 respectively. Currently, as a research scholar, he is pursuing a Ph.D. from Sarala Birla University. He has a 6 years of experience in the field of sales and Marketing in various organizations such as DTDC Express Limited, Byjus, Vodafone. In the future, this work will provide ideas on digital marketing.

Puja Mishra is working as an Assistant Professor in the Department of Management. She earned a PhD in Management from Ranchi University, Ranchi (Jharkhand). Prior to that, she obtained her MBA degree from BIT Mesra (Ranchi, Jharkhand). She has also qualified UGC -NET . She has more than eight years of teaching experience in management. She is active in research and has authored quality research papers and has presented her works in academic conferences and seminars. Her research interest is in organisational and human resources issues, in Indian work places.

Mallikarjun N. Mulimani, Selection Grade Librarian Government First Grade College Beedi, Tq.Khanapur. Dt. Belagavi. Dr. M. N. Mulimani joined as Chief Librarian Higher Education Academy, Dharwad in October 2017. He has completed his MLISc with second rank and secured Dr. S. R. Ranganathan Memorial Gold medal and did his Ph.D on "Cost effectiveness of UGC INFONET e- journals consortium accessed by selected three universities of Karnataka State" from KUD and his search for knowledge is added with his post-graduation in political science. In pursuit of practical knowledge he bagged Post Graduate Diploma in Library Automation and Networking certificate from University of Hyderabad for his professional proficiency. He is involved in many academic and research work as the coordinator of RUSA, IT and EDUSAT. He is the author of library and information science books and valuable contribution to research oriented national and international journals by way of articles and papers as many as 65. His work experience also includes editor in Chief of Indian Journal of Library and Information Technology (IJLIT) and presentation of papers in various conferences and workshops.

Satishkumar Naikar received his Master Degree in Library and Information Science from the Karnatak University, Dharwad in 2015. Completed Post Graduate Diploma in Library Automation and Networking from University of Hyderabad, Hyderabad in 2018. Cleared UGC-NET in the year 2018 conducted by University Grant Commission New Delhi and also cleared Karnataka SET in the year 2017 conducted by University of Mysore, Mysore. In 2015 he started as Assistant Librarian at Chetan Business School, Hubli and Woxsen School of Business, Hyderabad. Library Assistant at SVKM's Narsee Monjee Institute of Management Studies (NMIMS), Hyderabad, Assistant Librarian for the Institute of Integrated Learning in Management (IILM) University, Greater Noida, is currently the Assistant Librarian for the D Y Patil Deemed to be University, Navi Mumbai. Totally he has more than 07 years' experience in business school libraries and university libraries. He published 13 papers in national/international peer reviewed journals, conferences and edited book. His research areas are Information Technology, Library Automation, Academic Libraries, User Studies, Electronic Information Resources (EIR'S), RFID Technology.

Megha Paul received her Master Degree in Library and Information Science from the Assam University, Silchar in 2015. Completed Post Graduate Diploma in Library Automation and Networking from University of Hyderabad, Hyderabad in 2020. In 2016 she started working as an Assistant Librarian in Vivekananda Kendra Vidyalaya School, Silchar and as a Librarian in BBD Junior college, Silchar. Then in 2017 joined as an Executive Librarian at Woxsen University, Hyderabad. In 2022 she joined as a Librarian in Rockwell International School, Hyderabad and currently working here. She has more than 06 years' experience in different libraries. She published a paper in 1st International Conference on Transforming Library, Central Library CIT, Kokrajhar In Association with Department of Library & Information Science, Guwahati University, Guwahati, July 08th – 10th, 2017.

Piyush Ranjan is working as a Professor & Registrar with Jharkhand Rai University, Ranchi. Dr. Ranjan holds a double post-graduate degree in Management and Computer Application and also a double graduate degree in Physics and Computer Application. He has over 17+ years of experience in the corporate sector and academics. Apart from being an IT Consultant, he has also taught in various educational institutions in Delhi and other places. His area of expertise includes MIS, Operating System, Database Management System and Network Administration. His area of research includes the Environmental Impact of Microprocessor Technology, Threat of dumping Obsolete Computers, Sustainable Development of Computer Technology etc. Prof. Ranjan has contributed and edited chapters in various books both for National & International publishers and also published few books like 'Challenges to Higher Education', 'Online Learning', 'Changing Role of Teachers in Education' and many more. He is also on the Board of 'Advisory Editorial Member' of various National & International Journals and has conducted many workshops and FDP in institutes across India. He has also presented various papers in National & International Conferences organized by FMS Delhi, IIT Roorkee, ISB Hyderabad, BITS Pilani, IMT Ghaziabad, NIRMA University etc. He is also a recipient of various awards and achievements including "special acknowledgement Certificates" for the contribution in different Management Development Programs from All India Management Association (AIMA) for four consecutive years (2007- 2010). He has also been awarded as an "Innovative Academic Leader" in year 2017 for his outstanding and exemplary contribution to education and skill by Global Education and Skill Summit.

Sephalika Sagar is presently associated with Amity University of Jharkhand as Assistant Professor(Marketing). She has the privilege of 11 years of experiences in Academics. She is a Doctorate in Management from Ranchi University, Qualified in NET (Management), conducted by UGC, Professional Diploma in Digital Marketing,and Reviewer of Scopus Journal. She has published a number of research papers in various reputed national and international peer reviewed, scopus indexed, UGC recognized journals in several areas of marketing.

Ahmad Zam Hariro Samsudin is Associate Professor in the School of Information Science, College of Computing, Informatics and Mathematics Universiti Teknologi MARA Malaysia. His research interests currently focus on a number of areas including ontology, taxonomy, records management and information governance.

Muhammad Shobaruddin is an Associate Professor at the Department of Library and Information Science Faculty of Administrative Science at Brawijaya University, Indonesia. Since 2018 He serves as Head of the Department of Library and Information Science and is actively involved as a board in the Indonesian Library and Information Science Education Association. His research interests currently focus on a number of areas including information system in public sector, public communication, and public service and management.

Karan Pratap Singh was born in Bihar in 1986. He has completed his M.Com in Accounts from Patna University, Patna in 2007 and MBA in Finance and Business Analytics in 2016. He has cleared UGC- NET in 2019 .Presently pursuing PhD. in Management. This work provides an idea about the how digital marketing and celebrity endorsement influence the purchase intention of mutual fund.

L. G. Honey Singh was born in Ranchi, India, in 1994. She received her B.Com Degree from St. Xavier's college, Ranchi, Jharkhand, India, in 2016 and M.Com Degree in the field of Finance from St. Xavier's College, Jharkhand, India, in 2018 and she also completed her MBA Degree in the field of dual financial market in 2021. As a Research Scholar, she is currently doing a Ph.D. from Ranchi University in the field of Finance. In future, this work provides a ideas on herding behavior.

Priyanka Srivastava is presently associated with Sarala Birla University in the Department of CSE and also serving as Deputy Controller of Examinations. She is having 13+ years of experience in reputed educational organizations. She completed her Ph.D. from BIT, Mesra in the area of Digital Image Processing. The topic of her doctoral dissertation is "Investigation of NEAR System in terms of Image Resemblance". She did her Master in Information Technology from Birla Institute of Technology, Mesra. Apart from teaching she was also associated with Examination Department as 'Assistant Registrar (Examinations)' and also handled the work of SWAYAM as 'University SWAYAM Coordinator at Jharkhand Rai University. She is also associated with "Spoken Tutorial Project" by IIT Bombay. She has great interest in Research and Publications with few publications in reputed Journals indexed with SCI, SCOPUS, International Conference Proceedings and many more. She has been awarded with "BEST PAPER AWARD" twice while presenting her research article. She guided an M.Tech candidate and currently five research scholars are under her guidance.

Rani K. Swamy completed her Master Degree in Library and Information Science from Gulbarga University, Kalaburgi in the year 2022. Presently, she is serving the Assistant Librarian, Navodaya Medical College Hospital and Research Centre, Raichur. She research areas are Public libraries, Information Literacy, User Awareness and Academic Libraries.

Devesh Kumar Upadhyay, presently pursuing Ph.D. in applications of machine learning in psychiatry & medical science from Birla Institute of Technology, Mesra, Ranchi, has more than 5 years of experience in software development and hiring process in corporate world. He has completed his M.Tech. from Maharshi Dayanand University, Rohtak and MBA from Xavier Institute of Social Service, Ranchi. His area of Interests are artificial Intelligence, Machine learning, Big data and it's applications. he has published number of research articles in national and international journals in different areas of computer science and engineering, management and other fields.

Index

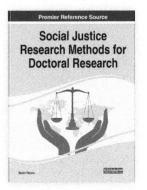

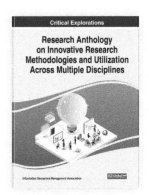

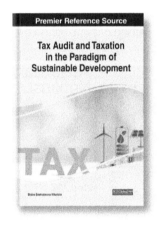

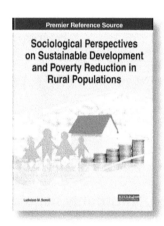

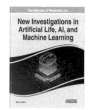

Milton Keynes UK
Ingram Content Group UK Ltd.
UKHW052000230224
438397UK00007B/56